ESSENTIALS
OF CLASSIC
ITALIAN
COOKING

ESSENTIALS
OF CLASSIC
ITALIAN
COOKING

by Marcella Hazan

Illustrated by Karin Kretschmann

ALFRED A. KNOPF

New York

2012

THIS IS A BORZOI BOOK
PUBLISHED BY ALFRED A. KNOPF, INC.

Library of Congress information available upon request

Manufactured in the United States of America

ISBN: 978-0-307-59795-3
30 29 28 27 26 25

Manufactured in the United States of America

For my students

MUCH OF THIS BOOK has been shaped by them. To their questions, I have sought to provide answers. Where they found obscurity, I have tried to bring clarity; what to them seemed difficult, I have tried to make simple. Their experiences and insights have become mine. To those who in the near quarter century that has gone by have followed me into my kitchen, first in my New York apartment, then in Bologna, finally in Venice, this work is dedicated, with affection and gratitude.

Contents

☙ *Preface* ❧

THOSE who are acquainted with *The Classic Italian Cook Book* and *More Classic Italian Cooking* may well wonder what those recipes are doing here, between a single pair of covers. I, for one, never imagined that some day my first two books would be reincarnated as one. But then, who could have expected them to journey as far as they have, becoming for so many people, in so many countries of the English-speaking world, a familiar reference to Italian cooking?

As volumes one and two, to use our working names for them, continued to go into new printings, my American editor, Judith Jones, and I thought it opportune to look them over and freshen them up, removing some recommendations that were no longer applicable, and where necessary, bringing recipes abreast of the many new ingredients available, and of the changes that had taken place in people's eating habits. It didn't appear to be much of an undertaking, just a little bit of housecleaning, but here we are three years later, with nearly every recipe completely rewritten, and many so substantially revised that they could well be considered new.

In the twenty years since *The Classic Italian Cook Book* was written, and in the fourteen since the publication of *More Classic Italian Cooking*, I have continued to cook from both books for my classes, for my husband, and for our friends. Perhaps without my always being fully conscious of it, the dishes continued to evolve, moving always toward a simpler, clearer expression of their primary flavors, and toward a steadily diminishing dependence on cooking fat. When I began systematically to go over each recipe for this book, I found myself rewriting each one to focus more sharply on what made the dish work, sometimes just to make one or two steps in the procedure more comprehensible, but often discovering that the recipe had to be wholly reshaped to make room for the perceptions and experiences gained in the intervening years of cooking and teaching.

In reviewing my work, I looked out for those recipes whose place in a book dedicated to classic principles of Italian cooking no longer seemed wholly earned, or whose successful execution depended on imponderables that no set of instructions could adequately convey. The few that fell into either category, I deleted. On the other hand, there were more than four dozen unpublished recipes that were the best of those I had come across and cooked with in recent years, a savory hoard that cried out to be included here. You will find them spread throughout the book, among the appetizers, soups, pastas, *risotti*, all the way to the desserts.

I have applied myself with all the diligence I could muster to reworking the section on yeast doughs, where you now have improved doughs for bread, new doughs for *focaccia* and pizza, and as an entirely fresh entry, one of the greatest of Italian regional loaves, Apulia's olive bread.

The microwave oven has become such a ubiquitous appliance that I had dearly hoped to incorporate here suggestions for its use but, I regret, those who like to cook by this method will have to look elsewhere. I have tried again and again, but the microwave does not produce for me the satisfying textures, the vigorous, well-integrated flavors that I look for in Italian cooking. This is aside from the fact that the oven's principal advantage, that of speed, declines precipitously when cooking for more than one. I believe with my whole heart in the act of cooking, in its smells, in its sounds, in its observable progress on the fire. The microwave separates the cook from cooking, cutting off the emotional and physical pleasure deeply rooted in the act, and not even with its swiftest and neatest performance can the push-button wizardry of the device compensate for such a loss.

Early on, when the full scope of the task of revision began to be visible, it became clear that the sensible approach was to pull the contents of *The Classic Italian Cook Book* and *More Classic Italian Cooking* together into a single broad-ranging volume. Having done so, the advantage became most apparent in the new pasta section: The chapters from the two earlier books have been consolidated and expanded to form one of the fullest and most detailed collections of recipes for pasta sauces and pasta dishes in print. It is preceded now by a completely reformulated introduction to homemade pasta that I hope will lead more cooks to discover how easily and quickly they can make homemade pasta in the classic Bolognese style, and how much better it is than any fresh pasta they can buy. Equally extensive are the sections on soups, *risotto*, fish, and vegetables, far more complete and more informative than in either of the two preceding books.

There is an entirely new chapter called Fundamentals, a mini-encyclopedia of Italian food. It is densely packed with information about cooking techniques and the herbs and cheeses used in an Italian kitchen, it has the recipes for several very useful basic sauces, and it tells how to choose and use such ingredients as balsamic vinegar, *bottarga*, extra virgin olive oil, *porcini* mushrooms, *radicchio*, truffles, dried pasta, different varieties of rice, and so on.

Both the revised and the newly added recipes in this book move on the same track, in pursuit not of novelty, but of taste. The taste they have been devised to achieve wants not to astonish, but to reassure. It issues from the cultural memory, the enduring world of generations of Italian cooks, each generation setting a place at table where the next one will feel at ease and at home. It is a pattern of cooking that can accommodate improvisation and fresh intuitions each time it is taken in hand, as long as it continues to be a pattern we can recognize, as long as its evolving forms comfort us with that essential attribute of the civilized life, familiarity.

Essentials of Classic Italian Cooking is meant to be used as a kitchen hand-book, the basic manual for cooks of every level, from beginners to highly accomplished ones, who want an accessible and comprehensive guide to the products, the techniques, and the dishes that constitute timeless Italian cooking.

Marcella Hazan
Venice, November 1991

ESSENTIALS OF CLASSIC ITALIAN COOKING

INTRODUCTION

Understanding Italian Cooking

ASK AN ITALIAN about Italian cooking and, depending on whom you approach, you will be told about Bolognese, Venetian, Roman, Milanese cooking or Tuscan, Piedmontese, Sicilian, Neapolitan. But *Italian* cooking? It would seem no single cuisine answers to that name. The cooking of Italy is really the cooking of regions that long antedate the Italian nation, regions that until 1861 were part of sovereign and usually hostile states, sharing few cultural traditions and no common spoken language—it was not until after World War II that Italian began to be the everyday language of a substantial part of the population—and practicing entirely distinct styles of cooking.

Take, for example, the cuisines of Venice and Naples, two cultures in whose culinary history seafood has had such a major role. Just as Venetians and Neapolitans cannot speak to each other in their native idiom and be understood, there is not a single dish from the light-handed, understated Venetian repertory that would be recognizable on a Neapolitan table, nor any of Naples's vibrant, ebulliently savory specialties that do not seem exotic in Venice.

Four hundred and fifty miles separate Venice and Naples but there are unbridgeable differences between Bologna and Florence, which are only sixty miles apart. In crossing the border between the two regional capitals, every aspect of cooking style seems to have turned over and, like an embossed coin, landed on its reverse side. Out of the abundance of the Bolognese kitchen comes cooking that is exuberant, prodigal with costly ingredients, wholly baroque in its restless exploration of every agreeable contrast of texture and flavor. On the other hand, the canny Florentine cook takes careful measure of all things and produces food that plays austere harmonies on unadorned, essential themes.

Bologna will stuff veal with succulent Parma ham, coat it with aged Parmesan, sauté it in butter, and conceal it all under an extravagant blanket of shaved white truffles. Florence takes a T-bone steak of noble size, grills it quickly over the incandescent embers of a wood fire, adding nothing but the aroma of olive oil and a grinding of pepper. Both can be triumphs.

The contrasts of Italian food's regional character are further sharpened by two dominant aspects of the landscape—the mountains and the sea.

Italy is a peninsula shaped like a full-length boot that has stepped up to the thigh into the Mediterranean and Adriatic seas. There it is fastened to the rest of Europe by an uninterrupted chain of the continent's tallest mountains, the Alps. At the base of the Alps lies Italy's only major plain, which spreads from Venice on the Adriatic coast westward through Lombardy and into Piedmont. This is the dairy zone of Italy, where the cooking fat is butter and the staple cereals are rice for *risotto* and cornmeal for *polenta*. It was only when the industries of the north began to attract labor from the south that *spaghetti* and other factory-made pasta appeared on the tables of Milan and Turin.

The plain ends its westward trek just before reaching the Mediterranean shore, cut off by the foothills of Italy's other great mountain chain, the Apennines. This chain stretches from north to south for the whole length of the country like the massive, protruding spine of some immense beast. On the eastern and western flanks, gently rounded hills slope toward the seas that surround the country. At the center, the land rises to form inhospitable stone peaks. Huddled between peaks and slopes are countless valleys, isolated from each other until they were connected by modern roads, giving birth, like so many Shangri-las, to wholly separate people, cultures, and cuisines.

Climatic zones, astonishing in their numbers and diversity for a country relatively small, have added their contributions to the variety of Italian food. Turin, capital of Piedmont, standing in the open plain at the foot of the windswept Alps, has winters more severe than Copenhagen, and one of the most robust cuisines of the nation. The coast just ninety miles to the west, sheltered by the Apennines' protecting slopes and bathed by soft Mediterranean breezes, enjoys the gentle weather synonymous with the Riviera. Here flowers thrive, olive groves flourish, fragrant herbs come up in every meadow and abound in every dish. It is no accident that this is the birthplace of *pesto*.

On the eastern side of the same Apennines that hug the Riviera coast lies the richest gastronomic region in Italy, Emilia-Romagna. Its capital, Bologna, is probably the only city in Italy whose name is instantly associated in the Italian mind not with monuments, not with artists, not with a heroic past, but with food.

Emilia-Romagna is almost evenly divided between mountainous land and flat, with the Apennines at its back and at its feet the southeastern corner of the great northern plain rolling out to meet the Adriatic. The Emilian plain is extraordinarily fertile land enriched by the alluvial deposits of the countless

Apennine torrents that have coursed through it toward the sea. It leads all Italy in the production of wheat, the same wheat with which Bologna's celebrated handmade pasta is produced. Italy's greatest cow's milk cheese, *parmigiano-reggiano,* is made here, taking its name from two Emilian cities, Parma and Reggio. The whey left over from cheesemaking is fed to hogs who, in turn, provide the hams for Parma prosciutto and meat for the finest pork products in the world.

Northern Italy stops at the southern border of Emilia-Romagna and, with Tuscany, Central Italy begins. From Tuscany down, the Apennines and their foothills in their southward march spread nearly from coast to coast, so that this part of Italy is prevalently mountainous. Two major changes take place in cooking. First, as it is simpler on a hillside to plant a grove of olive trees than to raise a herd of cows, olive oil supplants butter as the dominant cooking fat. Second, as we get farther away from Emilia-Romagna's fields, its homemade pasta of soft-wheat flour and eggs is replaced by the factory-made, hard-wheat and eggless macaroni of the south.

However much we roam, we shall not be able to say we have tracked down the origin of Italy's greatest cooking. It is not in the north, or the center, or the south, or the Islands. It is not in Bologna or Florence, in Venice or Genoa, in Rome or Naples or Palermo. It is in all of those places, because it is everywhere.

It is not the created, not to speak of "creative," cooking of restaurant chefs. It is the cooking that spans remembered history, that has evolved during the whole course of transmitted skills and intuitions in homes throughout the Italian peninsula and the islands, in its hamlets, on its farms, in its great cities. It is cooking from the home kitchen. Of course there have been—and there still are—aristocrats' homes, merchants' homes, peasants' homes, but however disparate the amenities, they have one vital thing in common: Food, whether simple or elaborate, is cooked in the style of the family. There is no such thing as Italian *haute cuisine* because there are no high or low roads in Italian cooking. All roads lead to the home, to *la cucina di casa*—the only one that deserves to be called Italian cooking.

FUNDAMENTALS

Where Flavor Starts

Flavor, in Italian dishes, builds up from the bottom. It is not a cover, it is a base. In a pasta sauce, a *risotto,* a soup, a fricassee, a stew, or a dish of vegetables, a foundation of flavor supports, lifts, points up the principal ingredients. To grasp this architectural principle central to the structure of much Italian cooking, and to become familiar with the three key techniques that enable you to apply it, is to take a long step toward mastering Italian taste. The techniques are known as *battuto, soffritto,* and *insaporire.*

BATTUTO

The name comes from the verb *battere,* which means "to strike," and it describes the cut-up mixture of ingredients produced by "striking" them on a cutting board with a chopping knife. At one time, the nearly invariable components of a *battuto* were lard, parsley, and onion, all chopped very fine. Garlic, celery, or carrot might be included, depending on the dish. The principal change that contemporary usage has brought is the substitution of olive oil or butter for lard, although many country cooks still depend on the richer flavor of the latter. However formulated, a *battuto* is at the base of virtually every pasta sauce, *risotto* or soup, and of numberless meat and vegetable dishes.

SOFFRITTO

When a *battuto* is sautéed in a pot or skillet until the onion becomes translucent and the garlic, if any, becomes colored a pale gold, it turns into a *soffritto.* This step precedes the addition of the main ingredients, whatever they may be. Although many cooks make a *soffritto* by sautéing all the components of the *battuto* at one time, it makes for more careful cooking to keep the onion and the garlic separate. The onion is sautéed first, when it becomes translucent the garlic is added, and when the garlic becomes colored, the rest of the *battuto.* The reasons are two: *one,* if you start by sautéing the onion, you are creating a richer base of flavor in which to sauté the *battuto; two,* because onion takes longer to sauté than garlic, if you were to put both in at the same time, by the time the onion became translucent the garlic would be too dark. If, however, your *battuto* recipe calls for *pancetta,* cook the onion and *pancetta* together to make use of the *pancetta*'s fat, thus reducing the need for other shortening.

An imperfectly executed *soffritto* will impair the flavor of a dish no matter how carefully all the succeeding steps are carried out. If the onion is merely stewed or incompletely sautéed, the taste of the sauce, or the *risotto,* or the vegetable never takes off and will remain feeble. If the garlic is allowed to become dark, its pungency will dominate all other flavors.

Note ❧ A *battuto* usually, but not invariably, becomes a *soffritto.* Occasionally, you combine it with the other ingredients of the dish as is, in its raw state, *a crudo,* to use the Italian phrase. This is a practice one resorts to in order to produce less emphatic flavor, such as, for example, in making a roast of lamb in which the meat cooks along with the *battuto a crudo* from the start. Another example is *pesto,* a true *battuto a crudo,* although, perhaps because it has traditionally been pounded with a pestle rather than chopped with a blade, it is not always recognized as such. Yet there are many Italian cooks who, in referring to any *battuto,* might say they are making a *pestino,* a "little pesto."

INSAPORIRE

The step that follows a *soffritto* is called *insaporire,* "bestowing taste." It usually applies to vegetables, inasmuch as, in Italian cooking, vegetables are the critical ingredient in most first courses—pastas, soups, *risotti*—and in many fricassees and stews, and often constitute an important course on their own. But the step may also apply to the ground meat that is going to be turned into a meat sauce or meat loaf, or to rice, when it is toasted in the *soffritto* as a preliminary to making *risotto.* As you become aware of it, you will spot it in countless recipes.

The technique of *insaporire* requires that you add the vegetables or other principal ingredients to the *soffritto* base and, over very lively heat, briskly sauté them until they have become completely coated with the flavor elements of the base, particularly the chopped onion. One can often trace the unsatisfying taste, the lameness of dishes purporting to be Italian in style, to the reluctance of some cooks to execute this step thoroughly, to their failure to give it enough time over sufficient heat, or even to their skipping it altogether.

SAUTÉING WITH BUTTER AND OIL

A *soffritto* is sometimes executed with olive oil as the only fat, but on those occasions when one might find the flavor of olive oil intrusive Italian cooks use butter together with neutral-tasting vegetable oil. Combining the two enables one to sauté at a higher temperature without scorching the butter or having to clarify it.

❦ *The Components* ❧

ANCHOVIES
Acciughe

Of all the ingredients used in Italian cooking, none produces headier flavor than anchovies. It is an exceptionally adaptable flavor that accommodates itself to any role one wishes to assign it. Chopped anchovy dissolving into the cooking juices of a roast divests itself of its explicit identity while it contributes to the meat's depth of taste. When brought to the foreground, as in a sauce for pasta or with melted mozzarella, anchovy's stirring call takes absolute command of our taste buds. Anchovies are indispensable to *bagna caôda,* the Piedmontese dip for raw vegetables, and to various forms of *salsa verde,* the piquant green sauces served with boiled meats or fish.

What anchovies to get and how to prepare them ❧ The meatier anchovies are, the richer and rounder is their flavor. The meatiest anchovies are the ones kept under salt in large tins and sold individually, by weight. One-quarter pound is, for most purposes, an ample quantity to buy at one time. Prepare the fillets as follows:

❦ Rinse the whole anchovies under cold running water to remove as much as possible of the salt used to preserve them.

❦ Take one anchovy at a time, grasping it by the tail and, with the other hand, use a knife gently to scrape off all its skin. After skinning it, remove the dorsal fin along with the tiny bones attached to it.

❦ Push your thumbnail into the open end of the anchovy opposite the tail and run it against the bone, opening the anchovy flat all the way to the tail. With your hand, loosen and lift away the spine, and separate the fish into two boneless fillets. Brush your fingertips over both sides of the fillets to detect and remove any remaining bits of bone.

❧ Rinse under cold running water, then pat thoroughly dry with paper towels. Place the fillets in a shallow dish. When one layer of fillets covers the bottom of the dish, pour over it enough extra virgin olive oil to cover. As you add fillets to the dish, pour olive oil over each layer. Make sure the top layer is fully covered by oil.

❧ If you are not going to use them within 2 or 3 hours, cover the dish and refrigerate. If the dish lacks a lid of its own use plastic wrap. The anchovies will keep for 10 days to 2 weeks, but they taste best when consumed during the first week. Prepared in this manner, the fillets are powerfully good as an appetizer or even a snack, when spread on a thickly buttered slice of crusty bread.

Note ❧ If you cannot find the salted whole anchovies described above and must buy prepared fillets, look for those packed in glass so you can choose the meatier ones. Do not be tempted by bargain-priced anchovies because the really good ones are never cheap, and the cheap ones are likely to be the really awful—mealy, salt-drenched—stuff that has given anchovies an undeserved bad name.

If you happen to be using canned anchovies, don't keep the leftover ones in the tin. Remove them, curl them into rolls, put them in a small jar or deep saucer, cover them with extra virgin olive oil, and refrigerate.

Do not use anchovy paste from a tube, if you can help it. It is harsh and salty and has very little of the warm, attractive aroma that constitutes the principal reason for using anchovies.

Cooking with anchovies ❧ On most occasions, anchovies are chopped fine so that they can more easily dissolve and merge their flavor with that of the other ingredients. Never put chopped anchovies into very hot oil because they will fry and harden instead of dissolving, and their flavor may turn bitter. Remove the pan from heat when adding the anchovies, putting it back on the burner only when, through stirring, the anchovies have begun to break down into a paste. If you can arrange to have another pot nearby with water boiling, place the pan with the anchovies over it, double-boiler fashion, and stir the anchovies until they dissolve.

BALSAMIC VINEGAR
Aceto Balsamico

Balsamic vinegar, a centuries-old specialty produced in the province of Modena, just north of Bologna, is made entirely from the boiled-down must—the concentrated, sweet juice—of white grapes. True balsamic vinegar is aged for decades in a succession of barrels, each made of a different wood.

How to judge it ❀ The color must be a deep, rich brown, with brilliant flashes of light. When you swirl the vinegar in a wine glass, it must coat the inside of the glass as would a dense, but flowing syrup, neither splotchy nor too thin. Its aroma should be intense, pleasantly penetrating. A sip of it will deliver balanced sweet and sour sensations, neither cloying nor too sharp, on a substantial and velvety body. It is never inexpensive, and it is too precious and rare ever to be put up in a container much larger than a perfume bottle. The label must carry, in full, the officially established appellation, which reads: *Aceto Balsamico Tradizionale di Modena.* All other so-called balsamic vinegars are ordinary commercial wine vinegar flavored with sugar or caramel, bearing no resemblance to the traditional product.

How to use it ❀ True balsamic vinegar is used sparingly. In a salad it never replaces regular vinegar; it is sufficient to add a few drops of it to the basic dressing of olive oil and pure wine vinegar. In cooking, it should be put in at the very end of the process or close to it so that its aroma will carry through into the finished dish. *Aceto balsamico* is marvelous over cut, fresh strawberries when they are tossed with it just before serving. Regrettably, balsamic vinegar has become a cliché of what is sometimes described as "creative" cooking, in somewhat the same way that tomato and garlic were once clichés of spaghetti-house Italian cooking. It should not be used so often or so indiscriminately that its flavor loses the power to surprise and its emphatic accents become tiresome with repetition.

BASIL
Basilico

The most useful thing one can know about basil is that the less it cooks, the better it is, and that its fragrance is never more seductive than when it is raw. It follows, then, that you will add basil to a pasta sauce only after it is done, when it is being tossed with the pasta. By the same consideration, that most concentrated of basil sauces, *pesto,* should always be used raw, at room temperature, never warmed up. Occasionally, one cooks basil in a soup or stew or other preparation, sacrificing some of the liveliness of its unfettered aroma in order to bond it to that of the other ingredients. If you are in doubt, however, or improvising, put it in at the very last moment, just before serving.

How to use basil ❀ Use only the freshest basil you can. Don't make do with blackened, drooping leaves. If you grow your own, pick only what you need that day, preferably plucking the leaves early in the morning before they've had too much sun. When you are ready to use the basil, rinse it quickly under cold running water or wipe the leaves with a dampened cloth. Unless the recipe calls for thin, julienned strips, it's best not to take a knife to basil. If you do not want to put the whole leaves in your dish, tear them into smaller pieces with your hands, rather than cutting them. Do not ever use dried or powdered basil. Many people freeze or preserve basil. I'd rather use it fresh and, if it isn't available, wait until its season returns.

BAY LEAVES
Alloro

Bay may be the most versatile herb in the Italian kitchen. It is used in pasta sauces, it aromatizes such different preserved foods as goat cheese in olive oil or sun-dried figs, it finds its way into most marinades for meat, it is the ideal herb for the barbecue: on a fish skewer, or over calf's liver, or even in the fire itself. There is no more agreeable match than bay leaves with pears cooked in red wine or with boiled chestnuts.

What to get ❀ Bay leaves dry beautifully and keep indefinitely. Buy only the whole leaves, not the crumbled or powdered, and keep them in a tightly closed glass jar in a cool cupboard. Before using, whether the leaves are dried or fresh, wipe each leaf lightly with a damp cloth.

Note ❀ If you have a garden or terrace or balcony, bay is a hardy perennial that grows quickly into a handsome plant with a nearly inexhaustible supply of leaves for the kitchen. If your winters are bitter and long, bring the bay indoors until spring.

BEANS
Fagioli

Legumes are used liberally throughout Italy, but they are nowhere treated with the affection they receive in the central regions of Tuscany, Abruzzi, Umbria, and Latium. Tuscans favor *cannellini,* or white kidney beans. Chick peas and fava beans triumph in Abruzzi and Latium. Umbria is celebrated for its lentils. In the north there is a pocket of bean adoration that rivals that of the center and it is in the Venetian northeast corner of the country, where perhaps the finest version of the classic bean soup—*pasta e fagioli*—is produced. The beans Venetians use are marbled pink and white versions of the cranberry or Scotch bean of which the most highly prized is the *lamon,* beautifully speckled when raw, dark red when cooked.

Some beans are available fresh for only a short time of the year and, outside Italy, some are rarely seen in their fresh-in-the-pod state. In their place you can use either canned or dried beans. The dried are much to be preferred, and not only because they are so much more economical than the canned. When properly cooked, dried beans have flavor and consistency that the bland, pulpy canned variety cannot match.

Cooking dried beans ❀ The instructions that follow are valid for all dried legumes that need to be precooked, such as white *cannellini* beans, Great Northern beans, red and white kidney beans, cranberry beans, chick peas, and fava beans. Lentils do not need to be precooked.

❀ Put the quantity of beans required by the recipe in a bowl and add enough water to cover by at least 3 inches. Put the bowl in some out-of-the-way corner of your kitchen and leave it there overnight.

❀ When the beans have finished soaking, drain them, rinse them in fresh cold water, and put them in a pot that will accommodate the beans and enough water to cover them by at least 3 inches. Put a lid on the pot and turn on the heat to medium. When the water comes to a boil, adjust the heat so that it simmers steadily, but gently. Cook the beans until tender, but not mushy, about 45 minutes to 1 hour. Add salt only when the beans are almost completely tender so that their skin does not dry and crack while cooking. Taste them periodically so you'll know when they are done. Keep the beans in the liquid that you cooked them in until you are ready to use them. If necessary, they can be prepared a day or two ahead of time and stored, always in their liquid.

BOTTARGA

This is the roe of the female thin-lipped gray mullet, which has been extracted with its membrane intact, salted, lightly pressed, washed, and dried in the sun. It has the shape of a long, flattened tear drop, usually varying in length between 4 and 7 inches, is of a dark, amber gold color, and usually comes in pairs. In the past it was always encased in wax but now it is more frequently vacuum-sealed in clear plastic. The finest *bottarga* comes from the mullet—*muggine* in Italian—taken from the brackish waters of Cabras, a lake off the western shore of Sardinia.

The flavor of good *bottarga* is delicately spicy and briny, very pleasantly stimulating on the palate. After peeling off its membrane, it can be sliced paper thin and added to green salads, or to boiled *cannellini*, or served as an appetizer on thin, toasted rounds of buttered bread with a slice of cucumber. It is delicious grated and tossed with pasta. *Bottarga* is never cooked.

Another kind of *bottarga* is that made from tuna roe; it is very much larger, a dark reddish brown in color, and shaped like a long brick. It is drier, sharper, more coarsely emphatic in flavor than mullet *bottarga,* for which it is a much cheaper, but not desirable substitute. Tuna *bottarga* is quite common throughout the countries on the eastern shores of the Mediterranean.

BREAD CRUMBS
Pan Grattato

The bread crumbs used in Italian cooking are made from good stale bread with the addition of no flavoring of any kind whatever. They must be very dry, or they will become gummy, particularly in those dishes where they are tossed with pasta. Once the bread has been ground into fine crumbs, dry the crumbs either by spreading them on a cookie sheet and baking them in a 375° oven for 15 minutes, or toasting them briefly in a cast-iron skillet.

BROTH
Brodo

The broth used by Italian cooks for *risotto,* for soups, and for braising meat and vegetables is a liquid to which meat, bones, and vegetables have given their flavor, but it is not a strong, dense reduction of those flavors. It is not stock, as the term is used in French cooking. It is light bodied and soft spoken, helping the dishes of which it is a part to taste better without calling attention to itself.

Italian broth is made principally with meat, together with some bones to give it a bit of substance. When I make broth I always try to have some marrow bones in the pot. The marrow itself makes a delicious appetizer later on grilled or toasted bread, seasoned with Horseradish Sauce, page 44.

The finest broth is that produced by a full-scale Bollito Misto, page 405. You may be reluctant, however, to undertake making *bollito misto* every time you need to replenish your supply of broth. If you are an active cook, you can collect and freeze meat for broth from the boning and preparation of different cuts of veal, beef, and chicken, stealing here and there a juicy morsel from a piece of meat before it is minced for a stuffing or for a meat sauce, or before it goes into a beef or a veal stew. Do not use lamb or pork, the flavor of which is too strong for broth. Use chicken giblets and carcasses most sparingly because their flavor can be disagreeably obtrusive. When ready to make broth, enrich the assortment with a substantial fresh piece of beef brisket or chuck.

Basic Homemade Meat Broth

1½ to 2 quarts

Salt
1 carrot, peeled
1 medium onion, peeled
1 or 2 stalks celery
¼ to ½ red or yellow bell
    pepper, cored and stripped
    of its seeds
1 small potato, peeled

1 fresh, ripe tomato OR a
    canned Italian plum
    tomato, drained
5 pounds assorted beef, veal,
    and chicken (the last
    optional) of which no
    more than 2 pounds may
    be bones

1. Put all the ingredients in a stockpot, and add enough water to cover by 2 inches. Set the cover askew, turn on the heat to medium, and bring to a boil. As soon as the liquid starts to boil, slow it down to the gentlest of simmers by lowering the heat.

2. Skim off the scum that floats to the surface, at first abundantly, then gradually tapering off. Cook for 3 hours, always at a simmer.

3. Filter the broth through a large wire strainer lined with paper towels, pouring it into a ceramic or plastic bowl. Allow to cool completely, uncovered.

4. When cool, place in the refrigerator for several hours or overnight until the fat comes to the surface and solidifies. Scoop up and discard the fat.

5. If you are using the broth within 3 days after making it, return the bowl to the refrigerator. If you expect to keep it any longer than 3 days, freeze it as described in the note below.

How to keep broth ❀ It is safe to keep broth in the refrigerator for a maximum of 3 days after making it, but unless you are certain you will use it that quickly, it is best to freeze it. It's impossible to overemphasize how convenient it always is to have frozen broth available. The most practical method is to freeze it in ice-cube trays, unmold it as soon as it is solid, and transfer the cubes to airtight plastic bags. Distribute the cubes among several containers, so that when you are going to use the broth you will open only as many bags as you need.

CAPERS
Capperi

Capers are the blooms, nipped while they are still tightly clenched buds, of a plant whose spidery branches hug stone walls and rocky hillsides throughout much of the Mediterranean region. Capers are used abundantly in Sicilian cooking, but no Italian kitchen should be without them. They have their assigned place in many classic preparations, in sauces for pasta, meat, fish, in stuffings, and their sprightly, pungent, yet not harsh flavor makes them one of those condiments that readily support the improvisational, casual style that characterizes much Italian cooking.

What to look for ❦ At one time I had a strong preference for the tiniest capers, the *nonpareil* variety from Provence. While they are certainly desirable, I'd now rather work with the larger capers from the islands off Sicily and the even larger ones from Sardinia, whose flavor has a more expansive, more stirring quality. Capers, particularly the Provençal ones, are usually pickled in vinegar. They have the advantage of lasting indefinitely, especially if refrigerated after being opened. The drawback is that the vinegar alters their flavor, making it sharper than it needs to be. In Italy, particularly in the South, capers are packed in salt, and they taste better. They are available in markets abroad as well, particularly in good ethnic groceries. Their disadvantage is that, before they can be used, they must be soaked in water 10 to 15 minutes and rinsed in several changes of water, otherwise they will be too salty. Nor can they be stored for as long as the vinegar-pickled kind because, when the salt eventually absorbs too much moisture and becomes soggy, they start to spoil. The color of the salt is an indication of the capers' state of preservation. It should be a clean white; if it is yellow the capers are rancid.

FONTINA

Fontina is made from the unpasteurized milk of cows that graze on mountain meadows in the Val d'Aosta, the Alpine region of Italy that adjoins France and Switzerland. *Fontina* has many imitators, both inside and outside Italy, but only the Val d'Aosta version has the sweet, distinctly nutty flavor that makes it probably the finest cheese of its kind. It is ideal for melting in a Piedmontese-style *fonduta,* or over gratinéed asparagus, or to bind a slice of prosciutto to a sautéed scallop of veal. Its buttery taste is exceptionally delicate but, unlike that of its imitators, not insignificant. It is ideal for cooking when you want the subtlest of cheese flavors.

GARLIC
Aglio

To equate Italian food with garlic is not quite correct, but it isn't totally wrong, either. It may strain belief, but there are some Italians who shun garlic, and many dishes at home and in restaurants are prepared without it. Nevertheless, if there were no longer any garlic, the cuisine would be hard to recognize. What would roast chicken be like without garlic, or anything done with clams, or grilled mushrooms, or *pesto,* or an uncountable number of stews and fricassees and pasta sauces?

When preparing them for Italian cooking, garlic cloves are always peeled. Once peeled, they may be used whole, mashed, sliced thin, or chopped fine, depending on how manifest one wants their presence to be. The gentlest aroma is that of the whole clove, the most unbuttoned scent is that exuded by the chopped. The least acceptable method of preparing garlic is squeezing it through a press. The sodden pulp it produces is acrid in flavor and cannot even be sautéed properly.

It is possible, and often desirable, for the fragrance to be barely perceptible, a result one can achieve by sautéing the garlic so briefly that it does not become colored, and then letting it simmer in the juices of other ingredients as, for example, when thin slices of it are cooked in a tomato sauce. On occasion, a more emphatic garlic accent may be appropriate, but never, in good Italian cooking, should it be allowed to become harshly pungent or bitter. When sautéing garlic, never take your eyes off it, never allow it to become colored a dark brown because that is when the offensive smell and taste develop. In a few circumstances, when the balance of flavors in a dish demand and support a particularly intense garlic flavor, garlic cloves may be cooked until they are the light brown color of walnut shells. For most cooking, however, the deepest color you should ever allow garlic to become is pale gold.

Choosing and storing ❧ Garlic is available all through the year, but it is best when just picked, in the spring. When young and fresh, the cloves are tender and moist, and the skin is soft and clear white. The flavor is so sweet that one can be careless about quantity. As it ages, and unfortunately, outside of the growing areas, older garlic is what one will find, it dries, losing sweetness and acquiring sharpness, its skin becoming flaky and brittle, its flesh wrinkled and yellow, like the color of old ivory. It is still good to cook with, but you must use it sparingly and cook it to an even paler color than you would the fresh. I have seen chefs split the clove to remove any part of it that may have turned green. I don't find this necessary, but I do discard the green shoot when it sprouts outside the clove.

Choose a head of garlic by weight and size. The heavier it feels in the hand, the fresher it's likelier to be, and large heads have bigger cloves that take longer to dry out. Use only whole garlic, do not be tempted by prepared chopped garlic, or garlic-flavored oils, or powdered garlic. All such products are too harsh for Italian cooking.

Keep garlic in its skin until you are ready to use it. Do not chop it long before you need it. Store garlic out of the refrigerator in a crock with a lid fitting loosely enough so air can flow through. There are perforated garlic crocks made that do the job quite well. Braids of garlic can look quite beautiful hanging in a kitchen, but the heads dry out fairly quickly and all you will have left at some point are empty husks.

MARJORAM
Maggiorana

It is the herb most closely associated with the aromatic cooking of Liguria, the Italian Riviera, where it is used in pasta sauces, in savory pies, in stuffed vegetables, and—possibly most triumphantly—in *insalata di mare,* seafood salad. Its bewitchingly spicy and flowery aroma vanishes almost entirely when marjoram is dried. One should make every possible effort to get it fresh or, failing that, frozen.

MORTADELLA

Imitation is the sincerest form of flattery but, in the case of *mortadella,* it has come closer to character assassination. The products that call themselves *mortadella* or go by the name of the city where it originated, Bologna, have completely obscured the merits of perhaps the finest achievement of the sausage-maker's art.

The name *mortadella* may derive from the mortar the Romans used to employ to pound sausage meat into a paste before stuffing it into its casing. Another explanation suggests that the origin of the name can be traced to the myrtle berries—*mirto* in Italian—that were once used to aromatize the mixture. The lean meat of which *mortadella* is composed—the shoulder and neck from carefully selected hogs—together with the jowl and other parts of the pig that the traditional formula requires, is, in fact, ground to a creamy consistency before it is studded with half-inch cubes of fine hogback mixed with a blend of spices and condiments that varies from producer to producer, and stuffed into the casing. Every step of the operation is critical in the making of *mortadella,* but the one that follows after it is cased is probably the one most responsible for the texture and fragrance that characterize a superior product. *Mortadella* is finished only when it has undergone a special cooking procedure. It is hung in a room where the temperature is kept at 175° to 190° Fahrenheit, and there it is slowly steamed for up to 20 hours.

Mortadella comes in all sizes, from miniatures of one pound to colossi of 200 or more pounds and 15 inches in diameter. The latter, for which a special beef casing must be used, is the most prized because it takes longer to cook and develops subtler, finer flavors. When it is cut open, the fragrance that rises from the glowing peach-pink meat of a choice, large, Bolognese *mortadella* is possibly the most seductive of any pork product.

Mortadella's uses ❀ In the cooking of Bologna, minced *mortadella* is used to enrich the flavor of the stuffing of *tortellini* and of ground meat dishes such as meat loaf. Cut into sticks, it is breaded and fried as part of a *fritto misto* or a warm *antipasto.* It is also served thickly sliced as part of an *antipasto* platter of cold meats. On a Bolognese table, you will often find a saucer of *mortadella* cut into half-inch cubes. Probably its greatest service to the nation has been in keeping alive generations of school children sent to class breakfastless, but with a roll in their satchel that is generously stuffed with sliced *mortadella* to bring sustenance to the traditional mid-morning interval.

BUFFALO-MILK MOZZARELLA
Mozzarella di Bufala

At one time, all mozzarella was *di bufala,* made from water buffalo milk. The buffalos graze on the pastures of Campania, the southern region of which Naples is the capital. Their milk is much creamier than cow's milk, and the cheese it produces is velvety in texture, pleasingly fragrant and, unlike other mozzarella, it has decided flavor, being sweet and, at the same time, delicately savory.

Pizza, when it was created in Naples, was always made with *mozzarella di bufala.* It is too expensive an ingredient today for commercial pizza, but it will immeasurably enhance homemade pizza, and such preparations as *parmigiana di melanzane.* It is, moreover, the mozzarella to choose, if you have the choice, for a *caprese* salad, which consists of mozzarella slices, sliced ripe tomatoes, and basil.

NUTMEG
Noce Moscata

We probably have the Venetians to thank for making nutmeg, along with other Eastern spices, available in Italy, but it is in Bolognese cooking that it has put its most tenacious roots. Nutmeg is indispensable to Bolognese meat sauce, and to the stuffings for its homemade pasta. It is used elsewhere too, such as in sauces with spinach and *ricotta,* in certain savory vegetable pies, in some desserts. One must use it carefully because, if a shade too much is added, the warmth of its musky flavor is lost in a dominant sensation of bitterness.

Use only whole nutmegs, which you can store in a tightly closed glass jar in a kitchen cabinet. Grate the nutmeg when needed, easily done on its special, small, curved grater. Any grater with very fine holes will do the job, however.

EXTRA VIRGIN OLIVE OIL
Olio d'Oliva Extra Vergine

Of all the grades of oil that can be marketed as olive oil, the only one a careful cook should look for is "extra virgin." To qualify as "virgin" an olive oil must be cold-processed, produced solely by the mechanical crushing of the whole olive and its pit, wholly excluding the use of chemical solvents or any other technique of extraction. The varying degrees of "virginity" are determined by the percentage of oleic acid contained. The highest grade, "extra virgin," is reserved for oils with 1 percent oleic acid or less. If the percentage of acid exceeds 4 percent, the oil must be rectified to lower the acid content and then it may no longer be labeled "virgin." Up until 1991, it was sold as "pure," a term that may have been technically accurate but did not seem to be an appropriate handle for the lowest marketable grade of olive oil.

Choosing an extra virgin olive oil ❀ Italian oils offer such a broad range of aromas and flavors that, when a representative selection is available, one can experiment with a view to choosing the oil that best supports one's own style of cooking. The oils produced on the Veneto side of Lake Garda and on the hills north of Verona are probably Italy's finest, certainly its most elegant: sweetly fragrant, nutty, with a gossamer touch on the palate. Those from Liguria are shier of flavor, but they have a thicker, more viscous feel. The oils from central Italy—of Tuscany and Umbria—are penetratingly fruity and, those of Tuscany in particular, even spicy and scratchy. The oils that come from further south have the scent of Mediterranean herbs—rosemary, oregano, thyme, with appley, almost sweet, pronouncedly fruity flavor. The only way to determine which one pleases one's palate most is to try as many as possible. The tasting qualities to look for, no matter what the other characteristics of the oil may be, are sensations of liveliness, freshness, and lightness. Avoid oils that taste fat, that feel sticky, that have earthy or moldy odors.

Storing olive oil 🌸 Olive oil is perishable, sensitive to air, light, and heat. The Italian ministry of agriculture recommends that it be used within a year and a half after it is bottled. It can be kept in its original container, if unopened, for that much time, or slightly longer, if stored in a cool, dark cupboard or in a wine cellar. Once opened, it should be used as soon as possible, certainly within a month or six weeks. Keep it in a bottle with a tight closure. Do not keep it in one of those oil cans with a spout unless you use it up rather quickly. If an opened bottle of oil has been around for some time, smell it before using it and, if it smells and tastes rancid, discard it or it will spoil the flavor of anything you cook.

Cooking with olive oil 🌸 It is sometimes suggested that while one should choose the very best oil one can for a salad, it's all right to use a lower grade for cooking. Such advice is flawed by a flagrant contradiction. One chooses an olive oil because of its flavor, and that flavor is no less critical to a pasta sauce, or to a dish of vegetables, than it is to a lettuce leaf. Once you have had spinach or mushrooms or a tomato sauce cooked in marvelous olive oil, you will not willingly have them any other way.

If taste is the overriding consideration, use the olive oil with the finest flavor as freely for cooking as for salads. If other factors, such as cost, must be given priority, cook with olive oil less often, replacing it with vegetable oil, but in those less frequent circumstances when you'll be turning to olive oil, cook with the best you can afford.

OLIVES
Olive

The olives used most commonly in Italian cooking are the glossy, round, black ones known in Italy as *greche,* Greek. They should not be confused with the other familiar variety of Greek olive, the purple Kalamata, elongated, tapering at the ends, whose flavor is ill suited to Italian dishes.

When cooking with olives, it's preferable to add the olives at the very last, when the sauce, the fricassee, the stew, or whatever you are making, is nearly done. Cooking olives a long time accentuates their bitterness.

OREGANO
Origano

Botanically speaking, oregano is closely related to marjoram, but its brasher scent is more closely associated with the cooking of the South, with pizza and with pizza-style sauces. It is excellent in some salads, with eggplant, with beans, and extraordinary in *salmoriglio,* the Sicilian sauce for grilled swordfish. Unlike marjoram, oregano dries perfectly.

PANCETTA

Pancetta, from *pancia,* the Italian for belly, is the distinctive Italian version of bacon. In its most common form, known as *pancetta arrotolata,* it is bundled jelly-roll fashion into a salami-like shape. To make *pancetta arrotolata,* the rind is first stripped away, then the meat is dressed with salt, ground black pepper, and a choice of other spices, which, depending on the packer, may include nutmeg, cinnamon, clove, or crushed juniper berries. It is moister than bacon because it is not smoked. When it has been cured for two weeks, it is tightly rolled up and tied, then wrapped in organic or, more commonly, artificial casing. At this point, it can be eaten as is, as one would eat prosciutto. It is more tender and considerably less salty than prosciutto. Its more important use, however, is in cooking, where its savory-sweet, unsmoked flavor has no wholly satisfactory substitute. Some Italians use a similarly cured, flat version of *pancetta* still attached to its rind, known as *pancetta stesa. Pancetta* is never smoked except in Italy's northeastern regions—Veneto, Friuli, Alto Adige—where a preference for flat, smoked bacon similar to North American slab bacon, is one of the legacies of a century of Austrian occupation.

PARMESAN
Parmigiano-Reggiano

Common usage bestows the name "Parmesan" on almost any cheese that can be grated over pasta, but the qualities of a true Parmesan—rich, round flavor and the ability to melt with heat and become inseparable from the ingredients to which it is joined—are vested in a cheese that has no rivals: *parmigiano-reggiano.*

What is parmigiano-reggiano? 🌸 The name is stringently protected by law. The only cheese that may bear it is produced—by a process unchanged in seven centuries—from the partly skimmed milk of cows raised in a precisely circumscribed territory mainly within the provinces of Parma and Reggio Emilia in the region of Emilia-Romagna. The totally natural process—nothing is added to the milk, but rennet; the long aging of eighteen months; the flora and the microorganisms that are specific to the pastureland of the production zone—all are contributors to the taste of *parmigiano-reggiano* and to the way it performs in cooking, qualities no other cheese can claim in the same measure.

How to buy it, how to store it 🌸 If you have the choice, do not buy a precut wedge of *parmigiano-reggiano,* but ask that it be cut from the wheel. To protect the cheese's special qualities, one must keep it from drying out. The more it is cut up, the more it loses moisture, until it begins to taste sharp and coarse. For the same reason, never buy any Parmesan in grated form and, at home, grate it only when you are ready to use it.

Take a careful look at the cheese you are about to buy. It should be a dewy, pale amber color, uniform throughout, without any dry white patches. In particular, look at the color next to the rind: If it has begun to turn white, the cheese has been stored badly and is drying out. If there is a broad chalk white rim next to the rind, the cheese is no longer in optimum condition. If there are no visible defects, ask to taste it. It should dissolve creamily in the mouth, its flavor nutty and mildly salty, but never harsh, sharp, or pungent.

When you have found an example of *parmigiano-reggiano* that meets all requirements, you might be well advised to buy a substantial amount. If it is more than you expect to use in two or three weeks' time, divide it into

two pieces, or more if it is exceptionally large. Each piece must be attached to a part of the rind. First wrap it tightly in wax paper, then wrap it in heavy-duty aluminum foil. Make sure no corners of cheese poke through the foil. Store on the bottom shelf of your refrigerator.

If you are keeping the cheese a long while, check it from time to time. If you find that the color has begun to lose its amber hue and is becoming chalkier, moisten a piece of cheesecloth with water, wring it until it is just damp, then fold it around the cheese. Wrap the cheese in foil and refrigerate for a day or two. Unwrap the Parmesan, discard the cheesecloth, rewrap the cheese in wax paper and aluminum foil, and return it to the refrigerator.

Note ❀ As a product of cow's milk, *parmigiano-reggiano* usually makes a more harmonious contribution to those preparations, and particularly to pasta sauces, that have a butter rather than an olive oil base. It is hardly ever grated on pasta or *risotto* that contain seafood, because seafood in Italy is nearly always cooked in olive oil. Like all rules, this one is meant to supply guidance rather than impose dogma. It should be applied with discrimination, taking account of exceptions, a notable one being *pesto,* which requires the use of both Parmesan and olive oil.

FLAT-LEAF PARSLEY
Prezzemolo

Italian parsley is the variety with flat, rather than curly, leaves. Italians are likely to say of someone whom they are always running into, "He—or she—is just like parsley." It is the fundamental herb of Italian cooking. It is found nearly everywhere, and there are comparatively few sauces for pasta, few soups, and few meat dishes that don't begin by sautéing chopped parsley with other ingredients. On many occasions, it is added again, raw, sprinkled over a finished dish that, without the fresh parsley fragrance hovering over it, might seem incomplete.

Curly parsley is not a satisfactory substitute, although it is better than no parsley at all. If you have difficulty finding Italian parsley, when you do come across it you might try buying a substantial quantity and freezing some of it. When the fall-out over Italy from Chernobyl made it impossible for a time to use any leaf vegetable or herb, I cooked with frozen parsley. It was not equivalent to the fresh, but it was acceptable. Indeed, we were thankful for it.

Note ❀ Do not get coriander—also known as *cilantro*—and Italian parsley mixed up. The leaves of the former are rounded at their tips, whereas parsley's come to sharp points. The aroma of coriander, which harmonizes so agreeably with Oriental and Mexican cooking, is jarring to the palate when forced into an Italian context.

PASTA

The shapes Italian pasta takes are varied beyond counting, but the categories an Italian cook works with are basically two: Factory-made, dried, flour and water macaroni pasta, and homemade, so-called "fresh," egg and flour pasta. There is not the slightest justification for preferring homemade pasta to the factory-made. Those who do deprive themselves of some of the most flavorful dishes in the Italian repertory. One pasta is not better than the other, they are simply different; different in the way they are made, in their texture and consistency, in the shapes to which they lend themselves, in the sauces with which they are most compatible. They are seldom interchangeable, but in terms of absolute quality, they are fully equal.

Factory-made macaroni pasta ❀ That most familiar of all pasta shapes, *spaghetti,* is in this category, along with *fusilli, penne, conchiglie, rigatoni,* and a few dozen others. The dough for factory pasta is composed of *semolina*— the golden yellow flour of hard wheat—and water. The shapes the dough is made into are obtained by extruding the dough through perforated dies. Once shaped, the pasta must be fully dried before it can be packaged. Aside from the quality of both the flour and the water, which is critically important to that of the finished product, the general factor that sets off exceptionally fine factory-made pasta from more common varieties is the speed at which it is produced. Great factory pasta is made slowly: The dough is kneaded at length; once kneaded, it is extruded through slow bronze dies rather than slippery, fast Teflon-coated ones. It is then dried gradually at an unforced pace. Such pasta is necessarily limited to small quantities; it is made only by a few artisan pasta makers in Italy, and it costs more than the industrial product of major brands.

Good-quality factory pasta should have a faintly rough surface, and an exceptionally compact body that maintains its firmness in cooking while swelling considerably in size. By and large, it is better suited than homemade "fresh" pasta to those sauces that have olive oil as their vehicle, such as seafood sauces and the broad variety of light, vegetable sauces. But, as some of the recipes bear out, there are also several butter-based sauces that marry well with factory pasta.

Homemade pasta ❀ Italians have fascinating ways of manipulating pasta dough at home: In Apulia, pinching it with the thumb to make *orecchiette;* on the Riviera, rolling it in the palm of the hand to make *trofie;* in Sicily, twisting it around a knitting needle to make *fusilli.* And there are many others. But the homemade pasta that enjoys uncontested recognition as Italy's finest is that of Emilia-Romagna, the birthplace of *tagliatelle, tagliolini*—also known as *capelli d'angelo* or angel hair, *cappelletti, tortellini, tortelli, tortelloni,* and *lasagne.*

The basic dough for homemade pasta in the Bolognese style consists of eggs and soft-wheat flour. The only other ingredient used is spinach or Swiss chard, required for making green pasta. No salt, no olive oil, no water are added. Salt does nothing for the dough, since it will be present in the sauce; olive oil imparts slickness, flawing its texture; water makes it gummy.

In the home kitchens of Emilia-Romagna, the dough is rolled out into a transparently thin circular sheet by hand, using a long, narrow hardwood pin. Girls used to begin to try their hand at it at the age of six or seven. Now that many have grown up without mastering their mothers' skill, they use the hand-cranked machine to reach comparable, if not equivalent, results. Instructions for both the rolling pin and the machine method appear later on in these pages.

Good homemade pasta is not as chewy as good factory pasta. It has a delicate consistency, and feels light and buoyant in the mouth. It has the capacity of absorbing sauces deeply, particularly the ones based on butter and those containing cream.

BLACK PEPPER
Pepe Nero

If a dish calls for ground or cracked pepper, black peppercorn berries are the only ones to use. White pepper is the same berry, but it is stripped of its skin, where much of the aroma and liveliness that makes pepper desirable resides. Although white pepper is actually feebler, it seems to taste sharper because it lacks the full, round aroma of the black. Once ground, that aroma fades rapidly, so it is imperative to grind pepper only when you need to use it, as the recipes in this book direct throughout. The variety of black pepper I have used is Tellicherry, whose warm, sweetly spiced flavor I find the most appealing.

DRIED PORCINI MUSHROOMS
Funghi Porcini Secchi

Even when fresh *porcini*—wild *boletus edulis* mushrooms—are available, the dried version compels consideration on its own terms not as a substitute, but as a separate, valid ingredient. Dehydration concentrates the musky, earthy fragrance of *porcini* to a degree the fresh mushroom can never equal. In *risotto,* in *lasagne,* in sauces for pasta, in stuffings for some vegetables, for birds, or for squid, the intensity of the aroma of dried *porcini* can be thrilling.

How to buy ❀ Dried *porcini* are usually marketed in small transparent packets, generally weighing slightly less than one ounce, one of which is sufficient for a *risotto* or a pasta sauce for four to six persons. They keep indefinitely, particularly if kept in a tightly sealed container in the refrigerator, so it pays to have a supply at hand that one can turn to on the inspiration of the moment. The dried *porcini* with the most flavor are the ones whose color is predominantly creamy. Choose the packet containing the largest, palest pieces and—unless you have no alternative—stay away from brown-black, dark mushrooms that appear to be all crumbs or little pieces. Dried morels, *chanterelles,* or *shiitake,* while they may be very good on their own terms, do not remotely recall the flavor of *porcini,* and are not a satisfactory substitute.

Note ❀ If you are traveling in Italy, particularly in the fall or spring, there is no more advantageous food purchase you can make than a bag of high-quality dried *porcini.* It is legal to bring them into the country and, if you refrigerate them in a tightly closed container, you can keep them for as long as you like.

How to prepare for cooking ❀ Before you can cook dried mushrooms, they must be reconstituted according to the following procedure:

❀ For ¾ to 1 ounce dried *porcini:* 2 cups barely warm water. Soak the mushrooms in the water for at least 30 minutes.

❀ Lift out the mushrooms by hand, squeezing as much water as possible out of them, letting it flow back into the container in which they had been soaking. Rinse the reconstituted mushrooms in several changes of fresh water. Scrape clean any places where soil may still be embedded. Pat dry with paper towels. Chop them or leave them whole as the recipe may direct.

❧ Do not throw out the water in which the mushrooms soaked because it is rich with *porcini* flavor. Filter it through a strainer lined with paper toweling, collecting it in a bowl or beaked pouring cup. Set aside to use as the recipe will subsequently instruct.

PROSCIUTTO

Prosciutto is a hog's hind thigh or ham that has been salted and air cured. Salt draws off the meat's excess moisture, a process the Italian word for which is *prosciugare,* hence the name prosciutto. A true prosciutto is never smoked. Depending on the size of the ham and other factors, the curing process may take from a few weeks to a year or more. Slow, unforced, wholly natural air-curing produces the delicate, complex aromas and sweet flavor that distinguish the finest prosciuttos. Parma ham, by which all others are judged, is aged a minimum of ten months, and particularly large examples may be aged one and a half years.

Slicing prosciutto ❦ Skillfully cured prosciutto balances savoriness with sweetness, firmness with moistness. To maintain that balance, each slice ought to maintain the same proportions of fat and lean meat that characterized the ham when it left the curing house. The regrettable practice of stripping away the fat from prosciutto subverts a carefully achieved balance of flavors and textures and elevates the salty over the sweet, the dry over the moist.

Sliced prosciutto ought to be consumed as soon as possible because, once cut, it quickly loses much of its alluring fragrance. If it must be kept for a length of time, each slice or each single layer of slices must be covered with wax paper or plastic wrap and the whole then tightly wrapped in aluminum foil. Plan on using it within the following twenty-four hours, if possible, and remove from the refrigerator at least a full hour before serving.

Cooking with prosciutto ❦ Prosciutto contributes huskier flavor to pasta sauces, vegetables, and meat dishes than any other ham. It also contributes salt, and one must be very judicious with what salt one adds when cooking with prosciutto. Sometimes none is needed. What is true when serving sliced prosciutto is even more pertinent when cooking with it: Do not discard any of the sweet, moist fat.

RADICCHIO

The crisp, bright-red vegetable responsible for adding the word *radicchio* to Americans' salad vocabulary is a part of the large chicory family, among whose many members are Belgian endive, escarole, and that bitter cooking green with long, loose saw-toothed leaves that resembles dandelion, *catalogna* or Catalonia. The familiar tight, round, colorful head vaguely resembling a cabbage, known in Italy as *radicchio rosso di Verona,* or *rosa di Chioggia,* is one of several varieties of red *radicchio* from the Veneto region. Another variety similar in shape, but with looser leaves of a mottled, marbleized pink hue is called *radicchio di Castelfranco.* Both the above are usually consumed raw, in salads. Those whose palate finds the bitterness of chicory that cooking brings out agreeably bracing, may also use them in soups, sauces, or as braised vegetables. A third *radicchio* is quite different in shape, somewhat resembling a Romaine lettuce, with loosely clustered, long, tapering, mottled red leaves. It is known as *radicchio di Treviso* or *variegato di Treviso.* It matures later than the previous two, usually in November; it is far less bitter than they are when cooked, hence, although it is frequently served as salad, it is also used in *risotto,* or in pasta sauces, or it is served on its own, either grilled or baked, basted liberally with olive oil. Another version is commonly known as *tardivo di Treviso,* "late-maturing" Treviso *radicchio,* and its season is end of November through January. Its long leaves are loosely spread and exceptionally narrow, more like slender stalks than leaves, with sharply pointed tips curled inwards. The stalk-like ribs are a dazzling white, their leafy fringes deep purple, and they spring away from the root like tongues of fire. It is an exceedingly beautiful vegetable. *Tardivo di Treviso* is the sweetest *radicchio* of all, a highly prized—and steeply priced—delicacy used either to make a luxuriously delicious salad or, best of all, cooked like *radicchio di Treviso* as described above.

Note ❧ If you cannot find either of the Treviso varieties, in any recipe that calls for cooking them you can satisfactorily substitute Belgian endive.

The striking red hues of Venetian *radicchio*s are achieved by blanching in the field. If left to grow naturally, *radicchio* would be green with rust-brown spots and it would be very bitter. Midway through its development, however, it is covered with loose soil, or straw, or dried leaves, or even sheets of black plastic. As it continues to grow in the absence of light, the lighter portions of the leaves become white and the darker, red.

Buying radicchio ❧ *Radicchio* is sweetest late in the year, most bitter in the summer. The stunted, small heads one sometimes sees in the market are of warm weather *radicchio,* and likely to be very astringent.

Note ❀ Although the whole, bright red leaf looks very attractive in a salad, *radicchio* can be made to taste sweeter by splitting the head in half, then shredding it fine on the diagonal. This is a secret learned from the *radicchio* growers of Chioggia. Do not discard the tender, upper part of the root just below the base of the leaves, because it is very tasty.

Radicchietto

Many varieties of small, green *radicchio,* some wild, some cultivated, are served in salads in Italy. Of the cultivated, the most popular is *radicchietto,* whose leaves slightly resemble *mâche* (in Italian, *dolcetta* or *gallinella*), but they are thinner, more elongated. The best *radicchietto* is that cultivated under the salty breezes that sweep through the farm islands in Venice's lagoon.

RICE
Riso

Choosing the correct rice variety is the first step in making one of the greatest dishes of the Northern Italian cuisine, *risotto.* What a grain of good *risotto* rice must be able to do are two essentially divergent things. It must partly dissolve to achieve the clinging, creamy texture that characterizes *risotto* but, at the same time, it must deliver firmness to the bite.

Of the several varieties of rice for *risotto* that Italy produces, three are exceptional: Arborio, Vialone Nano, Carnaroli. Arborio and Vialone Nano offer qualities at opposite ends of the scale.

Arborio ❀ It is a large, plump grain that is rich in amylopectin, the starch that dissolves in cooking, thus producing a stickier *risotto.* It is the rice of preference for the more compact styles of *risotto* that are popular in Lombardy, Piedmont, and Emilia-Romagna, such as *risotto* with saffron, or with Parmesan and white truffles, or with meat sauce.

Vialone Nano ❀ A stubby, small grain with more of another kind of starch, amylose, that does not soften easily in cooking, although Vialone Nano has enough amylopectin to qualify it as a suitable variety for *risotto.* It is the nearly unanimous choice in the Veneto, where the consistency of *risotto* is looser—*all'onda,* as they say in Venice, or wavy—and where people are partial to a kernel that offers pronounced resistance to the bite.

Carnaroli ❀ It is a new variety, developed in 1945 by a Milanese rice grower who crossed Vialone with a Japanese strain. There is far less of it produced than either Arborio or Vialone Nano, and it is more expensive, but it is unquestionably the most excellent of the three. Its kernel is sheathed in enough soft starch to dissolve deliciously in cooking, but it also contains more of the tough starch than any other *risotto* variety so that it cooks to an exceptionally satisfying firm consistency.

RICOTTA

The word *ricotta* literally means "recooked," and it names, as it describes, the cheese made when whey, the watery residue from the making of another cheese, is cooked again. The resulting product is milk white, very soft, granular, and mild tasting. It is a most resourceful ingredient in the kitchen: It can be used as part of a spread for canapés; it is combined with sautéed Swiss chard or spinach to make a meatless stuffing for *ravioli* and *tortelli;* again combined with Swiss chard or spinach, it can be used to make green *gnocchi;* it can be part of a pasta sauce; it is the key component of the batter for *ricotta* fritters, a marvelously light dessert; and, of course, there is *ricotta* cake, versions of which are beyond numbering.

Ricotta romana ❀ This is the archetypal *ricotta* from Latium, Rome's own home region. Originally, it was made solely from the whey remaining after making *pecorino,* ewe's milk cheese. Although some of it is still made that way, these days, in Latium as elsewhere, nearly all *ricotta* is made from whole or skimmed cow's milk. It is undeniably a richer product than the traditional one, but *ricotta* was not really intended to be rich. It was born as a poor by-product of cheesemaking, lean of texture, slightly tart in flavor, and it is those qualities that make it—and the dishes it is used for—uniquely appealing.

Ricotta salata ❀ This is *ricotta* to which salt has been added as a preservative. Since it is kept longer, it is not as moist as fresh *ricotta.* It can also be air cured or dried in an oven to render it a sharp-tasting grating cheese, somewhat reminiscent of the flavor of *romano.*

Buying ricotta ❀ One should look for *ricotta* in the same place one looks for other good cheese, in a cheese shop, in a food store with a specialized cheese department, or in a good Italian grocery. In any place, that is, that sells it loose, cutting it from a piece that looks as though it had been unmolded from a basket. Usually, it is not only fresher than the supermarket variety packed in plastic tumblers, but it is less watery, an important consideration when baking with *ricotta.*

Note ✺ If the only *ricotta* available to you is the plastic tumbler variety, and you intend to bake with it, the method described below will help you eliminate most of the excess liquid that would make the pastry crust soggy:

❀ Put the *ricotta* in a skillet and turn on the heat to very low. When the *ricotta* has shed its excess liquid, pour the liquid out of the pan, wrap the *ricotta* in cheesecloth, and hang it over a bowl or deep dish. The *ricotta* is ready to work with when it has stopped dripping.

ROMANO CHEESE
Pecorino Romano

The Italian for sheep is *pecora,* hence all cheese made from sheep's milk, such as *romano,* is called *pecorino.* The sheep antedates the cow in the domestic culture of Mediterranean peoples, and the first cheeses to be made were produced from ewe's milk. Today there are dozens of *pecorino* cheese of which *romano* is but one example. Some are soft and fresh, like a farmer's cheese, and there are others that mark every stage of a cheese's development, from the tenderness of a few weeks of age to the crumbliness and sharpness of a year and a half or more. The most stirring flavor and consistency of any table cheese may be that of a four-month-old *pecorino* from the Val d'Orcia, south of Siena, served with a few drops of olive oil and a coarse grating of black pepper.

Romano, on the other hand, is so sharp and pungent that only a singular palate is likely to find it agreeable as a table cheese. Its place is in the grater, and its use is with a limited group of pasta sauces that benefit from its piquancy. It is indispensable in *amatriciana* sauce, a little of it ought to be combined with Parmesan in *pesto,* and it is often the cheese to use in sauces for macaroni and other factory-made pasta that are made with such vegetables as broccoli, *rapini,* cauliflower, and olive oil.

In most instances where one would use *romano,* a better choice, if available, is another ewe's milk cheese, *fiore sardo,* a *pecorino* from Sardinia that has been aged twelve months or more. *Fiore,* while it delivers all the tanginess one looks for in *romano,* has none of its harshness.

ROSEMARY
Rosmarino

Next to parsley, rosemary is the most commonly used herb in Italy. Its aroma, which can quicken the most torpid appetites, is usually associated with roasts.

In Italian cooking, a sprig of rosemary is indispensable to the fully realized flavor of a roast chicken or rabbit. It is exceptionally good with pan-roasted potatoes, in some emphatically fragrant pasta sauces, in *frittate,* and in various breads, particularly flat breads like *focaccia.*

Using rosemary ✿ If at all possible, cook only with fresh rosemary. Grow your own, if you have a garden or terrace. It does particularly well with a sun-warmed wall at its back, putting out beautiful violet blue flowers twice a year. Some varieties have pink or white blooms. For the kitchen, snip off the tips of the younger, more fragrant branches.

If you have absolutely no access to fresh rosemary, use the dried whole leaves, a tolerable, if not entirely satisfactory, alternative. Powdered rosemary, however, is to be shunned.

SAGE
Salvia

A medicinal herb in antiquity, sage has been, since the Renaissance, one of Italy's favorite kitchen herbs. It is virtually inseparable from the cooking of game birds and, by logical extension, necessary to those preparations patterned after game dishes, such as *uccelli scappati,* "flown birds," sautéed veal or pork rolls with bacon. It is often paired with beans, as in the Tuscan *fagioli all'uccelletto, cannellini* beans with garlic and tomatoes, or, in Northern Italian cooking, in certain *risotti* with cranberry beans or soups with rice, beans, and cabbage. One of the most beguiling sauces for pasta or *gnocchi* is done simply by sautéing fresh sage leaves in butter.

Using sage ✿ If available, sage should be used fresh, as it always is in Italy. Otherwise, the same principle holds that applies to rosemary: Dried whole leaves are acceptable, powdered sage is not. Sage grows well if not subjected to extremes of cold or humidity and a mature plant will produce enough leaves from spring to fall to fill most kitchen requirements. It puts out beautiful purple blooms, but it is advisable to trim the flower-bearing tips of the branches to promote denser foliage.

Note ❀ When using either dried rosemary or dried sage leaves, chop the first or crumble the second to release flavor and use about half the quantity you would if they were fresh.

TOMATOES
Pomodori

The essential quality tomatoes must have is ripeness, achieved on the vine. Lacking it, all they have to contribute to cooking is acid. When truly ripe and fresh, they endow the dishes of many cuisines with dense, fruit-sweet, mouth-filling flavor. The flavor of fresh tomatoes is livelier, less cloying than that of the canned, but fully ripened fresh tomatoes for cooking are still not a common feature of North American markets, except for the six or eight weeks during the summer when they are brought in from nearby farms. When you are unable to get good fresh tomatoes, rather than cook with watery, tasteless ones, it's best to turn to the dependable canned variety.

What to look for in fresh tomatoes ❀ If there is a choice, the most desirable tomato for cooking is the narrow, elongated plum variety. It has fewer seeds than any other, more firm flesh and less watery juice. Because it has less liquid to boil down, it cooks faster, yielding that fresh, clear flavor that is characteristic of so many Italian sauces. If there are no plum tomatoes, measure the ones you have to choose from by the same standards. It doesn't matter whether they are large or small, if they are smoothly rounded or furrowed. What matters is that they be densely fleshed and ripe and that, in the pot, they produce tomato sauce, not tomato juice.

In Italy, there are other varieties of tomatoes, besides the plum, that are used for sauce. In Rome there is a marvelous, deeply wrinkled, small, round variety, locally called *casalini*. There are also perfectly smooth, round tomatoes, one kind about 2 inches in diameter that comes from Sicily, and then marvelous tiny ones, slightly bigger than cherry tomatoes, that come from Campania and are known as *pomodorini napoletani*. At the end of the season, both of the latter kind are detached from the plant together with part of the vine's branches and hung up in any cool part of the house. It's a practice that provides a source of ripe cooking tomatoes through most of the winter. There is no reason why it can't be adopted elsewhere. One important point to be aware of is that the variety should be of the kind that hangs firmly by its stem, that does not drop off. Air must circulate around the tomato, which must not sit on any surface or it will develop mold at the place of contact.

What to look for in canned tomatoes ❀ When buying canned tomatoes, if one has a choice one should look for whole, peeled plum tomatoes of the San Marzano variety imported from Italy. They are the best kind to use and, if possible, settle for no other. If your markets do not carry them, try any of the other whole peeled tomatoes, buying one can at a time until you find a brand that satisfies the following criteria: There should be no pieces, no sauce in the can, nothing but whole, firm-fleshed tomatoes, with a little of their juice. When cooked, there should be depth to their flavor, a satisfying fruity quality that is not too cloyingly sweet.

TRUFFLES
Tartufi

Italy produces excellent black truffles, just as France does, but unlike the French, Italians don't make much of a fuss over them. What they are capable of losing their heads over, and a substantial portion of their pocketbook, is the white truffle, which is found in no other country, or at least not with the characteristics of the Italian variety. The supremacy of the white truffle over the black, and—in terms of price by the ounce—over virtually every other food, is owed entirely to its aroma. One may describe it as related to that of garlic laid over a penetrating earthiness and combined with a pungent sensation that is like a whiff of some strong wine. But describing it cannot communicate its potency, the excitement it can bring to the plainest dish. In fact, only the most understated preparations are an appropriate foil for the commanding fragrance of white truffles.

What are truffles? ❀ They are underground fungi that develop, in a way no one has yet wholly understood, close to the roots of oaks, poplars, hazelnut trees, and certain pines. White truffles are found in Northern and Central Italy, in Piedmont, in Romagna, in the Marches, and in Tuscany. The most intensely aromatic and highly prized are the Piedmontese variety, from the hills near the town of Alba whose slopes also produce grapes for Italy's most majestic red wines, Barolo and Barbaresco. A great many of those truffles that claim the Alba name, however, actually come from the Marches, whose market town of Acqualagna advertises itself as the capital of the truffle.

White truffles begin to form in early summer and achieve maturity by the end of September, their season lasting until mid-January. There must be copious rain during late summer and early fall for truffles to achieve optimum quality, weather that could seriously compromise the grape harvest. Hence the saying, "*tartufo buono, vino cattivo,*" good truffles, poor wine.

The locations where truffles are likely to be found are a secret that truffle hunters guard tenaciously. Trained dogs help them unearth their prize, and a well-trained dog with a talented nose is held to be nearly priceless, never to be sold except in direst need. Night, when odors travel clearly, is the best time to hunt. In the fall, in the dark woods of truffle territory, what appear to be the tremblings of solitary fireflies are the flashlights of the truffle hunters.

Buying truffles ❀ Fresh white truffles should be very firm, with no trace of sponginess, and powerfully, inescapably fragrant. Buy them the same day you intend to use them because, from the moment they are dug out of the ground, truffles start to lose their precious aroma at an accelerating pace. If for any reason you must store them overnight, or longer, wrap them tightly in several layers of newspaper overlaid with aluminum foil, and keep them in a cool place, but preferably not the refrigerator. Some hold that the best way to keep a truffle is to bury it in rice in a jar. It certainly improves the rice, but it's uncertain how much good it does the truffle. The rice does protect it, absorbing undesirable moisture, but it also draws away very desirable aroma.

Preserved truffles are available in jars or cans. Jars have the advantage that they permit you to see what you are getting. Although they are never quite as scented as the fresh, some preserved truffles can be quite good. There is also paste made from white truffle fragments, packaged both in jars and tubes. I have always found the tube to be better. It can be used in sauce for pasta or over veal *scaloppine.* It is delicious spread over buttered toast, so much better than peanut butter.

How to clean ❀ Truffles exported to America have already been cleaned, but if you should buy them in Italy they will still be coated with dirt that must be carefully scraped away with a stiff brush. The most deeply embedded soil must be dislodged with a paring knife and a light touch. Finish cleaning by rubbing with a barely moistened cloth. Do not ever rinse in water.

How to use ❀ A whole white truffle, whether fresh or preserved, is sliced paper thin, using a tool that looks like a pocket *mandoline.* Lacking such a tool, one can use a potato peeler. The slices can be distributed, as generously as one's means will allow, over homemade *fettuccine* tossed with butter and Parmesan, over *risotto* also made with butter and Parmesan, over veal *scaloppine* sautéed in butter, on a traditional Piedmontese *fontina* cheese fondue, or over fried or scrambled eggs. Although one generally uses truffles thus, without cooking them, on the principle that there isn't anything cooking could do that could make them even better, an extraordinary expansion of flavor takes place when truffles are baked with slivers of *parmigiano-reggiano* cheese, particularly in a *tortino* or gratin consisting of layers of cheese, truffle, and sliced potatoes interspersed with dabs of butter.

TUNA
Tonno

In towns along both coasts of Italy, people used to buy the plentiful, cheap fresh tuna, boil it in water, vinegar, and bay leaves, drain it, and put it up, submerged in good olive oil, in large glass jars. It was one of the tastiest things one could eat. Acceptable canned tuna has long been universally available, and few cooks now bother to make their own.

Good canned Italian tuna packed in olive oil is delicious in sauces, both for pasta and for meats, and in salads, particularly when matched with beans. It used to be quite common on supermarket shelves, but it has been crowded off now by cheaper products packed in water. None of these is of any use in Italian dishes, least of all the wholly tasteless kind called light meat tuna.

Buying canned tuna ❀ For Italian cooking, only tuna packed in olive oil has the required flavor. The most advantageous way to buy it, is loose from a large can: It is juicier, more savory, and less expensive. Some ethnic grocers sell it thus, by weight. The alternative is buying smaller, individual cans of imported tuna packed in olive oil.

VEAL SCALOPPINE
Scaloppine di Vitello

Some of the most justifiably popular of all Italian dishes are those made with veal *scaloppine*. The problem is that it is exceptionally rare to find a butcher that knows how to slice and pound veal for *scaloppine* correctly. Even in Italy, I prefer to bring a solid piece of meat home and do it myself. It is, admittedly, one of the trickiest things to learn: It takes patience, determination, and coordination. If you do master it, however, you'll probably have better *scaloppine* at home than you have eaten anywhere.

The first requirement is not just good veal, but the right cut of veal. What you need is a solid piece of meat cut from the top round and when your relationship with the butcher enables you to obtain that, you are halfway to success.

Slicing ❀ What you must do at home is to cut the meat into thin slices across the grain. The ribbons of muscle in meat are tightly layered one over the other and form a pattern of fine lines. That pattern is the grain. If you take a close

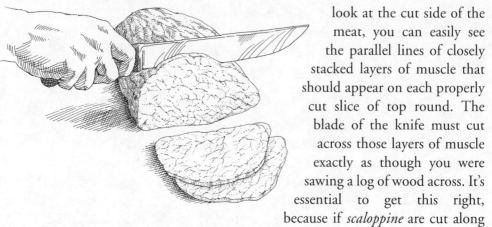

look at the cut side of the meat, you can easily see the parallel lines of closely stacked layers of muscle that should appear on each properly cut slice of top round. The blade of the knife must cut across those layers of muscle exactly as though you were sawing a log of wood across. It's essential to get this right, because if *scaloppine* are cut along the length of the grain, instead of across it, no matter how perfect they may look, they will curl, shrink, and toughen in the cooking.

Pounding ✸ Once cut, *scaloppine* must be pounded flat and thin so they will cook quickly and evenly. Pounding is an unfortunate word because it makes one think of pummeling or thumping. Which is exactly what you must not do. If all you do is bring the pounder down hard against the *scaloppine,* you'll just be mashing the meat between the pounder and the cutting board, breaking it up or punching holes in it. What you want to do is to stretch out the meat, thus thinning and evening it. Bring the pounder down on the slice so that it meets it flat, not on an edge, and as it comes down on the meat, slide it, in one continuous motion, from the center outward. Repeat the operation, stretching the slice in all directions until it is evenly thin throughout.

WATER
Acqua

Water is at the same time the most precious and most unobtrusive ingredient in Italian cooking, and its value is immense precisely because it is self-effacing. What water gives you is time, time to cook a meat sauce long enough without it drying out or becoming too concentrated, time for a roast to come around when using that superb Italian technique of roasting meat over a burner with the cover slightly askew, time for a stew or a fricassee or a glazed vegetable to develop flavor and tenderness. Water allows you to glean the tasty particles on the bottom of a pan without relying too much on such solvents as wine or stock that might tip the balance of flavor. When it has done its job and has been boiled away, water disappears without a trace, allowing your meats, your vegetables, your sauces to taste forthrightly of themselves.

Béchamel and Mayonnaise

Béchamel Sauce
Salsa Balsamella

BÉCHAMEL is a white sauce of butter, flour, and milk that helps bind the components of scores of Italian dishes: *lasagne,* gratins of vegetables, and many a *pasticcio* and *timballo*—succulent compounds of meat, cheese, and vegetables.

A smooth, luxuriantly creamy béchamel is one of the most useful preparations in the repertory of an Italian cook and it is easy to master, if you heed three basic rules. First, never allow the flour to become colored when you cook it with the butter, or it will acquire a burnt, pasty taste. Second, add the milk to the flour and butter mixture gradually and off heat to keep lumps from forming. Third, never stop stirring until the sauce is formed.

About 1⅔ cups medium-thick béchamel

2 cups milk	3 tablespoons all-purpose flour
4 tablespoons (½ stick) butter	¼ teaspoon salt

1. Put the milk in a saucepan, turn on the heat to medium low, and bring the milk just to the verge of boiling, to the point when it begins to form a ring of small, pearly bubbles.

2. While heating the milk, put the butter in a heavy-bottomed, 4- to 6-cup saucepan, and turn on the heat to low. When the butter has melted completely, add all the flour, stirring it in with a wooden spoon. Cook, while stirring constantly, for about 2 minutes. Do not allow the flour to become colored. Remove from heat.

3. Add the hot milk to the flour-and-butter mixture, no more than 2

Béchamel Sauce (continued)

tablespoons of it at a time. Stir steadily and thoroughly. As soon as the first 2 tablespoons of milk have been incorporated into the mixture, add 2 more, and continue to stir. Repeat this procedure until you have added ½ cup milk; you can now put in the rest of the milk ½ cup at a time, stirring steadfastly, until all the milk has been smoothly amalgamated with the flour and butter.

4. Place the pan over low heat, add the salt, and cook, stirring without interruption, until the sauce is as dense as thick cream. To make it even thicker, should a recipe require it, cook and stir a little longer. For a thinner sauce, cook it a little less. If you find any lumps forming, dissolve them by beating the sauce rapidly with a whisk.

Ahead-of-time note ❧ Béchamel takes so little time to prepare it is best to make just when you need it, so you can spread it easily while it is still soft. If you must make it in advance, reheat it slowly, in the upper half of a double boiler, stirring constantly as it warms up, until it is once again supple and spreadable. If you are making béchamel one day in advance, store it in the refrigerator in a tightly sealed container.

Increasing the recipe ❧ You can double or triple the quantities given above, but no more than that for any single batch. Choose a pan that is broader than it is tall so the sauce can cook more quickly and evenly.

Mayonnaise
Maionnese

HOMEMADE MAYONNAISE does marvelous things for the flavor of any dish of which it is a part and, with a little practice, you'll find it to be one of the easiest and quickest sauces you can produce.

After years of alternately using olive oil and vegetable oil, I have satisfied myself that, for a lighter sauce, vegetable oil is to be preferred. A good extra virgin olive oil brings a sharp accent to mayonnaise. It may even, as in the case of some Tuscan oils, make it bitter. One could resort to a thin, light-flavored olive oil, but why bother? Except when bolder flavor is required, as a few of the recipes in this book indicate, you might as well make vegetable oil your unvarying choice.

Be sure to start with all the ingredients at room temperature if you don't want to struggle to get your mayonnaise to mount. Even the bowl in which you will beat the eggs and the blades of the electric mixer should be run under hot water to warm them up.

Cautionary note 🌸 Homemade mayonnaise is made with raw eggs, which may transmit salmonella. I have made it dozens of times without encountering the problem, but if you are concerned about the possibility of salmonella poisoning, and particularly if you are planning to serve the mayonnaise to elderly people, or to very young children, or to someone who is immune deficient, use packaged, commercial mayonnaise.   *Over 1 cup*

The yolks of 2 eggs, brought to
    room temperature
Salt
From 1 to no more than 1⅓
    cups vegetable oil, depend-
ing on how much mayon-
    naise you want to make
2 tablespoons freshly squeezed
    lemon juice

1. Using an electric mixer set at medium speed, beat the egg yolks together with ¼ teaspoon salt until they become colored a pale yellow with the consistency of thick cream.

2. Add oil, *drop by drop,* while beating constantly. Stop pouring the oil every few seconds, without ceasing to beat, to make sure that all the oil you are adding is being absorbed by the egg yolks and none is floating free. Continue to dribble in oil, beating with the mixer.

3. When the sauce has become quite thick, thin it out slightly with a teaspoon or less of lemon juice, always continuing the beating action.

4. Add more oil, at a faster pace than at first, interrupting the pouring from time to time, while you continue beating, to allow the sauce to absorb the oil completely. As the sauce thickens, beat in a little more lemon juice, repeating the procedure from time to time until you have used up the 2 tablespoons. When the sauce has fully absorbed all the oil, the mayonnaise is done.

5. Taste and correct for salt and lemon juice. If you are planning to use the mayonnaise on fish, keep it on the tart side. Beat in any additions of salt and lemon juice with the mixer.

Food processor note 🌸 I don't see any advantage in using the food processor to make mayonnaise, except for its insignificantly faster speed. Mayonnaise out of the processor does not taste quite so good to me as that made with the mixer, and the processor's bowl is much more of a nuisance to clean.

Salsa Verde and Other Savory Sauces

Piquant Green Sauce
Salsa Verde

WHEN A *bollito misto*—mixed boiled meats—is served, this tart green sauce invariably accompanies it. But *salsa verde*'s uses are not limited to meat. It can also liven up the flavor of boiled or steamed fish. If you are going to use it for meat, make it with vinegar; if for fish, with lemon juice. The proportions of the ingredients given below seem to me well balanced, but they are subject to personal taste and may be adjusted, accentuating or deemphasizing one or more components as you may find desirable. The instructions below are based on the use of a food processor. If you are going to make the sauce by hand, please follow the slightly different procedure described in the note at the end.   *4 to 6 servings*

⅔ cup parsley leaves
2½ tablespoons capers
OPTIONAL: 6 flat anchovy fillets
½ teaspoon garlic chopped very
    fine
½ teaspoon strong mustard
½ teaspoon (depending on
    taste) red wine vinegar, if

the sauce is for meat, OR 1
tablespoon (depending on
taste) fresh lemon juice, if
for fish
½ cup extra virgin olive oil
Salt

Put all the ingredients into the food processor and blend to a uniform consistency, but do not overprocess. Taste and correct for salt and tartness. If you decide to add more vinegar or lemon juice, do so a little at a time, retasting each time to avoid making the sauce too sharp.

Hand-cut method ❦ Chop enough parsley to make 2½ tablespoons and enough capers for 2 tablespoons. Chop 6 flat anchovy fillets very fine, to as creamy a consistency as you can. Put the parsley, capers, and anchovies in a bowl together with the garlic and mustard from the ingredients list above. Mix thoroughly, using a fork. Add the vinegar or lemon juice, stirring it into the mixture. Add the olive oil, beating it sharply into the mixture to amalgamate it with the other ingredients. Taste and correct for salt and vinegar or lemon juice.

Ahead-of-time note ❀ Green sauce can be refrigerated in an airtight container for up to a week. Bring to room temperature and stir thoroughly before using.

Variation with Pickles and No Anchovies

What makes this alternative to classic *salsa verde* interesting is its chewier consistency, which is better achieved by hand-chopping than with the food processor.   *4 to 6 servings*

⅓ cup *cornichons* OR other fine cucumber pickles in vinegar
6 green olives in brine
½ tablespoon onion chopped very fine
⅛ teaspoon garlic chopped very fine

¼ cup chopped parsley
1½ tablespoons freshly squeezed lemon juice
½ cup extra virgin olive oil
Salt
Black pepper, ground fresh from the mill

1. Drain the pickles and chop them into pieces not finer than ¼ inch.
2. Drain and pit the olives, and chop them into ¼-inch pieces, like the pickles.
3. Put the pickles, olives, and all the other ingredients in a small bowl, and beat with a fork for a minute or two.

Warm Red Sauce
Salsa Rossa

WARM RED SAUCE is generally paired with green sauce, when that is served with boiled meats, to provide a mellow alternative to *salsa verde*'s tangy flavor. An exceptionally enjoyable way to use *salsa rossa* alone is alongside or over a breaded veal cutlet, page 375. It is very good, too, with grilled steak and delicious with hamburgers.   *4 servings*

3 meaty red or yellow bell peppers
5 medium yellow onions, peeled and sliced thin
¼ cup vegetable oil
A tiny pinch chopped hot chili pepper

2 cups canned imported Italian plum tomatoes, with their juice, OR 3 cups cut-up fresh tomatoes, if very ripe
Salt

Warm Red Sauce (continued)

1. Split the peppers lengthwise, and remove the core and seeds. Skin the peppers, using a peeler, and cut them into slices more or less ½ inch wide.

2. Put the onions and oil in a saucepan and turn on the heat to medium. Cook the onions, stirring, until wilted and soft, but not brown.

3. Add the peppers, and continue cooking over medium heat until both peppers and onions are very soft and their bulk has been reduced by half. Add the chili pepper, the tomatoes, and salt and continue cooking, letting the sauce simmer gently, for 25 minutes or so, until the tomatoes and oil separate and the fat floats free. Taste and correct for salt, and serve hot.

Ahead-of-time note 🌼 *Salsa rossa* can be prepared up to 2 weeks in advance and refrigerated in an airtight container. Reheat gently and stir thoroughly before serving.

Horseradish Sauce
Salsina di Barbaforte

Barbaforte, or *cren* as it is commonly known in northeastern Italy, makes an appetizing condiment not only for the boiled beef and other meats with which it is often served, but also for grilled lamb and steak, for boiled ham or cold turkey or chicken, for hamburgers and hot dogs. It is the most bracing seasoning you can have on a chicken or seafood salad. Horseradish in the Italian style does not have the acidic bite of other horseradish sauces because the vinegar is played down, replaced in large part by the silken touch of olive oil. The ideal tool for making the sauce is the food processor. Grinding a horseradish root is one of its kindest actions, effortlessly making a superbly uniform spread while saving cooks all the tears that accompany hand shredding on the grater.

About fresh horseradish 🌼 It looks like a root and, indeed, it is a root. Although, like all roots, it seems to have an unlimited life span, the fresher it is, the better. Its weight should not be too light in the hand, which would mean it has lost sap, and the skin should not be exceedingly dull nor feel too dusty-dry at the touch.   *About 1½ cups*

1½ pounds fresh whole
horseradish root
1 cup extra virgin olive oil
2 teaspoons salt
1½ tablespoons wine vinegar

OPTIONAL: 1½ teaspoons
balsamic vinegar
A 1¾- to 2-cup glass jar with a
tight-fitting cap

1. Pare all the brown rind away from the root, exposing the white horseradish flesh. A vegetable peeler with a swiveling blade is the easiest tool to use for the job. If there are stumps branching off from the root, detach them, if necessary, to get at the rind where they join the main root.

2. Rinse the pared root under cold running water, pat it dry with kitchen towels, and cut it into ½-inch pieces. Roots are hard stuff: Take a sharp, sturdy knife and use it with care.

3. Put the cut-up root in the bowl of a food processor fitted with the metal blade and begin processing. While the horseradish is being ground fine, pour the olive oil into the bowl, adding it in a thin stream. Add the salt and process a few more seconds. Add the wine vinegar and process for about 1 minute. If you like the sauce creamier, process it longer, but it is most satisfying when grainy and slightly chewy.

4. Remove the sauce from the processor bowl. If using the optional balsamic vinegar, beat it in at this point with a fork. Pour the sauce into a glass jar, packing it tightly, close securely, and refrigerate. It keeps well for several weeks.

Serving note ✸ At table, you may want to freshen and loosen the sauce with a little more olive oil.

Peppery Sauce for Boiled Meats
La Pearà

THE ORIGINS of *la pearà* can be traced to the Middle Ages, to the Venetian condiment known as *peverata,* a name that can be translated as "peppery" and accurately describes the flavor of the present-day sauce. The body of *la pearà* is formed by the slow swelling and massing of bread crumbs as broth is added to them a little at a time while they cook with butter and bone marrow. The slower the sauce cooks, the better it becomes. Calculate about 45 minutes to 1 hour of cooking time to achieve excellent results. Essential to the quality of the sauce is the quality of the broth; there is no satisfactory substitute here for good homemade meat broth.

La peparà is an earthy, substantial, creamy seasoning, a perfect accompaniment when served hot for mixed boiled meats, such as beef, veal, and chicken.   *About 1 cup*

1 cup beef marrow chopped
   very fine
1½ tablespoons butter
3 tablespoons fine, dry, unflavored bread crumbs
2 or more cups Basic Homemade Meat Broth, prepared
   as directed on page 15

Salt
Black pepper, ground fresh
   from the mill

1. Put the marrow and butter into a small saucepan. If you have one, a flameproof earthenware would be ideal for this kind of slow cooking, and enameled cast iron would be a suitable alternative. Turn on the heat to medium, and stir frequently, mashing the marrow with a wooden spoon.

2. When the marrow and butter have melted and begin to foam, put in the bread crumbs. Cook the crumbs for a minute or two, turning them in the fat.

3. Add ⅓ cup broth. Cook over slow heat, stirring with the wooden spoon while the broth evaporates and the crumbs thicken. Add 2 or 3 pinches of salt and a very liberal quantity of ground pepper.

4. Continue to add broth, a little at a time, letting it evaporate before adding more. Stir frequently, and keep the heat low. The final consistency should be creamy and thick, without any lumps. Taste and correct for salt and pepper. If the sauce is too dense for your taste, thin it by cooking it briefly with more broth. Serve hot over sliced boiled meat, or in a sauceboat on the side.

A Peppery Sauce for Roast Birds
La Peverada di Treviso

La peverada is one more descendant of the medieval *peverata* sauce referred to in the immediately preceding recipe for *la peparà*. The principal components are pork sausage and chicken livers, pounded or processed to a creamy consistency and cooked in olive oil with sautéed onion and white wine. All such sauces are subject to variations in the choice of ingredients: Garlic can take the place of onion, vinegar of wine, pickled green peppers for cucumber pickles. Once you have made the basic sauce, feel free to modify it along those lines, but be careful not to spike it with excessive tartness.

Peverada accompanies roast birds of all kinds, whether game or farm-raised. In Venice it is inseparable from roast duck, which is one of the dishes always present in the dinner taken aboard the boats that crowd the lagoon on the most important evening in the Venetian calendar, the Saturday in July on which the city celebrates its delivery from the plague.   *6 or more servings*

¼ pound mild pork sausage (see note)
¼ pound chicken livers
1 ounce cucumber pickles in vinegar, preferably *cornichons*
⅓ cup extra virgin olive oil, or less if the sausage is very fatty

1 tablespoon onion chopped very fine
Salt
Black pepper, ground fresh from the mill
1½ teaspoons grated lemon peel, carefully avoiding the white pith beneath it
⅔ cup dry white wine

Note ❧ Do not use so-called Italian sausages that contain fennel seeds. It is preferable to substitute good-quality breakfast sausage or mild pork salami.

1. Skin the sausage. Put the sausage meat, chicken livers, and pickles into a food processor and chop to a thick, creamy consistency.

2. Put the olive oil and onion in a small saucepan, turn on the heat to medium, and cook the onion until it becomes colored a pale gold. Add the chopped sausage mixture, stirring thoroughly to coat it well.

3. Add salt and liberal grindings of pepper. Stir well. Add the grated lemon peel, and stir thoroughly once again.

4. Add the wine, stir once or twice, then adjust heat to cook the sauce at a very gentle, steady simmer, and cover the pan. Cook for 1 hour, stirring occasionally. If you find the sauce becoming too dense or dry, add 1 or 2 tablespoons of water.

5. Serve hot over cut-up pieces or carved breast slices of roast birds.

Ahead-of-time note ❧ The sauce can be prepared up to a day or two in advance, and gently reheated, but its flavor is much better when it is used the same day it is made.

⊚ *Equipment* ⊚

The thing most cooks probably need least these days is another shopping list of cooking ware. Nearly all the kitchens I have seen, mine included, have more tools and pots and gadgets than are strictly needed. Nevertheless, there are certain pots and tools that, more efficiently than others, meet the fundamental requirements of the Italian way of cooking. They are few, but they are not to be overlooked and, since some of the items may be missing from an otherwise well-equipped kitchen, we had better see what they are.

THE SAUTÉ PAN

Sautéing is the foundation of most Italian dishes and a sauté pan is, by necessity, the workhorse of the Italian kitchen. It is a broad pan, 10 to 12 inches in diameter, with a flat bottom, sides 2 to 3 inches high that may be either straight or flaring, and it comes with a good-fitting lid. It should be the best-quality pot you can afford, of sturdy construction, capable of efficient transmission and retention of heat. Avoid nonstick surfaces that inhibit the full development of flavor a true sauté is designed to accomplish. A pan with these specifications will cook almost everything from the Italian repertory: pasta sauces, fricassees, stews, vegetables; it will handle cooking of any required speed, from a lazy simmer to hot deep-frying. You should own more than one such pan because you will encounter situations when it is convenient and time-saving to use them simultaneously for different procedures.

OTHER POTS

❈ You will find it helpful to supplement the sauté pan with skillets of varying dimensions. Bear in mind that, in Italian cooking, you need more broad, shallow pans than tall, narrow ones because, on a broad, shallow surface you can cook faster and bring ingredients to a more complete maturation of flavor.

❖ To boil pasta, a stockpot that accommodates 4 quarts of water comfortably, plus 1 to 1½ pounds pasta. It should be made of light-weight metal that transmits heat quickly and is easier to lift for draining. Indispensable companion to the pasta pot is a colander, with a self-supporting base.

❖ For *risotto,* I recommend either enameled cast iron, which retains heat evenly for the 25 minutes or so *risotto* needs to cook, or heavy steel ware in whose bottom several layers of metal are bonded together.

❖ Italian roasts are more frequently cooked on top of the stove than in the oven. The most practical shape of pot is an oval casserole that hugs the shape of the roast, with no waste of cooking liquid, such as broth or wine, and no waste of heat. Enameled cast iron is excellent material for this purpose, or heavy-bottomed, thick steel ware.

❖ An assortment of oven-to-table ware in various sizes and depths is needed for vegetables, for some fish dishes, and of course, for *lasagne.*

THE FOOD MILL

I don't recall ever seeing a kitchen in Italy that didn't have a food mill, not even the most modest peasant kitchen. What the food mill does, no other tool can equal. It purées cooked vegetables, legumes, fish, and other soft ingredients, separating unwanted seeds, skins, strings, and fish bones from the food being pulped through its perforated disks. Nor does it entirely break down the texture of that pulp, as the food processor would; instead, it preserves the lively, differentiated consistency so desirable for Italian dishes.

Food mills come with fixed perforated disks, or with interchangeable disks. The fixed disk usually has very small holes that make it useless for most Italian cooking. Of the interchangeable disks, the one you will need most often is the one with the largest holes, which is supplied only with those mills that have three disks. This is the only kind of food mill you should get, preferably made of stainless steel and fitted with very useful fold-away clamps on the bottom that let you rest the mill securely over a bowl or pot while you mash food through it.

OTHER TOOLS

❀ A Parmesan grater whose holes are neither so fine as to pulverize the cheese, nor so broad that it makes shreds or pellets of the Parmesan.

❀ A four-sided grater with different-size holes, including very fine ones for nutmeg.

❀ A peeler whose blade pivots on pins set at each end. The flesh of vegetables skinned with a peeler rather than by blanching or roasting is firmer and less watery and better for sautéing.

❀ Slotted spoons and spatulas. Immensely practical for removing food from a pan without any of the cooking fat, or for lifting food away temporarily from cooking juices that need to be boiled down.

❀ Long wooden spoons. Essential for stirring homemade pasta, particularly delicate stuffed pasta. Useful for all stirring, especially sauces, for mashing food while it is cooking, and for scraping tasty residues from the bottom of pans. Take care never to leave the spoon in the pan while food is cooking. Have several so you can discard those that become worn and hard to clean.

❀ Meat pounder. For flattening *scaloppine, braciole,* or chops. The best designed is the one that consists of a thick, heavy, stainless-steel disk with a short handle attached perpendicularly to its center.

BAKING NECESSITIES

❀ A single, large, heavy baking stone for bread, pizza, *sfinciuni,* and *focaccia.* Even when you are baking *focaccia* in a pan, as in this book, you will get better results if you slide the pan on top of a hot stone. The most practical size is one that is as large as your oven rack, or as close to it in size as possible.

❀ The wooden baker's peel for pizza and bread. I had always thought of it as a paddle, which is what it looks like, but I have found that real bakers call it a peel. Although you can improvise with a sheet of masonite or stiff cardboard or an unrimmed baking sheet, a paddle (peel) is easier and more fun to use. Mine is 16 by 14 inches, with an 8-inch handle. If you are going to have one, there is no point in getting a smaller one.

❀ For *focaccia,* rectangular baking pans made of dark carbon steel in two sizes, both the commonly available 9- by 13-inch size, and the professional-size one, 19 by 13 inches.

❀ Scrapers. The rectangular steel one with a large slot for your fingers to go through is particularly easy to handle, and most useful when you need to pick up a sticky mass of dough.

APPETIZERS

Cold Appetizers

Crostini Bianchi—Ricotta and Anchovy Canapés

For 28 canapés

½ pound fresh *ricotta*
1 tablespoon butter, softened to
  room temperature
8 flat anchovy fillets (preferably
  the ones prepared at home
  as described on page 9)

1 tablespoon extra virgin
  olive oil
Black pepper, ground fresh
  from the mill
7 slices good-quality, firm white
  toasting bread

1. Preheat oven to 400°.

2. If the *ricotta* is very moist, wrap it in cheesecloth, and hang it to drain over a sink or bowl for about 30 minutes. Put the *ricotta* and all the other ingredients, except for the bread, into the food processor, and chop to a creamy consistency.

3. Spread the bread out on a cookie sheet and bake in the preheated oven for a few minutes until it is toasted to a light gold.

4. Trim the bread slices of all the crust, cut each one in half, and then in half again, producing 4 squares from every slice. Spread the *ricotta* and anchovy cream over the bread and serve.

Ahead-of-time note ❦ You can prepare the *crostini* 2 or 3 hours in advance. Spread the *ricotta* and anchovy cream over the bread just before serving.

Hard-Boiled Eggs with Green Sauce

A SAVORY, attractive way to serve hard-boiled eggs whose yolks, after cooking, are blended with a piquant green sauce. *For 6 servings*

6 extra-large eggs

2 tablespoons extra virgin
olive oil

½ tablespoon chopped capers,
soaked and rinsed as
described on page 16
if packed in salt, drained if
in vinegar

1 tablespoon chopped parsley

3 flat anchovy fillets (preferably
the ones prepared at home

as described on page 9),
chopped very fine

¼ teaspoon chopped garlic

¼ teaspoon English or
Dijon-style mustard

Salt

A sweet red bell pepper,
diced not too fine

1. Put the eggs in cold water and bring to a boil. Cook at a slow boil for 10 minutes, then remove the eggs from the water and set aside to cool.

2. When cool, shell the eggs and cut them in half lengthwise. Carefully scoop out the yolks, taking care to leave the whites intact, and set aside the whites.

3. Put the yolks, olive oil, capers, parsley, anchovies, garlic, mustard, and a tiny pinch of salt in a bowl and, with a fork, mash all the ingredients into a creamy, uniform mixture. (If doing a large quantity for a party, you may want to blend them in a food processor.)

4. Divide the mixture into 12 equal parts and spoon into the cavities of the empty egg whites. Top with cubes of the diced red pepper.

Roasted Peppers and Anchovies

HERE, roasted peppers and anchovies steep together in olive oil, achieving a powerfully appetizing exchange of flavors: The peppers acquire spiciness while sharing their sweetness with the anchovies. The dish is most successful with the mellow anchovies one fillets and puts up in oil at home.

For 8 or more servings

Roasted Peppers and Anchovies (continued)

8 sweet red and/or yellow bell
  peppers
4 garlic cloves
16 large anchovy fillets (preferably the ones prepared at
  home as described on
  page 9)
Salt
Black pepper, ground fresh
  from the mill

Oregano
3 tablespoons capers, soaked
  and rinsed as described on
  page 16 if packed in salt,
  drained if packed in vinegar
¼ cup extra virgin olive oil

1. *Roasting the peppers:* The most delicious flavor and firmest consistency are attained when peppers are roasted over an open flame. It can be done on a charcoal-fired grill, in the broiler of an oven, or directly over the burner of a gas stove. The last is a very satisfactory method: The peppers can rest directly over the gas or, if you have one, on one of those grills or metal screens that are made specifically for cooking over gas burners. Whichever way you do them, roast the peppers until the skin is blackened on one side, then turn them with tongs until the skin is charred all over. Cook them as briefly as possible to keep the flesh firm. When done, put them in a plastic bag, twisting it tightly shut. As soon as they are cool enough to handle comfortably, remove the peppers from the bag and pull off the charred peel with your fingers.

2. Cut the peeled peppers lengthwise into broad strips about 2 inches wide. Discard all the seeds and pulpy inner core. Pat the strips as dry as possible with paper towels. Do not ever rinse them.

3. Mash the garlic cloves with a heavy knife handle, crushing them just enough to split them and to loosen the peel, which you will remove and discard.

4. Choose a serving dish that can accommodate the peppers 4 layers deep. Line the bottom with one layer. Over it place 4 or 5 anchovy fillets. Add a pinch of salt, a liberal grinding of black pepper, a light sprinkling of oregano, a few capers, and 1 garlic clove. Repeat the procedure until you have used all the ingredients. Over them pour the olive oil, adding more if necessary to cover the top layer of peppers.

5. Let the peppers marinate for at least 2 hours before serving. If you are serving them the same day, do not refrigerate them. If serving them a day or more than that, cover tightly with plastic film, and keep in the refrigerator until an hour or two before serving, allowing the dish to return to room tem-

perature before bringing it to the table. If keeping it over a day, after 24 hours remove and discard the garlic cloves.

Note ✹ Red and yellow peppers alone, roasted and skinned as described above, lightly salted, laid flat in a deep dish, and covered with extra virgin olive oil make a sensationally delicious appetizer. It would look most appealing on a buffet table, or take an important place in an assortment of dishes for a light lunch.

Roasted Eggplant with Peppers and Cucumber

WHAT MAKES THIS one of the freshest and most interesting ways to serve eggplant is the play of textures and flavors—the luscious softness of the roasted eggplant flesh against the crisp raw pepper, and the pungent eggplant flavor subsiding next to the cool, refreshing notes of the cucumber. It can be served as a salad appetizer, or as a spread on a thick slice of toast, or as a vegetable dish to accompany grilled meat.   *For 6 servings*

1½ pounds eggplant	1 tablespoon chopped parsley
½ teaspoon garlic chopped very fine	2 tablespoons extra virgin olive oil
½ cup sweet red bell pepper, diced into ⅓-inch cubes	2 tablespoons freshly squeezed lemon juice
¼ cup yellow bell pepper, diced like the red pepper	Black pepper, ground fresh from the mill
½ cup cucumber, diced like the bell pepper	Salt

1. Wash the eggplant and roast it over a charcoal grill or a gas burner or in the broiler of an oven. (See *roasting peppers,* page 54.) When the skin on the side next to the flame is blackened and the eggplant has become soft, turn it with a pair of tongs. When all the skin is charred and the entire eggplant is soft and looks as though it had deflated in the heat, remove from the fire and set aside to cool off.

2. When you can handle the eggplant comfortably, pick off as much of the skin as you can. If a few very small bits remain attached to the flesh it doesn't matter.

3. Cut the flesh into strips less than 1 inch wide. If there are many blackish seeds, remove them. Put the strips in a colander or a large strainer set

Roasted Eggplant (continued)

over a deep dish to allow all excess liquid to drain away for at least 30 minutes.

4. When you see no more liquid being shed, transfer the chopped eggplant to a mixing bowl and toss with all the remaining ingredients, except for the salt. Add salt just when ready to serve.

Marinated Carrot Sticks

For 4 servings

¼ pound carrots	Black pepper, ground fresh
1 garlic clove	from the mill
¼ teaspoon dried oregano	1 tablespoon red wine vinegar
Salt	Extra virgin olive oil

1. Peel the carrots, cut them into 2-inch lengths, and cook them in boiling salted water for about 10 minutes. The exact cooking time will vary depending on the thickness, youth, and freshness of the carrots. For this recipe, they must be cooked until tender, but firm because the marinade will soften them further. To cook them uniformly, put the thickest pieces into the water a few moments before the thin, tapered ones.

2. Drain and cut the carrots lengthwise into sticks about ¼ inch thick. Place in a small, but deep serving dish.

3. Mash the garlic clove with a heavy knife handle, crushing it just enough to split it and to loosen the skin, which you will remove and discard. Bury the peeled clove among the carrot sticks. Add the oregano, salt, a few grindings of pepper, the wine vinegar, and just enough olive oil to cover the carrots.

4. If serving them the same day, allow the carrots to steep in their marinade for at least 3 hours at room temperature. If making them for another day, cover tightly with plastic wrap, and refrigerate until 2 hours before serving, allowing them to come to room temperature before bringing to the table. If keeping for longer than a day, remove the garlic after 24 hours.

Carciofi alla Romana—Artichokes, Roman Style

THE STOUT, globe artichoke common to North American markets is but one of several varieties grown in Italy. It is, however, precisely the kind that

Romans use to prepare one of the glories of the *antipasto* table, *i carciofi alla romana,* one of the tenderest and most enjoyable of all artichoke dishes. In it, the artichoke is braised whole, with the stem on, and served thus, upside down, at room temperature. When you step into a Roman *trattoria,* if it is artichoke season, you will see them displayed on great platters bristling with their upended stems. The stem, when carefully trimmed, is the most delectable and concentrated part of the entire vegetable. The only exacting part of this recipe is, in fact, the trimming away of all the tough, inedible parts that usually make eating artichokes a chore. When you master the preparation of *carciofi alla romana,* you will be able to apply the same sound principles to a broad variety of other artichoke dishes.   *For 4 servings*

4 large globe artichokes
½ lemon
3 tablespoons parsley chopped
    very fine
1½ teaspoons garlic chopped
    very fine

6 to 8 fresh mint leaves,
    chopped fine
Salt
Black pepper, ground fresh
    from the mill
½ cup extra virgin olive oil

1. In preparing any artichoke it is essential to discard all the tough, inedible leaves and portions of leaves. When doing it for the first time it may seem wasteful to throw so much away, but it is far more wasteful to cook something that can't be eaten. Begin by bending back the outer leaves, pulling them down toward the base of the artichoke, and snapping them off just before you reach the base. Do not take the paler bottom end of the leaf off because at that

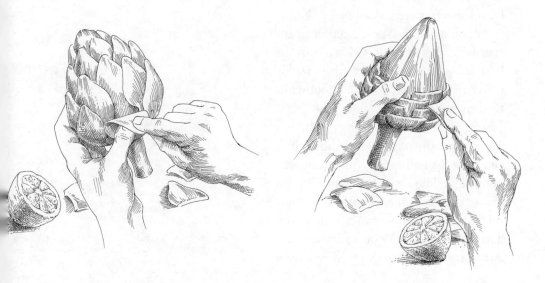

point it is tender and quite edible. As you take more leaves off and get deeper into the artichoke, the tender part at which the leaves will snap will be farther and farther from the base. Keep pulling off single leaves until you expose a central cone of leaves that are green only at the tip, and whose paler, whitish base is at least 1½ inches high.

Slice at least an inch off the top of that central cone to eliminate all of the tough green part. Take the half lemon and rub the cut portions of the artichoke, squeezing juice over them to keep them from discoloring.

Look into the exposed center of the artichoke, where you will see at the bottom very small leaves with prickly tips curving inward. Cut off all those little leaves and scrape away the fuzzy "choke" beneath them, being careful not to cut away any of the tender bottom. If you have a small knife with a rounded point, it will be easier for you to do this part of the trimming. Return to the outside of the artichoke and, where you have snapped off the outer leaves, pare away any of the tough green part that

remains. Be careful not to cut off the stem, which, for this dish, must remain attached.

Turn the artichoke upside down and you will notice, inspecting the bottom of the stem, that the stem consists of a whitish core surrounded by a layer of green. The green part is tough, the white, when cooked, soft and delicious, so you must pare away the green, leaving the white intact. Pare the stem thus all the way to the base of the artichoke, being careful not to detach it. Rub all the exposed cut surfaces with lemon juice.

2. In a bowl mix the chopped parsley, garlic, and mint leaves, and add salt and a few grindings of pepper. Set aside one-third of the mixture. Press the rest into the cavity of each artichoke, rubbing it well into the inner sides.

3. Choose a heavy-bottomed pot with a tight-fitting lid, such as enameled cast iron, tall enough to accommodate the artichokes, which are to go in standing. Put in the artichokes, tops facing down, stems pointing up. Rub the remaining herb and garlic mixture over the outside of the artichokes. Add all the olive oil, plus enough water to come up and cover one-third of the leaves, but *not* the stems.

4. Take a sufficient length of paper towels that, when doubled up, will completely cover the top of the pot. Or a muslin cloth will do as well. Soak the towels or cloth in water, and place over the top of the pot, covering it completely. Put the lid over the towels or cloth, then pull back over the lid any portion of them hanging down the sides of the pot.

5. Turn on the heat to medium and cook for 35 to 40 minutes. The artichokes are done when a fork easily pierces the thick part between the stem and the heart. Cooking times may vary depending on the freshness of the artichokes. If they are tough and take long to cook, you may have to add 2 or 3 tablespoons of water from time to time. If, on the other hand, they are very fresh and are cooked before all the water has simmered away, uncover the pot, remove the towels or muslin, and turn up the heat, quickly boiling away the

Artichokes, Roman Style (continued)

water. The edges of the leaves resting on the bottom of the pot may turn brown, but do not worry, it improves their flavor.

6. When done, transfer the artichokes to a serving platter, setting them down with their stems pointing up. Reserve the olive oil and other juices from the pot: They are to be poured over the artichokes only just before serving. If you were to pour the oil and juices over the artichoke when it is still hot, it would soak them up, making the artichoke greasy and sodden, and depriving it of the sauce with which later you want to accompany it.

The ideal serving temperature is when the artichokes are no longer hot, but have not yet cooled completely, when they are still faintly touched by the waning warmth of cooking. But they are excellent even later, at room temperature, as they are usually served in Rome. Plan to use them the same day, however; like all cooked greens, their flavor deteriorates in the refrigerator.

Mushroom, Parmesan Cheese, and White Truffle Salad

ONE OF THE happiest coincidences of autumn in Italy is the contemporaneous appearance of white truffles and wild mushrooms. Among the best things it leads to, and easiest to prepare, is this luxurious salad. Fortunately, the basic salad of mushrooms and *parmigiano-reggiano* is so good that one needn't forego it just because truffles may not be available or are too expensive. Just skip the truffles. If you can obtain fresh *porcini,* the wild *boletus edulis* mushroom, and if they are firm and sound (not wormy), by all means use them. If you cannot, of the cultivated mushrooms, the brown-skinned variety known as *cremini* is the most desirable to use because its flavor more closely recalls that of *porcini.* But if *cremini* are not available either, good-quality white button mushrooms are quite acceptable. What there can be no substitute for is the *parmigiano-reggiano* cheese and the olive oil. The latter should be a fruity extra virgin olive oil, if possible from the central Italian regions of Umbria or Tuscany. The oil absorbs flavor from the mushrooms, cheese, and the truffle, if any, and wiping the plate clean at the end with a good, crusty piece of bread may be the best part of all.

For 4 servings

½ pound firm, sound fresh
    mushrooms (see introduc-
    tory note above)
1 to 2 tablespoons freshly
    squeezed lemon juice
⅔ cup celery cut crosswise into
    ¼-inch slices
⅔ cup *parmigiano-reggiano*
    cheese, shaved into flakes
    with a vegetable peeler or
    on a *mandoline*

OPTIONAL: a 1-ounce or larger
    white truffle
3 tablespoons extra virgin olive
    oil (see introductory note
    above)
Salt
Black pepper, ground fresh
    from the mill

1. Wash the mushrooms quickly under cold running water. Do not let them soak. Pat them thoroughly dry with a cloth or paper towels. Cut them into very thin slices, about ⅛ inch thick, slicing them lengthwise so that the center slices have a part of both the stem and the cap.

2. Put the sliced mushrooms in a shallow bowl or platter and toss immediately with the lemon juice to keep them white. Add the sliced celery and the flakes of Parmesan cheese. If you own a truffle slicer, use it to slice the optional white truffle very thin into the bowl. Otherwise, use a vegetable peeler in a light sawing motion.

3. Toss with the olive oil, salt, and pepper. Serve promptly.

Tomatoes Stuffed with Shrimp

For 6 servings

6 large, round, ripe firm
    tomatoes
¾ pound small raw shrimp in
    the shell
1 tablespoon red wine vinegar
Salt
Mayonnaise, made as directed
    on page 40, using the yolk
    of 1 large egg, ½ cup
    vegetable oil, and 2½ to 3

tablespoons freshly
    squeezed lemon juice
1½ tablespoons capers, soaked
    and rinsed as described on
    page 16 if packed in salt,
    drained if packed in vinegar
1 teaspoon English or Dijon-
    style mustard
Parsley

1. Slice the tops off the tomatoes. With a small spoon, possibly a serrated grapefruit spoon, scoop out all the seeds, and remove some of the dividing

Tomatoes Stuffed with Shrimp (continued)

walls, leaving three or four large sections. Don't squeeze the tomato at any time. Sprinkle with salt, and turn the tomatoes upside down on a platter to let excess liquid drain out.

2. Rinse the shrimp in cold water. Fill a pot with 2 quarts of water. Add the vinegar and 1 tablespoon of salt, and bring to a boil. Drop in the shrimp and cook for just 1 minute (or more, depending on their size) after the water returns to a boil. Drain, shell, and devein the shrimp. Set aside to cool completely.

3. Set aside 6 of the best-looking, most regularly formed shrimp. Chop the rest not too fine, put them in a bowl, and mix them with the mayonnaise, capers, and mustard.

4. Shake off the excess liquid from the tomatoes without squeezing them. Stuff to the top with the shrimp mixture. Garnish each tomato with a whole shrimp and 1 or 2 parsley leaves. Serve at room temperature or even just slightly chilled.

Tomatoes Stuffed with Tuna

For 6 servings

6 large, round, ripe firm
   tomatoes
Salt
2 seven-ounce cans imported
   Italian tuna packed in olive
   oil
Mayonnaise, made as directed
   on page 40, using the yolk
   of 1 large egg, ½ cup
   vegetable oil, and 2 table-

spoons freshly squeezed
   lemon juice
2 teaspoons English or Dijon-
   style mustard
1½ tablespoons capers, soaked
   and rinsed as described on
   page 16 if packed in salt,
   drained if packed in vinegar
Garnishes as suggested below

1. Prepare the tomatoes for stuffing as described in Step 1 of the recipe for Tomatoes Stuffed with Shrimp on page 61.

2. Put the tuna in a mixing bowl and mash it to a pulp with a fork. Add the mayonnaise, holding back 1 or 2 tablespoons, the mustard, and capers. Using the fork, mix to a uniform consistency. Taste and correct for salt.

3. Shake off the excess liquid from the tomatoes without squeezing them. Stuff to the top with the tuna mixture.

4. Spread the remaining mayonnaise on top of the tomatoes, and garnish in any of the following ways: with an olive slice, a strip of red or yellow

pepper, a ring of tiny capers, or one or two parsley leaves. Serve at room temperature or slightly chilled.

In Carpione—Fried Marinated Fresh Sardines (or other fish)

Carpione, a magnificent variety of trout found only in Lake Garda, used to be so abundant that, when too many were caught to be consumed immediately, they were fried and then put up in a marinade of vinegar, onion, and herbs that preserved them for several days. *Carpione* has become so rare that few people today have seen one, let alone tasted its extraordinary flesh, but the practice has survived, applied to a large variety of fish, of both salt and fresh water. Similar methods are used in Venice, where they add raisins and pine nuts to the marinade and call it *in saor,* and in southern Italy, where it is called *a scapece* and the herb used is mint.

    The tastiest of all fish for the *in carpione* treatment is, for me, the fresh sardine. Unfortunately, one doesn't see it often in North American markets. Any fish, however, that can be fried whole, such as smelts, or a fillet of flat fish, such as sole, lends itself to this delectable preparation. Those who eat eel will find it particularly well suited to putting up *in carpione.* So, I suspect, would catfish, but I have never tried it.   *For 4 to 6 servings*

1 pound fresh sardines OR
    smelts OR other small fish
    OR ¾ pound fish fillets
Vegetable oil
An 8- to 9-inch skillet
½ cup flour, spread on a plate

Salt
Black pepper, ground fresh
    from the mill
1 cup onion sliced very thin
½ cup wine vinegar
4 whole bay leaves

    1. If using whole fish, gut it, scale it, and cut off the heads and the center back fins. If using fillets, cut them into 4 to 6 pieces. Wash the fish or fillets in cold water, and pat thoroughly dry with paper towels.

    2. Pour enough oil into the skillet to come 1 inch up its sides, and turn the heat on to medium-high. When the oil is hot, dredge both sides of the fish in the flour, and slip it into the pan. Do not crowd the pan. If necessary, you can fry the fish in two or more successive batches.

    3. Fry for about 2 minutes on each side until both sides have a nice brown crust.

    4. Using a slotted spoon or spatula, transfer the fish to a shallow serv-

Fried Marinated Fresh Sardines (continued)

ing platter, sprinkling it with salt and a few grindings of pepper. Choose a platter just large enough for the fish to form a single layer without overlapping.

5. When all the fish is fried, pour out and discard half the oil in the pan. Put the sliced onion into the same skillet and turn on the heat to medium-low. Cook at a gentle pace, stirring occasionally, until the onion is tender, but not colored.

6. Add the vinegar, turn up the heat, stir rapidly, and let it bubble for half a minute. Pour all the contents of the skillet over the fish. Top with the bay leaves.

7. Cover the platter with foil or with another platter. Allow the fish to steep in the marinade for at least 12 hours before serving. Turn it over once or twice during that period. It does not need to be refrigerated if you are going to have it within 24 hours. In the refrigerator it will keep for several days. Before bringing it to the table, remove it from the refrigerator an hour or two in advance to permit it to come to room temperature.

Cold Trout in Orange Marinade

OF THE MANY WAYS the Italian tradition has of putting up fried or sautéed fish in a marinade (see page 63), the most gently fragrant and the least acidic is the one given below, consisting of orange, lemon, and vermouth. It goes best with trout or other fine, freshwater fish. *For 6 servings*

3 trout, perch, or other fine freshwater fish, about ¾ pound each, gutted and scaled, but with heads and tails left on

½ cup extra virgin olive oil

½ cup flour, spread on a plate

2 tablespoons onion chopped very fine

1 cup dry white Italian vermouth

2 tablespoons chopped orange peel, using only the rind,

not the white pith beneath it

½ cup freshly squeezed orange juice

The freshly squeezed juice of 1 lemon

Salt

Black pepper, ground fresh from the mill

1½ tablespoons chopped parsley

OPTIONAL GARNISH: unpeeled orange slices

1. Wash the gutted, scaled fish in cold water and pat thoroughly dry with paper towels.

2. Put the oil in a skillet and turn on the heat to medium. When the oil is hot, lightly dredge both sides of the fish in flour and slip into the skillet. Don't overcrowd the pan; if all the fish does not fit loosely at one time, cook it in batches, dredging it in flour only at the moment you are ready to put it into the pan.

3. Brown the fish well on one side, then turn it and do the other, calculating about 5 minutes the first side and 4 minutes the second. Using a slotted spatula or spoon, transfer the fish when browned to a deep serving dish broad or long enough to accommodate all of it without overlapping. Do not pour out the oil in the skillet.

4. With a well-sharpened knife, make two or three skin-deep diagonal cuts on both sides of the fish. Be careful not to tear the skin, and avoid cutting into the flesh.

5. Put the chopped onion into the skillet that still contains the oil in which you cooked the fish. Turn on the heat to medium and cook the onion until it becomes colored a pale gold.

6. Add the vermouth and the orange peel. Let the vermouth bubble gently for about 30 seconds, stir, then add the orange juice, lemon juice, salt, and a few grindings of pepper. Let everything bubble for about half a minute, stirring two or three times. Add the chopped parsley, stir once or twice, then pour the entire contents of the skillet over the fish in the serving dish.

7. Allow the fish to steep in its marinade at room temperature for at least 6 hours before refrigerating. Plan to serve the fish no sooner than the following day. Do serve it within 3 days at the latest to enjoy its flavor at its freshest. Take it out of the refrigerator at least 2 hours before bringing to the table to allow it to come to room temperature. Before serving, garnish it, if you like, with fresh slices of orange.

Gamberetti all'Olio e Limone—Poached Shrimp with Olive Oil and Lemon Juice

WHEN VERY GOOD SHRIMP is simmered briefly, then steeped in olive oil and lemon juice and served before ever seeing the inside of the refrigerator, it makes one of those appetizers in the Italian seafood repertory that is as sublime in taste as it is in its simplicity. You'll find it on the menu of virtually every fish restaurant on the northern Adriatic. As in so many other Italian dishes where the principal elements are so few, the success of the preparation depends on the quality of its main ingredients: here, the shrimp and the olive oil. The first should be the juiciest and sweetest your fish market can provide, the latter the best estate-bottled Italian extra virgin olive oil you can find.

For 6 servings

1 stalk celery
1 carrot, peeled
Salt
2 tablespoons wine vinegar
1½ pounds choice small raw
    shrimp in the shell (if only
    larger shrimp are available,
    see note below)

½ cup extra virgin olive oil
¼ cup freshly squeezed
    lemon juice
Black pepper, ground fresh
    from the mill

1. Put the celery, carrot, 1 tablespoon of salt, and the vinegar in 3 quarts of water and bring to a boil.

2. When the water has boiled gently for 10 minutes, add the shrimp in their shells. If very tiny, the shrimp will be cooked just moments after the water returns to a boil. If medium-to-large, they will take 2 to 3 minutes longer.

3. When cooked, drain the shrimp, shell, and devein. If using medium-to-large shrimp, slice them lengthwise in half.

4. Put the shrimp in a shallow bowl and, while they are still warm, add the olive oil, lemon juice, and salt and pepper to taste. Toss well and allow to steep at room temperature for 1 hour before bringing to the table. Serve with good crusty bread to help wipe the plate clean of its delicious juices.

Note ✽ The dish is far better if never chilled, but if you are compelled to, you can prepare it a day in advance and refrigerate it under plastic wrap. Always return it to full room temperature before serving.

Insalata Russa—Shrimp Salad with Assorted Vegetables

IF YOU ARE SUSPICIOUS, as I am, of dishes that look too pretty, this is one dish whose lovely appearance you can make allowances for, because it tastes as good as it looks. It is, moreover, very simple to execute. It does take time to

clean, boil, and dice all the vegetables, but it can all be prepared and completed well in advance, whenever you feel like it and whenever you have the time. The only plausible explanation for this salad being called "Russian"—*russa*—is the presence of beets. *For 6 servings*

1 pound medium shrimp in the shell
1 tablespoon plus 2 teaspoons wine vinegar
¼ pound green beans
2 medium potatoes
2 medium carrots
⅓ of a 10-ounce package frozen peas, thawed
6 small canned whole red beets, drained
2 tablespoons capers, soaked and rinsed as described on page 16 if packed in salt, drained if in vinegar

2 tablespoons fine cucumber pickles, preferably *cornichons*, cut up
3 tablespoons extra virgin olive oil
Salt
Mayonnaise, made as directed on page 40, using the yolks of 3 eggs, 1¾ cups extra virgin olive oil (see note below), 3 tablespoons freshly squeezed lemon juice, and ⅜ teaspoon salt

Note ❀ Here is one of the uncommon occasions when the snappy flavor of good olive oil in mayonnaise is more desirable than the mildness of vegetable oil. Its density is also useful in pulling together the ingredients of the salad, making it more compact.

Shrimp Salad (continued)

1. Wash the shrimp. Bring water to a boil, add salt, and as it returns to a boil, put in the shrimp in their shells with 1 tablespoon of the vinegar. Cook for 4 minutes, less if the shrimp are small, then drain. When cool enough to handle, shell, and devein. Set the shrimp aside.

2. Snap both ends off the green beans and wash them in cold water. Bring water to a boil, add salt, drop in the beans, and drain them as soon as they are tender, but still firm.

3. Wash the potatoes with their skins on, put them in a pot with enough water to cover amply, bring to a boil, and cook until they are easily pierced with a fork. Drain and peel while still hot.

4. Peel the carrots, and cook them exactly as you cooked the beans, until tender, but still firm.

5. Drop the peas into salted, boiling water and cook not much longer than 1 minute. Drain and set aside.

6. Pat the beets as dry as possible with paper towels. When the cooked vegetables have cooled off, set aside a small quantity of each, including the beets but excepting the potatoes, which you will use later for the garnish. Cut up the rest as follows: the green beans into ⅜-inch lengths; the potatoes, carrots, and beets diced into ⅜-inch cubes. Put all the cut-up and diced vegetables, including the capers and cucumber pickles, in a mixing bowl.

7. Set aside half the shrimp. Dice the rest and add them to the bowl with the vegetables. Add the olive oil, 2 teaspoons wine vinegar, and salt and toss thoroughly. Add half the mayonnaise, and fold it into the mixture, distributing it evenly to coat the ingredients well. Taste and correct for salt.

8. Turn the contents of the bowl over onto a serving platter, preferably round. Shape it into a shallow, flat-topped, oval mound, pressing it with a rubber spatula to even it off and make the surface smooth. Spread the remaining mayonnaise over the mound, covering the entire surface and using the spatula to make it smooth.

9. Use the reserved vegetables and shrimp to decorate the mound in any way that you find attractive. One suggestion: Place a thin carrot disk on the center of the mound, and a pea in the center of the carrot. Use some of the shrimp to make a circle around the carrot, placing them on their side, nestling the tail of one over the head of the other. Over the rest of the mound scatter flowers, using carrots for the center button, beets for the petals, and green beans for the stems. Decorate the sides of the mound with the remaining shrimp, imbedding their bellies in the salad, heads toward the top, tails toward the bottom, backs arching away.

Ahead-of-time note ✳ You can make the salad up to 2 days in advance, refrigerating it under plastic wrap, but take it out in sufficient time to be able to serve it not too much colder than room temperature. Caution: If you are preparing the dish several hours or even a day in advance, use the beets in your decorative pattern at the last moment because their color tends to run.

Salmon Foam

LONG BEFORE the Norwegians raised salmon on farms and made it a commonplace ingredient in Italian markets, where it now costs far less than locally caught fish, it was better known to Italians in its canned form. Just as they have succeeded in elevating the status of canned tuna, Italian cooks produce excellent things with canned salmon, of which the recipe given here is one of the best examples.   *For 6 servings*

15 ounces canned salmon
¼ cup extra virgin olive oil
2 tablespoons freshly squeezed
    lemon juice
Salt

Black pepper, ground fresh
    from the mill
1½ cups very cold heavy
    whipping cream

1. Drain the salmon and look it over carefully, picking out any bones and bits of skin. Using a fork, crumble it in a mixing bowl. Add the oil, lemon juice, a pinch of salt, and a few grindings of pepper, and beat them with the fork into the salmon until you have obtained a smooth, homogeneous mixture.

2. Put the whipping cream into a cold mixing bowl and whip it until it is stiff. Gently fold the cream into the salmon mixture until it is wholly a part of it. Refrigerate covered with plastic wrap.

Chill for 2 hours before serving, but not longer than 24.

Optional garnish ✳ Spoon individual servings onto *radicchio* leaves, shaping the salmon foam into small, rounded mounds. Top each mound with a black olive—preferably not the Greek variety, but a milder one, such as the ones from California, and align half slices of lemon on either side of the olive, embedding them in the salmon.

Poached Tuna and Potato Roll

HUMBLE CANNED TUNA here undergoes a transformation into a dish as elegant in texture and flavor as it is in appearance. It is combined with mashed potatoes and cheese, shaped into a long roll, then poached in liquid lightly flavored with vegetables and white wine. When cold, it is served sliced, topped by caper mayonnaise.   *For 6 to 8 servings*

1 medium potato
2 seven-ounce cans imported
    Italian tuna packed in olive
    oil, drained
¼ cup freshly grated *parmi-
    giano-reggiano* cheese

1 whole egg plus the white
    of 1 egg
Black pepper, ground fresh
    from the mill
Cheesecloth

FOR THE POACHING LIQUID

½ medium yellow onion,
    sliced thin
1 stalk celery
1 carrot

The stems only of 6 parsley
    sprigs
Salt
1 cup dry white wine

MAYONNAISE MADE AS DIRECTED ON PAGE 40, USING

The yolk of 1 large egg
⅔ cup vegetable oil
2 tablespoons freshly squeezed
    lemon juice

½ teaspoon salt

AND INCORPORATING

2 tablespoons coarsely chopped
    capers, soaked and rinsed as
    described on page 16 if
    packed in salt, drained if in
    vinegar

1 anchovy fillet, chopped
    very fine

FOR THE GARNISH

Slivered black olives

1. Boil the potato with its peel on until it is tender. Drain, peel, and mash through a food mill or a potato ricer.

2. Mash the tuna in a bowl. Add the grated cheese, the whole egg plus the 1 white, a few grindings of pepper, and the mashed potato. Combine with the tuna into a homogeneous mixture.

3. Moisten a piece of cheesecloth, wring it until it is just damp, and lay it out flat on a work counter. Place the tuna mixture at one end of the cloth, and shape it with your hands into a salami-like roll, about 2½ inches in diameter. Wrap it in the cheesecloth, winding it around three or four times. Tie each end securely with string.

4. *To make the poaching liquid:* Put the sliced onion, celery stalk, carrot, parsley stems, a pinch of salt, and the wine in a saucepan, oval casserole, or a fish poacher. Put in the tuna roll and add enough water to cover by at least 1 inch. Cover the pot and bring to a boil. When the liquid boils, adjust the heat so that it subsides to the gentlest of simmers. Cook for 45 minutes.

5. Remove the tuna roll, taking care not to split it and lifting it up from both ends at the same time with spatulas. Unwrap it as soon as you are able to handle it. Set aside to cool completely.

Ahead-of-time note: ❀ The roll can be finished up to this point one or two days in advance. When it has cooled down completely, cover tightly with plastic wrap and refrigerate. Take it out in time for it to come to room temperature before proceeding with the next step.

6. Make the mayonnaise as directed above. When it is done, mix in the chopped capers and anchovy.

7. Cut the cold tuna roll into slices less than ½ inch thick. Arrange the slices on a serving platter, overlapping them slightly. Spread the mayonnaise over the tuna slices and garnish with the slivered olives. One way of doing it is to place the olives over the middle of each slice, running them in a straight line from one end of the platter to the other.

Poached Tuna and Spinach Roll

HERE IS ANOTHER preparation in which everyday canned tuna is endowed with a lovely presentation and flavor to match. (Also see Poached Tuna and Potato Roll on page 70.)   *For 8 servings*

Poached Tuna and Spinach Roll (continued)

1½ pounds fresh spinach

Salt

A 3½-ounce can imported Italian tuna packed in olive oil, drained

4 flat anchovy fillets (preferably the ones prepared at home as described on page 9), chopped fine

1½ slices good-quality white bread, trimmed of the crust

1½ cups milk

2 whole eggs

1½ cups freshly grated *parmigiano-reggiano* cheese

3 tablespoons fine, dry, unflavored bread crumbs

Black pepper, ground fresh from the mill

Cheesecloth

⅓ cup extra virgin olive oil

2 teaspoons freshly squeezed lemon juice

FOR THE GARNISH

1 lemon, sliced thin

1 small carrot, sliced into very thin rounds

1. Pull the spinach leaves from their stems and soak them in a basin in several changes of cold water until they are totally free of soil.

2. Cook the spinach in a covered pan with just the moisture clinging to the leaves and 2 teaspoons of salt to keep it green. When very tender, after 10 minutes of cooking or more, depending on how fresh and young the spinach is, drain it and let it cool.

3. When cool, take a fistful of spinach at a time, and squeeze it firmly until no more liquid runs out. When all the spinach has been squeezed dry, chop it very fine, and put it in a mixing bowl.

4. Chop the tuna and add it to the bowl, together with the anchovies.

5. Put the bread in a deep dish and pour the milk over it. Let it soak.

6. Break the eggs into the bowl with the spinach and tuna. Add the Parmesan, bread crumbs, salt, and liberal grindings of pepper.

7. Squeeze the soggy bread in your hand, letting all the milk run back into the dish. Add the bread to the bowl. Mix thoroughly into a homogeneous mixture.

8. Follow the directions in step 3 of the preceding recipe on page 71 to shape the tuna roll and wrap it in cheesecloth.

9. Put the roll in an oval pot or a fish poacher in which it will fit rather snugly. Add enough water to cover the roll, cover the pot, and turn on the heat to medium. When the water comes to a boil, adjust heat so that it maintains a steady, gentle simmer, and cook for 35 minutes.

10. Remove the roll from the pot, taking care not to split it and lifting it

up from both ends at the same time with spatulas. Let the roll cool slightly, then unwind and remove the cheesecloth. Let the roll cool completely to room temperature but do not refrigerate because it would adversely affect the flavor of the spinach.

11. Cut into slices less than ½ inch thick, and arrange the slices on a platter so they overlap slightly, like roof shingles. Drizzle with olive oil and lemon juice. Over each green slice place a thin slice of lemon with the skin on and on each lemon slice a tiny carrot disk.

⚙ *Warm Appetizers* ⚙

Bruschetta—Roman Garlic Bread

DIRECTLY from the Latin verb and into the modern vernacular of Rome comes the verb *bruscare,* which means to toast (as in a slice of bread), or roast (as with coffee beans); hence *bruschetta,* whose most important component, aside from the grilled bread itself, is olive oil.

On those brisk days that bridge the passage from fall to winter, and signal the release of the year's freshly pressed olive oil, toasting bread over a smoky fire and soaking it with spicy, laser-green newly minted oil is a practice probably as old as Rome itself. From Rome *bruschetta* spread through the rest of central Italy—Umbria, Tuscany, Abruzzi—and acquired other ingredients: invariably now, garlic and, here and there, tomatoes. Two versions of *bruschetta* follow.

Basic Bruschetta

For 6 to 12 servings

6 garlic cloves
12 slices good, thick-crusted
    bread, ½ to ¾ inch thick,
    3 to 4 inches wide
Extra virgin olive oil, fruity and
    young

Salt
Black pepper, ground fresh
    from the mill

1. Preheat a broiler or, even better, light a charcoal fire.
2. Mash the garlic cloves with a heavy knife handle, crushing them just enough to split them and to loosen the peel, which you will remove and discard.

Basic Bruschetta (continued)

3. Grill the bread to a golden brown on both sides.

4. As the bread comes off the grill, while it is still hot, rub one side of each slice with the mashed garlic.

5. Put the bread on a platter, garlicky side facing up, and pour a thin stream of olive oil over each slice, enough to soak it lightly.

6. Sprinkle with salt and a few grindings of pepper. Serve while still warm.

The Tomato Version

All the ingredients given in the recipe above plus

8 fresh, ripe plum tomatoes

8 to 12 fresh basil leaves OR a few pinches oregano

1. Wash the tomatoes, split them in half lengthwise, and with the tip of a paring knife pick out all the seeds you can. Dice the tomatoes into ½-inch cubes.

2. Wash the basil leaves, shake them thoroughly dry, and tear them into small pieces. (Omit this step if using oregano.)

3. After rubbing the hot grilled bread with garlic as directed in recipe above, top it with diced tomato, sprinkle with basil or oregano, add salt and pepper, and lightly drizzle each slice with olive oil. Serve while still warm.

Carciofi alla Giudia—Crisp-Fried Whole Artichokes

OF THE SUBSTANTIAL achievements of Jewish cooks in Italy, none is more justly celebrated than the fried artichokes of Rome, whose crisp outer leaves, looking like those of a dried chrysanthemum, curl around the tender, succulent interior.

The cooking is done in two stages. The first more slowly, at a lower temperature, giving the heat time to cook the artichokes thoroughly. The second with hotter oil, which is then excited by a sprinkling of cold water, to give the outer leaves their crisp finish. *For 6 servings*

6 medium artichokes, as young and fresh as possible	Black pepper, ground fresh from the mill
½ lemon	Vegetable oil
Salt	

1. Trim the artichokes exactly as directed in Step 1 of Artichokes, Roman Style, page 57, except that here you will cut off the stem, all but for a short stump. As you snap off the hard outer leaves, keep them progressively longer at the base, giving the artichoke's core the look of a thick, fleshy rosebud. Remember to cut off the inedible, tough tops, and to rub all cut parts with juice squeezed from the half lemon to keep them from turning black.

2. Turn the artichokes bottoms up, gently spread their leaves outward, and press them against a board or other work surface, flattening them as much as possible without going so far as to crack them. Turn right side up and sprinkle with salt and a few grindings of pepper.

3. Choose a deep skillet or sauté pan and pour enough oil into it to come 1½ inches up the sides of the pan. Turn the heat on to medium, and when the oil is hot slip in the artichokes, their bottoms facing up. Cook for 5 minutes or so, then turn them over. Turn them again, from time to time, as they cook. They are done when the thick part of the bottom feels tender at the pricking of a fork. It may take 15 minutes or longer, depending on how young and fresh the artichokes are. Regulate the heat to make sure the oil is not overheating and frying the artichokes too quickly.

4. When the artichokes are done, transfer them to a board or other work surface, their bottoms facing up, and press them with a wooden spoon or a spatula to flatten them some more.

5. Turn on the heat to high under the pan. Have a bowl with cold water near you by the stove. As soon as the oil is very hot, slip in the artichokes, their bottoms facing up. After frying them for just a few minutes, turn them over, dip your hand in the bowl of water, and sprinkle the artichokes. Stay at arm's length from the pan because the oil will sizzle and spatter.

6. As soon as the oil stops sputtering, transfer the artichokes face down to paper towels or to a cooling rack to drain. Serve with the leaves facing up. They are at their best when piping hot, but they are quite nice even a little later, at room temperature. Do not refrigerate or reheat.

Baked Stuffed Mushroom Caps

A KEY INGREDIENT in the stuffing of these mushrooms—which also has *pancetta,* garlic, egg, and marjoram—is reconstituted dried *porcini* mushrooms. As in many other recipes, their presence helps to transform the shy flavor of cultivated mushrooms into the effusive, dense one of the wild *boletus edulis.*   *For 6 servings*

A packet dried *porcini* mushrooms OR, if bought loose, about 1 ounce

¼ heaping cup crumb (the fresh, soft, crustless part of bread)

¼ cup milk

1 pound fresh, stuffing (large) mushrooms

¼ pound *pancetta*

4 flat anchovy fillets (preferably the ones prepared at home, as described on page 9)

4 fresh basil leaves, torn by hand into small pieces

A small garlic clove, chopped fine

1 egg

3 tablespoons parsley chopped fine

⅛ teaspoon dried marjoram OR ¼ teaspoon chopped fresh

Salt

Black pepper, ground fresh from the mill

½ cup dried, unflavored bread crumbs

⅓ cup extra virgin olive oil

1. Put the dried mushrooms in 2 cups of lukewarm water and let them soak for at least 30 minutes.

2. Put the soft crumb and milk together in a small bowl or deep dish and set aside to soak.

3. Wash the fresh mushrooms rapidly under cold running water, and pat them thoroughly dry with paper towels, taking care not to bruise them. Gently detach the stems without breaking the caps.

4. Line a wire strainer with a paper towel and place it over a small saucepan. Lift the *porcini* from their soak, but do not discard the liquid. Pour the liquid into the strainer, filtering it through the paper towel into the saucepan. Rinse the reconstituted *porcini* in several changes of cold water, making sure no grit remains attached to them. Add them to the saucepan and cook, uncovered, over lively heat until all the liquid has boiled away.

5. Preheat oven to 400°.

6. Chop the cooked reconstituted *porcini,* the fresh mushroom stems, the

pancetta, and anchovy fillets all very fine. It can be done by hand or in a food processor.

7. Put all the above chopped ingredients in a mixing bowl, adding the basil leaves and chopped garlic. Take the milk-soaked crumb into your hand, squeeze it gently until it stops dripping, and add it to the bowl. Break the egg into the bowl. Add the parsley, marjoram, salt, and several grindings of pepper, and thoroughly mix all the ingredients in the bowl with a fork until they are combined into a smooth, homogeneous mixture. Taste and correct for salt and pepper.

8. Stuff the mushroom caps with the mixture from the bowl. Put enough stuffing into each cap to make a rounded mound. Sprinkle the mounds with bread crumbs.

9. Choose a baking dish that will accommodate all the mushroom caps side by side in a single layer. Smear the bottom and sides of the dish with a little of the olive oil. Put the mushrooms in the dish, stuffed sides facing up. Crisscross the mushrooms with a thin stream of olive oil, lightly daubing the stuffing.

10. Place the dish in the uppermost level of the preheated oven and bake for 30 minutes, or until the mounds of stuffing have formed a light crust. After removing from the oven, allow them to settle for several minutes before serving.

Bagna Caôda—Hot Piedmontese Dip for Raw Vegetables

THE FLAVORS and sensations of the winter season are nowhere more affectingly celebrated than at a Piedmontese table when the *bagna caôda* is brought out: They are expressed by the austere taste of the cardoons, artichokes, scallions, and Jerusalem artichokes and others that form the classic assortment of dipping greens; by the cold of the raw vegetable softened by the heat of the sauce; by the spritzy, astringent impact of the newly racked wine that is its traditional accompaniment.

Caôda is the Piedmontese word for hot, and heat, in the sense of temperature, not spice, is an essential feature of this sauce. In Piedmont, table burners fed by candles keep *bagna caôda* at the desirable temperature, but any contraption whose purpose is to keep food hot, whether it is fed by candles, electricity, or canned heat, will do the job. Nonetheless, for esthetic reasons if for no others, an earthenware pot is what you want for your *bagna caôda* and, if you don't already own one, there may be no better reason than this to get one. *For 6 to 8 servings*

Hot Piedmontese Dip (continued)

¾ cup extra virgin olive oil

3 tablespoons butter

2 teaspoons garlic chopped very fine

8 to 10 anchovy fillets (preferably the ones prepared at home as described on page 9), chopped fine

Salt

1. Choose a pot over which you will subsequently be able to rest, double-boiler fashion, the saucepan in which you are making the *bagna caôda*. Put water in it and bring it to a lively simmer.

2. Put the oil and butter in the pot for *bagna caôda,* turn on the heat to medium-low, and heat the butter until it is thoroughly liquefied and just barely begins to foam. If you let it get past this stage, it will become too hot.

3. Add the garlic and sauté very briefly. It must not take on any color.

4. Place the *bagna caôda* pot over the pan with simmering water. Add the chopped anchovies and cook, stirring frequently with a wooden spoon while using the back of it to mash the anchovies, until they dissolve into a paste. Add salt, stir, and bring to the table over a warming apparatus. Serve with raw vegetables, as described below.

THE VEGETABLES FOR BAGNA CAÔDA

Cardoons They look like a large white celery, but taste more like artichoke, and are nearly synonymous with *bagna caôda*. Unfortunately, the cardoons sold in Italian markets in North America are much tougher and more bitter than their Piedmontese counterparts. You might try using just the heart, and discarding all the tough outer stalks. Wash the cardoon thoroughly and cut it into four sections, like a celery heart. Rub the cut parts with lemon juice to keep them from discoloring.

Artichokes You don't need to trim artichokes for *bagna caôda* as you do for other preparations. Rinse the artichoke in cold water and serve it whole or, if very large, cut it in half. If you cut it, rub the cut parts with lemon juice. To eat, one pulls off a leaf at a time, dips it, holding it by its tip, and bites off just the tender bottom.

Broccoli Not a Piedmontese vegetable, but very nice all the same. Cut off the florets and set them aside for any other recipe calling for broccoli. Serve just the stalks, after paring away the tough, outer skin.

Spinach Use only young, crisp spinach. Wash thoroughly in many changes of cold water until all traces of soil are gone. Serve with the stems because they provide a handy hold for dipping.

Sweet Red and Yellow Bell Peppers Wash in cold water and cut lengthwise into quarter sections. Remove the seeds and pulpy inner core.

Celery Cut in half, lengthwise or, if very thick, in quarters. Discard bruised or blemished outer stalks. Wash well in cold water.

Carrots Peel the carrots and cut them lengthwise into strips ½ inch thick.

Radishes Cut off the whiskery root tip, wash in cold water, and serve with the stems and leaves on.

Jerusalem Artichokes Soak them for a few minutes in cold water. Peel them using a potato peeler, but it isn't necessary to pare away every bit of the peel as it is edible.

Asparagus Certainly not a winter vegetable, although often available in some markets. It may be unorthodox, but it is also very good. Use the freshest asparagus possible, with the tightest buds. Pare away the tough, green skin from the base of the spear to the base of the bud. Remove any tiny leaves sprouting below the base of the bud. Wash in cold water.

Zucchini Not a winter vegetable either, but if it's there and it's good, why pass it up? Do choose only the freshest, glossiest, small young zucchini. Soak in a large bowl filled with cold water for at least 20 minutes. Rinse thoroughly under cold running water, rubbing briskly with your hands or a rough cloth to remove any grit still embedded in the skin. Trim away both ends. Cut lengthwise into pieces 1 inch thick.

OTHER VEGETABLES

In Piedmont, they also use turnips, and scallions. *Radicchio* and endive could be other suitable choices. The range is really only limited by what vegetables are edible raw, and which ones you like the best. Since they must be eaten raw, they should be as fresh and unblemished as you can obtain, and the broader the variety the more fun you will have with *bagna caôda*.

Ostriche alla Tarantina—Baked Oysters with Oil and Parsley

THE CITY of Taranto on the Ionian sea, whose waters bathe the instep of the Italian boot, has been celebrated since antiquity for its oyster beds. Oysters from France and Portugal now reach Italian tables, but for centuries most of the oysters consumed in Italy came from Taranto, and so did most of the recipes with oysters, such as the one below.   *For 6 servings*

Rock salt OR clean pebbles
36 live oysters, washed,
    scrubbed, shucked, and
    each placed on a half shell
1½ tablespoons fine, dry,
    unflavored bread crumbs

Black pepper, ground fresh
    from the mill
1½ tablespoons chopped
    parsley
¼ cup extra virgin olive oil
Freshly squeezed lemon juice

1. Preheat oven to 500°.

2. Choose a number of bake-and-serve dishes that will accommodate all the oysters in their half shells without overlapping. Spread the rock salt or pebbles on the bottom of the dishes; their purpose is both to keep the oysters from tipping and losing their juices and to retain heat after they are removed from the oven.

3. Put the oysters in their half shells side by side in the rock salt or pebbles. Top each oyster with a sprinkling of bread crumbs, some ground pepper, a little parsley, and a few drops of olive oil.

4. Place the baking dishes in the uppermost level of the preheated oven. Bake for 3 minutes. Before serving, moisten each oyster with a few drops of lemon juice.

Grilled Mussels and Clams on the Half Shell

For 4 to 6 servings

2 dozen littleneck clams, as
    small as possible
2 dozen mussels
3 tablespoons parsley chopped
    fine
½ teaspoon garlic chopped very
    fine

⅓ cup extra virgin olive oil
½ cup fine, dry, unflavored
    bread crumbs
4 ripe, fresh plum tomatoes
Lemon wedges

1. Soak the clams for 5 minutes in a basin or sink filled with cold water. Drain and refill the basin with fresh cold water, leaving in the clams. Vigorously scrub the clams one by one with a very stiff brush. Drain, refill the basin, and repeat the whole scrubbing operation. Do this 2 or 3 more times, always in fresh changes of water, until you see no more sand settling to the bottom of the basin. Discard any that, when handled, don't clamp shut.

2. Soak and scrub the mussels in cold water, following the procedure outlined above for the clams. In addition, pull away or cut off each mussel's protruding tuft of fibers. Discard any that, when handled, don't clamp shut.

3. Put the mussels and clams in separate pots, cover, and turn on the heat to high. As soon as they unclench their shells, remove them from the pot. Some shells will open up sooner than others, and the mussels will open up before the clams, so take care that each clam and mussel is removed from the pot as it opens up, otherwise it will become tough. Eventually every shell that contains a live mollusk will open. Those that never open are probably full of mud and should be discarded. Do not discard the clam juices in the pot just yet.

4. Detach the clam and mussel meat from the shells, setting aside half the clam shells and half the mussel shells and discarding the rest.

5. Rinse the clams one by one, swishing them around gently in their own juices still in the pan, to remove any remaining trace of sand.

6. Preheat the broiler.

7. Put the parsley, garlic, olive oil, and bread crumbs in a mixing bowl. Add the clam and mussel meat, mixing them with the ingredients until well coated. Let stand and marinate about 20 minutes.

8. Skin the tomatoes, using a potato peeler with a swiveling blade. Cut the tomatoes in half and remove all the seeds, picking them out with the point of a paring knife. Do not squeeze the tomatoes. Cut each one into 6 thin strips.

9. Wash the clam and mussel shells you set aside. In each shell place one of its respective mollusks. Distribute the marinade left over in the mixing bowl among all the clams and mussels. Top each clam with a strip of tomato. Place on the broiler pan and run under the hot broiler just long enough for a thin crust to form. Serve hot accompanied by lemon wedges.

Sautéed Scallops
with Garlic and Parsley

THE SUCCESS of this very tasty seafood appetizer rests on two recommendations: Buy the most tender, smallest scallops you can find and do not overcook them. *Canestrei,* as they are called in Venice, are no bigger than the nail on one's pinky. They are both tender and savory. If the small, sweet bay scallops are in season and available to you, those are the ones you should get. Deep-sea scallops are large, chewier, and less sweet, but they are a perfectly acceptable substitute if fresh.   *For 4 servings*

½ pound fresh bay scallops, OR large sea scallops cut into 3 or 4 pieces
2 tablespoons extra virgin olive oil
1 teaspoon garlic chopped fine
Salt
Black pepper, ground fresh from the mill
1 tablespoon parsley chopped fine

1 tablespoon chopped capers
2 tablespoons chopped home-made roasted peppers (see page 54)
1½ tablespoons fine, dry, unflavored bread crumbs
4 scallop shells, available in most cooking equipment shops, OR 4 small gratin dishes

1. Wash the scallops in cold water, drain, and pat thoroughly dry with kitchen towels.

2. Put the olive oil and garlic in a small saucepan, turn on the heat to medium. Cook and stir the garlic until it becomes colored a pale gold, but no darker. Then put in the scallops. Add salt and a few grindings of pepper, and turn up the heat. Cook at a brisk pace, stirring frequently, for a few seconds, until they lose their shiny raw color. Turn off the heat.

3. Preheat the broiler.

4. Add the parsley, capers, chopped peppers, and 1 tablespoon of bread crumbs to the scallops and mix well. Distribute the contents of the pan among the 4 shells or gratin dishes. Sprinkle with the remaining ½ tablespoon of bread crumbs.

5. Run the shells or gratin dishes under the preheated broiler for about 1 minute, or no longer than it takes to form a light brown crust over the scallops. Serve promptly.

Arrosticini Abruzzesi—
Skewered Marinated Lamb Tidbits

IN ABRUZZI, as in the other central Italian regions, Umbria, Latium, and Tuscany, the shepherd and his lambs are equally a feature of the landscape and of the gastronomic tradition. The recipe that follows is borrowed from the shepherds' own outdoor cooking, when they camp out with their flocks. Although it can be done indoors in a home broiler, it would be wonderful over the hot embers of a wood fire.   *For 4 servings*

½ pound boned lamb shoulder	Black pepper, ground fresh
1 garlic clove	from the mill
2 tablespoons extra virgin olive	½ teaspoon dried marjoram OR
oil	1 teaspoon fresh chopped
Salt	10 or 12 small skewers

1. Slice the meat into strips about ½ inch wide and 2 inches long. Do not trim away the fat, but try to have lean meat attached to some fat in as many pieces as possible. The fat will melt partly in the cooking, feeding the fire, and baste and sweeten the meat.

2. Mash the garlic with a heavy knife handle, crushing it enough to split it and loosen the peel, which you will remove and discard.

3. Put the meat in a bowl, adding the oil, salt, several grindings of pepper, marjoram, and garlic. Toss well, thoroughly coating the meat. Let the lamb marinate at room temperature for 2 hours, or in the refrigerator for 4 to 6 hours. Turn the lamb pieces from time to time. If refrigerated, take the meat out at least 30 minutes before cooking.

4. Preheat the broiler or light the coals or, even better, prepare a wood fire.

5. Turn the meat thoroughly one more time, then skewer it, piercing each strip in at least two places.

6. When the broiler or fire is hot, or the wood is reduced to hot embers, place the skewers as close as possible to the source of heat. If barbecuing, use very hot coals. Cook for 3 minutes on one side, then turn the skewers and cook for 2 to 3 minutes on the other. A small, fine crust should form on all sides of the meat. Serve at once.

SOUPS

ITALIAN SOUPS owe their character to two elements: the season and the place of origin.

The seasons determine the choice of vegetables, legumes, tubers, and herbs, which, except for those few fish soups that are more seafood courses than true soups, are usually prominently present, either as an accent or as the dominant ingredient.

The place shapes the style. A vegetable soup can tell you where you are in Italy almost as precisely as a map. There are the soups of the south, founded on tomato, garlic, and olive oil, often filled out with pasta; the soups of Tuscany and other central Italian regions that are fortified with beans and supported by thick slices of bread; the soups of the north, with rice; the fragrant ones of the Riviera, with lettuces and fresh herbs.

The one common link Italian soups have, the single distinguishing feature, is their substantiality. Some may be lighter than others; some may be thin; some thick. In some soups the beans or the potatoes may be puréed through a food mill. In no soup, however, is the texture, consistency, weight—the physical identity of the ingredients—wholly obliterated. There are no food processor soups, no cream-of-anything soups in the Italian repertory.

Minestrone alla Romagnola—Vegetable Soup, Romagna Style

AT HOME, in my native Romagna, this is the way we make minestrone. To seasonal vegetables we add the always available staples—carrots, onions, potatoes—and cook them in good broth over slow heat for hours. The result is a soup of dense, mellow flavor that recalls no vegetable in particular, but all of them at once.

Note that all the ingredients do not go into the pot at one time, but in a sequence that is indicated. By first sautéing the onion you produce the essential underlying flavor, which is then imparted to the other vegetables in turn. While one vegetable is cooking, you can peel and cut up another, a more efficient and less tedious method than preparing all the vegetables at once. If more convenient, you can of course have all the vegetables prepared before starting, but do observe the cooking intervals indicated in the recipe.

For 6 to 8 servings

1 pound fresh zucchini
½ cup extra virgin olive oil
3 tablespoons butter
1 cup onion sliced very thin
1 cup diced carrots
1 cup diced celery
2 cups peeled, diced potatoes
¼ pound fresh green beans
3 cups shredded Savoy cabbage
  OR regular cabbage
1½ cups canned *cannellini*
  beans, drained, OR ¾ cup
  dried white kidney beans,
  soaked and cooked as
  directed on page 13

6 cups Basic Homemade Meat
  Broth, prepared as directed
  on page 15, OR 2 cups
  canned beef broth plus 4
  cups water
OPTIONAL: the crust from a 1-
  to 2-pound piece of *parmigiano-reggiano* cheese,
  carefully scraped clean
⅔ cup canned imported Italian
  plum tomatoes, with their
  juice
Salt
⅓ cup freshly grated *parmigiano-reggiano* cheese

1. Soak the zucchini in a large bowl filled with cold water for at least 20 minutes, then rinse them clean of any remaining grit as described on page 530. Trim both ends on each zucchini and dice the zucchini fine.

2. Choose a stockpot that can comfortably accommodate all the ingredients. Put in the oil, butter, and sliced onion and turn on the heat to medium low. Cook the onion in the uncovered pot until it wilts and becomes colored a pale gold, but no darker.

3. Add the diced carrots and cook for 2 to 3 minutes, stirring once or twice. Then add the celery, and cook, stirring occasionally, for 2 or 3 minutes. Add the potatoes, repeating the same procedure.

4. While the carrots, celery, and potatoes are cooking, soak the green beans in cold water, rinse, snap off both ends, and dice them.

5. Add the diced green beans to the pot, and when they have cooked for 2 or 3 minutes, add the zucchini. Continue to give all ingredients an occasional stir and, after another few minutes, add the shredded cabbage. Continue cooking for another 5 to 6 minutes.

6. Add the broth, the optional cheese crust, the tomatoes with their juice, and a sprinkling of salt. If using canned broth, salt lightly at this stage, and taste and correct for salt later on. Give the contents of the pot a thorough

Vegetable Soup (continued)

stirring. Cover the pot, and lower the heat, adjusting it so that the soup bubbles slowly, cooking at a steady, but gentle simmer.

7. When the soup has cooked for 2½ hours, add the drained, cooked *cannellini* beans, stir well, and cook for at least another 30 minutes. If necessary, you can turn off the heat at any time and resume the cooking later. Cook until the consistency is fairly dense. Minestrone ought never to be thin and watery. If you should find that the soup is becoming too thick before it has finished cooking, you can dilute it a bit with some more homemade broth or, if you started with canned broth, with water.

8. When the soup is done, just before you turn off the heat, remove the cheese crust, swirl in the grated cheese, then taste and correct for salt.

Ahead-of-time note ✺ Minestrone, unlike most cooked vegetable preparations, is even better when reheated the following day. It will keep up to a week in a tightly sealed container in the refrigerator.

Summer Vegetable Soup with Rice and Basil, Milan Style

DURING Milan's hot summers, the *trattorie* make this minestrone first thing in the morning, pour it into individual soup plates, and display it on a table by the entrance alongside such other likely specialties of the day as an assortment of crisp vegetables for a *pinzimonio* (page 553), a cold poached bass, a Parma ham with sweet cantaloupes or, in late summer, with ripe, honey-oozing figs. By twelve-thirty or one o'clock, when the first lunch patrons are seated, the minestrone will have reached precisely the right temperature and consistency.

Because the flavor of vegetable soup improves upon reheating, you needn't make this minestrone entirely from scratch the same day you are going to serve it. You can cook the soup that constitutes its base a day or two earlier and take it out of the refrigerator when you are ready to begin. Bear in mind that once completed, cold minestrone needs at least one hour's settling time to cool down to the most desirable serving temperature. *For 4 servings*

2 cups Vegetable Soup, Romagna Style, from the recipe on page 84
½ cup rice, preferably Italian Arborio rice
Salt
Black pepper, ground fresh from the mill

¼ cup freshly grated *parmigiano-reggiano* cheese
8 to 10 fresh basil leaves, torn into several small strips
2 tablespoons extra virgin olive oil

1. Put the vegetable soup and 2 cups water in a pot and bring to a boil over medium heat. Add the rice, stirring it well with a wooden spoon.

2. When the soup returns to a boil, add salt and a few grindings of pepper. Stir, cover the pot, and turn the heat down to medium low. Stir from time to time. Begin to taste the rice for doneness after 12 minutes. Do not overcook it, because it will continue to soften later while the soup cools in the plate. When done, before turning off the heat, swirl in the grated cheese, then taste and correct for salt.

3. Ladle the soup into individual plates or bowls, add the torn up basil leaves, mix well, and set aside to rest. Serve at room temperature, drizzling each plate with a little bit of olive oil.

Note ❀ Do not serve the soup any later than the day it is made, and do not refrigerate it before serving.

Variation with Pesto

At the end of Step 2 in the preceding recipe, when the rice is done, swirl in 2 tablespoons of *pesto,* from the recipe on page 176. After ladling into the soup plates or individual bowls, omit the fresh basil leaves.

Spring Vegetable Soup

THIS IS lighter and fresher tasting than the more familiar versions of vegetable soup. It doesn't have, nor does it seek, the complex resonance of flavors that a minestrone achieves through lengthy cooking of an extensive assortment of vegetables. It is simply a sweet-tasting mix of artichokes and peas, supported by a base of potatoes, cooked with olive oil and garlic. *For 4 to 6 servings*

Spring Vegetable Soup (continued)

3 medium artichokes	Salt
1 tablespoon lemon juice	Black pepper, ground fresh
1 pound fresh peas, weighed	from the mill
unshelled, OR ½ of a 10-	3 tablespoons parsley chopped
ounce package frozen peas,	very fine
thawed	OPTIONAL: 1 slice per serving of
⅓ cup extra virgin olive oil	toasted crusty bread lightly
1 tablespoon garlic chopped	rubbed with garlic
fine	
1 pound boiling potatoes,	
peeled, washed, and cut	
into ¼-inch slices	

1. Trim the artichokes of their tough leaves and tops as described on pages 57–59. Cut them lengthwise in half, and remove the chokes and prickly inner leaves.

2. Cut the artichoke halves lengthwise into the thinnest possible slices, and put them in a bowl with enough water to cover, adding the lemon juice to the water.

3. If using fresh peas, shell them, and prepare some of the pods for cooking by stripping away their inner membranes, as described on page 93. It's not necessary to use all or even most of the pods, but do as many as you have patience for. The more of them that go into the pot, the sweeter the soup will taste.

4. Put the olive oil and garlic into a soup pot, turn on the heat to medium high, and sauté the garlic until it becomes colored a pale gold. Then add the sliced potatoes. Lower the heat to medium, cover the pot, and cook for about 10 minutes.

5. If using thawed frozen peas, set them aside for later and go now to Step 6 below. If using fresh peas, proceed as follows: Into the pot put the peas and the pods you have stripped, stir for 3 or 4 minutes to coat them, and add enough water to cover. Put a lid on the pot, reduce the heat to medium low, and cook for 20 minutes.

6. Drain the artichoke slices, rinsing off the acidulated water. Put them into the pot with salt and a few grindings of pepper. Cook the artichokes in the uncovered pot for 3 to 4 minutes, stirring them well.

7. Add enough water to top them, cover the pot, and make sure the heat is medium low. Cook the artichokes until very tender when prodded with a fork, about 30 minutes or so, depending on their freshness and youth.

8. If using frozen peas, add them now and cook for another 10 minutes.

9. Before turning off the heat, add the parsley and stir once or twice. Ladle the soup into individual plates over the optional slice of bread. Serve promptly.

Ahead-of-time note ❦ The soup may be cooked up through Step 8 several hours ahead of time. Reheat gently and finish as in Step 9.

Spinach Soup

For 5 or 6 servings

2 pounds fresh spinach OR 2 ten-ounce packages frozen whole leaf spinach, thawed
Salt
4 tablespoons (½ stick) butter
2 tablespoons chopped onion
2 cups Basic Homemade Meat Broth, prepared as directed on page 15, OR 1 cup

canned beef broth diluted with 1 cup water
2 cups milk
Whole nutmeg
5 tablespoons freshly grated *parmigiano-reggiano* cheese
Crostini, fried bread squares, made as directed on page 90

1.*If using fresh spinach:* Discard any wilted, bruised leaves, and trim away all the stems. Soak for several minutes in a basin or sink full of cold water, drain, and refill the basin or sink with fresh cold water, repeating the entire procedure several times until there are no more traces of soil in the water.

2. Put the spinach in a pan with no more water than what clings to its leaves. Add 1 tablespoon salt, cover the pan, turn the heat on to medium, and cook until tender, about 5 minutes or less, depending on the freshness and youth of the spinach.

3. Drain the spinach and, as soon as it is cool enough to handle, squeeze gently to force it to shed most of the moisture, and chop it rather coarse.

If using frozen spinach: Squeeze the moisture out of it when it has thawed, and chop it coarsely.

4. Put the butter and onion in a soup pot and turn on the heat to medium. Sauté the onion until it becomes colored a pale gold. Add the cooked fresh or the thawed spinach, and sauté in the uncovered pot for 2 to 3 minutes, stirring it to coat it well.

5. Add the broth, milk, and a tiny grating—no more than ⅛ teaspoon—of nutmeg, and bring to a simmer, stirring from time to time.

6. Add the grated Parmesan, stirring it thoroughly into the soup, taste and correct for salt, and turn off the heat.

7. Ladle into individual plates or bowls, and serve the *crostini* on the side.

Crostini

Crostini are the easy-to-make Italian equivalent of croutons, so delicious in many soups, particularly if you can manage to make them shortly before you are going to bring the soup to the table.   *For 4 servings*

4 slices good-quality white
  bread
Vegetable oil, enough to come

½ inch up the side of the
  pan

1. Trim the crust from the bread slices and cut them into ½-inch squares.
2. Put the oil in a medium-size skillet and turn on the heat to medium high. The oil should become hot enough so that the bread sizzles when it goes in. When you think it's ready, test it with one square. If it sizzles, put in as many pieces of bread as will fit without crowding the pan. It doesn't matter if they don't all go in at one time, because you can do two or more batches. Turn the heat down, because bread burns quickly if the oil gets too hot. Move the squares around in the pan with a long spoon or spatula, and as soon as they become colored a light gold remove them using a slotted spoon or spatula and place them on paper towels or a wire cooling rack to shed any excess oil.

If you are doing more than one batch, adjust the heat when necessary to avoid burning the bread. The oil must be kept hot enough, however, to brown the squares lightly and quickly.

Ahead-of-time note ❧ *Crostini* are at their best when made just before serving. They may be prepared several hours ahead of time, however, and kept at room temperature. Do not keep overnight because they are likely to acquire a stale, rancid taste.

Spinach or Escarole Soup with Rice

THE INGREDIENTS in either of these soups are so few that they must be well chosen in order to deliver the comforting flavor of which they are capable. Although, for the sake of practicality, alternatives are given for homemade meat broth, the hope here is that you ignore them, relying instead on the supply of good frozen broth that you try always to have on hand.

For 4 to 6 servings

1 head escarole OR 1 pound
    fresh spinach
Salt
4 tablespoons (½ stick) butter
2 tablespoons chopped onion
3½ cups Basic Homemade
    Meat Broth, prepared as
    directed on page 15, OR
    1 cup canned beef broth

diluted with 2½ cups water
    OR 2 bouillon cubes dis-
    solved with 3½ cups water
⅓ cup rice, preferably Italian
    Arborio rice
3 tablespoons freshly grated
    parmigiano-reggiano cheese

1. *If using escarole:* Detach all the leaves from the root end and discard any that are bruised, wilted, or discolored. Soak the others in several abundant changes of cold water until thoroughly free of soil. Drain and cut into strips about ½ inch wide. Set aside.

If using spinach: If the spinach leaves are still attached to their root, cut it off and discard it, separating each cluster into single leaves. Do not trim off the stems because both leaves and stems go into this soup. Soak the spinach clean in several changes of cold water as described on page 89.

Cook the spinach in a covered pan over medium heat, adding a pinch of salt to keep it green, but no other liquid than the water clinging to its leaves. When the water it sheds begins to bubble, cook for about 2 or 3 minutes longer.

Scoop up the spinach with a colander scoop or large slotted spoon. Do not discard any of the liquid remaining in the pan. As soon as the spinach is cool enough to handle, squeeze it gently, letting all the liquid it sheds run back into the pan. Set the spinach aside, reserving the liquid.

2. Put the butter and chopped onion in a large sauté pan, and turn on the heat to medium high. Sauté the onion until it becomes colored a light gold, then add the escarole or spinach.

If using escarole: Add a pinch of salt to help it maintain its color, stir it 2 or 3 times to coat it thoroughly, then add ½ cup of broth, turn the heat down to low, and cover the pan. Cook until the escarole is tender, approximately 25 to 45 minutes, depending on the freshness and youth of the green.

If using spinach: Sauté the spinach over lively heat in the onion and butter for a few minutes, stirring 2 or 3 times.

3. Transfer the entire contents of the pan to a soup pot, add all the broth and, if you were using spinach, 1 cup of the reserved spinach liquid. Cover the pot and turn on the heat to medium. When the broth comes to a boil, add the rice, and cover the pot again. Adjust the heat to cook at a steady, slow-bubbling boil, stirring from time to time until the rice is done. In

about 20 to 25 minutes, it should be firm to the bite, but tender, not chalky inside.

4. When the rice is done, swirl in the grated Parmesan and taste and correct for salt. Serve immediately.

Note ✥ The consistency of the soup should be dense, but still fairly runny on the spoon. If you find, while the rice is cooking, that it is becoming too thick, add a ladleful of water or of the spinach liquid, if available. But make sure not to dilute the soup too much.

Ahead-of-time note ✥ Once the rice is in the soup, it must be finished and served at once, otherwise the rice will become mushy. If you must cook it in advance, stop at the end of Step 2, and resume cooking when ready to serve. Do start the soup the same day you plan to have it, and do not refrigerate it.

Variation with Olive Oil and Garlic

For an alternative version of the same soup that invests it with an earthier flavor, substitute 3 tablespoons of extra virgin olive oil for the butter, and 2 teaspoons chopped garlic for the onion. Although the Parmesan cheese is still a good choice for the finishing touch, in its place you could do the following: After the soup is done and ladled into plates, drizzle a little fresh olive oil on each plate and sprinkle a few grindings of black pepper.

Risi e Bisi—Rice and Peas

ON APRIL 25, while all of Italy celebrates the day the country was liberated from Fascist and German rule, Venice celebrates its own most precious day, the birthday of St. Mark, patron saint of the republic that lasted 1,000 years. The tradition used to be that in honor of the apostle, on April 25th, one had one's first taste of the dish that for the remainder of the spring season became the favorite of the Venetian table, *risi e bisi*, rice and peas.

No alternative to fresh peas is suggested in the ingredients list, because the essential quality of this dish resides in the flavor that only good, fresh peas possess. To make peas taste even sweeter, many Italian families add the pods to the pot. If you follow the instructions below that describe how to prepare the pods for cooking, you will acquire a technique that will be useful in many other recipes that call for peas. The other vital component of the flavor of *risi e bisi* is homemade broth, for which no satisfactory substitute can be recommended.

Risi e bisi is not *risotto* with peas. It is a soup, albeit a very thick one. Some cooks make it thick enough to eat with a fork, but it is at its best when it is just runny enough to require a spoon. *For 4 servings*

2 pounds fresh, young peas, weighed with the pods
4 tablespoons (½ stick) butter
2 tablespoons chopped onion
Salt
3½ cups Basic Homemade Meat Broth, prepared as directed on page 15

1 cup Italian rice (see page 30)
2 tablespoons chopped parsley
½ cup freshly grated *parmigiano-reggiano* cheese

1. Shell the peas. Keep 1 cupful of the empty pods, selecting the crispest unblemished ones, and discard the rest.

2. Separate the two halves of each pod. Take a half pod, turning the glossy, inner, concave side that held the peas toward you. That side is lined by a tough, film-like membrane that you must pull off. Hold the pod with one hand, and with the other snap one end, pulling it down gently against the pod itself. You will find the thin membrane coming away without resistance. Because it is so thin, it is likely to break off before you have detached it entirely. Don't fuss over it: Keep the skinned portion of the pod, snap the other end of the pod and try to remove the remaining section of membrane. Cut off and discard those parts of any pod that you have been unable to skin completely. It's not necessary to end up with perfect whole pods since they will dissolve in the cooking anyway. Any skinned piece will serve the purpose, which is that of sweetening the soup. Add all the prepared pod pieces to the shelled peas, soak in cold water, drain, and set aside.

3. Put the butter and onion in a soup pot and turn on the heat to medium. Sauté the onion until it becomes colored a pale gold, then add the peas and the stripped-down pods, and a good pinch of salt to keep the peas green. Cook for 2 or 3 minutes, stirring to coat the peas well.

4. Add 3 cups of the broth, cover the pot, and adjust the heat so the broth bubbles at a slow, gentle boil for 10 minutes.

5. Add the rice and the remaining ½ cup of broth, stir, cover the pot again, and cook at a steady moderate boil until the rice is tender, but firm to the bite, about 20 minutes or so. Stir occasionally while the soup is cooking.

6. When the rice is done, stir in the parsley, then the grated Parmesan. Taste and correct for salt, then turn off the heat.

Rice and Smothered Cabbage Soup

GOOD LEFTOVERS make good soups, and this one makes use of the Smothered Cabbage, Venetian Style, on page 479. It's too good a soup, however, to have to wait for enough cabbage to be left over, so the recipe below is given on the assumption you will be starting from scratch.

Like *risi e bisi*, the Venetian rice and peas soup, which precedes this recipe, this one is fairly thick, but it is not quite a *risotto*. It should be runny enough to require a spoon.   *For 4 to 6 servings*

The smothered cabbage, made as directed on page 479 (It can be prepared 2 or 3 days ahead of time.)

3 cups Basic Homemade Meat Broth, prepared as directed on page 15, OR 1 cup canned beef broth diluted with 2 cups water OR 1½ bouillon cubes dissolved in 3 cups warm water

⅔ cup rice, preferably Italian Arborio rice

2 tablespoons butter

⅓ cup freshly grated *parmigiano-reggiano* cheese

Salt

Black pepper, ground fresh from the mill

1. Put the cabbage and broth into a soup pot, and turn on the heat to medium.

2. When the broth comes to a boil, add the rice. Cook uncovered, adjusting the heat so that the soup bubbles at a slow, but steady boil, stirring from time to time until the rice is done. It must be tender, but firm to the bite, and should take around 20 minutes. If while the rice is cooking, you find the soup becoming too thick, dilute it with a ladleful of homemade broth. If you are not using homemade broth, just add water. Remember that when finished, the soup should be rather dense.

3. When the rice is done, before turning off the heat, swirl in the butter and the grated Parmesan, stirring thoroughly. Taste and correct for salt, and add a few grindings of black pepper. Ladle the soup into individual plates, and allow it to settle just a few minutes before serving.

Minestrina Tricolore—Potato Soup with Carrots and Celery

WHEN I BECAME a wife and, by necessity, a cook, this was one of the first dishes I learned to make. Decades have gone by in which I have had my hand in uncounted dozens of other soups, but I turn still to this *minestrina*—little soup—for its charm, its delightful contrast of textures, its artless goodness, its never-failing power to please. *For 4 to 6 servings*

1½ pounds potatoes
2 tablespoons butter
3 tablespoons vegetable oil
3 tablespoons onion
    chopped fine
3 tablespoons carrot chopped
    fine
3 tablespoons celery
    chopped fine
5 tablespoons freshly grated
    parmigiano-reggiano cheese,
    plus additional cheese at the
    table

1 cup milk
2 cups Basic Homemade Meat
    Broth, prepared as directed
    on page 15, OR ½ cup
    canned beef broth diluted
    with 1½ cups water
Salt
2 tablespoons chopped parsley
Crostini, fried bread squares,
    made as directed on
    page 90

1. Peel the potatoes, rinse them in cold water, and cut them up in small pieces. Put them in a soup pot with just enough cold water to cover, put a lid on the pot, and turn on the heat to medium high. Boil the potatoes until they are tender, then purée them, with their liquid, through the large holes of a food mill back into the pot. Set aside.

2. Put the butter, oil, and chopped onion in a skillet and turn on the heat to medium. Sauté the onion until it becomes colored a pale gold. Add the chopped carrot and celery and cook for about 2 minutes, stirring the vegetables to coat them well. Don't cook them long enough to become soft because you want them noticeably crisp in the soup.

3. Transfer the entire contents of the skillet to the pot with the potatoes. Turn on the heat to medium, and add the grated Parmesan, the milk, and the broth. Stir and cook at a steady simmer for several minutes until the cooking fat floating on the surface is dispersed throughout the soup. Don't let the soup become thicker than cream in consistency. If that should happen, dilute it with equal parts of broth and milk. Taste and correct for salt. Off heat, swirl

Potato Soup with Carrots and Celery (continued)

in the chopped parsley, then ladle into individual plates or bowls. Serve with freshly grated Parmesan and *crostini* on the side.

Potato Soup with Smothered Onions

For 6 servings

2 pounds boiling potatoes	directed on page 15, OR ½
3 tablespoons butter	cup canned beef broth
3 tablespoons vegetable oil	diluted with 3 cups water
1½ pounds onions, sliced	3 tablespoons freshly grated
very thin	*parmigiano-reggiano* cheese,
Salt	plus additional cheese at the
3½ cups Basic Homemade	table
Meat Broth, prepared as	1 tablespoon chopped parsley

1. Peel the potatoes, cut them into ½-inch cubes, rinse in cold water, and set aside.

2. Put the butter, oil, all the sliced onions, and a healthy pinch of salt in a soup pot, and turn on the heat to medium. Do not cover the pot. Cook the onions at a slow pace, stirring occasionally, until they have wilted and become colored a pale brown.

3. Add the diced potatoes, turn up the heat to high, and sauté the potatoes briskly, turning them in the onions to coat them well.

4. Add the broth, cover the pot, and adjust the heat so that the broth comes to a slow, steady boil. When the potatoes are very tender, pulp most of them by mashing them against the side of the pot with a long wooden spoon. Stir thoroughly and cook for another 8 to 10 minutes. If you find the soup becoming too thick, add up to a ladleful of broth or, if you are not using homemade broth, add water.

5. Before turning off the heat, swirl in the grated Parmesan and the parsley, then taste and correct for salt. Ladle into individual plates or bowls and serve with additional grated cheese on the side.

Potato and Green Pea Soup

THE ENDEARING FLAVOR of this soup derives from a juxtaposition of sweetness and savoriness. The sweetness is largely owed to the peas, leading to the following consideration: If the fresh peas in the market are of the local, peak-of-season, young, and juicy variety, they are obviously your first choice; if they are mealy, very mature, out-of-town peas, you are better off with frozen ones.   *For 4 to 6 servings*

2 tablespoons butter
2 tablespoons vegetable oil
3 cups onion cut into very
   thin slices
Salt
2 garlic cloves, peeled and cut
   into paper-thin slices
3 cups potatoes, peeled and cut
   into very, very fine dice
Basic Homemade Meat Broth,
   prepared as directed on

page 15, enough to cover all
   ingredients by 2 inches, OR
   1 beef bouillon cube
2 pounds fresh peas, unshelled
   weight, OR 1 ten-ounce
   package frozen peas, thawed
Black pepper, ground fresh
   from the mill
Freshly grated *parmigiano-
   reggiano* cheese for the table

1. Choose a saucepan that can subsequently contain all the ingredients comfortably, put in the butter, oil, sliced onion, and a large pinch of salt, turn the heat on to low, and cover the pan. Cook the onion, turning it occasionally, until it becomes very soft and has shed all its liquid. Then uncover the pan, turn up the heat to medium, and cook, stirring once or twice, until all the liquid has bubbled away and the onion has become colored a tawny gold.

2. Add the sliced garlic and cook, stirring once or twice, until it becomes colored a pale gold. Add the potato dice, turning them several times during a minute or two to coat them well, then add enough broth to cover by 2 inches, or equivalent quantity of water together with a bouillon cube. Turn the heat down to cook at a slow, steady simmer, cover the pan, and cook for about 30 minutes.

3. Add the shelled fresh peas or thawed ones. If using fresh peas, cook another 10 minutes or more until they are done, replenishing the liquid if it falls below the original level. (Expect a substantial quantity of the fine potato dice to dissolve.) If using frozen peas, cook until they lose their raw taste, about 4 or 5 minutes. Taste and correct for salt. Add a few grindings of pepper, stir, and serve at once, with grated Parmesan on the side.

Ahead-of-time note ❧ You can make the soup a day in advance, and reheat it gently just before serving.

Potato Soup with Split Green Peas

For 6 servings

2 medium boiling potatoes
½ pound split dried green peas
5 cups Basic Homemade Meat
    Broth, prepared as directed
    on page 15, OR 1 cup
    canned beef broth diluted
    with 4 cups water OR 1
    bouillon cube dissolved in 5
    cups water
3 tablespoons butter

3 tablespoons vegetable oil
2 tablespoons chopped onion
3 tablespoons freshly grated
    parmigiano-reggiano cheese,
    plus additional cheese at the
    table
Salt
Crostini, fried bread squares,
    made as directed on
    page 90

1. Peel the potatoes and cut them up into small pieces. Rinse in cold water and drain.

2. Rinse the split peas in cold water and drain.

3. Put the potatoes and peas in a soup pot together with 3 cups of broth, cover, turn on the heat to medium, and cook at a gentle boil until both the potatoes and the peas are tender. Turn off the heat.

4. Purée the potatoes and peas with their liquid through a food mill back into the pot.

5. Put the butter and vegetable oil in a small skillet, add the chopped onion, turn on the heat to medium high. Cook the onion, stirring it, until it becomes colored a rich gold.

6. Pour the entire contents of the skillet into the pot with the potatoes and peas, add the remaining 2 cups of broth, cover, and turn on the heat to medium, adjusting it so that the soup bubbles at a steady, but slow boil. Cook, stirring from time to time, until any floating butter and oil has become evenly distributed into the broth.

7. Before turning off the heat, swirl in the grated Parmesan, then taste and correct for salt. Ladle into individual plates or bowls and serve with *crostini* on the side and additional grated Parmesan for the table.

Lentil Soup

For 4 servings

3 tablespoons butter

3 tablespoons vegetable oil

2 tablespoons onion chopped
    very fine

⅓ cup shredded *pancetta* OR
    prosciutto OR unsmoked
    country ham

2 tablespoons carrot chopped
    fine

2 tablespoons celery chopped
    fine

1 cup canned imported Italian
    plum tomatoes, cut up,
    with their juice

½ pound dried lentils

4 cups Basic Homemade Meat
    Broth, prepared as directed
    on page 15, OR 1 cup
    canned beef broth diluted
    with 3 cups water

Salt

Black pepper, ground fresh
    from the mill

3 tablespoons freshly grated
    parmigiano-reggiano cheese,
    plus additional cheese at the
    table

1. Put 2 tablespoons of the butter and all the oil in a soup pot, add the chopped onion and the *pancetta,* and turn on the heat to medium high. Do not cover the pot. Cook the onion, stirring it, until it becomes a deep gold.

2. Add the chopped carrot and celery. Cook at lively heat for 2 or 3 minutes, stirring occasionally.

3. Add the tomatoes with their juice, and adjust the heat so that they bubble gently, but steadily. Cook for about 25 minutes, stirring occasionally.

4. In the meantime, wash the lentils in cold water and drain them. Add the lentils to the pot, stirring thoroughly to coat them well, then add the broth, a pinch of salt, and a few grindings of pepper. Cover the pot, adjust the heat so that the soup cooks at a steady, gentle simmer, and stir from time to time. Generally, it will take about 45 minutes for the lentils to become tender, but each lot of lentils varies, so it is necessary to monitor their progress by tasting them. Some lentils will absorb more liquid than others. If necessary, add more broth while cooking or, if you are not using homemade broth, add water.

5. When the lentils are done, before turning off the heat, add the remaining tablespoon of butter and swirl in the grated Parmesan. Taste and correct for salt and pepper. Serve with additional grated Parmesan for the table.

Ahead-of-time note ❀ The soup can be made in advance, even in large batches, and frozen, if desired. When making it ahead of time, stop at the

Lentil Soup (continued)

end of Step 4, and add the butter and cheese only after reheating and just before serving.

Variation with Rice

The addition of rice provides a satisfying alternative to basic lentil soup.

For 6 servings

The Lentil Soup from the recipe on page 99, finished through Step 4

1½ cups Basic Homemade Meat Broth, prepared as directed on page 15, OR ½ cup canned beef broth diluted with 1 cup water

½ cup rice, preferably Italian Arborio rice

1 tablespoon butter

3 tablespoons freshly grated *parmigiano-reggiano* cheese, plus additional cheese at the table

Salt

Bring the soup to a boil, then add the broth. When the soup comes to a boil again, add the rice, stirring thoroughly with a wooden spoon. Cook at a steady, but moderate boil until the rice is tender, but still firm to the bite, approximately 20 minutes. If, while the rice is cooking, you find that it is absorbing too much liquid, add more homemade broth or water. When the rice is done, before turning off the heat, swirl in the tablespoon of butter and the grated Parmesan. Taste and correct for salt, if necessary. Serve with additional grated Parmesan on the side.

Lentil Soup with Pasta, Bacon, and Garlic

For 6 servings

Extra virgin olive oil, 2 tablespoons for cooking, plus more for stirring into the soup

¼ pound bacon chopped very fine

½ cup chopped onion

2 teaspoons chopped garlic

⅓ cup chopped celery

2 tablespoons chopped parsley

⅓ cup fresh, ripe, firm tomatoes, skinned raw with a

peeler, all seeds removed, and chopped, OR canned Italian plum tomatoes, cut up, with their juice

1 cup dried lentils

Salt

Black pepper, ground fresh from the mill

1½ cups short, tubular soup pasta

¼ cup freshly grated *romano* cheese (see note below)

Note 🌼 *Romano* is the most widely available export version of cheese made from ewe's milk. All such cheeses are known in Italian as *pecorino. Romano* is, regrettably, the sharpest of these, and if you should come across a better *pecorino* of grating consistency, such as *fiore sardo* or a Tuscan *cacciotta,* use it in place of *romano,* increasing the quantity to ⅓ cup, or more to taste.

1. Choose a saucepan that can later contain the lentils and pasta with sufficient water to cook them. Put in 2 tablespoons olive oil, the chopped bacon, onion, garlic, celery, and parsley, and turn on the heat to medium. Cook, stirring and turning the ingredients over often, until the vegetables become deeply colored, about 15 minutes. Add the chopped tomato, stir to coat it well, and cook for a few minutes until the fat floats free of the tomato.

2. Add the lentils, turning them over 3 or 4 times to coat them well, then add enough water to cover by 1 inch. Adjust heat so that the liquid simmers gently, and cook until the lentils are tender, about 25 to 30 minutes. Whenever the water level falls below the 1 inch above the lentils you started with, replenish with as much water as needed.

Ahead-of-time note 🌼 You can make the soup up to this point several hours or even a day or two in advance. Reheat thoroughly, adding water if necessary, before proceeding with the next step.

3. Add salt and several grindings of pepper, put in the pasta, and turn up the heat to cook at a brisk boil. Add more water if necessary to cook the pasta. When the pasta is done—it should be tender, but firm to the bite—the consistency of the soup should be more on the dense than on the thin side.

4. Taste and correct for salt and pepper. Add the grated cheese and about 1 tablespoon of olive oil, stir thoroughly, then take off heat and serve at once.

White Bean Soup with Garlic and Parsley

IF ONE really loves beans, all one really wants in a bean soup is beans. Why bother with anything else? Here there is very little liquid, and just enough olive oil and garlic to help the *cannellini* express the best of themselves. It can be made thick enough, if you allow the liquid to evaporate while cooking, to be served as a side dish, next to a good roast. But if you like it thinner, you only need add a little more broth or water.   *For 4 to 6 servings*

White Bean Soup (continued)

½ cup extra virgin olive oil
1 teaspoon chopped garlic
2 cups dried *cannellini* OR other
　white beans, soaked and
　cooked as directed on page
　13 and drained, OR 6 cups
　canned *cannellini* beans,
　drained
Salt
Black pepper, ground fresh
　from the mill

1 cup Basic Homemade Meat
　Broth, prepared as directed
　on page 15, OR ⅓ cup
　canned beef broth diluted
　with ⅔ cup water
2 tablespoons chopped parsley
OPTIONAL: thick grilled slices of
　crusty bread

1. Put the oil and chopped garlic in a soup pot and turn on the heat to medium. Cook the garlic, stirring it, until it becomes colored a very pale gold.

2. Add the drained cooked or canned beans, a pinch of salt, and a few grindings of pepper. Cover and simmer gently for 5 to 6 minutes.

3. Take about ½ cup of beans from the pot and purée them through a food mill back into the pot, together with all the broth. Simmer for another 5 to 6 minutes, taste, and correct for salt and pepper. Swirl in the chopped parsley, and turn off the heat.

4. Ladle over the grilled bread slices into individual soup bowls.

Pasta e Fagioli—Pasta and Bean Soup

THE CLASSIC bean variety for *pasta e fagioli* is the cranberry or Scotch bean, brightly marbled in white and pink or even deep red hues. When cooked, its flavor is unlike that of any other bean, subtly recalling that of chestnuts. In the spring and summer it is available fresh in its pod and many specialty or ethnic vegetable markets carry it. When very fresh, the pods are firm and brilliantly colored, but even if they are wilted and discolored, the beans inside are likely to be perfectly sound. You can open one or two pods just to make sure.

Cranberry beans can be frozen with great success and are better than the dried kind. If your market carries fresh cranberry beans in season, you could buy a substantial quantity, and freeze the shelled beans in tightly sealed plastic freezer bags. They can be cooked exactly like the fresh. When fresh cranberry beans are not available, the dried are a wholly satisfactory substitute and, if necessary, one may even use the canned. If you can't find cranberry beans in any form, you can substitute dried red kidney beans. *For 6 servings*

¼ cup extra virgin olive oil

2 tablespoons chopped onion

3 tablespoons chopped carrot

3 tablespoons chopped celery

3 or 4 pork ribs, OR a ham bone
    with some lean meat
    attached, OR 2 little pork
    chops

⅔ cup canned imported Italian
    plum tomatoes, cut up,
    with their juice, OR fresh
    tomatoes, if ripe and firm,
    peeled and cut up

2 pounds fresh cranberry beans,
    unshelled weight, OR 1 cup
    dried cranberry or red
    kidney beans, soaked and
    cooked as described on page
    13, OR 3 cups canned
    cranberry or red kidney
    beans, drained

3 cups (or more if needed)
    Basic Homemade Meat
    Broth, prepared as directed
    on page 15, OR 1 cup
    canned beef broth diluted
    with 2 cups water

Salt

Black pepper, ground fresh
    from the mill

Either *maltagliati* pasta, home-
    made with 1 egg and ⅔ cup
    flour, see pages 131 and
    137 for instructions,
    OR ½ pound small, tubular
    macaroni

1 tablespoon butter

2 tablespoons freshly grated
    parmigiano-reggiano cheese

1. Put the olive oil and chopped onion in a soup pot and turn on the heat to medium. Cook the onion, stirring it, until it becomes colored a pale gold.

2. Add the carrot and celery, stir once or twice to coat them well, then add the pork. Cook for about 10 minutes, turning the meat and the vegetables over from time to time with a wooden spoon.

3. Add the cut-up tomatoes and their juice, adjust the heat so that the juices simmer very gently, and cook for 10 minutes.

4. *If using fresh beans:* Shell them, rinse them in cold water, and put them in the soup pot. Stir 2 or 3 times to coat them well, then add the broth. Cover the pot, adjust the heat so that the broth bubbles at a steady, but gentle boil, and cook for 45 minutes to 1 hour, until the beans are fully tender.

If using cooked dried beans or the canned: Extend the cooking time for the tomatoes in Step 3 to 20 minutes. Add the drained cooked or canned beans, stirring them thoroughly to coat them well. Cook for 5 minutes, then add the broth, cover the pot, and bring the broth to a gentle boil.

5. Scoop up about ½ cup of the beans and mash them through a food mill back into the pot. Add salt, a few grindings of black pepper, and stir thoroughly.

6. Check the soup for density: It should be liquid enough to cook the

Pasta and Bean Soup (continued)

pasta in. If necessary, add more broth or, if you are using diluted canned broth, more water. When the soup has come to a steady, moderate boil, add the pasta. If you are using homemade pasta, taste for doneness after 1 minute. If you are using macaroni pasta, it will take several minutes longer, but stop the cooking when the pasta is tender, but still firm to the bite. Before turning off the heat, swirl in 1 tablespoon of butter and the grated cheese.

7. Pour the soup into a large serving bowl or into individual plates, and allow to settle for 10 minutes before serving. It tastes best when eaten warm, rather than piping hot.

Variation with Rice

The same soup is delicious with rice. Substitute 1 cup of rice, preferably Italian Arborio rice, for the pasta. Follow all other steps as given above.

Ahead-of-time note ❦ You can prepare the soup almost entirely in advance but stop at the end of Step 5. Add and cook the pasta or rice only when you are going to make the soup ready for serving.

Acquacotta—Tuscan Peasant Soup with Cabbage and Beans

WHEN YOU ARE HAVING a dish whose main ingredients are stale bread, water, onion, tomato, and olive oil, you are nourishing yourself as the once indigent Tuscan peasants did, when they could take sustenance only from those things that cost them nothing. If in the same dish, however, you find eggs, Parmesan cheese, and the aroma of lemons, then you know you have moved out of the farmyard and into the squire's great house. For a traditional Tuscan country dinner, this soup would precede other courses, but it is substantial enough to contemplate using it as the principal course of a simpler meal.

The great house this particular recipe comes from is Villa Cappezzana, whose mistress, Countess Lisa Contini Bonacossi, is not only one of the most gifted of Tuscan cooks, but fortunately, one of the most hospitable. Equally fortunate for the guests that are always turning up at Cappezzana, among the red wines her husband Ugo and son Vittorio make are two that in Tuscany stand out for their refinement, Carmignano and Ghiaie della Furba.

For 6 servings

4 cups onion sliced rather thick, about ⅓ inch
Salt

½ cup extra virgin olive oil
3 cups celery chopped fine, the leaves included

3 cups Savoy cabbage shredded
   very fine
2 cups kale leaves, chopped
   very fine
1 cup fresh, ripe, firm tomato,
   skinned raw with a peeler,
   seeds removed, and cut into
   ¼-inch dice
8 fresh basil leaves, torn into
   2 or 3 pieces
1 bouillon cube
⅓ cup dried *cannellini* beans,
   soaked and cooked as
   directed on page 13 and
   drained

Black pepper, ground fresh
   from the mill
An oven-to-table ceramic
   casserole with a lid
12 thin toasted slices day-old
   Tuscan-style or other good
   country bread OR Olive Oil
   Bread, made as directed on
   page 635
⅓ cup freshly grated
   parmigiano-reggiano cheese
⅓ cup freshly squeezed
   lemon juice
6 eggs

1. Choose a saucepan that can subsequently contain all the vegetables and beans and enough water to cover by 2 inches. Put in the onion, some salt, ¼ cup olive oil, and turn on the heat to medium. Cook the onion, turning it over occasionally, until it wilts. Add the chopped celery, turning it over to coat it well, and cook for 2 or 3 minutes, stirring occasionally. Add the Savoy cabbage, turn it over well, cook for 2 or 3 minutes. Add the chopped kale leaves, turning them over and cooking them briefly as just described. Add the diced tomato and the basil, turning them over once or twice, then add the bouillon cube with enough water to cover by about 2 inches. Cover tightly and cook for at least 2 and possibly 3 hours, replenishing the water when necessary to maintain its original level.

Ahead-of-time note ✿ You may complete the soup up to this point several hours or even a day in advance. When keeping it overnight, if you have a cold place to store it, it would be preferable to use it instead of the refrigerator, which tends to give cooked greens a somewhat sour taste. Reheat completely before proceeding with the next step.

   2. Preheat oven to 400°.

   3. Put the drained, cooked beans and several grindings of pepper in the pot with the vegetables, stir, taste, and correct for salt and pepper.

   4. Line the bottom of the ceramic casserole with the sliced bread. Pour over it the remaining ¼ cup olive oil, then the vegetable broth from the pot, then all the vegetables and beans in the pot. Sprinkle over it half the grated Parmesan.

   5. Put the lemon juice in a small skillet together with 1½ inches or more

Tuscan Peasant Soup (continued)

of water, and turn the heat on to medium. When the liquid comes to a simmer, adjust the heat to maintain it thus without letting it come to a fast boil. Break 1 egg into a saucer and slide it into the pan. Spoon a little of the simmering liquid over the egg as it cooks. When, in about 3 minutes, the egg white becomes set and turns a dull, flat color, but the yolk is still runny, retrieve the egg with a slotted spoon and slide it over the vegetables in the casserole. Repeat the procedure with the other 5 eggs, placing the eggs side by side.

6. Sprinkle salt and the remaining Parmesan cheese over the eggs. Cover the casserole and place in the preheated oven for 10 minutes. After taking the dish out of the oven, uncover and let the contents settle for several minutes before serving. When serving, make sure each guest gets some of the bread from the bottom of the dish and an egg.

La Jota—Beans and Sauerkraut Soup

FOR MOST of the twentieth century, the city of Trieste has clung passionately to its Italian identity, but its cooking, such as this stout bean soup with potatoes, sauerkraut, and pork, often speaks with the earthy accent of its Slavic origins.

An ingredient that contributes much to the delightful consistency of the soup is fresh, unsmoked pork rind, preferably coming from the jowl. It is, unfortunately, rather difficult to obtain except from specialized pork butchers. If you can persuade your butcher to get some for you and you have to buy more than you need for this recipe, you can freeze the rest and use it on another occasion. If no rind of any kind is available to you, use fresh pig's feet, which are easier to find, or the fresh end of the shoulder known as pork hock.

When completed, *jota* is enriched with a final flavoring called *pestà:* salt pork so finely chopped that it is nearly reduced to a paste, hence the name. Although the components here are different, the procedure recalls the practice of adding flavored oils to some Tuscan bean soups.   *For 8 servings*

FOR THE SOUP

2 pounds fresh cranberry beans, unshelled weight, OR 1 cup dried cranberry beans or red kidney beans, soaked and cooked as described on page 13

¼ pound bacon

1 pound sauerkraut, drained

½ teaspoon cumin

1 medium potato

¾ pound fresh pork jowl, OR pig's feet, OR pork hock, see remarks above

Salt

3 tablespoons coarse cornmeal

Note ❀ If unfamiliar with cranberry beans, see page 102.

FOR THE PESTÀ, THE SAVORY FINISH

¼ cup salt pork chopped fine to a pulp either with a knife or in the food processor

1 tablespoon onion chopped very fine

1 teaspoon garlic chopped very fine

Salt

1 tablespoon flour

1. *If using fresh beans:* Shell, rinse, and cook them in water as described on page 103. Set aside in their cooking liquid.

If using cooked dried beans: Reserve for later, together with their liquid, and begin with Step 2.

2. Cut the bacon into 1-inch strips, put it in a saucepan, and turn on the heat to medium. Cook for 2 to 3 minutes, then add the drained sauerkraut and the cumin, stir thoroughly to coat well with bacon fat, and cook for 2 minutes.

3. Add 1 cup water, cover the pan, turn the heat down to very low, and cook for 1 hour. At that time the sauerkraut should be substantially reduced in bulk and there should be no liquid in the pan. If some liquid is still left, uncover the pan, turn up the heat to medium, and boil it away.

4. Peel the potato, cut it up into small chunks, rinse in cold water and drain.

Beans and Sauerkraut Soup (continued)

5. *If using fresh pork jowl or other fresh pork rind:* While the sauerkraut is slowly stewing and/or the fresh beans are cooking, put the pork rind in a soup pot with 1 quart of water and bring to a boil. Boil for 5 minutes, drain, discarding the cooking liquid, and cut the rind into ¾- to 1-inch-wide strips. Do not be alarmed if it is tough. It will soften to a creamy consistency in subsequent cooking.

Return the rind to the soup pot, add the cut-up potato, 3 cups of water, and a large pinch of salt. Cover the pot and adjust heat so that the water bubbles at a slow, but steady boil for 1 hour.

If using fresh pig's feet or pork hock: Put the pork, potato, and salt in a soup pot with enough water to cover by 2 inches, put a lid on the pot, and adjust heat so that the water bubbles at a slow, but steady boil for 1 hour. Take the pork out of the pot, bone it, cut it into ½-inch strips, and put it back into the pot.

6. Add the cooked fresh or dried beans with all their liquid, cover, adjust heat so that the liquid bubbles at a steady, but slow simmer, and cook for 30 minutes.

7. Add the sauerkraut, cover the pot again, and continue to cook, always at a steady simmer, for 1 more hour.

8. Add the cornmeal in a thin stream, stirring it thoroughly into the soup. Add 2 cups water, cover, and cook for 45 minutes more, always at a slow, steady simmer. Stir from time to time.

9. When the soup is nearly done, prepare the *pestà:* Put the chopped salt pork and onion in a skillet or small saucepan, and turn on the heat to medium. Sauté the onion until it becomes colored a pale gold. Add the chopped garlic and sauté it until it becomes colored a very pale gold. Add a large pinch of salt and pour in the flour, one teaspoon at a time, stirring it thoroughly until it becomes colored a rich gold.

10. Add the *pestà* to the soup, stirring it in thoroughly, and simmer for another 15 minutes or so. Allow the soup to settle for a few minutes before serving.

Ahead-of-time note ❀ Although La Jota requires hours of slow cooking, these can be staggered and scheduled at your convenience because the soup should be served a day or two after it has been made to give its flavors time to develop fully and merge. You can interrupt its preparation whenever you have completed one of its major steps. Allow the soup to cool, refrigerate it, and on the following day resume cooking where you left off. Prepare and add the *pestà,* however, only when ready to serve.

Novara's Bean and Vegetable Soup

THIS MONUMENTALLY dense minestrone from Piedmont, the northwestern region of Italy at the foot of the Alps, has at least two lives. It is a deeply satisfying vegetable soup, and it is also the base for one of the most robust of *risotti: La paniscia,* see page 252.

If you are making the recipe to use it in *la paniscia,* there will be some soup left over, because only part of it will go into the *risotto.* But the leftover soup can be refrigerated, and, a few days later, when its flavor will be even richer, you can expand it with pasta and broth for yet a different version.

For 4 to 6 servings

¼ pound pork rind OR fresh side pork (pork belly)

⅓ cup vegetable oil

1 tablespoon butter

2 medium onions, sliced very thin, about 1 cup

1 carrot, peeled, washed, and diced

1 large stalk of celery, washed and diced

2 medium zucchini, washed as described on page 530, then trimmed of both ends and diced

1 cup shredded red cabbage

1 pound fresh cranberry beans, unshelled weight, OR 1 cup

dried cranberry or red kidney beans, soaked as described on page 13 and drained but *not* cooked

⅓ cup canned imported Italian plum tomatoes, cut up, with their juice

Salt

Black pepper, ground fresh from the mill

3 cups Basic Homemade Meat Broth, prepared as described on page 15, OR 1 cup canned beef broth diluted with 2 cups water

Freshly grated *parmigiano-reggiano* cheese for the table

1. Cut the pork into strips about ½ inch long and ¼ inch wide.

2. Put the oil, butter, onion, and pork into a soup pot, and turn on the heat to medium. Stir from time to time.

3. When the onion becomes colored a deep gold, add all the diced vegetables, the shredded cabbage, and the shelled fresh beans or the drained, soaked dried beans. Stir well for about a minute to coat all ingredients thoroughly.

4. Add the cut-up tomatoes with their juice, a pinch of salt, and several grindings of pepper. Stir thoroughly once again, then put in all the broth. If there should not be enough to cover all the ingredients by at least 1 inch, make up the difference with water.

Novara's Bean and Vegetable Soup (continued)

5. Cover the pot, turn the heat down to low, adjusting it so the soup cooks at a very slow simmer. Cook for at least 2 hours. Expect the consistency, when done, to be rather thick. Taste and correct for salt and pepper.

If you have made it to serve as a soup and not as a component of *la paniscia,* ladle it into individual plates or bowls, let it settle a few minutes, and bring to the table along with freshly grated Parmesan.

Bean and Red Cabbage Soup

As MUCH as a cabbage soup, this is a full-bodied pork and beans dish, part of that corpulent Mediterranean family of bean and meat dishes of which *cassoulet* is also a member. You should not hesitate to take some freedom with the basic recipe, varying its proportions of sausage, beans, and cabbage to suit your taste. The recipe as it is given here will produce a robust course in which soup, meat, and vegetable are combined and can become a meal in itself. Increasing the amount of sausage will make it even heartier. On the other hand, you can eliminate the sausage altogether, substituting it with a piece of fresh pork on the bone, and augment the quantity of broth to turn it into a soupier dish that can serve as the first course of a substantial country menu.

For 6 servings

¾ pound pork rind OR fresh
    pig's feet OR pork hock
¼ cup extra virgin olive oil
½ teaspoon chopped garlic
2 tablespoons chopped onion
2 tablespoons *pancetta* shredded
    very fine
1 pound shredded red cabbage,
    about 4 cups
⅓ cup chopped celery
3 tablespoons canned imported
    Italian plum tomatoes,
    drained
A pinch of thyme
3 cups (or more) Basic Home-
    made Meat Broth, prepared
    as directed on page 15,

    OR 1 cup canned beef broth
    diluted with 2 cups water
Salt
Black pepper, ground fresh
    from the mill
½ pound mild fresh pork
    sausage that does not
    contain fennel seeds or
    other herbs
1 cup dried *cannellini* OR other
    white kidney beans, soaked
    and cooked as directed on
    page 13, OR 3 cups canned
    cannellini beans, drained
OPTIONAL: thick slices of grilled
    or toasted crusty bread

FOR THE FINISHING TOUCH OF FLAVORED OIL

2 to 3 garlic cloves, lightly
    mashed with a knife handle
    and peeled
3 tablespoons extra virgin olive
    oil

½ teaspoon chopped dried
    rosemary leaves OR a small
    sprig of fresh rosemary

1. *If you are using pork rind:* Put the rind in a small saucepan, add enough cold water to cover by about 1 inch, and bring to a boil. Cook for 1 minute, then drain and, when cool enough to handle, cut the rind into strips about ½ inch wide and 2 to 3 inches long.

If you are using fresh pig's feet or hock: Put the feet or hock in a saucepan with enough water to cover by about 2 inches, put a lid on the pot, and cook at a moderate boil for 45 minutes to 1 hour.

Remove the pork from the pot, bone it, cut it into strips approximately ½ inch wide and set aside.

2. Put the olive oil in a soup pot together with the chopped onion and *pancetta,* and turn on the heat to medium. Cook the onion, stirring, until it becomes translucent, then add the garlic, and cook it, stirring from time to time, until it becomes lightly colored.

3. Add the shredded cabbage, chopped celery, pork rind or feet or hock, the drained tomato, and a pinch of thyme. Cook over medium-low heat until the cabbage has completely wilted. Stir thoroughly from time to time.

4. Add the broth, salt, and several grindings of pepper, cover the pot, and turn the heat down to very low. Cook for about 2½ hours. This phase may be spread over 2 days, stopping the cooking and refrigerating the soup whenever you need to. The soup develops even deeper flavor when reheated and cooked in this manner.

5. Uncover the pot and, off heat, tilting it slightly, draw off as much of the fat as possible floating on the surface. If the soup is refrigerated after completing Step 4, the fat will be even easier to remove because it will have formed a thin, but firm layer on top. Return the pot to the burner, and bring its contents to a slow simmer.

6. Pierce the sausages at two or three points with a toothpick or sharp fork, put them in a small skillet, and turn on the heat to medium low. Brown them well on all sides, using just the fat they themselves shed. Add just the browned sausages, but none of the fat in the skillet, to the pot.

7. Purée half the drained cooked or canned beans into the pot, stirring thoroughly. Cover and continue to simmer for 15 minutes.

Bean and Red Cabbage Soup (continued)

8. Add the remaining whole beans and correct the density of the soup, if desired, by adding a little more homemade broth or water. Cover and simmer for 10 minutes more. If you are making the dish ahead of time and stopping at this point, bring the soup to a simmer for a few minutes before proceeding with the next and final steps.

9. To make the flavored oil, put the mashed, peeled garlic cloves and the 3 tablespoons of olive oil in a small skillet and turn on the heat to medium. When the garlic becomes colored a light nut brown, add the chopped rosemary or the whole sprig, turn off the heat, and stir two or three times. Pour the oil through a strainer into the pot, discarding the garlic and rosemary. Simmer the soup for another few minutes.

10. Transfer the soup to a large serving bowl to bring to the table. Something made of earthenware in a deep terra-cotta color would be quite handsome. Put the optional grilled bread slices into individual plates or bowls and ladle a first serving of soup over them.

Chick Pea Soup

THERE IS a sweet depth of flavor to chick peas that distinguishes them from all other legumes. In the countries on the eastern edge of the Mediterranean they continue to be popular after more than 5,000 years of cultivation. Soup is one of the tastiest things one can do with chick peas. This one is lovely on its own, and it can be varied adding either rice or pasta. Unlike canned kidney beans, which can be mushy, canned chick peas can be very good and, if you don't mind the slightly higher cost, you needn't bother with soaking and cooking dried chick peas.   *For 4 to 6 servings*

4 whole garlic cloves, peeled
⅓ cup extra virgin olive oil
1½ teaspoons dried rosemary
    leaves, crushed fine almost
    to a powder, OR a small
    sprig of fresh rosemary
⅔ cup canned imported Italian
    plum tomatoes, cut up,
    with their juice
¾ cup dried chick peas, soaked
    and cooked as directed on

page 13, OR 2¼ cups
    canned chick peas, drained
1 cup Basic Homemade Meat
    Broth, prepared as directed
    on page 15, OR 1 bouillon
    cube dissolved in 1 cup
    water
Salt
Black pepper, ground fresh
    from the mill

1. Put the garlic and olive oil in a pot that can subsequently accommodate all the ingredients, and turn on the heat to medium. Sauté the garlic cloves until they become colored a light nut brown, then remove them from the pan.

2. Add the crushed rosemary leaves or the fresh sprig, stir, then put in the cut-up tomatoes with their juice. Cook for about 20 to 25 minutes or until the oil floats free from the tomatoes.

3. Add the drained cooked or canned chick peas and cook for 5 minutes, stirring them thoroughly with the juices in the pan.

4. Add the broth or the dissolved bouillon cube, cover, and adjust heat so that the soup bubbles at a steady, but moderate boil for 15 minutes.

5. Taste and correct for salt. Add a few grindings of pepper. Let the soup bubble uncovered for another minute, then serve promptly.

Ahead-of-time note ❀ The soup can be made in advance and refrigerated for at least a week in a tightly sealed container. If making it ahead of time, do not add any salt or pepper until you reheat it just before serving.

Version with Rice

For 8 servings

The Chick Pea Soup made from the preceding recipe
3 cups (or more) Basic Home-made Meat Broth, prepared as directed on page 15, OR 2 bouillon cubes dissolved with 3 cups water

1 cup rice, preferably Italian Arborio rice
1 tablespoon extra virgin olive oil
Salt

1. Purée all but a quarter cupful of the chick pea soup through the larger holes of a food mill into a soup pot. Add the rest of the soup, all the broth or dissolved bouillon, and bring to a steady, but moderate boil.

2. Add the rice, stir, cover the pot, and cook, letting the soup bubble steadily, but moderately, until the rice is tender, but still firm to the bite. Check after about 10 to 12 minutes to see if more liquid is needed. If the soup is becoming too dense, add more homemade broth or water. When the rice is done, swirl in the olive oil, then taste and correct for salt. Let the soup settle for two or three minutes before serving.

Chick Pea Soup (continued)

Version with Pasta

The Chick Pea Soup made from the recipe on page 112

2 cups (or more) Basic Home-made Meat Broth, prepared as directed on page 15, OR 2 bouillon cubes dissolved with 2 cups water

Either *maltagliati* pasta, home-made with 1 egg and ⅔ cup flour, see pages 131 and 137 for instructions, OR ½ pound small, tubular macaroni

2 tablespoons freshly grated *parmigiano-reggiano* cheese

1 tablespoon butter

Salt

1. Purée one-third of the chick pea soup through the larger holes of a food mill into a soup pot. Add the rest of the soup and all the broth or dissolved bouillon and bring to a steady, but moderate boil.

2. Add the pasta, stir, cover the pot, and continue to cook at a moderate boil. If you are using homemade pasta, taste after 1 minute for doneness. If you are using macaroni pasta, it will take several minutes longer, but stop the cooking when the pasta is tender, but still firm to the bite. If, while the pasta is cooking, you find the soup needs more liquid, add a little more homemade broth or water.

3. When the pasta is done, turn off the heat, swirl in the grated Parmesan and the butter, taste, and correct for salt. Serve immediately.

Barley Soup in the Style of Trent

ONE OF THE outstanding features of the cooking of the northeastern region of Friuli and the neighboring Trentino is barley soup. The one given below owes its exceptional appeal to the successive layers of flavor laid down by the sautéed onion and ham, by the rosemary and parsley, and by the diced potato and carrot, which provide the ideal base for the wonderfully fortifying quality of barley itself.   *For 4 servings*

1¼ cups pearl barley

¼ cup plus 2 tablespoons extra virgin olive oil

½ cup chopped onion

⅓ cup prosciutto OR *pancetta* OR country ham OR boiled unsmoked ham, chopped fine

½ teaspoon dried rosemary
    leaves OR 1 teaspoon fresh
    chopped very fine
1 tablespoon chopped parsley
1 medium potato
2 small carrots or 1 large
1 bouillon cube

Salt
Black pepper, ground fresh
    from the mill
2 to 3 tablespoons freshly
    grated *parmigiano-reggiano*
    cheese

1. Put the barley in a soup pot, add enough water to cover by 3 inches, put a lid on the pot, bring the water to a slow, but steady simmer, and cook for 1 hour or until the barley is fully tender but not mushy.

2. While the barley is cooking, put all the oil and the chopped onion in a small skillet, and turn on the heat to medium. Sauté the onion until it becomes colored a pale gold, and add the chopped ham, cooking it for 2 to 3 minutes and stirring it from time to time. Add the rosemary and parsley, stir thoroughly, and after a minute or less, turn off the heat.

3. Peel both the potato and carrot, rinse in cold water, and dice them fine (they should yield approximately ⅔ cup each).

4. When the barley is done, pour the entire contents of the skillet into the pot, add the diced potato and carrot, the bouillon cube, salt, and several grindings of pepper. Add a little more water if the soup appears to be too dense. It should be neither too thick nor too thin. Cook at a steady simmer for 30 minutes, stirring from time to time.

5. Off heat, just before serving, swirl the grated cheese into the pot. Serve promptly.

Ahead-of-time note ✹ The soup may be prepared one or two days in advance, but add the grated cheese only when you reheat it.

Broccoli and Egg Barley Soup

THE BARLEY in this soup is a coarse-grained homemade pasta product that is described in the pasta chapter, and it seems to have just the texture and consistency one wants here. One can, however, substitute cooked true barley, or, less satisfactorily, the small, grainy boxed soup pasta. One of the charms of this soup is the way the broccoli stems and florets are used, both sautéed in garlic and olive oil, but the first puréed to provide body, while the florets become delicious bite-size pieces, their tenderness in lively contrast to the chewy firmness of the pasta or real barley.   *For 6 servings*

Broccoli and Egg Barley Soup (continued)

A medium bunch fresh broccoli
Salt
⅓ cup extra virgin olive oil
1 teaspoon chopped garlic
2 cups Basic Homemade Meat
　　Broth, prepared as directed
　　on page 15
⅔ cup *manfrigul,* homemade
　　pasta barley, made as

described on page 138, OR
cooked barley (see page
115), OR ½ cup small,
coarse, boxed soup pasta
1 tablespoon chopped parsley
Freshly grated *parmigiano-
reggiano* cheese at the table

1. Detach the broccoli florets from the stalks. Trim away about ½ inch from the tough butt end of the stalks. With a sharp paring knife, peel away the dark green skin on the stalks and on the thicker stems of the florets. Split very thick stems in two lengthwise. Soak all the stalks and florets in cold water, drain, and rinse in fresh cold water.

2. Bring 3 quarts of water to a boil. Add 2 tablespoons of salt, which will keep the broccoli green, and put in the stalks. When the water returns to a boil, wait 2 minutes, then add the florets. If they float to the surface, dunk them from time to time to keep them from losing color. When the water returns to a boil again, wait 1 minute, then retrieve all the broccoli with a colander scoop or slotted spoon. Do not discard the water in the pot.

3. Choose a sauté pan that can accommodate all the stalks and florets without overlapping. Put in the oil and garlic, and turn on the heat to medium. Sauté the garlic until it becomes colored a light gold. Add all the broccoli, some salt, and turn the heat up to high. Cook for 2 to 3 minutes, stirring frequently.

4. Using a slotted spoon, transfer the broccoli florets to a plate and set aside. Do not discard the oil from the pan.

5. Put the broccoli stalks into a food processor, run the steel blade for a moment, then add all the oil from the pan plus 1 tablespoon of the water in which the broccoli had been blanched. Finish processing to a uniform purée.

6. Put the puréed stalks into a soup pot, add the broth, and bring to a moderate boil. Add the pasta or the cooked barley. Cook at a steady, gentle boil until the pasta is tender, but firm. Depending on the thickness and freshness of the pasta, it should take about 10 minutes. You will probably need to dilute the soup as it cooks, because it tends to become too dense. To thin it out use some of the reserved water in which the broccoli had been blanched. Take care not to make the soup too runny.

7. While the pasta is cooking, separate the floret clusters into bite-size pieces. As soon as the pasta is done, put in the florets, continue cooking for about 1 minute, add the chopped parsley, and stir. Taste and correct for salt, and serve the soup promptly with the grated Parmesan on the side.

Passatelli—Egg and Parmesan Strands in Broth

WHERE THE PROVINCE of Bologna stops, traveling southeast toward the Adriatic, the territory known as Romagna begins. A style of cooking is practiced here that, while it may bear a superficial resemblance to the Bolognese, holds more dear such values as lightness and delicacy. This simplest of soups is a good example of that approach and those virtues.

In Romagna a slightly concave, perforated disk with handles is used to produce the *passatelli* strands from the egg and Parmesan mixture, but it is possible to duplicate the result fairly closely using that essential tool of an Italian kitchen, a food mill. *For 6 servings*

7 cups Basic Homemade Meat Broth, prepared as directed on page 15

¾ cup freshly grated *parmi-giano-reggiano* cheese, plus additional cheese at the table

⅓ cup fine, dry, unflavored bread crumbs

Whole nutmeg

The grated peel of 1 lemon

2 eggs

Note ✹ The flavor of good homemade meat broth is so vital to this soup that no commercial substitute should be used.

1. Bring the broth to a steady, slow boil in an uncovered pot. In the meantime, combine the grated Parmesan, bread crumbs, a tiny grating—no more than ⅛ teaspoon—of nutmeg, and grated lemon peel on a pastry board or other work surface, making a mound with a well in the center. Break the eggs into the well, and knead all the ingredients to form a well-knit, tender,

Egg and Parmesan Strands in Broth (cont.)

granular dough, somewhat resembling *polenta,* cooked cornmeal mush. If the mixture is too loose and moist, add a little more grated Parmesan and bread crumbs.

2. Fit the disk with large holes into your food mill. When the broth begins to boil, press the *passatelli* mixture through the mill directly into the boiling broth. Keep the mill as high above the steam rising from the pot as you can. Cook at a slow, but steady boil for 1 minute or 2 at the most. Turn off the heat, allow the soup to settle for 4 to 5 minutes, then ladle into individual plates or bowls. Serve with grated Parmesan on the side.

Stuffed Lettuce Soup

EASTER on the Italian Riviera is a time for roast baby lamb and stuffed lettuce soup. In the traditional version of this soup, the hearts of small lettuce heads are scooped out and replaced by a mixture of herbs, soft cheese, chicken, veal, calf's brains, and sweetbreads. The much simpler version below, omitting the brains and sweetbreads, comes from a friend's kitchen in Rapallo, and is immensely satisfying. *For 4 to 6 servings*

½ pound veal, any cut as long as it is all solid meat

1 whole chicken breast, boned and skinned

4 tablespoons (½ stick) butter

Salt

Black pepper, ground fresh from the mill

1½ tablespoons chopped onion

1 tablespoon celery chopped very fine

1 tablespoon carrot chopped very fine

2 tablespoons fresh *ricotta*

½ cup freshly grated *parmigiano-reggiano* cheese, plus additional cheese for each serving

1 teaspoon fresh marjoram OR
   ¾ teaspoon dried
1 tablespoon chopped parsley
1 egg yolk
3 heads Boston lettuce
4 cups Basic Homemade Meat

Broth, prepared as directed
on page 15
For each serving: 1 slice of
bread toasted dark or
browned in butter

1. Cut the veal and the chicken into 1-inch pieces.

2. Put all the butter in a large sauté pan and turn on the heat to medium. When the butter foam begins to subside, put in the veal with a pinch or two of salt and one or two grindings of pepper. Cook and turn the veal to brown it evenly on all sides, then transfer it to a plate, using a slotted spoon or spatula.

3. Put the chicken pieces in the pan, with a little salt and pepper, and cook briefly, just until the meat loses its raw shine. Transfer it to the plate with the veal.

4. Put the chopped onion into the pan and cook it at medium heat, stirring it, until it becomes colored a pale gold. Add the celery and carrot, stir from time to time, and cook the vegetables until they are tender. Pour the vegetables along with all the juices in the pan into a bowl.

5. Chop the cooked veal and chicken pieces very fine, using a knife or the food processor. Add the minced meat to the bowl.

6. Put the *ricotta*, the ½ cup grated Parmesan, the marjoram, parsley, and egg yolk into the bowl and mix thoroughly until all ingredients are smoothly amalgamated. Taste and correct for salt and pepper.

7. Discard any of the bruised or blemished outer leaves of the lettuce. Pull off all the others one by one, taking care not to rip them, and gently rinse them in cold water. Save the very small leaves at the heart to use on another occasion in a salad.

8. Bring 1 gallon of water to a boil, add 1 tablespoon of salt, and put in 3 or 4 lettuce leaves. Retrieve them after 5 or 6 seconds, using a colander scoop or skimmer.

9. Spread the leaves flat on a work surface. Cut away any part of the central rib that is not tender. On each leaf, place about 1 tablespoon of the mixture from the bowl, giving it a narrow sausage shape. Roll up the leaf, wrapping it completely around the stuffing. Gently squeeze each rolled up leaf in your hand to tighten the wrapping, and set it aside.

10. Repeat the above operation with the remaining leaves, doing them 3 or 4 at a time. No additional salt is needed when blanching them. When the leaves get smaller, slightly overlap 2 leaves to make a single wrapper.

11. When all the leaves have been stuffed, place them side by side in a

Stuffed Lettuce Soup (continued)

soup pot or large saucepan. Pack them tightly, leaving no space between them, and make as many layers as is necessary. Choose a dinner plate or flat pot lid just small enough to fit inside the pan and rest it on the top layer of stuffed lettuce rolls to keep them in place while cooking.

12. Pour in enough broth to cover the plate or lid by about 1 inch. Cover the pot, bring the broth to a steady, very gentle simmer, and cook for 30 minutes from the time the broth starts to simmer.

13. At the same time, pour the remaining broth—there should be no less than 1½ cups left—into a small saucepan, cover, and turn on the heat to low.

14. When the stuffed lettuce rolls are done, transfer them to individual plates or bowls, placing them over a single slice of toasted or browned bread. Handle gently to keep the rolls from unwrapping. Pour over them any of the broth remaining in the larger pot and all the hot broth from the small saucepan. Sprinkle some grated Parmesan over each plate and serve at once.

Clam Soup

THE FLAVOR of most Italian dishes is usually within reach of those who understand and practice the simplicity and directness of Italian methods. When it comes to seafood, however, one must sometimes take a more round-about route to approach comparable results. The clams of my native Romagna, once so plentiful and cheap that in our dialect they were called *povrazz—poveracce* in Italian—meaning they were food for the poor, come out of the sea with so much natural, peppery flavor that next to nothing needs to be added when cooking them. North American clams, on the other hand, need all the help they can get. Thus, in the recipe that follows you will find shallots and wine and chili pepper, all of which you would very likely dispense with if you were making the dish somewhere on the Adriatic coast.

Note ✽ In Italy, no cook book or cook will ever advise you to discard any clams that don't open while cooking. Clams stay clamped shut because they are alive. The most reluctant ones to loosen their hold and unclench their shells are the most vigorously alive of all. When eating them raw on the half shell, how does anyone know which ones would not have opened in the pot? The clams you should discard are those that stay open when you handle them before cooking, because they are dead.   *For 4 servings*

3 dozen small littleneck clams live in their shells
½ cup extra virgin olive oil
1½ tablespoons shallots OR onions chopped very fine
2 teaspoons garlic chopped very fine
2 tablespoons parsley chopped very fine

¼ teaspoon cornstarch dissolved in ⅔ cup dry white wine
⅛ teaspoon chopped hot red chili pepper
For each serving: 1 thick slice of crusty bread, grilled

1. Soak the clams for 5 minutes in a basin or sink filled with cold water. Drain and refill the basin with fresh cold water, leaving in the clams. Vigorously scrub the clams one by one with a very stiff brush. Drain, refill the basin, and repeat the whole scrubbing operation. Do this 2 or 3 more times, always in fresh changes of water, until you see no more sand settling to the bottom of the basin. Discard any that, when handled, don't clamp shut.

2. Choose a broad enough pot that can later accommodate all the clams in layers no more than 2 or 3 deep. Put in the olive oil and chopped shallots or onion and turn on the heat to medium. Sauté until the shallots or onion become translucent, and add the garlic. Sauté the garlic until it becomes colored a pale gold, then add the parsley. Stir once or twice, and add the wine and the chili pepper. Cook at lively heat for about 2 minutes, stirring frequently, then put all the clams in the pot.

3. Stir 2 or 3 times, trying to turn over as many of the clams as you can, then cover the pot, keeping the heat at high. Check the clams frequently, moving them around with a long-handled spoon. Some clams will open sooner than others. Using a pair of tongs or a slotted spoon, pick up the clams as they open and put them into a serving bowl.

4. When all the clams have opened and have been transferred to the serving bowl, turn off the heat and, tipping the pot to one side, ladle the juices out of the pot and over the clams. Take care not stir up the juices or to scoop

them up from the bottom, where there may be sand. Bring the bowl to the table promptly together with a slice of grilled bread for each diner's soup plate.

Clam and Pea Soup

CLAMS MARRY WELL with green vegetables, and when good fresh peas are around this can be an especially sweet and lively soup. If raw peas are stale and floury, however, it may be wiser to settle for the frozen variety. *For 6 servings*

3 dozen small littleneck clams live in their shells
3 pounds fresh peas, unshelled weight, OR 3 ten-ounce packages frozen peas, thawed
⅓ cup extra virgin olive oil
½ cup chopped onion
1½ teaspoons chopped garlic
2 tablespoons chopped parsley

⅔ cup canned imported Italian plum tomatoes, cut up, with their juice
Salt
Black pepper, ground fresh from the mill
Crostini, fried bread squares, made as directed on page 90

1. Soak and scrub the clams as directed on page 121. Discard any open clams that do not clamp shut at your touch.

2. Put the clams in a pot broad enough to accommodate them in layers no more than 2 or 3 deep, add ½ cup of water, cover tightly, and turn on the heat to high. Check the clams frequently, moving them around with a long-handled spoon, bringing up to the top the clams from the bottom. As soon as the first clams start to open, transfer these with tongs or a slotted spoon to a bowl. When the last clam has unclenched its shell and you have taken it out of the pot, turn off the heat, and leave the pot's lid on.

3. Detach all the clam meat from the shells, discarding the shells. Dip each clam in the juices in the pot to rinse off any grains of sand clinging to it; dip it in and out very gently, without stirring up the pot juices.

4. Cut each clam up into 2 or 3 pieces, putting them all in a small, clean bowl.

5. Pour back into the pot any of the juices that collected in the original bowl to which you had transferred the clams in their shells.

6. Set a strainer over a bowl or pouring cup and line it with a paper towel. Filter all the juices in the pot, straining them through the paper towel.

7. Pour just enough of the filtered juices over the cut-up clam meat to keep it moist, and reserve the rest.

8. *If using fresh peas:* Shell them and prepare a cupful of the pods for cooking as described on page 93. Soak in cold water, drain, rinse, and set aside.

If using thawed frozen peas: Move on to the next step.

9. Choose a deep, large sauté pan, put in the oil, the chopped onion, and turn on the heat to medium. Cook and stir the onion until it becomes translucent, then add the chopped garlic. Stir once or twice. When the garlic becomes colored a deep gold, add the chopped parsley, stir well, then add the cut-up tomatoes with their juice. Add salt and a few grindings of pepper and cook for 10 minutes, stirring occasionally.

10. Put in the shelled fresh peas and the prepared pods, or the thawed frozen peas, add the filtered clam juices and, if necessary, enough water to cover the peas by about 1 inch. Cover the pot and adjust heat to cook at a gentle, but steady simmer. If using fresh peas, it may take 10 minutes or more for them to become tender, depending on their freshness and youth. If using thawed peas, cook for just 1 or 2 minutes. Taste and correct for salt and pepper.

11. Add the cut-up clams with any remaining juices. Cook no longer than the few seconds necessary to warm them through, or they will become tough. Ladle into individual soup bowls and serve at once with *crostini.*

Mussel Soup

For 4 servings

2 pounds mussels live in their shells

⅓ cup extra virgin olive oil

1½ teaspoons garlic chopped fine

1 tablespoon parsley chopped coarse

1 cup canned imported Italian plum tomatoes, drained and cut up

⅛ teaspoon chopped hot red chili pepper

For each serving: 1 thick slice of grilled or browned in the oven crusty bread, lightly rubbed with a peeled mashed garlic clove

1. Wash and clean the mussels as described on page 81. Discard any that do not clamp shut at the touch.

2. Choose a pot that can comfortably accommodate all the mussels in

Mussel Soup (continued)

their shells. Put in the oil and chopped garlic, and turn on the heat to medium. Sauté the garlic until it has become colored a light gold. Add the parsley, stir thoroughly once, then put in the cut-up tomatoes and the chili pepper. Cook, uncovered, at a gentle, but steady simmer for about 25 minutes, or until the oil floats free of the tomatoes.

3. Put in all the mussels in their shells, cover the pot, and raise the heat to high. Check the mussels frequently, moving them around with a long-handled spoon and bringing up to the top the mussels from the bottom. Cook until all the mussels have opened their shells.

4. Put a slice of the grilled, garlicky bread on the bottom of each individual soup bowl, ladle the mussels with their sauce and juices over it, and serve at once.

Squid and Artichoke Soup

IN THE ITALIAN RIVIERA, whether one is cooking meat or seafood, the principal concern is marrying it to the right vegetable. An example is this soup of squid and artichokes, a match as fresh as it is beautiful, mingling pearly white rings and moss-green slivers, gifts of the deep and of the sun.   *For 4 servings*

1 pound fresh OR frozen whole
    squid, thawed, preferably
    with sacs under 5 inches
    long
½ cup extra virgin olive oil
1 teaspoon garlic chopped very
    fine
3 tablespoons chopped parsley
Black pepper, ground fresh
    from the mill

1 cup dry white wine
1 large or 2 medium artichokes
The juice of ½ lemon
Salt
For each serving: 1 thick slice of
    grilled or browned in the
    oven crusty bread, rubbed
    lightly with a peeled
    mashed garlic clove

1. Clean the squid as described on pages 317–319. Cut the sacs into narrow rings, ¼ inch broad or less. Separate the larger tentacle clusters in two, and cut in half all tentacles that are longer than 1 inch.

2. Put the oil and garlic into a soup pot and turn the heat on to medium. Cook, stirring from time to time, until the garlic becomes lightly colored. Add the parsley, stir once or twice, add the squid, stir to coat well, add liberal grindings of pepper and the wine, and turn all ingredients over once or

twice. If the liquid is not sufficient to cover the squid by at least 1½ inches, add as much water as necessary. When the liquid begins to simmer, cover the pot and turn down the heat to medium low.

3. Cook for 40 minutes or more until the squid rings feel tender when prodded with a fork. Whenever the level of liquid falls below 1½ inches above the squid, add more water.

4. While the squid cooks, clean the artichoke as described on pages 57–59. Cut it lengthwise into the very thinnest possible slices, leaving on part of the stem wherever possible. Put the sliced artichoke in a bowl with enough cold water to cover and the juice of ½ lemon.

5. When the squid is tender, add salt and stir well. Drain the artichoke slices, rinse them in cold water, and add them to the pot. Add enough water to cover the ingredients by 2 inches. Add a little more salt, stir thoroughly, and cover the pot again. Cook until the artichoke is tender, about 15 minutes, more or less, depending on the artichoke. Taste and correct for salt and pepper.

6. Put a slice of the garlicky bread in each individual soup bowl, pour soup over it, and serve at once.

PASTA

The Essentials of Cooking Pasta

The pot Use a lightweight pot, such as enameled aluminum, that will transmit heat quickly and be easy to handle when full of pasta and boiling water.

The colander An ample colander with feet attached should be waiting, resting securely in the kitchen sink or a large basin.

Water Pasta needs lots of water to move around in, or it becomes gummy. Four quarts of water are required for a pound of pasta. Never use less than 3 quarts, even for a small amount of pasta. Add another quart for each half pound, but do not cook more than 2 pounds in the same pot. Large quantities of pasta are difficult to cook properly, and pots with that much water are heavy and dangerous to handle.

Salt For every pound of pasta, put in no less than 1½ tablespoons of salt, more if the sauce is very mild and undersalted. Add the salt when the water comes to a boil. Wait until the water returns to a full, rolling boil before putting in the pasta.

Olive oil Never put oil in the water except when cooking stuffed homemade pasta. In the latter case, a tablespoon of oil in the pot reduces the friction and keeps the stuffed pasta from splitting.

Calculating servings One pound of factory-made, boxed dry pasta should produce 4 to 6 servings, depending on what follows the pasta. For approximate servings of fresh pasta, see the section on homemade pasta, page 130.

Putting the pasta in the pot The pasta goes in after the boiling water has been salted and has returned to a full boil. Put all the pasta in at one time and cover the pot briefly to hasten the water's return to a boil. Watch it to avoid it boiling over and extinguishing the gas flame. When the water has once again returned to a boil, cook either uncovered or with a lid on largely askew. Using a long wooden spoon, stir the pasta the moment it goes into the water, and frequently thereafter while it is cooking.

❧ If you are cooking long dried pasta such as *spaghetti* or *perciatelli,* when you drop it in the pot, use a long wooden spoon to bend the strands and submerge them completely. Do not break up spaghetti or any other long pasta into smaller pieces.

❧ If you are using homemade pasta, gather all of it in a dish towel, tightly hold one end of the towel high above the boiling water, loosen the bottom end, and let the pasta slide into the pot.

Al dente ❧ Pasta must be cooked until it is firm to the bite, *al dente.* The firmness of *spaghetti* and other dried factory pasta is different from that of *fettuccine* and other homemade pasta. The latter can never be as firm and chewy as the former, but that does not mean one should allow it to become yieldingly soft: It should always offer some resistance to the bite. When it does not, pasta becomes leaden, it loses buoyancy and its ability to deliver briskly the flavors of its sauce.

Draining ❧ The instant pasta is done, and not a second later, you must drain it, pouring it out of the pot and into the colander. Give the colander a few vigorous sideways and up-and-down shakes to drain all the water away.

Saucing and tossing ❧ Have the sauce ready when the pasta is done. Do not let drained pasta sit in the colander waiting for the sauce to be finished or reheated. Transfer cooked, drained pasta without a moment's delay to a warm serving bowl. The instant it's in the bowl, start tossing it with the sauce. If grated cheese is called for, add some of it immediately, and toss the pasta with it. The heat will melt the cheese, which can then fuse creamily with the sauce.

In the sequence of steps that lead to producing a dish of pasta and getting it to the table, none is more important than tossing. Up to the time you toss, pasta and sauce are two separate entities. Tossing bridges the separation and makes them one. The oil or butter must coat every strand thoroughly and evenly, reach into every crevice, and with it carry the flavors of the components of the sauce. However marvelous a sauce may be, it cannot merely sit on top of or at the bottom of the bowl. If it is not broadly and uniformly distributed, the pasta for which it is intended will have little flavor.

When you add the sauce, toss rapidly, using a fork and spoon or two forks, bringing the pasta up from the bottom of the bowl, separating it, lifting it, dropping it, turning it over, swirling it around and around. If the sauce clings thickly together, separate it with the fork and spoon so that it can be spread evenly.

When the sauce is butter-based, add a dollop of fresh butter and give the pasta one or two last tosses. If the sauce has an olive oil base, follow the same procedure, using fresh olive oil instead of butter.

Note ✿ Fresh pasta is more absorbent than factory-made pasta, and more butter or oil is usually required.

Serving ✿ Once the pasta is sauced, serve it promptly, inviting your guests and family to put off talking and start eating. The point to remember is that from the moment the pasta is done, there should be no pauses in the sequence of draining, saucing, serving, and eating. Cooked, hot pasta must not be allowed to sit, or it will turn into a clammy, gluey mass.

❦ *Factory-Made Pasta* ❦

THE BOXED, dry pasta one refers to as factory-made includes such familiar shapes as *spaghetti, penne,* and *fusilli.* These cannot be made as successfully at home as they are in commercial pasta plants with industrial equipment. Dry pasta from factories is not necessarily less fine than the fresh pasta one can make at home. On the contrary, for many dishes, factory-made pasta is the better choice, although for some others, one may want the particular attributes of homemade pasta. The differences between the two categories of pasta and their general applications are discussed on pages 25–26.

❦ *How to Make Fresh Pasta at Home* ❦
The Machine Method and the Rolling-Pin Method

UNLESS you happen to live in Emilia-Romagna, in whose towns and cities there are still a few shops selling pasta made by hand, you can make far better fresh pasta, either by the rolling-pin method or the machine method, than you can buy or eat anywhere.

It needs to be said, however, that the two methods are not merely separate ways of reaching the same objective. Pasta rolled by hand is quite unlike the fresh pasta made with a machine. In hand-rolled pasta, the dough is thinned by stretching it, with a rapid succession of hand motions, over the length of a yard-long wooden dowel. In the machine method, the dough is squeezed between two cylinders until it reaches the desired thinness.

The color of hand-stretched pasta is demonstrably deeper than that thinned by machine; its surface is etched by a barely visible pattern of intersecting ridges and hollows; when cooked, the pasta sucks in sauce and exudes moistness. On the palate it has a gossamer, soft touch that no other pasta can duplicate. But learning the rolling-pin method is, unfortunately, not just a question of following instructions but rather of learning a craft. The instructions must be executed again and again with great patience, and mastered by a pair of nimble, willing hands until the motions are performed through intuition rather than deliberation.

The machine, on the other hand, requires virtually no skill to use. Once you have learned to combine eggs and flour into a dough that is neither too moist nor too dry, all you do is follow a series of extraordinarily simple, mechanical steps and you can produce fine fresh pasta inexpensively, at home, at the very first attempt.

The flour ✹ In Italy, the classic fresh egg pasta produced in the Bolognese style is made with a flour known as 00, *doppio zero*. It is a talcum-soft white flour, less strong in gluten than American all-purpose flour of either the bleached or unbleached variety. When, outside of Italy, I make fresh pasta at home, I have found that unbleached all-purpose flour does the most consistently satisfying job: It is easy to work with; the pasta it produces is plump and has marvelous texture and fragrance.

Confusion exists over the merits of *semolina*, which is milled from durum, the strongest of wheats. In Italian it is called *semola di grano duro*, and you will find it listed on all Italian packages of factory-made pasta. It is the only suitable flour for industrially produced pasta, but I do not prefer it for home use. To begin with, its consistency is often grainy, even when it is sold as pasta flour, and grainy *semolina* is frustrating to work with. Even when it is milled to the fine, silky texture you need, you must use a machine to roll it out; to try to do it with a rolling pin is to face a nearly hopeless struggle. My advice is to leave *semolina* flour to factories and to commercial pasta makers: At home use unbleached all-purpose flour.

PASTA BY THE MACHINE METHOD

The machine ✹ The only kind of pasta machine you should consider is the kind that has one set of parallel cylinders, usually made of steel, for kneading and thinning the dough, and a double set of cutters, one broad for *fettuccine*,

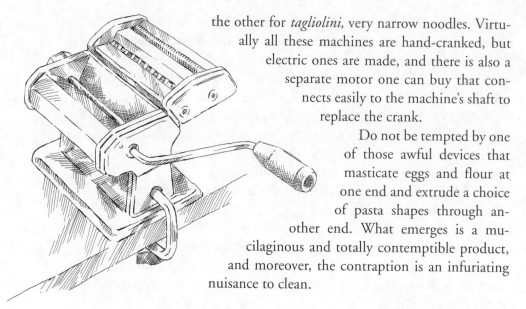

the other for *tagliolini,* very narrow noodles. Virtually all these machines are hand-cranked, but electric ones are made, and there is also a separate motor one can buy that connects easily to the machine's shaft to replace the crank.

Do not be tempted by one of those awful devices that masticate eggs and flour at one end and extrude a choice of pasta shapes through another end. What emerges is a mucilaginous and totally contemptible product, and moreover, the contraption is an infuriating nuisance to clean.

For yellow pasta dough ❀ 1 cup unbleached flour and 2 large eggs produce about ¾ pound homemade pasta, which will yield 3 standard portions or 4 of appetizer dimensions. Use the above as an approximate ratio of flour to eggs, which you may need to alter depending on the absorption capacity of the eggs, and sometimes, even on the humidity or lack thereof in the kitchen.

Note ❀ If making dough for stuffed yellow pasta, add ½ tablespoon of milk to the above proportions.

For green pasta dough ❀ 1½ cups unbleached flour, 2 large eggs, and either ½ of a 10-ounce package of frozen leaf spinach, thawed, ·OR ½ pound fresh spinach. The yield is approximately 1 pound of green pasta, which produces 4 standard portions.

If using thawed frozen spinach, cook it in a covered pan with ¼ teaspoon salt until it is tender and loses its raw taste. If using fresh spinach, wash it and cook it as described on page 89. Drain either kind of spinach of all liquid, and when cool enough to handle, squeeze it in your hands to force it to shed any remaining liquid. Chop very fine with a knife, but not in a food processor, which draws out too much moisture.

Note ❀ Outside of spinach, no other coloring can be recommended as an alternative to basic yellow pasta. Other substances have no flavor, and therefore have no gastronomic interest. Or, if they do contribute flavor, such as that of the deplorable black pasta whose dough is tinted with squid ink, its taste is not fresh. Pasta does not need to be dressed up, except in the colors and aromas of its sauce.

Combining the eggs and flour ❀ Because no one can tell in advance exactly how much flour one needs, the sensible method of combining eggs and flour is by hand, which permits you to adjust the proportion of flour as you go along.

Pour the flour onto a work surface, shape it into a mound, and scoop out a deep hollow in its center. Break the eggs into the hollow. If making green dough, also add the chopped spinach at this point.

Beat the eggs lightly with a fork for about 1 minute as though you were making an omelet. If using spinach, beat for a minute or so longer. Draw some of the flour over the eggs, mixing it in with the fork a little at a time, until the eggs are no longer runny. Draw the sides of the mound together with your hands, but push some of the flour to one side, keeping it out of the way until you find you absolutely need it. Work the eggs and flour together, using your fingers and the palms of your hands, until you have a smoothly integrated mixture. If it is still moist, work in more flour.

When the mass feels good to you and you think it does not require any more flour, wash your hands, dry them, and run a simple test: Press your thumb deep into center of the mass; if it comes out clean, without any sticky matter on it, no more flour is needed. Put the egg and flour mass to one side, scrape the work surface absolutely clear of any loose or caked bits of flour and of any crumbs, and get ready to knead.

Kneading ❀ The proper kneading of dough may be the most important step in making good pasta by machine, and it is one of the secrets of the superior fresh pasta you can make at home. Dough for pasta can be kneaded in a machine, but it isn't really that much quicker than doing it by hand, and it is far less satisfactory, particularly when kneaded in a food processor.

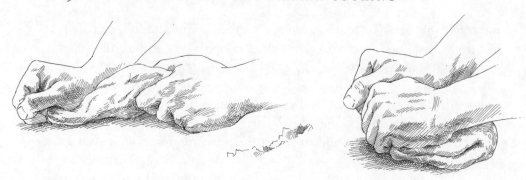

Return to the mass of flour and eggs. Push forward against it using the heel of your palm, keeping your fingers bent. Fold the mass in half, give it a half turn, press hard against it with the heel of your palm again, and repeat the operation. Make sure that you keep turning the ball of dough always in the same direction, either clockwise or counterclockwise, as you prefer. When you have kneaded it thus for 8 full minutes and the dough is as smooth as baby skin, it is ready for the machine.

Note ❀ If you are working with a large mass, you can divide it into 2 or more parts and finish kneading one before taking on the other. Keep any part of the mass you are not working with or of the dough you have finished kneading tightly covered in plastic wrap.

Thinning ❀ Cut each ball of dough made with 2 eggs into 6 equal parts. In other words, the pieces of dough you end up with for thinning should be three times as many as the eggs you used.

Spread clean, dry, cloth dish towels over a work counter near where you'll be using the machine. If you are making a lot of pasta you'll need a lot of counter space and a lot of towels.

Set the pair of smooth cylinders, the thinning rollers, at their widest opening. Flat-ten one of the pieces of dough by pum-meling it with your palm, and run it through the machine. Fold the dough

twice into a third of its length, and feed it by its narrow end through the machine once again. Repeat the operation 2 or 3 times, then lay the flattened strip of pasta over a towel on the counter. Since you are going to have a lot of strips, start at one end of the counter, leaving room for the others.

Take another piece of dough, flatten it with your hand, and run it through the machine exactly as described above. Lay the strip next to the previously thinned one on the towel, but do not allow them to touch or overlap, because they are still moist enough to stick to each other. Proceed to flatten all the remaining pieces in the same manner.

Note ✽ This is the procedure to follow if you are going to cut the pasta into noodles. If you plan to use it for *raviolini* or other stuffed shapes, please see the stuffed pasta note on the next page.

Close down the opening between the machine's rollers by one notch. Take the first pasta strip you had flattened and run it once through the rollers, feeding it by its narrow end. Do not fold it, but spread it flat on the cloth towel, and move on to the next pasta strip in the sequence.

When all the pasta strips have gone through the narrower opening once, bring the rollers closer together by another notch, and run the strips of pasta through them once again, following the procedure described above. You will find the strips becoming longer, as they get thinner, and if there is not enough room to spread them out on the counter, you can let them hang over the edge. Continue thinning the strips in sequence, progressively closing down the opening between the rollers one notch at a time, until the pasta is as thin as you want it. This step-by-step thinning procedure, which commercial makers of fresh pasta greatly abbreviate or skip altogether, is responsible, along with proper kneading, for giving good pasta its body and structure.

Stuffed pasta note ❦ Pasta dough to be used as a wrapper for stuffing should be soft and sticky. You must, therefore, make the following change in the sequence described above: Take just one piece of dough at a time through the entire thinning process, cut it, and stuff it as the recipe you've chosen describes. Then go on to the next piece. Keep all the pieces of dough waiting to be thinned out tightly wrapped in plastic wrap.

Drying ❦ For all cut pasta, *fettuccine, tagliolini, pappardelle,* and so on, allow the strips spread on the towels to dry for 10 minutes or more, depending on the temperature and ventilation of your kitchen. From time to time, turn the strips over. The pasta is ready for cutting when it is still pliant enough that it won't crack when cut, but not so soft and moist that the strands will stick to each other. Pasta requires no additional drying except for the purpose of storing it (see page 136).

Cutting flat pasta ❦ Use the broader set of cutters on the machine to make *fettuccine,* and the narrower ones for *tonnarelli* (see below) or *tagliolini.* When the pasta strips are sufficiently, but not excessively, dried, feed them through the cutter of choice. As the ribbons of noodles emerge from the cutter, separate them and spread them out on the cloth towels. To cook, gather the pasta in a single towel, as described in The Essentials of Cooking Pasta, pages 126-127, and slide it into boiling, salted water.

SPECIAL NOODLE CUTS

❧ *Tonnarelli* One of the most interesting shapes is this thin, square noodle from central Italy, which goes superbly well with an exceptional variety of sauces. It is also known as *maccheroni alla chitarra* because of the guitar-like tool used in central Italy for cutting it. It is as thick as it is broad. Its firmer body gives it the substance and "bite" of factory pasta, while its surface maintains the texture and affinity for delicate sauces of all homemade pasta.

The machine does a perfect job of making *tonnarelli.* The dough for *tonnarelli* must be left thicker than that for *fettuccine* and other noodles. To obtain the square cross-section this noodle must have, the thickness of the pasta strip should be equal to the width of the narrower grooves of the machine's cutter. On most machines, the last

thinning setting for *tonnarelli* is the second before the last. To make sure, run some dough through that setting and make sure that its thickness equals the width of the narrower cutting grooves.

❀ *Pappardelle* In Bologna, the city where homemade pasta reigns supreme, this eye-filling broad noodle is one of the favorite cuts. Its larger surface accepts substantial sauces, whether made with meat or vegetables or a combination of both. It has to be cut by hand, because the machine has no cutters for *pappardelle*. Cut the rolled-out pasta strips into ribbons about 6 inches long and 1 inch wide. A pastry wheel is the most efficient tool to use for the purpose, and the fluted kind yields the most attractive results.

❧ *Tagliatelle* When you use the broader cutters of the pasta machine, what you get is *fettuccine*. *Tagliatelle*, the classic Bolognese noodle and the best suited to Bolognese meat sauce, is a little broader and must be cut by hand. When the thinned strips of pasta are dry enough to cut, but still soft enough to bend without cracking, fold them up loosely along their length, making a flat roll about 3 inches wide at its sides. With a cleaver or similar knife,

cut the roll into ribbons about ¼ inch wide. Cut parallel to the original length of the pasta strip so that when you unroll the *tagliatelle* the noodle will be the full length of the strip.

Drying noodles for long storage ❧ It is often assumed that fresh pasta must be soft. Nothing could be more misleading. It is indeed soft the moment it's made, and it is perfectly all right to cook it while it is still in that state. But if one waits it will dry; it is a natural process and there is no reason to interfere with it. On the contrary, all the artificial methods by which fresh pasta is kept soft—sprinkling it with cornmeal, wrapping in plastic, refrigerating it—are not merely unnecessary, they actually undermine the quality of the pasta and ought to be shunned. When cooked, properly dried fresh pasta delivers all the texture and flavor it had originally. The limp product marketed as "fresh" pasta does not.

Once dried, fresh homemade

noodles can be stored for weeks in a cupboard, just like a box of *spaghetti*. As the noodles are cut, gather several strands at a time and curl them into circular nest shapes. Allow them to dry totally before storing them because, if any moisture remains when they are put away, mold will develop. To be safe, let the nests dry on towels for 24 hours. When dry, place them in a large box or tin, interleaving each layer of nests with paper towels. Handle carefully because they are brittle. Store in a dry cupboard, not in the refrigerator.

Note ❦ Allow slightly more cooking time for dried fresh pasta.

SOUP PASTA

It is in its cuts for soup that homemade pasta, with its light egg flavor and gentler consistency, clearly emerges as more desirable than the boxed factory-made kind.

❧ *Maltagliati* It is the best pasta you can use for thick soups, especially bean soups. Its name means "badly cut," because its irregular lozenge shape is not that of a long, even-sided ribbon. Fold the pasta strips into flat rolls, as described above for *tagliatelle*. Instead of cutting the roll straight as you would for regular noodles, cut it on the bias, cutting off first one corner, then the other. This leaves the pasta roll coming to a sharp point in the center of its cut end. Even off that end with a straight cut across, then cut off the corners once more as before. When you have finished cutting one roll, unfold and loosen the *maltagliati* immediately so they don't stick to each other.

Every time you make pasta, it is a good idea to use some of the dough for *maltagliati*. It can be dried for long storage, as described above, and you will have it available any time you want to add it to a soup.

❧ *Quadrucci* They are little squares, as their Italian name tells us, and they are made by first cutting the pasta into *tagliatelle* widths then, instead of unfolding the noodles, cutting them crosswise into squares. *Quadrucci* are particularly lovely in a fine homemade meat broth with peas and sautéed chicken livers.

❀ *Manfrigul* It is pasta chopped into small, barley-like nuggets, a specialty of Romagna, the northeastern coastal area on the Adriatic. Its robust, inimitable chewiness contributes enjoyable textural contrast to soup.

Prepare kneaded dough as described above, on page 131. Flatten the dough with the palm of your hand to a thickness of about 2 inches. Cut it into the thinnest possible slices and spread these on a clean, dry, cloth towel. Turn them once or twice and allow them to dry until they lose their stickiness, but not so dry that they become brittle. Depending on the temperature and ventilation in the kitchen, it may take between 20 and 30 minutes. Cut one of the slices to see whether the dough is still sticky. If not, transfer all the sliced dough to a cutting board and dice it very fine with a sharp knife.

Note ❀ *Manfrigul* can be chopped in the food processor, using the steel blade. Pulse the motor on and off to ensure fairly even chopping. Stop when you reach the consistency of very tiny pellets. When done, part of the dough will have become pulverized. Discard it by emptying the processor's bowl into a fine strainer and shaking the powdered dough away.

Keeping manfrigul: It keeps so well that it is a good idea to have a supply always on hand. Spread on a dry, clean, cloth towel and let it dry out thoroughly. It takes about 12 hours, so you may want to leave it out overnight. Store it in a cupboard in a closed glass jar.

Use *manfrigul* in vegetable soups, or in any soup where you might use rice or barley. It is also excellent on its own, in Basic Homemade Meat Broth, prepared as directed on page 15, served with grated Parmesan.

STUFFED AND SHAPED PASTA

For all the shapes given below, work only with soft, moist, just-made dough. Before beginning, read the instructions given in the Stuffed Pasta Note on page 134. The softness of dough that has just been rolled out makes it easier to shape, and its stickiness is necessary to produce a tight seal that will keep the stuffing from leaking during the cooking.

❧ *Tortellini* The dumplings that in Bologna are called *tortellini*, in Romagna—the provinces of Ravenna, Forlì, and Rimini—are called *cappelletti*. The fillings may vary, but the method for making the wrappers is the same. Trim the strips of pasta dough into rectangular bands 1½ inches wide. Do not discard the trimmings, but press them into one of the balls of dough to be thinned out later.

Cut the bands into 1½-inch squares. Put about ¼ teaspoon of whatever filling the recipe calls for in the center of each square. Fold the square diagonally in half, forming two triangles, one above the other. The edges of the top half of the triangle should stop short of meeting those of the bottom half by about ⅛ inch. Press the edges firmly together with your fingertip, sealing them tightly.

Pick up the triangle by one of the corners of its long side, the folded over side. Pick up the other end with the other hand, holding it between thumb and forefinger. The triangle should now be facing you, its long side parallel to the kitchen counter, its tip pointing straight up. Without letting go of the end, slip the index finger of one hand around the back of the triangle, and as you turn the fingertip toward you let it come up against the base of the triangle pushing it upward in the direction of the tip. As you do this, the triangle's peak should tip toward you and fold over the base. With the same motion, bring together the two corners you are holding, form-

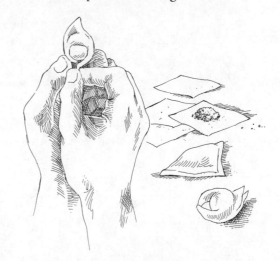

ing a ring around the tip of your forefinger which should still be facing you. Lap one corner over the other, pressing them firmly togeter to close the ring securely. Slip the *tortellino* off your finger, and place it on a clean, dry, cloth towel.

As you continue to make them, lay all the *tortellini* in rows on the towel, making sure they do not touch or they will stick to each other and tear when separated. Although they are ready for cooking immediately, it's likely that you will be making them a few hours or even a day ahead of time. When making them in advance, turn them from time to time, so that they dry evenly on all sides. Do not let them touch until the dough has become leather hard, or you will end up with torn *tortellini*.

Suggestion: ❀   Before making *tortellini* for the first time, cut facial tissue into a number of squares 1½ by 1½ inches, and practice on them until you feel you're doing it right.

❀ *Tortelloni, Tortelli, Ravioli* They are called by different names, and they may vary in size and in their stuffing, but they are all one shape: square. To make them, trim soft, freshly made pasta dough into a long rectangle that is exactly twice the width of the dumpling the recipe calls for.

Assume, as an example, that the recipe requires *tortelloni* with 2-inch wide sides. Cut the dough into a long rectangle 4 inches broad. Put dots of stuffing down 2 inches apart. The distance between the

dots must always be the same as the width of the dumpling, in this case 2 inches. The dotted row of stuffing runs parallel to the edges of the rectangle and is set back 1 inch—half the width of the dumpling—from one edge. (This is much easier to do than it is to try to visualize. Try it first with paper cut to size, and you'll see.)

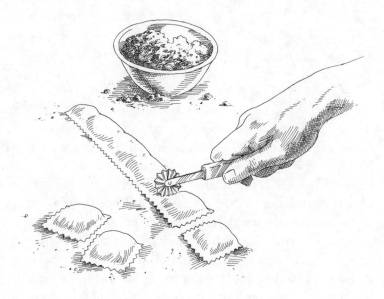

Once the rectangle is dotted with stuffing, bring the edge farther from the row of dots over it and join it to the other edge, thus creating a long tube that encloses the stuffing. Use a fluted pastry wheel to trim the joined edges and both ends of the tube, to seal it all around. With the same wheel, cut across the tube between every mound of stuffing, separating it into squares. Spread the squares out on clean, dry, cloth towels, making sure they do not touch while the dough is still soft. If they do they will stick to one another and tear when you try to pull them apart. If you are not cooking them right away, turn the squares over from time to time while they are drying.

❀ *Garganelli Garganelli,* a hand-turned, grooved tubular pasta, is a specialty of Imola and other towns in Romagna. Its floppy shape, somewhat reminiscent of factory-made *penne,* and its texture, which is that of homemade pasta, combine to offer unique and delicious sensations when matched with a congenial sauce. Although it is not stuffed, *garganelli* must be made with soft, fresh dough, like the *tortellini* and *tortelloni* above.

In Romagna, *garganelli* is made with the help of a small, loom-like tool called *pettine,* or comb. As a substitute, you can use a clean, new hair comb with teeth at least 1½ inches long. An Afro comb would do the job. You also need a small dowel or a smooth, perfectly round pencil ¼ inch in diameter and 6 to 7 inches long.

Cut soft, fresh dough into 1½-inch squares. Lay the comb flat on the counter, its teeth pointing away from you. Lay a pasta square diagonally on the comb so that one corner points toward you, another toward the tips of the comb's teeth. Place the dowel or pencil on the square and parallel to the comb. Curl the corner of the square facing you around the dowel and, with gentle downward pressure, push the dowel away from you and off the comb. Tip the dowel on its end and a small, ridged tube of pasta will slide off. Spread the *garganelli* on a clean, dry, cloth towel, making sure they do not touch each other. *Garganelli* cannot be made long in advance and dried like other pasta because they will crack while cooking. They are best cooked immediately, but if you cannot do that, plunge them in boiling water for a few seconds, drain immediately, toss with olive oil, and spread on a tray to cool.

❦ *Stricchetti* This is the shape known as "bow ties" in English or *farfalline* in standard Italian; *stricchetti* is in the dialect of Romagna, where the shape probably originated. It is the easiest of all pasta shapes to form by hand. Cut soft, freshly made pasta dough into rectangles 1 by 1½ inches. Pinch each rectangle at the middle of its long sides, bringing the sides together, and squeezing them fast. There is also a slightly more complicated method that has the advantage of producing a smaller mound in the center. Place your thumb in the middle of the rectangle, and fold the center of one of the long sides toward it; replace the thumb with the tip of your index finger, and with your thumb, bring the center of the other side of the rectangle to meet it. Squeeze tightly to fasten the fold.

Drying stuffed and shaped pasta ❦ *Tortellini, ravioli,* and the other stuffed or shaped pasta described above can be stored for at least a week once fully dry and leather hard. Allow the pasta to dry out for 24 hours, turning it from time to time, before putting it away. It can be stored in a cupboard, as is done in Italy, but if you'd rather refrigerate the stuffed pasta, you can do so. Make certain it has dried thoroughly first, or mold will develop.

PASTA BY THE ROLLING-PIN METHOD

The necessary equipment ❦ To make pasta by hand you need a large, steady table and a pasta rolling pin. For cutting the pasta after it is rolled out, it would be helpful to have a Chinese cleaver, which is what most closely resembles the kind of knife used in Bologna.

A depth of 24 inches is sufficient for the table, but the longer it is, the easier it is to work with. Three feet would be adequate, and 4½ would be ideal.

The best material for the table's top is wood, either solid hardwood planking or butcher block. Formica or Corian is satisfactory. The least desirable material is marble, whose coldness inhibits the dough, making it inelastic.

If the top is wood, make sure the edge near you is not sharply angular, because it would cut a sheer sheet of pasta hanging over it. If it is not smooth and rounded, sand it to make it so. Laminated tops usually don't present this problem because the edge is either covered by a molding or it is finished blunt.

The rolling pin for pasta is narrower and longer than pastry pins. Its classic dimensions are 1½ inches in diameter and 32 inches in length. It's not easy to come by outside of Emilia-Romagna, although some particularly well-stocked kitchen equipment stores occasionally carry it. A good lumber-supply house can cut you one from a hardwood dowel whose thickness can vary from 1½ to 2 inches. Sand the ends of the dowel to make them perfectly smooth.

Curing and storing a rolling pin: Wash it with soap and water, then rinse all the soap away under cold running water. Dry thoroughly with a soft cloth. Allow the pin to become completely dry in a moderately warm room.

Moisten a cloth with any neutral-tasting vegetable oil and with it rub the entire surface of the pin. Don't put on too much oil, it should be a very light coating. When the oil has seeped into the wood, rub the pin with flour.

To maintain the pin in good condition, repeat the "cure" once every dozen times the pin is used.

Store the pin hanging free to keep it from warping. Screw an eye hook into one end, and suspend the pin from a hook set into a wall or inside a cupboard. Take care not to dent the pin because any unevenness in its surface may tear the pasta.

Before you pick up the rolling pin, read through all the following instructions carefully. The movements with the pin are like a ballet of the hands and they should be learned as a dancer learns a part. Before your hands can take over and their action become intuitive, the logic and sequence of the motions must unfold clearly in the mind.

The dough ✿ Prepare a kneaded ball of dough exactly as described on pages 131–132, in the section on Pasta by the Machine Method.

Suggestion: When making pasta by hand for the first time, you'll find it easier to start with green pasta dough, see page 130. It is softer and easier to stretch.

Relaxing the dough ✿ Even when you have become accomplished in the use of the pin, it is desirable to let the kneaded dough rest and relax its gluten before rolling it out. When it is fully kneaded, wrap the ball of dough in plastic wrap, and let it rest at room temperature for at least 15 minutes or as much as 2 hours.

The first movement ✿ Remove the plastic wrap from the ball of dough and place the dough within comfortable reach in the center of the work table. Flatten it slightly by pounding it two or three times smartly with the palm of your hand.

Place the rolling pin across the flattened top of the ball, about one-third of the way in toward its center. The pin must be parallel to the edge of the table near you.

Open out the ball of dough by pushing the pin forcefully forward, letting it roll lightly backward to its starting point, and pushing it forward again, repeating the operation 4 or 5 times. Do not at any time allow the pin to roll onto or past the far edge of the dough.

Turn the dough a full quarter turn, and repeat the above operation. Continue to turn the gradually flatter disk of dough a full quarter turn at first, then gradually less, but always in the same direction. If you are doing it correctly, the ball will spread into an evenly flattened, regularly circular shape. When it has been opened up to a diameter of about 8 to 9 inches, proceed to the next movement.

The second movement ❀ You will now begin to stretch the dough. Hold the near edge of the dough down with one hand. Place the rolling pin at the opposite, far edge of the dough, laying it down parallel to your side of the table. One hand will be working the pin while the other will act as a stop, holding down the edge of the dough nearest you.

Curl the far edge of the dough around the pin. Begin to roll the pin toward you, taking up as much dough as needed to fit snugly under the pin. Hold the near edge of the dough still with your other hand. Roll the pin toward you, then use the heel of your palm to push it back. Do not *roll* it back, but *push,* making the sheet of dough taut between your two hands, and stretching it. This should be done very rapidly, in a continuous and fluid motion. Do not put any downward pressure whatsoever into the movement. Do not let the hand working the pin rest on the dough longer than 2 or 3 seconds on the same spot.

Keep rolling the pin toward you, stopping, pushing it forward to stretch the dough, taking up more dough with it, rolling it toward you, stopping, stretching, repeating the sequence several times until you have taken up all the dough on the pin. Then, while the dough is curled around the pin, rotate the pin a full half turn—180°—so that it points toward you, and unfurl the dough, opening it up flat.

Repeat the rolling and stretching operation described above until the dough is once again completely wrapped around the pin. Rotate the pin another 180° in the same direction as before, uncurl the dough from it, and repeat the operation once again. Continue this procedure until the sheet of dough has been stretched to a diameter of about 12 inches. Proceed immediately to the next movement.

The third movement 🌼 This is the decisive step, the one in which you'll stretch the sheet of dough to nearly double its preceding diameter, when it ceases to be merely dough and becomes pasta. When your hands have mastered the rhythmic and pressureless execution of this movement, you will have acquired one of the most precious of culinary crafts: handmade pasta in the Bolognese tradition.

The circle of dough lies flat before you on the table. Place the rolling pin at its far end, parallel to the edge of the table near you. Curl the end of the dough around the center of the pin and roll the pin toward you, taking up with it about 4 inches of the sheet of dough. Cup both your hands lightly over the center of the pin, keeping your fingers from touching it. Roll the

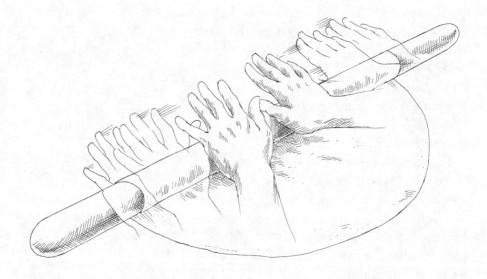

pin away from you and then toward you, taking up with it no more than the original 4 inches of dough. At the same time that you are rolling the pin back and forth, slide your hands apart from each other and toward the ends of the pin, and back to the center, quickly repeating the motion a number of times.

As your hands move away from the center, let the heels of your palms brush against the surface of the dough, dragging it, pulling it, in fact stretching it toward the ends of the pin. At the same time that you are sliding your hands from the center toward the ends, you must roll the pin toward you. Bear in mind that there is some pressure in this motion but it is directed sideways, not downward. If you press down on the dough it won't stretch because it will stick to the pin.

When the hands move back toward the center they should float over the dough, barely skimming it. You want to stretch the dough outward, toward the ends of the pin, and not drag it back toward the center. At the same time that you are bringing your hands back to the center of the pin, roll it forward, away from you.

Your hands must flit out and back very rapidly, touching the dough only with the heel of the palm, applying pull as they move outward, never weight. And all this while, you must also rock the pin forward and back.

Take up another few inches of dough on the pin and repeat the combined motion: The hands moving out and in, the pin rocking forward and back.

When you have taken up and stretched all but the last few inches of dough, rotate the pin 180º, unfurl the sheet of dough opening it up flat, and start again from the far end, repeating the entire stretching operation described above.

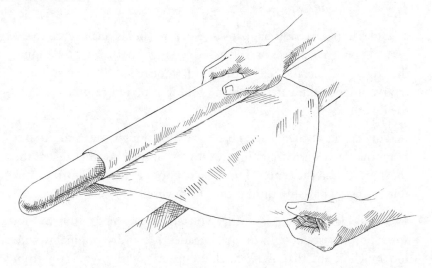

As the sheet of dough becomes larger, let it hang over the near side of the table. It will act as a counterweight and contribute to the stretching action. But do not lean against it, because you might break it. As you take up dough on the rolling pin, you will allow the end of the sheet to slide gradually back onto the table.

When you have rotated the pasta sheet a complete turn and it is all fully stretched, open it up flat on the table and use the rolling pin to iron out any creases.

The entire third movement should be executed in 10 minutes or less for a standard quantity of pasta dough.

Suggestions:

❧ Thinning out a ball of dough into a sheer sheet of pasta is a race against time. Dough can be stretched as long as it is soft and pliable, but its flexibility is short-lived. The moment dough begins to dry out, it refuses to give and starts to crack. From the very beginning, you must work on developing speed.

❧ Do not make pasta while the oven is turned on, or near a hot radiator, or in a draft. All these cause dough to dry out.

❧ Work with the dough within easy reach of your arms to exercise better control of your movements.

❧ Before you begin rolling out real dough, it might be helpful to try out the stretching motion, using a circular sheet of oilcloth or non-sticky plastic.

Problems: Their Causes and Possible Solutions

❧ Holes in the pasta. It happens to everyone, occasionally even to experts. Usually it's not serious. Patch the dough, narrowly overlapping the edges of the tears. Seal with slightly moistened fingertips, if necessary. Smooth the patch with the rolling pin, and resume working the dough.

❧ Tiny cracks at the edges. This means the dough began to dry out faster than you were stretching it. Or you thinned out the edge of the sheet more than the center. The sheet cannot be stretched further, but if it is already passably thin, it can still be used.

❧ The dough falls apart. Either you are letting it dry out by not stretching it fast enough, or you kneaded it too dry originally, with too much flour, that is. A fatal symptom. Start over again from scratch, taking special care, when kneading, to produce dough that is tender and elastic.

❧ You cannot get the pasta thin enough. Basically it's a question of practice and perseverance. Reread the descriptions of the stretching movements. Work faster. There may also be technical reasons: The dough has not been kneaded long or thoroughly enough; it has too much flour; you didn't let it rest after kneading; the kitchen may be too hot, too dry, too draughty.

❧ The sheet sticks to itself or to the rolling pin. You may be putting downward pressure into your stretching motion. Or you have kneaded the dough too soft, with insufficient flour. In this case, you may be able to rescue the dough by sprinkling flour over it and spreading it uniformly over the sheet.

❧ The pasta is too thick for *fettuccine* or *tortellini,* but looks too good to throw away. Cut it into *maltagliati, quadrucci,* or *manfrigul,* pages 137–138, and use in soup. If very thick, allow adequate time when cooking.

Drying handmade pasta ❧ Spread a dry, clean, cloth towel on a table or work counter and lay the sheet of pasta flat over the towel, making sure there are no creases. Let one-third of the sheet hang over the edge of the table or counter. After about 10 minutes, rotate the sheet to let a different part of it hang. Another 10 minutes and rotate it again. Total drying time depends on the softness of the dough and the temperature and ventilation in the room. The dough must lose enough of its moisture so that it will not stick to itself when folded and cut, but it must not dry out too much or it will become brittle and crack. It is usually ready when the surface of the pasta begins to have a leathery look.

Cutting handmade pasta ❧ When the dough has reached a desirable stage of dryness, roll up the sheet on the pasta pin, remove the towel from the counter, and unroll the pasta from the pin, laying it flat on the work surface. Pick up the edge of the sheet farthest from you, and fold the sheet loosely about 3 inches in from the edge. Fold it again, and again, until the whole sheet has been folded into a long, flat, rectangular roll about 3 inches wide.

With a cleaver or other suitable knife, cut the roll across into ribbons, ¼ inch wide for *tagliatelle,* a little narrower for *fettuccine.* Unfold the ribbons and spread out on a dry, clean, cloth towel. See pages 134–136 for instructions on drying pasta for long-term storage, and for other cuts.

Using handmade pasta for tortellini *and other shapes* ❧ If you are going to make stuffed pasta and other shapes that require soft dough, do not let the pasta sheet dry. Refer to remarks on dough for stuffed pasta, page 138.

Trim one end of the pasta sheet to give it a straight edge. (Save the trimmings to cut into soup squares.) Cut off a rectangular strip from the sheet; if you are making *tortellini,* the strip should be 1½ inches wide; if you are making *tortelloni* or other square shapes, the strip should be twice the width of the shape required by the recipe.

Move the remaining sheet of dough to one side, and cover it with plastic wrap to keep it from drying. Use the strip to make *tortellini,* or any of the other shapes described on pages 139–142. When the one strip has been turned into the desired shape, cut off another identical strip from the main sheet, remembering afterward to keep the main sheet covered in plastic wrap.

★ *Pasta Sauces* ★

TOMATO SAUCES

For a long time, Italian dishes abroad had been characterized by such a heavy-handed use of tomato that, for the many who had begun to discover refine-ment and infinite variety in the regional cuisines of Italy, the color red and any taste of tomato in a sauce came to represent a coarse and discredited style of cooking. The moment for a major reassessment may be at hand.

There is nothing inherently crude about tomato sauce. Quite the con-trary: No other preparation is more successful in delivering the prodigious satisfactions of Italian cooking than a competently executed sauce with toma-toes; no flavor expresses more clearly the genius of Italian cooks than the freshness, the immediacy, the richness of good tomatoes adroitly matched to the most suitable choice of pasta.

The sauces that are grouped immediately below are those in which toma-toes have a dominant role. They are followed by a broad selection of recipes that shift their focus from tomatoes to other vegetables, to cheese, to fish, to meat, illustrating the unrestricted choice of ingredients on which a pasta sauce can be based.

The basic cooking method ♘ Pasta sauces may cook slowly or rapidly, they may take 4 minutes or 4 hours, but they always cook by evaporation, which concentrates and clearly defines their flavor. Never cook a sauce in a covered pan, or it will emerge with a bland, steamed, weakly formulated taste.

Tasting a sauce and correcting for salt ♘ A sauce must be sufficiently savory to season pasta adequately. Blandness is not a virtue, tastelessness is not a joy. Always taste a sauce before tossing the pasta with it. If it seems barely salty enough on its own, it's not salty enough for the pasta. Remember it must have flavor enough to cover a pound or more of cooked, virtually unsalted pasta.

When tomato is the main ingredient: If they are available, use fresh, nat-urally and fully ripened, plum tomatoes. Varieties other than the plum may be used, if they are equally ripe and truly fruity, not watery. If completely sat- isfactory fresh tomatoes are not available, it is better to use canned imported Italian plum tomatoes. If your local grocers do not carry these, experiment with other canned varieties until you can determine which has the best flavor and consistency. A brief discussion of fresh and canned tomatoes as a com- ponent of Italian cooking appears on pages 34–35.

Cooking-time note ❀ For all the tomato sauces that follow, the cooking time given is indicative. If you make a larger quantity of sauce, it will take longer; if the pot is broad and shallow, the sauce will cook faster, if it is deep and narrow, it will cook more slowly. You alone can tell when it's ready. Taste it for density: It should be neither too thick nor too watery, and for flavor the tomato must lose its raw taste, without losing sweetness or freshness.

Freezer note ❀ Wherever indicated, tomato sauces may be frozen success- fully. After thawing, simmer for 10 minutes before tossing with pasta.

Reminder ❀ If the sauce has butter, always toss the pasta with an additional tablespoon of fresh butter; if it has olive oil, drizzle with raw olive oil while tossing.

Making Fresh Tomatoes Ready for Sauce

Unless the recipe indicates otherwise, fresh, ripe tomatoes must be prepared to use for sauce following one of the two methods given below. The blanch- ing method can lead to a meatier, more rustic consistency. The food mill method produces a silkier, smoother sauce.

The blanching method ❀ Plunge the tomatoes in boiling water for a minute or less. Drain them and, as soon as they are cool enough to handle, skin them, and cut them up in coarse pieces.

The food mill method ❀ Wash the tomatoes in cold water, cut them length- wise in half, and put them in a covered saucepan. Turn on the heat to medium and cook for 10 minutes. Set a food mill fitted with the disk with the largest holes over a bowl. Transfer the tomatoes with any of their juices to the mill and purée.

Tomato Sauce with Onion and Butter

THIS IS THE SIMPLEST of all sauces to make, and none has a purer, more irresistibly sweet tomato taste. I have known people to skip the pasta and eat the sauce directly out of the pot with a spoon.   *For 6 servings*

2 pounds fresh, ripe tomatoes, prepared as described on page 151, OR 2 cups canned imported Italian plum tomatoes, cut up, with their juice

5 tablespoons butter

1 medium onion, peeled and cut in half

Salt

1 to 1½ pounds pasta

Freshly grated *parmigiano-reggiano* cheese for the table

Recommended pasta ❦ This is an unsurpassed sauce for Potato Gnocchi, page 260, but it is also delicious with factory-made pasta in such shapes as *spaghetti, penne,* or *rigatoni.* Serve with grated Parmesan.

Put either the prepared fresh tomatoes or the canned in a saucepan, add the butter, onion, and salt, and cook uncovered at a very slow, but steady simmer for 45 minutes, or until the fat floats free from the tomato. Stir from time to time, mashing any large piece of tomato in the pan with the back of a wooden spoon. Taste and correct for salt. Discard the onion before tossing the sauce with pasta.

Note ❦ May be frozen when done. Discard the onion before freezing.

Tomato Sauce with Olive Oil and Chopped Vegetables

THE CARROT AND CELERY in this sauce are put in *a crudo,* which means without the usual separate and preliminary sautéeing procedure, along with the tomatoes. The sweetness of carrot and the fragrance of celery contribute depth to the fresh tomato flavor of the sauce.   *For 6 servings*

2 pounds fresh, ripe tomatoes, prepared as described on page 151, OR 2 cups canned imported Italian plum tomatoes, cut up, with their juice

⅔ cup chopped carrot
⅔ cup chopped celery
⅔ cup chopped onion
Salt
⅓ cup extra virgin olive oil
1 to 1½ pounds pasta

Recommended pasta ❀ This is an all-purpose sauce for most cuts of factory-made pasta, particularly *spaghettini* and *penne.*

1. Put either the prepared fresh tomatoes or the canned in a saucepan, add the carrot, celery, onion, and salt, and cook with no cover on the pan at a slow, steady simmer for 30 minutes. Stir from time to time.

2. Add the olive oil, raise the heat slightly to bring to a somewhat stronger simmer, and stir occasionally, while reducing the tomato to as much of a pulp as you can with the back of the spoon. Cook for 15 minutes, then taste and correct for salt.

Note ❀ May be frozen when done.

Variation with Marjoram and Two Cheeses

The above sauce, cooked through to the end, plus the following:

Marjoram, 2 teaspoons if fresh, 1 if dried
2 tablespoons freshly grated *parmigiano-reggiano* cheese

2 tablespoons freshly grated *romano* cheese
2 teaspoons extra virgin olive oil

1. While the sauce is simmering, add the marjoram, stir thoroughly, and simmer for another 5 minutes.

2. Off heat, swirl in the grated Parmesan, then the *romano,* then the 2 teaspoons of olive oil. Toss immediately with the pasta.

Recommended pasta ❀ Excellent with *spaghetti,* but even better with the thicker, hollow shape, *bucatini* or *perciatelli.*

Tomato Sauce (continued)

Variation with Rosemary and Pancetta

The basic sauce above, cooked through to the end, plus the following:

2 teaspoons dried rosemary
   leaves, chopped very fine,
   OR a small sprig of fresh
   rosemary

½ cup *pancetta* sliced thin and
   cut into narrow julienne
   strips

1. While the sauce is simmering, put the olive oil in a small skillet and turn on the heat to medium high. When the oil is hot, add the rosemary and the pancetta. Cook for about 1 minute, stirring almost constantly with a wooden spoon.

2. Transfer the entire contents of the skillet to the saucepan with the tomato sauce, and simmer for 15 minutes, stirring occasionally.

Recommended pasta ❀ A shape with crevices or hollows, such as *ruote di carro* ("cartwheels"), or *conchiglie,* or *fusilli,* would be a good choice.

Tomato Sauce with
Sautéed Vegetables and Olive Oil

THIS IS A DENSER, darker sauce than the preceding two, cooked longer over a base of sautéed vegetables.   *For 6 servings*

2 pounds fresh, ripe tomatoes,
   prepared as described on
   page 151, OR 2 cups canned
   imported Italian plum
   tomatoes, cut up, with their
   juice

⅓ cup extra virgin olive oil
⅓ cup chopped onion
⅓ cup chopped carrot
⅓ cup chopped celery
Salt
1 to 1½ pounds pasta

Recommended pasta ❀ Most factory-made pasta will carry this sauce well, in particular substantial shapes such as *rigatoni,* ridged *penne,* or *bucatini.*

1. *If using fresh tomatoes:* Put the prepared tomatoes in an uncovered saucepan and cook at a very slow simmer for about 1 hour. Stir from time to time, mashing any pieces of tomato against the sides of the pan with the back of a wooden spoon. Transfer to a bowl with all their juices.

If using canned tomatoes: Proceed with Step 2, and add the tomatoes where indicated in Step 3.

2. Wipe the saucepan dry with paper towels. Put in the olive oil and the chopped onion, and turn on the heat to medium. Cook and stir the onion until it becomes colored a very pale gold, add the carrot and celery, and cook at lively heat for another minute, stirring once or twice to coat the vegetables well.

3. Add the cooked fresh tomatoes or the canned, a large pinch of salt, stir thoroughly, and adjust heat to cook in the uncovered pan at a gentle, but steady simmer. If using fresh tomatoes, cook for 15 to 20 minutes; if using the canned, simmer for 45 minutes. Stir from time to time. Before turning off the heat, taste and correct for salt.

Note ✽ May be frozen when done.

Tomato Sauce with Heavy Cream

For 6 servings

⅓ cup butter
3 tablespoons each onion, carrot, celery, all chopped very fine
2½ pounds fresh, ripe tomatoes, prepared by the food mill method described on page 151, OR 2½ cups

canned imported Italian plum tomatoes, with their juice
Salt
½ cup heavy whipping cream
1 to 1½ pounds pasta
Freshly grated *parmigiano-reggiano* cheese for the table

Recommended pasta ✽ Here is an ideal tomato sauce for stuffed fresh pasta in such versions as Tortelloni Stuffed with Swiss Chard, Prosciutto, and Ricotta, page 211, Tortelli Stuffed with Parsley and Ricotta, page 210, Green Tortellini with Meat and Ricotta Stuffing, page 208, or Spinach and Ricotta Gnocchi, page 262. Serve with grated Parmesan.

1. Put all the ingredients except for the heavy cream into a saucepan and cook, uncovered, at the merest simmer for 45 minutes. Stir from time to time with a wooden spoon. At this point, if using canned tomatoes, purée them through a food mill back into the saucepan.

Note ✽ May be frozen up to this point.

Tomato Sauce with Heavy Cream (continued)

2. Adjust heat so that the simmer picks up a little speed. Add the heavy cream. Stir thoroughly and cook for about 1 minute, continuing to stir always.

Tomato Sauce with Garlic and Basil

THIS IS ONE of many versions of the sauce Romans call *alla carrettiera*. The *carrettieri* were the drivers of the mule- or even hand-driven carts in which wine and produce were brought down to Rome from its surrounding hills, and the sauces for their pasta were improvised from the least expensive, most abundant, ingredients available to them.   *For 4 servings*

1 large bunch fresh basil
2 pounds fresh, ripe tomatoes, prepared as described on page 151, OR 2 cups canned imported Italian plum tomatoes, drained and cut up
5 garlic cloves, peeled and chopped fine

5 tablespoons extra virgin olive oil
Salt
Black pepper, ground fresh from the mill
1 pound pasta

Note ❀ Do not be alarmed by the amount of garlic this recipe requires. Because it simmers in the sauce, it is poached, rather than browned, and its flavor is very subdued.

Recommended pasta ❀ The ideal shape for tomato *alla carrettiera* is thin spaghetti—*spaghettini*—but regular *spaghetti* would also be satisfactory.

1. Pull all the basil leaves from the stalks, rinse them briefly in cold water, and shake off all the moisture using a colander, a salad spinner, or simply by gathering the basil loosely in a dry cloth towel and shaking it two or three times. Tear all but the tiniest leaves by hand into small pieces.

2. Put the tomatoes, garlic, olive oil, salt, and several grindings of pepper into a saucepan, and turn on the heat to medium high. Cook for 20 to 25 minutes, or until the oil floats free from the tomato. Taste and correct for salt.

3. Off heat, as soon as the sauce is done, mix in the torn-up basil, keeping aside a few pieces to add when tossing the pasta.

Amatriciana—Tomato Sauce with Pancetta and Chili Pepper

THE ROMAN TOWN of Amatrice, with which this sauce is identified, offers a public feast in August whose principal attraction is undoubtedly the celebrated *bucatini*—thick, hollow spaghetti—*all'Amatriciana*. No visitor should pass up, however, the pear-shaped salamis called *mortadelle*, the *pecorino*—ewe's milk cheese—or the *ricotta*, also made from ewe's milk. They are among the best products of their kind in Italy.

When making Amatriciana sauce, some cooks add white wine before putting in the tomatoes; I find the result too acidic, but you may want to try it.   *For 4 servings*

2 tablespoons vegetable oil
1 tablespoon butter
1 medium onion chopped fine
A ¼-inch-thick slice of
    pancetta, cut into strips ½
    inch wide and 1 inch long
1½ cups canned imported
    Italian plum tomatoes,
    drained and cut up

Chopped hot red chili pepper,
    to taste
Salt
3 tablespoons freshly grated
    parmigiano-reggiano cheese
2 tablespoons freshly grated
    romano cheese
1 pound pasta

Recommended pasta ❀ It's impossible to say "*all'amatriciana*" without thinking "*bucatini.*" The two are as indivisible as Romeo and Juliet. But other couplings of the sauce, such as with *penne* or *rigatoni* or *conchiglie,* can be nearly as successful.

1. Put the oil, butter, and onion in a saucepan and turn on the heat to medium. Sauté the onion until it becomes colored a pale gold, then add the *pancetta.* Cook for about 1 minute, stirring once or twice. Add the tomatoes, the chili pepper, and salt, and cook in the uncovered pan at a steady, gentle simmer for 25 minutes. Taste and correct for salt and hot pepper.

2. Toss the pasta with the sauce, then add both cheeses, and toss thoroughly again.

Tomato Sauce with Porcini Mushrooms

For 4 servings

2 tablespoons shallot OR onion
    chopped fine
2½ tablespoons butter
1 tablespoon vegetable oil
2 tablespoons *pancetta,* pro-
    sciutto, OR unsmoked ham,
    cut into ¼-inch-wide strips
1½ cups fresh, ripe tomatoes,
    peeled and chopped, OR
    canned imported Italian
    plum tomatoes, cut up,
    with their juice
A small packet OR 1 ounce
    dried *porcini* mushrooms,

reconstituted as described
    on page 27
The filtered water from the
    mushroom soak, see page
    28 for instructions
Salt
Black pepper, ground fresh
    from the mill
1 pound pasta
Freshly grated *parmigiano-
    reggiano* cheese for the table

Recommended pasta ❧ *Conchiglie, penne,* ridged *ziti,* or a substantial fresh pasta such as *tonnarelli* or *pappardelle,* see pages 134 and 135. Serve with grated Parmesan.

1. Put the shallot or onion into a saucepan together with all the butter and oil, and turn on the heat to medium. Cook and stir the shallot or onion until it becomes colored a pale gold. Add the strips of *pancetta* or ham, and cook for 1 or 2 minutes, stirring from time to time.

2. Add the cut-up tomatoes with their juice, the reconstituted mushrooms, the strained liquid from the mushroom soak, salt, and several grindings of pepper. Adjust heat so that the sauce bubbles at a gentle, but steady simmer. Cook in the uncovered pan for about 40 minutes, until the fat and the tomato separate, stirring occasionally.

3. After tossing the pasta with the sauce, serve with freshly grated Parmesan on the side.

Mushroom Sauce with Ham and Tomato

For 4 to 6 servings

¾ pound fresh white mush-
rooms
⅓ cup extra virgin olive oil
2 garlic cloves, peeled and
lightly mashed
⅓ cup boiled unsmoked ham
cut into very narrow
julienne strips, ⅛ inch wide
or less
A small packet OR 1 ounce
dried *porcini* mushrooms,
reconstituted as described
on page 27

The filtered water from the
mushroom soak, see page
28 for instructions
2 tablespoons chopped parsley
Salt
Black pepper, ground fresh
from the mill
1 cup canned imported Italian
plum tomatoes, chopped
fine, with their juice
1 pound pasta

Recommended pasta ❀ Short shapes of factory-made pasta: *maccheroncini, penne, ziti, conchiglie,* or *fusilli.*

1. Wash the fresh white mushrooms very rapidly under cold running water. Pat them thoroughly dry with a soft towel and cut them into very thin lengthwise slices, leaving the caps attached to the stems.

2. Put the oil and mashed garlic cloves into a large sauté pan and turn on the heat to medium high. Cook and stir the garlic until it becomes colored a light nut brown, then remove it from the pan.

3. Add the ham strips, stir once or twice, then add the reconstituted *porcini* mushrooms and their filtered water. Cook at lively heat until all the mushroom liquid has evaporated.

4. Add the fresh mushrooms, the chopped parsley, salt, and a few grindings of pepper. Stir for about half a minute, add the tomatoes and their juice, and stir thoroughly once again to coat all ingredients. Adjust the heat so that the sauce bubbles at a steady pace in the uncovered pan, and cook for 25 minutes or so until the oil separates and floats free.

Note ❀ Do not expect the fresh mushrooms to be firm; they are being cooked in the manner of *porcini* and, like *porcini,* they will be very tender when done.

Eggplant Sauce with Tomato
and Red Chili Pepper

For 4 servings

About 1 pound eggplant
Salt
Vegetable oil for frying the
    eggplant
3 tablespoons extra virgin olive
    oil
1½ teaspoons chopped garlic

2 tablespoons chopped parsley
1¾ cups canned imported
    Italian plum tomatoes, cut
    up, with their juice
Chopped hot red chili pepper,
    to taste
1 pound pasta

Recommended pasta ❁ No other shape carries this sauce as well as *spaghettini,* thin factory-made *spaghetti.*

1. Trim and slice the eggplant, steep it in salt, and fry it following the complete directions on page 494. Set aside to drain on a cooling rack or on a platter lined with paper towels.

2. Put the olive oil and garlic in a saucepan, and turn on the heat to medium. Cook and stir the garlic until it becomes lightly colored. Add the parsley, tomatoes, chili pepper, and salt, and stir thoroughly. Adjust heat so that the sauce simmers steadily but gently, and cook for about 25 minutes, until the oil separates and floats free.

3. Cut the fried eggplant into slivers about ½ inch wide. Add to the sauce, cooking it another 2 or 3 minutes, while stirring once or twice. Taste and correct for salt and hot pepper.

Ahead-of-time note ❁ You can fry the eggplant a day or two in advance of making the sauce, or make the entire sauce in advance and refrigerate it for up to 3 or 4 days before reheating.

Eggplant and Ricotta Sauce, Sicilian Style

For 6 servings

About 1 to 1½ pounds eggplant
Salt
Vegetable oil
⅓ cup extra virgin olive oil
½ cup onion sliced very thin
1½ teaspoons chopped garlic
2 cups fresh, ripe Italian plum
    tomatoes, skinned with a
    peeler, split lengthwise to
    pick out the seeds, and cut
    into narrow strips

Black pepper, ground fresh
    from the mill
3 tablespoons freshly grated
    romano cheese
3 tablespoons fresh *ricotta*
8 to 10 fresh basil leaves
1 to 1½ pounds pasta
Freshly grated *parmigiano-*
    reggiano cheese for the table

Recommended pasta ✽ I love this sauce with *ruote di carro,* "cartwheels," and it is also good with *fusilli* or *rigatoni.* Nor can you go wrong with plain old *spaghetti.*

    1. Cut off the eggplant's green spiky cap. Peel the eggplant and cut it into 1½-inch cubes. Put the cubes into a pasta colander set over a basin or large bowl, and sprinkle them liberally with salt. Let the eggplant steep for about 1 hour so that the salt can draw off most of its bitter juices.

    2. Scoop up a few of the eggplant cubes and rinse them in cold running water. Wrap them in a dry cloth towel, and twist it to squeeze as much moisture as possible out of them. Spread them out on another clean, dry towel, and proceed thus until you have rinsed all the eggplant cubes.

    3. Put enough vegetable oil in a large frying pan to come ½ inch up the sides of the pan, and turn on the heat to medium high. When the oil is quite hot, slip in as many of the eggplant pieces at one time as will fit loosely in the pan. If you can't fit them all in at one time, fry them in two or more batches. As soon as the eggplant feels tender when prodded with a fork, transfer it with a slotted spoon or spatula to a cooling rack or to a platter lined with paper towels to drain.

    4. Pour off the oil and wipe the pan clean with paper towels. Put in the olive oil and the sliced onion and turn on the heat to medium high. Sauté the onion until it becomes colored a light gold, then add the chopped garlic and cook for only a few seconds, stirring as you cook.

    5. Add the strips of tomato, turn up the heat to high, and cook for 8 to 10 minutes, stirring frequently, until the oil floats free from the tomato.

Eggplant and Ricotta Sauce (continued)

6. Add the eggplant and a few grindings of pepper, stir, and turn the heat down to medium. Cook for just a minute or two more, stirring once or twice. Taste and correct for salt.

7. Toss the cooked and drained pasta with the eggplant sauce, add the grated *romano,* the *ricotta,* and the basil leaves. Toss again, mixing all ingredients thoroughly into the hot pasta, and serve at once, with the grated Parmesan on the side.

Spinach Sauce
with Ricotta and Ham

For 4 to 6 servings

2 pounds fresh spinach OR 2 ten-ounce packages frozen leaf spinach, thawed
¼ pound butter
2 ounces unsmoked boiled ham, chopped
Salt

Whole nutmeg
½ cup fresh *ricotta*
½ cup freshly grated *parmigiano-reggiano* cheese, plus additional cheese at the table
1 to 1½ pounds pasta

Recommended pasta ❦ Ridged *penne, maccheroncini,* or *rigatoni.*

1. *If using fresh spinach:* Pull the leaves from the stems, and discard the stems. Soak, rinse, and cook the spinach and gently squeeze the moisture from it exactly as described on page 89. Chop it rather fine and set aside.

If using thawed frozen spinach: With your hands, squeeze the moisture from it, chop it fine, and set aside.

2. Put half the butter in a sauté pan and turn on the heat to medium high. When the butter foam begins to subside, add the ham, turn it two or three times, then add the spinach and liberal pinches of salt. Bear in mind that aside from the *ricotta,* which has no salt, the spinach is the principal component of the sauce and must be adequately seasoned. Sauté the spinach over lively heat, turning it frequently, for about 2 minutes.

3. Off heat, mix in the nutmeg, grated—no more than ⅛ teaspoon.

4. Toss the cooked and drained pasta with the contents of the pan, plus the *ricotta,* the remaining butter, and the ½ cup grated Parmesan. Serve at once, with grated Parmesan on the side.

Peas, Bacon, and Ricotta Sauce

IN MOST of Italy, bacon is not used as commonly in cooking as its spicier, unsmoked version, *pancetta,* except for the northeast of the country, where it prevails. In the same territory, the *ricotta* is very mild, the fresh peas from the farm islands of the Venetian lagoon are very sweet, and the sauce they make together has considerable charm.   *For 4 servings*

1 pound fresh, young peas, unshelled weight, OR ½ of a 10-ounce package tiny frozen peas, thawed
¼ pound bacon, preferably lean, slab bacon
Salt
¼ pound fresh *ricotta*

1 tablespoon butter
⅓ cup freshly grated *parmi- giano-reggiano* cheese, plus additional cheese at the table
Black pepper, ground fresh from the mill
1 pound pasta

Recommended pasta ❀ First choice goes to *conchiglie* for the deftness with which its hollows catch the sauce, but both *fusilli* and *rigatoni* are excellent alternatives.

1. *If using fresh peas:* Shell them, discard the pods, rinse them in cold water, and cook them in a small amount of simmering water until they are just tender. The time varies greatly depending on the freshness and youth of the peas.

If using thawed frozen peas: Begin the sauce at Step 2.

2. Cut the bacon into short, narrow strips. Put it into a small sauté pan, and turn on the heat to medium. Cook until it becomes very lightly browned, but not crisp, and the fat melts. Pour off all but 2 tablespoons of bacon fat from the pan.

3. Put the cooked fresh peas or the thawed frozen peas in the pan with the bacon. Cook at medium heat for about 1 or 2 minutes, stirring to coat the peas thoroughly.

4. Put the *ricotta* in the bowl the pasta will subsequently be tossed in, and crumble it with a fork. Add the butter.

5. Cook and drain the pasta, and put it in the bowl, tossing it immediately with the ricotta and the butter. Rapidly warm up the peas and bacon, and pour the entire contents of the pan onto the pasta. Toss thoroughly, add the grated Parmesan and 2 or 3 grindings of pepper, toss once or twice again, and serve at once, with more grated cheese on the side.

Peas, Peppers, and Prosciutto Sauce with Cream

PEAS AND PROSCIUTTO make one of the most light-handed pasta sauces with cream. In the version below, peppers are added, increasing the vivaciousness of the sauce with their aroma, their texture, their ripe red color.

For 4 to 6 servings

3 meaty, ripe red bell peppers
3 tablespoons butter
A ½-inch-thick slice of prosciutto OR country ham, OR
   plain boiled unsmoked
   ham, about 6 ounces, diced
   very fine
1 cup tiny frozen peas, thawed
1 cup heavy whipping cream

Salt
Black pepper, ground fresh
   from the mill
1 cup freshly grated
   parmigiano-reggiano cheese,
   plus additional cheese at the
   table
1 to 1½ pounds pasta

Recommended pasta ✿ There is no more appropriate sauce than this one for *garganelli,* the handmade tubular macaroni on page 141. It would also go quite well with short, tubular factory-made pasta such as *maccheroncini* or *penne.*

1. Roast and skin the peppers, and remove their seeds as described on page 54. When you have thoroughly dried them, patting them with paper towels, cut them into ¼-inch squares and set aside.

2. Put the butter and diced prosciutto into a sauté pan and turn on the heat to medium. Cook for a minute or less, stirring frequently.

3. Add the thawed peas, and cook for another minute, stirring to coat them well.

4. Add the little squares of peppers, stirring for half a minute or less.

5. Add the cream, salt, and several grindings of pepper, and turn up the heat to high. Cook, stirring constantly, until the cream thickens.

6. Toss the sauce with cooked, drained pasta, swirling in the grated Parmesan. Serve immediately, with additional grated cheese.

Roasted Red and Yellow Pepper
Sauce with Garlic and Basil

ROASTING PEPPERS is one way of separating them from their skin, but in this magnificent Neapolitan sauce the peeler is the better way. When roasted, peppers become soft and partly cooked, but to be sautéed successfully, as they need to be here, the peppers must be raw and firm, as they are when skinned with a peeler. *For 4 servings*

3 meaty bell peppers, some red, some yellow	Salt
16 to 20 fresh basil leaves	2 tablespoons butter
2 tablespoons extra virgin olive oil	⅔ cup freshly grated *parmigiano-reggiano* cheese
4 garlic cloves, peeled	1 pound pasta

Recommended pasta ❀ Ridged *rigatoni* would be best here, but other tubular pasta, such as *penne, ziti,* or *maccheroncini,* would also be good.

1. Wash the peppers in cold water. Cut them lengthwise along their crevices. Scoop away and discard their seeds and pulpy core. Peel the peppers, using a swiveling-blade peeler and skimming them with a light, sawing motion. Cut the peppers lengthwise into strips about ½ inch broad, then shorten the strips, cutting them in two.

2. Rinse the basil leaves in running cold water, and gently pat them dry with a soft towel or paper towels, without bruising them. Tear the larger leaves by hand into smaller pieces.

3. Choose a sauté pan that can subsequently accommodate all the peppers without crowding them. Put in the olive oil and the garlic cloves, and turn on the heat to medium high. Cook and stir the garlic until it becomes colored a light nut brown, then remove it and discard it.

4. Put the peppers in the pan, and continue to cook at lively heat for another 15 minutes, stirring frequently. The peppers are done when they are tender, but not mushy. Add an adequate amount of salt, stir, and take off heat. Gently reheat when you'll be getting ready to toss the pasta.

5. When you are nearly ready to drain and toss the pasta, melt the butter in a small saucepan at low heat. It should be just runny, not sizzling.

6. Toss the cooked drained pasta with the contents of the sauté pan, then add the melted butter, the grated Parmesan, and the basil and toss thoroughly once more. Serve at once.

Zucchini Sauce with Basil
and Beaten Egg Yolk

For 4 servings

1 pound fresh zucchini
Vegetable oil for frying
3 tablespoons butter
1 teaspoon all-purpose flour,
    dissolved in ⅓ cup milk
Salt
1 egg yolk, beaten lightly with a
    fork (see warning about
    salmonella poisoning,
    page 41)

½ cup freshly grated *parmi-
    giano-reggiano* cheese
¼ cup freshly grated *romano*
    cheese
⅔ cup fresh basil leaves torn by
    hand into several pieces OR
    equal amount of chopped
    parsley
1 pound pasta

Recommended pasta ❧ The clinging zucchini strips and the creamy consistency of the sauce make it particularly suitable for curly shapes, such as both kinds of *fusilli*—the short, stubby ones and the long, corkscrew strands.

1. Soak the zucchini for at least 20 minutes in cold water, then wash it free of all grit, as described on page 530. Drain it, trim away both ends, and cut the zucchini into sticks about 3 inches long and ⅛ inch thick. Pat them thoroughly dry with paper towels.

2. Put enough oil in a frying pan to come ½ inch up the sides of the pan, and turn on the heat to medium high. When the oil is hot enough that a zucchini strip sizzles when dropped in, put in as many strips at one time as will fit without being crowded. If all the zucchini do not fit in at one time, cook it in two or more batches. Fry the zucchini until it becomes colored a light brown, but no darker, turning it from time to time. As each batch is done, transfer it to a cooling rack or a plate lined with paper towels to drain.

Ahead-of-time note ❧ You can fry the zucchini several hours in advance of cooking the pasta and completing the sauce.

3. When the pasta is nearly ready to drain and toss, pour out the oil from the frying pan, wipe it clean and dry with paper towels, put in 2 tablespoons of the butter, and turn on the heat to medium. When the butter foam begins to subside, turn the heat down to medium low, and stir in the flour-and-milk mixture, a little bit at a time. Cook, stirring constantly, for half a minute. Add a pinch of salt, all the fried zucchini strips, and cook for about 1 minute, turning the zucchini over to coat thoroughly.

4. Off heat, vigorously swirl in the remaining tablespoon of butter and the egg yolk.

5. Toss the cooked drained pasta with the sauce, add both grated cheeses, toss thoroughly once again, add the torn-up basil leaves, toss once more, then serve immediately.

Fried Zucchini Sauce with Garlic and Basil

For 4 servings

1½ pounds fresh, young
    zucchini
Salt
10 to 12 fresh basil leaves
½ cup all-purpose flour
Vegetable oil for frying
3 garlic cloves, peeled

4 tablespoons (½ stick) butter
½ cup freshly grated *parmi-giano-reggiano* cheese, plus
    additional cheese at the
    table
1 pound pasta

Recommended pasta ❀ Fresh pasta's flavor seems to be particularly congenial to this sauce. *Fettuccine* would be the preferred shape, made as described on page 134. Such boxed pasta shapes as *fusilli* or *spaghetti* would also work well here.

1. Soak the zucchini for at least 20 minutes in cold water, then wash it free of all grit, as described on page 530. Drain it, trim away both ends, and cut the zucchini into sticks about 2½ inches long and no more than ¼ inch thick.

2. Put the zucchini in a freestanding pasta colander set over a large bowl, and sprinkle liberally with salt. Toss the zucchini 2 or 3 times to distribute the salt evenly, and let stand for at least 2 hours. Check the bowl occasionally, and if the liquid that collects in it comes up high enough to reach the zucchini, empty the bowl.

3. When 2 or more hours have elapsed, remove the zucchini and pat thoroughly dry with paper towels. Rinse and dry the colander, which you will need again.

4. Rinse the basil in cold water. Pat dry with paper towels and tear the leaves by hand into smaller pieces. Set aside.

5. When you are ready to fry, set the colander over a platter, and put the zucchini back in it. Dust the zucchini with the flour, shaking the colander to coat them evenly and to shed excess flour.

Fried Zucchini Sauce (continued)

6. Put enough vegetable oil in a frying pan to come ¼ to ½ inch up its sides. Add the garlic and turn the heat on to high. When the oil is quite hot, put in as many zucchini sticks at one time as will fit loosely in the pan. Check the garlic and as soon as it begins to turn brown, remove it and discard it. Turn the zucchini sticks, cooking them until they become colored a golden brown all over, then transfer them to a cooling rack to drain or to a platter lined with paper towels. Continue adding zucchini to the pan in as many batches as necessary until it is all done to a golden brown.

Ahead-of-time note ☙ The sauce may be prepared several hours in advance up to this point, but do not refrigerate the zucchini.

7. When the pasta is nearly ready to be drained, melt the butter in the upper part of a double boiler and keep it warm. If you are using soft, freshly made pasta, melt the butter before dropping the pasta in the pot.

8. Toss cooked drained pasta with the warm melted butter, add the fried zucchini, the basil, and the grated cheese and toss thoroughly again. Serve at once with additional grated Parmesan on the side.

Smothered Onions Sauce

THE SWEET PUNGENCY of onion is the whole story of this sauce. To draw out its character, the onion is first stewed very slowly for almost an hour, until it is meltingly soft and sweet. Then it is browned to bring its flavor to a sharper, livelier edge.

If you have no problems in using lard, it will considerably enrich the sauce. You may, however, use butter as a substitute.   *For 4 to 6 servings*

Either 2 tablespoons lard OR 2
  tablespoons butter with 2
  tablespoons extra virgin
  olive oil
1½ pounds onions, sliced very
  thin, about 6 cups
Salt

Black pepper, ground fresh
  from the mill
½ cup dry white wine
2 tablespoons chopped parsley
⅓ cup freshly grated *parmigiano-reggiano* cheese
1 to 1½ pounds pasta

Recommended pasta ☙ *Spaghetti* is an excellent choice, but an even better one may be homemade *tonnarelli*, see instructions on page 134. This is a rather dense sauce and if using homemade pasta, which is more absorbent than *spaghetti,* you should start with ½ tablespoon more lard or 1 tablespoon more butter when making the sauce.

1. Put the lard or butter and olive oil, and the onions with some salt in a large sauté pan. Cover and turn on the heat to very low. Cook for almost an hour until the onions become very soft.

2. Uncover the pan, raise the heat to medium high, and cook the onions until they become colored a deep, dark gold. Any liquid the onions may have shed must now boil away.

3. Add liberal grindings of pepper. Taste and correct for salt. Bear in mind that onions become very sweet when cooked in this manner and need an adequate amount of seasoning. Add the wine, turn the heat up, and stir frequently while the wine bubbles away. Add the parsley, stir thoroughly, and take off heat.

Ahead-of-time note ❀ You can cook the sauce entirely in advance up to the point where you add the parsley. When you are nearly ready to toss it with the pasta, reheat the sauce over medium heat and add the parsley just before draining the pasta.

4. Toss with cooked drained pasta, adding the grated Parmesan. As you toss, separate the onion strands somewhat to distribute them as much as possible throughout the pasta. Serve immediately.

Butter and Rosemary Sauce

THE TASTIEST PART of an Italian meat roast is what is left over: The rosemary-saturated garlicky juices, the bits of brown that have fallen off the meat. They usually end up tossed with pasta, which is then known as *la pasta col tocco d'arrosto,* "with a touch of the roast." If you don't have leftovers to fall back on, you can make a mock and meatless "touch of the roast" sauce as in the quick recipe here in which the presence of rosemary and garlic summons up all the fragrance of the original.
For 4 to 6 servings

Butter and Rosemary Sauce (continued)

3 to 4 garlic cloves
6 tablespoons butter, cut into
    small pieces
3 sprigs of fresh rosemary
1 beef bouillon cube, crushed

⅓ cup freshly grated
    parmigiano-reggiano cheese,
    plus additional cheese at the
    table
1 pound pasta

Recommended pasta ❀ This sauce probably tastes best of all with *tonnarelli*, the square fresh noodle, made as described on page 134. But it can also be used with unqualified success on *fettuccine* or *spaghetti*.

1. Mash the garlic cloves with the back of a knife handle, crushing them just enough to split and loosen the peel, which you will discard. Put the garlic, butter, and rosemary in a small saucepan and turn on the heat to medium. Cook, stirring frequently, for 4 to 5 minutes.

2. Add the crushed bouillon cube. Cook and stir until the bouillon has completely dissolved.

3. Pour the sauce through a fine wire strainer over cooked drained pasta. Toss thoroughly to coat the pasta well. Add the grated Parmesan and toss once more. Serve at once with additional grated cheese on the side.

"Aio e Oio"—Roman Garlic and Oil Sauce

For 4 servings

1 pound pasta
Salt
⅓ cup extra virgin olive oil
2 teaspoons garlic chopped very
    fine

Chopped hot red chili pepper,
    to taste
2 tablespoons chopped parsley

Recommended pasta ❀ Romans say "*spaghetti aio e oio*" as though it were one word, and they would as soon expect another pasta to be in the combination as the moon to change its course. If any substitution may hesitantly be suggested, it is *spaghettini*, thin *spaghetti*, which takes very well to the coating of garlic and oil.

1. Cook the *spaghetti* in boiling water to which an extra measure of salt has been added. There is no salt in the sauce itself because salt does not dis-

solve well in olive oil, so the pasta must be abundantly salted before it is tossed.

2. While the pasta is cooking, put the olive oil, garlic, and chopped hot pepper in a small saucepan, and turn on the heat to medium low. Cook and stir the garlic until it becomes colored a pale gold. Do not let it become brown.

3. Toss the cooked drained pasta with the entire contents of the saucepan, turning the strands over and over in the oil to coat them evenly. Taste and, if necessary, correct for salt. Add the chopped parsley, toss once again, and serve immediately.

"Aio e Oio" Raw Version

For 4 servings

4 garlic cloves
Salt
⅓ cup extra virgin olive oil
Chopped hot red chili pepper,
    to taste

1 pound pasta
2 tablespoons chopped parsley

1. Mash each garlic clove lightly with a knife handle, crushing it just enough to split it and loosen the skin, which you will loosen and discard.
2. Put the garlic, salt, olive oil, and chili pepper in a warm bowl, the one in which you will subsequently toss the pasta and turn all ingredients over two or three times.
3. Cook the pasta with an extra measure of salt. When done *al dente*, drain and toss it in the bowl with the raw garlic and oil. Thoroughly turn the strands in the oil again and again to coat them well. Taste and correct for salt. Add the chopped parsley, toss again, and serve immediately.

"Aio e Oio" Raw Version, with Fresh Tomatoes and Basil

To all the ingredients in the immediately preceding recipe except for the parsley, which you'll omit, add ¼ pound, or slightly more, fresh, very ripe, but firm plum tomatoes, and a few fresh basil leaves.

Skin the tomatoes raw, using a swiveling-blade peeler, split them in half, scoop out the seeds, then dice them very fine. Put the tomatoes in the bowl where the pasta will later be tossed, together with one or two large pinches of

"Aio e Oio" with Tomatoes and Basil (continued)

salt and the garlic, olive oil, and chili pepper from the preceding recipe. Cook the pasta with an average amount of salt. Toss the cooked drained pasta in the bowl, separating and turning the strands over and over in the oil.

Recommended pasta ✿ For both raw versions of *aio e oio,* thin *spaghetti, spaghettini,* is the pasta of choice.

Cauliflower Sauce with Garlic, Oil, and Chili Pepper

For 4 to 6 servings

1 head cauliflower, about 1½ pounds
½ cup extra virgin olive oil
2 large garlic cloves, peeled and chopped
6 flat anchovy fillets (preferably the ones prepared at home
as described on page 9), chopped very fine
Chopped hot red chili pepper, to taste
Salt
2 tablespoons chopped parsley
1 to 1½ pounds pasta

Recommended pasta ✿ *Penne,* the quill-shaped macaroni, either in the smooth or ridged version, would be the most appealing choice.

1. Strip the cauliflower of all its leaves except for a few of the very tender inner ones. Rinse it in cold water and cut it in two.

2. Bring 4 to 5 quarts of water to boil, put in the cauliflower, and cook it until it is tender, but not mushy, about 25 to 30 minutes. Prod it with a fork to test for doneness. When cooked, drain and set aside.

3. Put water in a saucepan, and bring it to a lively simmer.

4. Put the oil and garlic in a medium sauté pan, turn on the heat to medium, and cook until the garlic becomes colored a light, golden brown. Remove the pan from the burner, place it over the saucepan of simmering water, and add to it the chopped anchovies. Cook, stirring and mashing the anchovies with the back of a wooden spoon against the sides of the pan to dissolve them as much as possible into a paste. Return the sauté pan to the burner over medium heat and cook for another half minute, stirring frequently.

5. Add the drained, boiled cauliflower, breaking it up quickly with a fork into pieces not bigger than a small nut. Turn it thoroughly in the oil to coat it well, mashing some of it to a pulp with the back of the spoon.

6. Add the chopped chili pepper and salt. Turn up the heat, and cook for a few minutes more, stirring frequently.

Ahead-of-time note ✿ You can prepare the sauce several hours in advance up to this point. Do not refrigerate it. Reheat it gently when the pasta is nearly ready to be drained and tossed.

7. Toss with cooked drained pasta. Add the chopped parsley, toss once or twice again, then serve immediately.

Broccoli and Anchovy Sauce

For 6 servings

A large bunch fresh broccoli, about 1 pound
⅓ cup extra virgin olive oil
6 flat anchovy fillets (preferably the ones prepared at home as described on page 9), chopped very fine

Chopped hot red chili pepper, to taste
1½ pounds pasta
2 tablespoons freshly grated *parmigiano-reggiano* cheese
¼ cup freshly grated *romano* cheese

Recommended pasta ✿ A chewy, handmade pasta from Apulia known as *orecchiette*—it looks like miniature saucers—is the natural match for this earthy broccoli sauce. *Orecchiette* can be made at home, see the instructions on page 233, but it is also available in shops that specialize in imported Italian products. An excellent alternative to *orecchiette* is *fusilli* or *conchiglie*.

1. Detach the broccoli florets from the stalks, but do not discard the stalks. Following the detailed instructions on page 116, pare the stalks, wash the stalks and florets, and cook them in salted, boiling water until just tender when prodded with a fork.

2. Drain the broccoli, break up the florets into smaller pieces, and cut the stalks into large dice. Set aside.

3. Put water in a saucepan, and bring it to a lively simmer.

4. Put the oil in a sauté pan and turn on the heat to low. When the oil begins to warm up, place the pan over the saucepan of simmering water, double-boiler fashion, and add the chopped anchovies. Cook, stirring and mashing the anchovies with the back of a wooden spoon to dissolve them as much as possible into a paste.

Ahead-of-time note ✿ The sauce may be prepared a few hours in advance up to this point, but do not refrigerate the cooked broccoli.

5. Return the sauté pan to the burner over medium heat. If you were making the first part of the sauce in advance, reheat the anchovies gently, stir-

Broccoli and Anchovy Sauce (continued)

ring with a wooden spoon. Add the broccoli florets, the diced stalks, and the hot chili pepper. Cook the broccoli for 4 to 5 minutes, turning it from time to time to coat it well.

6. Toss the entire contents of the pan with cooked drained pasta. Add both grated cheeses, and toss thoroughly once again. Serve immediately.

Tomato and Anchovy Sauce

For 4 servings

1 teaspoon garlic chopped very
    fine
⅓ cup extra virgin olive oil
4 flat anchovy fillets (preferably
    the ones prepared at home
    as described on page 9),
    chopped coarse
1½ cups canned imported
    Italian plum tomatoes, cut
    up, with their juice

Salt
Black pepper, ground fresh
    from the mill
1 pound pasta
2 tablespoons chopped parsley

Recommended pasta ❀ First choice would be thin *spaghetti, spaghettini,* to which the only satisfactory alternative is the thicker, standard *spaghetti.*

1. Put water in a saucepan, and bring it to a lively simmer.

2. Put the garlic and oil in a sauté pan or another saucepan, turn the heat on to medium, and cook and stir the garlic until it becomes colored a very pale gold.

3. Place the pan with the garlic and oil over the saucepan of simmering water, double-boiler fashion. Add the chopped anchovies, stirring and mashing them against the sides of the pan with the back of a wooden spoon until they begin to dissolve into a paste. Return the pan with the anchovies to the burner over medium heat and cook for half a minute or less, stirring constantly. Add the tomatoes, salt, and a few grindings of pepper, and adjust heat so that the sauce cooks at a gentle, but steady simmer for 20 to 25 minutes or until the oil floats free from the tomatoes. Stir from time to time.

Ahead-of-time note ❀ The sauce may be prepared several hours in advance and gently reheated when the pasta is nearly ready to be drained and tossed. Do not refrigerate.

4. Toss cooked drained pasta with the entire contents of the saucepan,

turning the strands so that they are thoroughly coated. Add the chopped parsley, toss once more, and serve immediately.

PESTO

Pesto may have become more popular than is good for it. When I see what goes by that name, and what goes into it, and the bewildering variety of dishes it is slapped on, I wonder how many cooks can still claim acquaintance with *pesto*'s original character, and with the things it does best.

Pesto is the sauce the Genoese invented as a vehicle for the fragrance of a basil like no other, their own. Olive oil, garlic, pine nuts, butter, and grated cheese are the only other components. *Pesto* is never cooked, or heated, and while it may on occasion do good things for vegetable soup, it has just one great role: to be the most seductive of all sauces for pasta.

It is unlikely that any *pesto* will taste quite like the one made with the magically scented basil of the Italian Riviera. But never mind, as long as you have fresh basil, and use no substitute for basil, you can make rather wonderful *pesto* anywhere.

Genoese cooks insist that if it isn't made in a mortar with a pestle, it isn't *pesto*. Linguistically at least, they are correct, because the word comes from the verb *pestare,* which means to pound or to grind, as in a mortar. They are probably right gastronomically, too, and out of respect for the merits of the tradition, the mortar method is described below. It would be a greater pity, however, to pass up making *pesto* at home because one has not the time or inclination to use the mortar. The nearly effortless and very satisfactory food processor method is therefore also given.

Note ✸ The *pecorino* cheese known as *fiore sardo,* which is used in the Riviera for making *pesto,* is much less harsh than *romano.* But up to now at least, *romano* is the one that is available. In the recipes given here, the proportion of *romano* to *parmigiano-reggiano* is less than what you will want to use if you can get *fiore sardo.*

Pesto by the Food Processor Method

For 6 servings

FOR THE PROCESSOR

2 cups tightly packed fresh basil
    leaves
½ cup extra virgin olive oil
3 tablespoons pine nuts

2 garlic cloves, chopped fine
    before putting in the
    processor
Salt

FOR COMPLETION BY HAND

½ cup freshly grated *parmi-giano-reggiano* cheese
2 tablespoons freshly grated
    romano cheese

3 tablespoons butter, softened
    to room temperature

1½ pounds pasta

1. Briefly soak and wash the basil in cold water, and gently pat it thoroughly dry with paper towels.

2. Put the basil, olive oil, pine nuts, chopped garlic, and an ample pinch of salt in the processor bowl, and process to a uniform, creamy consistency.

3. Transfer to a bowl, and mix in the two grated cheeses by hand. It is worth the slight effort to do it by hand to obtain the notably superior texture it produces. When the cheese has been evenly amalgamated with the other ingredients, mix in the softened butter, distributing it uniformly into the sauce.

4. When spooning the *pesto* over pasta, dilute it slightly with a tablespoon or two of the hot water in which the pasta was cooked.

Freezing pesto ❀ Make the sauce by the food processor method through to the end of Step 2, and freeze it without cheese and butter in it. Add the cheese and butter when it is thawed, just before using.

Pesto by the Mortar Method

For 6 servings

A large marble mortar with a
　hardwood pestle
2 garlic cloves
2 cups tightly packed fresh basil
　leaves
3 tablespoons pine nuts
Coarse sea salt
½ cup freshly grated *parmigiano-reggiano* cheese

2 tablespoons freshly grated
　romano cheese
½ cup extra virgin olive oil
3 tablespoons butter, softened
　to room temperature
1½ pounds pasta

1. Lightly mash the garlic with a heavy knife handle, just enough to split and loosen the skin, which you will remove and discard.

2. Briefly soak and wash the basil leaves in cold water, and pat them gently but thoroughly dry with paper towels.

3. Put the basil, garlic, pine nuts, and coarse salt into the mortar. Using the pestle with a rotary movement, grind all the ingredients against the side of the mortar. When they have been ground into a paste, add both grated cheeses, and grind them evenly into the mixture, using the pestle.

4. Add the olive oil, in a very thin stream, beating it into the mixture with a wooden spoon. When all the oil has been incorporated, beat in the butter with the spoon, distributing it evenly.

5. When spooning the *pesto* over pasta, dilute it slightly with a tablespoon or two of the hot water in which the pasta was cooked.

Recommended pasta ✹ *Spaghetti* is perfect with *pesto* and so are the Potato Gnocchi on page 260. In Genoa, a homemade noodle locally called *trenette* is the classic pasta for *pesto*. It is virtually identical to *fettuccine,* and if you'd like to serve *pesto* on fresh pasta, follow the instructions for making *fettuccine* on page 134. Even more appealing, if less orthodox than *fettuccine,* would be another kind of homemade noodle, *tonnarelli,* page 134.

Pasta and Pesto with Potatoes and Green Beans

WHEN SERVING *pesto* on *spaghetti* or noodles, the full Genoese treatment calls for the addition of boiled new potatoes and green beans. When all its components are right, there is no single dish more delicious in the entire Italian pasta repertory.

For 6 servings

Pasta and Pesto (continued)

3 small, new potatoes
½ pound young green beans
1½ pounds pasta

The pesto from the preceding
  recipe

1. Boil the potatoes with their skins on, peel them when done, and slice them thin.

2. Snap both ends from the green beans, wash them in cold water, and cook them in salted boiling water until tender—not overcooked, but not too hard either. Drain and set aside.

3. Cook *spaghetti* or *fettuccine* for 6. When draining the pasta, hold back some of its cooking water, and add 2 tablespoonfuls of it to the *pesto*.

4. Toss the cooked drained pasta with the potatoes, green beans, and *pesto*. Serve immediately.

Pesto with Ricotta

The slightly sour, milky flavor of *ricotta* brings lightness and vivacity to *pesto*. To the ingredients in the basic food processor recipe on page 176, add 3 tablespoons fresh *ricotta* and reduce the amount of butter to 2 tablespoons. As in the basic recipe, mix the grated cheese, the *ricotta,* and the butter into the processed ingredients by hand in another bowl. Serves 6.

Recommended pasta ✹ The homemade *lasagne*-like *piccagge* described on page 221 are the traditional and most interesting choice. But even if you settle for *spaghetti,* you are not likely to be disappointed.

Black Truffle Sauce

WHEN THIS RECIPE was first published in *More Classic Italian Cooking,* the cost of the ingredients and the powerfully sensual quality of the dish led me to scale the quantities down to serve two persons. It still seems to me that its pleasures are of the kind that are best savored *a due,* in the company of just one other. If you'd rather have a crowd, increase the recipe, but each time you double the truffles, add only half again as much anchovies.   *For 2 servings*

3 ounces black truffles, preferably fresh
1 or 2 garlic cloves

3 tablespoons extra virgin olive
  oil, plus a little more oil for
  the pasta

1 flat anchovy fillet (preferably
    the kind prepared at home
    as described on page 9),
    chopped very fine

Salt
½ pound pasta

Recommended pasta ✿ Thin *spaghetti, spaghettini.*

1. *If using fresh truffles:* Clean them with a stiff brush, wipe them with a moist cloth, and pat thoroughly dry.

If using canned truffles: Drain them and pat them dry. Save their liquid to use in a risotto, or a meat sauce.

2. Grate the truffles to a very fine-grained consistency, using the smallest holes of a flat-sided grater. Some Japanese stores sell a very sharp metal grater that does the job extremely well.

3. Mash the garlic lightly with a knife handle, enough to split it and loosen the skin, which you will remove and discard.

4. Put water in a narrow saucepan and bring it to a lively simmer.

5. Put the olive oil and the garlic in another small saucepan, earthenware if possible, turn on the heat to medium, and cook until the garlic becomes colored a light nut brown.

6. Discard the garlic, remove the pan from the burner, and place it, double-boiler fashion, over the pan with simmering water. Add the chopped anchovy, and stir it with a wooden spoon, using the back of it to mash it against the sides of the pan. After a minute or two, place the pan over the burner again, turning the heat on to low, and stir constantly, for a few minutes, until the anchovy is almost entirely dissolved into paste.

7. Add the grated truffles, stir thoroughly once or twice, taste and, if necessary, correct for salt. Stir quickly once more and turn the heat off.

8. Toss cooked and drained *spaghettini* with the entire contents of the pan. Drizzle a few drops of raw olive oil over the pasta and serve at once.

Tuna Sauce with Tomatoes and Garlic

For 4 to 6 servings

4 tablespoons extra virgin olive oil

½ teaspoon garlic chopped very fine

1½ cups canned imported Italian plum tomatoes, cut up, with their juice

12 ounces imported Italian tuna packed in olive oil, see Tuna, page 37

Salt

Black pepper, ground fresh from the mill

1 tablespoon butter

1 to 1½ pounds pasta

3 tablespoons chopped parsley

Recommended pasta ❀ *Spaghetti* or short, tubular macaroni, such as *penne* or *rigatoni.*

1. In a saucepan or small sauté pan put the olive oil and the chopped garlic, turn on the heat to medium, and cook until the garlic becomes colored a pale gold. Add the cut-up tomatoes with their juice, stir to coat the tomatoes well, and adjust heat to cook at a gentle, but steady simmer for about 25 minutes, until the oil floats free from the tomatoes.

Ahead-of-time note ❀ The sauce can be prepared up to this point several hours or even a day or two in advance. When ready to use, reheat gently.

2. Drain the tuna and crumble it with a fork. Turn off the heat under the tomatoes, and add the tuna, mixing thoroughly to distribute it evenly. Taste and, if necessary, correct for salt. Add a few grindings of pepper, the 1 tablespoon of butter, and mix well once again.

3. Toss with cooked drained pasta. Add the chopped parsley, toss again, and serve at once.

Clam Sauce with Tomatoes

ITALIAN CLAMS, particularly the common, small round ones from the Adriatic are very savory, and little or nothing needs to be done to build up their flavor. Clams from other seas are blander, and you must look for help from external sources to approximate the natural spiciness of a clam sauce you'd be likely to experience in Italy. That explains the presence in the recipe that follows of anchovies and chili pepper. *For 4 servings*

1 dozen small littleneck clams

3 tablespoons extra virgin olive oil, plus a little more for the pasta

1½ teaspoons garlic chopped fine

2 tablespoons chopped parsley

2 cups canned imported Italian plum tomatoes, cut up, with their juice, OR fresh,

ripe tomatoes, peeled and chopped

1 flat anchovy fillet (preferably the kind prepared at home as described on page 9), chopped very fine

Salt

Chopped hot red chili pepper, to taste

1 pound pasta

Recommended pasta 🌸 *Spaghettini*, thin *spaghetti*, takes to clam sauces more successfully than other shapes. A close enough second is *spaghetti*.

1. Wash and scrub the clams as described on page 121. Discard those that stay open when handled. Put them in a pan broad enough so that the clams don't need to be piled up more than 3 deep, cover the pan, and turn on the heat to high. Check the clams frequently, turning them over, and remove them from the pan as they open their shells.

2. When all the clams have opened up, detach their meat from the shells, and gently swish each clam in its own juices in the pan to rinse off any sand. Unless they are exceptionally small, cut them up in 2 or even 3 pieces. Put them aside in a small bowl.

3. Line a strainer with paper towels, and filter the clam juices in the pan through the paper into a bowl. Spoon some of the filtered juice over the clam meat to keep it moist.

4. Put the olive oil and garlic in a saucepan, turn on the heat to medium, and cook until the garlic has become colored a pale gold. Add the parsley, stir once or twice, then add the cut up tomatoes, their juice, the chopped anchovy, and the filtered clam juices. Stir thoroughly for a minute or two, then adjust heat to cook at a gentle, but steady simmer for 25 minutes, or until the oil floats free from the tomatoes.

Ahead-of-time note 🌸 The sauce may be prepared several hours in advance up to this point. Reheat gently when preparing to toss it with pasta.

5. Taste and correct for salt, add the chopped chili pepper, stir two or three times, then remove the pan from heat. Add the cut-up clams, stirring them into the sauce to coat them well. Toss thoroughly with cooked, drained *spaghettini* or *spaghetti*. Drizzle a few drops of raw olive oil over the pasta and serve at once.

White Clam Sauce

EVERYWHERE in Venice—or in Italy for that matter—one can eat *spaghetti* with clams, but none tastes like the dish Cesare Benelli makes at Al Covo, the restaurant he owns with his Texan wife, Diane. Cesare's genial variation on this timeless theme consists of holding back the natural juices of the just-opened clams, draining the pasta while it is still underdone, then finishing the cooking of it in a skillet together with the clam juice. The pasta, by the time it becomes fully cooked, drinks up all the fresh clam juices, achieving a density and richness of flavor no other version of the dish can match.

For 4 servings

1½ dozen littleneck clams
5 tablespoons extra virgin olive
    oil
2 large garlic cloves, peeled and
    sliced paper thin
1½ tablespoons chopped
    parsley
Chopped fresh hot chili pepper,
    2 teaspoons, or to taste
1 fresh, ripe, firm plum tomato,
    cut into ½-inch dice with

its skin on, but drained of
    juice and all seeds removed
½ cup dry white wine
1 pound dry pasta
6 fresh basil leaves, torn into 2
    or 3 pieces

Recommended pasta ❀ The recommendations for Clam Sauce with Tomatoes on page 181 are equally valid here. If you should want to use fresh, homemade *fettuccine* instead of the recommended *spaghettini,* bear in mind that it will cook much faster than boxed, dry factory pasta. Before cooking it, put the clam juice in the skillet and boil away half of it, so that when you will be adding the *fettuccine* to the pan it will take less time to cook down all the juice.

1. Wash and scrub the clams as described on page 121, discarding those that stay open when handled. Heat up the clams to open them, following the directions in the preceding recipe in Step 1 for Clam Sauce with Tomatoes, page 181.

2. When all the clams have opened up, take them out of the pan, using a slotted spoon. Try not to stir up the juices in the pan any more than you must. Detach the clam meat from its shell, and gently swish each clam in the pan juices to rinse off any sand. Unless they are exceptionally small, cut them up in 2 or even 3 pieces. Put them in a small bowl, pour 2 tablespoons olive oil

over them, cover the bowl tightly with plastic wrap, and set it aside for later. Do not refrigerate.

3. Line a strainer with paper towels, and filter the clam juices in the pan through the paper and into another bowl. Set aside for later.

4. Choose a skillet or sauté pan broad enough to contain the pasta later. Put in 3 tablespoons olive oil and the sliced garlic, and turn on the heat to medium high. Cook the garlic, stirring it, for just a few seconds, without letting it become colored, then add the parsley and the chili pepper. Stir once or twice, and add the diced tomato. Cook the tomato for 1 to 2 minutes, stirring it from time to time, then add the wine. Simmer the wine for about 20 to 30 seconds, letting it reduce, then turn off the heat.

5. Cook the pasta in abundant boiling salted water until it is very firm to the bite, barely short of being fully cooked. When you bite a piece off, it should feel slightly stiff and the narrowest of chalk-white cores should be showing in the center of the strand.

6. Turn the heat on to high under the skillet or sauté pan, drain the pasta and transfer it immediately to the pan. Add all the filtered clam juice, and cook, tossing and turning the pasta, until all the juice has evaporated.

If the pasta was not too underdone when you drained it, it should now be perfectly cooked. Taste it and, in the unlikely event it needs more cooking after the clam juices have evaporated and been absorbed, add a small amount of water.

7. As soon as the pasta is done, before you turn the heat off, add the cut-up clams with all the oil in the bowl and the torn basil leaves, toss in the pan 2 or 3 times, then transfer to a warm platter and serve at once.

Sardinian Bottarga Sauce

THE FLAVORS of Sardinia, like its landscape and the features of its people, are unlike anything you may find on mainland Italy. Intensity and force are some of the qualities that come to mind. The provocatively musky taste of *bottarga di muggine*—dried mullet roe, see page 13 for a full description—is consistent with the sensations, so titillating for the palate, that after a sojourn on the island we begin to recognize as distinctively Sardinian.

There are two main schools of thought on how to use *bottarga*. One maintains that, as with all fish products, olive oil should be used exclusively. Others feel that butter softens and sweetens the roe's vigorous flavor. My friend Daniel Berger of the Metropolitan Museum, a long-time devotee and dazzling practitioner of Italian cooking, uses oil to make the sauce and butter to toss it. After working with several approaches, I have found butter alone satisfies me best. Danny's suggestion of scallions I fully endorse, although strict fidelity to traditional practice would suggest onions.

Note ❦ Because fine mullet *bottarga* is expensive, I have scaled the recipe to produce enough for two. I don't think of *bottarga* as a condiment for a crowd, but you can easily double or triple the recipe to serve four or six.

For 2 servings

1 ounce mullet *bottarga,* sliced, then chopped, following directions given below, to produce ¼ loosely packed cup

⅔ cup scallions, both leaves and bulbs cut into very thin rounds, OR chopped onion

Salt

Butter, 1½ tablespoons for cooking onion, plus 1 tablespoon to toss the pasta

½ pound pasta

1 tablespoon parsley chopped fine

¼ teaspoon lemon peel grated without digging into the white pith

OPTIONAL: a tiny amount of chopped hot red chili pepper, to taste

Recommended pasta ❦ In Sardinia, it would be *malloreddus,* a small, *gnocchi-*shaped pasta made from hard, *semolina* flour. You can successfully replace *malloreddus* with *spaghettini,* thin *spaghetti,* preferably of high-quality, imported Italian pasta. If you would like to have the sauce with homemade pasta, it would be very good with *tonnarelli,* the thick, square noodle. Instructions for making *tonnarelli* are on page 134.

1. Weigh the *bottarga* roe and cut off 1 ounce of it. Strip away the membrane enveloping it. Use a swiveling-blade peeler to slice it paper thin, then chop it as fine as you are able with a knife. If you hold the tip of the blade down on the cutting board, and rock the knife up and down over the *bottarga,* you will be able in seconds to grind it down to very fine soft grains. (If you are making more than this recipe calls for, you can use the food processor.)

2. Put the scallions or onion in a small saucepan together with a large pinch of salt and 1½ tablespoons butter. Turn on the heat to medium and cook, stirring from time to time, until the scallions or onion become lightly colored.

3. As soon as the pasta is cooked, drain it and put it in a warm serving bowl together with 1 tablespoon of butter. Add all the contents of the

saucepan, toss 2 or 3 times, then add the parsley, the grated lemon peel, the optional chili pepper, and the ground *bottarga,* and toss again thoroughly to coat the pasta strands with an even distribution of sauce. Serve at once.

Note ✺ The chili pepper is, to my mind, unnecessary and competes with the flavor of *bottarga.* Many people do enjoy it, however, so it is up to you to decide.

Scallop Sauce with Olive Oil, Garlic, and Hot Pepper

THE SMALLEST—and perhaps the tastiest—of several varieties of scallop found in Italian waters is called *canestrelli,* smaller, when shelled, than the nail of a child's little finger. When fresh, North American scallops are exceptionally good too, particularly the sweet ones known as bay scallops, but they are larger than *canestrelli,* and should be cut up so that, like *canestrelli,* there will be more little pieces available to carry the seasoning.   *For 6 servings*

1 pound fresh bay OR deep sea
    scallops
½ cup extra virgin olive oil
1 tablespoon garlic chopped
    very fine
2 tablespoons chopped parsley
Chopped hot red chili pepper,
    to taste

Salt
1 to 1½ pounds pasta
½ cup dry, unflavored bread
    crumbs, lightly toasted in
    the oven or in a skillet

Recommended pasta ✺ As in so many other seafood sauces, *spaghettini,* thin *spaghetti,* is the most congenial shape, but *spaghetti* is an equally valid choice.

1. Wash the scallops in cold water, pat thoroughly dry with a cloth towel, and cut up into pieces about ⅜ inch thick.

2. Put the olive oil and garlic in a saucepan, turn on the heat to medium, and cook, stirring, until the garlic becomes colored a light gold. Add the parsley and hot pepper. Stir once or twice, then add the scallops and one or two large pinches of salt. Turn the heat up to high, and cook for about 1½ minutes, stirring frequently, until the scallops lose their shine and turn a flat white. Do not overcook the scallops or they will become tough. Taste and correct for salt and hot pepper. If the scallops should shed a lot of liquid, remove them from the pan with a slotted spoon, and boil down the watery

Scallop Sauce (continued)

juices. Return the scallops to the pan, turn them over quickly, then turn off the heat.

3. Toss thoroughly with cooked drained *spaghettini,* add the bread crumbs, toss again, and serve at once.

Fish Sauce

THIS SAUCE is based on the observation that the sweetest, most flavorful morsels in a fish are trapped within its head and that all that stands in the way of one's enjoyment of that savory meat is the bony matter that surrounds it. When the heads are mashed through a food mill, all their flavor is extracted, and the pesky, little bones are left behind. It's the same technique used to heighten the flavor of fish soup, see page 310.

Most markets dealing in whole, fresh fish have available the heads they usually take off when preparing fish for their customers. If you stand high in the dealer's esteem, he may let you have a few heads for nothing, but even if you must pay for them, the cost should be quite modest.   *For 8 servings*

1½ to 2 pounds assorted fresh fish heads, from such fish as sea bass, red snapper, or porgie	1½ cups canned imported Italian plum tomatoes, cut up, with their juice
⅔ cup extra virgin olive oil	Salt
⅓ cup chopped onion	Black pepper, ground fresh from the mill
1 tablespoon chopped garlic	1½ pounds pasta
¼ cup chopped parsley	2 tablespoons butter
⅓ cup dry white wine	

Recommended pasta ❀ *Spaghetti* is an ideal carrier for the full flavor of the sauce, but other very good choices are short, tube-shaped macaroni, such as *penne* and *rigatoni.*

1. Wash all the fish heads in cold water, then set aside to drain in a colander.

2. Choose a sauté pan that can subsequently accommodate all the fish heads without stacking or overlapping them. Put in the olive oil and the chopped onion, turn on the heat to medium, and cook the onion, stirring, until it is translucent. Add the garlic and sauté until it becomes colored a pale

gold. Add half the chopped parsley (2 tablespoons), stir once or twice, then put in the fish heads.

3. Turn the heads over to coat them well, then add the wine, letting it come to a lively simmer. When it has bubbled away for a minute or less, add the cut-up tomatoes with their juice, salt, and black pepper, and stir, turning over all the ingredients in the pan. Adjust heat to cook at a gentle simmer for 15 minutes.

4. Remove the heads from the pan. With a small spoon, scoop out as much of the meat as comes away easily, particularly at the cheeks and the throat, putting it aside in a small bowl or saucer for later.

5. Loosen and discard all the larger bones. Fit the food mill with the disk with the largest holes and mash the remainder of the heads through it, letting the pulp drop into the sauté pan.

Ahead-of-time note ❀ Everything can be prepared several hours in advance up to this point. Pour a little bit of the sauce from the pan over the meat from the fish heads that had been set aside and cover the bowl or saucer with plastic wrap.

6. Turn the heat on again, adjusting it to cook at a very gentle simmer. Cook for about 20 minutes, stirring frequently, until the sauce thickens to a dense, creamy consistency. Add the small pieces of meat you had scooped out of the heads, stir, and cook for 5 minutes more.

7. Toss cooked drained pasta with the entire contents of the pan, add the remaining chopped parsley and the butter, toss again, and serve at once.

Sicilian Sardine Sauce

THE COOKING of Sicily dazzles us with its fluent use of a more vivid vocabulary of ingredients than any other cuisine in Italy is accustomed to command. Take Palermo's *pasta con le sarde*—pasta with sardines—a dish that takes the fragrances of saffron and of wild mountain fennel, the pungencies of sardines and anchovies, the nectar of raisins, and the toasty quality of nuts, and merges them into a full-throated chorus of appetite-stirring harmony.

To achieve a reasonable facsimile of *pasta con le sarde,* one must be prepared to make substantial compromises: Fresh sardines, although they do exist, make rare and unpredictable appearances and may have to be replaced by canned sardines; outside of northern California, where wild fennel can be found from spring through summer, we have to make do with the tops of cultivated *finocchio.* *For 4 to 6 servings*

Sicilian Sardine Sauce (continued)

1 pound fresh sardines OR 8 ounces, net weight, drained choice canned sardines packed in olive oil

2 cups *finocchio* leaf tops (see note below) OR 1¾ cups fresh wild fennel

Salt

1 tablespoon black raisins

½ cup extra virgin olive oil

2 tablespoons chopped onion

4 flat anchovy fillets (preferably the ones prepared at home as described on page 9), chopped fine

⅓ cup *pignoli* (pine nuts)

1½ tablespoons tomato paste, dissolved in 1 cup luke-warm water together with a large pinch of powdered saffron OR ½ teaspoon crumbled saffron threads

Black pepper, ground fresh from the mill

1 to 1½ pounds pasta

½ cup dry, unflavored bread crumbs, lightly toasted in the oven or in a skillet

Note ❀ Vegetable markets usually sell *finocchio* with the tops trimmed away, so you must arrange in advance for them to be kept for you.

Recommended pasta ❀ We should do as Palermo does, and choose the thick, hollow *spaghetti* that in Sicily is called *u pirciatu*. It is the same shape as the one identified on boxes as *bucatini* or *perciatelli*.

1. *If using fresh sardines:* Snap off the head of the fish, pulling away with it most of the intestines.

Remove the center back fin together with the little bones that are attached to it by pulling it off starting at the tail end.

Hold the sardine with one hand, slip the thumbnail of the other hand into the belly cavity, and run it against the spine all the way to the tail. This will open up the sardine completely flat, exposing the spine.

Slip the nails of your thumb and forefinger under the spine, and work it loose. Lift the spine, freeing it from the flesh, but do not snap it off. Pull the spine toward the tail, and pull it sharply away from the body of the fish, taking the tail with it.

Wash the boned, butterflied sardine under cold running water, rinsing away any remaining portion of the guts or any loose bones.

When all the sardines are done, lay them flat on a large cutting board, propping up one end of the board to let the fish drain.

If using canned sardines: Begin the recipe with the next step.

2. Wash the *finocchio* tops or the wild fennel in cold water. Bring 4 to 5 quarts of water to a boil, add salt, and as the water resumes boiling put in the greens. Cook for 10 minutes with a cover set on askew. Off heat, retrieve the cooked fennel greens using a colander spoon, but do not pour out the water in the pot. Save it for cooking the pasta later.

3. When cool enough to handle, squeeze the greens gently in your hand to force moisture out, then chop them.

4. Soak the raisins in several changes of cold water for no less than 15 minutes, then drain them and chop them.

5. Put water in a saucepan and bring it to a lively simmer.

6. Choose a sauté pan that can subsequently accommodate all the ingredients except the pasta. Put in the olive oil and chopped onion, and turn on the heat to medium. Cook the onion, stirring, until it becomes translucent. Place the sauté pan over the pot with simmering water, add the anchovies, and stir them constantly with a wooden spoon, mashing them from time to time with the back of the spoon.

7. When the anchovies are nearly dissolved to a paste, return the pan to the burner over medium heat, add the greens, and cook for 5 minutes, stirring from time to time.

8. *If using fresh sardines:* Clear some space in the pan by pushing its contents to one side with the wooden spoon. Into the cleared area, put as many sardines as will fit flat without overlapping. Cook them briefly on one side, then on the other, less than a minute for each side. Push the cooked sardines to one side of the pan, clearing room to cook more sardines, continuing in this fashion until all the sardines have been done.

If using canned sardines: Proceed directly to the next step.

9. Add the *pignoli,* the chopped raisins, the tomato paste and saffron solution, salt, and a few grindings of black pepper, and turn over all ingredients to season them evenly. Continue to cook at medium heat, letting all the liquid in the pan bubble away. If using canned sardines, add them at this point, turning them over in the sauce two or three times, then remove from heat.

Sicilian Sardine Sauce (continued)

Ahead-of-time note 🐟 The sauce can be prepared several hours in advance up to this point, but if you are using canned sardines, put them in only when reheating the sauce to toss it with the pasta.

10. Bring the water in which you cooked the fennel greens to a boil, add a little salt, and in it cook the pasta.

11. Toss the sardine sauce with the cooked drained pasta. Add the bread crumbs and toss again. Allow the pasta to settle several minutes before serving.

Baked Pasta con le Sarde with Toasted Almonds

1. Prepare the sardine sauce, following the instructions in the basic recipe above.

2. If using fresh sardines, purchase an additional ¼ pound, clean them and butterfly them as described in the basic recipe, and sauté them in a separate pan in hot olive oil, cooking them just long enough to brown them lightly on each side. Transfer them to a cooling rack or to a paper-lined platter to drain.

3. Blanch ¼ cup of shelled almonds, as described on page 570, toast them for a few minutes in an oven preheated to 350°, and process to a very coarse consistency or chop roughly by hand. (Leave the oven turned on to 350°.)

4. Choose a 10-cup bake-and-serve dish (13 inches by 9 inches, if rectangular), and smear with butter.

5. Cook the pasta in the fennel-greens cooking water as described in the basic recipe, draining it while it is still slightly undercooked, a few degrees firmer than *al dente*. Line the bottom of the baking dish with a layer of pasta, spread over it some of the sardine sauce, and sprinkle with bread crumbs. Top with another layer of pasta, sauce, and bread crumbs, proceeding thus until you have used up all the pasta and sauce. Reserve some of the bread crumbs. If using fresh sardines, distribute the separately browned sardines over the top layer, skin side up. Sprinkle with the chopped up toasted almonds and the bread crumbs. Drizzle very lightly with olive oil. Bake in the 350º oven for 5 minutes. After removing it from the oven, allow the pasta to settle for several minutes before serving it.

Pink Shrimp Sauce with Cream

For 6 servings with tortellini *or 4 servings with flat noodles*

½ pound medium shrimp,
    unshelled weight
⅓ cup extra virgin olive oil
2 garlic cloves, peeled and
    chopped fine
1½ tablespoons tomato paste
    dissolved in ½ cup dry
    white wine

Salt
Black pepper, ground fresh
    from the mill
½ cup heavy cream
The *tortellini* from page 139
    OR 1 pound other pasta
2 tablespoons chopped parsley

Recommended pasta ❧ The ideal combination for this elegant and lively sauce is Tortellini with Fish Stuffing, page 209. It will also suit other home-made pasta cuts, such as *fettuccine,* page 134, or *pappardelle,* page 135.

1. Shell the shrimp, cut them in half lengthwise, removing the vein, and rinse under cold running water.

2. Put the olive oil and the chopped garlic in a saucepan, and turn on the heat to medium. Cook the garlic, stirring it, until it becomes colored a very pale gold, then add the tomato paste and wine solution. Pour it in all at once quickly to avoid spattering. Cook for 10 minutes, stirring from time to time.

3. Add the shrimp, salt, and liberal grindings of pepper, and turn up the heat to medium high. Cook for 2 minutes or so, turning the shrimp over frequently to coat well. Remove the pan from heat.

4. With a slotted spoon, retrieve about ⅔ of the shrimp from the pan, and purée them in the food processor or blender.

5. Return the puréed shrimp to the pan. Turn on the heat to medium, add the cream, and cook for about 1 minute, stirring constantly, until the cream thickens. Taste and correct for salt and pepper.

6. Toss the sauce with cooked drained pasta. Add the chopped parsley, toss again, and serve at once.

Butter and Parmesan Cheese Sauce

THE BASIC WHITE SAUCE of butter and Parmesan has, for generations, eclipsed all others among families of northern Italy as the favorite way of seasoning pasta. The sauce is produced by the heat of the pasta itself as it melts the raw cheese and the butter, and by the care with which the pasta is tossed to fuse both ingredients to itself and to each other. It is perhaps the best sauce for developing and mastering that skill of tossing, which is essential to the success of any pasta dish.   *For 4 servings*

1 pound pasta
1 cup freshly grated
    parmigiano-reggiano cheese

4 tablespoons (½ stick) choicest
    quality butter

Recommended pasta ❧ Butter and cheese is equally good with homemade pasta and with boxed, dry pasta. Try it with Tortelloni Stuffed with Swiss Chard, Prosciutto, and Ricotta, page 211, or with *spaghetti*. Always serve with additional grated cheese on the side.

1. Put hot, just-cooked, and drained pasta in a preheated serving bowl. Add about 4 tablespoonfuls of grated cheese and toss rapidly and thoroughly, turning all the pasta in the cheese, which will begin to melt and cling.

2. Add half the butter and another 4 tablespoonfuls of cheese, and toss thoroughly and quickly again.

3. Add the remaining cheese, and turn the pasta over with it three or four times.

4. Add the remaining butter, toss until all the butter has melted, and serve at once with additional cheese at the table.

Butter and Sage Sauce

IN ITALY, this sauce is called burro oro e salvia, "golden butter and sage," because to become fully impregnated with the penetrating sage fragrance, the butter must be heated until it becomes colored a rich gold. *For 4 to 6 servings*

4 to 5 tablespoons choicest
    quality butter
6 to 8 whole sage leaves,
    preferably fresh

1 pound pasta
Freshly grated *parmigiano-
    reggiano* cheese for the table

Recommended pasta ❧ Butter and sage works best with homemade pasta, either a noodle cut such as *fettuccine,* page 134, or stuffed pasta, such as Tortelli Stuffed with Parsley and Ricotta, page 210. It would also be very good with Potato Gnocchi, page 260.

Put the butter in a small skillet and turn on the heat to medium. When the butter foam subsides, and the butter's color is a tawny gold but not yet brown, add the sage leaves. Cook for a few seconds, turning the sage leaves over once, then pour the contents of the pan over cooked, drained pasta. Toss thoroughly, and serve immediately with grated Parmesan on the side.

Cream and Butter Sauce

THIS IS THE SAUCE that has become known to diners throughout the world as *all'Alfredo,* after the Roman restaurateur who popularized it. If a fat, fresh white truffle should come your way, one of the best uses for it is to shave it over pasta tossed with Alfredo's sauce. *For 4 to 6 servings*

1 cup heavy whipping cream
2 tablespoons choicest quality butter
1¼ pounds homemade *fettuccine,* page 134, OR *tortellini,* page 139, OR green *tortellini,* page 208
⅔ cup freshly grated *parmigiano-reggiano* cheese, plus

additional cheese at the table
Salt
Black pepper, ground fresh from the mill
Whole nutmeg

Recommended pasta ❀ No other sauce is a better vehicle for the virtues of homemade pasta, and in particular for *fettuccine.* It is also quite blissful with *tortellini.*

1. Choose any flameproof ware suitable for tossing and serving the pasta in later. Put in ⅔ cup of the heavy cream and all the butter, turn on the heat to medium, and cook for less than a minute, just until the cream and butter have thickened. Turn off the heat.

2. Cook the pasta, draining it while it is still very firm and even slightly underdone, a degree or so firmer than *al dente.* Freshly made *fettuccine* will take just seconds.

3. Transfer the drained pasta to the pan containing the butter and cream, turn on the heat to low, and toss the pasta thoroughly, bringing it up and around from the bottom, coating all the strands with the cream and butter sauce.

4. Add the remaining ⅓ cup of cream, the ⅔ cup of grated Parmesan, a pinch of salt, a few grindings of pepper, and a very tiny grating—less than ⅛

Cream and Butter Sauce (continued)

teaspoon—of nutmeg. Toss again briefly until the *fettuccine* are well coated. Taste and correct for salt and serve immediately from the pan, with additional grated Parmesan on the side.

Gorgonzola Sauce

THE ONLY COMPLICATION attendant on this sauce is finding the right *gorgonzola*. If you have a good, conscientious cheese dealer, ask to be notified when a fresh wheel of *gorgonzola* arrives from Italy. Once cut, the cheese does not improve, it becomes dry, crumbly, and yellowish. When it is at its peak, it is a warm white color, creamily soft and even runny.

Do not use *gorgonzola* straight out of the refrigerator, because the cold stunts its flavor and aroma. If you are going to use it the same day you've bought it, do not refrigerate it at all. If you have had it a day or two, take it out of the refrigerator at least 6 hours before using it.   *For 6 servings*

¼ pound *gorgonzola* (see prefatory remarks above), kept at room temperature for 6 hours
⅓ cup milk
3 tablespoons butter
Salt
½ cup heavy whipping cream
1¼ pounds pasta
⅓ cup freshly grated *parmi-giano-reggiano* cheese, plus additional cheese at the table

Recommended pasta ✳ Although it is excellent over such factory-made pasta shapes as *rigatoni* and *penne*, gorgonzola sauce is at its best with homemade pasta—*fettucine*, page 134, or *garganelli*, page 141, and with Potato Gnocchi, page 260.

1. Choose flameproof serving ware that can subsequently accommodate all the pasta. Put in the *gorgonzola*, milk, butter, and one or two pinches of salt, and turn on the heat to low. Stir with a wooden spoon, mashing the cheese with the back of the spoon and, as it begins to dissolve, incorporating it with the milk and butter. Cook for a minute or two until the sauce has a dense, creamy consistency. Take off the heat until the moment you are nearly ready to drain the pasta. Bear in mind that if you are using freshly made pasta, it will cook in just a few seconds and the sauce needs to be reheated for about 1 minute.

2. Shortly before the pasta is cooked, add the heavy cream to the sauce

and stir over medium-low heat until it is partly reduced. Add the cooked drained pasta (if you are doing *gnocchi,* add sauce to the *gnocchi* as each batch is retrieved from the pot and transferred to a warm platter; see page 262), and toss with the sauce. Add the ⅓ cup grated Parmesan and toss thoroughly to melt it. Serve immediately, directly from the pan, with additional grated cheese on the side.

Mushroom, Ham, and Cream Sauce

For 6 to 8 servings

¾ pound fresh mushrooms, either white button OR *cremini*

3 tablespoons butter

2 tablespoons shallot OR onion chopped fine

Salt

Black pepper, ground fresh from the mill

6 ounces boiled unsmoked ham, cut into very narrow julienne strips

6 tablespoons heavy whipping cream

The homemade *fettuccine* suggested below

FOR TOSSING THE PASTA

2 tablespoons butter

6 tablespoons heavy whipping cream

½ cup freshly grated *parmi-giano-reggiano* cheese, plus

additional cheese at the table

Recommended pasta ❀ The loveliest match here would be with *paglia e fieno,* "straw and hay," yellow and green *fettuccine.* For the amount of sauce above, follow the basic proportions given for yellow pasta dough and green pasta dough on page 130, to make approximately 10 ounces of the former and 1 pound of the latter. Of course, the sauce would taste equally good with either yellow or green pasta alone. In this case, double the quantity of either yellow or green *fettuccine.*

  1. Slice off and discard the ends of the mushroom stems. Wash the mushrooms very rapidly under running cold water, then pat them thoroughly dry with a soft towel. Dice into ¼-inch cubes and set aside.

  2. Choose a sauté pan or skillet that can subsequently accommodate the mushrooms without crowding. Put in the butter and chopped shallot or

Mushroom, Ham, and Cream Sauce (continued)

onion, turn on the heat to medium, and cook the shallot or onion until it has become colored a pale gold.

3. Turn up the heat to high and add the diced mushrooms. Stir thoroughly to coat well, and when the mushrooms have soaked up all the butter, turn the heat down to low, add salt and a few grindings of pepper, and turn the mushrooms over 2 or 3 times.

4. As soon as the mushrooms release their liquid, which should happen quickly, turn the heat up to high and boil the liquid away, stirring frequently.

5. Turn the heat down to medium, add the ham, and stir while it cooks for about a minute or less. Add the cream, and cook just long enough for the cream to become reduced and slightly thickened. Taste and correct for salt and pepper. Turn off the heat and set the sauce aside.

6. Choose an enameled cast-iron pan or other flameproof serving ware that can later contain all the pasta without piling it high. Put in the 2 tablespoons butter and 6 tablespoons cream for tossing the pasta, and turn on the heat to low. When the butter melts, stir to amalgamate it with the cream, then turn off the heat.

7. *If using both green and yellow fettuccine:* Spinach pasta cooks faster than yellow pasta, so the two must be boiled in separate pots of salted water. Drop the yellow *fettuccine* into their pot first, stir them with a wooden spoon, count to 3, then drop the spinach pasta into the other pot.

If using only one kind of pasta: Drop it into boiling salted water.

8. Turn the heat on to low under the mushroom sauce.

9. Drain the pasta when done to a very firm *al dente,* even slightly undercooked, consistency, bearing in mind that it will continue to soften during the final phase of preparation. Transfer to the serving pan containing butter and cream. Turn on the heat to low, and toss the noodles, turning them thoroughly to coat them well. Add half the mushroom sauce, tossing it with the noodles. Add the ½ cup grated Parmesan, toss again, and turn off the heat. Pour the remainder of the mushroom sauce over the pasta and serve at once, with additional grated Parmesan on the side.

Red and Yellow
Bell Pepper Sauce with Sausages

THERE WAS A RESTAURANT in Bologna, Al Cantunzein, that had a standing challenge for its patrons: It would continue to bring to the table different courses of homemade pasta until the customer called a stop. Its claim was that on any day it could serve between thirty and forty different pastas, but I don't know of anyone who succeeded in making the restaurant prove it. Al Cantunzein thrived until the late 1970s, when it was destroyed by student violence. It was rebuilt, but it was never the same again. It survives through its creations, some of which are now part of the classic homemade pasta repertory, such as *scrigno di venere*—page 227—and this perfect summer sauce for *pappardelle*.   *For 6 to 8 servings*

3 meaty bell peppers, 1 red, 2 yellow
4 tablespoons extra virgin olive oil
2 tablespoons chopped onion
4 sweet sausages without fennel seeds, chili pepper, or other strong seasonings, cut into ½-inch pieces, about 1½ cups

Salt
Black pepper, ground fresh from the mill
1 cup canned imported Italian plum tomatoes, drained and cut up
The fresh *pappardelle* suggested below OR 1½ pounds boxed dry pasta

FOR TOSSING THE PASTA

1 tablespoon butter
⅔ cup freshly grated *parmigiano-reggiano* cheese, plus

additional cheese at the table

Recommended pasta ❀ Yellow and green broad egg noodles, *pappardelle,* is what this sauce was created for and no other pasta combination seems quite so perfect. Make *pappardelle* as described on page 135, using a dough made from 2 large eggs and approximately 1 cup flour for the yellow noodles, and for the green noodles, 1 large egg, ¾ to 1 cup flour, and a tiny fistful of cooked spinach. See the instructions for pasta dough on pages 131–134. Cook the yellow and green pasta separately, as described on page 196.

Although it may not be quite so sublime a match, boxed, dry, factory

Bell Pepper Sauce with Sausages (continued)

pasta would be delicious with this sauce. Try such shapes as *rigatoni,* or *ruote di carro,* cartwheels.

1. Split the peppers into 4 sections, discard the seeds and cores, and peel them, using a swiveling-blade peeler. Cut them into more or less square 1-inch pieces.

2. Put the olive oil and the chopped onion in a sauté pan, and turn on the heat to medium high. Cook and stir the onion until it becomes colored a pale gold. Put in the sausages, cook them for about 2 minutes, then add the peppers, and cook them for 7 or 8 minutes, turning them occasionally. Add salt and pepper, and stir well.

3. Add the tomatoes to the pan and cook them at a lively simmer for about 15 or 20 minutes, until the oil floats free of the tomatoes.

Ahead-of-time note ❀ The sauce may be prepared up to this point a few hours before serving. Do not refrigerate it. Reheat gently just before tossing with pasta.

4. Empty the entire contents of the pan over cooked drained pasta and toss thoroughly. Add the butter and grated Parmesan, toss one more time, and serve at once, with additional grated cheese on the side.

Embogoné—Cranberry Beans, Sage, and Rosemary Sauce

IN THE ANCIENT stonecutters' town of San Giorgio, high in the hills of Valpolicella, north of Verona, the cooking skills of the Dalla Rosa family have been celebrated by townspeople and visitors for at least four generations. One of the dishes for which people now trek to their *trattoria* is pasta sauced with one of the fundamental elements of cooking in the Veneto, cranberry beans. Cranberry beans are essential to *pasta e fagioli* but no one, before some unidentified and forgotten Dalla Rosa, had put them to such delicious use with pasta.

According to Lodovico Dalla Rosa, the word *embogoné* comes from the dialect word for snails, *bogoni.* He surmised that the beans as they turn to sauce in the skillet, in their roundness and slow motion, must have reminded the originator of the dish of snails that had slipped out of their shells.

Note ❀ If you are not acquainted with cranberry beans, please see the explanation that accompanies Pasta and Bean Soup on page 102.   *For 4 servings*

3 pounds fresh cranberry beans,
unshelled weight, OR 1½
cups dried cranberry OR red
kidney beans, soaked and
cooked as described on
page 13
Extra virgin olive oil, 1 tablespoon for the sauce, 2
tablespoons for tossing the
pasta
¼ pound *pancetta* chopped very
fine to a pulp
⅓ cup onion chopped fine
1 teaspoon garlic chopped fine
Chopped sage leaves, 1 teaspoon if fresh, ½ teaspoon
if dried
Chopped rosemary, 1 teaspoon
if fresh, ½ teaspoon if dried
Salt
Black pepper, ground fresh
from the mill ·
The fresh *pappardelle* suggested
below OR 1 pound boxed
dry pasta
½ cup freshly grated *parmigiano-reggiano* cheese, plus
additional cheese at the
table

Recommended pasta ❀ *Pappardelle,* broad homemade egg noodles, is what the Trattoria Dalla Rosa serves this sauce on, and I don't see how one could improve on the taste of this large noodle wrapped around the substantial bean sauce. Make *pappardelle* as described on page 135, using a dough made from 3 large eggs and approximately 1⅔ cups unbleached flour.

A substantial shape of boxed, dry, factory pasta would also be a good choice. Try *rigatoni.*

1. If using fresh beans, put them in a pot with 2 inches of water to cover. Cover the pot, turn on the heat to low, and cook until tender, about 1 hour or less.

2. Put 1 tablespoon of olive oil, the chopped *pancetta,* and the onion in a sauté pan and turn on the heat to medium high. Cook, stirring occasionally, until the onion becomes translucent. Add the garlic, sage, and rosemary and cook another minute or so, then turn the heat down to minimum.

3. Drain the cooked fresh or dried beans, reserving their cooking liquid. Put the beans in the pan and mash most of them—about three-fourths the total amount—with the back of a wooden spoon. Add about ½ cup of the bean cooking liquid to the pan to make the sauce somewhat runnier. Add salt and several grindings of pepper, and stir thoroughly.

4. Drain the pasta the moment it's cooked and toss it immediately in a warm serving bowl with the contents of the pan; add the remaining 2 table-spoons of olive oil, sprinkle with freshly grated Parmesan, toss once more, and serve at once. If you should find the sauce too dense, thin it with a little more of the bean cooking liquid.

Asparagus Sauce with Ham and Cream

For 4 to 6 servings

1½ pounds fresh asparagus
Salt
1 to 1¼ pounds pasta
6 ounces boiled unsmoked ham
2 tablespoons butter

1 cup heavy whipping cream
⅔ cup freshly grated *parmigiano-reggiano* cheese, plus
additional cheese at the
table

Recommended pasta ❀ Small, tubular macaroni are the most compatible with this sauce. Use such boxed, dry pasta shapes as *penne, maccheroncini,* or *ziti,* or the homemade *garganelli,* described on page 141.

1. Cut off 1 inch or more from the butt ends of the asparagus to expose the moist part of each stalk. Pare the asparagus and wash it as described on page 466.

2. Choose a pan that can accommodate all the asparagus lying flat. Put in enough water to come 2 inches up the sides of the pan, and 1 tablespoon salt. Turn on the heat to medium high and when the water boils, slip in the asparagus, and cover the pan. Cook for 4 to 8 minutes after the water returns to a boil, depending on the freshness and thickness of the stalks. Drain the asparagus when it is tender, but firm. Wipe the pan dry with paper towels and set aside for later use.

3. When the asparagus is cool enough to handle, cut off the spear tips at their base, and cut the rest of the stalks into lengths of about ¾ inch. Discard any part of the stalk that is still woody and tough.

4. Cut the ham into long strips about ¼ inch wide. Put the ham and the butter into the pan where you cooked the asparagus, turn on the heat to medium low, and cook for 2 to 3 minutes without letting the ham become crisp.

5. Add the cut-up asparagus spear tips and stalks, turn up the heat to medium high, and cook for 1 to 2 minutes, turning all the asparagus pieces in the butter to coat them well.

6. Add the cream, turn the heat down to medium, and cook, stirring constantly, for about half a minute, until the cream thickens. Taste and correct for salt.

7. Turn out the entire contents of the pan over cooked and drained pasta, toss thoroughly, add the ⅔ cup grated Parmesan, toss again, and serve at once, with additional grated cheese on the side.

Sausages and Cream Sauce

For 4 servings

½ pound sweet sausage
    containing no fennel seed,
    chili pepper, or other strong
    seasonings
1½ tablespoons chopped onion
2 tablespoons butter
1 tablespoon vegetable oil

Black pepper, ground fresh
    from the mill
⅔ cup heavy whipping cream
Salt
1 pound pasta
Freshly grated *parmigiano-*
    reggiano cheese at the table

Recommended pasta ✸ In Bologna, where this sauce is popular, they use it on thin, curved, tubular macaroni called "crab grass," or *gramigna*. It is a perfect sauce for those shapes of pasta whose twists or cavities can trap little morsels of sausage and cream. *Conchiglie* and *fusilli* are the best examples.

1. Skin the sausage and crumble it as fine as possible.

2. Put the chopped onion, butter, and vegetable oil in a small saucepan, turn the heat on to medium, and cook until the onion becomes colored a pale gold. Add the crumbled sausage and cook for 10 minutes. Add a few grindings of pepper and all the cream, turn the heat up to medium high, and cook until the cream has thickened, stirring once or twice. Taste and correct for salt.

3. Toss the sauce with cooked drained pasta and serve at once with grated Parmesan on the side.

Prosciutto and Cream Sauce

For 4 servings

¼ pound sliced prosciutto OR
    country ham
3 tablespoons butter
½ cup heavy whipping cream
1 pound pasta

¼ cup freshly grated
    parmigiano-reggiano cheese,
    plus additional cheese at the
    table

Recommended pasta ✸ The sauce works equally well with homemade *fettuccine* or *tonnarelli*, page 134, or with green *tortellini*, page 241, and with short, tubular macaroni such as *penne* or *rigatoni*.

Prosciutto and Cream Sauce (continued)

1. Shred the prosciutto or ham into narrow strips. Put it into a saucepan with the butter, turn on the heat to medium, and cook it for about 2 minutes, turning it from time to time, until it is browned all over.

2. Add the heavy cream and cook, stirring frequently, until you have thickened and reduced it by at least one-third.

3. Toss the sauce with cooked drained pasta, add the ¼ cup grated Parmesan, toss again, and serve at once with additional grated cheese on the side.

Carbonara Sauce

AN ITALIAN food historian claims that during the last days of World War II, American soldiers in Rome who had made friends with local families would bring them eggs and bacon and ask them to turn them into a pasta sauce. The historian notwithstanding, how those classic American ingredients, bacon and eggs, came to be transformed into *carbonara* has not really been established, but there is no doubting the earthy flavor of the sauce: It is unmistakably Roman.

Most versions of *carbonara* use bacon smoked in the American style, but in Rome one can sometimes have the sauce without any bacon at all, but with salted pork jowl in its place. It is so much sweeter than bacon, whose smoky accents tend to weary the palate. Pork jowl is hard to get outside Italy, but in its place one can use *pancetta,* which supplies comparably rounded and mellow flavor. You can make the sauce either way, with bacon or *pancetta,* and you could try both methods to see which satisfies you more.

For 6 servings

½ pound *pancetta,* cut as a single ½-inch-thick slice, OR its equivalent in good slab bacon

4 garlic cloves

3 tablespoons extra virgin olive oil

¼ cup dry white wine

2 large eggs (see warning about salmonella poisoning, page 41)

¼ cup freshly grated *romano* cheese

½ cup freshly grated *parmigiano-reggiano* cheese

Black pepper, ground fresh from the mill

2 tablespoons chopped parsley

1¼ pounds pasta

Recommended pasta ❀ It is difficult to imagine serving *carbonara* on anything but *spaghetti.*

1. Cut the *pancetta* or slab bacon into strips not quite ¼ inch wide.

2. Lightly mash the garlic with a knife handle, enough to split it and loosen the skin, which you will discard. Put the garlic and olive oil into a small sauté pan and turn on the heat to medium high. Sauté until the garlic becomes colored a deep gold, and remove and discard it.

3. Put the strips of *pancetta* or bacon into the pan, and cook until they just begin to be crisp at the edges. Add the wine, let it bubble away for 1 or 2 minutes, then turn off the heat.

4. Break the 2 eggs into the serving bowl in which you'll be subsequently tossing the pasta. Beat them lightly with a fork, then add the two grated cheeses, a liberal grinding of pepper, and the chopped parsley. Mix thoroughly.

5. Add cooked drained *spaghetti* to the bowl, and toss rapidly, coating the strands well.

6. Briefly reheat the *pancetta* or bacon over high heat, turn out the entire contents of the pan into the bowl, toss thoroughly again, and serve at once.

Bolognese Meat Sauce

Ragù, as the Bolognese call their celebrated meat sauce, is characterized by mellow, gentle, comfortable flavor that any cook can achieve by being careful about a few basic points:

❀ The meat should not be from too lean a cut; the more marbled it is, the sweeter the *ragù* will be. The most desirable cut of beef is the neck portion of the chuck.

❀ Add salt immediately when sautéing the meat to extract its juices for the subsequent benefit of the sauce.

❀ Cook the meat in milk before adding wine and tomatoes to protect it from the acidic bite of the latter.

❀ Do not use a *demiglace* or other concentrates that tip the balance of flavors toward harshness.

❀ Use a pot that retains heat. Earthenware is preferred in Bologna and by most cooks in Emilia-Romagna, but enameled cast-iron pans or a pot whose heavy bottom is composed of layers of steel alloys are fully satisfactory.

Bolognese Meat Sauce (continued)

❦ Cook, uncovered, at the merest simmer for a long, long time; no less than 3 hours is necessary, more is better.

2 heaping cups, for about 6 servings and 1½ pounds pasta

1 tablespoon vegetable oil	1 cup whole milk
3 tablespoons butter plus 1	Whole nutmeg
tablespoon for tossing the	1 cup dry white wine
pasta	1½ cups canned imported
½ cup chopped onion	Italian plum tomatoes, cut
⅔ cup chopped celery	up, with their juice
⅔ cup chopped carrot	1¼ to 1½ pounds pasta
¾ pound ground beef chuck	Freshly grated *parmigiano-*
(see prefatory note above)	*reggiano* cheese at the table
Salt	
Black pepper, ground fresh	
from the mill	

Recommended pasta ❦ There is no more perfect union in all gastronomy than the marriage of Bolognese *ragù* with homemade Bolognese *tagliatelle*, page 136. Equally classic is Baked Green Lasagne with Meat Sauce, Bolognese Style, page 215. *Ragù* is delicious with *tortellini*, page 139, and irreproachable with such boxed, dry pasta as *rigatoni, conchiglie,* or *fusilli.* Curiously, considering the popularity of the dish in the United Kingdom and countries of the Commonwealth, meat sauce in Bologna is never served over *spaghetti.*

1. Put the oil, butter, and chopped onion in the pot, and turn the heat on to medium. Cook and stir the onion until it has become translucent, then add the chopped celery and carrot. Cook for about 2 minutes, stirring the vegetables to coat them well.

2. Add the ground beef, a large pinch of salt, and a few grindings of pepper. Crumble the meat with a fork, stir well, and cook until the beef has lost its raw, red color.

3. Add the milk and let it simmer gently, stirring frequently, until it has bubbled away completely. Add a tiny grating—about ⅛ teaspoon—of nutmeg, and stir.

4. Add the wine, let it simmer until it has evaporated, then add the tomatoes and stir thoroughly to coat all ingredients well. When the tomatoes begin to bubble, turn the heat down so that the sauce cooks at the laziest of simmers, with just an intermittent bubble breaking through to the surface. Cook,

uncovered, for 3 hours or more, stirring from time to time. While the sauce is cooking, you are likely to find that it begins to dry out and the fat separates from the meat. To keep it from sticking, continue the cooking, adding ½ cup of water whenever necessary. At the end, however, no water at all must be left and the fat must separate from the sauce. Taste and correct for salt.

5. Toss with cooked drained pasta, adding the tablespoon of butter, and serve with freshly grated Parmesan on the side.

Ahead-of-time note ❀ If you cannot watch the sauce for a 3- to 4-hour stretch, you can turn off the heat whenever you need to leave, and resume cooking later on, as long as you complete the sauce within the same day. Once done, you can refrigerate the sauce in a tightly sealed container for 3 days, or you can freeze it. Before tossing with pasta, reheat it, letting it simmer for 15 minutes and stirring it once or twice.

Variation of Ragù with Pork

Pork is an important part of Bologna's culture, its economy, and the cuisine, and many cooks add some pork to make their *ragù* tastier. Use 1 part ground pork, preferably from the neck or Boston butt, to 2 parts beef, and make the meat sauce exactly as described in the basic recipe above.

Chicken Liver Sauce

For 4 to 6 servings

½ pound fresh chicken livers
2 tablespoons chopped shallot
    OR onion
1 tablespoon vegetable oil
2 tablespoons butter
¼ teaspoon garlic chopped very
    fine
3 tablespoons diced *pancetta* OR
    prosciutto
4 to 5 whole sage leaves

¼ pound ground beef chuck
Salt
Black pepper, ground fresh
    from the mill
1 teaspoon tomato paste,
    dissolved in ¼ cup dry
    white vermouth
1¼ pounds homemade pasta
Freshly grated *parmigiano-*
    reggiano cheese at the table

Recommended pasta ❀ Here we have a magnificent sauce for *pappardelle*, the eye- and mouth-filling homemade broad noodles, instructions for which

Chicken Liver Sauce (continued)

appear on page 135. It can also be combined with the Molded Parmesan Risotto with Chicken Liver Sauce on page 257.

1. Remove any greenish spots and particles of fat from the chicken livers, rinse them in cold water, cut each liver into 3 or 4 pieces, and pat them thoroughly dry with paper towels.

2. Put the shallot or onion in a saucepan or small sauté pan together with the oil and butter; turn on the heat to medium. Cook and stir the shallot or onion until it becomes translucent. Add the chopped garlic and cook it briefly, not long enough to become colored, then add the diced *pancetta* or prosciutto, and the sage. Stir well, cooking for about a minute or less, then add the ground beef, a large pinch of salt, and a few grindings of pepper. Crumble the meat with a fork and cook it until it has lost its raw, red color.

3. Add the cut-up chicken livers, turn the heat up to medium high, stir thoroughly, and cook briefly, just until the livers have lost their raw, red color.

4. Add the tomato paste and vermouth mixture, and cook for 5 to 8 minutes, stirring from time to time. Taste and correct for salt.

5. Turn out the entire contents of the pan over cooked drained pasta, toss well, coating all the strands, and serve at once with grated Parmesan on the side.

Special Pasta Dishes

Tortellini
with Meat and Cheese Filling

About 200 tortellini

FOR THE STUFFING

¼ pound pork, preferably from the neck OR Boston butt
6 ounces boned, skinless chicken breast
2 tablespoons butter
Salt
Black pepper, ground fresh from the mill

3 tablespoons *mortadella* chopped very fine
1¼ cups fresh *ricotta*
1 egg yolk
1 cup freshly grated *parmigiano-reggiano* cheese
Whole nutmeg

FOR THE PASTA

Homemade yellow pasta dough, made as directed on page 129 for the machine method, OR page 143 for the hand-rolled method, using 4 large eggs, approximately 2 cups unbleached flour, and 1 tablespoon milk

Recommended sauce 🌸 The traditional way of serving *tortellini* is in broth, calculating about 2½ quarts homemade meat broth for cooking and serving 100 *tortellini*, approximately 6 portions. Not as traditional, but very good all the same is Cream and Butter Sauce, page 193, or Tomato Sauce with Heavy Cream, page 155, or Bolognese Meat Sauce, page 203. Calculate about 2 dozen *tortellini* per person when serving them with sauce. In all the above instances, serve with grated Parmesan.

1. Dice the pork and the boned, skinless chicken breast into ½-inch cubes.

2. Put the butter in a skillet and turn on the heat to medium. When the butter foam begins to subside, add the cubed pork, one or two pinches of salt, and a few grindings of pepper. Cook for 6 or 7 minutes, turning it to brown it evenly on all sides. Using a slotted spoon, remove it from the skillet and set aside to cool.

3. Add the chicken pieces to the skillet with a pinch of salt and a few grindings of pepper. Brown the chicken on all sides, cooking it about 2 minutes. Remove it from the skillet with a slotted spoon and set aside to cool with the pork.

4. When cool enough to handle, chop the pork and chicken together to a grainy, slightly coarse consistency. It is all right to use the food processor, but do not reduce the meat to a pulp.

5. Put the chopped meat in a bowl and add the *mortadella, ricotta,* egg yolk, grated Parmesan, and a tiny grating—about ⅛ teaspoon—of nutmeg. Mix thoroughly until all ingredients are evenly amalgamated. Taste and correct for salt.

6. Make yellow pasta dough as directed on page 130 for the machine method, or page 144 for the hand-rolled method. Cut it into *tortellini,* following the instructions on page 139, and stuff them with the above mixture. When boiling the pasta, add 1 tablespoon olive oil to the water.

Green Tortellini
with Meat and Ricotta Stuffing

About 130 tortellini, *5 to 6 servings*

FOR THE STUFFING

¼ pound pork, preferably from
  the neck OR Boston butt
¼ pound veal shoulder
1 tablespoon butter
Salt
Black pepper, ground fresh
  from the mill

1 tablespoon *mortadella*
  chopped very fine
½ cup fresh *ricotta*
⅓ cup freshly grated
  parmigiano-reggiano cheese
1 egg yolk
Whole nutmeg

FOR THE PASTA

Homemade green pasta dough,
  made as directed on page
  129 for the machine
  method, OR page 143 for
  the hand-rolled method,
  using 2 large eggs, ⅓

package frozen leaf spinach
  OR 6 ounces fresh spinach,
  salt, approximately 1½ cups
  unbleached flour, and 1
  tablespoon milk

Recommended sauce ◉ Prosciutto and Cream Sauce, page 29; Cream and
Butter Sauce, page 193; Tomato Sauce with Heavy Cream, page 155. Always
serve with grated Parmesan.

1. Cut the pork and veal into thin slices, then into 1-inch pieces more or
less square. Keep the two meats separate.

2. Put the butter and pork in a small skillet, and turn on the heat to medium low. Cook for 5 minutes, browning the meat on both sides and turning
it frequently.

3. Add the veal, and cook it for 1½ minutes or less, browning it on both
sides. Add salt, a few grindings of pepper, stir thoroughly to coat well, then
remove all the meat from the pan, using a slotted spoon so that all the fat remains behind.

4. When cool enough to handle, chop the pork and veal together to a
grainy, slightly coarse consistency. It is all right to use the food processor, but
do not reduce the meat to a pulp.

5. Put the chopped meat in a bowl, and add the *mortadella, ricotta,*
grated cheese, egg yolk, and a tiny grating—about ⅛ teaspoon—of nutmeg.

Mix thoroughly until all ingredients are evenly amalgamated. Taste and correct for salt and pepper.

6. Make green pasta dough as directed on page 130 for the machine method, or page 144 for the hand-rolled method. Cut it, stuff it with the above mixture, and shape it into *tortellini,* following the instructions on page 139. When boiling the pasta, add 1 tablespoon olive oil to the water.

Tortellini with Fish Stuffing

About 140 tortellini, *6 servings*

FOR THE STUFFING

1 small onion
1 medium carrot
1 small celery stalk
A 1-pound piece of fish, in a
    single slice if possible,
    preferably sea bass, OR other
    fish with comparable
    delicate flavor and juicy
    flesh
2 tablespoons wine vinegar
Salt

2 egg yolks
3 tablespoons freshly grated
    parmigiano-reggiano cheese
⅛ teaspoon dried marjoram OR
    a few fresh leaves
Whole nutmeg
Black pepper, ground fresh
    from the mill
2 tablespoons heavy whipping
    cream

FOR THE PASTA

Homemade yellow pasta dough,
    made as directed on page
    129 for the machine
    method, OR page 143 for
    the hand-rolled method,

using 3 large eggs, approximately 1⅔ cups unbleached
flour, and 1 tablespoon
milk

Recommended sauce ❀ Pink Shrimp Sauce with Cream, page 191, or Tomato Sauce with Heavy Cream, page 155. You can serve it with or without grated cheese.

1. Peel the onion and carrot, and rinse the carrot and celery under cold water.

2. Put enough water in a pan to cover the fish at a later point. Add the onion, carrot, and celery, and bring to a boil.

Tortellini with Fish Stuffing (continued)

3. Add the fish, vinegar, and salt, and cover the pan. When the water returns to a boil, adjust the heat so that the fish cooks at a gentle, steady simmer. Cook about 8 minutes, depending on the thickness of the fish.

4. Using a slotted spoon or spatula, transfer the fish to a platter. Remove the skin, any gelatinous matter, the center bone, and carefully pick out all the small bones you may find. Do not be concerned about keeping the piece of fish whole, because you will shortly have to break it up for the stuffing.

5. Put the fish in a bowl and mash it with a fork. Add the egg yolks, grated Parmesan, marjoram, a tiny grating—about ⅛ teaspoon—of nutmeg, just a few grindings of pepper, and the heavy cream. Mix all ingredients with a fork until they are evenly amalgamated. Taste and correct for salt.

6. Make yellow pasta dough as directed on page 130 for the machine method, or page 144 for the hand-rolled method. Cut it, stuff it with the fish mixture, and shape it into *tortellini,* following the instructions on page 139. When boiling the pasta, add 1 tablespoon olive oil to the water.

Tortelli Stuffed with Parsley and Ricotta

About 140 tortelli, *6 servings*

FOR THE STUFFING

½ cup chopped parsley
1½ cups fresh *ricotta*
1 cup freshly grated
   parmigiano-reggiano cheese

Salt
1 egg yolk
Whole nutmeg

FOR THE PASTA

Homemade yellow pasta dough, made as directed on page 129 for the machine method, OR page 143 for the hand-rolled method, using 3 large eggs, 1⅔ cups unbleached flour, and 1 tablespoon milk

Recommended sauce ● First choice goes to the Cream and Butter Sauce on page 193, second to Tomato Sauce with Heavy Cream, page 155. Serve with grated Parmesan.

1. Put the parsley, *ricotta,* grated Parmesan, salt, egg yolk, and a tiny grat-

ing—about ¼ teaspoon—of nutmeg into a bowl and mix with a fork until all ingredients are evenly combined. Taste and correct for salt.

2. Make yellow pasta dough as directed on page 130 for the machine method, or page 144 for the hand-rolled method. Cut it for square *tortelli* with 2-inch sides, following the instructions on page 140, and stuff with the *ricotta* and parsley mixture. When boiling the pasta, add 1 tablespoon of olive oil to the water.

Tortelloni Stuffed with Swiss Chard, Prosciutto, and Ricotta

About 140 tortelloni, *6 servings*

FOR THE STUFFING

2 pounds Swiss chard, if the stalks are very thin, OR 2½ pounds, if the stalks are broad, OR 2 pounds fresh spinach
Salt
2½ tablespoons onion chopped very fine
3½ tablespoons chopped

prosciutto OR *pancetta* OR unsmoked boiled ham
3 tablespoons butter
1 cup fresh *ricotta*
1 egg yolk
⅔ cup freshly grated *parmigiano-reggiano* cheese
Whole nutmeg

FOR THE PASTA

Homemade yellow pasta dough, made as directed on page 129 for the machine method, OR page 143 for the hand-rolled method,

using 3 large eggs, approximately 1⅔ cups unbleached flour, and 1 tablespoon milk

Recommended sauce ✾ Butter and Sage Sauce, page 192, Butter and Parmesan Cheese Sauce, page 191, or Tomato Sauce with Heavy Cream, page 155. Serve with grated Parmesan.

1. Pull the Swiss chard leaves from the stalks, or the spinach from its stems, and discard any bruised, wilted, or discolored leaves. If you have a mature chard with large, white stalks, save the stalks and use them in Swiss Chard Stalks Gratinéed with Parmesan Cheese, page 489. Soak the leaves in

Tortelloni Stuffed with Swiss Chard (continued)

a basin of cold water, lifting out the chard and changing the water several times, until there is no trace of soil at the bottom of the basin.

2. Gently scoop up the leaves without shaking them and put them in a pot with just the water that clings to them. Add large pinches of salt to keep the vegetable green, cover the pot, turn on the heat to medium, and cook until tender, about 12 minutes or so, depending on the freshness of the chard or spinach. Drain, and as soon as it is cool enough to handle, squeeze it gently to drive out as much moisture as possible, and chop it very fine.

3. In a small sauté pan put the onion, prosciutto, and butter and turn on the heat to medium. Cook, stirring, until the onion becomes translucent, then add the chopped chard or spinach. Cook for 2 to 3 minutes, until all the butter has been absorbed.

4. Turn out all the contents of the pan into a bowl. Add the *ricotta,* egg yolk, grated Parmesan, and a tiny grating—about ⅛ teaspoon—of nutmeg, and mix with a fork until all ingredients have been evenly combined. Taste and correct for salt.

5. Make yellow pasta dough as directed on page 130 for the machine method, or page 144 for the hand-rolled method. Cut it for square *tortelloni* with 2-inch sides, following the instructions on page 140, and stuff them with the vegetable mixture. When boiling the pasta, add 1 tablespoon of olive oil to the water.

Cappellacci—Ravioli Filled with Sweet Potatoes

WHEN YOU SAY *cappellacci* in Italy, it is understood you are talking about a square pasta dumpling with a furtively sweet pumpkin-based filling. It is a specialty of the northeastern section of Emilia-Romagna, in particular of the city of Ferrara.

The pumpkin used there, known as *zucca barucca,* is sweet and juicy with a satiny flesh. It has no equivalent among other squashes. When I first set down the recipe in *The Classic Italian Cook Book,* I found that I could most closely recreate the filling in North America not with any of the local pumpkin varieties, none of which is comparable in flavor and texture to *zucca barucca,* but by using sweet potato instead.

You must choose the right kind of sweet potato: Not the one with the pale, grayish yellow skin, but the dark-skinned one with a reddish-orange flesh, sometimes mistakenly called a yam. When cooked, it is lusciously sweet and moist, quite as good for *cappellacci* as the best *zucca barucca.*

About 140 cappellacci, *6 servings*

FOR THE FILLING

1¾ pounds orange-fleshed sweet potatoes, see prefatory remarks above

A pair of imported Italian *amaretti* cookies

1 egg yolk

3 tablespoons chopped prosciutto

1½ cups freshly grated *parmigiano-reggiano* cheese

3 tablespoons parsley chopped very fine

Whole nutmeg

Salt

FOR THE PASTA

Homemade yellow pasta dough, made as directed on page 129 for the machine method, OR page 143 for the hand-rolled method, using 3 large eggs, approximately 1⅔ cups unbleached flour, and 1 tablespoon milk

Recommended sauce ❊ Butter and Parmesan Cheese Sauce, page 191, or Cream and Butter Sauce, page 193. Serve with grated Parmesan.

1. Preheat oven to 450°.

2. Bake the potatoes in the middle level of the hot oven. After 20 minutes turn the thermostat down to 400° and cook for another 35 to 40 minutes, until the potatoes are very tender when prodded with a fork.

3. Turn off the oven. Remove the potatoes and split them in half lengthwise. Return the potatoes to the oven, cut side facing up, leaving the oven door slightly ajar. Remove after 10 minutes, when they will have dried out some.

4. Reduce the *amaretti* cookies to a powder using the food processor or a pestle and mortar.

5. Peel the potatoes and purée them through a food mill into a bowl. Add the powdered cookies, egg yolk, prosciutto, grated Parmesan, parsley, a tiny grating—about ⅛ teaspoon—of nutmeg, and salt. Mix with a fork until all ingredients are evenly combined.

6. Make yellow pasta dough as directed on page 130 for the machine method, or page 144 for the hand-rolled method. Cut it for square *ravioli* with 2-inch sides, following the instructions on page 140, and stuff them with the sweet potato mixture. When boiling the pasta, add 1 tablespoon of olive oil to the water.

Baked Rigatoni
with Bolognese Meat Sauce

For 6 servings

1½ pounds *rigatoni*

Salt

The Bolognese Meat Sauce,
    made with the recipe on
    page 203

A medium-thick Béchamel
    Sauce, prepared as directed
    on page 39, using 2 cups
    milk, 4 tablespoons

(½ stick) butter, 3 table-
    spoons flour, and
¼ teaspoon salt

6 tablespoons freshly grated
    parmigiano-reggiano cheese

An oven-to-table ceramic
    baking dish

Butter for smearing and dotting
    the dish

1. Preheat oven to 400°.

2. Cook the *rigatoni* in abundant, boiling salted water. Drain when exceptionally firm, a shade less cooked than *al dente* because it will undergo additional cooking in the oven. Transfer to a mixing bowl.

3. Add the meat sauce, béchamel, and 4 tablespoons grated Parmesan to the pasta. Toss thoroughly to coat the pasta well and distribute the sauces uniformly.

4. Lightly smear the baking dish with butter. Put in the entire contents of the bowl, leveling it with a spatula. Top with 2 tablespoons grated Parmesan and dot with butter. Put the dish on the uppermost rack of the preheated oven and bake for 10 minutes, until a little bit of a crust forms on top. After taking it out of the oven, allow the *rigatoni* to settle for a few minutes before bringing to the table.

LASAGNE

Properly made *lasagne* consists of several layers of delicate, nearly weightless pasta spaced by layers of savory, but not overbearing filling made of meat or artichokes or mushrooms or other fine mixtures. The only pasta suitable for *lasagne* is paper-thin dough freshly made at home. If you have not mastered rolling out pasta by hand, the machine method described on page 129 does a fully satisfactory job with nearly no effort.

It might take a little more time to run pasta dough through a machine than to go to the market and buy a box of the ready-made kind, but there is nothing packed in a box that can lead to the flavor of the *lasagne* you can produce in your kitchen. Using clunky, store-bought *lasagne* may save a little time, but you will be sadly shortchanged by the results.

Baked Green Lasagne
with Meat Sauce, Bolognese Style

For 6 servings

The full amount of Bolognese
Meat Sauce from the recipe
on page 203
Béchamel Sauce, prepared as
directed on page 39, using
3 cups milk, 6 tablespoons
butter, 4½ tablespoons
flour, and ¼ teaspoon salt
Homemade green pasta dough,
made as directed on page
129 for the machine
method, OR page 143 for
the hand-rolled method,

using 2 large eggs, ⅓
package frozen leaf spinach
OR 6 ounces fresh spinach,
salt, and approximately 1½
cups unbleached flour
1 tablespoon salt
2 tablespoons butter plus more
for greasing a 9- by 12-inch
bake-and-serve *lasagne* pan,
no less than 2½ inches high
⅔ cup freshly grated
parmigiano-reggiano cheese

1. Prepare the meat sauce and set aside or, if using sauce you've previously frozen, thaw about 2½ cups, reheat gently and set aside.

2. Prepare the béchamel, keeping it rather runny, somewhat like sour cream. When done, keep it warm in the upper half of a double boiler, with the heat turned to very low. If a film should form on top, just stir it when you are ready to use it.

3. Make green pasta dough either by the machine method, page 130, or by the hand-rolled method, page 144. Roll it out as thin as it will come by either method. If making the dough by machine, leave the strips as wide as they come from the rollers, and cut them into 10-inch lengths. If making it by hand, cut the pasta into rectangles 4½ inches wide and 10 inches long.

4. Set a bowl of cold water near the range, and lay some clean, dry cloth towels flat on a work counter. Bring 4 quarts of water to a rapid boil, add 1 tablespoon salt, and as the water returns to a boil, slip in 4 or 5 of the cut pasta strips. Cook very briefly, just seconds after the water returns to a boil after you dropped in the pasta. Retrieve the strips with a colander scoop or slotted spatula, and plunge them into the bowl of cold water. Pick up the strips, one at a

Baked Green Lasagne (continued)

time, rinse them under cold running water, and rub them delicately, as though you were doing fine hand laundry. Squeeze each strip very gently in your hands, then spread it flat on the towel to dry. When all the pasta is cooked in this manner, 4 or 5 strips at a time, and spread out to dry, pat it dry on top with another towel.

Explanatory note ❀ The washing, wringing, and drying of pasta for *lasagne* is something of a nuisance, but it is necessary. You first dip the partly cooked pasta into cold water to stop the cooking instantly. This is important because if *lasagne* pasta is not kept very firm at this stage it will become horribly mushy later when it is baked. And you must afterward rinse off the moist starch on its surface, or the dough will become glued to the towel on which it is laid out to dry, and tear when you are ready to use it.

5. Preheat the oven to 400°.

6. Thickly smear the bottom of a *lasagne* pan with butter and about 1 tablespoon of béchamel. Line the bottom of the pan with a single layer of pasta strips, cutting them to fit the pan, edge to edge, allowing no more than ¼ inch for overlapping.

7. Combine the meat sauce and the béchamel and spread a thin coating of it on the pasta. Sprinkle on some grated Parmesan, then add another layer of pasta, cutting it to fit as you did before. Repeat the procedure of spreading the sauce and béchamel mixture, then sprinkling with Parmesan. Use the trimmings of pasta dough to fill in gaps, if necessary. Build up to at least 6 layers of pasta. Leave yourself enough sauce to spread very thinly over the top-most layer. Sprinkle with Parmesan and dot with butter.

Ahead-of-time note ❀ The *lasagne* may be completed up to 2 days in advance up to this point. Refrigerate under tightly sealing plastic wrap.

8. Bake on the uppermost rack of the preheated oven until a light, golden crust forms on top. It should take between 10 and 15 minutes. If after the first few minutes you don't see any sign of a crust beginning to form, turn up the oven another 50° to 75°. Do not bake longer than 15 minutes altogether.

9. Remove from the oven and allow to settle for about 10 minutes, then serve at table directly from the pan.

Lasagne with Mushrooms and Ham

For 6 servings

1½ pounds fresh, firm, white
    button mushrooms
3 tablespoons vegetable oil
3 tablespoons butter plus more
    butter for greasing and
    dotting a 9- by 12-inch
    bake-and-serve *lasagne* pan,
    no less than 2½ inches high
⅓ cup onion chopped very fine
Two small packets OR 2 ounces
    dried *porcini* mushrooms,
    reconstituted as described
    on page 27
The filtered water from the
    mushroom soak, see page
    28 for instructions
⅓ cup canned imported Italian
    plum tomatoes, drained
    and chopped
2 tablespoons chopped parsley
Salt
Black pepper, ground fresh
    from the mill

Homemade yellow pasta dough,
    made as directed on page
    129 for the machine
    method, OR page 143 for
    the hand-rolled method,
    using 3 large eggs and
    approximately 1⅔ cups
    unbleached flour
¾ pound unsmoked boiled
    ham
Béchamel Sauce, prepared as
    directed on page 39, using
    2 cups milk, 4 tablespoons
    butter, 3 tablespoons flour,
    and ¼ teaspoon salt
⅔ cup freshly grated
    parmigiano-reggiano cheese,
    plus additional cheese at the
    table

1. Rinse the fresh mushrooms rapidly under cold running water. Drain and wipe thoroughly dry with a soft cloth or paper towels. Cut them very thin in lengthwise slices, leaving the stems attached to the caps.

2. Choose a sauté pan that can subsequently accommodate all the fresh mushrooms without crowding. Put in the oil, the 3 tablespoons of butter, and the chopped onion, and turn the heat on to medium.

3. Cook, stirring, until the onion becomes translucent. Put in the reconstituted dried *porcini,* the filtered water from their soak, the chopped tomatoes, and the parsley. Stir thoroughly to coat all ingredients, set the cover on the pan slightly ajar, and turn the heat down to medium low.

4. When the liquid in the pan has completely evaporated, put in the sliced fresh mushrooms, salt, and a few grindings of pepper, and turn the heat

Lasagne with Mushrooms and Ham (continued)

up to high. Cook, uncovered, for 7 to 8 minutes until all the liquid thrown off by the fresh mushrooms has evaporated. Taste and correct for salt and pepper, stir, turn off the heat, and set aside.

5. Make yellow pasta dough either by the machine method, page 130, or by the hand-rolled method, page 144. Following the instructions in the recipe for green *lasagne* on pages 215–216, cut the dough into *lasagne* strips, parboil them, and spread them out to dry on cloth towels.

6. Preheat oven to 400°.

7. Cut the ham into very thin, julienne strips.

8. Make the béchamel sauce. When done, keep it warm in the upper half of a double boiler, with the heat turned to very low. If a film should form on top, just stir it when you are ready to use it.

9. Thickly smear the bottom of the *lasagne* pan with butter and a little bit of béchamel. Line the bottom with a single layer of pasta strips, cutting them to fit the pan, edge to edge, allowing no more than ¼ inch for overlapping.

10. Combine the mushrooms with all but 2 or 3 tablespoons of béchamel, then spread a thinly distributed layer of the mixture over the pasta. Scatter a few strips of ham over the sauce, then sprinkle with a little grated Parmesan. Cover with another pasta layer, cutting it to fit as you did before; use the trimmings of pasta dough to fill in gaps, if necessary. Repeat the sequence of mushroom and béchamel mixture, ham, and grated cheese. Continue building up layers of pasta and filling up to a minimum of 6 layers of pasta. Over the topmost layer spread only the remaining béchamel, sprinkle on the rest of the Parmesan, and dot with about 2 tablespoons of butter.

Ahead-of-time note ✿ The *lasagne* may be completed up to 2 days in advance up to this point. Refrigerate under tightly sealing plastic wrap.

11. Bake on the uppermost rack of the preheated oven until a light, golden crust forms on top. It should take between 10 and 15 minutes. If after the first few minutes you don't see any sign of a crust beginning to form, turn up the thermostat another 50° to 75°. Do not bake longer than 15 minutes altogether.

12. Remove from the oven and allow to settle for about 10 minutes, then serve at table directly from the pan, with grated Parmesan on the side.

Lasagne with Artichokes

For 6 servings

4 to 5 medium artichokes
½ lemon
Salt
3 tablespoons butter plus more
   butter for greasing and
   dotting a 9- by 12-inch
   bake-and-serve *lasagne* pan,
   no less than 2½ inches high
Béchamel Sauce, prepared as
   directed on page 39, using
   2 cups milk, 4 tablespoons
   (½ stick) butter, 3 table-

spoons flour, and ¼ tea-
   spoon salt
Homemade yellow pasta dough,
   made as directed on page
   129 for the machine
   method, OR page 143 for
   the hand-rolled method,
   using 3 large eggs and
   approximately 1⅔ cups
   unbleached flour
⅔ cup freshly grated
   parmigiano-reggiano cheese

1. Trim the artichokes of all their tough parts following the detailed in-structions on pages 57–59. As you work, rub the cut artichokes with the lemon to keep them from turning black.

2. Cut each trimmed artichoke lengthwise into 4 equal sections. Remove the soft, curling leaves with prickly tips at the base, and cut away the fuzzy "choke" beneath them. Cut the artichoke sections lengthwise into the thinnest possible slices, and put them in a bowl with water mixed with the juice of the half lemon.

Ahead-of-time note ❀ You can prepare the artichokes up to this point sev-eral hours in advance.

3. Drain the artichokes and rinse thoroughly in fresh water, then put them into a sauté pan with salt, the 3 tablespoons of butter and enough water to cover, and turn on the heat to medium. Cook at a gentle, but steady sim-mer until all the water has bubbled away and the artichokes have become lightly browned. Prod the artichokes with a fork. If not fully tender, add a little water and continue cooking a while longer, letting all the water evapo-rate. When the artichokes are done, turn the entire contents of the pan out into a bowl, and set aside.

4. Make the béchamel, keeping it at medium density, like thick cream. Set aside 4 or 5 tablespoons of it, and combine the rest with the artichokes in the bowl.

5. Make yellow pasta dough either by the machine method, page 130,

Lasagne with Artichokes (continued)

or by the hand-rolled method, page 144. Following the instructions in the recipe for green *lasagne* on pages 215–216, cut the dough into *lasagne* strips, parboil them, and spread them out to dry on cloth towels.

6. Preheat oven to 400°.

7. Thickly smear the bottom of the *lasagne* pan with butter and a little bit of béchamel. Line the bottom with a single layer of pasta strips, cutting them to fit the pan, edge to edge, allowing no more than ¼ inch for overlapping.

8. Over the pasta spread a thin, even coating of the artichoke and béchamel mixture, and top with a sprinkling of grated Parmesan. Cover with another pasta layer, cutting it to fit as you did before; use the trimmings of pasta dough to fill in gaps, if necessary. Continue to alternate layers of pasta with coatings of béchamel and artichoke, always sprinkling with cheese before covering with a new layer of dough. Do not build up fewer than 6 layers of pasta.

9. Over the top layer spread the 4 or 5 tablespoons of béchamel you had set aside. Dot with butter, and sprinkle with the remaining grated Parmesan.

Ahead-of-time note ❧ The *lasagne* may be completed up to a day in advance up to this point. Refrigerate under tightly sealing plastic wrap.

10. Bake on the uppermost rack of the preheated oven until a light, golden crust forms on top. It should take between 10 and 15 minutes. If after the first few minutes you don't see any sign of a crust beginning to form, turn up the thermostat another 50° to 75°. Do not bake longer than 15 minutes altogether.

11. Remove from the oven and allow to settle for about 10 minutes, then serve at table directly from the pan, with grated Parmesan on the side.

Lasagne with Ricotta Pesto

ON THE Italian Riviera they make a flat pasta that is much broader than the broadest noodles, but a little smaller than the classic *lasagne* of Bologna. Unlike Bolognese *lasagne,* it is only boiled, rather than blanched and baked. In the Genoese dialect it is called *piccagge,* which means napkin or dish cloth. *Piccagge* is almost invariably served with *ricotta pesto,* making it one of the lightest and freshest pasta dishes for summer.   *For 6 servings*

Homemade yellow pasta dough, made as directed on page 129 for the machine method, OR page 143 for the hand-rolled method, using 3 large eggs and approximately 1⅔ cups unbleached flour

The Pesto with Ricotta, produced with the recipe on page 178
2 tablespoons salt
1 tablespoon extra virgin olive oil
Freshly grated *parmigiano-reggiano* cheese at the table

1. Make yellow pasta dough either by the machine method, page 130, or by the hand-rolled method, page 144. Cut the dough into rectangular strips about 3½ inches wide and 5 inches long. Spread them out on a counter lined with clean, dry, cloth towels.

2. Make the *ricotta pesto,* following the directions on page 178.

3. Bring 4 to 5 quarts water to a boil. Add 2 tablespoons salt and 1 tablespoon olive oil. As the water returns to a boil, put in half the pasta. (It's not advisable to put it all in at one time, because the broad strips may stick to each other.)

4. As soon as the first batch of pasta is done *al dente,* retrieve it with a colander spoon or skimmer, and spread it out on a warm serving platter. Take a spoonful of hot water from the pasta pot and use it to thin out the *pesto.* Spread half the *pesto* over the pasta in the platter.

5. Drop the remaining pasta into the pot, drain it when done, spread it on the platter over the previous layer of pasta, cover with the remaining *pesto,* and serve at once with grated Parmesan on the side.

Note 🌸 If the pasta is very fresh, you can cook it in two batches as suggested above, because it will cook so quickly that the first batch will not have had time to get cold by the time the second batch is done. If it is on the dry side, it will take longer to cook, so you must do the two batches simultaneously in two separate pots.

Cannelloni with Meat Stuffing

THOSE SOFT, rolled up bundles of pasta, meat, and cheese called *cannelloni* are one of the most graceful and pleasing ways to use homemade pasta dough. It's not the least bit difficult to do, and the result can be invariably successful if one bears in mind a single basic principle. Do not think of *cannelloni* as a tube enclosing a single sausage-like lump of stuffing. Before rolling up the pasta, the stuffing mixture should be spread over it in a filmy, adherent layer not much thicker than the pasta itself. Then the dough is rolled up jelly-roll fashion with the filling evenly distributed throughout.   *For 6 servings*

Béchamel Sauce, prepared as
    directed on page 39,
    using 2 cups milk,

4 tablespoons (½ stick)
    butter, 3 tablespoons flour,
    and ¼ teaspoon salt

FOR THE FILLING

1 tablespoon butter
1½ tablespoons onion chopped
    fine
6 ounces ground beef chuck
Salt
½ cup chopped unsmoked
    boiled ham

1 egg yolk
Whole nutmeg
1½ cups freshly grated
    parmigiano-reggiano cheese
1¼ cups fresh *ricotta*

FOR THE SAUCE

2 tablespoons butter
1 tablespoon onion chopped
    fine
6 ounces ground beef chuck

Salt
½ cup canned imported Italian
    plum tomatoes, chopped,
    with their juice

FOR THE PASTA

Homemade yellow pasta dough,
    made as directed on page
    129 for the machine
    method, OR page 143 for
    the hand-rolled method,
    using 3 large eggs and

approximately 1⅔ cups
    unbleached flour

Salt

A rectangular, 9- by 13-inch
    bake-and-serve dish

⅓ cup freshly grated
    parmigiano-reggiano cheese

3 tablespoons butter, plus more
    for smearing

1. Prepare the béchamel sauce, making it rather thin, the consistency of sour cream. When done, keep it warm in the upper half of a double boiler, with the heat turned to very low. Stir it just before using.

2. *To make the filling:* Put the tablespoon of butter and chopped onion in a small sauté pan, turn on the heat to medium, and cook the onion until it becomes translucent. Add the ground beef. Turn the heat down to medium low, crumble the meat with a fork, and cook it without letting it brown. After it loses its raw, red color, cook for 1 more minute, stirring two or three times.

3. Transfer the meat to a mixing bowl, using a slotted spoon so as to leave all the melted fat in the pan. Add one or two pinches of salt, the chopped ham, the egg yolk, a tiny grating—about ⅛ teaspoon—of nutmeg, the grated Parmesan, the *ricotta,* and ¼ cup of the béchamel sauce. Mix with a fork until all ingredients are evenly combined. Taste and correct for salt.

4. *To make the sauce:* Put the 2 tablespoons butter and the chopped onion in a saucepan, turn on the heat to medium, and cook the onion until it becomes colored a pale gold. Add the meat, crumbling it with a fork. Turn the heat down to medium low, cook the meat until it loses its raw color, add salt, and the chopped tomatoes with their juice, and adjust the heat so that the sauce cooks at the slowest of simmers. Cook for 45 minutes, stirring from time to time. Taste and correct for salt.

5. *To make the pasta:* Prepare the yellow pasta dough by machine, page 130, or by hand, page 144, rolling it out as thin as it will come by either method. Cut the pasta into rectangles 3 inches by 4 inches.

6. Bring water to a boil. On a nearby work counter, spread clean, dry, cloth towels. Set a bowl of cold water not too far from the stove. Following the instructions in the recipe for green *lasagne,* pages 215–216, parboil, rinse, and spread the pasta strips on the cloth towels.

7. Preheat the oven to 400°.

8. Thickly butter the bottom of the baking dish.

9. *To make the cannelloni:* Spread 1 tablespoon of béchamel sauce on a dinner plate. Place one of the pasta strips over the béchamel, rotating it to coat all its underside. On the pasta's top side, spread about a tablespoon of filling, enough to cover thinly, but leaving an exposed ½-inch border all around. Roll up the pasta softly, jelly-roll fashion, starting from its narrower

Cannelloni with Meat Stuffing (continued)

side. Place the roll in the pan, its overlapping edge facing down. Proceed until you have used up all the pasta or all the filling. From time to time spread more béchamel on the bottom of the dinner plate, but keep some in reserve. It's all right to fit the *cannelloni* tightly into the baking dish, but do not overlap them.

10. Spread the meat sauce over the *cannelloni,* coating them uniformly. Spread the remaining béchamel over the sauce, sprinkle with the grated Parmesan, and dot with butter.

Ahead-of-time note ✸ The *cannelloni* may be completed up to two days in advance up to this point. Refrigerate under tightly sealing plastic wrap.

11. Bake on the topmost rack of the preheated oven until a light, golden crust forms on top. It should take between 10 and 15 minutes, but do not bake longer than 15 minutes. After removing from the oven, allow the *cannelloni* to settle for at least 10 minutes, then serve at table directly from the baking dish.

Sliced Pasta Roll
with Spinach and Ham Filling

IN ITALY we call it a *rotolo;* it starts out as a large jelly roll of pasta wrapped around a delicious spinach and ham filling, wrapped in cheesecloth and boiled, then when cold, sliced, sauced, and briefly browned in a hot oven. It's a marvelous dish for a buffet table, quite as captivating in flavor as it is in appearance.   *For 6 servings*

Tomato Sauce with Onion and
    Butter, ½ the quantity

produced with the recipe
on page 152

FOR THE FILLING

2 pounds fresh spinach OR 2
    ten-ounce packages frozen
    leaf spinach, thawed
Salt
2 tablespoons onion chopped
    very fine
3 tablespoons butter

3 tablespoons prosciutto
    chopped fine
1 heaping cup fresh *ricotta*
1 cup freshly grated
    parmigiano-reggiano cheese
Whole nutmeg
1 egg yolk

FOR THE PASTA

Homemade yellow pasta dough,
    made as directed on page
    129 for the machine
    method, OR page 143 for
    the hand-rolled method,

using 3 large eggs and
    approximately 1⅔ cups
    unbleached flour

Cheesecloth
Salt
Béchamel Sauce, prepared as
    directed on page 39,
    using 1 cup milk, 2 table-
    spoons butter, 1½ table-

spoons flour, and ⅛ tea-
    spoon salt
⅓ cup freshly grated
    parmigiano-reggiano cheese
About 2 tablespoons butter for
    dotting the baking dish

1. Prepare the tomato sauce as directed on page 152, using only half the recipe.

2. *If using fresh spinach:* Soak it in several changes of water, and cook it with salt until tender, as described on page 89. Drain it, and as soon as it is cool enough to handle, squeeze it gently in your hands to drive out as much moisture as possible. Chop it rather coarse, and set aside.

If using thawed frozen leaf spinach: Cook in a covered pan with salt for about 5 minutes. Drain it, when cool squeeze all the moisture out of it that you can, and chop it coarse.

3. Put the chopped onion and butter for the filling in a skillet or small sauté pan, turn on the heat to medium, and sauté the onion until it becomes colored a pale gold. Add the chopped prosciutto. Cook it for about half a minute, stirring to coat it well, then add the chopped spinach. Stir thoroughly

Sliced Pasta Roll (continued)

once or twice and cook for 2 minutes or more until the spinach absorbs all the butter.

4. Turn out all the contents of the pan into a bowl, add the *ricotta,* the 1 cup grated Parmesan, a tiny grating—about ⅛ teaspoon—of nutmeg, and the egg yolk. Mix well with a fork until all the ingredients of the filling are evenly combined. Taste and correct for salt.

5. Prepare the yellow pasta dough by machine, page 130, or by hand, page 144, rolling it out as thin as it will come by either method.

6. *If making pasta by machine:* You must join all the pasta strips to make a single large sheet. Lightly moisten the edge of one strip with water, then place the edge of another strip over it, overlapping it by very little, about ⅛ inch. Run your thumb along the whole length of the edge, pressing down hard on the two edges to bond them together. Smooth the bumps out with a pass or two of a rolling pin. Repeat the operation with another pasta strip, continuing until all the dough has been joined to form a single sheet. Even off the irregular fringes with a pastry wheel or knife.

If making pasta by hand: When you have rolled out a single thin sheet of pasta proceed to the next step.

7. Spread the spinach filling over the pasta, starting about 3 inches in from the edge close to you. Spread it thinly to cover all the sheet of dough except for the 3-inch border near you and a ¼-inch border along the other sides. Lift the edge of the 3-inch border and fold the whole width of the border over the filling. Fold again and again until the whole sheet of pasta has been loosely rolled up.

8. Wrap the pasta tightly in cheesecloth, tying both ends securely with kitchen string. If you do not have a fish poacher, choose a pot that can subsequently accommodate the pasta in 3 to 4 quarts of water. Bring the water to a boil, add 1 tablespoon salt and when the water resumes boiling, slip in the pasta roll. Adjust heat to cook at a steady but moderate boil for 20 minutes. Lift the pasta out supporting it with two spoons or spatulas to make sure it does not split in the middle. Remove the cheesecloth while the pasta is still hot, and set the roll aside to cool.

9. Preheat oven to 400°.

10. While the pasta is cooling, make the béchamel sauce, bringing it to a medium thickness. When done, mix it with the tomato sauce prepared earlier.

11. When the pasta is cool and firm, slice it like a roast into ¾-inch slices.

12. Choose a bake-and-serve dish that can accommodate the pasta slices in a single layer. Lightly smear the bottom of the dish with sauce. Place the

pasta slices in the dish, arranging them so that they overlap slightly, roof shingle fashion. Pour the rest of the sauce and béchamel mixture over the pasta, sprinkle with the ⅓ cup grated Parmesan, and dot lightly with butter.

Ahead-of-time note ❀ The dish can be assembled completely up to this point several hours in advance, but not overnight. Do not refrigerate because cooked spinach acquires a sour, metallic taste in the refrigerator.

13. Bake on the uppermost rack of the oven for 10 to 15 minutes, until a light golden crust forms on top. Remove from the oven and allow to settle for 10 minutes before bringing to the table. Serve directly from the baking dish.

Pasta Wrappers Filled with Spinach Fettuccine, Porcini Mushrooms, and Ham

BEFORE the student riots of the late 1970s demolished it, Al Cantunzein, in Bologna, was probably the greatest pasta restaurant that has ever existed. Among the thirty or forty pastas it served, the most sublime was called *scrigno di venere,* Venus's jewel case. The "case" was formed by a small handkerchief-sized wrapper of yellow pasta pulled around a collection of edible "jewels": green *fettuccine,* ham, wild mushrooms, truffles.

The recipe, while not particularly troublesome from the point of view of technique, requires a substantial amount of organization to assemble. Reading it through carefully first will help you put it together smoothly later.

For 6 servings

Pasta Wrappers (continued)

FOR THE FETTUCCINE

Homemade green pasta dough, made as directed on page 129 for the machine method, OR page 143 for the hand-rolled method, using 2 large eggs, ⅓ package frozen leaf spinach OR 6 ounces fresh spinach, salt, and approximately 1½ cups unbleached flour

TO SAUCE THE FETTUCCINE

3 tablespoons butter
2 tablespoons chopped shallots OR onion
Two small packets OR 2 ounces dried *porcini* mushrooms, reconstituted as described on page 27
The filtered water from the mushroom soak, see page 28 for instructions

⅔ cup unsmoked boiled ham, cut into ¼-inch strips
1 cup heavy whipping cream
⅓ cup freshly grated *parmigiano-reggiano* cheese
OPTIONAL: ½ ounce (or more if affordable) fresh OR canned white truffle

THE PASTA WRAPPERS

Homemade yellow pasta dough made as directed on page 129 for the machine method, OR page 143 for the hand-rolled method, using 3 large eggs and approximately 1⅔ cups unbleached flour

THE BÉCHAMEL SAUCE

Béchamel Sauce, prepared as directed on page 39, using 3 cups milk, 6 tablespoons butter, 4½ tablespoons flour, and ¼ teaspoon salt

Salt
6 gratin pans, preferably earthenware, about 4½ inches in diameter

Butter for greasing the pans
Wooden toothpicks

1. Make green pasta dough either by machine, page 132, or by hand, pages 144–147. Cut it into *fettuccine,* either using the wide-grooved cutters of the

pasta machine, or cutting it by hand. See pages 134 and 149 for complete details. Spread the *fettuccine* loosely on a counter lined with clean, dry, cloth towels.

2. To make the sauce: Put 3 tablespoons of butter in a saucepan or small sauté pan together with the chopped onion or shallot, turn on the heat to medium, and cook the onion or shallot, stirring, until it becomes colored a pale gold. Add the reconstituted dried mushrooms and the filtered water from their soak. Cook at a simmer until all the mushroom liquid has evaporated.

3. Add the ham, cook half a minute or so, stirring once or twice to coat it well, then add the heavy cream. Cook until the cream has thickened somewhat, then turn off the heat and set aside.

4. Make the pasta wrappers: Prepare the yellow pasta dough by machine, page 132, or by hand, pages 144-147, rolling it out as thin as it will come by either method.

5. *If making pasta by machine:* You must join all the pasta strips to make a single large sheet. Lightly moisten the edge of one strip with water, then place the edge of another strip over it, overlapping it by very little, about ⅛ inch. Run your thumb along the whole length of the edge, pressing down hard on the two edges to bond them together. Smooth the bumps out with a pass or two of a rolling pin. Repeat the operation with another pasta strip, continuing until all the dough has been joined to form a single sheet.

If making pasta by hand: When you have rolled out a single thin sheet of pasta proceed to the next step.

6. Lay the sheet of dough flat on a counter lined with dry, cloth towels, and let it dry for about 10 minutes.

7. To make the wrappers, you must cut the pasta into disks 8 inches in diameter. Look for a pot cover of that size, or a plate, or use a compass to trace 6 eight-inch disks on the pasta dough. Detach the disks from the pasta sheet, spreading them on the cloth towels. (The leftover pasta can be cut and dried to cook in soup on another occasion.)

8. Prepare the béchamel sauce, making it rather thin, the consistency of sour cream. When done, keep it warm in the upper half of a double boiler, with the heat turned to very low. Stir it just before using.

9. Place a bowl of cold water near the range and bring 4 quarts of water to a boil in a soup pot. Add 1 tablespoon salt, and as the water resumes boiling, drop in 2 of the pasta disks. When they have cooked for no more than half a minute, retrieve them with a colander spoon, or other spoon, dip them in the bowl of cold water, then rinse them under cold running water, wringing them gently, and spread them out flat on the cloth towel. Repeat the operation until you have done all 6 pasta disks.

Pasta Wrappers (continued)

10. Turn the heat on to low under the mushroom and ham sauce, stirring it once or twice while you are reheating it. If using canned truffles, add the juice from the can to the sauce.

11. Add more water to the soup pot to replenish what has boiled away, and when the water comes to a lively boil, drop in the green *fettuccine*. Drain the pasta when slightly underdone, a little firmer than *al dente*. Toss it immediately with the ham and mushroom sauce. Add the grated Parmesan, and toss again. If using truffle, slice it very thin over the pasta; if you don't have a truffle slicer, use a swiveling-blade peeler or a *mandoline*. Divide the *fettuccine* into 6 equal portions, keeping to one side 6 individual strands.

12. Preheat oven to 450°.

13. Thickly smear the bottom of the gratin pans with butter. Spread some béchamel sauce on a large platter. Place one of the pasta disks over the béchamel, rotating it to coat all its underside. Thinly spread a little more béchamel on its top side. Place the disk in a gratin pan, centering it and letting its edges hang over the sides.

Put one of the 6 portions of *fettuccine* in the center of the disk, making sure it has its share of sauce. Keep the *fettuccine* loose, don't tamp them down. Mix in a little béchamel.

Pick up the edges of the disk and fold them toward the center with a spiral movement, thus sealing the pasta wrapper. Fasten the folds at the top with a toothpick, then wrap one of the *fettuccine* strands you had set aside around the toothpick.

Repeat the entire procedure until you have filled and sealed all 6 wrappers.

Ahead-of-time note 🌸 You can prepare the wrappers several hours in advance up to this point. They can be done in the morning for the evening, but not overnight, and they are not to be refrigerated.

14. Place the gratin pans on the uppermost rack of the preheated oven. Bake until a light brown crust forms on the edge of the wrapper folds, about 8 minutes. Do not bake longer than 10 minutes.

15. Transfer each wrapper from the gratin pan to a soup plate, lifting carefully with 2 metal spatulas. Remove the toothpick without dislodging the single strand of *fettuccine.* Allow to rest for at least 5 minutes before serving.

Pizzoccheri

Pizzoccheri are short, broad, taupe-colored noodles made principally of soft buckwheat flour. They are a specialty of Valtellina, on the Swiss border, where in cool, Alpine valleys buckwheat grows well. Because buckwheat is so soft, it must be stiffened with some wheat flour, in the proportions given below.

As you will see when you follow the recipe, the preparation of *pizzoccheri* has three parts: The pasta is cooked along with potatoes and vegetables, it is then tossed with sage- and garlic-scented butter and topped with sliced, soft cheese, and finally briefly gratinéed in the oven.

The vegetable may be either Savoy cabbage or Swiss chard stalks. My preference is for the Swiss chard. Only the stalks go into this recipe, but the detached leafy tops can be boiled, tossed with olive oil and lemon juice, and served as salad, as described on page 561, or else sautéed with garlic and served as a vegetable as described on page 490. Valtellina's own tender and savory cheese is not available elsewhere, but an excellent replacement is *fontina.*

For 6 servings

FOR THE PIZZOCCHERI

Homemade pasta dough, made as directed on page 129 for the machine method, OR page 143 for the hand-rolled method, using 3 large eggs and approximately 1¼ cups fine-grained buckwheat flour, ½ cup plus 1 tablespoon unbleached flour, 1 tablespoon milk, 1 tablespoon water, and ½ teaspoon salt

Pizzoccheri (continued)

THE OTHER INGREDIENTS

3 to 3½ cups Swiss chard stalks (leafy tops completely removed), cut into pieces 2 to 3 inches long and about ½ inch wide

Salt

1 cup potatoes, preferably new, peeled and sliced ¼ inch thick

4 tablespoons (½ stick) butter

4 large garlic cloves, lightly mashed with a knife handle and peeled

2 dried or 3 fresh sage leaves

A 12- to 14-inch oven-to-table baking dish and butter to smear it

¼ pound imported Italian *fontina* cheese, sliced into thin slivers

⅔ cup freshly grated *parmigiano-reggiano* cheese

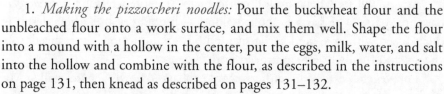

1. *Making the pizzoccheri noodles:* Pour the buckwheat flour and the unbleached flour onto a work surface, and mix them well. Shape the flour into a mound with a hollow in the center, put the eggs, milk, water, and salt into the hollow and combine with the flour, as described in the instructions on page 131, then knead as described on pages 131–132.

2. Roll out the dough, either by the machine method, page 132, or by the hand method, pages 144–147, keeping it somewhat thicker than you would for *fettuccine.* Let it dry for 2 or more minutes until it is no longer so moist that it will stick to itself when folded and cut, but without letting it get so brittle that it will crack.

3. Loosely fold the machine-made strips or hand-rolled sheet of dough into a loose flat roll as you would for cutting *tagliatelle,* see page 136. Cut the rolled-up dough into 1-inch wide ribbons, and cut each ribbon diagonally in the middle to obtain diamond-shaped noodles that are 1 inch wide and about 3 to 3½ inches long. Unfold the noodles and spread them out on top of a counter lined with clean, dry cloth towels.

Ahead-of-time note ● The pasta can be prepared up to this point days or even weeks ahead of time. See page 136 for instructions on drying pasta for storage. Bear in mind when cooking it later that dried pasta takes longer than the freshly made.

Cooking the Pasta

1. Preheat oven to 400°.
2. Wash the cut-up Swiss chard stalks in cold water.
3. Bring 4 quarts of water to a boil, add 2 tablespoons salt, and as soon as the water resumes boiling put in the chard. When the chard has cooked for 10 minutes, put in the potatoes, setting the pot's cover on slightly askew.
4. While the chard and potatoes are cooking, put 4 tablespoons of butter and the mashed garlic in a small skillet and turn on the heat to medium. Cook the garlic, stirring, until it becomes colored a light nut brown, discard it, and put in the sage leaves. Turn the leaves over in the hot butter once or twice, then remove the pan from heat.
5. Thinly smear the baking dish with butter.
6. When both the chard and the potatoes are tender—test each by prodding it with a fork—drop the pasta into the same pot. Cook the pasta until it is slightly underdone, very firm to the bite, *molto al dente.* If freshly made, it will take just a few seconds. Drain it immediately together with the chard and potatoes, and transfer all ingredients to the buttered baking dish.
7. Over the pasta pour the garlic and sage butter, tossing thoroughly to coat the noodles well.
8. Add the sliced *fontina* and grated Parmesan, mixing them into the pasta and vegetables. Level off the contents of the dish, and place on the uppermost rack of the preheated oven. Remove after 5 minutes, allow to settle for another 2 or 3, then serve at table directly from the dish.

Orecchiette

APULIA, the region that extends over the entire heel and half the instep of the boot-shaped Italian peninsula, has a strong tradition of homemade pasta. Unlike the *tortellini, tagliatelle,* and *lasagne* of Emilia-Romagna, Apulian pasta is made with water instead of eggs, and the flour is mostly from their native hard-wheat variety, rather than from the soft wheat of the Emilian plain. Apulian dough is chewier, firmer, more rustic in texture. It is perfectly suited to the strongly accented sauces of the region.

The best-known shape of Apulian pasta is *orecchiette,* "little ears," small disks of dough given their ear-like shape by a rotary pressure of the thumb. In the recipe that follows, hard-wheat flour is mixed with standard, unbleached flour to make a dough easier to work.   *For 6 servings*

1 cup *semolina,* the yellow flour
   from hard wheat, ground
   very fine
2 cups all-purpose unbleached
   flour

½ teaspoon salt
Up to 1 cup lukewarm water

1. Combine the *semolina,* the all-purpose flour, and salt on your work counter, making a mound with a well in the center. Add a few tablespoons of water at a time, incorporating it with the flour until it has absorbed as much water as it can without becoming stiff and dry. The consistency must not be sticky, but it can be somewhat softer than egg pasta.

2. Scrape away any crumbs of flour from the work surface, wash and dry your hands, and knead the mass for about 8 minutes, until it is smooth and elastic. Refer to the description of hand kneading pasta dough on pages 131–132.

3. Wrap the dough in plastic wrap and let it rest about 15 minutes.

4. Pull off a ball about the size of a lemon from the kneaded mass, rewrapping the rest of the dough. Roll the ball into a sausage-like roll about ½ inch thick. Slice it into very thin disks, about ¹⁄₁₆ inch, if you are able. Place a disk in the cupped palm of one hand, and with a rotary pressure of the thumb of the other hand, make a hollow in the center, broadening the disk to a width of about 1 inch. The shape should resemble a shallow mushroom cap, slightly thicker at its edges than at its center. Repeat the procedure until you have used up all the dough.

5. If you are not using the *orecchiette* immediately, spread them out to dry on clean, dry cloth towels, turning them over from time to time. When they are fully dry, after about 24 hours, you can store them in a box in a kitchen cupboard for a month or more. They are cooked like any other pasta but will take longer than conventional fresh egg pasta.

Recommended sauce ✱ The most suitable is the Broccoli and Anchovy Sauce on page 173. Other good choices are Tomato and Anchovy Sauce, page 174, and Cauliflower Sauce with Garlic, Oil, and Chili Pepper, page 172.

❧ *Matching Pasta to Sauce* ❧

THE SHAPES pasta takes are numbered in the hundreds, and the sauces that can be devised for them are beyond numbering, but the principles that bring pasta and sauce together in satisfying style are few and simple. They cannot be ignored by anyone who wants to achieve the full and harmonious expression of flavor of which Italian cooking is capable.

Even if you have done everything else right when producing a dish of pasta—you have carefully made fine fresh pasta at home or bought the choicest quality imported Italian boxed, dry pasta; you have cooked a ravishing sauce from the freshest ingredients; you have boiled the pasta in lots of hot water, drained it perfectly *al dente,* deftly tossed it with sauce—your dish might not be completely successful unless you have given thought to matching pasta type and shape to a congenial sauce.

The two basic pasta types you'll be considering are the boxed, factory-made, eggless dry kind and homemade, fresh, egg pasta. When well made, one is quite as good as the other, but what you can do with the former you would not necessarily want to do with the latter.

The exceptional firmness, the compact body, the grainier texture of factory-made pasta makes it the first choice when a sauce is based on olive oil, such as most seafood sauces and the great variety of light, vegetable sauces. That is not to say, however, that you must pass up all butter-based sauces. Boxed, dry pasta can establish a most enjoyable liaison with some of them, but the result will be different, weightier, more substantial.

When you use factory-made pasta, your choice of sauce will be affected by the shape. *Spaghettini,* thin *spaghetti,* is usually the best vehicle for an olive oil–based seafood sauce. Many tomato sauces, particularly when made with butter, work better with thicker *spaghetti,* in some cases with the hollow strands known as *bucatini* or *perciatelli.* Meat sauces or other chunky sauces nest best in larger hollow tubes such as *rigatoni* and *penne,* or in the cupped shape of *conchiglie. Fusilli* are marvelous with a dense, creamy sauce, such as the Sausages and Cream Sauce on page 201, which clings to all its twists and curls.

Factory-made pasta carries sauce firmly and boldly; homemade pasta absorbs it deeply. Good, fresh pasta made at home has a gossamer touch on the palate, it feels light and buoyant in the mouth. Most olive oil sauces obliterate its fine texture, making it slick, and strong flavors deaden it. Its most pleasing match is with subtly constituted sauces, be they with seafood, meat, or vegetable, generally based on butter and often enriched by cream or milk.

The following table illustrates some of the pleasing combinations that the sauces appearing in this volume lend themselves to with a variety of pasta types.

Factory-Made Boxed, Dry Pasta

PASTA SHAPE	RECOMMENDED SAUCE
bucatini (also known as *perciatelli*) (thick, hollow strands)	❀ Tomato with Olive Oil and Chopped Vegetables, Variation with Marjoram and Two Cheeses, page 153 ❀ Tomato with Sautéed Vegetables and Olive Oil, page 154 ❀ Amatriciana: Tomato with Pancetta and Chili Pepper, page 157 ❀ Sicilian Sardine, page 187
ruote di carro (cartwheels), *conchiglie* (shells), *fusilli* (corkscrews, either short and stubby or long and thin)	❀ Tomato with Olive Oil and Chopped Vegetables, Variation with Rosemary and Pancetta, page 154 ❀ Amatriciana: Tomato with Pancetta and Chili Pepper, page 157 ❀ Tomato with Porcini Mushrooms, page 158 ❀ Mushroom with Ham and Tomato, page 159 ❀ Peas, Bacon, and Ricotta, page 163 ❀ Broccoli and Anchovy, page 173 ❀ Sausages and Cream, page 201 ❀ Bolognese Meat, page 203 ❀ Eggplant and Ricotta, Sicilian Style, page 161
Also specially good with *fusilli*:	❀ Fried Zucchini with Garlic and Basil, page 167 ❀ Zucchini with Basil and Beaten Egg Yolk, page 166
maccheroncini (short, narrow tubes), and *penne* (quills)	❀ Tomato with Onion and Butter, page 152 ❀ Tomato with Olive Oil and Chopped Vegetables, page 153 ❀ Tomato with Sautéed Vegetables and Olive Oil, page 154 ❀ Amatriciana: Tomato with Pancetta and Chili Pepper, page 157

PASTA SHAPE	RECOMMENDED SAUCE
maccheroncini and *penne*	❈ Tomato with Porcini Mushrooms, page 158
	❈ Mushroom with Ham and Tomato, page 159
	❈ Spinach with Ricotta and Ham, page 162
	❈ Peas, Peppers, and Prosciutto with Cream, page 164
	❈ Roasted Red and Yellow Pepper with Garlic and Basil, page 165
	❈ Cauliflower with Garlic, Oil, and Chili Pepper, page 172
	❈ Tuna with Tomatoes and Garlic, page 180
	❈ Fish, page 186
	❈ Gorgonzola, page 194
	❈ Asparagus with Ham and Cream, page 200
	❈ Prosciutto and Cream, page 201
rigatoni (broad, short tubes)	❈ Tomato with Onion and Butter, page 152
	❈ Tomato with Sautéed Vegetables and Olive Oil, page 154
	❈ Amatriciana: Tomato with Pancetta and Chili Pepper, page 157
	❈ Eggplant and Ricotta, Sicilian Style, page 161
	❈ Spinach with Ricotta and Ham, page 162
	❈ Peas, Bacon, and Ricotta, page 163
	❈ Roasted Red and Yellow Pepper with Garlic and Basil, page 165
	❈ Tuna with Tomatoes and Garlic, page 180
	❈ Fish, page 186
	❈ Gorgonzola, page 194
	❈ Red and Yellow Bell Pepper with Sausages, page 197
	❈ Prosciutto and Cream, page 201
	❈ With Bolognese Meat Sauce, page 203

Factory-Made Boxed, Dry Pasta (continued)

PASTA SHAPE	RECOMMENDED SAUCE
spaghetti, sometimes known as *vermicelli*	❀ Tomato with Onion and Butter, page 152
	❀ Tomato with Olive Oil and Chopped Vegetables, Variation with Marjoram and Two Cheeses, page 153
	❀ Eggplant and Ricotta, Sicilian Style, page 161
	❀ Fried Zucchini with Garlic and Basil, page 167
	❀ Smothered Onions, page 168
	❀ Butter and Rosemary, page 169
	❀ Aio e Oio: Roman Garlic and Oil, page 170
	❀ Pesto, page 176
	❀ Pesto with Ricotta, page 178
	❀ Tuna with Tomatoes and Garlic, page 180
	❀ Scallop with Olive Oil, Garlic, and Hot Pepper, page 185
	❀ Fish, page 186
	❀ Butter and Parmesan Cheese, page 191
	❀ Carbonara, page 202
spaghettini, thin *spaghetti,* sometimes known as *vermicellini*	❀ Tomatoes with Olive Oil and Chopped Vegetables, page 153
	❀ Tomato with Garlic and Basil, page 156
	❀ Eggplant with Tomato and Red Chili Pepper, page 160
	❀ Aio e Oio, Raw Version, with Fresh Tomatoes and Basil, page 171
	❀ Tomato and Anchovy, page 174
	❀ Black Truffle, page 178
	❀ Clam with Tomatoes, page 180
	❀ White Clam, page 182
	❀ Sardinian Bottarga, page 183
	❀ Scallop with Olive Oil, Garlic, and Hot Pepper, page 185
ziti (narrow, short tubes), see *penne,* above	

Homemade Fresh* Pasta

*Note ✵ When, in this book, the word "fresh" is applied to pasta, it means pasta produced by home techniques, almost invariably using a dough that contains eggs. It does not mean pasta kept artificially soft with cornmeal or through vacuum-packaging or by other methods. Fresh pasta may indeed be quite dry, and good, naturally dried fresh pasta is absolutely to be preferred to the spuriously soft variety available commercially.

PASTA SHAPE	RECOMMENDED SAUCE
capelli d'angelo, angel hair	In Italy, these very thin noodles are served only in meat or chicken broth
cappellacci, pumpkin-filled *ravioli*	✤ Butter and Parmesan Cheese, page 191 ✤ Cream and Butter, page 193
fettuccine	✤ Fried Zucchini with Garlic and Basil, page 167 ✤ Butter and Rosemary, page 169 ✤ Pesto, page 176 ✤ White Clam, page 182 ✤ Pink Shrimp with Cream, page 191 ✤ Butter and Sage, page 192 ✤ Cream and Butter, page 193 ✤ Gorgonzola, page 194 ✤ Mushroom, Ham, and Cream, page 195 ✤ Prosciutto and Cream, page 201
garganelli, hand-turned macaroni	✤ Peas, Peppers, and Prosciutto with Cream, page 164 ✤ Gorgonzola, page 194 ✤ Asparagus with Ham and Cream, page 200
lasagne	✤ With Meat Sauce, Bolognese Style, page 215 ✤ With Mushrooms and Ham, page 217 ✤ With Artichokes, page 219 ✤ With Ricotta Pesto, page 221
maltagliati, short, irregularly cut soup noodles	✤ With all soups that call for pasta, and particularly apt with *pasta e fagioli,* Pasta and Beans, page 102

Homemade Fresh Pasta (continued)

PASTA SHAPE	RECOMMENDED SAUCE
orecchiette	❋ Broccoli and Anchovy, page 173
pappardelle, broad noodles	❋ Tomato with Porcini Mushrooms, page 158
	❋ Pink Shrimp with Cream, page 191
	❋ Red and Yellow Bell Pepper with Sausages, page 197
	❋ Cranberry Beans, Sage, and Rosemary, page 198
	❋ Chicken Liver, page 205
pizzoccheri, short buckwheat noodles	❋ Tossed with sage, and garlic, and gratinéed with soft cheese, pages 231-233
tagliatelle noodles, broader than *fettuccine*	❋ Bolognese Meat Sauce, page 203
tonnarelli, thick, square noodles	❋ Tomato with Porcini Mushrooms, page 158
	❋ Smothered Onions, page 168
	❋ Butter and Rosemary, page 169
	❋ Pesto, page 176
	❋ Sardinian Bottarga, page 183
	❋ Prosciutto and Cream, page 201
tortellini	❋ Tomato with Heavy Cream, page 155
	❋ Pink Shrimp with Cream, page 191 (when the *tortellini* is filled with fish)
	❋ Cream and Butter, page 193
	❋ Prosciutto and Cream, page 201 (most desirable with green *tortellini*)
	❋ Bolognese Meat Sauce, page 203
	❋ When it is the classic meat-filled *tortellini* made with yellow dough, the traditional service is in meat broth
tortelloni	❋ Tomato with Heavy Cream, page 155
	❋ Butter and Parmesan Cheese, page 191
	❋ Butter and Sage, page 192

Here are some varieties of cut pasta.

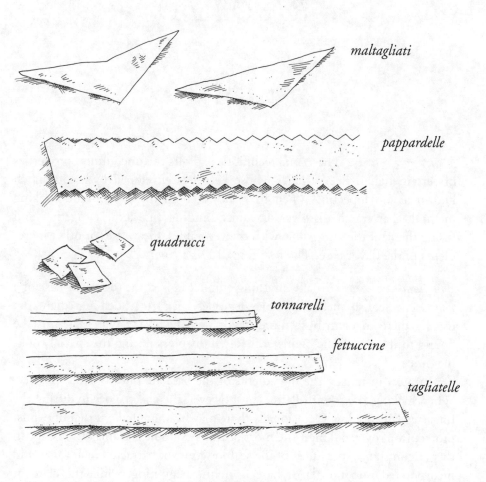

maltagliati

pappardelle

quadrucci

tonnarelli

fettuccine

tagliatelle

RISOTTO

Defining risotto 🌸 The *risotto* technique exploits the uncommon properties of certain Italian rice varieties whose kernel is enveloped by a soft starch known as amylopectin. When it is subjected to the appropriate cooking method, that starch dissolves, creamily binding the kernels together and fusing them, at the same time, with the vegetables, meat, fish, or other ingredients in the flavor base. The resulting dish is a *risotto.*

The flavor base 🌸 Virtually anything edible can become the flavor base of a *risotto:* cheese, fish, meat, vegetables, legumes, even fruit. Such ingredients are usually there to contribute more flavor than texture, flavor that must be bound to the rice as the grains' soft starch dissolves during the special cooking process.

In most instances, the ingredients of the base are put in before the rice. When making *risotto* with Parmesan, however, the cheese goes in during the final stage of cooking. Occasionally there may be an ingredient that one must protect from overcooking. The most obvious example is clams or mussels. In that circumstance, the juices of the seafood must be extracted in advance and incorporated into the flavor base from the beginning, while the clam or mussel meat itself can be stirred into the rice when it is nearly done.

The cooking method 🌸 The ingredients of a *risotto*'s flavor base usually rest on a foundation of chopped onion sautéed in butter. In some infrequent instances, olive oil replaces the butter, and garlic may be added.

Raw, unwashed Italian rice is added to the hot butter or oil base, and it is lightly toasted in it. Immediately thereafter, a ladleful of cooking liquid is added to the pot. The rice is stirred until the liquid is gone, partly through absorption, partly through evaporation. More liquid is added, and the procedure is repeated, until the rice is done.

It is only through the gradual administration of small quantities of liquid, through its simultaneous absorption and evaporation, and through constant stirring, that the rice's soft starch is transformed into a clinging agent, pulling the grains together and fastening on them the taste of the flavor base. Rice that is not stirred, that stews in too much liquid, that cooks in a covered pot, may turn into a perfectly agreeable dish, but it is not *risotto,* and will not taste like *risotto.*

The cooking liquid ❀ All the flavors that the cooking liquid starts out with become more concentrated and intense as it evaporates. Bearing that in mind, when the recipe requires broth you will use a fine, mild meat broth made by boiling mainly beef and veal, with next to no bones and very little chicken. Pure chicken broth becomes distractingly sharp, and so does stock produced in the French manner. Neither is a desirable vehicle for cooking *risotto.*

Water is the best choice for seafood *risotto.* Fish *fumets,* or broths enriched with shellfish carcasses, become too emphatic as they cook down, thus upsetting a *risotto*'s balance of flavors.

Liquids that issue from the ingredients in the flavor base should be retained, such as the juices released by clams or mussels, the water used to reconstitute dried mushrooms, and the vegetable-flavored liquid left from the preliminary blanching of asparagus or other greens.

Wine may be added, but it must not be the sole liquid used.

Note ❀ The quantity of liquid suggested in the recipes that follow is approximate. In actual cooking, you should be prepared to use more, or sometimes less, as the *risotto* itself requires. When cooking with broth, if you have used up the broth before the rice is fully cooked, continue with water.

How long to cook ❀ Some Italian cooks like the grains in *risotto* to be exceptionally firm, and suggest cooking times between 18 and 20 minutes. At that stage, the center of the kernel is chalky hard. If you find a chalky sensation unappealing, as I do, expect to cook the rice another 5 to 10 minutes, for a total of 25 minutes to half an hour.

The pace at which *risotto* cooks can vary considerably, however. It is affected by the receptivity to moisture of the specific rice you are using, by the amount of liquid you add at a time, by the speed at which the liquid evaporates.

It is prudent to begin to taste the rice after 20 minutes' cooking, so you can begin to judge how much further it has to go, and how much more liquid you are going to need. Never cook rice until it is soft at the center. It should be tender, but still firm to the bite.

The pot ❀ It must transmit and retain sufficient heat to cook the rice at a very lively pace without scorching it. Pure aluminum and other light-weight ware are not suitable. Heavy-bottomed pots made of steel-jacketed alloys are the sturdiest, and the most practical for professional cooking, but for home use an enameled cast-iron pot is a pleasure to work with.

Rice varieties ❀ Imported Italian varieties are the only ones on which one can rely for a completely successful *risotto*. Of the many that are grown, the best are Arborio, Vialone Nano, and Carnaroli. Please see page 30 in the section on ingredients for a detailed description of their individual characteristics.

Risotto styles ❀ All *risotto* can be grouped into two basic styles that differ in the consistency at which they aim. There is the compact, more tightly knit, somewhat stickier style of Piedmont, Lombardy, and Emilia-Romagna and the looser, runny style of the Veneto, known as *all'onda*, "wavy." You obtain the former by evaporating all the cooking liquid as the rice finishes cooking, and the latter by bringing the rice to the desired degree of doneness while it is still rather moist.

The Piedmontese/Milanese/Bolognese style is more compatible with substantial flavor bases founded on cheese, sausage, game, and wild mushrooms, whereas the Venetian *risotto all'onda* achieves great delicacy with seafood and spring vegetables.

Serving temperature ❀ Among the myths associated with *risotto* there is the one that you must eat it piping hot, as it comes from the pot. Unlike pasta, *risotto* tastes better when it has rested on your plate a minute or so. When Italians are served *risotto*, they often spread it on their plate from the center toward the rim, to dissipate some of the steam.

Risotto with Parmesan Cheese

THIS BASIC white *risotto* is the simplest way to prepare the dish, and for many, the finest. Good as it is, it can be even better when blanketed by shaved white truffles.   *For 6 servings*

5 cups Basic Homemade Meat
Broth, prepared as directed
on page 15, OR 1 cup
canned beef broth diluted
with 4 cups water

3 tablespoons butter

2 tablespoons vegetable oil

2 tablespoons onion chopped
very fine

2 cups Arborio OR other
imported Italian *risotto* rice

½ heaping cup freshly grated
parmigiano-reggiano cheese

OPTIONAL: ½ ounce (or more if
affordable) fresh OR canned
white truffle

Salt, if required

1. Bring the broth to a very slow, steady simmer on a burner near where you'll be cooking the *risotto*.

2. Put 1 tablespoon of butter, the vegetable oil, and the chopped onion in a broad, sturdy pot, and turn on the heat to medium high. Cook and stir the onion until it becomes translucent, then add the rice. Stir quickly and thoroughly until the grains are coated well.

3. Add ½ cup of simmering broth and cook the rice, stirring constantly with a long wooden spoon, wiping the sides and bottom of the pot clean as you stir, until all the liquid is gone. You must never stop stirring and you must be sure to wipe the bottom of the pot completely clean frequently, or the rice will stick to it.

4. When there is no more liquid in the pot, add another ½ cup, continuing always to stir in the manner described above. Maintain heat at a lively pace.

5. Begin to taste the rice after 20 minutes of cooking. It is done when it is tender, but firm to the bite. As it approaches that stage, gradually reduce the amount of liquid you add, so that when it is fully cooked, it is slightly moist, but not runny.

6. When the rice is about 1 or 2 minutes away from being fully cooked, add all the grated Parmesan and the remaining butter. Stir constantly to melt the cheese and wrap it around the grains. Off heat, taste and correct for salt, stirring after adding salt.

7. Transfer to a platter and serve promptly. Shave the optional white truffle over it, using either a truffle slicer or a swiveling-blade vegetable peeler. Some prefer to shave the truffle over each individual portion.

Risotto with Saffron, Milanese Style

For 6 servings

5 cups Basic Homemade Meat Broth, prepared as directed on page 15, OR 1 cup canned beef broth diluted with 4 cups water

2 tablespoons diced beef marrow, *pancetta,* or prosciutto

3 tablespoons butter

2 tablespoons vegetable oil

2 tablespoons onion chopped very fine

2 cups Arborio or other imported Italian *risotto* rice

⅓ teaspoon powdered saffron OR ½ teaspoon chopped saffron strands dissolved in 1 cup hot broth or water

Black pepper, ground fresh from the mill

⅓ cup freshly grated *parmigiano-reggiano* cheese, plus additional cheese at the table

Salt, if required

1. Bring the broth to a very slow, steady simmer on a burner near where you'll be cooking the *risotto.*

2. Put the diced marrow, *pancetta,* or prosciutto, 1 tablespoon of butter, the vegetable oil, and the chopped onion in a broad, sturdy pot, and turn on the heat to medium high. Cook and stir the onion until it becomes translucent, then add the rice. Stir quickly and thoroughly until the grains are coated well.

3. Add ½ cup of simmering broth, and cook the rice following the directions in Steps 3 and 4 of the basic white *risotto* recipe on page 245.

4. When the rice has cooked for 15 minutes, add half the dissolved saffron. Continue to stir, and when there is no more liquid in the pot, add the remaining saffron.

5. Finish cooking the rice, stirring always, until it is tender, but firm to the bite, and there is no more liquid in the pot.

6. Off heat, add a few grindings of pepper, the remaining butter, all the grated Parmesan, and stir thoroughly until the cheese melts and clings to the rice. Taste and correct for salt. Transfer to a platter and serve promptly with additional grated cheese on the side.

Risotto with Porcini Mushrooms

For 6 servings

5 cups Basic Homemade Meat Broth, prepared as directed on page 15, OR 1 cup canned beef broth diluted with 4 cups water

2 tablespoons butter

2 tablespoons vegetable oil

2 tablespoons onion chopped very fine

2 cups Arborio or other imported Italian *risotto* rice

A small packet OR 1 ounce dried *porcini* mushrooms, reconstituted as described on page 27

The filtered water from the mushroom soak, see page 28 for instructions

Black pepper, ground fresh from the mill

⅓ cup freshly grated *parmigiano-reggiano* cheese, plus additional cheese at the table

Salt, if required

1. Bring the broth to a very slow, steady simmer on a burner near where you'll be cooking the *risotto*.

2. Put 1 tablespoon of the butter, the vegetable oil, and the chopped onion in a broad, sturdy pot, and turn on the heat to medium high. Cook and stir the onion until it becomes translucent, then add the rice. Stir quickly and thoroughly until the grains are coated well.

3. Add ½ cup of simmering broth, and cook the rice following the directions in Steps 3 and 4 of the basic white *risotto* recipe on page 245.

4. When the rice has cooked for 10 minutes, add the reconstituted mushrooms and ½ of their filtered water. Continue to stir and when there is no more liquid, add more of the mushroom water, stirring, letting it evaporate, and adding more, until you have used it all up.

5. Finish cooking the rice with broth or, if you have no more broth, with water. Cook the rice until it is tender, but firm to the bite, with no more liquid remaining in the pot.

6. Off heat, add a few grindings of pepper, the remaining 1 tablespoon of butter, and all the grated Parmesan, and stir thoroughly until the cheese melts and clings to the rice. Taste and correct for salt. Transfer to a platter and serve promptly with additional grated cheese on the side.

Risotto with Asparagus

For 6 servings

1 pound fresh asparagus	2 tablespoons vegetable oil
Salt	2 tablespoons onion chopped
Enough Basic Homemade Meat	very fine
Broth, prepared as directed	2 cups Arborio or other import-
on page 15, OR canned beef	ed Italian *risotto* rice
broth diluted with water to	Black pepper, ground fresh
provide at least 6 cups	from the mill
cooking liquid when added	¼ cup freshly grated
to the water used for blanch-	*parmigiano-reggiano* cheese
ing the asparagus	1 tablespoon parsley chopped
3 tablespoons butter	very fine

1. Cut off 1 inch or more from the butt end of the asparagus spears to expose the moist part of each stalk, then pare the asparagus and wash it as described on page 466.

2. Choose a pan that can accommodate all the asparagus lying flat. Put in enough water to come 2 inches up the sides of the pan, and 1 tablespoon salt. Turn on the heat to medium high and when the water boils, slip in the asparagus and cover the pan. Cook for 4 to 5 minutes after the water returns to a boil, depending on the freshness and thickness of the stalks. Drain the asparagus when tender, but still firm, without discarding their water. Set aside to cool.

3. When the asparagus is cool enough to handle, cut off the tips of the spears about 1¼ to 1½ inches from the top and set aside, and cut the rest of the spears into ½-inch pieces, discarding any portion of the bottoms that seems particularly tough and stringy.

4. Add enough broth to the asparagus blanching water to make about 6 cups, and bring it to a very slow, steady simmer on a burner near where you'll be cooking the *risotto*.

5. Put 1 tablespoon of butter, the vegetable oil, and the chopped onion in a broad, sturdy pot, turn on the heat to medium high, and cook the onion, stirring, until it becomes translucent. Add the cut-up asparagus stalks, but not the spear tips. Cook for a minute or so, stirring thoroughly to coat the asparagus well.

6. Add the rice, stirring quickly and thoroughly until the grains are coated well. Add ½ cup of the simmering broth and asparagus water, and cook

the rice following the directions in Steps 3 and 4 of the basic white *risotto* recipe on page 245.

7. Cook the rice until it is tender, but firm to the bite, with barely enough liquid remaining to make the consistency somewhat runny. Off heat, add the reserved asparagus tips, a few grindings of pepper, the remaining 2 tablespoons of butter, and all the grated Parmesan, and stir thoroughly until the cheese melts and clings to the rice. Taste and correct for salt. Mix in the chopped parsley. Transfer to a platter and serve promptly.

Risotto with Celery

WHEN WORKING with this recipe, do not discard all the leafy celery tops because some will be cooked with the *risotto* from the start to accentuate the celery aroma. Part of the stalk goes in later to retain some of its textural interest.

For 6 servings

5 cups Basic Homemade Meat
    Broth, prepared as directed
    on page 15, OR 1 cup
    canned beef broth diluted
    with 4 cups water
3 tablespoons butter
2 tablespoons vegetable oil
½ cup chopped onion
2 cups celery stalk diced very
    fine

1 tablespoon chopped leafy tops
    of the celery heart
Salt
2 cups Arborio or other import-
    ed Italian *risotto* rice
Black pepper, ground fresh
    from the mill
⅓ cup freshly grated
    parmigiano-reggiano cheese
1 tablespoon chopped parsley

1. Bring the broth to a very slow, steady simmer on a burner near where you'll be cooking the *risotto*.

2. Put 2 tablespoons of the butter, the vegetable oil, and the chopped onion in a broad, sturdy pot, turn on the heat to medium high. Cook and stir the onion until it becomes translucent, then add half the diced celery stalk, all the chopped leaves, and a pinch of salt. Cook for 2 or 3 minutes, stirring frequently to coat the celery well.

3. Add the rice, stirring quickly and thoroughly until the grains are coated well. Add ½ cup of simmering broth, and cook the rice following the directions in Steps 3 and 4 of the basic white *risotto* recipe on page 245.

4. When the rice has cooked for 10 minutes, add the remaining diced celery, and continue to stir and add broth as needed, a little at a time.

5. Cook the rice until it is tender, but firm to the bite, with barely enough

Risotto with Celery (continued)

liquid remaining to make the consistency somewhat runny. Off heat, add a few grindings of pepper, the remaining 1 tablespoon of butter, and all the grated Parmesan, and stir thoroughly until the cheese melts and clings to the rice. Taste and correct for salt. Mix in the chopped parsley. Transfer to a platter and serve promptly.

Risotto with Zucchini

For 6 servings

4 medium or 6 small zucchini	2 tablespoons butter
2 tablespoons vegetable oil	2 cups Arborio or other import-
3 tablespoons onion chopped	ed Italian *risotto* rice
coarse	Black pepper, ground fresh
½ teaspoon garlic chopped very	from the mill
fine	¼ cup freshly grated
Salt	*parmigiano-reggiano* cheese,
5 cups Basic Homemade Meat	plus additional cheese at the
Broth, prepared as directed	table
on page 15, OR 1 cup	1 tablespoon chopped parsley
canned beef broth diluted	
with 4 cups water	

1. Soak the zucchini in cold water, scrub them clean, and cut off both ends as described in greater detail on page 530. Cut the cleaned zucchini into disks ½ inch thick.

2. Put all the vegetable oil and the chopped onion in a broad, sturdy pot, and turn on the heat to medium high. Cook and stir the onion until it becomes translucent, then add the chopped garlic. When the garlic becomes lightly colored, add the sliced zucchini, and turn the heat down to medium low. Cook for about 10 minutes, turning the zucchini from time to time, then add a pinch of salt. Continue cooking until the zucchini become colored a rich gold, another 15 minutes or so.

Ahead-of-time note ✸ The recipe may be cooked several hours or a day or two in advance up to this point. If resuming the same day, do not refrigerate the zucchini. When refrigerating, store tightly covered with plastic wrap.

3. Bring the broth to a very slow, steady simmer on a burner near where you'll be cooking the *risotto*.

4. Add 1 tablespoon butter to the zucchini and turn on the heat to high.

Add the rice, stirring quickly and thoroughly until the grains are coated well.

5. Add ½ cup of simmering broth, and cook the rice following the directions in Steps 3 and 4 of the basic white *risotto* recipe on page 245.

6. Cook the rice until it is tender, but firm to the bite, with barely enough liquid remaining to make the consistency somewhat runny. Off heat, add a few grindings of pepper, the remaining tablespoon of butter, and all the grated Parmesan, and stir thoroughly until the cheese melts and clings to the rice. Taste and correct for salt. Mix in the chopped parsley. Transfer to a platter and serve promptly with grated Parmesan on the side.

Risotto with Spring Vegetables, Tomato, and Basil

For 6 servings

1 medium or 2 small zucchini
5 cups Basic Homemade Meat
    Broth, prepared as directed
    on page 15, OR 1 cup
    canned beef broth diluted
    with 4 cups water
3 tablespoons butter
2 tablespoons vegetable oil
⅓ cup chopped onion
⅓ cup carrot diced very fine
⅓ cup celery diced very fine
Salt

2 cups Arborio or other im-
    ported Italian *risotto* rice
½ cup shelled fresh young peas
    OR thawed frozen peas
1 ripe, firm, fresh tomato,
    skinned raw with a peeler,
    seeded, and diced fine
⅓ cup freshly grated
    parmigiano-reggiano cheese
6 or more fresh basil leaves,
    washed and shredded by
    hand

1. Soak the zucchini in cold water, scrub them clean, and cut off both ends as desribed in greater detail on page 530. Dice them very fine.

2. Bring the broth to a very slow, steady simmer on a burner near where you'll be cooking the *risotto*.

3. Put 2 tablespoons of the butter, all the vegetable oil, and the chopped onion in a broad, sturdy pot, turn on the heat to medium high, and cook the onion until it becomes colored a fine golden brown.

4. Add the diced carrot and celery, and cook for about 5 minutes, stirring from time to time to coat them well. Add the diced zucchini, one or two pinches of salt, and cook for 8 minutes more, stirring occasionally.

Risotto with Spring Vegetables (continued)

5. Using a slotted spoon or skimmer, remove half the vegetables in the pot, and set aside. Turn on the heat to high. Add the rice, stirring quickly and thoroughly until the grains are coated well. If using fresh peas, add now.

6. Add ½ cup of simmering broth, and cook the rice following the directions in Steps 3 and 4 of the basic white *risotto* recipe on page 245.

7. When the rice has cooked for 20 to 25 minutes, add the cooked vegetables you had set aside earlier, the diced tomato, and the thawed frozen peas, if you are not using the fresh. Cook the rice until it is tender, but firm to the bite, with barely enough liquid remaining to make the consistency somewhat runny. Off heat, add the remaining tablespoon of butter, and all the grated Parmesan, and stir thoroughly until the cheese melts and clings to the rice. Taste and correct for salt. Mix in the shredded basil. Transfer to a platter and serve promptly.

Paniscia—Risotto with Vegetables and Red Wine

Paniscia is a merger of two lusty dishes: A *risotto,* cooked with red wine, and a generously endowed minestrone, the mighty vegetable soup from Novara, described on page 109.

In Novara, one of the ingredients of the dish is soft salami made from donkey meat, *salam d'la duja.* To replace, look for a high-quality, tender salami that is neither too spicy nor too garlicky. To hew as closely as possible to the original character of *la paniscia,* the wine should be a good Piedmontese red, a Spanna, a fine Barbera, a Dolcetto. Should you be unable to find them, look for a good Zinfandel, a Shiraz, or a Côte du Rhône.   *For 6 servings*

¼ cup vegetable oil
3 tablespoons chopped onion
¼ cup tender, mild salami chopped fine (see prefatory remarks above)
2 cups Arborio or other imported Italian *risotto* rice
2 cups dry red wine (see prefatory remarks above)
2½ cups Novara's Bean and Vegetable Soup, produced

with the recipe on page 109.
1 tablespoon butter
Black pepper, ground fresh from the mill
Salt
Freshly grated *parmigiano-reggiano* cheese at the table

1. Put all the vegetable oil, the chopped onion, and salami in a broad, sturdy pot, turn on the heat to medium high, and cook, stirring from time to time, until the onion becomes colored a deep gold.

2. Add the rice, stirring quickly and thoroughly until the grains are coated well. Add ½ cup of wine, and cook the rice following the directions in Steps 3 and 4 of the basic white *risotto* recipe on page 245. Add more wine, a little at a time, when needed. When you have used up the wine, switch to warm water.

3. When the rice has cooked for 15 minutes, add the bean and vegetable soup, mixing it in thoroughly. Continue cooking the rice with a half cupful of water at a time, stirring always. Cook the rice until it is tender, but firm to the bite, with barely enough liquid remaining to make the consistency somewhat runny. Off heat, add the tablespoon of butter and several liberal grindings of pepper, taste and correct for salt, stir well, and transfer to a serving platter. Allow to settle for a few minutes, then serve with grated Parmesan on the side.

Risotto with Clams

For 6 servings

3 dozen littleneck clams, the smallest you can find
1 tablespoon onion chopped fine
5 tablespoons extra virgin olive oil
2 teaspoons garlic chopped fine
2 tablespoons chopped parsley

2 cups Arborio or other imported Italian *risotto* rice
⅓ cup dry white wine
Chopped hot red chili pepper, to taste
Salt
Black pepper, ground fresh from the mill

1. Wash and scrub the clams as described on page 121. Discard those that stay open when handled. Put them in a pan broad enough so that the clams don't need to be piled up more than 3 deep, cover the pan, and turn on the heat to high. Check the clams frequently, turning them over, and removing them from the pan as they open their shells.

2. When all the clams have opened up, detach their meat from the shells and, unless they are exceptionally small, cut them up in 2 or even 3 pieces. Put the clam meat in a bowl and cover with its own juices from the pan. To be sure, as you are doing this, that any sand is left behind, tip the pan and gently spoon up the liquid from the top.

Risotto with Clams (continued)

3. Let the clams rest for 20 or 30 minutes, so that they may shed any sand still clinging to their meat, then retrieve them gently with a slotted spoon. Set them aside in a small bowl. Line a strainer with paper towels, and filter the clam juices through the paper into a separate bowl.

Ahead-of-time note ❀ The steps above may be completed 2 or 3 hours in advance. When doing so, spoon some of the filtered juice over the clam meat to keep it moist.

4. Bring 5 cups of water to a very slow, steady simmer on a burner near where you'll be cooking the *risotto*.

5. Put the chopped onion and 3 tablespoons of the olive oil in a broad, sturdy pot, and turn on the heat to medium high. Cook and stir the onion until it becomes translucent, then add the garlic. When it becomes colored a pale gold, add 1 tablespoon of the parsley, stir, then add the rice. Stir quickly and thoroughly for 15 or 20 seconds, until the grains are coated well.

6. Add the wine, and cook the rice following the directions in Steps 3 and 4 of the basic white *risotto* recipe on page 245. When all the wine is gone, add the filtered clam juices, and when these have evaporated, continue with the water you have kept simmering, adding a ½ cup of it at a time when needed. At any point, while the rice is cooking, add chopped hot chili pepper, salt, and a few grindings of black pepper.

7. Cook the rice until it is tender, but firm to the bite, with barely enough liquid remaining to make the consistency somewhat runny. Add the clams, the remaining tablespoon of parsley, and the remaining 2 tablespoons of olive oil, mixing them thoroughly with the *risotto*. Transfer to a platter, and serve promptly.

Risotto with Beef, Rosemary, Sage, and Barolo Wine, Alba Style

For 6 servings

5 cups Basic Homemade Meat Broth, prepared as directed on page 15, OR 1 cup canned beef broth diluted with 4 cups water

3 tablespoons butter

3 tablespoons *pancetta* chopped very fine

1½ teaspoons garlic chopped very fine

Chopped rosemary leaves, 1½ teaspoons if fresh, ¾ teaspoon if dried

Chopped sage leaves, 2 teaspoons if fresh, 1 teaspoon if dried

¼ pound ground beef chuck

Salt

Black pepper, ground fresh from the mill

1⅓ cups Barolo wine (see note below)

2 cups Arborio or other imported Italian *risotto* rice

⅓ cup freshly grated *parmigiano-reggiano* cheese, plus additional cheese at the table

Note ❀ Barolo, perhaps Italy's greatest red wine, and certainly its most profound in flavor, can satisfactorily be replaced in this preparation by its closest relative, Barbaresco. For other substitutions, look for wines derived from the same distinctive *nebbiolo* grape, such as Gattinara, Spanna, Carema, or Sfursat. You could try still other red wines, and although you might well make an excellent *risotto* with them, it would not be *this risotto*.

1. Bring the broth to a very slow, steady simmer on a burner near where you'll be cooking the *risotto*.

2. Put 1 tablespoon of butter, the *pancetta*, and the garlic in a broad, sturdy pot, turn on the heat to medium high, and stir from time to time as you cook. When the garlic becomes colored a very pale gold, add the rosemary and sage, cook, and stir for a few seconds, then add the ground meat. Crumble the meat with a fork, and turn it over several times to brown and coat it well, adding salt and a generous grinding of pepper.

3. When the meat has been well browned, add 1 cup of the red wine. Cook at a simmer, letting the wine bubble away until it becomes reduced to a film on the bottom of the pan.

Risotto with Beef (continued)

4. Turn up the heat, and add the rice. Stir quickly and thoroughly until the grains are coated well.

5. Add ½ cup of simmering broth, and cook the rice following the directions in Steps 3 and 4 of the basic white *risotto* recipe on page 245. When the rice is just about done, but still rather firm, after approximately 25 minutes, add the remaining wine, and finish cooking, stirring constantly, until all the wine has evaporated.

6. Off heat, add the 2 tablespoons of butter and the grated Parmesan, and stir thoroughly, turning the *risotto* over and over until the cheese has been well distributed and has melted. Taste and correct for salt. Transfer to a platter and serve promptly, with additional grated cheese on the side.

Risotto with Bolognese Meat Sauce

For 6 servings

5 cups Basic Homemade Meat
  Broth, prepared as directed
  on page 15, or 1 cup
  canned beef broth diluted
  with 4 cups water
1¼ cups Bolognese Meat Sauce,
  prepared from the recipe on
  page 203

2 cups Arborio or other imported Italian *risotto* rice
1 tablespoon butter
¼ cup freshly grated
  parmigiano-reggiano cheese,
  plus additional cheese at
  the table
Salt, if required

1. Bring the broth to a very slow, steady simmer on a burner near where you'll be cooking the *risotto.*

2. Put the meat sauce in a broad, sturdy pot, turn on the heat to medium, and bring it to a steady, gentle simmer. Add the rice and stir thoroughly for about 1 minute until the grains are coated well.

3. Add ½ cup of simmering broth and cook the rice following the directions in Steps 3 and 4 of the basic white *risotto* recipe on page 245.

4. Finish cooking the rice with broth or, if you have no more broth, with water. Cook the rice until it is tender, but firm to the bite, with no more liquid remaining in the pot.

5. Off heat, swirl in the tablespoon of butter and all the grated Parmesan, and stir thoroughly until the cheese melts and clings to the rice. Taste and correct for salt. Transfer to a platter and serve promptly with grated cheese on the side.

Risotto with Sausages

For 6 servings

5 cups Basic Homemade Meat Broth, prepared as directed on page 15, OR 1 cup canned beef broth diluted with 4 cups water
2 tablespoons onion chopped fine
2 tablespoons butter
2 tablespoons vegetable oil
¾ pound mild, sweet pork sausage, cut into disks about ⅓ inch thick

¼ cup dry white wine
2 cups Arborio or other imported Italian *risotto* rice
Black pepper, ground fresh from the mill
3 tablespoons freshly grated *parmigiano-reggiano* cheese
Salt, if required

1. Bring the broth to a very slow, steady simmer on a burner near where you'll be cooking the *risotto*.

2. Put the chopped onion, 1 tablespoon of the butter, and the vegetable oil in a broad, sturdy pot, and turn on the heat to medium high. Cook and stir the onion until it becomes translucent, then add the sliced sausage. Cook until the sausage is browned well on both sides, then add the wine, stirring from time to time. When the wine has bubbled away completely, add the rice, stirring quickly and thoroughly until the grains are coated well.

3. Add ½ cup of simmering broth, and cook the rice following the directions in Steps 3 and 4 of the basic white *risotto* recipe on page 245.

4. Finish cooking the rice with broth or, if you have no more broth, with water. Cook the rice until it is tender, but firm to the bite, with no more liquid remaining in the pot.

5. Off heat, add a few grindings of pepper, the remaining tablespoon of butter, and all the grated Parmesan, and stir thoroughly until the cheese melts and clings to the rice. Taste and correct for salt. Transfer to a platter and serve promptly.

Molded Parmesan Risotto with Chicken Liver Sauce

THIS GRACEFUL presentation, suitable for a buffet table or a holiday dinner, can be adapted to a variety of combinations aside from the chicken livers suggested below. Bolognese Meat Sauce (page 203), Veal Stew with Sage, White

Wine, and Cream or Sautéed Sweetbreads with Tomatoes and Peas (pages 377 and 441), Fresh Mushrooms with Porcini, Rosemary, and Tomatoes (page 511), are just a few of the preparations that would look and taste good within the ring of white *risotto*.   *For 6 servings*

Risotto with Parmesan Cheese, produced by the recipe on page 244, using just 1 tablespoon butter and 1 tablespoon oil, and omitting the butter in Step 6

Chicken Liver Sauce, produced by the recipe on page 205, reducing the butter to just 1 tablespoon
A 6-cup ring mold
Butter for smearing the mold

Smear the mold lightly with butter. As soon as the *risotto* is done, spoon it all into the mold, tamping it down. Invert the mold over a serving platter, shake it and lift it away, leaving a ring of *risotto* on the plate. Pour the chicken liver sauce or another suitable preparation into the center of the ring, and serve promptly.

Boiled Rice with Parmesan, Mozzarella, and Basil

Butter and cheese melting in a bowl of hot, boiled rice is one of the unsung joys of the Italian table. The version given below is tossed with butter, Parmesan, mozzarella, and basil.   *For 4 servings*

4 tablespoons (½ stick) butter
6 ounces mozzarella, preferably imported buffalo-milk mozzarella
Salt
1½ cups white rice, preferably Arborio

⅔ cup freshly grated *parmigiano-reggiano* cheese
4 to 6 fresh basil leaves, shredded by hand

1. Bring the butter to room temperature and cut it into small pieces.
2. Shred the mozzarella on the largest holes of the grater or, if it is too soft to grate, cut it up very fine with a chopping knife.
3. Bring 3 quarts of water to a boil, add a tablespoon of salt, and as the water resumes boiling, add the rice. Stir immediately with a wooden spoon for about 5 or 10 seconds. Cover the pot and adjust heat to cook at a moder-

ate, but constant boil, until the rice is tender, but *al dente,* firm to the bite. It should take between 15 and 20 minutes, depending on the rice variety. Stir from time to time while the rice cooks.

4. Drain the rice and transfer to a warm serving bowl. Add the shredded mozzarella, mixing it in quickly and thoroughly so that the heat of the rice can string it out. Promptly add the grated Parmesan and stir well so that it can dissolve and cling to the rice. Add the butter, stir once more to melt and distribute it, add the shredded basil leaves, stir again, and serve immediately.

GNOCCHI

THE WORD *gnocco* in Italian means a little lump, such as the one that might be raised by sharply knocking your head against a hard object. Gastronomically speaking however, *gnocchi* should be anything but lumpish. Whether they are made of potatoes, *semolina* flour, or spinach and *ricotta,* as in the recipes that follow, the essential characteristic of well-made *gnocchi* is that they be fluffy and light.

Potato Gnocchi

GOOD COOKS in the Veneto, where cloud-light *gnocchi* are as much a part of the tradition as creamy *risotto,* are loath to add eggs to the potato dough. Some people do use eggs because the dough becomes easier to handle, but that method, which is called *alla parigina,* "Paris style," results in a tougher, more rubbery product.

The choice of potato is critical. Neither a baking potato, such as the Idaho, nor any kind of new potato, is suitable. The first is too mealy and the second is too moist, and if you use either, *gnocchi* are likely to collapse while cooking. The only reliable potato for *gnocchi* is the more or less round, common kind known as a "boiling" potato. In Italy, where there are no baking potatoes, and both new and old are of the boiling, waxy variety, you would ask for "old" potatoes if you are making *gnocchi.*   *For 6 servings*

1½ pounds boiling potatoes
1½ cups unbleached all-
    purpose flour

Recommended sauce ✺ *Gnocchi* take well to many sauces, but three particularly happy choices are Tomato Sauce with Onion and Butter, page 152; Pesto, page 176; and Gorgonzola Sauce, page 194.

1. Put the potatoes with their skins on in a pot of abundant water, and bring to the boil. Cook until tender. Avoid testing them too often by puncturing with a fork because they may become waterlogged. When done, drain them and pull off their skins while hot. Purée them through a food mill and onto a work surface while they are still warm.

2. Add most of the flour to the puréed potatoes and knead into a smooth mixture. Some potatoes absorb less flour than others, so it is best not to add all the flour until you know exactly how much they will take. Stop adding flour when the mixture has become soft and smooth, but still slightly sticky.

3. Dust the work surface lightly with flour. Divide the potato and flour mass into 2 or more parts and shape each of them into a sausage-like roll about 1 inch thick. Slice the rolls into pieces ¾ inch long. While working with *gnocchi,* dust your hands and the work surface repeatedly with flour.

4. You must now shape the *gnocchi* so that they will cook more evenly and hold sauce more successfully. Take a dinner fork with long, slim tines, rounded if possible. Working over a counter, hold the fork more or less parallel to the counter and with the concave side facing you.

With the index finger of your other hand, hold one of the cut pieces against the inside curve of the fork, just below the tips of the prongs. At the same time that you are pressing the piece against the prongs, flip it away from the tips and in the direction of the fork's handle. The motion of the finger is flipping, not dragging. As the piece rolls away from the prongs, let it drop to the counter. If you are doing it correctly, it will have ridges on one side formed by the 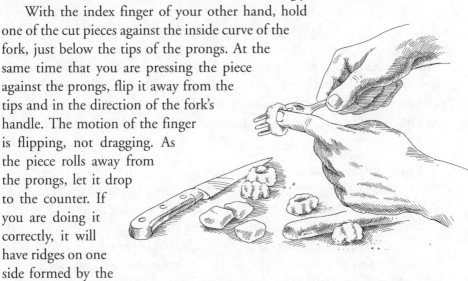 tines and a depression on the other formed by your fingertip. When *gnocchi* are shaped in this manner, the middle section is thinner and becomes more tender in cooking, while the ridges become grooves for sauce to cling to.

5. Choose, if possible, a broad pan of about 6 quarts' capacity and approximately 12 inches in diameter. The broader the better because it will accommodate more *gnocchi* at one time. Put in about 4 quarts of water, bring to a boil, and add salt. Before putting in the whole first batch of *gnocchi,* drop in just 2 or 3. Ten seconds after they have floated to the surface, retrieve them

Potato Gnocchi (continued)

and taste them. If the flavor is too floury, you must add 2 or 3 seconds to the cooking time; if they are nearly dissolved, you must subtract 2 or 3 seconds. Drop in the first full batch of *gnocchi,* about 2 dozen. In a short time they will float to the surface. Let them cook the 10 seconds, or more, or less, that you have determined they need, then retrieve them with a colander scoop or a large slotted spoon, and transfer to a warm serving platter. Spread over them some of the sauce you are using and a light sprinkling of grated Parmesan. Drop more *gnocchi* in the pot and repeat the whole operation. When all the *gnocchi* are done, pour the rest of the sauce over them and more grated Parmesan, turn them rapidly with a wooden spoon to coat them well, and serve at once.

Note ❦ If the potatoes you work with produce *gnocchi* dough that dissolves or collapses in cooking, you must add 1 whole egg to the puréed potatoes.

Spinach and Ricotta Gnocchi

WHEN YOU EAT the spinach and *ricotta gnocchi* in the recipe given below it will remind you of the stuffing of spinach- or chard-filled *tortelloni* without the pasta around it. As the instructions that follow will show, they can be served like potato *gnocchi,* or as soup dumplings, or gratinéed like *semolina gnocchi.*

For 4 servings

1 pound fresh spinach OR 1 ten-ounce package frozen leaf spinach, thawed	Salt
	¾ cup fresh *ricotta*
	⅔ cup all-purpose flour
2 tablespoons butter	2 egg yolks
1 tablespoon onion chopped very fine	1 cup freshly grated *parmigiano-reggiano* cheese, plus additional cheese at the table
2 tablespoons chopped pro-sciutto OR for milder flavor, boiled unsmoked ham	Whole nutmeg

Recommended sauce ❦ Tomato Sauce with Heavy Cream on page 155 may be the most appealing, both in flavor and appearance; another excellent combination is with Butter and Sage Sauce, page 192. Spinach and Ricotta Gnocchi are delicious as soup dumplings, served in Basic Homemade Meat Broth, page 15.

1. *If using fresh spinach:* Soak it in several changes of water, and cook it with salt until tender, as described on page 89. Drain it, and as soon as it is cool enough to handle, squeeze it gently in your hands to drive out as much moisture as possible, chop it rather coarse, and set aside.

If using thawed frozen leaf spinach: Cook in a covered pan with salt for about 5 minutes. Drain it, when cool squeeze all the moisture out of it that you can, and chop it coarse.

2. Put the butter and onion in a small skillet, and turn the heat on to medium. Cook and stir the onion until it becomes colored pale gold, then add the chopped prosciutto or ham. Cook for just a few seconds, long enough to stir 2 or 3 times and coat the meat well.

3. Add the cooked, chopped spinach and some salt, and cook for about 5 minutes, stirring frequently.

4. Turn out the entire contents of the skillet into a bowl, and when the spinach has cooled down to room temperature, add the *ricotta* and flour, and stir with a wooden spoon, mixing the ingredients well. Add the egg yolks, grated Parmesan, and a tiny grating—about ⅛ teaspoon—of nutmeg, and mix with the spoon until all the ingredients are evenly amalgamated. Taste and correct for salt.

5. Make small pellets of the mixture, shaping them quickly by rolling them in the palm of your hand. Ideally they should be no bigger than ½ inch across, but if you find it troublesome to make them that small, you can try for ¾ inch. The smaller the better, because they cook more quickly and favor a better distribution of sauce. If the mixture sticks to your palm, dust your hands lightly with flour.

6. *If serving with sauce:* Drop the *gnocchi,* a few at a time, into 4 to 5 quarts of boiling, salted water. When the water returns to a boil, cook for 3 or 4 minutes, then retrieve them with a colander scoop or a large slotted spoon, and transfer to a warm serving platter. Spread over them some of the sauce you are using. Drop more *gnocchi* in the pot and repeat the whole operation. When all the *gnocchi* are done, pour the rest of the sauce over them, turn them rapidly to coat them well, and serve at once, with grated Parmesan on the side.

If serving in soup: Bring 2 quarts of Basic Homemade Meat Broth, prepared as directed on page 15, to a boil. Drop in all the *gnocchi* and cook for 3 to 4 minutes after the broth returns to a boil. Ladle into soup plates and serve with grated Parmesan on the side. When served in soup, *gnocchi* go further, and the recipe above should produce 6 satisfactory servings.

Gratinéed Spinach and Ricotta Gnocchi

For 4 servings

The *gnocchi* from the recipe on
  page 262
A bake-and-serve dish
3 tablespoons butter plus more
  butter for greasing the pan

½ cup freshly grated
  parmigiano-reggiano cheese,
  plus additional cheese at
  the table

1. Preheat oven to 375°.

2. Thickly smear the baking dish with butter.

3. Drop the *gnocchi,* a few at a time, into 4 to 5 quarts of boiling, salted water. When the water returns to a boil, cook for 2 or 3 minutes, then retrieve them with a colander scoop or a large slotted spoon, and transfer to the baking dish. Drop more *gnocchi* in the pot and repeat the procedure described above, until you have got all the *gnocchi* cooked and in the baking dish.

4. Melt the 3 tablespoons of butter in a small saucepan and pour it over the *gnocchi,* distributing it evenly. Sprinkle the ½ cup grated Parmesan on top.

5. Bake on the uppermost rack of the preheated oven until the cheese melts, about 5 minutes. Remove from the oven and allow to settle for several minutes, then serve at table directly from the baking dish with grated Parmesan on the side.

Baked Semolina Gnocchi

THE BATTER for *semolina gnocchi,* which in Italy are often called *gnocchi alla romana,* uses the yellow, coarsely ground flour of hard or *durum* wheat.

The problem some cooks have with *semolina gnocchi* is that in the baking, the batter runs together and they become shapeless. This usually happens because it has not been cooked long enough with the milk. I have found the batter requires at least 15 minutes of cooking and stirring for it to acquire, and later maintain, the necessary consistency.   *For 6 servings*

1 quart milk
1 cup *semolina,* coarsely ground
  yellow hard-wheat flour

1 cup freshly grated
  parmigiano-reggiano cheese
Salt

3 egg yolks, lightly beaten in a
    saucer
2 tablespoons butter

An oven-to-table baking dish
    and butter to smear it
¼ pound prosciutto OR bacon
    OR boiled ham, cut into
    small strips

1. Put the milk in a heavy-bottomed saucepan and turn on the heat to medium low. If possible slip a flame-tamer under the pot. When the milk forms a ring of tiny, pearly bubbles, but before it comes to a boil, turn down the heat to low, and add the *semolina* flour, pouring it out of a clenched fist in a very thin, slow stream and, with a whisk in your other hand, beating it into the milk.

2. When all the *semolina* has gone into the pot, stir it with a long-handled wooden spoon. Stir continuously and with thoroughness, bringing the mixture up from the bottom and loosening it from the sides of the pot. Be prepared for some resistance because the flour and milk mixture quickly becomes very dense. In little more than 15 minutes and less than 20, the mixture forms a mass that comes cleanly away from the sides of the pot.

3. Remove from heat, let it cool just slightly, for about a minute, then add two-thirds of the grated Parmesan, 2 teaspoons of salt, the egg yolks, and the 2 tablespoons of butter to the batter. Mix immediately and rapidly to avoid having the egg yolks set.

4. Moisten a laminated or marble surface with cold water, and turn the *gnocchi* batter out over it, using a spatula to spread it to an even thickness of about ⅜ inch. Dip the spatula in cold water from time to time as you use it. Let the batter cool completely.

5. Preheat oven to 400°.

6. When the batter has cooled off completely, cut it into disks, using a 1½-inch biscuit cutter or a glass of approximately the same diameter. Moisten the tool from time to time in cold water as you use it. (Do not discard the trimmings, see the note below.)

7. Smear the bottom of a bake-and-serve dish lightly with butter. On the bottom, arrange the *gnocchi* in a single layer, overlapping them roof-tile fashion. On top spread the prosciutto or bacon or ham strips, sprinkle with the remaining grated Parmesan, and dot sparingly with butter. Bake on the

Baked Semolina Gnocchi (continued)

uppermost rack of the preheated oven for 15 minutes, until a light, golden crust has formed and the prosciutto or bacon or ham has become crisp. After removing from the oven, allow to settle for 5 minutes before bringing to the table and serving directly from the baking dish. If you find that the underside of the *gnocchi* has fused together, it is perfectly all right, as long as the top side maintains its shape.

Ahead-of-time note 🍲 *Semolina gnocchi* can be completely prepared and assembled in their baking dish up to 2 days in advance. Cover tightly with plastic wrap before refrigerating. Keep the trimmings, too, in the refrigerator, in a tightly sealed container.

Making Fritters from the Trimmings

Knead the trimmings together briefly into a ball up to a day or two before you plan to use them. When you are ready to make the fritters, divide the ball into croquette-size pieces, adding a pinch of salt and shaping them into short, plump forms tapered at both ends, about 2½ inches in length. Roll them in dry, unflavored bread crumbs and fry them in hot vegetable oil until they form a light crust all over. Serve as you would croquettes, or French fried potatoes, as though it were an accompanying vegetable, without any sauce.

CRESPELLE

WHAT ITALIANS CALL *crespelle* are very thin pancakes made from a batter of milk, flour, and eggs sautéed in butter. Italians work with them as if they were pasta wrappers, stuffing them with savory meat, cheese, or vegetable fillings. A basic recipe for making *crespelle* is given below, but any method you are comfortable with that produces thin, plain, unsweetened *crêpes* is satisfactory.

Crespelle

16 to 18 crespelle

THE BATTER

1 cup milk

¾ cup all-purpose flour

2 eggs

⅛ teaspoon salt

FOR COOKING THE CRESPELLE

1 to 1½ tablespoons butter

An 8-inch nonstick skillet

1. Put the milk in a bowl and add the flour gradually, sifting it through a sieve if possible, while you mix steadily with a fork or whisk to avoid making lumps. When you have added all the flour, beat the mixture until it is evenly blended.

2. Add the eggs, one at a time, beating them in rapidly with a fork. When both eggs have been incorporated into the batter, add the salt, stirring to distribute it.

3. Lightly smear the bottom of the skillet with some of the butter. Turn on the heat under the pan to medium low.

4. Give the batter a good stirring, and pour 2 tablespoons of it into the pan. Tilt and rotate the pan to distribute the batter evenly.

5. As soon as the batter sets and becomes firm and speckled brown, slip a spatula underneath it and flip it over to cook the other side. Stack the finished *crespelle* on a plate.

Crespelle (continued)

6. Coat the bottom of the skillet with a tiny amount of butter, and repeat the procedure described above until you've used up all the batter. Remember to stir the batter each time before pouring it into the pan.

Ahead-of-time note ❀ You can make *crespelle* several hours in advance, or even days. If you are doing them days ahead of time, interleave them with wax paper before refrigerating. If you are keeping them longer than 3 days, freeze them.

Baked Crespelle
with Bolognese Meat Sauce

For 4 to 6 servings

Crespelle (thin pancakes) produced with the recipe on page 267
Béchamel Sauce, prepared as directed on page 39, using 1 cup milk, 2 tablespoons butter, 1½ tablespoons flour, and ¼ teaspoon salt
1¼ cups Bolognese Meat Sauce, prepared as described on page 203
Whole nutmeg

Flameproof ware for baking and serving
Butter for smearing and dotting the baking dish
⅓ cup freshly grated *parmigiano-reggiano* cheese

1. Prepare the béchamel sauce, making it rather thin, the consistency of sour cream. When done, keep it warm in the upper half of a double boiler, with the heat turned to very low. Stir it just before using.

2. After making or reheating the meat sauce, draw off with a spoon any fat that may float on the surface. Put 1 cup of the sauce in a bowl, add ¼ cup béchamel, and a tiny grating—about ⅛ teaspoon—of nutmeg. Mix well to combine the ingredients evenly.

3. Preheat oven to 450°.

4. Choose a baking dish that can subsequently accommodate all the rolled up *crespelle* in a single layer. Lightly smear the bottom of the baking dish with butter. Lay one of the pancakes flat on a platter or a clean work surface, and spread a heaping tablespoon of the meat sauce filling over it, leaving uncovered a ½-inch border all around. Roll up the pancake, folding it

loosely and keeping it flat. Place on the bottom of the baking dish, its over-lapping edge facing down. Proceed in this manner until you have filled and rolled up all the *crespelle* and arranged them in the dish in a single layer without packing them in too tight.

5. Mix the remaining ¼ cup meat sauce with the ½ cup béchamel, and spread it over the *crespelle*. Sprinkle with the grated Parmesan, and dot lightly with butter.

6. Bake on the uppermost rack of the preheated oven for 5 minutes, then turn on the broiler and run the dish under it for less than a minute, just long enough for a light crust to form on top. Let the *crespelle* settle for a few minutes, then serve at table directly from the baking dish.

Baked Crespelle with Spinach, Prosciutto, and Parmesan Filling

For 4 to 6 servings

Crespelle (thin pancakes), produced with the recipe on page 267

1 pound fresh spinach OR 1 ten-ounce package frozen leaf spinach, thawed

Béchamel Sauce, prepared as directed on page 39, using 2 cups milk, 4 tablespoons (½ stick) butter, 3 tablespoons flour, and ¼ teaspoon salt

1 tablespoon butter plus more for greasing and dotting the baking dish

3 tablespoons onion chopped very fine

½ cup chopped prosciutto

1¼ cups freshly grated *parmigiano-reggiano* cheese

Whole nutmeg

Salt

Flameproof ware for baking and serving

1. *If using fresh spinach:* Soak it in several changes of water, and cook it with salt until tender, as described on page 89. Drain it, and as soon as it is cool enough to handle, squeeze it gently in your hands to drive out as much moisture as possible, chop it rather coarse, and set aside.

If using thawed frozen leaf spinach: Cook in a covered pan with salt for about 5 minutes. Drain it, when cool squeeze all the moisture out of it that you can, and chop it coarse with a knife, not in the food processor.

2. Prepare the béchamel sauce, making it rather thin, the consistency of sour cream. When done, keep it warm in the upper half of a double boiler, with the heat turned to very low. Stir it just before using.

Baked Crespelle with Spinach (continued)

3. Put the butter and chopped onion in a skillet or small sauté pan, and turn on the heat to medium. Cook and stir the onion until it begins to be colored a pale gold, then add the chopped prosciutto. Cook for less than a minute, stirring to coat it well. Add the chopped spinach, stir, and cook for another 2 minutes or so, turning it over 2 or 3 times to coat it thoroughly.

4. Turn out the entire contents of the pan into a bowl, add 1 cup of the grated Parmesan, a tiny grating—about ⅛ teaspoon—of nutmeg, ⅔ cup of béchamel, and a pinch of salt. Mix until all the ingredients are evenly combined. Taste and correct for salt.

5. Preheat oven to 450°.

6. Choose a baking dish that can subsequently accommodate all the rolled up *crespelle* in a single layer. Lightly smear the bottom of the baking dish with butter. Lay one of the pancakes flat on a platter or a clean work surface, and spread a heaping tablespoon of filling over it, leaving uncovered a ½-inch border all around. Roll up the pancake, folding it loosely and keeping it flat. Place on the bottom of the baking dish, its overlapping edge facing down. Proceed in this manner until you have filled and rolled up all the *crespelle,* and arranged them in the dish in a single layer without packing them in too tight.

7. Spread the remaining béchamel over the *crespelle.* Make sure the sauce covers the ends of the rolled up pancakes and fills some of the space between them. Sprinkle with the remaining ¼ cup grated Parmesan, and dot lightly with butter.

8. Bake on the uppermost rack of the preheated oven for 5 minutes, then turn on the broiler and run the dish under it for less than a minute, just long enough for a light crust to form on top. Let the *crespelle* settle for a few minutes, then serve at table directly from the baking dish.

Layered Crespelle with Tomato, Prosciutto, and Cheese

HERE THIN PANCAKES are assembled in the form of a pie and layered in the manner of *lasagne,* with an earthy filling whose robustness benefits from the moderating delicacy of the *crespelle*—and vice versa.

The "pie" should be no more than 8 or 9 layers thick. If you need to increase the recipe, distribute the additional *crespelle* among 2 or more baking pans.   *For 4 to 6 servings*

8 to 9 *crespelle* (thin pancakes) made with the recipe on page 267, using half the recipe, or *crêpes* made by any other comparable method

FOR THE FILLING

A tomato sauce made using:
  3 tablespoons extra virgin olive oil
  1 teaspoon chopped garlic
  1½ tablespoons chopped parsley
  ⅔ cup canned imported Italian plum tomatoes, cut up, with their juice
  Salt

A 9-inch round cake pan
Butter for greasing the pan
½ cup prosciutto shredded very fine
¼ cup freshly grated *parmigiano-reggiano* cheese
½ cup mozzarella, preferably imported Italian buffalo-milk mozzarella, diced very, very fine

1. Make the pancakes and set aside.

2. Preheat oven to 400°.

3. *To make the filling:* Put the olive oil and garlic into a small sauté pan, turn on the heat to medium, and cook the garlic, stirring, until it becomes colored a pale gold. Add the parsley. Cook just long enough to stir once or twice, then add the cut-up tomatoes with their juice and a pinch of salt. Adjust heat to cook at a steady simmer for about 15 minutes, stirring from time to time, until the tomato liquid has been reduced and has separated from the fat. Turn off heat.

4. Lightly smear the baking pan with butter. Choose the largest among the *crespelle* you made and place it on the bottom of the pan. Coat it thinly with tomato sauce, bearing in mind you'll need enough sauce to repeat the

Layered Crespelle (continued)

procedure 8 times. Over the sauce sprinkle some shredded prosciutto, grated Parmesan, and diced mozzarella, and cover with another pancake. Proceed thus until you have used up all the *crespelle* and their filling. Leave just enough sauce with which to dab the topmost pancake and grated Parmesan to sprinkle over it.

5. Bake on the uppermost rack of the preheated oven for 15 minutes. Transfer to a serving platter, without turning the *crespelle* "pie" over, but loosening it with a spatula and sliding it out of the pan. Allow to settle a few minutes before serving, or serve at room temperature.

POLENTA

Pasta has become so universally accepted as the national dish of Italy that it is difficult to believe that not much farther into the past than two generations ago, pasta was as foreign to certain Italian regions as it might have been to, say, Lapland. For a quarter of a millennium, in the Veneto and Friuli, as well as in much of Lombardy, it was *polenta,* more than any other food, that sustained life. Preparing it was a ritual, eating it was like receiving a sacrament.

It was made then, as it is today, in an unlined copper kettle, the *paiolo,* once kept hanging on a hook in the center of the fireplace. The hearth could often accommodate a bench on which the family sat as they watched the stream of cornmeal go glittering into the boiling kettle, and waited for the tireless stirring of the cook to transform it into a meal. When, three quarters of an hour later, the cornmeal became *polenta,* the golden mass was poured steaming onto a circular board. To a nineteenth-century Milanese novelist describing the scene, it looked like a harvest moon coming through the mist.

Polenta can be used in many ways, in a first or second course, as a side dish, or as an appetizer.

When Piping Hot and Soft

❋ With butter and grated Parmesan cheese melted into it, it can be eaten alone. A creamy *gorgonzola,* softened at room temperature for 4 to 6 hours, is marvelous when mashed into hot, very soft *polenta* together with some butter and Parmesan.

❋ It can provide a bed for warm steamed shrimp or other seafood that has been tossed with a little raw garlic, chopped very, very fine, and extra virgin olive oil.

❋ It goes with any stewed, braised, or roasted meat or fowl. It is the ultimate accompaniment for squab, pigeons, or quail. Whenever *polenta* is served soft and warm, it is desirable to have enough juices available from the meat it accompanies to sauce it lightly.

When Allowed to Cool

❀ It can be sliced and grilled and served, as in Venice, alongside a *fritto misto di pesce,* a mixed fry of seafood and vegetables.

❀ It can be sliced and baked like *lasagne,* with a variety of fillings.

❀ It can be cut into thin sticks or wedges, fried crisp in vegetable oil, and served with salads, or alongside Sautéed Calf's Liver and Onions, Venetian Style, page 438, or with aperitifs, before dinner.

There is both yellow and white *polenta,* depending on whether one uses meal from yellow or white corn, but yellow *polenta* is more common. The cornmeal itself may be either fine-grained or coarse. Coarse-grained yellow cornmeal is more robustly satisfying in texture and flavor, and it is the one suggested in the recipes below.

Making Polenta

About 4 cups

7 cups water
1 tablespoon salt
1⅔ cups coarse-grained import-
    ed Italian yellow cornmeal

An 8- to 10-cup bowl, prefer-
    ably steel or copper

1. Bring the water to a boil in a large, heavy pot.

2. Add the salt, keep the water boiling at medium-high heat, and add the cornmeal in a very thin stream, letting a fistful of it run through nearly closed fingers. You should be able to see the individual grains spilling into the pot. The entire time you are adding the cornmeal, stir it with a whisk, and make sure the water is always boiling.

3. When you have put in all the meal, begin to stir with a long-handled wooden spoon, stirring continuously and with thoroughness, bringing the mixture up from the bottom, and loosening it from the sides of the pot. Continue to stir for 40 to 45 minutes. The cornmeal becomes *polenta* when it forms a mass that pulls cleanly away from the sides of the pot.

Note on consistency ❀ As it begins to cool, *polenta* should be thick, and when moved, firm enough to quiver. From an Italian point of view, it is least appealing when it is as thin and runny as breakfast oatmeal.

4. Moisten the inside of the bowl with cold water. Turn the *polenta* out of

the pot and into the bowl. After 10 to 15 minutes, turn the bowl over onto a wooden block or a large round platter, unmolding the *polenta,* which will have a dome-like shape.

5. If serving it soft and hot, serve it at once. You may, if you wish, scoop out the upper central portion of the dome and fill it with whatever you have prepared to go with the *polenta*—sausages, pork ribs, a veal, beef, or lamb stew, fricasseed chicken, and so on.

Note ❀ If you are going to let it become completely cold and firm and later slice it, do not put the hot *polenta* in a bowl, but spread it flat on a board to a thickness of about 3 inches.

Ahead-of-time note ❀ If you are planning to slice *polenta* and grill it, bake it, or fry it, you *must* make it several hours in advance. It will keep for several days in the refrigerator. If you are refrigerating it for a few days, keep it whole, in one piece, and wrap it tightly with foil or plastic wrap.

Cleaning the pot ❀ After emptying the *polenta* from the pot, fill it with cold water and set it aside to soak overnight. In the morning most of the cornmeal film attached to the pot lifts off easily. If you are using an Italian-made unlined copper *polenta* pot, after emptying it in the morning and scraping away all the loosened residues, clean it with ¼ cup of vinegar and some salt. Rinse with plain water, without using any detergent, and wipe dry. Whenever you use an unlined copper pot, go over it again with vinegar and salt, and rinse thoroughly with plain water before each use.

Variation: Polenta by the No-Stirring Method

Stirring *polenta* in an open pot for the entire time it cooks undoubtedly yields the best product, mostly in terms of pure fragrance, and to a certain, but lesser extent in terms of overall flavor. It is nonetheless possible to make very good *polenta* with hardly any stirring. It will take the same amount of time, but it will free you from the stove for the better part of an hour. Use exactly the same ingredients in the basic recipe above, and proceed as follows:

1. Bring the water to a boil in a large, heavy pot.

2. Add the salt, keep the water boiling at medium-high heat, and add the cornmeal in a very thin stream, letting a fistful of it run through nearly closed fingers. You should be able to see the individual grains spilling into the pot. The entire time you are adding the cornmeal, stir it with a whisk, and make sure the water is always boiling.

3. When you have put in all the meal, stir with a long-handled wooden spoon for 2 minutes, then cover the pot. Adjust heat so that the water bub-

bles at a lively simmer, but not at a full boil. When the *polenta* has cooked for 10 minutes, uncover and stir for 1 full minute, then cover again. After another 10 minutes, stir again, then cover, let cook another 10 minutes, stir once more, and in 10 minutes, repeat the procedure.

4. Forty minutes will have elapsed, and the *polenta* will need another 5 minutes to shed its graininess and come together into a soft, creamy mass. Just before you take it off heat, stir it vigorously for about 1 minute, loosening it from the pot. Turn it out of the pot into a moistened bowl, and proceed as described in the basic recipe, page 274.

Instant Polenta

IT IS SO EASY and it takes such little time to make *polenta* using the instant product, that I wish I could regard it more favorably. Unfortunately, if you are acquainted with the texture and flavor of *polenta* cooked by the conventional slow method, you might not be wholly satisfied by the results the short-cut brings.

Not to be completely discouraging, I would recommend you rely on the instant *polenta* when you plan to integrate *polenta* with other savory ingredients, such as in the layered *polenta* described on page 277, or with a juicy dish of sausages, in which its shortcomings would become negligible. If it is to stand on its own, however, next to a fine roast quail, for example, you'd be likely to enjoy traditional *polenta* more.   *4 heaping cups*

6½ cups water   2 cups imported Italian instant
1 tablespoon salt   *polenta* flour

1. Bring the water to a boil.
2. Add the salt, wait for the water to resume a fast boil, then add the *polenta* flour in a thin stream. Stir it with a whisk or wooden spoon as you add it. Continue stirring for 1 full minute, cover the pot, and cook for 15 minutes, longer than most instructions on the packages indicate. Stir for 1 minute before turning it out of the pot and into a moistened bowl, as described in the basic recipe on page 274.

Baked Polenta
with Bolognese Meat Sauce

Polenta is used here as though it were pasta for *lasagne:* It is sliced, layered with meat sauce and béchamel, and baked.   *For 6 servings*

Béchamel Sauce, prepared as
    directed on page 39, using
    2 cups milk, 4 tablespoons

(½ stick) butter, 3 tablespoons flour, and ¼ tea-
spoon salt

Polenta, produced with the
    recipe on page 276, allowed

to become cold and firm for
slicing

A *lasagne* pan and butter for
    smearing it
2 cups Bolognese Meat Sauce,
    prepared with the recipe on
    page 203

⅔ cup freshly grated
    parmigiano-reggiano cheese

1. Prepare the béchamel sauce, making it rather thin, the consistency of sour cream. When done, keep it warm in the upper half of a double boiler, with the heat turned to very low. Stir it just before using.

2. Preheat oven to 450°.

3. Slice the cold *polenta* into layers about ½ inch thick, watching both sides of the mass as you cut to be sure to produce even slices.

4. Smear the *lasagne* pan lightly with butter. Cover with a layer of *polenta,* patching with more *polenta* where necessary to fill in gaps. Combine the meat sauce and the béchamel, spread some of it over the *polenta,* then add a sprinkling of grated Parmesan. Cover with another layer of *polenta,* repeating the entire procedure, leaving just enough of the béchamel and meat sauce mixture and grated cheese for a light topping over the next and final layer of *polenta.* Dot sparingly with butter.

5. Bake on the uppermost rack of the preheated oven for about 10 to 15 minutes, until a light brown crust has formed on top. After removing from the oven, allow to settle for a few minutes before serving.

FRITTATE

Defining frittate 🕸 A *frittata* may be described as an open-faced Italian omelet. Like an omelet, it consists of eggs cooked in butter with a variety of fillings. But the texture, appearance, and cooking procedure of a *frittata* are quite unlike those of other types of omelets. Instead of being creamy or runny, it is firm and set, although never to the point of being stiff and dry. It is not folded over into a thick, padded, tapered shape, but consists of a single thin layer, round in shape like the bottom of the pan in which it was made. The variable ingredients that determine the flavor of a *frittata* are mixed with the eggs while these are raw and become an integral part of them. *Frittate* are always cooked very slowly, over low heat.

Making a frittata 🕸 The basic method consists of the following steps:

1. Break the eggs into a bowl and beat them with a fork or whisk until the yolks and whites are evenly blended. Add the vegetables, cheese, or other flavor components required by the specific recipe, and mix thoroughly until all the ingredients are evenly combined.

2. Turn on your broiler. (See note below.)

3. Melt the butter in a skillet, preferably with non-stick surface, over medium heat. Do not let the butter become colored, but as soon as it begins to foam, pour the egg mixture—stirring it with a fork while tipping it out of the bowl—into the pan. Turn the heat down to very low. When the eggs have set and thickened, and only the surface is runny, run the skillet under the broiler for a few seconds. Take it out as soon as the "face" of the *frittata* sets, before it becomes browned.

Note 🕸 A *frittata* must be cooked on both sides and running it under a broiler, as described above, is the method I find most satisfactory. I have seen people flip a *frittata* in the air, like a flapjack, and continue cooking it over the stove. Others turn it over onto a plate, and slide it back into the pan. Or, if you like working with the oven, you can do it entirely there: Pour the mixture into a buttered baking pan, preferably round, and put it into a preheated 350° oven for 15 minutes, or until the *frittata* is no longer runny.

4. When ready, loosen the *frittata* with a spatula, slide it onto a platter, and cut it into serving wedges, like a pie.

Serving a frittata ❀ *Frittate* taste equally good when hot, warm, or at room temperature. They are at their least appealing cold out of the refrigerator. When cut into pie-like wedges, a *frittata* or an assortment of them will enrich an *antipasto* platter, make a very nice sandwich, travel beautifully to any picnic, or become a welcome addition to any buffet table.

Pan size ❀ All the *frittate* that follow were made in a 10-inch non-stick skillet. The pan must have a metal, flameproof handle so you can place it under the broiler.

Frittata with Cheese

For 4 to 6 servings

6 eggs
Salt
Black pepper, ground fresh
    from the mill

1 cup freshly grated
    parmigiano-reggiano OR
    Swiss cheese
2 tablespoons butter

Beat the eggs in a bowl and add the salt, a few grindings of pepper, and the grated Parmesan or Swiss cheese. Mix thoroughly until evenly blended. Melt the butter in the pan and when it begins to foam add the egg mixture and make the *frittata* following the basic method described on pages 278–279.

Frittata with Onions

LIKE A large part of Italian cooking, particularly that of the North, this *frittata* rests on a foundation of browned onions. If you want to, you can build on it, adding vegetables, herbs, sausages, or shrimp, according to your inclination or what you happen to have on hand. Anything may be added, but nothing need be because it is complete and satisfying just as it is.

For 4 to 6 servings

Frittata with Onions (continued)

4 cups onion sliced very thin	⅔ cup freshly grated
3 tablespoons extra virgin olive	*parmigiano-reggiano* cheese
oil	Black pepper, ground fresh
Salt	from the mill
5 eggs	2 tablespoons butter

1. Put the onions, olive oil, and some salt into a large sauté pan, turn the heat on to low, and cover the pan. Cook until the onions wilt and become greatly diminished in bulk, then uncover and continue cooking until the onions become colored a rich golden brown.

Ahead-of-time note ◉ You can cook the onions up to this point several hours or even a day or two in advance. You do not need to refrigerate them if you are going to use them later the same day. Let them come to room temperature before mixing them with the eggs.

2. Beat the eggs in a bowl and add the onions, grated Parmesan, salt, and a few grindings of pepper. When adding the onions, drain them of oil by using a slotted spoon or spatula to transfer them from the pan. Mix thoroughly. Melt the butter in the pan, and when it begins to foam, add the egg mixture and make the *frittata* following the basic method described on pages 278–279.

Frittata with Zucchini and Basil

For 4 to 6 servings

1 cup onion sliced very thin	Black pepper, ground fresh
¼ cup extra virgin olive oil	from the mill
Salt	6 to 8 fresh basil leaves, torn
3 medium zucchini (see note	into pieces, OR 1 tablespoon
below)	parsley chopped fine
5 eggs	2 tablespoons butter
⅔ cup freshly grated	
parmigiano-reggiano cheese	

Note ◉ If you have just made the stuffed zucchini on page 537, or any other stuffed zucchini dish, use the leftover cores of 6 to 8 zucchini for this *frittata*.

1. Put the onion, olive oil, and some salt into a large sauté pan, turn the

heat on to low, and cover the pan. Cook until the onion wilts and becomes greatly diminished in bulk, then uncover and continue cooking until the onion becomes colored a rich golden brown.

2. While the onion is cooking, soak the zucchini in cold water, scrub them clean, and cut off both ends, as described in greater detail on page 530. Cut the cleaned zucchini into disks ¼ inch thin. If you are using leftover cores, chop them into coarse pieces.

3. When the onion is done, add salt and the zucchini. Cook over medium heat until the zucchini have become colored a light nut brown, or if you are using the cores, until they have become a light brown, creamy pulp. Off heat, tip the pan, push the zucchini and onion toward the upended edge of the pan, and spoon off the oil that collects at the bottom. When drained of oil, transfer the vegetables to a bowl until their heat abates.

4. Make the *frittata* following the basic method described on pages 278–279, adding the grated Parmesan, the zucchini and onion, a pinch of salt, and a few grindings of pepper to the beaten egg. After mixing thoroughly to combine the ingredients well, add the torn-up basil or chopped parsley.

Frittata with Tomato, Onion, and Basil

For 4 to 6 servings

3 cups onion sliced very thin
¼ cup extra virgin olive oil
Salt
1 cup fresh, ripe plum tomatoes, skinned raw with a peeler, seeded, and chopped, OR canned imported Italian plum tomatoes, drained and chopped

5 eggs
2 tablespoons freshly grated *parmigiano-reggiano* cheese
Black pepper, ground fresh from the mill
½ cup fresh basil, torn into very small pieces
2 tablespoons butter

1. Put the onion, olive oil, and some salt into a large sauté pan, turn the heat on to low, and cover the pan. Cook until the onion wilts and becomes greatly diminished in bulk, then uncover and continue cooking until the onion becomes colored a rich golden brown.

2. Add the tomatoes and salt, turn the ingredients over thoroughly to coat well, and adjust heat to cook at a steady simmer for about 15 or 20 minutes, until the oil floats free of the tomatoes. Tip the pan, push the tomatoes and

Frittata with Tomato, Onion, and Basil (continued)

onion toward the upended edge of the pan, and spoon off the oil that collects at the bottom. When drained of oil, transfer the vegetables to a bowl until their heat abates.

Ahead-of-time note ❀ You can cook the onion and tomatoes up to this point several hours or even a day or two in advance. You do not need to refrigerate them if you are going to use them later the same day. If refrigerated, bring them to room temperature before proceeding with the *frittata*.

3. Beat the eggs in a bowl and add the tomatoes and onion, a pinch of salt, the grated Parmesan, and a few grindings of pepper. After mixing thoroughly to combine the ingredients well, add the torn-up basil. Melt the butter in the pan, and when it begins to foam, add the egg mixture and make the *frittata* following the basic method described on pages 278–279.

Frittata with Artichokes

For 6 servings

2 medium artichokes	Salt
½ lemon	Black pepper, ground fresh
1 teaspoon garlic chopped very	from the mill
fine	5 eggs
2 tablespoons extra virgin olive	¼ cup freshly grated
oil	*parmigiano-reggiano* cheese
2 tablespoons parsley chopped	2 tablespoons butter
very fine	

1. Trim the artichokes of all their tough parts following the detailed instructions on pages 57–59. As you work, rub the cut artichokes with the lemon to keep them from turning black.

2. Cut each trimmed artichoke lengthwise into 4 equal sections. Remove the soft, curling leaves with prickly tips at the base, and cut away the fuzzy "choke" beneath them. Cut the artichoke sections lengthwise into the thinnest possible slices, and squeeze the lemon over them to moisten them with juice.

3. Put the garlic and olive oil in a skillet, and turn on the heat to medium. Sauté the garlic until it has become colored a pale gold, add the sliced artichokes, the parsley, salt, and 2 or 3 grindings of pepper. Cook for about 1 minute, turning the artichokes over at least once completely to coat them

well. Add ⅓ cup water, put a lid on the pan, and cook until the artichokes are very tender, 15 minutes or more depending on their youth and freshness. If the artichokes reach tenderness quickly, there may still be liquid in the pan; uncover and boil it away while moving the artichokes around. If, on the other hand, the artichokes take long to cook, the liquid may become insufficient, in which case you must replenish it with 2 or 3 tablespoons of water as needed. Tip the pan, push the artichokes toward the upended edge of the pan, and spoon off the oil that collects at the bottom. When drained of oil, transfer to a bowl until their heat abates.

4. Beat the eggs in a bowl and add the artichokes, a pinch of salt, the grated Parmesan, and a few grindings of pepper. Melt the butter in the pan, and when it begins to foam, add the egg mixture and make the *frittata* following the basic method described on pages 278–279.

Frittata with Asparagus

For 4 to 6 servings

1 pound fresh asparagus	⅔ cup freshly grated
5 eggs	*parmigiano-reggiano* cheese
Salt	2 tablespoons butter
Black pepper, ground fresh	
from the mill	

1. Trim the spears, peel the stalks, and cook the asparagus as described on page 466. Do not overcook it, but drain it when it is still firm to the bite. Set aside to cool, then cut into ½-inch lengths.

2. Beat the eggs in a bowl and add the asparagus, 2 or 3 large pinches of salt, a few grindings of pepper, and the grated Parmesan. Melt the butter in the pan, and when it begins to foam, add the egg mixture and make the *frittata* following the basic method described on pages 278–279.

Frittata with Green Beans

For 4 to 6 servings

½ pound fresh green beans
Salt
5 eggs
Black pepper, ground fresh
   from the mill

1 cup freshly grated
   parmigiano-reggiano cheese
2 tablespoons butter

1. Snap the ends off the green beans, wash them in cold water, and drain. Bring 3 quarts water to a boil, add ½ tablespoon salt, and when the water resumes boiling, drop in the green beans. Cook, uncovered, at a moderate, but steady boil, until the beans are firm to the bite, but tender, 5 minutes or substantially longer, depending on how fine and young the beans are. Drain immediately and chop into coarse pieces. Set aside to let their heat abate.

2. Beat the eggs in a bowl and add the chopped beans, salt, a few grindings of pepper, and the grated Parmesan. Mix thoroughly. Melt the butter in the pan, and when it begins to foam, add the egg mixture and make the *frittata* following the basic method described on pages 278–279.

Frittata with Pan-Fried Onions and Potatoes

THE ONION-AND-POTATO mix for this *frittata* is based on the potatoes from the recipe on page 520. They are diced very fine and when pan-roasted produce a wonderful, crackling crust. Here they are paired with sautéed onions, and the combination of the crisp and the tender becomes exceptionally pleasing.

From 4 to 6 servings

The browned, diced potatoes
   made with ¼ cup vegetable
   oil and 2 cups potatoes,
   diced very fine, as described
   on page 520
1 cup onion sliced fine

5 eggs
Salt
Black pepper, ground fresh
   from the mill
2 tablespoons butter

1. When the potatoes have formed a golden crust all over, use a slotted spoon or spatula to transfer them to a cooling rack or a platter lined with paper towels.

2. Put the sliced onion in the same pan still containing the same oil used for cooking the potatoes. Turn the heat on to low, and cover the pan. Cook until the onion wilts and becomes greatly diminished in bulk, then uncover and continue cooking until the onion becomes colored a rich golden brown. Transfer to a bowl or plate, using a slotted spoon or spatula, to let their heat abate. Pour out the oil from the pan and wipe it clean so that you can use it for making the *frittata*.

3. Beat the eggs in a bowl and add the potatoes and onion, salt, and a few grindings of pepper. Mix thoroughly. Melt the butter in the pan, and when it begins to foam, add the egg-and-potato mixture and make the *frittata* following the basic method described on pages 278–279.

Frittata with Pasta

THE MOST DESIRABLE kind of pasta to use in a *frittata* is the dry, factory-made kind, because of its firm body, and the most appropriate shape is *spaghetti*, because of the bond its strands form with beaten eggs. You must cook the pasta and sauce it before you can mix it with the eggs. The recipe below uses one of the purest of *spaghetti* dishes, one tossed with butter, cheese, and parsley; if you are making pasta *frittata* for the first time, you will find this a good one to start with, to get the feeling, look, and taste of the finished dish. On subsequent occasions you can improvise all you like, saucing the *spaghetti* with tomato and basil, with fried eggplant, or fried zucchini. Except for clams or other shellfish, which would become dry, any sauce that works well on *spaghetti* works well in a *frittata*.   *For 4 servings*

½ pound *spaghetti*
Salt
Butter, 2 tablespoons for
   tossing the *spaghetti*, 1
   tablespoon for cooking the
   frittata

⅓ cup freshly grated
   parmigiano-reggiano cheese
2 tablespoons chopped parsley
3 eggs
Black pepper, ground fresh
   from the mill

1. Drop the *spaghetti* into 3 to 4 quarts boiling, salted water and cook until very firm to the bite. It should be a bit more *al dente*—more underdone—than you usually cook it because it will undergo further cooking in the *frittata*. Drain, and toss immediately and thoroughly with 2 tablespoons of butter, the grated cheese, and the parsley. Set aside until its heat abates somewhat.

Frittata with Pasta (continued)

2. Add the tossed, sauced *spaghetti,* salt, and a few grindings of pepper to the beaten egg, mixing thoroughly to distribute the egg evenly over the pasta. Put the 1 tablespoon butter in a skillet, turn the heat on to medium, and when the butter foam begins to subside, but before it darkens, put in the pasta and egg mixture.

3. Turn on the broiler.

4. Cook the *frittata* on top of the stove for 3 to 4 minutes without touching the pan. Then tilt the pan slightly, bringing its edge closer to the flame of the burner. Keep the pan in this position for about 1 minute, then rotate it a shade less than a full quarter turn, always keeping it tilted so that its edge is close to the flame. Repeat the procedure until you have come around full circle. Take a look at the underside of the *frittata,* lifting the edge gently with a spatula, to make sure it has formed a fine, golden crust all around; if it has not, cook a little longer where needed.

5. Run the pan under the broiler until the top side has formed a lightly colored crust. When ready, loosen the *frittata* with a spatula, slide it onto a platter, and cut it into serving wedges, like a pie.

Stuffed Spaghetti Frittata with Tomato, Mozzarella, and Ham

THERE IS a substantial and interesting difference between this *frittata* and the preceding one, as well as between it and every other *frittata:* Here there are two layers of *frittata* sandwiching a filling of tomatoes, mozzarella, and ham.

For 4 servings

½ pound *spaghetti*
Salt
Butter, 2 tablespoons for
    tossing the *spaghetti,* 1
    tablespoon for cooking the
    frittata
⅓ cup freshly grated
    parmigiano-reggiano cheese
2 tablespoons chopped parsley
2 tablespoons extra virgin olive
    oil
2 tablespoons chopped onion

½ cup canned imported Italian
    plum tomatoes, drained
    and cut up
½ cup mozzarella, preferably
    buffalo-milk mozzarella,
    diced very, very fine
½ cup boiled unsmoked ham
    chopped or diced very fine
3 eggs
Black pepper, ground fresh
    from the mill

1. Cook, drain, and toss the *spaghetti* with butter, cheese, and parsley exactly as described in the preceding recipe on page 285.

2. Put the olive oil and onion into a small saucepan, and turn on the heat to medium. Cook and stir the onion until it becomes colored a golden brown, then add the cut-up drained tomatoes and salt. Cook for about 20 minutes, until the oil floats free of the tomato. Take off heat.

3. When the tomatoes have cooled, mix in the diced mozzarella and ham. Tip the pan and spoon off most of the oil.

4. Add the tossed sauced *spaghetti,* salt, and a few grindings of pepper to the beaten egg, mixing thoroughly to distribute the egg evenly over the pasta. Put the 1 tablespoon butter in a skillet, turn the heat on to medium, and when the butter foam begins to subside, but before it darkens, put in just *half* the pasta and egg mixture, spreading it uniformly over the bottom of the pan. Then over it pour the tomato and mozzarella from the saucepan, spreading it evenly, and stopping a little short of the *frittata*'s edge. Pour in the remaining half of the *spaghetti* and egg mixture and cover the *frittata* in the pan, spreading it out to the edges of the pan. Finish cooking the *frittata,* following the directions in the preceding recipe for Frittata with Pasta, page 285.

FISH AND SHELLFISH

Grilled Fish, Romagna Style

LONG BEFORE my native region of Romagna, on the northern Adriatic shore, became known for its string of beach towns and their all-night discos, it was famous for its fish. Romagna's fishermen are unsurpassed in the art of grilling. Their secret, aside from the freshness of their catch, is to steep fish in a marinade of olive oil, lemon juice, salt, pepper, rosemary, and bread crumbs for an hour or more before broiling it. It's a method that works well with all fish, sweetening its natural sea flavor and keeping the flesh from drying out over the fire.   *For 4 or more servings*

2½ to 3 pounds whole fish,
    gutted and scaled, OR fish
    steaks
Salt
Black pepper, ground fresh
    from the mill
¼ cup extra virgin olive oil
2 tablespoons freshly squeezed
    lemon juice
A small sprig of fresh rosemary
    OR ½ teaspoon dried leaves
    chopped very fine

⅓ cup fine, dry, unflavored
    bread crumbs
OPTIONAL: a charcoal or wood-
    burning grill
OPTIONAL: a small branch of
    fresh bay leaves or several
    dried leaves

1. Wash the fish or the fish steaks in cold water, then pat thoroughly dry with paper towels.

2. Sprinkle the fish liberally with salt and pepper on both sides, put it on a large platter, and add the olive oil, lemon juice, and rosemary. Turn the fish two or three times to coat it well. Add the bread crumbs, turning the fish once or twice again until it has an even coating of oil-soaked bread crumbs. Marinate for 1 or 2 hours at room temperature, turning and basting the fish from time to time.

3. If using charcoal or wood, light the charcoal in time for it to form white ash before cooking, or the wood long enough in advance to reduce it to hot embers. If using an indoor gas or electric grill, preheat it at least 15 minutes before you are ready to cook.

4. Place the fish 4 to 5 inches from the source of heat. Do not discard its marinade. If cooking on charcoal or with wood, throw the bay leaves into the fire, otherwise omit. Grill on both sides until done, turning the fish once. Depending on the thickness of the fish steaks or the size of the whole fish, it may take between 5 and 15 minutes. While cooking, baste the top with the marinade. Serve piping hot from the grill.

Grilled Swordfish Steaks, Sicilian Salmoriglio Style

WHEREVER IN THE WORLD you may be when having fish prepared in the *salmoriglio* style, you might think you are breathing the pungent summer air of the Mediterranean. Olive oil, lemon juice, and oregano make a beguilingly fragrant amalgam that is brushed on smoking hot fish the moment it's lifted from the grill. The fish of choice is swordfish, as it would be on Sicily's eastern shore, but other steak fish such as tuna, halibut, mako shark, or tilefish are acceptable alternatives. The Sicilian practice of using rather thin slices is ideal because it makes it possible to keep the fish on the grill such a brief time that it doesn't have a chance to dry out.   *For 4 to 6 servings*

OPTIONAL: a charcoal grill
Salt
2 tablespoons freshly squeezed
    lemon juice
2 teaspoons chopped fresh
    oregano OR 1 teaspoon
    dried

¼ cup extra virgin olive oil
Black pepper, ground fresh
    from the mill
2 pounds fresh swordfish OR
    other fish steaks, sliced no
    more than ½ inch thick

1. If using charcoal, light it in time for it to form white ash before cooking. If using an indoor gas or electric grill, preheat it at least 15 minutes before you are ready to cook.

2. Put a liberal amount of salt, about 1 tablespoon, into a small bowl, add the lemon juice, and beat with a fork until the salt has dissolved. Add the oregano, mixing it in with the fork. Trickle in the olive oil, drop by drop, beating it in with the fork to blend it with the lemon juice. Add several grindings of pepper, stirring to distribute it evenly.

3. When the broiler or charcoal is ready, place the fish close to the source

Grilled Swordfish Steaks (continued)

of heat so that it cooks quickly at high heat. Grill it for about 2 minutes on one side, then turn it and grill the other side for 1½ to 2 minutes. It doesn't need to become brown on the surface.

4. Transfer the fish to a large, warm serving platter. Prick each steak with a fork in several places to let the sauce penetrate deeper. Use a spoon to beat and, at the same time, to pour the *salmoriglio* mixture of oil and lemon juice over the fish, spreading it evenly all over. Serve at once, spooning some sauce from the platter over each individual portion.

Note ✹ Freshness is essential to the fragrance of *salmoriglio* sauce. Do not prepare it long in advance. It is so simple and quick to do that you can make it while the grill is warming up.

Grilled Shrimp Skewers

THERE IS no other way I have ever come across that produces grilled shrimp as juicy as these. The coating of olive oil–soaked bread crumbs is what does it. When preparing it, bear in mind that there should be enough oil to film the shrimp, but not so much to drench them, enough bread crumbs to absorb oil and keep it from running, but not so much to bread them and form a thick crust.   *For 4 to 6 servings*

2 pounds medium shrimp, unshelled weight

3½ tablespoons extra virgin olive oil

3½ tablespoons vegetable oil

⅔ cup fine, dry, unflavored bread crumbs

½ teaspoon garlic chopped very fine

2 teaspoons parsley chopped very fine

Salt

Black pepper, ground fresh from the mill

Skewers

OPTIONAL: a charcoal grill

1. Shell the shrimp and remove their dark vein. Wash in cold water and pat thoroughly dry with cloth kitchen towels.

2. Put the shrimp in a roomy bowl. Add as much of the olive and vegetable oil, in equal parts, and of the bread crumbs as you need to coat the shrimp evenly, but lightly all over. You may not require all the oil indicated in the ingredients list, but if you have a large number of very small shrimp you

may need even more. When you increase the quantity, use olive and vegetable oil in equal parts.

3. Add the chopped garlic, parsley, salt, and pepper, and toss thoroughly to coat the shrimp well. Allow them to steep in their coating a minimum of 20 to 30 minutes, or up to 2 hours, at room temperature.

4. Preheat the broiler at least 15 minutes before you are ready to cook, or light the charcoal in time for it to form white ash before cooking.

5. Skewer the shrimp tightly, curling one end of each shrimp inward so that the skewer goes through at three points, preventing the shrimp from slipping as you turn the skewer on the grill.

6. Cook the shrimp briefly, close to the source of heat. Depending on their size and the intensity of the fire, about 2 minutes on one side and 1½ on the other, just until they form a thin, golden crust. Serve piping hot.

Grilled Shrimp, Cannocchie Style

THE PRAWN-LIKE crustaceans with a broad, flat body and mantis-like front claws that Italians call *cannocchie,* are found in the Adriatic, and nowhere else in the Western Hemisphere to my knowledge. (A closely related variety is caught off the coast of Japan, where it is known as *shako.*) The exceptionally tender, sweet, and salty flesh resembles that of no other shellfish. Restaurants in Venice serve *cannocchie* steamed, shelled, and dressed with olive oil and lemon juice. The name of the dish, *cannocchie con olio e limone,* is one every visitor to Venice who cares about eating well should memorize before arrival.

The way the fishermen of my town prepare *cannocchie* is rarely if ever found on a restaurant menu. They split the back of the shell along its whole length, marinate the shrimp in olive oil, bread crumbs, salt, and a prodigal quantity of black pepper, and grill them over very hot charcoal or wood embers. But how they are cooked is only half the story, it's how you eat them. You pick one up with your fingers, spread the shell open with your lips, and suck in the meat. In Romagna we call it eating *col bacio,* with a kiss. And a most savory kiss it is, as you lick from the shell its peppery coating of oil-soaked crumbs enriched by the charred flavor of the shell itself.

The shrimp in this recipe is prepared in the manner of *cannocchie,* and should be eaten in the same lip-smacking style. It's advisable to serve it with a plentiful supply of paper napkins.   *For 4 to 6 servings*

2 pounds medium to large
   unshelled shrimp
Round wooden toothpicks
1 cup unflavored bread crumbs
Salt

⅓ cup extra virgin olive oil
Black pepper, ground fresh
   from the mill
OPTIONAL: a charcoal or wood-
   burning grill

1. Wash the unshelled shrimp in cold water, then pat thoroughly dry with cloth kitchen towels.

2. Using scissors, cut the shell of each shrimp along the back and for its entire length down to the tail. Run a single toothpick into each shrimp, inserting it between the flesh of the belly and the shell. This is to straighten the shrimp and to keep it from curling while it cooks so that when done it resembles *cannocchie.*

3. When all the shrimp is prepared, put it in a bowl and add all the other ingredients. Be liberal with both salt and pepper. Turn the shrimp to coat it thoroughly, forcing a little of the marinade under the shell where it is cut. Let steep at room temperature for at least ½ hour, or as long as 2 hours, turning it from time to time.

4. If using charcoal or wood, light the charcoal in time for it to form

white ash before cooking, or the wood long enough in advance to reduce it to hot embers. If using an indoor gas or electric grill, preheat it at least 15 minutes before you are ready to cook.

5. If using charcoal or wood, put the shrimp in a hinged, double grill and close the grill tightly. If using an indoor broiler, place it on the broiler's grilling pan. Cook very close to the source of heat, about 2 minutes on one side and 1½ minutes on the other, or slightly more if the shrimp is very thick. When done, serve at once, with plenty of paper napkins available.

Shrimp Fried in Leavened Batter

THERE ARE MANY frying batters, each suited to a different objective. For a thin eggshell-like crust of matchless crispness, try the flour-and-water batter on page 530. For a crisp coating that is also light and fluffy, try the yeast batter given below. It is a favorite of cooks from Rome down to Palermo who use it for frying small shellfish and vegetables.

Skewering each shrimp, or 2 at a time if very small, with a toothpick as described in the recipe is not absolutely necessary, but it has its advantages. If you are using tiny shrimp, which would be the most desirable ones for this dish, it keeps them from forming lumps of two or three as they fry and permits them to maintain a clearly defined and attractive shape. And it is very helpful to have one end of the toothpick to hold on to when dipping the shrimp in the batter. *For 4 servings*

1 pound unshelled shrimp, as small as possible	½ package active dry yeast (about 1¼ teaspoons), dissolved in 1 cup luke-warm water
OPTIONAL: round wooden toothpicks	
2 eggs	1 cup flour
Salt	Vegetable oil for frying

1. Shell the shrimp and remove their dark vein. Wash in several changes of cold water and pat thoroughly dry with cloth kitchen towels.

2. OPTIONAL: Bend each shrimp following its natural curve, causing the head and tail to meet and slightly overlap. Skewer it with a toothpick holding tail and head in place.

3. Break both eggs into a bowl, add a large pinch of salt, and beat them well with a fork. Add the dissolved yeast, then add the flour, shaking it through a strainer, while beating the mixture steadily with a fork.

4. Put enough oil in a frying pan to come ¼ inch up its sides and turn on the heat to high. To determine when the oil is hot enough for frying, plop a drop of batter into it: If it stiffens and instantly comes to the surface, the oil is ready.

5. Dip the shrimp into the batter, letting the excess flow back into the bowl, and slip it into the pan. Do not put in any more shrimp at one time than will fit loosely without crowding the pan. As soon as the shrimp has formed a rich, golden crust on one side, turn it and do the other side. Using a slotted spoon or spatula, transfer the fried shrimp to a cooling rack to drain, or place it on a platter lined with paper towels.

6. Stir the batter with the fork, dip more shrimp, and repeat the procedure described above, until all the shrimp are done. Sprinkle with salt and serve promptly.

Fried Tidbits of Swordfish
or Other Fish

HERE WE HAVE an excellent Sicilian method to use when working with fish that tends to become dry. The fish is soaked for about 1 hour in an olive oil and lemon juice marinade, then it is fried. The cooking goes very fast because the fish is sliced thin and cut into bite-size morsels. When it comes out of the pan it is nearly as moist and tender as when it came out of the sea.

For 4 servings

2 pounds fresh swordfish OR
    other fish steaks, sliced ½
    inch thick
Salt
Black pepper, ground fresh
    from the mill
⅓ cup extra virgin olive oil

3 tablespoons parsley chopped
    very, very fine
¼ cup freshly squeezed lemon
    juice
2 eggs
Vegetable oil for frying
1 cup flour, spread on a plate

1. Cut the fish steaks into pieces that are more or less 2 by 3 inches.

2. Put a liberal quantity of salt and pepper into a broad bowl or deep platter, add the olive oil, parsley, and lemon juice, and beat with a fork until the ingredients are evenly blended. Put in the fish, turning the pieces over several times in the oil and lemon juice mixture to coat them well. Let the fish marinate at least 1 hour, but no more than 2, at room temperature, turning it from time to time.

3. Retrieve the fish from its marinade, and pat the pieces thoroughly dry with paper towels.

4. Break the eggs into a deep dish, beating them with a fork until the yolks and whites combine.

5. Pour enough vegetable oil into a frying pan to come between ¼ and ½ inch up its sides and turn on the heat to high.

6. While the oil heats up, dip a few pieces of fish into the beaten eggs. Pick up one of the pieces, let the excess egg flow back into the dish, and dredge the piece on both sides in the flour. Holding the piece by one end with your fingertips, dip a corner of it into the pan. If the oil around it bubbles instantly, it is hot enough and you can slip in the whole piece. Dredge more egg-coated fish in the flour and add it to the pan, but do not crowd the pan.

7. When the fish has formed a light golden crust on one side, turn it. When crust forms on the other side, transfer the fish, using a slotted spoon or spatula, to a cooling rack to drain, or place on a large plate lined with paper towels. When there is room in the pan, add more fish. When it is all done, sprinkle with salt and serve at once.

Pan-Roasted Mackerel with Rosemary and Garlic

HERE FISH is cooked by the same method one uses for making a roast of veal in Italy, and for the same reasons. The slow cooking in a covered pan keeps the flesh tender and juicy, its flavor uplifted by the fragrance of rosemary and garlic.   *For 4 servings*

4 small mackerel, about ¾
    pound each, gutted and
    scaled, but with heads and
    tails on
⅓ cup extra virgin olive oil
4 garlic cloves, peeled
A small sprig of rosemary OR 1
    teaspoon dried leaves,
    crumbled

Salt
Black pepper, ground fresh
    from the mill
Freshly squeezed juice of
    ½ lemon

1. Wash the fish under cold running water, then pat thoroughly dry with paper towels. Make 3 parallel, diagonal cuts on both sides of each fish, cutting no deeper than the skin.

Pan-Roasted Mackerel (continued)

2. Put the olive oil and garlic in an oval roasting pan, if you have one, or a sauté pan or other pot where the fish can subsequently fit side by side. Turn on the heat to medium, and cook the garlic until it becomes colored a pale gold. Put in the fish and the rosemary. Brown the fish well on both sides. Keep loosening it from the bottom with a metal spatula to keep it from sticking, and turn it over carefully to make sure it doesn't break up. Put salt and pepper on both its sides.

3. Add the lemon juice, cover with a tight-fitting lid, turn the heat down to low, and cook for about 10 to 12 minutes, until the flesh feels tender when prodded with a fork. Serve promptly when done.

Sautéed Snapper or Other Whole Fish with Mushrooms

FISH AND MUSHROOMS in Italy have a strong common bond, the garlic and olive oil with which they are customarily cooked. Both fish and mushrooms come together quite naturally in this recipe, but they are fully cooked independently and if you want to omit the mushrooms, the fish stands well on its own.

For 4 servings

FOR THE MUSHROOMS

½ pound fresh, firm white button mushrooms, cooked as described on page 509, with 2 tablespoons extra

virgin olive oil, 1 teaspoon chopped garlic, 2 teaspoons chopped parsley, and salt

FOR THE FISH

A 2- to 2½-pound whole fish, such as red snapper or sea bass, gutted and scaled, but with head and tail on
1 large or 2 small garlic cloves
2 tablespoons extra virgin olive oil
2 tablespoons onion chopped fine
2 tablespoons chopped carrot

2 teaspoons chopped parsley
1 whole fresh bay leaf OR ½ dried, crumbled fine
⅓ cup dry white wine
1 flat anchovy fillet, chopped fine, to a pulp
Salt
Black pepper, ground fresh from the mill

1. Wash the scaled and gutted fish under cold running water, then pat it thoroughly dry with paper towels.

2. Lightly mash the garlic with a heavy knife handle, just enough to split its skin and peel it.

3. Choose a sauté pan just large enough to accommodate the fish later, put in the olive oil and onion, and turn on the heat to medium-low. Cook the onion, stirring, until it becomes translucent, add the chopped carrot, and cook for about 2 minutes, stirring thoroughly to coat it well. Add the garlic and cook it, stirring, until it becomes lightly colored. Add the parsley, stir thoroughly once or twice, then put in the bay leaf, the wine, and the anchovy. Cook, stirring frequently, mashing the anchovy against the sides of the pan with the back of a wooden spoon until the wine has evaporated by half.

4. Put in the fish, season both fish and vegetables with salt and pepper, and cover the pan, setting the lid slightly ajar. Cook for about 8 minutes, depending on the thickness of the fish, turn it over carefully, using two spatulas or a large fork and spoon to keep it from breaking apart, sprinkling salt and pepper on the side you have just turned over. Cook for 5 minutes more, always with a cover on ajar, then add the optional mushrooms. Cover the pan, and let the fish and mushrooms cook together for no more than a minute. Serve promptly.

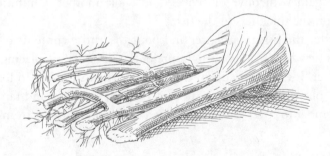

Sautéed Snapper or Bass with Finocchio, Sicilian Style

For 4 servings

2 small snappers OR sea bass, about 1¼ pounds each, scaled and gutted, OR an equivalent fillet of larger fish

2 large *finocchi*
¼ cup extra virgin olive oil
Salt
Black pepper, ground fresh from the mill

Sautéed Snapper or Bass with Finocchio (continued)

1. Wash the fish in cold water, inside and out. If using a fish fillet, separate it into two halves, remove the bones, but leave the skin on.

2. Cut off the *finocchio* tops down to the bulbs, and discard them. Trim away any bruised, discolored portion of the bulbs. Cut the bulbs lengthwise into thin slices less than ½ inch thick. Soak them in cold water for a few minutes and rinse.

3. Choose a sauté pan that can subsequently accommodate all the fish. Put in the olive oil, the sliced *finocchio,* salt, about ½ cup water, and turn on the heat to medium. Cover the pan and cook for 30 minutes or more, depending on the freshness of the *finocchio,* until it is completely wilted and very tender. If after 20 minutes, the *finocchio* appears still to be hard when prodded with a fork, add ¼ cup water.

4. When the *finocchio* is tender, uncover the pan, and turn up the heat to boil away completely any liquid left in the pan. Turn the *finocchio* slices frequently until they become colored a deep gold on both sides. Add a few grindings of pepper, turn the heat down to medium, and push the *finocchio* to one side to make room for the fish in the pan.

5. Put in the fish, skin side down if you are using fish fillet, sprinkle with liberal pinches of salt and grindings of pepper, and spoon some of the oil in the pan over it. Cover and cook for 6 to 7 minutes. Then gently turn the fish over, baste again with olive oil, cover, and cook another 5 minutes or so, depending on the thickness of the fish.

6. Transfer the fish to a platter and pour the entire contents of the pan over it. If using whole fish, you might prefer to fillet it before placing it in the serving platter. It's not difficult to do: Separate the fish into two lengthwise halves, pick out the bones, use a spoon to detach the head and tail, and it's done. Remember to cover with all the *finocchio* slices and juices from the pan.

Porgies or Other Small Fish Pan-Roasted with Marjoram and Lemon

PAN-ROASTING—the method that is neither sautéing nor braising, but something in between—is one of the basic techniques of the Italian kitchen for cooking fish as well as meat, chicken, and smaller birds. It is more controlled cooking than oven-roasting, combining the slow concentration of flavor that takes place in the dry air of the oven with the juiciness and superior texture one can achieve on top of the stove.

The recipe below is most successful with small, whole fish, but firm-fleshed, thick fillets with the skin on can also be used.   *For 4 to 6 servings*

4 small or 3 medium whole
    fish, such as porgies, bass,
    pompano, about ¾ to 1
    pound each, scaled and
    gutted, but with head and
    tail on
3 garlic cloves
3 tablespoons butter
2 tablespoons vegetable oil

1 cup flour, spread on a plate
1 teaspoon fresh marjoram
    leaves OR ½ teaspoon dried
Salt
Black pepper, ground fresh
    from the mill
1 tablespoon freshly squeezed
    lemon juice

1. Wash the fish inside and out in cold water, then pat thoroughly dry with paper towels.

2. Lightly mash the garlic with a heavy knife handle, just hard enough to split the skin, and peel it.

3. Choose a lidded sauté pan or deep skillet that will subsequently be able to accommodate all the fish without overlapping. Put in the butter and oil and turn on the heat to medium high.

4. When the butter and oil are quite hot, dredge the fish in flour on both sides, and put it in the pan together with the garlic and marjoram. If using thick fillets, put them in skin side down first.

5. Brown the fish for about 1½ minutes on each side. Add liberal pinches of salt, black pepper, and the lemon juice, cover the pan, and turn the heat down to medium. Cook for about 10 minutes, depending on the thickness of the fish, turning the fish over after 6 minutes or so.

6. Transfer to a warm serving platter, lifting the fish gently with two metal spatulas to keep it from breaking up, pour all the juices in the pan over it, and serve at once.

Halibut or Other Fish Steaks
Sauced with White Wine and Anchovies

For 4 servings

2 pounds halibut OR other fish
  steaks in slices 1 inch thick
½ cup extra virgin olive oil
⅔ cup flour, spread on a plate
1½ cups onion chopped fine
3 tablespoons chopped parsley
Salt
⅔ cup dry white wine

1 or 2 flat anchovy fillets
  (preferably the ones prepared at home as described
  on page 9), chopped to
  a pulp
Black pepper, ground fresh
  from the mill

1. Wash the fish steaks in cold water, then pat them thoroughly dry with paper towels. Do not tear or remove the skin that encircles them.

2. Choose a sauté pan that can subsequently accommodate all the fish without overlapping. Put in half the olive oil and turn on the heat to medium.

3. Dredge the fish in the flour on both sides. When the oil is hot, slip the steaks into the pan, and cook them about 5 minutes on one side and 4 minutes or less on the other. Take off heat, and draw off and discard most of the oil in the pan.

4. Put the remaining ¼ cup of oil and the chopped onion into a small saucepan, turn on the heat to medium, and cook the onion, stirring, until it becomes colored a very pale gold. Add the chopped parsley and a pinch of salt, stir quickly once or twice, then add the wine and the anchovies. Cook, stirring constantly with a wooden spoon, using the back of the spoon from time to time to mash the anchovies against the side of the pan.

5. When most of the wine has evaporated, pour the contents of the saucepan over the fish in the sauté pan. Add some pepper. Turn on the heat to medium, and cook for about 2 minutes, spooning the sauce over the fish to baste it once or twice.

6. Lift the steaks with a broad spatula or possibly two, one in either hand, gently transferring them to a warm serving platter, taking care that they do not break up. Pour all the contents of the pan over the fish and serve at once.

Sautéed Swordfish or Salmon Steaks
with Capers and Vinegar, Stimpirata Style

In Siracusa, Sicily, this flavorful preparation is applied principally to swordfish and occasionally to fresh tuna. When, many years ago, I began working with it, I looked for other fish, at that time more commonly available outside Sicily, that would respond to the savory *stimpirata* treatment. The most successful substitute was one most unlike the original Sicilian varieties, salmon. On reflection, one need not be surprised because no other fish has salmon's ability to handle with aplomb such a diversity of flavors in its sauces, from the most shy to the most emphatic.

For this recipe, if you should decide to turn to salmon, you may use either thin steaks or fillets. Swordfish, tuna, or other fish such as shark, grouper, tilefish, or red snapper should be in steak form, sliced very thin.

For 4 to 6 servings

3 tablespoons extra virgin olive oil

¼ cup onion chopped very thin

6 tablespoons celery chopped very fine

2 tablespoons capers, soaked and rinsed as described on page 16 if packed in salt, drained if in vinegar

Vegetable oil for sautéing the fish

2 pounds swordfish, salmon, or other fish steaks (see recommendations above), sliced ½ inch thick, or salmon fillets

⅔ cup flour, spread on a plate

Salt

Black pepper, ground fresh from the mill

¼ cup good-quality wine vinegar, preferably white

1. Put the 3 tablespoons of olive oil in a sauté pan, and turn the heat on to medium. Cook and stir the onion until it becomes colored a pale gold, then add the chopped celery. Cook, stirring from time to time, until the celery is tender, 5 or more minutes. Add the capers and cook for about half a minute, stirring steadily. Turn off the heat.

2. Put enough vegetable oil in a frying pan to come ½ inch up the sides and turn on the heat to medium high. When the oil is hot, dredge the fish on both sides in the flour and slip it into the pan. Do not crowd the pan at one time with more fish than will fit comfortably without overlapping. Cook the fish briefly, about 1 minute per side or a little longer if thicker than ½ inch, then transfer it to a platter, using a slotted spoon or spatula. When all the fish is done, add salt and a few grindings of pepper.

Sautéed Swordfish or Salmon Steaks (continued)

3. Turn on the heat to medium under the pan with the celery and capers. When the contents of the pan begin to simmer, add the sautéed fish from the platter, turn it gently to coat it with sauce, then add the vinegar. Let the vinegar bubble for a minute or so, then transfer the entire contents of the pan to a warm platter and serve at once.

Sweet and Sour Tuna Steaks, Trapani Style

ANOTHER SAVORY item from Sicilian cooking's remarkable seafood repertory, this sliced fresh tuna is simple to do and wonderfully appetizing, its sweet and sour flavor a luscious blend that is neither cloying nor bitingly tart.

For 6 servings

2½ pounds fresh tuna, cut into
    ½-inch-thick steaks
3 cups onion sliced very,
    very thin
⅓ cup extra virgin olive oil
Salt
1 cup flour, spread on a plate

Black pepper, ground fresh
    from the mill
2 teaspoons granulated sugar
¼ cup red wine vinegar
⅓ cup dry white wine
2 tablespoons chopped parsley

1. Remove the skin circling the tuna steaks, wash them in cold water, and pat thoroughly dry with paper towels.

2. Choose a sauté pan broad enough to accommodate later all the steaks in a single layer without overlapping. Put in the sliced onion, 2 tablespoons of olive oil, 1 or 2 large pinches of salt, and turn on the heat to medium low. Cook until the onion has wilted completely, then turn up the heat to medium and continue cooking, stirring from time to time, until the onion becomes colored a deep golden brown.

3. Using a slotted spoon or spatula, transfer the onion to a small bowl. Add the remaining 2 tablespoons of olive oil to the pan, turn the heat up to medium high, dredge the tuna steaks in flour on both sides, and slip them into the pan. Cook them for 2 to 3 minutes, depending on their thickness, then sprinkle with salt and pepper, add the sugar, vinegar, wine, and onions, turn the heat up to high, and cover the pan. Cook at high heat for about 2 minutes, uncover the pan, add the parsley, turn the fish steaks over once or twice, then transfer them to a warm serving platter.

4. If there are thin juices left in the pan, boil them down and at the same

time scrape loose with a wooden spoon any cooking residue sticking to the bottom. If, on the other hand, there is no liquid in the pan, add 2 tablespoons of water and boil it away while loosening the cooking residues. Pour the contents of the pan over the tuna, and serve at once.

Shrimp with Tomatoes and Chili Pepper

For 4 to 6 servings

¼ cup extra virgin olive oil
3 tablespoons chopped onion
2 teaspoons chopped garlic
Chopped hot red chili pepper,
   to taste
3 tablespoons chopped parsley
1⅔ cups canned imported
   Italian plum tomatoes, cut

up, with their juice (see
   fresh tomato note below)
Salt
1½ to 2 pounds unshelled
   medium shrimp
Grilled or oven-browned slices
   of crusty bread

Note ✸ If in season and available, use the same amount of fresh, ripe plum tomatoes, skinned with a peeler and diced very fine.

1. Put the olive oil and onion in a sauté pan, turn on the heat to medium, and cook the onion until it becomes translucent. Add the garlic and chopped chili pepper. When the garlic becomes colored a pale gold, add the parsley, stir once or twice, then add the cut-up tomatoes with their juice together with liberal pinches of salt. Stir thoroughly to coat the tomatoes well, and adjust heat to cook at a steady simmer. Stir from time to time and cook for about 20 minutes, until the oil floats free from the tomatoes.

Ahead-of-time note ✸ The recipe may be completed several hours or even a day in advance up to this point. Refrigerate the sauce if you are not using it the same day. Bring to a simmer when you are ready to add the shrimp.

2. Shell the shrimp and remove their dark vein. If they are larger than medium size, split them in half lengthwise. Wash in several changes of cold water, then pat thoroughly dry with paper towels.

3. Add the shrimp to the simmering sauce, turning them 2 or 3 times to coat them well. Cover the pan and cook for about 2 to 3 minutes, depending on the thickness of the shrimp. Taste and correct for salt and chili pepper. Serve at once with crusty bread to dunk in the sauce.

Note ✸ It's possible that the shrimp may shed liquid that will make the sauce thin and runny. Should this happen, uncover the pan, transfer the shrimp to a warm, deep serving platter using a slotted spoon or spatula, turn the heat under the pan up to high, and boil down the sauce until it regains its original density. Pour over the shrimp and serve at once.

Baked Sea Bass or Other
Whole Fish Stuffed with Shellfish

IN THIS PREPARATION, a whole bass is stuffed with shellfish, onions, olive oil, and lemon juice; it is then tightly sealed in foil or parchment paper and baked in the oven, where it braises in its own juices and those released by the stuffing. It emerges from the cooking with its flesh extraordinarily moist and saturated with a medley of sea fragrances.

The most agreeable way to serve the fish is whole, with the head and tail on, but completely boned. If you have an obliging fish dealer, he would know how to do it for you. If he is not that obliging, you can settle for having him fillet the fish, splitting it into two halves, removing the head and tail along with the bones, but leaving the skin on. Another solution is for you to bone it yourself, which is really not all that difficult as you will see from the instructions below.

Boning fish while leaving it whole ☙ A slit will be made in the fish's belly when it is gutted at the store. With a sharp knife, extend the slit the whole length of the fish, head to tail. The entire backbone will then be exposed, along with the rib bones embedded in the upper part of the belly. With your fingertips and with the help of a paring knife, pry all the rib bones loose, detach them, and discard them. Use the same technique to loosen the backbone, separating it from the flesh attached to it. Carefully bend the head without detaching it, until the backbone snaps off. Do the same at the tail end. You can now lift off the entire backbone, and your whole, boneless fish is ready to be stuffed.   *For 6 or more servings*

1 dozen clams
1 dozen mussels
6 medium raw shrimp
2 garlic cloves
1 small onion
2 tablespoons chopped parsley
Freshly squeezed juice of
   1 lemon
½ cup extra virgin olive oil
Salt

Black pepper, ground fresh
   from the mill
⅓ cup fine, dry, unflavored
   bread crumbs
A 4- to 5-pound whole sea bass,
   red snapper, or small
   salmon, or similar fish,
   boned as described above
Heavy-weight cooking parchment or foil

1. Wash and scrub the clams and mussels as described on page 81. Discard those that stay open when handled. Put them in a pan broad enough so that they don't need to be piled up more than 3 deep, cover the pan, and turn on the heat to high. Check the mussels and clams frequently, turning them over, and promptly removing them from the pan as they open their shells.

2. When all the clams and mussels have opened up, detach their meat from the shells. Put the shellfish meat in a bowl and cover it with its own juices from the pan. To be sure, as you are doing this, that any sand is left behind, tip the pan and gently spoon off the liquid from the top.

3. Let the clam and mussel meat rest for 20 or 30 minutes, so that it may shed any sand still clinging to it, then retrieve it gently with a slotted spoon, and put it in a bowl large enough to contain later all the other ingredients except for the fish. Line a strainer with paper towels, and filter the shellfish juices through the paper into the bowl.

Ahead-of-time note ❀ The steps above may be completed 2 or 3 hours in advance.

4. Shell the shrimp and remove their dark vein. Wash in cold water and pat thoroughly dry with cloth kitchen towels. If using very large shrimp, slice them in half, lengthwise. Add them to the bowl.

5. Mash the garlic lightly with a heavy knife handle, just hard enough to split its skin and peel it. Add it to the bowl.

6. Slice the onion as fine as possible. Add it to the bowl.

7. Put all the other ingredients listed, except for the fish, into the bowl. Toss thoroughly to coat all the shellfish well.

8. Preheat oven to 475°.

9. Wash the fish in cold water inside and out, then pat thoroughly dry with paper towels.

10. Lay a double thickness of aluminum foil or cooking parchment on the bottom of a long, shallow baking dish, bearing in mind that there must be enough to close over the whole fish. Pour some of the liquid in the mixing bowl over the foil or parchment, tipping the baking dish to spread it evenly. Place the fish in the center and stuff it with all the contents of the bowl, reserving just some of the liquid. If you have opted for having the fish split into two fillets, sandwich the contents of the bowl between them. Use the liquid you just reserved to moisten the skin side of the fish. Fold the foil or parchment over the fish, crimping the edges to seal tightly throughout, and tucking the ends under the fish.

11. Bake in the upper third of the preheated oven for 35 to 45 minutes, depending on the size of the fish. After removing it from the oven, let the fish rest for 10 minutes in the sealed foil or parchment. If the baking dish is not presentable for the table, transfer the still-sealed fish to a platter. With scissors, cut the foil or parchment open, trimming it down to the edge of the dish. Don't attempt to lift the fish out of the wrapping, because it is boneless and will break up. Serve it directly from the foil or parchment, slicing the fish across as you might a roast, pouring over each portion some of the juices.

Baked Bluefish Fillets
with Potatoes, Garlic, and Olive Oil, Genoese Style

IN GENOESE COOKING, there is a large repertory of dishes in which the lead role is taken each time by a different player, while the supporting cast remains the same. The regulars are potatoes, garlic, olive oil, and parsley; the star may be fish, shrimp, small octopus, meat, or fresh *porcini* mushrooms. The recipe that follows illustrates the general procedure.

In Genoa one would have used the fresh-caught silvery anchovies of the Riviera. I have found Atlantic bluefish to be a successful replacement, so good in fact that one may even prefer it. Where bluefish is unobtainable, the fillets of any firm-fleshed fish may be substituted.   *For 6 servings*

1½ pounds boiling potatoes
A bake-and-serve dish, approximately 16 by 10 inches,

preferably enameled cast-iron ware
½ cup extra virgin olive oil

1 tablespoon chopped garlic	2 bluefish fillets with the skin
¼ cup chopped parsley	on, approximately 1 pound
Salt	each, OR the equivalent in
Black pepper, ground fresh	other thick, firm fish fillets
from the mill	

1. Preheat oven to 450°.

2. Peel the potatoes, and slice them very thin, barely thicker than chips. Wash them in cold water, then pat them thoroughly dry with cloth kitchen towels.

3. Put all the potatoes into the baking dish, half the olive oil, half the garlic, half the parsley, several liberal pinches of salt, and black pepper. Toss the potatoes 2 or 3 times to coat them well, then spread them evenly over the bottom of the dish.

4. When the oven reaches the preset temperature, put the potatoes in the uppermost third of it and roast them for 12 to 15 minutes, until they are about halfway done.

5. Take out the dish, but do not turn off the oven. Put the fish fillets skin side down over the potatoes. Mix the remaining olive oil, garlic, and parsley in a small bowl, and pour the mixture over the fish, distributing it evenly. Sprinkle with liberal pinches of salt and black pepper. Return the dish to the oven.

6. After 10 minutes, take the dish out, but do not turn off the oven. Use a spoon to scoop up some of the oil at the bottom of the dish, and baste the fish with it. Loosen those potatoes that have become browned and are stuck to the sides of the dish, moving them away. Push into their place slices that are not so brown. Return the dish to the oven and bake for 5 to 8 more minutes, depending on the thickness of the fish fillets.

7. Remove the dish from the oven and allow to settle a few minutes. Serve directly from the baking dish, scraping loose all the potatoes stuck to the sides—they are the most delectable bits—and pouring the cooking juices over each portion of fish and potatoes.

Bass or Other Whole Fish
Baked with Artichokes

For 4 servings

4 medium artichokes
½ lemon
¼ cup extra virgin olive oil
3 tablespoons freshly squeezed
    lemon juice
Salt
Black pepper, ground fresh
    from the mill
A 2- to 2½-pound sea bass
    OR red snapper OR similar

fine-fleshed fish, scaled and
    gutted, but with head and
    tail on
An oval or rectangular bake-
    and-serve dish
A small sprig of fresh rosemary
    OR 1 teaspoon dried leaves,
    chopped very fine

1. Preheat oven to 425°.

2. Trim the artichokes of all their tough parts following the detailed instructions on pages 57–59. As you work, rub the cut artichokes with the lemon to keep them from turning black.

3. Cut each trimmed artichoke lengthwise into 4 equal sections. Remove the soft, curling leaves with prickly tips at the base, and cut away the fuzzy "choke" beneath them. Cut the artichoke sections lengthwise into wafer-thin slices, and squeeze the lemon over them to moisten them with juice that will protect them against discoloration.

4. Put the olive oil, lemon juice, several pinches of salt, and a few gridings of pepper in a small bowl, beat briefly with a fork or whisk, and set aside.

5. Wash the fish in cold water, inside and out, pat thoroughly dry with paper towels, and place it in the baking dish, which ought to be just large enough to contain it.

6. Add the sliced artichokes, the oil and lemon juice mix, and the rosemary. If using chopped dried rosemary, distribute it evenly over the fish. Turn the artichoke slices over to coat them well with the oil mixture, and stuff some of them into the fish's cavity. Tilt the dish in a see-saw motion to distribute the oil and lemon juice evenly, and spoon some of the liquid over the fish. Place in the upper third of the preheated oven.

7. After 15 minutes, spoon the liquid in the dish over the fish, and move the artichoke slices around a bit. Continue to bake for another 10 to 12 minutes. Remove from the oven and allow the fish to settle for a few minutes. Serve at table directly from the baking dish.

Note ❀ If you have difficulty finding a whole small fish as indicated in the list of ingredients, and do not want to increase the recipe by using a much bigger fish, buy a 2-pound fillet with the skin on cut from grouper or other large fish. First bake the artichoke slices alone, along with the oil and lemon juice. After 20 minutes, put the fish skin side down in the baking dish, and spoon over it some of the artichokes to cover. Cook for 15 minutes, basting it midway with the juices in the dish.

Baked Fillet of Sole with Tomato, Oregano, and Hot Pepper

GRILLING or crisp-frying, which are the most characteristic Italian methods of handling sole, are successful only with European sole, in particular the small, very firm-fleshed, nutty variety caught in the northern Adriatic. When flatfish from either the Atlantic or Pacific is grilled or fried, its consistency is unsatisfyingly flaky, and its flavor listless, drawbacks that can be minimized by a less brisk cooking mode and a stimulating sauce, as in the baked fillets of the recipe that follows. *For 6 servings*

⅔ cup onion sliced very thin
3 tablespoons extra virgin olive oil
½ teaspoon garlic chopped very fine
1 cup canned imported Italian plum tomatoes, cut up, with their juice
Salt
2 tablespoons capers, soaked and rinsed as described on page 16 if packed in salt, drained if in vinegar
2 teaspoons fresh oregano OR 1 teaspoon dried
Black pepper, ground fresh from the mill, OR chopped hot red chili pepper, to taste
2 pounds gray sole fillets OR other flatfish fillets
A bake-and-serve dish

1. Preheat oven to 450°.
2. Put the onion and olive oil in a sauté pan, turn on the heat to medium, and cook the onion until it softens and becomes colored a light gold. Add the garlic. When the garlic becomes colored a very pale gold, add the cut-up tomatoes with their juice and a few pinches of salt, and stir thoroughly to coat well. Cook at a steady simmer for about 20 minutes, until the oil floats free of the tomatoes. Add the capers, oregano, and ground black or chopped chili pepper, stir two or three times, cook for about a minute longer. Take off heat.

Baked Fillet of Sole (continued)

3. Wash the fish fillets in cold water and pat thoroughly dry with paper towels. The fish will be placed in the baking dish with the fillets folded so they meet edge to edge, and in a single layer where they slightly overlap. Choose a bake-and-serve dish just large enough to accommodate them, and smear the bottom with a tablespoon of the tomato sauce. Dip each fillet in the sauce in the pan to coat both sides, then fold it and arrange it in the baking dish as described just above. Pour the remaining sauce over the fish, and place the dish on the uppermost rack of the preheated oven. Bake for about 5 minutes, or slightly more, depending on the thickness of the fillets, but taking care not to overcook them.

4. If, when you remove the dish from the oven you find that the fish has shed some liquid, diluting the sauce, tip the dish, spoon off all the sauce and liquid into a small saucepan, turn the heat on to high, and reduce the sauce to its original density. Pour the sauce over the fish and serve immediately, directly from the baking dish.

My Father's Fish Soup

EVERY VILLAGE on Italy's long coastlines makes *zuppa di pesce,* fish soup. On the Adriatic side it is likely to be called *brodetto,* on the Tuscan coast *caciucco,* on the Riviera *ciuppin,* but there are not enough names around to attach to every variation of the dish. Each town makes it in its distinctive style, of which each family in the town usually has its own version.

I have never had a better *zuppa di pesce* than the one my father used to make. His secret was to extract the flavor of the tastiest part of any fish, the head, and use it as a base to enrich the soup. We lived in a town facing the best fishing grounds of the Adriatic, and he would bring home from the market a large variety of small fish and crustaceans, up to a dozen different kinds, using them to make a soup of many-layered flavor. Most of us now have to make do with a small variety of large fish, but the basic principle of the soup is so efficacious that it can be applied successfully to all firm, white-fleshed fish and shellfish in almost any combination, even to just a single fish, as will be shown in another recipe (see page 314).

Note ❀ You need at least 3 or 4 heads for this recipe, so if you won't be buying that many whole fish, ask your dealer for extra heads. Make sure you have a food mill with interchangeable disks; the disk with the largest holes is indispensable for puréeing the heads.

Do not use dark-fleshed fish such as bluefish or mackerel whose flavor is too strong for the delicate balance of this recipe. Do not use eel, which is too fat. Always use some squid, whose flavor contributes depth and intensity. Firm flatfish, such as turbot or halibut, are fine, but sole, sand dab, and flounder are flimsy in consistency and unsatisfying in taste.

Although this is called a soup, it is more of a stew, and no spoon is needed. The juices are usually soaked up with grilled or toasted slices of bread.

About 8 servings

3 to 4 pounds assorted fish (see note above), scaled and gutted
½ pound or more unshelled shrimp
1 pound whole squid OR ¾ pound cleaned squid, sliced into rings
1 dozen littleneck clams
1 dozen mussels
3 tablespoons chopped onion
⅓ cup extra virgin olive oil

1½ teaspoons chopped garlic
3 tablespoons chopped parsley
½ cup dry white wine
1 cup canned imported Italian plum tomatoes, cut up, with their juice
Salt
Black pepper, ground fresh from the mill, OR chopped hot red chili pepper, to taste
Grilled or toasted slices of crusty bread

1. Wash all the fish inside and out in cold water, and pat dry with paper towels. Cut off the heads and set them aside. Cut any fish longer than 6 to 7 inches into pieces about 3½ inches long.

2. Shell the shrimp, wash in cold water, remove their dark vein, and pat dry.

3. If cleaning the squid yourself, follow the directions on pages 317–319. Slice the sac into rings a little less than ½ inch wide, and separate the cluster of tentacles into two parts. Whether cleaning it yourself or using it already cleaned, wash all parts in cold water and pat thoroughly dry with cloth or paper towels.

4. Wash and scrub the clams and mussels as described on page 81. Discard those that stay open when handled. Put them in a pan broad enough so that they don't need to be piled up more than 3 deep, cover the pan, and turn on the heat to high. Check the mussels and clams frequently, turning them over, and promptly removing them from the pan as they open their shells.

5. When all the clams and mussels have opened up, detach their meat from the shells. Put the shellfish meat in a bowl and cover it with its own juices from the pan. To be sure, as you are doing this, that any sand is left behind, tip the pan and gently spoon off the liquid from the top.

My Fathers's Fish Soup (continued)

6. Choose a sauté pan that can later accommodate all the fish in a single layer. Put in the onion and olive oil, and turn on the heat to medium. Cook and stir the onion until it becomes translucent, then add the garlic. When the garlic becomes colored a pale gold, add the parsley, stir 2 or 3 times, then add the wine. Let the wine bubble away and when it has evaporated by about half, add the cut-up tomatoes with their juice. Stir to coat well, turn the heat down, and cook at a gentle simmer for about 25 minutes, until the oil floats free of the tomatoes.

7. Add the fish heads to the pan, a liberal pinch of salt, either the black pepper or the hot chili pepper, cover the pan, adjust heat to medium, and cook for 10 to 12 minutes, turning the heads over after 6 minutes.

8. Retrieve the heads and spread them on a plate. Loosen and detach all the meat and pulp you find attached to the larger bones, and discard the bones. It's a messy job that must be done with your hands, but it will make it much simpler subsequently to mash the heads through the food mill if you have already removed the larger, harder bones. When you have eliminated as many bones as possible, purée what remains on the plate through a food mill fitted with the disk that has the largest holes. Do not use a processor or blender. Put the puréed fish in the pan, add the squid rings and tentacles, cover, and adjust heat to cook at a slow, intermittent simmer for about 45 minutes, until the squid is tender enough to be easily pierced by a fork. If during this time, the juices in the pan become much reduced and appear to be insufficient, add about ⅓ cup water.

9. While the squid is cooking, retrieve the clam and mussel meat from its juices, carefully lifting it with a slotted spoon, and put it aside. Line a strainer with paper towels, and filter the shellfish juices through the paper and into a bowl. Spoon a little of the juice over the clam and mussel meat to keep it moist.

10. When the squid is tender, add the fish to the pan, holding back the smallest and most delicate pieces for about 2 minutes, then add a little more salt, and all the filtered clam and mussel liquid. Cover and cook over medium heat for about 5 minutes, turning the fish over carefully once or twice. Add the shelled shrimp. Cook for another 2 or 3 minutes, then add the clam and mussel meat, turning it into the soup gently, so as not to break up the fish, and cook for 1 more minute.

11. Carefully transfer the contents of the pan to a serving bowl or deep platter and serve at once, preferably accompanied by thick, grilled slices of good, crusty bread.

Halibut over Squid Sauce

WHEN YOUNG and locally caught, halibut is a fish of exceptionally fine texture. It is rather short on flavor, however, and can become dry in cooking. The preparation described here preserves all of the fish's natural moisture, and overcomes a shyness in taste by being cooked over a tender, densely savory stew of squid braised with tomato and white wine. The same method can be applied with equal success to other fish steaks, such as mako shark or monkfish.   *For 6 to 8 servings*

2 pounds whole squid OR
   1½ pounds cleaned squid,
   sliced into narrow rings
⅔ cup onion chopped fine
½ cup extra virgin olive oil
2 tablespoons garlic chopped
   fine
3 tablespoons parsley chopped
   fine
⅔ cup dry white wine
1½ cups fresh, ripe, firm
   tomatoes skinned raw with

a peeler and chopped
   OR canned imported Italian
   plum tomatoes, cut up with
   their juice
Salt
Chopped hot red chili pepper,
   to taste
3 pounds halibut, cut into
   steaks 1 inch thick,
   OR other fish steaks (see
   recommendations above)

1. If cleaning the squid yourself, follow the directions on pages 317–319. Slice the sac into rings a little less than ½ inch wide, and separate the cluster of tentacles into two parts. Whether cleaning it yourself or using it already cleaned, wash all parts in cold water and pat thoroughly dry with cloth or paper towels.

2. Choose a sauté pan that can later accommodate all the fish steaks in a single layer without overlapping. Put in the onion and olive oil, and turn on the heat to medium high. Cook the onion, stirring once or twice, until it becomes colored a pale gold, then add the garlic. As soon as the garlic becomes colored a very pale gold, add 2 tablespoons parsley, stir quickly once or twice, then put in all the squid.

3. Turn the squid over completely 2 or 3 times, coating it thoroughly. Cook it for 3 or 4 minutes, then add the wine. When the wine has simmered for about 20 to 30 seconds and partly evaporated, add the tomatoes with their juice, turning all the ingredients over completely. When the tomatoes begin to bubble, turn the heat down to minimum and put a lid on the pan. Cook

Halibut over Squid Sauce (continued)

until the squid feels tender when prodded with a fork, about 1 hour. If in the interim, the cooking juices become insufficient, replenish with up to ½ cup water when needed. Add salt and chili pepper, and cook for 1 or 2 minutes longer, while stirring frequently.

Ahead-of-time note ✿ You can complete the recipe up to this point several hours in advance. Reheat the squid gently, but completely before proceeding with the next step.

4. Put the fish steaks over the squid, in a single layer without overlapping. Sprinkle with salt, turn the heat up to medium, and cover the pan. Cook for about 3 minutes, then turn the steaks over and cook another 2 minutes or so. The fish should be cooked all the way through so that it is no longer gelatinous, but you must stop the cooking while it is still moist. Taste and correct for salt and chili pepper. Transfer the entire contents of the pan to a warm platter, and serve at once.

Grilled, sliced *polenta* would be very pleasant accompanying this dish. See Polenta (page 274).

A Single Fish
Cooked Fish-Soup Style

IF YOU LIKE the spirited taste of fish soup, but you don't want to cook up a large assortment of fish because there are only four or fewer at table, here is a way of preparing just one fish in a simplified *zuppa di pesce* style. The procedure is analogous to that employed in My Father's Fish Soup (page 310), except for puréeing the heads, which is omitted. The result is fresh and lively flavor that allows the character of the single fish to stand out. Almost any white-fleshed fish is suitable: sea bass, red snapper, mahimahi, monkfish, flounder. Or fish steaks, cut from halibut, grouper, tilefish, mako shark, or swordfish.

For 4 servings (If cooking for 2, use a smaller fish and halve the other ingredients.)

A 2½- to 3-pound whole fish, scaled and gutted, but with head and tail on, OR 1½ to 2 pounds fish steaks (see recommended varieties above)

¼ cup extra virgin olive oil

½ cup chopped onion

1 teaspoon chopped garlic

2 tablespoons chopped parsley

½ cup dry white wine

¾ cup canned imported Italian plum tomatoes, chopped, with their juice

Salt

Black pepper, ground fresh from the mill, OR chopped hot red chili pepper, to taste

1. Wash the fish inside and out in cold water, then pat thoroughly dry with paper towels.

2. Choose a sauté pan that can later accommodate the whole fish or the fish steaks in a single layer. Put in the olive oil and the onion, turn on the heat to medium, and cook the onion until it becomes translucent. Add the garlic. When the garlic becomes colored a pale gold, add the parsley, stir once or twice, then put in the white wine.

3. Let the wine simmer for about a minute, then add the chopped tomatoes with their juice. Cook at a moderate, but steady simmer in the uncovered pan, stirring from time to time, for about 15 or 20 minutes, until the oil floats free from the tomatoes.

4. Put in the whole fish or the steaks without overlapping them. Sprinkle liberally with salt, add several grindings of black pepper or the hot chili pepper, cover the pan, and turn the heat down to medium low.

5. If using a whole fish, cook it about 10 minutes, then turn it over and cook it about 8 minutes more. If using fish steaks, cook each side about 5 minutes, or more if very thick.

6. Transfer to a warm serving platter, handling the fish gently with two spatulas or a large fork and spoon, being careful that it does not break up. Pour all the contents of the pan over it, and serve at once.

All-Shellfish and Mollusks Soup

For 6 servings

2 pounds whole squid
   OR 1½ pounds cleaned
   squid, sliced into rings
2 dozen live littleneck clams in
   the shell
1 dozen live mussels in the shell
½ cup extra virgin olive oil
½ cup chopped onion
1 tablespoon chopped garlic
3 tablespoons chopped parsley
1 cup dry white wine

1½ cups canned imported
   Italian plum tomatoes, cut
   up, with their juice
1 pound unshelled raw shrimp
Salt
Black pepper, ground fresh
   from the mill, OR chopped
   hot red chili pepper, to taste
1 pound fresh sea scallops
Thick, grilled or oven-toasted
   slices of crusty bread

1. If cleaning the squid yourself, follow the directions on pages 317–319. Slice the sac into rings a little less than ½ inch wide, and separate the cluster of tentacles into two parts. Whether cleaning it yourself or using it already cleaned, wash all parts in cold water and pat thoroughly dry with cloth or paper towels.

2. Wash and scrub the clams and mussels as described on page 81. Discard those that stay open when handled.

3. Put the olive oil and chopped onion in a deep saucepan, turn on the heat to medium high, and cook the onion until it is translucent. Add the chopped garlic. When the garlic becomes colored a pale gold, add the chopped parsley. Stir rapidly once or twice, then add the wine. Let the wine bubble for about half a minute, then add the cut-up tomatoes with their juice. Cook at a steady simmer for 10 minutes, stirring once or twice.

4. Put in the squid rings and tentacles, cover the pan leaving the cover slightly askew, and cook at a gentle simmer for about 45 minutes, or until the squid is very tender when prodded with a fork. If the liquid in the pan should become insufficient to continue cooking before the squid is done, add about ½ cup water. Make sure, however, that the water has boiled away before adding the other ingredients.

5. While the squid is cooking, shell the shrimp, remove the dark vein, and wash in cold water. If larger than small to medium size, divide the shrimp in half lengthwise.

6. When the squid is tender, add liberal pinches of salt, several grindings of black pepper or the chopped chili pepper, and the washed clams and mus-

sels in their shells. Turn the heat up to high. Check the mussels and clams frequently, and move them around, bringing to the top the ones from the bottom. The moment the first mussels or clams begin to unclench their shells, add the shrimp and the scallops. Cook until the last clam or mussel has opened up. Transfer the soup to a serving bowl and bring to the table at once, with the grilled or toasted bread on the side.

Squid

FRIED *calamari,* to use the Italian word by which squid has become popular, appears on the menus of restaurants of nearly every gastronomic persuasion. But frying is merely one of the many delectable uses to which you can put *calamari.* No other food that comes from the sea is more versatile to work with. It can be baked, braised, grilled, stewed, or made into soup. It can be congenially paired with potatoes and with a great number of other vegetables. When very small, it can be cooked whole, but when larger, its sac can either be sliced into rings or employed as nature's most perfectly conceived container for stuffing. Only outside Italy, however, is its ink used much. To the Italian palate, the harsh, pungent ink is the least desirable part of the squid. As Venetian cooks have shown, it's only the mellow, velvety, warm-tasting ink of cuttlefish—*seppie*—that is suitable for pasta sauce, *risotto,* and other black dishes.

Cooking times ❀ Squid's most vulnerable quality is its tenderness, which it has when raw, but loses when improperly cooked. To stay tender, squid must be cooked either very briefly, over a strong flame, as when it is fried or grilled, or for a long time—45 minutes or more—over very gentle heat. Any other cooking procedure produces a consistency that closely resembles that of thick rubber bands.

How to clean and prepare for cooking ❀ Fishmongers are now doing a competent job of cleaning squid, and if your market offers that service, you should take advantage of it. Nevertheless, it is useful to understand how squid is cleaned because you never know how thorough your fishmonger may have been, and you will particularly want to go over his work when you will be using the sac whole for stuffing. It is possible, moreover, that cleaned squid is not available and you have to do the job yourself.

❀ Put the squid in a bowl, fill it with cold water, and let soak for a minimum of 30 minutes.

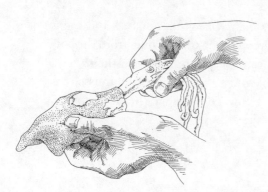

❊ Take a squid, hold the sac in one hand, and with the other, firmly pull off the tentacles, which will come away with the squid's pulpy insides to which they are attached.

❊ Cut the tentacles straight across just above the eyes, and discard everything from the eyes down.

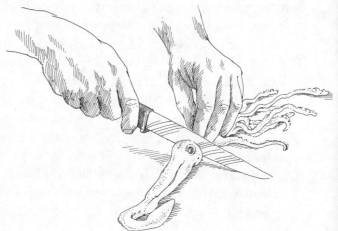

❊ Squeeze off the small, boney beak at the base of the tentacles.

❊ If dealing with tentacles from a large squid, try to pull off as much of their skin as you easily can. Wash the tentacles in cold water and pat thoroughly dry with cloth or paper towels.

❊ Grasp the exposed end of the cellophane-thin, quill-like bone in the sac and pull it away.

❧ Peel off all the partly mottled skin enveloping the sac. If using the whole sac to make stuffed squid, cut a tiny opening—no larger than ¼ inch—at the tip of the sac, hold the large open end of the sac under a faucet, and let cold water run through it. If slicing the sac into rings, first slice it, then wash the rings in cold water. Drain and pat thoroughly dry with cloth or paper towels.

Fried Calamari

For 4 servings, or more if served as an appetizer

2½ pounds whole squid
  OR 2 pounds cleaned squid,
  sliced into rings
Vegetable oil for frying

1 cup flour, spread on a plate
A spatter screen
Salt

1. If cleaning the squid yourself, follow the directions on pages 317–319. Slice the sac into rings a little less than ½ inch wide, and separate the cluster of tentacles into two parts. Whether cleaning it yourself or using it already cleaned, wash all parts in cold water and pat thoroughly dry with cloth or paper towels.

2. Pour enough oil into a frying pan to come 1½ inches up the sides, and turn on the heat to high.

3. When the oil is very hot—test it with 1 *calamari* ring, if it sizzles it's ready—put the rings and tentacles into a large strainer, pour flour over them, shake off the excess flour, grab a handful of squid at a time, and slip it into the pan. Do not crowd the pan; fry the *calamari* in two or more batches, depending on the size of the pan. Squid may burst while frying, spraying hot oil. Hold the spatter screen over the pan to protect yourself.

4. The moment the *calamari* is done to a tawny gold on one side, turn it and do the other side. When done, use a slotted spoon or spatula to transfer it to a cooling rack to drain or spread on a platter lined with paper

Fried Calamari (continued)

towels. When all the *calamari* is cooked and out of the pan, sprinkle with salt and serve at once while still piping hot.

Note 🍪 If the squid rings are rather small, they are fully cooked the moment they become colored a light gold. If they are medium to large in size, they will take just a few seconds longer.

Squid with Tomatoes and Peas,
Tuscan Style

For 4 to 6 servings

2½ pounds small to medium whole squid
OR 2 pounds cleaned squid, sliced into rings
1½ tablespoons onion chopped very fine
3 tablespoons extra virgin olive oil
1½ teaspoons garlic chopped fine
1 tablespoon chopped parsley
¾ cup fresh, ripe tomatoes, peeled and coarsely chopped, OR canned imported Italian plum tomatoes, coarsely chopped, with their juice
Salt
Black pepper, ground fresh from the mill
2 pounds unshelled fresh peas OR 1 ten-ounce package frozen peas, thawed

1. If cleaning the squid yourself, follow the directions on pages 317–319. Slice the sac into rings a little less than ½ inch wide, and separate the cluster of tentacles into two parts. Whether cleaning it yourself or using it already cleaned, wash all parts in cold water and pat thoroughly dry with cloth or paper towels.

2. Put the onion and olive oil in a large saucepan, and turn on the heat to medium. Cook and stir the onion until it becomes colored a pale gold, then add the garlic. When the garlic becomes lightly colored, add the parsley, stir once or twice, then add the tomatoes. Stir thoroughly to coat well and cook at a steady simmer for 10 minutes.

3. Add the squid to the pot, cover, and adjust heat to cook at a slow simmer for 35 to 40 minutes. Add a few pinches of salt, some grindings of pepper, and stir thoroughly.

4. *If using fresh peas:* Shell them, add them to the pot, stir thoroughly, cover, and continue to cook at a slow simmer until the squid feels tender when prodded with a fork. It may take another 20 minutes depending on the squid's size. Taste a ring to be sure it is fully cooked.

If using frozen peas: Add the thawed peas when the squid is tender, stir thoroughly, and cook for another 3 or 4 minutes.

5. Taste and correct for salt and pepper, transfer to a warm, deep serving platter, and serve promptly.

Ahead-of-time note ✺ You can stop the cooking at the end of Step 3 and resume it several hours or even a day later. Bring to a simmer before adding the peas. You may even complete the dish a day or two in advance, reheating it very gently before serving. It tastes sweetest, however, when prepared and eaten the same day.

Alternative Uses for Squid and Tomatoes

Omit the peas from the above recipe, and when the squid is done, chop it coarsely in the food processor. You can then use it as a sauce for such pasta shapes as *spaghettini* or *rigatoni,* or as the flavor base of a *risotto* made following the general procedure described in Risotto with Clams, page 253.

Squid and Potatoes, Genoa Style

For 6 servings

3 pounds small to medium
  whole squid OR 2½ pounds
  cleaned squid, sliced into
  rings
5 tablespoons extra virgin olive
  oil
2 teaspoons chopped garlic
1½ tablespoons chopped
  parsley
⅓ cup dry white wine

1 cup canned imported Italian
  plum tomatoes, cut up,
  with their juice
½ teaspoon chopped fresh
  marjoram or oregano
  OR ¼ teaspoon dried
1¼ pounds boiling potatoes
Salt
Black pepper, ground fresh
  from the mill

Note ❀ Marjoram is what a Genoese cook would use and it should be your first choice if you prefer a lighter fragrance. With oregano, the dish assumes an emphatically accented style that can be rather enjoyable.

1. If cleaning the squid yourself, follow the directions on pages 317–319. Slice the sac into rings a little less than ½ inch wide, and separate the cluster of tentacles into two parts. Whether cleaning it yourself or using it already cleaned, wash all parts in cold water and pat thoroughly dry with cloth or paper towels.

2. Put the oil, garlic, and parsley in a sauté pan, turn the heat on to high, and cook the garlic until it becomes colored a light nut brown. Put in all the squid. Use a long-handled fork to turn the squid, looking out for any that may pop, spraying drops of hot oil; do not hunch over the pan.

3. When the squid turns a dull, flat white, add the wine, and let it bubble away for about 2 minutes. Add the cut-up tomatoes with their juice, the marjoram or oregano, and stir thoroughly. Cover the pan and adjust the heat to cook at a slow simmer.

4. While the squid is cooking, peel the potatoes and cut them up into irregular pieces about 1½ inches thick. When the squid has cooked for about 45 minutes and is tender, add salt, the potatoes, and several grindings of pepper, stir thoroughly to coat well, and cover the pan again. Cook, always at a slow simmer, until the potatoes are tender, about 20 to 30 minutes. Taste and correct for salt and pepper and serve promptly.

Ahead-of-time note ❀ The dish may be prepared entirely in advance, and kept for a day or two. Reheat gently before serving. If possible, eat it the same day it is cooked, when its flavor has not been impaired by refrigeration.

Stuffed Whole Squid Braised with Tomatoes and White Wine

For 6 servings

6 whole squid with sacs measuring 4½ to 5 inches in length, not including the tentacles

FOR THE STUFFING

1 egg
Approximately 1 tablespoon extra virgin olive oil
2 tablespoons parsley chopped fine
½ teaspoon chopped garlic
2½ tablespoons freshly grated *parmigiano-reggiano* cheese

¼ cup fine, dry unflavored bread crumbs
Salt
Black pepper, ground fresh from the mill

Darning needle and cotton thread OR strong, round toothpicks

THE BRAISING INGREDIENTS

Extra virgin olive oil for cooking
4 whole garlic cloves, peeled
½ cup canned imported Italian plum tomatoes, chopped, with their juice

½ teaspoon garlic chopped fine
¼ cup dry white wine

1. When stuffing squid it is preferable to clean it yourself, both to make sure the sac is thoroughly clean and that it is not cut or torn, which might cause it to come apart in cooking. Pull off the tentacles as described on page 318 and proceed to clean the squid following the directions given there. If it has been cleaned for you, look the sac over, wash out the inside thoroughly, and remove any of the skin that might have been left on. Wash in cold water and pat thoroughly dry with cloth or paper towels.

2. Chop the tentacles very fine either with a knife or in the processor, and put them in a bowl.

3. *To make the stuffing:* In a saucer beat the egg lightly with a fork, and add it to the bowl with the tentacles. Into the same bowl put all the ingredients that go into the stuffing and mix with a fork until they are uniformly blended. There should be just enough olive oil in the mixture to make it

Stuffed Whole Squid (continued)

slightly glossy. If it doesn't have this gloss on the surface, add a little more oil.

4. Divide the stuffing into 6 equal parts and spoon it into the squid sacs. Stuff the sacs only two-thirds full, because as they cook they shrink and if they are packed tightly they may burst. Sew up the opening with a darning needle and cotton thread, making absolutely certain that when you are finished with the needle you take it out of the kitchen lest it disappear into the sauce. Sewing them up is the best way to close squid sacs, but if you are not comfortable with it, you can stitch the edges of the opening together with a strong, round, sharply pointed toothpick.

5. Choose a sauté pan that can later contain all the sacs in a single layer. Pour in enough olive oil to come ¼ inch up the sides, turn on the heat to medium high, and put in the whole peeled garlic cloves. Cook, stirring, until the garlic becomes colored a golden nut brown, remove it from the pan, and put in all the stuffed squid. Brown the squid sacs all over, then add the chopped tomatoes with their juice, the chopped garlic, and the wine. Cover the pan and adjust the heat to cook at a slow simmer. Cook for 45 to 50 minutes, or until the squid feels tender when prodded with a fork.

6. When done, transfer the squid to a cutting board using a slotted spoon or spatula. Let it settle a few minutes. If you have sewn up the sacs, slice away just enough squid from that end to dispose of the thread. If you have used toothpicks, remove them. Cut the sacs into slices about ½ inch thick. Arrange

the slices on a warm serving platter. Bring the sauce in the pan to a simmer, then pour it over the sliced squid, and serve immediately.

Ahead-of-time note 🌸 If necessary, the dish can be finished 3 or 4 days in advance. Reheat it as follows: Preheat oven to 300°. Transfer the squid slices and their sauce to a bake-and-serve dish, add 2 or 3 tablespoons of water, and place on the middle rack of the preheated oven. Turn and baste the slices as they warm up, handling them gently to keep them from breaking apart. Serve when warmed all the way through.

Squid with Porcini Mushroom Stuffing

For 4 servings

A small packet OR 1 ounce dried *porcini* mushrooms, reconstituted as described on page 27

The filtered water from the mushroom soak, see page 28 for instructions

4 whole squid with sacs measuring 4½ to 5 inches in length, not including the tentacles

Black pepper, ground fresh from the mill

Salt

2 teaspoons chopped garlic

2 tablespoons chopped parsley

⅓ cup fine, dry unflavored bread crumbs

Extra virgin olive oil: 1 tablespoon for the stuffing plus 3 tablespoons for cooking

Darning needle and cotton thread OR strong, round toothpicks

½ cup dry white wine

1. Thoroughly rinse the reconstituted dried *porcini* in several changes of cold water, then chop them very fine. Put them in a small saucepan together with the filtered liquid from their soak, turn on the heat to medium high, and cook until all the liquid has boiled away.

2. Prepare the squid for cooking as described in the preceding recipe for Stuffed Whole Squid Braised with Tomatoes and White Wine, page 323. Chop the tentacles very fine.

3. Put the chopped tentacles into a bowl together with the mushrooms, several grindings of pepper, salt, the chopped garlic, parsley, bread crumbs, and 1 tablespoon of olive oil. Mix thoroughly with a fork until all the ingredients are uniformly blended.

4. Set aside 1 tablespoon of the mixture, and divide the rest into 4 equal parts, spooning it into the squid sacs. Stuff the sacs and close them with

Squid with Porcini Mushroom Stuffing (continued)

needle and thread or with toothpicks, as described in Step 4 of the preceding recipe. If any stuffing is left over, add it to the tablespoon you had set aside.

5. Choose a sauté pan that can subsequently accommodate all the stuffed squid in a single layer. You can squeeze them in quite snugly because they will shrink in cooking. Put 3 tablespoons of olive oil in the pan and turn on the heat to high. When the oil is very hot, put in the squid. Brown them all over, add a pinch of salt, a grinding of pepper, the white wine, and the stuffing mixture that you had set aside. Quickly turn the squid sacs once or twice, turn the heat down to cook at a very slow, intermittent simmer, and cover the pan.

6. Cook for 45 minutes or more, depending on the size and thickness of the squid, turning the sacs from time to time. The squid is done if it feels tender when gently prodded with a fork.

7. Transfer to a cutting board, let settle a few minutes, then slice and arrange on a platter as in Step 6 of the preceding recipe.

8. Add 1 or 2 tablespoons of water to the pan, and boil it away while scraping loose all the cooking residues from the bottom of the pan. Spoon the contents of the pan over the squid, together with any juices left on the cutting board, and serve at once.

CHICKEN, SQUAB, DUCK, AND RABBIT

Roast Chicken with Lemons

IF THIS WERE a still life its title could be "Chicken with Two Lemons." That is all that there is in it. No fat to cook with, no basting to do, no stuffing to prepare, no condiments except for salt and pepper. After you put the chicken in the oven you turn it just once. The bird, its two lemons, and the oven do all the rest. Again and again, through the years, I meet people who come up to me to say, "I have made your chicken with two lemons and it is the most amazingly simple recipe, the juiciest, best-tasting chicken I have ever had." And you know, it is perfectly true.

For 4 servings

A 3- to 4-pound chicken
Salt
Black pepper, ground fresh
    from the mill

2 rather small lemons

1. Preheat oven to 350°.
2. Wash the chicken thoroughly in cold water, both inside and out. Remove all the bits of fat hanging loose. Let the bird sit for about 10 minutes on a slightly tilted plate to let all the water drain out of it. Pat it thoroughly dry all over with cloth or paper towels.
3. Sprinkle a generous amount of salt and black pepper on the chicken, rubbing it with your fingers over all its body and into its cavity.
4. Wash the lemons in cold water and dry them with a towel. Soften each lemon by placing it on a counter and rolling it back and forth as you put firm downward pressure on it with the palm of your hand. Puncture the lemons in at least 20 places each, using a sturdy round toothpick, a trussing needle, a sharp-pointed fork, or similar implement.

Roast Chicken with Lemons (continued)

5. Place both lemons in the bird's cavity. Close up the opening with toothpicks or with trussing needle and string. Close it well, but don't make an absolutely airtight job of it because the chicken may burst. Run kitchen string from one leg to the other, tying it at both knuckle ends. Leave the legs in their natural position without pulling them tight. If the skin is unbroken, the chicken will puff up as it cooks, and the string serves only to keep the thighs from spreading apart and splitting the skin.

6. Put the chicken into a roasting pan, breast facing down. Do not add cooking fat of any kind. This bird is self-basting, so you need not fear it will stick to the pan. Place it in the upper third of the preheated oven. After 30 minutes, turn the chicken over to have the breast face up. When turning it, try not to puncture the skin. If kept intact, the chicken will swell like a balloon, which makes for an arresting presentation at the table later. Do not worry too much about it, however, because even if it fails to swell, the flavor will not be affected.

7. Cook for another 30 to 35 minutes, then turn the oven thermostat up to 400°, and cook for an additional 20 minutes. Calculate between 20 and 25 minutes' total cooking time for each pound. There is no need to turn the chicken again.

8. Whether your bird has puffed up or not, bring it to the table whole and leave the lemons inside until it is carved and opened. The juices that run out are perfectly delicious. Be sure to spoon them over the chicken slices. The lemons will have shriveled up, but they still contain some juice; do not squeeze them, they may squirt.

Ahead-of-time note ◉ If you want to eat it while it is warm, plan to have it the moment it comes out of the oven. If there are leftovers, they will be very tasty cold, kept moist with some of the cooking juices and eaten not straight out of the refrigerator, but at room temperature.

Oven-Roasted Chicken with Garlic and Rosemary

For 4 servings

A 3½-pound chicken
2 sprigs of fresh rosemary
   OR 1 heaping teaspoon
    dried leaves
3 garlic cloves, peeled

Salt
Black pepper, ground fresh
   from the mill
2 tablespoons vegetable oil

1. Preheat oven to 375°.

2. Wash the chicken inside and out with cold water, and pat thoroughly dry with cloth or paper towels.

3. Put one of the fresh rosemary sprigs, or half the dried leaves, inside the bird's cavity together with all the garlic, salt, and pepper.

4. Rub 1 tablespoon of the oil over the chicken's skin, and sprinkle with salt and pepper. Strip the leaves from the remaining sprig of rosemary, and sprinkle them over the bird, or sprinkle the remaining dried leaves. Put the chicken together with the remaining tablespoon of oil in a roasting pan, and place it on the middle rack of the preheated oven. Every 15 minutes, turn and baste it with the fat and cooking juices that collect in the pan. Cook until the thigh feels very tender when prodded with a fork, and the meat comes easily off the bone, about 1 hour or more.

5. Transfer the chicken to a warm serving platter. Tip the roasting pan and spoon off all but a small amount of fat. Place the pan over the stove, turn the heat on to high, add 2 tablespoons of water, and while it boils away, use a wooden spoon to scrape loose any cooking residues stuck to the bottom. Pour the pan juices over the chicken and serve at once.

Pan-Roasted Chicken with Rosemary, Garlic, and White Wine

For 4 servings

1 tablespoon butter
2 tablespoons vegetable oil
A 3½-pound chicken, cut into
    4 pieces
2 or 3 garlic cloves, peeled
1 sprig of fresh rosemary
    broken in two OR ½ tea-
    spoon dried rosemary leaves

Salt
Black pepper, ground fresh
    from the mill
½ cup dry white wine

1. Put the butter and oil in a sauté pan, turn on the heat to medium high, and when the butter foam begins to subside, put in the chicken quarters, skin side down.

2. Brown the chicken well on both sides, then add the garlic and rosemary. Cook the garlic until it becomes colored a pale gold, and add salt, pepper, and the wine. Let the wine simmer briskly for about 30 seconds, then adjust heat to cook at a slow simmer, and put a lid on the pan, setting it slightly ajar. Cook until the bird's thigh feels very tender when prodded with a fork,

Pan-Roasted Chicken (continued)

and the meat comes easily off the bone, calculating between 20 and 25 minutes per pound. If while the chicken is cooking, you find the liquid in the pan has become insufficient, replenish it with 1 or 2 tablespoons water as needed.

3. When done, transfer the chicken to a warm serving platter, using a slotted spoon or spatula. Remove the garlic from the pan. Tip the pan, spooning off all but a little of the fat. Turn the heat up to high, and boil the water away while loosening cooking residues from the bottom and sides with a wooden spoon. Pour the pan juices over the chicken and serve at once.

Chicken Fricassee, Cacciatora Style

Cacciatora means hunter's style, and since there has always been a hunter in nearly every Italian household, every Italian cook prepares a dish with a claim to that description. Making generous allowances for the uncounted permutations in the dishes that go by the *cacciatora* name, what they generally consist of is a chicken or rabbit fricassee with tomato, onion, and other vegetables. And that is exactly what this is. *For 4 to 6 servings*

A 3- to 4-pound chicken, cut into 6 to 8 pieces
2 tablespoons vegetable oil
Flour, spread on a plate
Salt
Black pepper, ground fresh from the mill
⅓ cup onion sliced very thin
⅔ cup dry white wine
1 sweet yellow or red bell pepper, seeds and core removed and cut into thin julienne strips
1 carrot, peeled and cut into thin disks
½ stalk celery sliced thin crosswise
1 garlic clove, peeled and chopped very fine
⅔ cup canned imported Italian plum tomatoes, chopped coarse, with their juice

1. Wash the chicken in cold water and pat thoroughly dry with cloth or paper towels.

2. Choose a sauté pan that can subsequently accommodate all the chicken pieces without crowding them. Put in the oil and turn the heat on to medium high. When the oil is hot, turn the chicken in the flour, coat the pieces on all sides, shake off excess flour, and slip them into the pan, skin side down. Brown that side well, then turn them and brown the other side. Transfer them to a warm plate, and sprinkle with salt and pepper.

3. Turn the heat back on to medium high, put in the sliced onion, and cook the onion until it has become colored a deep gold. Add the wine. Let it simmer briskly for about 30 seconds while using a wooden spoon to scrape loose the browning residues on the bottom and sides of the pan. Return the browned chicken pieces to the pan, except for the breasts, which cook faster and will go in later. Add the bell pepper, carrot, celery, garlic, and the chopped tomatoes with their juice. Adjust heat to cook at a slow simmer, and put a lid on the pan to cover tightly. After 40 minutes add the breast and continue cooking at least 10 minutes more until the chicken thighs feel very tender when prodded with a fork, and the meat comes easily off the bone. Turn and baste the chicken pieces from time to time while they are cooking.

4. When the chicken is done, transfer it to a warm serving platter, using a slotted spoon or spatula. If the contents of the pan are on the thin, watery side, turn the heat up to high under the uncovered pan, and reduce them to an appealing density. Pour the contents of the pan over the chicken and serve at once.

Ahead-of-time note ✿ The dish can be cooked through to the end up to a day in advance. Let the chicken cool completely in the pan juices before refrigerating. Reheat in a covered pan at a slow simmer, turning the chicken pieces until they are warmed all the way through.

Chicken Cacciatora, New Version

THIS APPROACH to the *cacciatora* style is even simpler than the preceding one. There is less wine, no flour, and there are no other vegetables except for tomatoes and onion, which in this version are present in more prominent proportions, bestowing on the chicken a sweeter, fruitier flavor, somewhat like that of a very fresh pasta sauce. Also note that here olive oil replaces vegetable oil.

For 4 to 6 servings

A 3- to 4-pound chicken, cut
  into 6 to 8 pieces
2 tablespoons extra virgin
  olive oil
1 cup onion sliced very thin
2 garlic cloves, peeled and
  sliced very thin
Salt
Black pepper, ground fresh
  from the mill

⅓ cup dry white wine
1½ cups fresh, very ripe, firm
  meaty tomatoes, skinned
  raw with a peeler and
  chopped, OR canned
  imported Italian plum
  tomatoes, cut up, with their
  juice

Chicken Cacciatora, New Version (continued)

1. Wash the chicken in cold water and pat thoroughly dry with cloth or paper towels.

2. Choose a sauté pan that can subsequently contain all the chicken pieces without crowding them. Put in the olive oil and the sliced onion, and turn on the heat to medium. Cook the onion, turning it occasionally, until it becomes translucent.

3. Add the sliced garlic and the chicken pieces, putting them in skin side facing down. Cook until the skin forms a golden crust, then turn the pieces and do the other side.

4. Add salt and several grindings of pepper, and turn the chicken pieces over 2 or 3 times. Add the wine, and let it simmer away until about half of it has evaporated.

5. Add the cut-up tomatoes, turn down the heat to cook at an intermittent simmer, and cover the pan, putting the lid on slightly askew. Turn and baste the chicken pieces from time to time while they are cooking. Whenever you find that the liquid in the pan becomes insufficient, add 2 tablespoons of water. Cook until the chicken thighs feel very tender when prodded with a fork, and the meat comes easily off the bone, about 40 minutes.

Ahead-of-time note ❧ The recommendations in the preceding *cacciatora* recipe are applicable here.

Chicken Fricassee with Porcini Mushrooms, White Wine, and Tomatoes

For 4 servings

A 3½-pound chicken, cut into 4 pieces
2 tablespoons vegetable oil
Salt
Black pepper, ground fresh from the mill
½ cup dry white wine
A small packet OR 1 ounce dried *porcini* mushrooms,
reconstituted as described on page 27 and cut up
The filtered water from the mushroom soak, see page 28 for instructions
¼ cup canned imported Italian plum tomatoes, chopped coarse, with their juice
1 tablespoon butter

1. Wash the chicken in cold water and pat thoroughly dry with cloth or paper towels.

2. Put the oil in a sauté pan, turn on the heat to medium high, and when

the oil is very hot, slip in the chicken pieces, skin side down. Brown them well on that side, then turn them and brown the other side. Sprinkle with salt and pepper, turn them once, then add the wine. Let the wine simmer briskly for 30 seconds as you scrape loose browning residue from the bottom and sides of the pan with a wooden spoon.

3. Add the chopped reconstituted *porcini,* the filtered water from their soak, and the chopped tomatoes with their juice. Turn over all ingredients then adjust heat to cook at a slow simmer, and put a lid, slightly ajar, on the pot. Cook until the bird's thighs feel very tender when prodded with a fork, and the meat comes easily off the bone, about 50 minutes. Turn the chicken pieces from time to time while they are cooking.

4. When the chicken is done, transfer it to a warm serving platter. Tip the pan and spoon off all but a little of the fat. If the juices in the pan are too thin, boil them down over high heat. Swirl into them the 1 tablespoon of butter, then pour all the contents of the pan over the chicken and serve at once.

Chicken Fricassee with Red Cabbage

IN THIS FRICASSEE, chicken pieces cook smothered in red cabbage, which keeps them tender and invests them with some of its own sweetness. By the time the chicken is done, the cabbage dissolves into a dense, clinging sauce.

For 4 servings

1 cup onion sliced very thin
¼ cup extra virgin olive oil plus
   1 tablespoon
2 garlic cloves, peeled and each
   cut into 4 pieces
4 cups red cabbage shredded
   fine, about 1 pound

A 3- to 4-pound chicken, cut
   into 8 pieces
½ cup dry red wine
Black pepper, ground fresh
   from the mill
Salt

1. Put the sliced onion, the ¼ cup oil, and the garlic in a sauté pan, turn the heat on to medium, and cook the garlic until it becomes colored a deep gold. Add the shredded cabbage. Stir thoroughly to coat well, sprinkle with salt, stir again, adjust heat to cook at a gentle simmer, and put a lid on the pan. Cook the cabbage for 40 minutes or more, turning it over from time to time, until it has become very tender and considerably reduced in bulk.

Ahead-of-time note ❁ The dish can be prepared up to this point even 2 or 3 days in advance. Reheat completely in a covered pan before proceeding to the next step.

Chicken Fricassee with Red Cabbage (continued)

2. Wash the chicken pieces in cold water, and pat thoroughly dry with cloth or paper towels.

3. In another pan, put in 1 tablespoon of olive oil, turn on the heat to medium, and, after warming up the oil very briefly, put in all the chicken pieces skin side down in a single layer. Turn the chicken after a little while to brown the pieces equally on both sides, then transfer them to the other pan, all except the breast, which you'll hold aside until later. Turn the chicken over in the cabbage, add the wine and a few grindings of pepper, cover the pan, putting the lid on slightly ajar, and continue cooking at a slow, steady simmer. From time to time turn the chicken pieces over, sprinkling them once with salt. After 40 minutes add the breasts. Cook for about 10 minutes more, until the chicken is tender all the way through and the meat comes easily off the bone. You will no longer be able to recognize the cabbage as such; it will have become a dark, supple sauce for the chicken. Transfer the entire contents of the pan to a warm platter and serve at once.

Fricasseed Chicken with Rosemary and Lemon Juice

For 4 servings

A 3- to 4-pound chicken, cut into 8 pieces

2 tablespoons vegetable oil

1 tablespoon butter

1 sprig of fresh rosemary OR 1 teaspoon dried leaves

3 garlic cloves, peeled

Salt

Black pepper, ground fresh from the mill

⅓ cup dry white wine

2 tablespoons freshly squeezed lemon juice

Lemon peel with none of the white pith, cut into 6 thin julienne strips

1. Wash the chicken pieces in cold water, and pat thoroughly dry with cloth or paper towels.

2. Choose a sauté pan that can subsequently accommodate all the chicken pieces without overlapping. Put in the oil and butter, turn the heat on to medium high, and when the butter foam begins to subside, put in the chicken, skin side down. Brown the chicken on both sides, then add the rosemary, garlic, salt, and pepper. Cook for 2 or 3 minutes, turning the

chicken pieces from time to time, then remove the breast and set aside.

3. Add the wine, let it bubble at a brisk simmer for about 20 seconds, then adjust the heat to cook at a very slow simmer, and put a lid on the pan slightly ajar. After 40 minutes return the breast to the pan. Cook for 10 minutes more at least, until the thighs of the chicken feel very tender when prodded with a fork, and the meat comes easily off the bone. While it's cooking, check the liquid in the pot from time to time. If it becomes insufficient, replenish with 2 or 3 tablespoons water.

4. When the chicken is done, remove from heat and transfer the pieces to a warm serving platter, using a slotted spoon or spatula. Tip the pan and spoon off all but a little bit of the fat. Add the lemon juice and lemon peel, place the pan over medium-low heat, and use a wooden spoon to scrape loose cooking residues from the bottom and sides. Pour the pan juices over the chicken and serve at once.

Fricasseed Chicken with Egg and Lemon, Marches Style

LIKE THE LAMB CHOPS on page 413, this chicken is cooked, then tossed with a raw mixture of beaten egg yolks and lemon juice, which the heat of the meat seizes on to form a clinging, satiny coat. *For 4 servings*

A 3- to 4-pound chicken, cut
    into 8 pieces
4 tablespoons (½ stick) butter
3 tablespoons onion chopped
    very fine
Salt
Black pepper, ground fresh
    from the mill
1 cup Basic Homemade Meat
    Broth, prepared as directed

on page 15, OR 1 bouillon
    cube dissolved in 1 cup
    water
2 egg yolks (see warning about
    salmonella poisoning,
    page 41)
¼ cup freshly squeezed
    lemon juice

1. Wash the chicken pieces in cold water, and pat thoroughly dry with cloth or paper towels.

2. Choose a sauté pan that can later accommodate all the chicken pieces without overlapping. Put in the butter and chopped onion, turn the heat on to medium, and cook the onion until it becomes colored a pale gold. Turn the

Fricasseed Chicken, Marches Style (continued)

heat up a little, and put in the chicken, skin side down. Brown the pieces thoroughly on both sides.

3. Add salt and pepper, turn the chicken pieces over, then remove the breasts from the pan. Add all the broth, adjust heat to cook at a very gentle simmer, and cover the pan with the lid on well ajar. After 40 minutes, return the breast to the pan and cook for at least 10 minutes more, until the thighs feel very tender when prodded with a fork, and the meat comes easily off the bone. While it's cooking, turn the chicken from time to time. If the broth should become insufficient, add 2 or 3 tablespoons water when needed. When the chicken is done, however, there should be no liquid left in the pan. If you find watery juices in the pan, uncover, turn the heat up to high, and boil them away, turning the chicken pieces frequently as you do so. Take the pan off heat, leaving the chicken in.

4. Put the egg yolks in a small bowl and beat them lightly with a fork or whisk while slowly adding the lemon juice. Pour the mixture over the chicken pieces, tossing to coat them well. Transfer the entire contents of the pan to a warm platter, and serve at once.

Grilled Chicken alla Diavola, Roman Style

IN ROME they call this the devil's chicken because of the diabolical quantity of the crushed black peppercorns that are used. Actually, although it is indeed peppery, its most striking quality is its fragrance, a medley of the aromas of the grill, of the black pepper, and of lemon.

For this preparation, the chicken must be split open and pounded flat. The butcher can easily do it, but so can you, following the directions in the recipe. Before it is grilled it must be rubbed with peppercorns, and marinated for at least 2 hours in lemon juice and olive oil. It's an ideal dish for a cookout because you can prepare the chicken in the kitchen, put it with its marinade in one of those plastic bags with an airtight closure, and take it

with you. By the time your fire is ready later in the day, the chicken will be
ready too. *For 4 to 6 servings*

A 3½-pound chicken
1 tablespoon black peppercorns
⅓ cup freshly squeezed
    lemon juice
2 tablespoons extra virgin
    olive oil

OPTIONAL: a charcoal or wood-
    burning grill
Salt

1. The chicken must be flattened either by you or the butcher into a shape
that will look more like that of a butterfly than of a bird. If you are doing
it, place the chicken on a work counter with the breast facing down. Using
a cleaver or a chopping knife, split it open along the entire backbone. Crack
the breastbone from behind, spreading the chicken as flat as you can with
your hands. Turn it over with its breast facing you. Make cuts where the wings
and legs join the body, without detaching them, but for the purpose of
spreading them out flat. Turn the chicken over, the breast facing down again,
and pound it as flat as you can, using a meat pounder or the flat side of a
cleaver.

2. Wrap the peppercorns in a towel and crack them with a mallet, a meat
pounder, or a hammer. If you have a mill that can crack peppercorns very
coarse, you can use that instead. Put the chicken in a deep dish, and rub the
cracked peppercorns into it, covering as much of it as you can. Pour the
lemon juice and olive oil over it, and let steep for 2 to 3 hours, turning it and
basting it from time to time.

3. If cooking the chicken in an indoor broiler, preheat it at least 15 minutes in advance. If using charcoal, light it in sufficient time to form a coat
of white ash; if using wood, in time to produce a substantial quantity of
embers.

4. Sprinkle the chicken with salt, and place it on the broiler pan, if
indoors, on the grill, if outdoors, with the skin side facing the source of heat.
Cook until the skin becomes colored brown, then baste it with a little of its
marinade, and turn it over. Turn the bird from time to time until it is fully
cooked. The thigh must feel very tender when prodded with a fork. The
cooking time varies considerably, depending on the intensity of the fire, and
on the chicken itself. Should you run out of liquid from the marinade before
the chicken is done, baste it with fresh olive oil. When it is ready, sprinkle
with fresh-cracked pepper, and serve at once.

Filleting Breasts of Chicken

BREAST OF CHICKEN has a delicate texture and fine, mild flavor comparable to that of veal *scaloppine*. *Scaloppine* are pounded thin to permit the most rapid cooking; boned chicken breast is too fragile to be pounded, but it can be converted into *scaloppine*-like slices by filleting. When you use the method described here, chicken breasts can become an inexpensive but no less fine alternative to veal, adaptable to the numerous ways one can prepare *scaloppine*.

1. A chicken breast is sold covered by two layers of skin, the fatty, yellow outer one, and a very thin, membrane-like inner layer. When you pull these away with your fingers you will find them attached at the breastbone and at the sides of the breast where the rib cage was connected. Cut them loose from both places and discard them.

2. Run a finger along the upper part of the breast where the wing used to be attached. Feel for an opening. You will find one where your fingertip can enter without any resistance: It is the space between the two muscles, a large one and a small one, that lie cupped, one over the other, and that constitute each half of the breast. You must detach them, one at a time. Detach the larger muscle first, severing it with a knife from the side of the breast that adjoined the rib cage, then cutting it loose from the breastbone. Repeat the procedure with the smaller muscle, then bone the other half of the breast in the same manner. You now have two separate pieces from each side of the

breast: one piece flatter, larger, and triangular; the other smaller, rounder, and tapered.

3. The smaller, tapered piece has a white tendon that protrudes slightly from one end. It must be pulled out. Grasp the protruding tip of the tendon, using a bit of paper or the corner of a cloth towel because it is slippery. With the other hand press the knife blade against the muscle near the tendon, angling the blade to keep the edge from cutting. While pressing firmly with the knife, pull at the tendon, which will come out easily. Remove the tendon from the other small muscle in the same manner. Nothing more needs to be done to these pieces.

4. Place the larger muscle on a cutting board, with the side that was next to the bone facing down. Hold it flat with the palm of one hand. With the other hand take a sharp knife and slice the breast, moving the blade parallel to the cutting board, thus dividing the piece into two equal slices half its original thickness. Repeat the procedure with the other large muscle. You now have, from each whole breast, six tender fillets ready for cooking.

Ahead-of-time note You can prepare the fillets several hours or even a day or two in advance. Wrap in plastic wrap before refrigerating.

Rolled Fillets of Breast of Chicken
with Pork and Rosemary Filling

For 4 to 6 servings

2 garlic cloves
2 tablespoons vegetable oil
½ pound ground pork
Salt
Black pepper, ground fresh
    from the mill
2 teaspoons fresh rosemary
    leaves OR 1 teaspoon dried

2 whole chicken breasts, filleted
    as directed on pages
    338–339
2 tablespoons butter
Sturdy round toothpicks
½ cup dry white wine

1. Lightly mash the garlic with a heavy knife handle, just hard enough to split the skin, which you will remove and discard. Put the garlic in a skillet together with the oil, turn on the heat to medium, and cook the garlic until it has become colored a pale gold. Add the ground pork, salt, pepper, and the rosemary leaves. Cook for about 10 minutes, stirring and crumbling the meat with a fork. Discard the garlic and, using a slotted spoon or spatula, transfer the meat to a plate.

2. Lay the chicken fillets flat on a work surface and sprinkle with salt and pepper. Spread the pork filling over the fillets, and roll up each fillet tightly. Fasten each roll with a toothpick inserted lengthwise.

Ahead-of-time note ❀ The rolls can be prepared up to this point several hours in advance.

3. Spoon off most of the fat from the pan in which you cooked the pork. (If you made the chicken rolls some time in advance, degrease the pan at that time, and reserve the juices in the pan for when you are ready to resume cooking.) Add the butter, turn the heat on to medium high, and when the butter foam begins to subside, slip in the chicken rolls. Cook them briefly, about 1 minute altogether, turning them to brown them all over. Transfer to a warm serving platter, using a slotted spoon or spatula, and remove the toothpicks.

4. Add the wine to the skillet, and while it simmers briskly for about half a minute, use a wooden spoon to scrape loose cooking residues from the bottom and sides of the pan. Pour the cooking juices over the chicken rolls and serve at once.

Sautéed Fillets of Breast of Chicken with Lemon and Parsley, Siena Style

For 4 to 6 servings

1 tablespoon vegetable oil
4 tablespoons (½ stick) butter
3 whole chicken breasts, filleted
  as directed on pages
  338–339
Salt
Black pepper, ground fresh
  from the mill

The freshly squeezed juice of 1
  lemon
3 tablespoons chopped parsley
Garnish: 1 lemon, sliced thin

1. Put the oil and 3 tablespoons of the butter in a skillet and turn on the heat to medium high. When the butter foam subsides, slip in as many of the chicken fillets as will fit loosely. Cook them briefly on both sides, less than 1 minute altogether. Transfer the fillets to a warm plate, using a slotted spoon or spatula, and sprinkle with salt and pepper. Repeat the procedure until all the fillets are done.

2. Add the lemon juice to the skillet, and let it simmer briskly over medium heat for about 20 seconds, while scraping loose cooking residues from the bottom and sides of the pan, using a wooden spoon. Add the chopped parsley and the remaining tablespoon of butter, stir rapidly for 4 or 5 seconds, then turn the heat down to low and return the fillets to the pan together with any juices they may have shed in the plate. Turn them over in the pan juices 2 or 3 times, then transfer, together with the juices, to a warm platter. Garnish with the thin slices of lemon, and serve at once.

Boning a Whole Chicken

A WHOLE CHICKEN with its bones removed makes a beautiful natural casing for any stuffing. It is great fun to bring it to the table—its chicken shape less angular, more voluptuous, but intact—and to carve from it, without any effort, perfect, solid, boneless slices.

You will find nothing baffling about boning a chicken. Equipped with patience, a small, sharp knife, and of course, a chicken, you could easily figure it out for yourself. Nearly all of the bird's carcass—backbone, ribs, and breastbone—conveniently comes away in one piece once it has been loosened

Boning a Whole Chicken (continued)

from the flesh. The thigh and drumstick bones must be removed separately, and you must start with those. The wings are not worth fussing with: Their bones can be left in place.

What you must be careful about is never to cut or tear the skin, except for a single, long incision down the back, which you must make to get to the bones and which you will later sew up. Chicken skin is wonderfully strong and elastic, when intact. But any breach will spread into a yawning gap. To keep your knife from slipping and puncturing the skin, always turn the blade's cutting edge away from the skin and toward the bone you are working on.

When you have finished boning, you'll be faced with what looks like a hopelessly confused and floppy mass that in no way resembles a chicken. Don't panic. When the stuffing goes where the bones used to be, the bird will fill out in all the right places and look absolutely lovely.

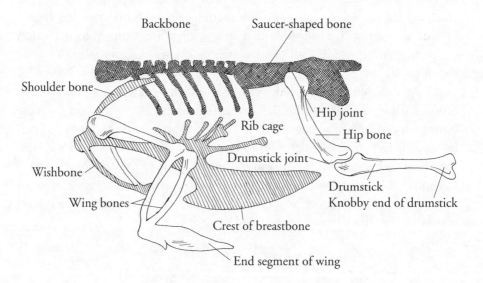

1. You will need a very sharp knife with a short blade. Place the chicken with the breast down, facing the work counter, and make a single, straight cut from the neck all the way down to the tail, probing deeply enough to reach the backbone.

2. Do one whole side of the bird at a time. Begin at the neck, detaching the flesh from the bones by prying it loose with your fingers and, where necessary, cutting it from the bone with the knife. Always angle the blade's cutting edge toward the bone and away from the skin. Continue thus as you work your way down the chicken's back.

3. When you have passed the midway point and are approaching the small of the back, you will find a small saucer-shaped bone filled with meat. Pull the meat away with your fingers, cutting it loose with the knife when necessary. Further on you will come to the hip joint. Use your fingers to loosen as much of the meat around it as you can, then sever the joint from the carcass with poultry shears. With one hand, hold the end of the chicken's leg, and with the other, pull the meat away from the hip bone. When you come to long white filaments—the tendons—sever them at the bone with your knife.

4. The next joint you must deal with is the one connecting the hip bone to the drumstick. Hold the hip bone in one hand, the drumstick in the other, and snap off the hip bone at the joint. You can now remove the hip bone completely, using your knife to scrape it loose from any meat still attached to it. Whenever the knife is in your hand, always think about the skin, taking care not to tear it or pierce it.

5. Next, you must remove the drumstick bone. Start at the thick, fleshy end and loosen the meat from the bone, pulling it away with your fingers when it will give, detaching it with the knife when necessary. Sever the tendons at the bone, leaving them attached to the flesh. Work your way gently to the knobby end of the drumstick, taking care not to split the skin. As you continue to pull the meat away from the bone, you will find this part of the chicken turning itself inside out like a glove. When you are about ½ inch away from the drumstick's knob, make a circular cut, cutting skin, meat, and tendons clear through to the bone. Grasp the bone by its knob and push it back through the leg until it slips out at the other end.

6. Return to the upper part of the back. Pulling with your fingers and scraping against the bone with the knife, free the flesh from the rib cage, moving toward the breastbone. When you reach the breastbone, leave the skin attached to the bone's crest for the time being.

7. Joined to the wing you will find the shoulder bone. Pry the meat loose from it, using your fingers when you can and the knife when you need to, then sever the bone at the joint where it meets the wing, and remove it. With poultry shears, cut off the end segment of the wing. Do not bother to remove the bones from that part of the wing still attached to the body.

8. Bone the other side of the bird, repeating the procedure described above, until the chicken is attached to its carcass only at the crest of the breastbone.

9. Turn the chicken over so that the breast faces you and the carcass rests on the counter. Pick up the two loose sides of the bird's flesh, and lift them above the carcass, holding them with one hand. With the knife, carefully free the skin from its hold on the crest of the breastbone. You must be at your

Boning a Whole Chicken (continued)

most careful here, because the skin is very thin where it is attached to the bone, and you can easily make a slit. Keep the cutting edge and the point of the knife turned away from the skin, scraping the blade along the bone's surface. When you have completely loosened the flesh, discard the carcass. Your boned chicken is ready for the stuffing.

Ahead-of-time note ❀ The entire boning operation may be completed a day before stuffing the chicken.

Pan-Roasted Whole Boned Chicken with Beef and Parmesan Stuffing

For 6 servings

⅔ cup crumb, the soft, crustless part of bread, cut into 1-inch pieces

½ cup milk

1 pound ground beef, preferably chuck

2 tablespoons parsley chopped very fine

½ teaspoon garlic chopped very fine

Salt

Black pepper, ground fresh from the mill

⅔ cup freshly grated *parmigiano-reggiano* cheese

A 3- to 4-pound chicken, boned as directed on pages 341–344

Trussing needle and string OR a darning needle and strong cotton thread

¼ cup vegetable oil

1 tablespoon butter

½ cup dry white wine

1. Put the cut-up crumb and the milk in a deep dish and let the bread steep for 10 or 15 minutes.

2. Put the ground beef, parsley, garlic, salt, pepper, and grated Parmesan into a bowl and mix thoroughly until the ingredients are evenly combined.

3. Gently squeeze the soaked crumb in your hand until it no longer drips milk. Add to the ground beef mixture, and softly knead with your hands until the ingredients are smoothly amalgamated.

4. Place the boned chicken skin side down on a work counter. Use some of the stuffing mixture to fill the places in the legs where the bones used to be. Take the rest of the mixture and shape it into an oval mass about as long

as the chicken. Put it in the center of the chicken, and bring the bird's skin around and over it, covering the stuffing completely. One edge of the skin should overlap the other by approximately 1 inch. Mold the mass under the skin with your hands to restore the chicken as closely as possible to its original shape.

5. Sew up the skin, starting at the neck and working down toward the tail. Use a sort of overcast stitch, looping the stitches over the edge of the skin. Don't expect to do a perfectly neat job when you get to the tail, but do the best you can, making sure you sew up all openings. When done, put the needle safely out of harm's way.

6. Choose a heavy-bottomed or enameled cast-iron pot that can subsequently contain the chicken snugly. Put in the oil and butter and turn on the heat to medium. When the butter foam begins to subside, put in the chicken, the stitched side facing down. Brown it well all over, handling the bird gently when you turn it. Add the wine, and when it has simmered briskly for about 30 seconds, sprinkle with salt and pepper, adjust heat to cook at a very slow simmer, and put a lid on the pot, setting it slightly askew. Calculate about 20 minutes per pound of stuffed chicken for cooking time. Turn the chicken occasionally while it cooks. If the cooking liquid should become insufficient, add 1 or 2 tablespoons water as needed.

7. Transfer the chicken to a carving board or large platter, letting it settle for a few minutes.

8. Spoon off all but a little bit of the fat in the pot. Add 1 or 2 tablespoons water, turn the heat up to high, and while boiling away the water use a wooden spoon to scrape loose cooking residues from the bottom and sides. Pour the pot juices into a warm saucer or small sauceboat.

Pan-Roasted Whole Boned Chicken (continued)

9. Carve the chicken at the table, starting at the neck, making thin slices. Pour a few drops of the warm pot juices over each slice when serving. If serving the bird cold—at room temperature, that is—omit the juices.

Pan-Roasted Squab Pigeons

THE CLASSIC METHOD for cooking feathered game relies heavily on the aroma of fresh sage, as does this recipe. Also contributing intensity of flavor is the bird's own liver, which is stuffed into the cavity. The birds are roasted in the unmistakable Italian style, in a partly covered pan over the stove, rather than in the oven, and cooked until they are tender through and through, the meat ready to fall off the bone.

For 4 to 6 servings (A generous portion would be 1 squab per person. When preceded by a substantial first course, ½ squab is adequate, the rest divided up for possible second helpings.)

4 fresh squab, about 1 pound
    each, plucked thoroughly
    clean (if the squab don't
    come with the livers,
    add 4 fresh chicken livers)
1 dozen fresh sage leaves
Pancetta, cut into 4 thin strips,
    1½ inches long and ½ inch
    wide

Salt
Black pepper, ground fresh
    from the mill
1 tablespoon butter
2 tablespoons vegetable oil
⅔ cup dry white wine

1. Remove any organs from the birds' interior, discarding the hearts and gizzards, but keeping the livers. Wash the squab inside and out in cold running water, and pat thoroughly dry on the inside as well as the outside with cloth or paper towels. Stuff the cavity of each bird with 2 sage leaves, 1 strip of *pancetta,* 1 liver, a couple of pinches of salt, and grindings of black pepper.

2. Choose a sauté pan that can subsequently contain the squab without overlapping. Put in the butter and oil, turn the heat on to medium high, and when the butter foam subsides, add the remaining 4 sage leaves, then the squab. Brown the birds all over, sprinkle with salt and pepper, turn them over once or twice, then add the wine. Let the wine bubble briskly for 20 to 30 seconds, then adjust heat to cook at a slow simmer, and put a lid slightly ajar on the pan. Cook until the squab thighs feel very tender when prodded with a fork and the meat comes easily off the bone, approximately 1 hour. Turn the birds once every 15 minutes. If the liquid in the pan becomes insufficient, add 2 or 3 tablespoons of water as needed.

3. Transfer the squab when done to a warm serving platter. If serving ½ a bird per person, halve them with poultry scissors. Tip the pan and spoon off some of the fat. Add 2 tablespoons of water, turn the heat up to high, and while boiling away the water, scrape the bottom and sides of the pan with a wooden spoon to loosen cooking residues. Pour the pan juices over the squab and serve at once.

Roast Duck

THE AIM of this recipe was, when using birds with more fat than one finds on ducks in Italy, to transform them to the savory leanness of their Italian counterparts. The procedure used is borrowed in part from Chinese cooking. The duck is given a brief preliminary dunking in boiling water, and then thor-

Roast Duck (continued)

oughly gone over with a hair dryer. The first step opens the skin's pores wide, the second ensures that they stay open. When the bird roasts in the oven later, the fat melts and slowly runs off through the open pores, leaving the flesh succulent, but not greasy, while allowing the skin to become deliciously crisp. It's a method recommended not for wild ducks, but for those farm-raised ducklings thickly engirdled by fat.

The gravy is produced by the duck's own cooking juices that are flavored by a classic mixture of sage, rosemary, and mashed duck livers. Since ducklings do not have quite as much liver as we need, add either a chicken liver or even better, an extra duck liver, if you can obtain it from your butcher.

For 4 servings

Rosemary leaves, chopped very fine, 2 teaspoons if fresh, 1 teaspoon if dried

Sage leaves, chopped or crumbled very fine, 1 tablespoon if fresh, 1½ teaspoons if dried

Salt

Black pepper, ground fresh from the mill

⅔ cup duck liver, or duck and chicken liver (see remarks above) chopped very fine

A 4½- to 5-pound fresh duckling

A hand-held hair dryer

1. Combine the rosemary, sage, salt, and pepper, and divide the mixture into two parts.

2. Put the chopped liver and one of the halves of the above herb mixture into a bowl, and mix with a fork to an evenly blended consistency.

3. In a pot large enough to contain the duck completely covered in water, bring sufficient water to a boil.

4. Preheat oven to 450°.

5. If the bird still contains the gizzard, remove and discard it. Also remove the gobs of fat on either side of the cavity. When the water comes to a boil, put in the duck. After the water returns to a boil, leave the duck in another 5 to 7 minutes, then take it out. Drain the bird well, and pat it dry inside and out with paper towels. Turn on the hair dryer and direct hot air over the whole skin of the duck, for 6 to 8 minutes. (Please refer to the introductory remarks for an explanation of this procedure.)

6. Rub the remaining herb mixture, the part not combined with the liver, into the skin of the duck.

7. Spread the herb and liver mixture inside the bird's cavity.

8. Put the bird on a roasting rack, breast side up, and place the rack in a

shallow baking pan. Tuck up the tail with a toothpick so that the cavity will not spill its filling. Roast in the upper third of the preheated oven. After 30 minutes, turn the thermostat down to 375° and cook the duck for at least 1 hour more, until the skin becomes crisp.

9. Take the duck out of the oven and transfer it temporarily to a deep dish. Remove the toothpick from the tail to let all the liquid inside the cavity run into the dish. Collect this liquid and put it into a small saucepan, together with ¼ cup fat drawn from the roasting pan. Scrape away the herb and liver mixture still adhering to the duck's cavity and add it to the saucepan. Turn on the heat to low, and stir the contents of the pan until you have obtained a fairly dense gravy.

10. Detach the bird's wings and drumsticks, and either cut the breast into 4 pieces, or if you prefer, into several thin slices. Put the duck on a warm serving platter, pour the gravy over it, and serve immediately. If you prefer to carve the duck at table, English style, serve the gravy separately, in a sauceboat.

Rabbit with Rosemary and White Wine

MY FATHER lived in town, but like many Italians, he had a farm. It was the custom that on his periodic visits of inspection, the family that worked it for him, the *contadini*—the peasant farmers—would kill a chicken or rabbit and cook it for dinner. Here is the way they used to do rabbit. Without browning, it is stewed in very little besides its own juices. It is then simmered in white wine with some rosemary and a touch of tomato.   *For 4 to 6 servings*

A 3- to 3½-pound rabbit, cut into 8 pieces	Salt
⅓ cup extra virgin olive oil	Black pepper, ground fresh from the mill
¼ cup celery diced fine	1 bouillon cube and 2 table-
1 garlic clove, peeled	spoons tomato paste,
⅔ cup dry white wine	dissolved in ⅓ cup warm
2 sprigs of fresh rosemary OR 1½ teaspoons dried leaves	water

1. Soak the rabbit in abundant cold water overnight, in an unheated room in cold weather or in the refrigerator. Rinse in several changes of cold water, then pat thoroughly dry with cloth or paper towels.

2. Choose a sauté pan that can contain all the rabbit pieces without over-

Rabbit with Rosemary (continued)

lapping. Put in the oil, celery, garlic, and the rabbit, cover tightly, and turn the heat on to low. Turn the meat occasionally, but do not leave it uncovered.

3. You will find that at the end of 2 hours, the rabbit has shed a considerable amount of liquid. Uncover the pan, turn the heat up to medium, and cook until all the liquid has simmered away, turning the rabbit from time to time. Add the wine, rosemary, salt, and pepper. Allow the wine to simmer briskly until it has evaporated, then pour the dissolved bouillon cube and tomato paste mixture over the meat. Cook at a steady, gentle simmer for another 15 minutes or more, until the juices in the pan have formed a dense little sauce, turning the rabbit pieces over from time to time. Transfer the entire contents of the pan to a warm platter and serve promptly.

Ahead-of-time note You can finish cooking the rabbit several hours or a day in advance. Reheat in a covered pan over low heat, adding 2 or 3 tablespoons of water. Turn the rabbit pieces from time to time until they are warmed all the way through.

VEAL

Pan-Roasted Veal with Garlic, Rosemary, and White Wine

FOR ITALIAN FAMILIES, this exquisitely simple dish is the classic way to cook a roast. It is a perfect illustration of the basic pan-roasting method used by home cooks in Italy, conducted entirely over a burner. Its secret lies in slow, watchful cooking, in a partly covered pot, carefully monitoring the amount of liquid so that there is just enough to keep the meat from sticking to the pan, but not so much that it dilutes its flavor. No other technique produces a more savory or succulent roast, and it is as successful with birds and lamb as it is with veal.

For 6 servings

3 medium garlic cloves
2 pounds boned veal roast (see note below)
A sprig of rosemary OR 1 teaspoon dried rosemary leaves

2 tablespoons vegetable oil
2 tablespoons butter
Salt
Black pepper, ground fresh from the mill
⅔ cup dry white wine

Note ❀ A juicy, flavorful, and not expensive cut for this roast would be boned, rolled shoulder of veal.

1. Lightly mash the garlic with a knife handle, hitting it just hard enough to split the skin, which you will remove and discard.

2. If the meat is to be rolled up, put the garlic, rosemary, and a few grindings of pepper on it while it is flat, then roll it, and tie it securely. If it is a solid piece from the round, pierce it at several points with a sharp, narrow-bladed knife and insert the garlic and distribute here and there the sprig of rosemary, divided into several pieces, or the dried leaves.

3. Choose a heavy-bottomed or enameled cast-iron pot, possibly oval-shaped, just large enough to hold the meat. Put in the oil and butter, turn on

Pan-Roasted Veal (continued)

the heat to medium high, and when the butter foam begins to subside, put in the meat and brown it deeply all over. Sprinkle with salt and pepper.

4. Add the wine and, using a wooden spoon, loosen the browning residues sticking to bottom and sides of the pot. Adjust heat so that the wine barely simmers, set the cover on slightly ajar, and cook for 1½ to 2 hours, until the meat feels very tender when prodded with a fork. Turn the roast from time to time while it is cooking and, if there is no liquid in the pot, add 2 or 3 tablespoons of water as often as needed.

5. When done, transfer the roast to a cutting board. Should there be no juices left in the pan, put in ¼ cup of water, turn the heat up to high, and boil the water away while loosening the cooking residues stuck to the bottom and sides. If on the other hand, you have ended up with too much liquid in the pan—there should be about a spoonful or slightly less of juice per serving—reduce it over high heat. Turn off the heat.

Ahead-of-time note ❀ The cooking can be completed up to this point several hours in advance. Reheat gently in a covered pan with 1 or 2 tablespoons of water if necessary.

6. Cut the roast into slices about ¼ inch thick. Arrange them on a warm platter, spoon the cooking juices over them, and serve at once.

Rolled-Up Breast of Veal with Pancetta

THE BREAST is one of the juiciest and tastiest, as well as one of the least expensive, cuts of veal. The rib bones it is attached to must be removed so that the meat can be rolled, but if you have the butcher do it for you, don't leave the bones behind because they are an excellent addition to homemade meat broth.

If you'd like to try boning the meat yourself—and it is quite simple—proceed as follows: Lay the breast on a work counter, ribs facing down, and slip the blade of a sharp knife between the meat and the bones, working all the meat loose in a single, flat piece. Remove bits of gristle and loose patches of skin, but do not detach the one layer of skin that adheres to and covers the breast.

For 4 to 6 servings

Breast of veal in a single piece, 4½ to 5 pounds with the bones, yielding approximately 1¾ pounds of meat when boned either by the butcher or as described above

Salt

Black pepper, ground fresh from the mill

¼ pound *pancetta,* sliced very, very thin

2 or 3 garlic cloves, peeled

A sprig or two of rosemary OR 1 teaspoon dried rosemary leaves

Trussing string

1 tablespoon vegetable oil

2 tablespoons butter

½ cup dry white wine

1. Lay the boned meat flat, skin side facing down, sprinkle with salt and pepper, spread the sliced *pancetta* over it, add the garlic cloves, spaced well apart, and top with rosemary. Roll the meat up tightly, jelly-roll fashion, and tie it firmly with trussing string.

2. Choose a heavy-bottomed or enameled cast-iron pot, possibly oval-shaped, just large enough for the meat. Put in the oil and butter, turn on the heat to medium high, and when the butter foam begins to subside, put in the meat and brown it deeply all over. Sprinkle with salt and add the wine.

3. Let the wine come to a boil, turn the meat in it, and after a few seconds, turn down the heat so that the wine will bubble at a very slow, intermittent simmer. Set the cover on slightly ajar, and cook for 1½ to 2 hours, until the meat feels very tender when prodded with a fork. Turn the breast from time to time while it is cooking and, if there is no liquid in the pot, add 2 or 3 tablespoons of water as often as is necessary.

4. Transfer the meat to a cutting board. Add 2 tablespoons of water to the juices in the pot, turn up the heat to high, and boil the water away while using a wooden spoon to scrape loose the cooking residues from the bottom and sides. Turn off the heat.

Ahead-of-time note ✿ Follow the recommendations for Pan-Roasted Veal with Garlic, Rosemary, and White Wine on page 351.

5. Cut the breast into slices a little less than ½ inch thick. If you leave the trussing strings on, it will be easier to cut the breast into compact slices, but make sure you pick out all the bits of string after slicing. Look for and discard the 2 garlic cloves, arrange the slices on a warm serving platter, pour the pot juices over them, and serve at once.

Pan-Roasted Breast of Veal

ALTHOUGH THIS HAD long been one of my favorite meat dishes, it was so simple and straightforward that I took it for granted, and it escaped my notice as a recipe to record. The late James Beard had it with me at Bologna's Diana restaurant when he came, in the mid-1970s, to observe the course I was then teaching. It was he who was so taken with it that he urged me to set the recipe down.

The whole breast, with the bones in, is pan-roasted on top of the stove in the classic Italian manner, with no liquid but a small amount of cooking fat, a little wine, and its own juices. It is far simpler to do than any of the fancy stuffed things one sometimes does with breast of veal, and it produces an impressive roast with a rich brown color, and astonishingly tender, savory meat.

For 4 servings

3 tablespoons extra virgin
    olive oil
3 whole garlic cloves, peeled
3½ pounds breast of veal with
    rib bones in
2 sprigs of fresh rosemary
    OR 1 teaspoon dried leaves

Salt
Black pepper, ground fresh
    from the mill
⅔ cup dry white wine

1. Choose a sauté pan that can subsequently accommodate the meat lying flat. Put in the oil and garlic, and turn on the heat to medium.

2. When the oil is quite hot, put in the breast, skin side facing down. The oil should sizzle when the meat goes in. Add the rosemary. Brown the meat deeply on one side, then on the other. Add salt and pepper, cook a minute or two longer, turning the breast 2 or 3 times, then add the wine. When the wine has bubbled briskly for 20 or 30 seconds, turn the heat down to low, and cover the pan, setting the lid slightly ajar.

3. Turn the meat from time to time while it cooks. If you find it sticking, loosen it with the help of 2 or 3 tablespoons of water and check the heat to make sure you are cooking at a very gentle pace. The veal is done when it feels very tender when prodded with a fork and has become colored a lovely brown all over. Expect it to take 2 to 2½ hours.

4. Transfer the breast to a cutting board with the ribs facing you. Use a sharp boning knife to work the bones loose, pull them away, and discard them. Carve the meat into thin slices, cutting it on the diagonal. Put the sliced meat on a warm serving platter.

5. Tip the pan, and spoon off some of the fat. Turn the heat on to medium, put in 2 or 3 tablespoons of water, and boil it away while using a wooden spoon to scrape loose cooking residues from the bottom and sides. Pour the pan juices over the veal and bring to the table promptly.

Ossobuco—Braised Veal Shanks, Milanese Style

Ossobuco, oss bus in Milan's dialect, means "bone with a hole." The particular bone in question is that of a calf's hind shank, and the ring of meat that circles it is the sweetest and most tender on the entire animal. To be sure that it is as meltingly tender on the plate as Nature had intended, be guided by the following suggestions:

❀ Insist that the shank come from the meatier hind leg only. If you are buying it in a supermarket and are in doubt, look for one of the butchers who is usually on hand during the day, and ask him.

Braised Veal Shanks (continued)

❧ Have the *ossobuco* cut no thicker than 1½ inches. It is the size at which it cooks best. Thick *ossobuco,* however impressive it looks on the plate, rarely cooks long and slowly enough, and it usually ends up being chewy and stringy.

❧ Make sure the butcher does not remove the skin enveloping the shanks. It not only helps to hold the *ossobuco* together while it cooks, but its creamy consistency makes a delectable contribution to the final flavor of the dish.

❧ Be prepared to give *ossobuco* time enough to cook. Slow, patient cooking is essential if you want to protect the shank's natural juiciness.

Note ❦ When you are buying a whole shank, ask the butcher to saw off both ends for you. You don't want them in the *ossobuco* because they don't have much meat, but they make a splendid addition to the assorted components of a homemade meat broth. *For 6 to 8 servings*

1 cup onion chopped fine
⅔ cup carrot chopped fine
⅔ cup celery chopped fine
4 tablespoons (½ stick) butter
1 teaspoon garlic chopped fine
2 strips lemon peel with none
  of the white pith beneath it
⅓ cup vegetable oil
8 1½-inch-thick slices of veal
  hind shank, each tied
  tightly around the middle
Flour, spread on a plate
1 cup dry white wine
1 cup Basic Homemade Meat
  Broth, prepared as directed
on page 15, OR ½ cup
  canned beef broth with
  ½ cup water
1½ cups canned imported
  Italian plum tomatoes,
  coarsely chopped, with
  their juice
½ teaspoon fresh thyme
  OR ¼ teaspoon dried
2 bay leaves
2 or 3 sprigs of parsley
Black pepper, ground fresh
  from the mill
Salt

1. Preheat oven to 350°.

2. Choose a pot with a heavy bottom or of enameled cast iron that can subsequently accommodate all the veal shanks in a single layer. (If you do not have a single pot large enough, use two smaller ones, dividing the ingredients into two equal halves, but adding 1 extra tablespoon of butter for each

pot.) Put in the onion, carrot, celery, and butter, and turn on the heat to medium. Cook for about 6 to 7 minutes, add the chopped garlic and lemon peel, cook another 2 or 3 minutes until the vegetables soften and wilt, then remove from heat.

3. Put the vegetable oil in a skillet and turn on the heat to medium high. Turn the veal shanks in the flour, coating them all over and shaking off the excess flour.

Note ❀ Do not flour the veal, or anything else that needs to be browned, in advance because the flour will become soggy and make it impossible to achieve a crisp surface.

When the oil is quite hot—it should sizzle when the veal goes in—slip in the shanks and brown them deeply all over. Remove them from the skillet using a slotted spoon or spatula, and stand them side by side over the chopped vegetables in the pot.

4. Tip the skillet and spoon off all but a little bit of the oil. Add the wine, reduce it by simmering it over medium heat while scraping loose with a wooden spoon the browning residues stuck to the bottom and sides. Pour the skillet juices over the veal in the pot.

5. Put the broth in the skillet, bring it to a simmer, and add it to the pot. Also add the chopped tomatoes with their juice, the thyme, the bay leaves, parsley, pepper, and salt. The broth should have come two-thirds of the way up to the top of the shanks. If it does not, add more.

6. Bring the liquids in the pot to a simmer, cover the pot tightly, and place it in the lower third of the preheated oven. Cook for about 2 hours or until the meat feels very tender when prodded with a fork and a dense, creamy sauce has formed. Turn and baste the shanks every 20 minutes. If, while the *ossobuco* is cooking, the liquid in the pot becomes insufficient, add 2 tablespoons of water at a time, as needed.

7. When the *ossobuco* is done, transfer it to a warm platter, carefully remove the trussing strings without letting the shanks come apart, pour the sauce in the pot over them, and serve at once. If the pot juices are too thin and watery, place the pot over a burner with high heat, boil down the excess liquid, then pour the reduced juices over the *ossobuco* on the platter.

Gremolada

If you wish to observe *ossobuco* tradition strictly, you must add an aromatic mixture called *gremolada* to the shanks, when they are nearly done. I never

Gremolada (continued)

do it myself, but some people like it, and if you want to try it, here is what it consists of:

1 teaspoon grated lemon peel, taking care to avoid the white pith	¼ teaspoon garlic chopped very, very fine 1 tablespoon chopped parsley

Combine the ingredients evenly and sprinkle the mixture over the shanks while they are cooking but when they are done, so that the *gremolada* cooks with the veal no longer than 2 minutes.

Ahead-of-time note ✸ *Ossobuco* can be completely cooked a day or two in advance. It should be reheated gently over the stove, adding 1 or 2 tablespoons of water, if needed. If you are using the *gremolada,* add it only when reheating the meat.

Ossobuco in Bianco—Tomato-Less Braised Veal Shanks

THE LIGHT-HANDED and delicately fragrant *ossobuco* of this recipe is quite different from the robust Milanese version. The tomato and vegetables and herbs of the traditional preparation are absent, and it is cooked in the slow Italian pan-roasted style, entirely on top of the stove.   *For 6 to 8 servings*

¼ cup extra virgin olive oil 2 tablespoons butter 8 1½-inch-thick slices of veal hind shank, each tied tightly around the middle Flour, spread on a plate Salt Black pepper, ground fresh from the mill	1 cup dry white wine 2 tablespoons lemon peel with none of the white pith beneath it, chopped very fine 5 tablespoons chopped parsley

1. Choose a large sauté pan that can subsequently accommodate all the shanks snugly without overlapping. (If you do not have a single pan that broad, use two, dividing the butter and oil in half, then adding 1 tablespoon of each for each pan.) Put in the oil and butter, and turn on the heat to

medium high. When the butter foam begins to subside, turn the shanks in the flour, coating them on both sides, shake off excess flour, and slip them into the pan.

2. Brown the meat deeply on both sides, then sprinkle with salt and several grindings of pepper, turn the shanks, and add the wine. Adjust heat to cook at a very slow simmer, and cover the pan, setting the lid slightly ajar.

3. After 10 minutes or so, look into the pan to see if the liquid has become insufficient to continue cooking. If, as is likely, this is the case, add ⅓ cup warm water. Check the pan from time to time, and add more water as needed. The total cooking time will come to 2 or 2½ hours: The shanks are done when the meat comes easily away from the bone and is tender enough to be cut with a fork. When done, transfer the veal to a warm plate, using a slotted spoon or spatula.

4. Add the chopped lemon peel and parsley to the pan, turn the heat up to medium, and stir for about 1 minute with a wooden spoon, loosening cooking residues from the bottom and sides, and reducing any runny juices in the pan. Return the shanks to the pan, turn them briefly in the juices, then transfer the entire contents of the pan to a warm platter and serve at once.

Ahead-of-time note 🍲 The light, fragrant flavor of this particular *ossobuco* does not withstand refrigeration well, so it is not advisable to prepare it very long in advance. It can certainly be made early on the day it is to be served; reheat it in the pan it was cooked in, covered, over low heat, for 10 or 15 minutes until the meat is warmed all the way through. If the juices in the pan become insufficient, replenish with 1 or 2 tablespoons water.

Stinco—Braised Whole Veal Shank, Trieste Style

Stinco is Italian for what Trieste's dialect calls *schinco,* a veal shank slowly braised whole, then served carved off the bone in very thin slices. It comes from the same part of the hind leg that Milan uses for *ossobuco,* whose succulent quality it shares, but unlike *ossobuco,* it is not made with tomatoes. The anchovies that are part of the flavor base dissolve and become undetectable, but they contribute subtly to the depth of taste that is the distinctive feature of this dish. *Stinco,* or *schinco,* tastes best when cooked entirely over the stove in the classic Italian pan-roasting method.

Braised Whole Veal Shank (continued)

For 8 servings

2 whole veal shanks (see note
  below)
2 garlic cloves
3 tablespoons vegetable oil
3 tablespoons butter
½ cup chopped onion
Salt

Black pepper, ground fresh
  from the mill
⅓ cup dry white wine
6 flat anchovy fillets (preferably
  the ones prepared at home
  as described on page 9)

Note ❧ The shanks must come from the hind leg. Have the joint at the broad end of the shank sawed off flat so that the bone can be brought to the table standing up, surrounded by the carved slices. Also have the butcher take off enough of the bone at the narrow end to expose the marrow, which, at table, can be picked out with a narrow implement and is most delectable.

1. Stand the shanks on their broad ends and, with a sharp knife, loosen the skin, flesh, and tendons at the narrow end. This will cause the meat, as it cooks, to come away from the bone at that end, and to gather in a plump mass at the base of the shank, giving the *stinco* a shape like that of a giant lollypop. If you find this difficult to do when the meat is raw, try it after 10 minutes' cooking, when it becomes much easier.

2. Lightly mash the garlic with a knife handle, just hard enough to split the skin, which you will loosen and discard.

3. You will need a heavy-bottomed pot, preferably oval in shape, that can subsequently snugly accommodate both shanks. Put in the oil and butter, turn on the heat to medium high, and when the butter foam begins to subside, put in both shanks.

4. Turn the shanks over to brown the veal deeply all over, then lower the heat to medium and add the chopped onion, nudging it in between the meat to the bottom of the pot.

5. Cook the onion, stirring, until it becomes colored gold. Add the garlic, salt, pepper, and wine. Let the wine simmer for about 1 minute, turning the shanks once or twice, then add the anchovy fillets, turn the heat down to very low, and cover the pot, setting the lid slightly ajar. Cook for about 2 hours, until the meat feels very tender when prodded with a fork. Turn the veal over from time to time. Whenever there is so little liquid in the pot that the meat begins to stick to the bottom, add ⅓ cup water and turn the shanks.

6. When the veal is done, lay the shank down on a cutting board, and carve the meat into thin slices, cutting at an angle, diagonally toward the bone. Stand the carved bones on their broader end on a warm serving platter and spread the slices of meat at their base.

7. Pour ⅓ cup water into the pot in which you cooked the meat, turn the heat up to high, and boil away the water using a wooden spoon to loosen all cooking residues from the bottom and sides. Pour the pot juices over the slices of veal and serve at once.

Ahead-of-time note ❀ The entire dish can be made several hours in advance. When doing so, instead of pouring the pot juices over the veal, put the sliced meat into the pot together with the bones. Reheat over gentle heat just before serving, turning the slices in the juice. Arrange on a warm platter as described above, and serve at once. Use the dish the same day you make it, because its flavor will deteriorate if kept overnight.

Veal Scaloppine with Marsala

For 4 servings

2 tablespoons vegetable oil
2 tablespoons butter
1 pound veal *scaloppine,* cut from the top round, and flattened as described on page 38

Flour, spread on a plate
Salt
Black pepper, ground fresh from the mill
½ cup dry Marsala wine

1. Put the oil and 1 tablespoon butter in a skillet and turn on the heat to medium high.

2. When the fat is hot, dredge both sides of the *scaloppine* in flour, shake off excess flour, and slip the meat into the pan. Brown them quickly on both sides, about half a minute per side if the oil and butter are hot enough. Transfer them to a warm plate, using a slotted spoon or spatula, and sprinkle with salt and pepper. (If the *scaloppine* don't all fit into the pan at one time without overlapping, do them in batches, but dredge each batch in flour just before slipping the meat into the pan; otherwise the flour will become soggy and make it impossible to achieve a crisp surface.)

3. Turn the heat on to high, add the Marsala, and while it boils down, scrape loose with a wooden spoon all browning residues on the bottom and sides. Add the second tablespoon of butter and any juices the *scaloppine* may have shed on the plate. When the juices in the pan are no longer runny and have the density of sauce, turn the heat down to low, return the *scaloppine* to the pan, and turn them once or twice to baste them with the pan juices. Turn out the entire contents of the pan onto a warm platter and serve at once.

Veal Scaloppine with Marsala and Cream

IN THIS VARIATION on the classic veal and Marsala theme, cream is introduced to soften the wine's emphatic accent without robbing it of any of its flavor. It becomes a rather more gentle dish than it is in its standard edition.

For 4 servings

1 tablespoon vegetable oil	Flour, spread on a plate
2 tablespoons butter	Salt
1 pound veal *scaloppine*, cut from the top round, and flattened as described on page 38	Black pepper, ground fresh from the mill ½ cup dry Marsala wine ⅓ cup heavy whipping cream

1. Put the oil and butter into a skillet, turn on the heat to medium high, and when the butter foam begins to subside, dredge the *scaloppine* in flour and cook them exactly as described in Step 2 of Veal Scaloppine with Marsala, page 361.

2. Turn the heat on to high, put into the pan any juices the *scaloppine* may have shed on the plate and the Marsala. While the wine boils down, scrape loose with a wooden spoon all browning residues on the bottom and sides. Add the cream and stir constantly until the cream is reduced and bound with the juices in the pan into a dense sauce.

3. Turn the heat down to medium, return the *scaloppine* to the pan, and turn them once or twice to coat them well with sauce. Turn out the entire contents of the pan onto a warm platter and serve at once.

Veal Scaloppine with Lemon

For 4 servings

1 tablespoon vegetable oil	Black pepper, ground fresh from the mill
3 tablespoons butter	2 tablespoons freshly squeezed lemon juice
1 pound veal *scaloppine*, cut from the top round, and flattened as described on page 38	2 tablespoons parsley chopped very fine
Flour, spread on a plate	½ lemon, sliced very thin
Salt	

1. Put the oil and 2 tablespoons of butter into a skillet, turn on the heat to medium high, and when the butter foam begins to subside, dredge the *scaloppine* in flour and cook them exactly as described in Step 2 of Veal Scaloppine with Marsala, page 361.

2. Off heat, add the lemon juice to the skillet, using a wooden spoon to scrape loose the browning residues on the bottom and sides. Swirl in the remaining tablespoon of butter, put in any juices the *scaloppine* may have shed in the plate, and add the chopped parsley, stirring to distribute it evenly.

3. Turn on the heat to medium and return the *scaloppine* to the pan. Turn them quickly and briefly, just long enough to warm them and coat them with sauce. Turn out the entire contents of the pan onto a warm platter, garnish the platter with lemon slices, and serve at once.

Note ❀ One sometimes sees *scaloppine* with lemon topped with a sprinkling of fresh chopped parsley. It's perfectly all right as long as you don't make the sauce with parsley. The color of cooked parsley contrasts unappetizingly with that of the fresh. If you use one, omit the other.

Veal Scaloppine with Mozzarella

For 4 servings

½ pound mozzarella, preferably buffalo-milk mozzarella
2 tablespoons butter
1 tablespoon vegetable oil
1 pound veal *scaloppine,* cut from the top round, and flattened as described on page 38
Salt
Black pepper, ground fresh from the mill

1. Slice the mozzarella into the thinnest slices you are able to, making sure you end up with 1 slice for every *scaloppine.*

2. Choose a sauté pan that can subsequently accommodate all the *scaloppine* without overlapping. (If you do not have a single pan that large, use two, dividing the butter and oil in half, then adding 1 tablespoon of each for each pan.) Put in the butter and oil, and turn on the heat to high.

3. When the butter foam begins to subside, put in the *scaloppine.* Brown them quickly on both sides, about 1 minute altogether if the fat is hot enough. Sprinkle with salt and turn the heat down to medium.

4. Place a slice of mozzarella on each of the *scaloppine,* and sprinkle with pepper. Put a cover on the pan for the few seconds it will take for the

Veal Scaloppine with Mozzarella (continued)

mozzarella to soften. Using a slotted spoon or spatula, transfer the veal to a warm serving platter, the mozzarella-topped side facing up.

5. Add 1 or 2 tablespoons water to the pan, turn the heat up to high, and while the water boils away, scrape the cooking residues from the bottom and sides with a wooden spoon. Pour the few dark drops of pan juices over the *scaloppine*, stippling the mozzarella, and serve at once.

Veal Scaloppine with Tomato, Oregano, and Capers

For 4 servings

2½ tablespoons vegetable oil
3 garlic cloves, peeled
1 pound veal *scaloppine*, cut from the top round, and flattened as described on page 38
Flour, spread on a plate
Salt
Black pepper, ground fresh from the mill
⅓ cup dry white wine

½ cup canned imported Italian plum tomatoes, chopped, with their juice
1 tablespoon butter
1 teaspoon fresh oregano OR ½ teaspoon dried
2 tablespoons capers, soaked and rinsed as described on page 16 if packed in salt, drained if in vinegar

1. Put the oil and garlic in a skillet, turn on the heat to medium, and cook the garlic until it becomes colored a light nut brown. Remove it from the pan and discard it.

2. Turn up the heat to medium high, dredge the *scaloppine* in flour, and cook them exactly as described in Step 2 of Veal Scaloppine with Marsala, page 361, transferring them to a warm plate when done.

3. Over medium-high heat, add the wine, and while the wine simmers use a wooden spoon to loosen all cooking residues on the bottom and sides. Add the chopped tomatoes with their juice, stir to coat well, add the butter and any juices the *scaloppine* may have shed on the plate, stir, and adjust heat to cook at a steady, but gentle simmer.

4. In 15 or 20 minutes, when the fat floats free of the tomatoes, add the oregano and capers, stir thoroughly, then return the *scaloppine* to the pan and turn them in the tomato sauce for about a minute until they are warm again. Turn out the entire contents of the pan onto a warm platter and serve at once.

Veal Scaloppine with Ham, Anchovies, Capers, and Grappa

For 4 servings

3 tablespoons butter

4 flat anchovy fillets (preferably the ones prepared at home as described on page 9), chopped very fine

¼ pound boiled unsmoked ham, sliced ¼ inch thick and diced fine

1½ tablespoons capers, soaked and rinsed as described on page 16 if packed in salt, drained if in vinegar, and chopped

1 tablespoon vegetable oil

Flour, spread on a plate

1 pound veal *scaloppine,* cut from the top round, and flattened as described on page 38

Salt

Black pepper, ground fresh from the mill

3 tablespoons *grappa* (see note below)

¼ cup heavy whipping cream

Note ✸ *Grappa* is a pungently fragrant distilled spirit made from pomace, a residue of winemaking. It is usually obtainable in stores stocking Italian wines, but it can be substituted with *marc,* a French spirit made like *grappa.* If neither is available, use *calvados,* French apple brandy, or a good grape brandy.

1. Put half the butter into a small saucepan, turn on the heat to very low, and add the chopped anchovies. Stir constantly as the anchovies cook, mashing them to a pulp against the sides of the pan with a wooden spoon. When the anchovies begin to dissolve, add the diced ham and chopped capers, and turn up the heat to medium. Stir thoroughly to coat well, cook for about 1 minute, then remove the pan from heat.

2. Put the oil and remaining butter in a skillet, and turn on the heat to medium high. When the butter foam begins to subside, dredge the *scaloppine* in flour and cook them exactly as described in Step 2 of Veal Scaloppine with Marsala, page 361.

3. Tip the skillet and spoon off most of the fat. Return to medium-high heat, add the *grappa,* and while it simmers quickly use a wooden spoon to loosen all cooking residues on the bottom and sides. Add the ham and anchovy mixture from the saucepan to the skillet and any juices the *scaloppine* may have shed on the plate, and stir thoroughly to combine all ingredients evenly. Add the cream, and reduce it briefly while stirring.

Veal Scaloppine with Ham (continued)

4. Return the *scaloppine* to the skillet, and turn them in the hot sauce for about a minute until they are completely warm again. Turn out the entire contents of the pan onto a warm platter and serve at once.

Veal Scaloppine in Parchment with Asparagus and Fontina Cheese

For 4 servings

½ pound fresh asparagus

2 tablespoons butter plus butter for dotting the finished dish

1½ tablespoons vegetable oil

1 pound veal *scaloppine,* cut from the top round, and flattened as described on page 38

Flour, spread on a plate

A baking dish

Cooking parchment or heavy-duty aluminum foil

Salt

Black pepper, ground fresh from the mill

6 ounces *fontina* cheese

⅓ cup dry Marsala wine

1. Trim the asparagus spears, peel the stalks, and cook the asparagus as described on page 466. Do not overcook it, but drain it when it is still firm to the bite. Set it aside until you come to the directions for cutting it later in this recipe.

2. Put the butter and oil in a sauté pan, and turn on the heat to high. When the butter foam begins to subside, take as many *scaloppine* as will fit loosely at one time in the pan, dredge them on both sides in the flour, shaking off excess flour, and slip them into the pan. Brown the veal briefly on both sides, altogether a minute or less if the fat is very hot, then transfer to a plate using a slotted spoon or spatula. Add another batch of *scaloppine* to the pan, and repeat the above procedure until you have browned all the meat.

3. Preheat oven to 400°.

4. Choose a baking dish that can subsequently accommodate all the *scaloppine* snugly, but without overlapping. Line it with cooking parchment or a piece of heavy aluminum foil large enough to extend well beyond the edges of the dish. When working with foil, take care not to tear it or pierce it. Lay the *scaloppine* flat in the dish, and sprinkle them with salt and pepper.

5. Cut the asparagus diagonally into pieces that are no longer than the

scaloppine. If any part of the stalk is thicker than ½ inch, divide it in half. Top each of the *scaloppine* with a layer of asparagus pieces. Sprinkle lightly with salt.

6. Cut the cheese into the thinnest slices you can. Do not worry if the slices are irregular in shape, they will fuse into one when the cheese melts. Cover the layer of asparagus with one of cheese slices.

7. Pour off and discard all the fat from the pan in which you browned the veal, but do not wipe the pan clean. Add to it any juices that the *scaloppine* may have shed on the plate and the Marsala. Turn on the heat to medium high, and scrape loose with a wooden spoon the browning residues on the bottom and sides, while reducing the juices in the pan to about 3 tablespoons.

8. Spoon the juices over the layer of cheese, distributing them evenly. Dot lightly with butter. Take a sheet of parchment or foil large enough to extend past the edge of the baking dish and lay it flat over the *scaloppine.* Bring together the edges of the lower sheet of parchment or foil and those of the upper sheet, crimping them to make a tight seal. Put the baking dish on the uppermost rack of the preheated oven and leave it in for 15 minutes, just long enough for the cheese to melt.

9. Take the dish out of the oven, and open the parchment or foil wrap, taking care to direct the outrushing steam away from you so as not to be scalded by it. Cut away the parchment or foil all around the dish and serve as is or gently lift the *scaloppine* out using a broad metal spatula, and transfer them to a warm serving platter without turning them over. Spoon the juices in the baking dish over them, and serve at once.

Messicani—Stuffed Veal Rolls with Ham, Parmesan, Nutmeg, and White Wine

For 4 servings

⅓ cup crumb, the soft, crustless part of bread, preferably from good Italian or French bread

⅓ cup milk

2 ounces boiled unsmoked ham, chopped fine

2 ounces pork, ground or chopped fine

1 egg

⅓ cup freshly grated *parmigiano-reggiano* cheese

Salt

Black pepper, ground fresh from the mill

Whole nutmeg

1 pound veal *scaloppine,* cut from the top round, and flattened as described on page 38

Sturdy round toothpicks

2 tablespoons butter

1 tablespoon vegetable oil

Flour, spread on a plate

⅓ cup dry white wine

½ cup Basic Homemade Meat Broth, prepared as directed on page 15, OR ½ bouillon cube dissolved in ½ cup water

1. Put the crumb and milk in a small bowl. When the bread has soaked up the milk, mash it to a creamy consistency with a fork, and pour off all excess milk.

2. Add the chopped ham, pork, egg, grated Parmesan, salt, pepper, a tiny grating of nutmeg—about ⅛ teaspoon—and the bread and milk mush, and mix with a fork until all ingredients are evenly combined. Turn the mixture out on a work surface and divide into as many parts as you have *scaloppine.*

3. Lay the *scaloppine* flat on a work surface. Coat each with one of the parts of the stuffing mixture, spreading it evenly over the meat. Roll the meat up into a sausage-like roll, and fasten it with a toothpick inserted lengthwise to allow the roll to be turned easily later when cooking.

4. Choose a sauté pan that can subsequently accommodate all the veal rolls in a single layer, put in the butter and oil, and turn on the heat to medium high. Dredge the rolls in flour all over, and when the butter foam subsides, slip them into the pan.

5. Brown the meat deeply all over, then add the wine. When the wine has bubbled away for a minute or so, sprinkle with salt, put in the broth, cover the pan, and turn the heat down to cook at a gentle simmer.

6. When the veal rolls have cooked all the way through, in about 20 min-

utes, transfer them to a warm platter. If the juices in the pan are thin and runny, turn the heat up to high and reduce them, while scraping loose with a wooden spoon cooking residues from the bottom and sides of the pan. If on the other hand, they are too thick and partly stuck to the pan, add 1 or 2 tablespoons water, and while the water boils away, scrape loose all cooking residues. Pour the pan juices over the veal rolls, and serve at once.

Veal Rolls with Pancetta and Parmesan

For 4 servings

1 pound veal *scaloppine,* cut from the top round, and flattened as described on page 38
¼ pound *pancetta,* sliced very, very thin
5 tablespoons freshly grated *parmigiano-reggiano* cheese
Sturdy round toothpicks
2 tablespoons butter

2 tablespoons vegetable oil
Salt
Black pepper, ground fresh from the mill
½ cup dry white wine
⅔ cup fresh, ripe tomatoes, peeled and chopped, OR canned Italian plum tomatoes, cut up, with their juice

1. Trim the *scaloppine* so that they are approximately 5 inches long and 3½ to 4 inches wide. Try not to end up with bits of meat left over that you can't use. It does not really matter if some pieces are irregular: It's better to use them than to waste them.

2. Lay the *scaloppine* flat and over each spread enough *pancetta* to cover. Sprinkle with grated Parmesan and roll up the *scaloppine* tightly into compact rolls. Fasten the rolls with a toothpick inserted lengthwise so that the meat can be turned in the pan. If any *pancetta* is left over, chop it very fine and set aside.

Veal Rolls with Pancetta (continued)

3. Put 1 tablespoon of butter and all the oil in a skillet and turn on the heat to medium high. When the butter foam begins to subside, put in the veal rolls, and turn them to brown them deeply all over. Transfer to a warm plate, using a slotted spoon or spatula, remove all the toothpicks, and sprinkle the meat with salt and pepper.

4. If you had set aside some chopped *pancetta,* put it in the skillet and cook it over medium heat for about 1 minute, then add the wine. Let the wine simmer steadily for 1½ to 2 minutes while using a wooden spoon to loosen cooking residues from the bottom and sides of the pan. Add the tomatoes, stir thoroughly, and adjust heat to cook for a minute or so at a steady simmer until the fat separates from the tomato.

5. Return the veal rolls to the pan, warming them up for a few minutes and turning them in the sauce from time to time. Take off heat, swirl in the remaining tablespoon of butter, then turn out the entire contents of the pan onto a warm platter and serve at once.

Ahead-of-time note ❧ These veal rolls don't take that long to do and they taste best when served the moment they are made. If you must make them in advance, cook them through to the end up to several hours ahead of time, then reheat gently in their sauce.

Veal Rolls with Anchovy Fillets and Mozzarella

For 6 servings

8 flat anchovy fillets (preferably the ones prepared at home as described on page 9)

3 tablespoons butter

¼ cup chopped parsley

⅓ cup canned imported Italian plum tomatoes, drained of juice

Black pepper, ground fresh from the mill

½ pound mozzarella, preferably imported buffalo-milk mozzarella

1½ pounds veal *scaloppine,* cut from the top round, and flattened as described on page 38

Salt

Thin kitchen twine

Flour, spread on a plate

½ cup dry Marsala wine

1. Chop the anchovies very, very fine, put them in a small saucepan with 1 tablespoon of butter, turn on the heat to very low, and while the anchovies are cooking, mash them with a wooden spoon against the side of the pan to reduce them to a pulp.

2. Add the chopped parsley, the tomatoes, a few grindings of pepper, and turn up the heat to medium. Cook at a steady simmer, stirring frequently, until the tomato thickens and the butter floats free.

3. Cut the mozzarella into the thinnest slices you can, possibly about ⅛ inch.

4. Lay the *scaloppine* flat on a platter or work surface, sprinkle with a tiny pinch of salt, and spread the tomato and anchovy sauce over them, stopping short of the edges to leave a margin of about ¼ inch all around. Top with sliced mozzarella. Roll up the *scaloppine*, push the meat in at both ends to plug them, and truss with kitchen twine, running the string once around the middle of the rolls, and once lengthwise so as to loop it over both ends.

5. Choose a skillet that can subsequently accommodate all the rolls without crowding them, put in the remaining 2 tablespoons of butter and turn the heat on to medium high. When the butter foam begins to subside, turn the veal rolls in the flour, shake off excess flour, and slip them into the pan. Cook for a minute or two, turning them, until they are browned deeply all over. If a little cheese oozes out of the rolls, it does no harm; it will help enrich the sauce. Transfer the meat to a warm plate, snip off the strings, and remove them, being careful not to undo the rolls.

6. Add the Marsala to the pan, bring it to a lively simmer for about 2 minutes, and while it is reducing use a wooden spoon to loosen cooking residues from the bottom and sides. Return the veal rolls to the pan, turn them gently in the sauce 2 or 3 times, then transfer the entire contents of the pan to a warm serving platter and serve at once.

Veal Roll with Spinach and Prosciutto Stuffing

A SINGLE, large slice of veal is covered with spinach, sautéed with onion and prosciutto, rolled up tightly, and pan-roasted with white wine. When it is sliced, the alternating layers of veal and stuffing make an attractive spiral pattern, but what is more important is that it is juicy and savory, tasting as good as it looks.

To produce the dish, you need a single, large, one-pound slice of veal, preferably cut from the broadest section of the top round, and flattened by

Veal Roll with Spinach (continued)

your cooperative butcher to a thickness of no more than ⅜ inch. The breast of veal, which is usually employed to make large rolls, does not lend itself well to this recipe because of its uneven thickness.   *For 4 servings*

1½ pounds fresh spinach	A 1-pound slice of veal, prefer-
Salt	ably from the top round
3 tablespoons butter	(see remarks above),
2 tablespoons vegetable oil	pounded flat to a thickness
2 tablespoons onion chopped	of ⅜ inch
very fine	Thin kitchen twine
¼ pound prosciutto OR *pancetta*	½ cup dry white wine
chopped very fine	⅓ cup heavy whipping cream
Black pepper, ground fresh	
from the mill	

1. Pull the leaves from the spinach, discarding all the stems. Soak the spinach in a basin of cold water, dunking it repeatedly. Carefully lift out the spinach, empty the basin of water together with the soil that has settled to the bottom, refill with fresh water, and repeat the entire procedure as often as necessary until the spinach is completely free of soil.

2. Cook the spinach in a covered pan over medium heat with just the water that clings to its leaves and 1 tablespoon of salt to keep it green. Cook for 2 minutes after the liquid shed by the spinach comes to a boil, then drain at once. As soon as it is cool enough to handle, squeeze as much moisture as you can out of the spinach, chop it very fine with a knife, not in the food processor, and set it aside.

3. Put 1 tablespoon of butter, 1 tablespoon of oil, all the onion, and all the prosciutto or *pancetta* into a small sauté pan, and turn on the heat to medium. Cook the onion until it becomes colored a rich, golden brown, and add the chopped spinach and several grindings of pepper. Stir thoroughly to coat well, and cook for 20 or 30 seconds, then remove from heat. Taste and, if necessary, correct for salt.

4. Lay the veal slice flat on a work surface. Spread the spinach mixture over it, spreading it evenly. Lift one end of the slice to look for the way the grain of the meat runs, then curl up the veal tightly with the grain parallel to the length of the roll. When you slice the roll after cooking, you will easily obtain even, compact slices because you will be cutting across the grain. Tie the roll securely into a salami-like shape with kitchen twine.

5. Choose a pot, oval if possible, in which the roll will fit snugly. Put in

the remaining butter and oil, turn on the heat to medium high, and as soon as the butter foam begins to subside, put in the veal roll. Brown it deeply all over, then sprinkle with salt and pepper, turn the roll once or twice, and add the wine. When the wine has simmered briskly for 15 or 20 seconds, turn the heat down to low, and cover the pot with the lid set slightly ajar.

6. Cook for about 1½ hours, turning the roll from time to time, until the meat feels very tender when prodded with a fork.

Ahead-of-time note ❧ You can complete the recipe up to this point several hours in advance. Before proceeding, reheat gently, adding 1 tablespoon water if needed. Do not refrigerate at any time or the spinach will acquire a sour taste.

Uncover the pot, add the cream, turn the heat up, and use a wooden spoon to loosen cooking residues from the bottom and sides of the pot. Remove from heat as soon as the cream thickens a bit and becomes colored a light nut brown.

7. Transfer the roll to a warm platter. Snip off and remove the kitchen twine. Cut the roll into thin slices, pour over it the juices from the pot, and serve at once.

Sautéed Breaded Veal Chops, Milanese Style

SOME ITALIAN DISHES are so closely associated with their place of origin that they have appropriated its name for their own. To Italians a *fiorentina* means "T-bone steak," and a breaded veal chop is *una milanese:* No other description is required. It can be debated whether *ossobuco* or the veal chop *milanese* is Milan's best-known gastronomic export. The latter has certainly been appropriated by many other cuisines, most notably in Austria, where it was taken off the bone to become the national dish, *wiener schnitzel.*

The classic Milanese chop is a single-rib chop that has been pounded very thin, with the rib trimmed entirely clean to give the bone the appearance of a handle. (Do not discard the trimmings from the bone. Add them to the assortment of meats for homemade broth, or if you have enough of them, grind them and make meatballs.) Before pounding the chop flat, a Milanese butcher will knock off the corner where the rib meets the bone. Your own butcher can do this easily, but so can you: Use a meat cleaver to crop the corner, then pound the chop's eye thin, following the method for flattening *scaloppine* described on page 37.

Sautéed Breaded Veal Chops (continued)

When the chop is taken from a large animal, there may be too much meat on a single rib to flatten. Before pounding it, it should be sliced horizontally into two chops, one attached to the rib, the other not.   *For 6 servings*

2 eggs
6 veal chops, with either 6 or 3
    ribs, depending on the size,
    the bones trimmed clean
    and the meat flattened (see
    explanatory remarks above)

1½ cups fine, dry, unflavored
    bread crumbs spread on a
    plate
2 tablespoons butter
2 tablespoons vegetable oil
Salt

1. Lightly beat the eggs in a deep dish, using a fork or a whisk.

2. Dip each chop in the egg, coating both sides and letting excess egg flow back into the plate as you pull the chop away. Turn the meat in the bread crumbs as follows: Press the chop firmly against the crumbs, using the palm of your hand. Tap it 2 or 3 times, then turn it and repeat the procedure. Your palm should come away dry, which means the crumbs are adhering to the meat.

3. Choose a sauté pan that can subsequently accommodate the chops without overlapping. If you don't have a large enough pan, you can use a smaller one, and do the chops in 2 or even 3 batches. Put in the butter and oil, turn on the heat to medium high, and when the butter foam begins to subside, slip in the chops. Cook until a dark golden crust forms on one side, then turn them and do the other side, altogether about 5 minutes, depending on the thickness of the chops. Transfer to a warm platter and sprinkle with salt. Serve promptly when all the chops are done.

Variation in the Sicilian Style, with Garlic and Rosemary

To the ingredients in the above recipe for Sautéed Breaded Veal Chops, Milanese Style, add the following:

Rosemary leaves, chopped very
    fine, 1 tablespoon if fresh, 2
    teaspoons if dried

4 garlic cloves, lightly mashed
    with a knife handle and
    peeled

Use the basic recipe, varying it as follows:

1. Sprinkle the chops with chopped rosemary after dipping them into the egg, but *before* coating them with bread crumbs.

2. Put the garlic into the pan at the same time with the butter and oil and remove it as soon as it becomes colored a light nut brown, either before or after you have begun sautéing the chops.

Adapting the Milanese Style to Veal and Other Cutlets

THE ITALIAN for cutlet, *cotoletta,* describes not the type of meat, but the method by which it is cooked. The method is the one described above in Sautéed Breaded Veal Chops, Milanese Style, page 373. To make *cotolette—* or cutlets—follow it exactly, simply replacing the chops with veal *scaloppine,* or thin slices of beef, or sliced chicken or turkey breast, or even sliced eggplant. When using meat sliced very thin, as for example *scaloppine,* the cooking time must be very brief, just long enough to form a light crust on both sides of the cutlet.

Serving Suggestion for Breaded Veal Cutlets ✽ They are delicious, either hot or at room temperature, with a combination of Fried Eggplant, page 493, and Oven-Browned Tomatoes, page 527, both also good either hot or at room temperature.

Sautéed Veal Chops with Sage and White Wine

For 4 servings

3 tablespoons vegetable oil	Salt
4 veal loin chops less than 1 inch thick	Black pepper, ground fresh from the mill
Flour, spread on a plate	⅓ cup dry white wine
12 dried sage leaves	1 tablespoon butter

1. Choose a skillet that can subsequently accommodate all the chops at one time without overlapping. If you don't have a pan large enough, choose a smaller one in which you can do the chops in 2 batches. Put in the vegetable oil, and turn on the heat to medium high.

2. When the oil becomes hot, turn both sides of the chops in the flour, shaking off any excess flour, and slip the veal into the pan together with the sage leaves. Cook for about 8 minutes, turning the chops two or three times to cook both sides evenly. The chops are done when the meat is rosy pink. Don't cook them much longer or they will become dry. Transfer

Sautéed Veal Chops with Sage (continued)

to a warm plate with a slotted spoon or spatula, and sprinkle with salt and pepper.

3. Tip the skillet and spoon off most of the oil. Add the wine and simmer it over medium-high heat until it is reduced to a slightly syrupy consistency. While it simmers, scrape with a wooden spoon to loosen cooking residues from the bottom and sides of the pan. When the wine has simmered away almost completely, turn the heat down to low and stir in the butter. Return the chops to the skillet briefly, turning them in the pan juices, then transfer the entire contents of the pan to a warm platter and serve at once.

Sautéed Veal Chops with Garlic, Anchovies, and Parsley

For 4 servings

2 tablespoons butter

1 teaspoon garlic chopped
    coarse

2 flat anchovy fillets (preferably
    the ones prepared at home
    as described on page 9),
    chopped very, very fine

2 tablespoons chopped parsley

3 tablespoons vegetable oil

4 veal loin chops less than 1
    inch thick

Flour, spread on a plate

Salt

Black pepper, ground fresh
    from the mill

1. Put the butter and garlic in a small saucepan and turn on the heat to medium. Cook the garlic until it becomes colored a pale gold, then turn the heat down to very low, and put in the chopped anchovies. Cook, stirring the anchovies with a wooden spoon and mashing them against the sides of the pan, until they begin to dissolve into a paste. Add the chopped parsley, stir and cook for about 20 seconds, then remove from heat.

2. Choose a sauté pan that can subsequently accommodate all the chops without overlapping. Put in the vegetable oil and turn on the heat to medium high. When the oil becomes hot, turn both sides of the chops in the flour, shaking off any excess flour, and slip the veal into the pan. Cook for about 8 minutes, turning the chops two or three times to cook both sides evenly. The chops are done when the meat is rosy pink. Don't cook them much longer or they will become dry. Transfer to a warm plate with a slotted spoon or spatula, and sprinkle with salt and pepper.

3. Turn the heat on to medium, add 2 or 3 tablespoons of water, and, as you boil it away, scrape loose the cooking residues in the pan. Return the chops to the pan, and immediately pour the anchovy and parsley sauce over them. Turn the chops just once or twice, then transfer the entire contents of the pan to a warm platter and serve at once.

Veal Stew with Sage,
White Wine, and Cream

THE MOST DESIRABLE cuts for an Italian veal stew are the shoulder and the shanks. Avoid the round or the loin, which are too lean for the prolonged cooking a stew requires, becoming dry and stringy.

For 4 to 6 servings

1 tablespoon vegetable oil	18 dried sage leaves
1½ tablespoons butter	⅔ cup dry white wine
1½ pounds boned veal shoulder or shank, cut into cubes of approximately 1½ inches	Salt
	Black pepper, ground fresh from the mill
Flour, spread on a plate	⅓ cup heavy whipping cream
2 tablespoons chopped onion	

1. Put the oil and butter in a sauté pan and turn on the heat to high. When the butter foam begins to subside, turn the veal cubes in the flour, coating them on all sides, shake off excess flour, and put them in the pan. Cook the meat, turning it, until all sides are deeply browned. Transfer it to a plate using a slotted spoon or spatula. (If the meat doesn't fit loosely into the pan all at one time, brown it in batches, but dip the cubes in flour only when you are ready to slip them into the pan.)

2. Turn the heat down to medium, and put the chopped onion in the pan together with the sage leaves. Cook the onion until it becomes colored a pale

Veal Stew with Sage (continued)

gold, return the meat to the pan, and add the wine, bringing it to a lively simmer while scraping the bottom and sides of the pan with a wooden spoon to loosen the browning residues. After half a minute or less, adjust the heat to cook at a gentle simmer, add salt, several grindings of pepper, and cover the pan. Cook for 45 minutes, turning and basting the meat from time to time. If the liquid in the pan becomes insufficient, replenish it when needed with 1 or 2 tablespoons of water.

3. Add the heavy cream, turn the meat thoroughly to coat it well, cover the pan again, turn the heat down to low, and cook for another 30 minutes, or until the veal feels very tender when prodded with a fork. Taste and correct for salt. Transfer the entire contents of the pan to a warm platter and serve at once.

Ahead-of-time note ❦ Like most stews, this one can be prepared several days in advance and refrigerated until needed. Reheat it gently until the meat has been warmed through and through, either on the stove or in a preheated 325° oven. Add 2 tablespoons of water when reheating.

Veal Stew with Tomatoes and Peas

For 4 to 6 servings

1 tablespoon vegetable oil
1½ tablespoons butter
1½ pounds boned veal shoulder
    or shank, cut into 1½-inch
    cubes
Flour, spread on a plate
2 tablespoons chopped onion
Salt
Black pepper, ground fresh
    from the mill

1 cup canned imported Italian
    plum tomatoes, chopped
    coarse, with their juice
2 pounds fresh peas in their
    pods (please see note),
    OR 1 ten-ounce package
    frozen small peas, thawed

Note ❦ If you are using fresh peas, you will add to their sweetness and that of the stew by utilizing some of the pods. It is an optional procedure, however, and if you choose to, you can omit it.

1. Put the oil and butter in a heavy-bottomed pot or in enameled cast-iron ware, and turn on the heat to high. When the fat is hot, turn the veal cubes in the flour, coating them on all sides, shake off excess flour, and put them in the pan. Cook the meat, turning it, until all sides are deeply browned.

Transfer it to a plate using a slotted spoon or spatula. (If the meat doesn't fit loosely into the pan all at one time, brown it in batches, but dip the cubes in flour only when you are ready to slip them into the pan.)

2. Turn the heat down to medium, and put the chopped onion in the pan. Cook the onion until it becomes colored a pale gold, return the meat to the pan, add salt, pepper, and the chopped tomatoes with their juice. When the tomatoes begin to bubble, adjust heat so that they simmer slowly, and cover the pot. Turn the meat from time to time.

3. *If using fresh peas:* Shell them, and prepare some of the pods for cooking by stripping away their inner membrane as described on page 93. It's not necessary to use all or even most of the pods, but do as many as you have patience for. When the meat has cooked for about 50 minutes, add the peas and pods.

If using frozen peas: Add them to the pot when the meat has cooked for about an hour.

Cover the pot again, and continue cooking for about 1 or 1½ hours, until the veal feels very tender when prodded with a fork. If you are using fresh peas, taste them to make sure they are done; if you have to cook them longer, it will do the stew absolutely no harm. Frozen peas don't need much cooking, but the longer they cook along with the veal the more their flavor becomes an integral part of the stew. Taste and correct for salt before serving.

Ahead-of-time note ❦ Please follow the suggestions on page 378.

Veal Stew with Mushrooms

For 4 to 6 servings

3 tablespoons butter
2½ tablespoons vegetable oil
1½ pounds boned veal shoulder or shank, cut into 1½-inch cubes
Flour, spread on a plate
½ cup onion chopped fine
1 large garlic clove, peeled and chopped fine
½ cup dry white wine
½ cup canned imported Italian plum tomatoes, cut up, with their juice

1 or 2 sprigs of fresh rosemary
    OR 1 teaspoon dried leaves, chopped fine
4 or 5 fresh sage leaves
    OR 2 or 3 dried whole leaves
2 tablespoons chopped parsley
Salt
Black pepper, ground fresh from the mill
½ pound fresh, white button mushrooms

Veal Stew with Mushrooms (continued)

1. Put 2 tablespoons of butter and 2 tablespoons of vegetable oil in a medium sauté pan, and turn on the heat to medium high. When the butter foam begins to subside, turn the veal cubes in the flour, coating them on all sides, shake off excess flour, and put them in the pan. Cook the meat, turning it, until all sides are deeply browned. Transfer it to a plate using a slotted spoon or spatula. (If the meat doesn't fit loosely into the pan all at one time, brown it in batches, but dip the cubes in flour only when you are ready to slip them into the pan.)

2. Turn the heat down to medium, put in the chopped onion, cook, stirring, until it becomes translucent, then add the garlic. Cook the garlic until it becomes slightly colored, add the wine, and let it bubble for a few seconds. Return the meat to the pan, then add the cut-up tomatoes with their juice, the rosemary, sage, and parsley, liberal pinches of salt, and several grindings of pepper. Adjust heat to cook at a steady, but gentle simmer, and cover the pan. Cook for 1 hour and 15 minutes or more, turning the meat from time to time, until the veal is tender enough to be cut with a fork.

3. While the meat is cooking, prepare the mushrooms. Wash them rapidly in cold running water, pat dry with a soft towel, and cut them into irregular ½-inch pieces.

4. Choose a skillet or sauté pan just large enough to contain them snugly, but without overlapping. Put in the remaining 1 tablespoon of butter and ½ tablespoon vegetable oil, and turn on the heat to medium. When the butter foam subsides, put in the cut-up mushrooms, and turn up the heat to high. Cook, turning them frequently, until they stop throwing off liquid and the liquid they have already shed has entirely evaporated. They are now ready for the stew.

5. When the stew has cooked for at least 1 hour, put in the mushrooms, tossing them thoroughly with the meat, and cover the pan with the lid slightly ajar. Cook for another 30 minutes or so and, when the meat feels very tender when tested with a fork, transfer the entire contents of the pan to a warm platter, and serve at once.

Ahead-of-time note ✿ The dish may be completed several hours in advance the same day you are going to eat it, and reheated gently just before serving.

Skewered Veal Cubes and Pork Sausage
Pan-Roasted with Sage and White Wine

THE STYLE in which these tasty skewers are made is called *all'uccelletto* in Italian because it is the treatment one reserves for *uccelletti,* small birds: pan-roasting with *pancetta* and sage. Ideally, they should be served as one would serve such birds, over hot, soft *polenta.*   *For 6 servings*

1¼ pounds mild pork sausage made without strong spices or herbs

20 whole sage leaves, fresh if possible

1 pound boneless shank or shoulder of veal, cut into 1½-inch cubes

½ pound *pancetta* in a single slice, unrolled and cut into 1½-inch pieces

Approximately 12 skewers, 6 to 8 inches long

3 tablespoons vegetable oil

⅔ cup dry white wine

1. Cut the sausages into pieces 1½ inches long. Skewer the ingredients alternating 1 piece of sausage, 1 fresh sage leaf, 1 piece of veal, and 1 piece of *pancetta.* At the end you may run short of some of the components, but make sure there is at least one of each kind on every skewer. If using dried sage leaves, do not skewer them because they will crumble. Put them loose in the pan later, as directed in the next step.

2. Choose a sauté pan broad enough to contain the skewers. Put in the oil, turn on the heat to medium, and when the oil is hot, put in the skewers. If using dried sage, add all of it to the pan now. Turn the skewers, browning the meat deeply on all sides. If the pan cannot accommodate all of the skewers at one time without stacking them, put them in in batches, removing one batch as you finish browning it, and putting in another.

3. If you have browned the skewers in batches, return them all to the pan, one above the other if necessary to fit them in. Add the wine, turn up the heat just long enough to make the wine bubble briskly for 15 or 20 seconds, then turn the heat down to low and cover the pan, setting the lid slightly ajar.

4. Cook for 25 minutes or so, turning the skewers from time to time and bringing to the top any that may be on the bottom, until the veal feels sufficiently tender when prodded with a fork. It does not need to become quite as soft as stewed veal or *ossobuco.* When done, transfer the skewers to a warm serving platter, using tongs or a slotted spoon or spatula.

5. Tip the pan and spoon off all but about 2 tablespoons of fat. Pour ⅓ cup water into the pan and boil it away over high heat, while using a wooden spoon to scrape loose cooking residues from the bottom and sides. Pour the reduced juices over the skewers and serve at once.

Vitello Tonnato—Cold Sliced Veal with Tuna Sauce

ITALY'S MOST CELEBRATED contribution to the cold table, *vitello tonnato,* is a dish as versatile as it is lovely. It is an ideal meat course for a summer menu, an exceedingly elegant *antipasto* for an elaborate dinner, and a most successful party dish for small or large buffets.

I have seen dishes described as *vitello tonnato* served with the sliced veal prettily fanned out and a little mound of sauce on the side. This defeats the very purpose of the dish, which is to give the tuna sauce time to infiltrate the veal so that the flavors of one and the delicate texture of the other become fully integrated. The meat must macerate with the sauce for at least 24 hours before it can be served.

Some cooks braise the veal with white wine, but I find that wine contributes more tartness than is needed here. Veal can become dry; to keep it tender and juicy, cook it in just enough boiling water to cover, determining in advance the exact amount of water needed by the simple expedient described in the recipe. Three other important points to remember in order to keep the meat moist are, first, put the veal into water only when the water has come to a full boil; second, never add salt to the water; third, allow the meat to cool completely while immersed in its own broth.

If delicacy of flavor and texture are the paramount considerations, veal is the only meat to use. Breast of turkey and pork loin, however, offer excellent alternatives at considerably less cost. *For 6 to 8 servings*

FOR POACHING THE MEAT

2 to 2½ pounds lean veal roast, preferably the top round, firmly trussed, OR turkey breast OR pork loin
1 medium carrot, peeled

1 stalk celery without the leaves
1 medium onion, peeled
4 sprigs parsley
1 dried bay leaf

FOR THE TUNA SAUCE

Mayonnaise prepared as
  described on page 40,
    using 2 egg yolks, 1¼ cups
  extra virgin olive oil (see
  note below), 2 tablespoons
  freshly squeezed lemon
  juice, and ¼ teaspoon salt
1 seven-ounce can imported
  tuna packed in olive oil
5 flat anchovy fillets (preferably
  the ones prepared at home
  as described on page 9)

1 cup extra virgin olive oil
3 tablespoons freshly squeezed
  lemon juice
3 tablespoons capers, soaked
  and rinsed as described on
  page 16 if packed in salt,
  drained if in vinegar

Note ❀ This is one of the rare instances in which olive oil in mayonnaise is really to be preferred. Its intense flavor gives the dish greater depth. Please see warning about salmonella poisoning on page 41. If you would like to omit the mayonnaise, make the sauce doubling the quantity of tuna, adding 1 anchovy fillet, 1 cup olive oil, and 2 tablespoons lemon juice.

SUGGESTED GARNISH

Thin slices of lemon
Pitted black olives cut into
  narrow wedges
Whole capers

Whole parsley leaves
Anchovy fillets

1. In a pot just large enough to contain the veal (or the turkey breast or pork loins), put in the meat, carrot, celery, onion, parsley, bay leaf, and just enough water to cover. Now *remove the meat and set it aside.* Cover the pot and bring the water to a boil, then put in the meat and when the water resumes boiling, cover the pot, adjust heat to cook at a gentle, steady simmer, and cook for 2 hours. (If it's turkey breast, cook it about 1 hour less.) Remove the pot from heat and allow the meat to cool in its broth.

2. Make the mayonnaise.

3. Drain the canned tuna, and put it into a food processor together with the anchovies, olive oil, lemon juice, and capers. Process until you obtain a creamy, uniformly blended sauce. Remove the sauce from the processor bowl and fold it gently, but thoroughly into the mayonnaise. No salt may be required because both the anchovies and capers supply it, but taste to be sure.

Cold Sliced Veal with Tuna Sauce (continued)

4. When the meat is quite cold, retrieve it from its broth, place it on a cutting board or other work surface, snip off and remove the trussing strings, and cut it into uniformly thin slices.

5. Smear the bottom of a serving platter with some of the tuna sauce. Over it spread a single layer of veal (or turkey or pork) slices, meeting edge to edge without overlapping. Cover with sauce, then make another layer of meat slices, and cover again with sauce. Repeat the procedure until you have used up all the meat, leaving yourself with enough sauce to blanket the topmost layer.

6. Cover with plastic wrap and refrigerate for at least 24 hours. It will keep well for at least a week. Bring to room temperature before serving. When you remove the plastic wrap, use a spatula to even off the top, and garnish with some or all of the suggested garnish ingredients in an agreeable pattern.

BEEF

La Fiorentina—Grilled
T-Bone Steak, Florentine Style

ONE OF ITALY'S two prized breeds of cattle for meat—*Chianina* beef—is native to Tuscany. Its only rival in the country is Piedmont's *Razza Piemontese*. The latter is the tenderer of the two and sweet as cream, whereas the Tuscan is firmer and tastier. *Chianina* grows rapidly to great size so that it is butchered when the steer is a grown calf, *vitellone* in Italian. To Italians who love beef, a T-bone grilled in the Florentine style is the ultimate steak. It owes some of its appeal, of course, to the distinctive flavor of the meat, but as much again can be attributed to the Florentine way of preparing it which can be applied successfully to a fine, well-aged steak anywhere.   *For 2 servings*

A charcoal or wood-burning
    grill
Black peppercorns, ground very
    coarse or crushed with a
    pestle in a mortar
1 T-bone beef steak, 1½ inches
    thick, brought to room
    temperature

Coarse sea salt
OPTIONAL: a lightly crushed
    and peeled garlic clove
Extra virgin olive oil

1. Light the charcoal in time for it to form white ash before cooking, or the wood long enough in advance to reduce it to hot embers.

2. Rub the coarsely ground or crushed peppercorns into both sides of the meat.

3. Grill the steak to the degree desired, preferably very rare, approximately 5 minutes on one side and 3 on the other. After turning it, sprinkle salt on the grilled side. When the other side is done, turn it over and sprinkle salt on it.

4. When the steak is cooked to your taste, and while it is still on the grill,

Grilled T-Bone Steak (continued)

rub the optional garlic clove over the bone on both sides, then drizzle the meat very lightly on both sides with a few drops of olive oil. Transfer to a warm platter and serve at once.

Note ✿ I have seen cooks rub the steak with oil *before* putting it on the grill, but the scorched oil imparts a taste of tallow to the meat that I prefer to avoid.

Pan-Broiled Steaks with Marsala and Chili Pepper

For 4 servings

Extra virgin olive oil
4 sirloin steaks or equivalent
  boneless cut, ¾ inch thick,
  brought to room temperature before cooking
Salt
Black pepper, ground fresh
  from the mill
½ cup dry Marsala wine
½ cup dry red wine

1½ teaspoons garlic chopped
  fine
1 teaspoon fennel seeds
1 tablespoon tomato paste,
  diluted with 2 tablespoons
  water
Chopped hot red chili pepper,
  to taste
2 tablespoons chopped parsley

1. Choose a skillet that can subsequently accommodate all the steaks in a single layer. Put in just enough olive oil, tilting the pan in several directions, to coat the bottom well. Turn the heat on to high and when the oil is hot enough that a slight haze forms over it, slip in the steaks. Cook them to taste, preferably rare, approximately 3 minutes on one side and 2 on the other. When done, turn off the heat, transfer the steaks to a warm platter, and sprinkle with salt and a few grindings of pepper.

2. Turn the heat on to medium high under the skillet, and put in the Marsala and the red wine. Let the wines bubble for about half a minute, while scraping the pan with a wooden spoon to loosen any cooking residues stuck to the bottom and sides.

3. Add the garlic, cook just long enough to stir 2 or 3 times, add the fennel seeds, stir for a few seconds, then add the diluted tomato paste and chopped chili pepper to taste. Turn the heat down to medium and cook, stirring frequently, for a minute or so, until a dense, syrupy sauce is formed.

4. Return the steaks to the pan for no longer than it takes to turn them 2 or 3 times in the sauce. Transfer the steaks and their sauce to a warm serving platter, top with the chopped parsley, and serve at once.

Pan–Broiled Thin Beef Steaks with Tomatoes and Olives

THE STEAKS for this dish are very thin slices of beef that are made even thinner by pounding to bring cooking time down to a minimum. Most butchers will pound them for you, but if you must flatten them yourself, follow the method described in the section on veal *scaloppine,* page 38. Notch the edges of the slices, after pounding, to keep them from curling in the pan.

For 4 servings

½ medium onion sliced very thin
2 tablespoons olive oil
2 medium garlic cloves, peeled and sliced very thin
⅔ cup fresh, ripe tomatoes, peeled and chopped, OR canned imported Italian plum tomatoes, coarsely chopped, with their juice
Oregano, ½ teaspoon if fresh, ¼ teaspoon if dried

Salt
Black pepper, ground fresh from the mill
1 dozen black, round Greek olives, pitted and quartered
Vegetable oil
1 pound boneless beef steaks, preferably chuck, sliced less than ½ inch thick, flattened as described above, and brought to room temperature before cooking

1. Put the sliced onion and the olive oil in a sauté pan, turn on the heat to medium low, and cook the onion, letting it gradually wilt. When it becomes colored a pale gold, add the garlic. Cook the garlic until it becomes very lightly colored, then add the tomatoes with their juice and the oregano. Stir thoroughly to coat well, adjust heat so that the tomatoes cook at a steady simmer, and cook for about 15 minutes, until the oil floats free of the tomatoes. Add salt, a few grindings of pepper, and the olives, stir thoroughly, and cook for 1 more minute. Turn the heat down to minimum.

Ahead-of-time note ❀ The recipe can be completed up to this point several hours or even a day in advance. Stop short of putting in the olives, adding them only after reheating the sauce, before it is combined with the steaks.

Pan-Broiled Thin Beef Steaks (continued)

2. Heat a heavy skillet, preferably cast iron, until it is hot, then quickly grease the bottom with a cloth towel soaked in vegetable oil. Put in the beef slices, cooking both sides just the few seconds necessary to brown them. Sprinkle with salt and pepper as you turn them.

3. Transfer the meat to the pan with the tomato sauce, and turn it 2 or 3 times. Put the steaks on a warm serving platter, turning out the sauce over them, and serve at once.

Pan-Fried Thin Beef Steaks, Cacciatora Style

For 4 servings

3 tablespoons extra virgin
   olive oil
½ cup onion sliced very thin
4 pan-frying beef steaks, cut less
   than ½ inch thick from
   chuck or the round
1 cup flour, spread on a plate
Salt
Black pepper, ground fresh
   from the mill
A small packet OR 1 ounce
   dried *porcini* mushrooms,

reconstituted as described
   on page 27 and chopped
   into coarse pieces
The filtered water from the
   mushroom soak, see page
   28 for instructions
½ cup dry red wine
½ cup canned imported Italian
   plum tomatoes, cut up,
   with their juice

1. Choose a sauté pan that can subsequently accommodate all the steaks without overlapping. Put in the olive oil and sliced onion, and turn on the heat to medium.

2. Cook until the onion becomes translucent, then dredge the steaks on both sides in the flour, and put them in the pan, turning the heat up to high. Cook the meat about 1 minute on each side, sprinkle it with salt and a few grindings of pepper, and transfer it with a slotted spoon to a warm plate.

3. Add the cut-up reconstituted mushrooms and the filtered water from their soak to the pan, turn the heat down to medium, and cook until the mushroom liquid has completely evaporated. Stir from time to time.

4. Add the wine and let it simmer away for a minute or so, stirring frequently, then put in the tomatoes with their juice and adjust heat to cook at a slow, but steady simmer. Add salt and pepper, correcting seasoning to taste,

and stir from time to time. Cook for about 10 or 15 minutes, until the oil floats free from the tomatoes.

5. Turn the heat up to high, return the steaks to the pan together with any juices they may have shed in the plate, and turn them once or twice to reheat them in the sauce, but for no longer than 20 or 30 seconds. Transfer the meat and the entire contents of the pan to a warm platter and serve at once.

Pan-Fried Beef Braciole Filled with Cheese and Ham

VERY THIN matched slices of beef are coupled here, bracketing a filling of cheese and ham. What holds them together is a coating of flour, egg, and bread crumbs that sets as it is cooked and joins the edges. The cheese in the filling also does its part by melting and clinging to the meat.   *For 4 servings*

1 pound *braciole* steaks, sliced as thin as possible (see note below)	4 thin slices prosciutto OR boiled unsmoked ham
Salt	1 egg
Black pepper, ground fresh from the mill	Whole nutmeg
4 very thin slices of *fontina* cheese	Vegetable oil
	1 cup flour, spread on a plate
	Fine, dry, unflavored bread crumbs, spread on a plate

Note ❧ *Braciole* steaks come from the center cut of the top or bottom round. If they are taken from the broadest section of the round, the slices will be very long, about 10 to 12 inches. In this case, you only need 4 slices, which you will then cut in half. If the slices are from the narrower end section, you'll need 8 of them, which you will leave whole. If they are any thicker than ¼ inch, have your butcher flatten them some, or do it yourself as described on page 38.

1. Pair off the *braciole* slices that are closest in size and shape. Place one above the other and, if necessary, trim the edges so that the slice above matches the one below it as closely as possible, without large gaps or overlaps.

2. In between each pair of *braciole* sprinkle salt and pepper, and put a slice of *fontina* and one of prosciutto. Center the *fontina* so that it does not come too close to the edges of the meat. Fold the prosciutto over, if necessary, so that it does not protrude beyond the edge of the *braciole*. Line up the upper

Pan-Fried Beef Braciole (continued)

and lower half of each pair of meat slices so that they coincide as closely as possible.

Ahead-of-time note ❊ The *braciole* can be prepared up to this point several hours in advance on the same day you plan to cook them.

3. Break the egg into a small bowl, and beat it lightly with a fork, adding a tiny grating of nutmeg—about ⅛ teaspoon—and a pinch of salt.

4. Choose a skillet that can subsequently accommodate the *braciole* without overlapping, put in enough oil to come ¼ inch up the sides, and turn on the heat to high.

5. Turn each pair of *braciole* in the flour, handling them carefully to avoid their coming apart. Make sure the edges are sealed with flour, then dip them in the beaten egg and dredge them in the bread crumbs.

6. As soon as the oil is quite hot, slip the *braciole* into the pan. The oil is ready when it sizzles if you dip one end of a *braciola* into it. Brown them well on one side, turn them carefully, and do the other side. When you have thoroughly browned both sides, place them briefly on a cooling rack to drain or on a plate lined with paper towels, then transfer to a warm platter and serve at once.

Farsumauro—Stuffed Large Braciole, Sicilian Style

THERE ARE many versions of *farsumauro* in Southern Italy and in Sicily that vary depending on the variety of sausages, cheeses, and herbs that a cook may choose to put into the stuffing. The recipe given below is more restrained than most I have had, partly out of necessity—there are no satisfactory substitutes available outside Sicily for the local cheeses and pork products—and partly out of choice: It seems to me that even in this simplified rendering it is rich and savory enough.

The large slice of meat that constitutes the wrapping for the stuffing, can either be rolled up jelly-roll fashion or sewn up forming a *calzone*-like bundle. The latter is the method I recommend because I find it keeps the filling tender and succulent.   *For 6 servings*

Approximately 1½ pounds beef *braciole,* cut either in 1 large slice from the center section of the top or

bottom round, ½ inch thick, OR 2 smaller slices of the same thickness

Needle and thin trussing string
¾ pound not too lean
    ground pork
1 medium garlic clove, peeled
    and chopped fine
2 tablespoons chopped parsley
1 egg
2 tablespoons freshly grated
    parmigiano-reggiano cheese

Salt
Black pepper, ground fresh
    from the mill
2 tablespoons butter
2 tablespoons vegetable oil
⅔ cup flour, spread on a plate
1 cup dry white wine

1. If using a single large slice of meat, fold it in half, and stitch its edges together, leaving enough of an opening for putting in the stuffing. If using 2 slices, place one on top of the other and stitch 3 of the sides, leaving one narrow side open, like a pillowcase. Put the needle safely distant from the work area.

2. Put the ground pork, garlic, parsley, egg, grated Parmesan, salt, and pepper into a bowl, and mix with a fork until all the ingredients are evenly combined.

3. Place the mixture inside the sewn-up *braciole* wrapper, distributing it evenly. Get the needle and string out again and sew up the remaining opening. The *farsumauro* may look rather floppy at this stage, but it will tighten up in cooking. Put the needle safely out of the kitchen.

4. Choose a sauté pan, or a roasting pan preferably oval in shape, that can subsequently snugly accommodate the meat roll. Put in the butter and oil and turn on the heat to medium high.

5. Turn the meat in the flour to coat it all over, and when the butter foam begins to subside, put the meat in the pan. Brown the meat roll well all over.

6. When you have browned the meat, sprinkle with salt and pepper, and add the wine. Let the wine simmer for about half a minute, turn the heat down to medium low, and cover the pan, setting the lid slightly ajar. Cook for 1 to 1½ hours, turning the meat from time to time. There ought to be sufficient liquid in the pan to keep the meat from sticking, but if you should find the opposite, add 2 to 3 tablespoons of water, as needed. The total cooking time may appear to be abnormally long, but think of this as comparable to a pot roast that needs to cook slowly and at length so that it can become very soft, while its flavors acquire intensity and complexity.

7. With a slotted spoon or spatula, transfer the *farsumauro* roll to a cutting board. Cut the *farsumauro* into slices ½ inch thick. Pick out the bits of string (or let people do it on their own plates). Spread the slices on a warm platter.

8. There should be fat floating on top of the juices in the pan. Tip the pan

Stuffed Large Braciole (continued)

and spoon off about two-thirds of the fat. If the juices are rather dense, add 1 or 2 tablespoons water to the pan, turn the heat on to high, and, while boiling away the water, scrape loose the cooking residues stuck to the bottom and sides, using a wooden spoon. If the juices should be thin and runny, reduce them over high heat, while loosening the cooking residues on the bottom and sides of the pan. Pour the contents of the pan over the sliced *farsumauro* and serve at once.

Beef Rolls with Red Cabbage and Chianti Wine

For 4 servings

3 tablespoons extra virgin olive oil

1 tablespoon garlic chopped very fine

4 to 5 cups red cabbage shredded very fine

Salt

Black pepper, ground fresh from the mill

1 pound beef round, sliced extra thin, preferably by machine

6 ounces sliced boiled unsmoked ham

6 ounces sliced Italian *fontina* OR comparable tender, fine-flavored cheese

Round sturdy toothpicks

⅔ cup Chianti or other fruity, full-bodied, dry red wine

1. Choose a sauté pan that can later accommodate all the beef rolls without overlapping. Put in 2 tablespoons olive oil and the garlic, and turn on the heat to medium. Cook the garlic, stirring occasionally, until it becomes colored a very pale gold.

2. Add the shredded cabbage, salt, and liberal grindings of pepper, turn the cabbage over completely a few times to coat it well, put a cover on the pan, and turn the heat down to low. Cook, stirring from time to time, until the cabbage becomes very soft and has become reduced to half its original bulk, approximately 45 minutes.

3. While the cabbage is cooking, assemble the beef rolls. If the meat is not truly thin, flatten it some more with a meat pounder. Trim the slices into shapes more or less square with sides approximately 3 to 4½ inches long, and lay them flat on a platter or work surface. Over each square place a slice of

ham and a slice of cheese, neither of which should protrude beyond the edge of the beef. Roll up each square and fasten it with 1 or 2 toothpicks or tie it with string like a miniature roast.

4. When the cabbage is done, transfer it to a plate, using a slotted spoon or spatula. Put the remaining 1 tablespoon olive oil in the same pan, turn on the heat to high, and put in the beef rolls. Turn them as they cook to brown them all over.

Ahead-of-time note ✸ You can cook the rolls up to this point several hours in advance, and reheat them briefly before proceeding to the next step. You may also cook the dish through to the end, and when ready to serve it a few hours later, reheat it gently in its juices.

5. Return the cabbage to the pan, add the wine, and a little more salt and pepper. When the wine has bubbled for about 15 seconds, turn the heat down to low and put a cover on the pan. Cook until the wine has been totally reduced, about 10 minutes. Serve promptly in a warm platter with all the juices of the pan.

Note ✸ It's possible that some of the cheese will run out of the beef rolls while they are cooking. It's not a cause for concern; mix the cheese into the cabbage, thus enriching the sauce for the beef.

Pot Roast of Beef Braised in Red Wine

For 6 servings

Vegetable oil
4 pounds boneless beef roast, preferably chuck
1 tablespoon butter
3 tablespoons onion chopped very fine
3 tablespoons carrot chopped very fine
2 tablespoons celery chopped very fine
1½ cups dry red wine (see note below)
1 cup or more Basic Home-made Meat Broth, prepared

as directed on page 15, OR ½ cup canned beef broth plus ½ cup or more water
1½ tablespoons chopped canned imported Italian plum tomatoes
A pinch of dried thyme
¼ teaspoon fresh marjoram or ⅛ teaspoon dried
Salt
Black pepper, ground fresh from the mill

Pot Roast of Beef Braised in Red Wine (continued)

Wine note ❧ This pot roast is a version of Piedmont's *stracotto al Barolo* and an ideal rendition of it would call for Barolo in the pot as well as Barolo in your glass. If you must make a substitution, try to use another Piedmontese red, such as Barbaresco or a fine Barbera. Other suitable choices: Rhône wine, California Syrah or Zinfandel, or Shiraz from Australia or South Africa.

1. Preheat oven to 350°.

2. Put in just enough vegetable oil in a skillet, tilting the pan in several directions, to coat the bottom well. Turn the heat on to high and when the oil is hot enough that a slight haze forms over it, slip in the meat. Brown it well all over, then transfer it to a platter and set aside. Set the skillet aside for later use, without cleaning it.

3. Choose a pot with a tight-fitting lid just large enough to accommodate the meat later. Put in 2 tablespoons of vegetable oil, the butter, and the onion, turn on the heat to medium, and cook the onion until it becomes colored a pale gold. Add the carrot and celery. Stir thoroughly to coat well, cook for 4 to 5 minutes, then put in the browned meat.

4. Pour the wine into the skillet in which the meat was browned, turn on the heat to medium high, and allow the wine to bubble briskly for a minute or less, while scraping the pan with a wooden spoon to loosen cooking residues stuck to the bottom and sides. Add the contents of the skillet to the pot with the meat.

5. Add the homemade broth or diluted canned broth to the pot. It should come two-thirds of the way up the sides of the meat, but if it doesn't, add more homemade broth or water. Add the tomatoes, thyme, marjoram, salt, and several grindings of pepper. Turn the heat on to high, bring the contents of the pot to a boil, then cover the pot and put it on the middle rack of the preheated oven. Cook for about 3 hours, turning the meat every 20 minutes or so, basting it with the liquid in the pot, which should be cooking at a slow, steady simmer. If it is not simmering, turn up the oven thermostat. On occasion it may happen that all the liquid in the pot has evaporated or been absorbed before the meat is done. If this should occur, add 3 to 4 tablespoons of water. Cook until the meat feels very tender when prodded with a fork.

6. Remove the meat to a cutting board. If the liquid in the pot should be too thin and it has not been reduced to less than ⅔ cup, put the pot on a burner, turn the heat on to high, and boil down the juices, while scraping up any cooking residues stuck to the pot. Taste the juices and correct for salt and pepper. Slice the meat, put the slices on a warm platter, arranging them so they overlap slightly, pour the pot juices over them, and serve at once.

Pot Roast of Beef Braised
in Amarone Wine

AMARONE is Verona's unique and great red wine. It is made from grapes that, after they are harvested, have been put aside to shrivel for 3 or 4 months before they are crushed. Their concentrated juice produces a dry wine of intense flavor, splendid as an accompaniment to meat dishes of substance, sumptuous to sip on its own at the end of a meal, and extraordinary as the braising liquid for a pot roast of beef. No other wine delivers comparable taste sensations. It should not be difficult to find in any shop that stocks good Italian wine, but should you be compelled to make a substitution, look for any unfortified, fine, dry red wine with an alcohol content of at least 14 percent.

For 4 to 6 servings

2 tablespoons chopped *pancetta*

2 tablespoons extra virgin
    olive oil

2 pounds beef chuck

¾ cup onion chopped very fine

½ cup celery chopped fine

2 garlic cloves, lightly mashed
    and peeled

Salt

Black pepper, ground fresh
    from the mill

1¾ cups Amarone wine (see
    introductory note above)

1. Choose a heavy-bottomed pot with a tight-fitting lid just large enough to accommodate the meat later. Put in the chopped *pancetta* and the olive oil, turn the heat on to medium high, and cook the *pancetta* for about 1 minute, stirring it once or twice. Put in the meat, turn it to brown it well all over, then remove it from the pot.

2. Add the chopped onion to the pot and cook it, stirring it once or twice, until it becomes colored a pale gold.

3. Return the meat to the pot, adding the celery, garlic, salt, liberal grindings of pepper, and ½ cup of the Amarone. Cover the pot, keeping the lid slightly askew, and turn the heat down to minimum. Cook for 3 hours over very slow heat. Turn the meat from time to time and add the rest of the Amarone, a little bit at a time. If, before the 3 hours are up, all the wine in the pot has evaporated, add 2 or 3 tablespoons of water, as needed, to keep the roast from sticking. The meat is fully cooked if it feels extremely tender when tested with a fork.

4. Take the meat out of the pot and let it rest on a cutting board for about

Pot Roast of Beef Braised in Amarone Wine (continued)

10 minutes. Slice it very thin, then put the slices back in the pot and turn them in the small amount of sauce that will have formed.

Ahead-of-time note ✖ You can complete the recipe up to this point several hours before serving. When ready to serve, warm the meat in its sauce over very low heat. If the roast has absorbed all the sauce, add 1 or 2 tablespoons of water while reheating.

Beef Roast Braised with Onions

WHAT IS REMARKABLE about this roast is that it is braised with only the juices that flow from the onions on which the meat rests. Eventually the juices vanish, the meat becomes tenderly impregnated with sweet onion flavor, and the onions themselves turn deliciously brown.

The only fat used is the *pancetta* with which the beef is larded. If you don't have a larding needle, push strips of *pancetta* into the meat using a chopstick of the traditional hard Chinese rather than the soft, breakable Japanese kind, or any other blunt, narrow stick, or similar object. Pierce the meat following the direction of its grain.   *For 4 to 6 servings*

¼ pound *pancetta* OR salt pork in a single piece
2 pounds boneless beef roast, preferably the brisket
5 cloves
4 medium onions sliced very, very thin
Salt
Black pepper, ground fresh from the mill

1. Preheat oven to 325°.

2. Cut the *pancetta* or salt pork into narrow strips about ¼ inch wide. Use half the strips to lard the meat with a larding needle, or by an alternative method as suggested in the introductory remarks above.

3. Insert the cloves at random into any 5 of the places where the *pancetta* was inserted.

4. Choose a heavy-bottomed pot just large enough to accommodate the roast snugly. Spread the sliced onion on the bottom of the pot, over it distribute the remaining strips of *pancetta* or salt pork, then put in the meat. Season liberally with salt and pepper, and cover tightly. If the lid does not provide a tight fit, place a sheet of aluminum foil between it and the pot. Put on the uppermost rack of the preheated oven.

5. Cook for about 3½ hours, until the meat feels very tender when prodded with a fork. Turn the roast after the first 30 minutes, and every 30 to 40 minutes thereafter. You will find that the color of the meat is dull and unlovely at first, but as it finishes cooking and the onions become colored a dark brown it develops a rich, dark patina.

6. When done, slice the meat and arrange the slices on a warm platter. Pour the contents of the pan and the juices left on the cutting board over the meat, and serve at once.

Beef Tenderloin with Red Wine

For 4 servings

3 garlic cloves
1 tablespoon vegetable oil
2 tablespoons butter
4 beef fillets, cut 1 inch thick
⅔ cup flour, spread on a plate
Salt
Black pepper, ground fresh
   from the mill

⅔ cup full-bodied dry red wine
   (follow suggestions in wine
   note to recipe Pot Roast of
   Beef Braised in Red Wine,
   page 394)

1. Lightly mash the garlic cloves with a knife handle, just hard enough to split the peel, which you will loosen and discard.

2. Choose a sauté pan that can later accommodate the 4 fillets without overlapping. Put in the oil and butter, and turn on the heat to medium high.

3. Dredge both sides of the meat in flour. As soon as the butter foam begins to subside, put in the fillets and the mashed garlic cloves. Brown the meat deeply on both sides, then transfer to a plate, using a slotted spoon or spatula. Season with salt and liberal grindings of pepper.

4. Add the wine to the pan and let it boil away completely while using a wooden spoon to loosen the cooking residues on the bottom and sides of the pan. When the wine has boiled away, return the fillets to the pan. Cook them in the pan juices for about 1 minute on each side, then transfer the fillets with all the cooking juices to a warm platter, and serve at once.

Beef Stew with Red Wine and Vegetables

THE FRESH, clean taste of this stew is uncomplicated by herbs and seasonings other than salt and pepper. To make it, you need good red wine, olive oil, and a few vegetables. In reading through the recipe you will notice that the vegetables are put in at different stages: the onions first, because they must cook alongside the meat from the beginning, suffusing it with sweetness; the carrots after a while; the celery later yet to keep its sprightly fragrance from being submerged; and at the very last, the peas. *For 4 to 6 servings*

Vegetable oil

2 pounds boneless beef chuck, cut into 1½- to 2-inch stewing cubes

1½ cups sturdy red wine, preferably a Barbera from Piedmont

1 pound small white onions

4 medium carrots

4 meaty celery stalks

1½ pounds fresh peas, unshelled weight, OR 1½ ten-ounce packages frozen peas, thawed

¼ cup extra virgin olive oil

Salt

Black pepper, ground fresh from the mill

1. Put enough vegetable oil into a small sauté pan to come ¼ inch up the sides, and turn on the heat to medium high. When the oil is quite hot, put in the meat, in successive batches if necessary not to crowd the pan. Brown the meat to a deep color on all sides, transfer it to a plate, using a slotted spoon or spatula, put another batch of meat in the pan, and repeat the above procedure until all the meat has been well browned.

2. Pour the fat out of the pan, pour in ½ cup of wine, and simmer it for a few moments while using a wooden spoon to loosen the browning residues from the bottom and sides of the pan. Remove from heat.

3. Peel the onions and cut a cross into each at the root end. Peel the carrots, wash them in cold water, and cut them into sticks about ½ inch thick and 3 inches long. Cut the celery stalks into pieces about 3 inches long, and split these in half lengthwise, peeling away or snapping down any strings. Wash the celery in cold water. Shell the peas.

4. Choose a heavy-bottomed pot with a tight-fitting lid that can later accommodate all the ingredients of the recipe. Put in the browned meat cubes, the contents of the browning pan, the onions, olive oil, and the remaining cup of wine. Cover tightly and turn on the heat to low.

5. When the meat has cooked for 15 minutes, add the carrots, turning them over with the other ingredients. After another 45 minutes, add the celery, and give the contents of the pan a complete turn. If using fresh peas, add them after another 45 minutes. If there is very little liquid in the pot, put in ½ to ⅔ cup water to help the peas cook, unless these are exceptionally young and fresh, in which case they will need less liquid. After 15 minutes, add a few pinches of salt, liberal grindings of pepper, and turn over the contents of the pot. Continue cooking until the meat feels tender when prodded with a fork. If you are using frozen peas, add the thawed peas when the meat is already tender, and let them cook in the stew for about 15 minutes. Altogether, the stew should take about 2 hours to cook, depending on the quality of the meat. Taste and correct for salt and pepper before serving.

Ahead-of-time note ❀ Like all stews, this one will have excellent flavor when prepared a day or two in advance. Reheat gently just before serving.

Meatballs and Tomatoes

For 4 servings

A slice of good-quality white
    bread
⅓ cup milk
1 pound ground beef, prefer-
    ably chuck
1 tablespoon onion chopped
    very fine
1 tablespoon chopped parsley
1 egg
1 tablespoon extra virgin olive
    oil
3 tablespoons freshly grated
    parmigiano-reggiano cheese

Whole nutmeg
Salt
Black pepper, ground fresh
    from the mill
Fine, dry, unflavored bread
    crumbs, spread on a plate
Vegetable oil
1 cup fresh, ripe tomatoes,
    peeled and chopped,
    OR canned imported Italian
    plum tomatoes, chopped
    up, with their juice

1. Trim away the bread's crust, put the milk and bread in a small saucepan, and turn on the heat to low. When the bread has soaked up all the milk, mash it to a pulp with a fork. Remove from heat and allow to cool completely.

2. Into a bowl put the chopped meat, onion, parsley, the egg, the tablespoon of olive oil, the grated Parmesan, a tiny grating of nutmeg—about ⅛

Meatballs and Tomatoes (continued)

teaspoon—the bread and milk mush, salt, and several grindings of black pepper. Gently knead the mixture with your hands without squeezing it. When
all the ingredients are evenly combined, shape it gently and without squeezing into balls about 1 inch in diameter. Roll the balls lightly in the bread
crumbs.

3. Choose a sauté pan that can subsequently accommodate all the meatballs in a single layer. Pour in enough vegetable oil to come ¼ inch up the
sides. Turn on the heat to medium high and when the oil is hot, slip in the
meatballs. Sliding them in with a spatula will avoid splashing hot oil out of
the pan. Brown the meatballs on all sides, turning them carefully so they
won't break up.

4. Remove from heat, tip the pan slightly and with a spoon, remove as
much of the fat as floats to the surface. Return the pan to the burner over
medium heat, add the chopped tomatoes with their juice, a pinch of salt, and
turn the meatballs over once or twice to coat them well. Cover the pan and
adjust the heat to cook at a quiet, but steady simmer for about 20 to 25 minutes, until the oil floats free of the tomatoes. Taste and correct for salt and
serve at once.

Ahead-of-time note ❀ The dish can be cooked entirely in advance and stored
in a tightly covered container in the refrigerator for several days. Reheat gently before serving.

Winter Meatballs with Savoy Cabbage

For 4 to 6 servings

⅓ cup milk

A slice of good-quality white
    bread, trimmed of its crust

1 pound ground beef, prefer-
    ably chuck

2 ounces *pancetta* chopped very
    fine

1 egg

Salt

Black pepper, ground fresh
    from the mill

1 tablespoon chopped parsley

2 tablespoons onion chopped
    very fine

3 tablespoons freshly grated
    parmigiano-reggiano cheese

1 cup fine, dry, unflavored
    bread crumbs, spread on a
    plate

Vegetable oil

1¼ to 1½ pounds Savoy
    cabbage

2 tablespoons extra virgin
    olive oil

2 teaspoons chopped garlic
⅔ cup canned imported Italian
  plum tomatoes, drained

and cut up into coarse
pieces

1. Put the milk and bread in a small saucepan, and turn on the heat to low. When the bread has soaked up all the milk, mash it to a pulp with a fork. Remove from heat and allow to cool completely.

2. Put the ground meat, chopped *pancetta,* egg, salt, pepper, parsley, onion, grated Parmesan, and the bread and milk mush into a bowl. Gently knead the mixture with your hands without squeezing it. When all the ingredients are evenly combined, shape it gently and without squeezing into balls about 1½ inches in diameter. Roll the balls lightly in the bread crumbs.

3. Choose a sauté pan that can subsequently accommodate all the meatballs in a single layer. Pour in enough vegetable oil to come ¼ inch up the sides. Turn on the heat to medium high and when the oil is hot, slip in the meatballs. Sliding them in with a spatula will avoid splashing hot oil out of the pan. Brown the meatballs on all sides, turning them carefully so they won't break up. When they are done, remove them from the pan with a slotted spoon or spatula and transfer them to a cooling rack to drain or to a platter lined with paper towels. Pour the oil from the pan, and wipe the pan dry with paper towels.

4. Discard any of the cabbage's bruised or blemished leaves. Detach the other leaves from the core, discarding the core, and shred them into strips about ¼ inch wide.

5. Put the olive oil and chopped garlic into the sauté pan, and turn on the heat to medium. Cook and stir the garlic until it becomes colored gold, then add all the shredded cabbage. Turn it over 2 or 3 times to coat it well, cover the pan, and turn the heat down to the minimum.

6. Cook for 40 minutes to 1 hour, turning the cabbage from time to time, until it has become very soft and it is reduced to one-third its original bulk. Add a liberal amount of salt and ground pepper, bearing in mind that the cabbage is very sweet and needs considerable seasoning. Taste and correct seasoning to suit.

7. Turn up the heat to medium, uncover the pan, and continue to cook the cabbage. When it becomes colored a light nut brown, add the cut-up tomatoes, stir to coat well, and cook for about 15 minutes. Return the meatballs to the pan, turning them over 2 or 3 times in the cabbage and tomatoes. Cover the pan, turn the heat down to low, and cook for 10 to 15 minutes, turning the contents over from time to time. Transfer the entire contents of the pan to a warm platter and serve at once.

Beef Patties Baked
with Anchovies and Mozzarella

For 6 servings

½ slice of good-quality white
    bread
3 tablespoons milk
1½ pounds ground beef,
    preferably chuck
1 egg
Salt
Fine, dry, unflavored bread
    crumbs, spread on a plate
Vegetable oil
A bake-and-serve dish
Butter for greasing the dish

6 whole canned imported
    Italian plum tomatoes,
    drained of juice,
    OR fresh tomatoes (see note)
Oregano, 1 teaspoon if fresh, ½
    teaspoon if dried
6 slices mozzarella, each cut ¼
    inch thick
12 flat anchovy fillets (prefer-
    ably the ones prepared at
    home as described on
     page 9)

Note ❀ You can use fresh plum tomatoes if they are at the height of their season and very ripe and meaty.

1. Preheat oven to 400°.

2. Trim away the bread's crust, put the milk and bread in a small saucepan, and turn on the heat to low. When the bread has soaked up all the milk, mash it to a pulp with a fork. Remove from heat and allow to cool completely.

3. Put the chopped meat in a bowl, add the cooled bread and milk mush, the egg, and some salt, and gently knead the mixture with your hands without squeezing it. When all the ingredients are evenly combined, shape it gently and without squeezing into 6 patties about 1½ inches high. Dredge the patties in the bread crumbs.

4. Choose a sauté pan that can subsequently accommodate all the patties in a single layer. Pour in enough vegetable oil to come ¼ inch up the sides. Turn on the heat to medium high and when the oil is hot, slip in the patties. Sliding them in with a spatula will avoid splashing hot oil out of the pan. Brown the patties on both sides, cooking them about 2 minutes on one side and 1 minute on the other. Turn them carefully to avoid their breaking up.

5. While the meat is being browned, smear a bake-and-serve dish with butter. When the patties are ready, transfer them to the dish, using a slotted spoon or spatula.

6. If using fresh tomatoes, skin them raw with a peeler. Split the tomatoes in half lengthwise, scoop out their seeds, cut from each tomato a strip ½ inch wide, and set it aside to use for garnish. Cover each patty with both halves of a tomato, sprinkle with salt and oregano, top with a slice of mozzarella, and over the mozzarella place 2 anchovy fillets, crossing each other. Where the crossed anchovies meet, place the reserved strip of tomato.

Ahead-of-time note ✾ The baking dish with the patties may be prepared several hours in advance, before proceeding to the final step.

7. Put the baking dish on the uppermost rack of the preheated oven and bake for 10 minutes or more until the mozzarella melts. Serve at table directly from the baking dish.

Tuscan Meat Roll with White Wine and Porcini Mushrooms

For 4 to 6 servings

A 2- by 2-inch slice of good-quality white bread, trimmed of all the crust

2 tablespoons milk

1 pound ground beef, preferably chuck

1 tablespoon onion chopped very, very fine

Salt

Black pepper, ground fresh from the mill

2 tablespoons chopped prosciutto OR *pancetta* OR boiled unsmoked ham

⅓ cup freshly grated *parmi-giano-reggiano* cheese

1 teaspoon chopped garlic

1 egg yolk

Fine, dry, unflavored bread crumbs, spread on a plate

1 tablespoon butter

2 tablespoons vegetable oil

⅓ cup dry white wine

A small packet OR 1 ounce dried *porcini* mushrooms, reconstituted as described on page 27, and chopped into coarse pieces

The filtered water from the mushroom soak, see page 28 for instructions

⅔ cup canned imported Italian plum tomatoes, chopped, with their juice, OR fresh, ripe tomatoes, peeled and chopped

1. Put the bread and milk in a small saucepan, and turn on the heat to low. When the bread has soaked up all the milk, mash it to a pulp with a fork. Remove from heat and allow to cool completely.

Tuscan Meat Roll (continued)

2. Put the ground meat in a bowl and crumble it with a fork. Add the bread and milk mush, the chopped onion, salt, pepper, the chopped prosciutto, *pancetta,* or ham, the grated Parmesan, the garlic, and the egg yolk, and gently knead the mixture with your hands without squeezing it.

3. When all the ingredients are evenly combined, shape the meat into a firmly packed ball. Place the ball on any flat work surface and roll it into a salami-like cylinder about 2½ inches thick. With your palm, tap it sharply in several places to drive out any air bubbles. Turn the roll in the bread crumbs until it is evenly coated all over.

4. Choose a heavy-bottomed pot—possibly an oval or a rectangular roaster—that can snugly accommodate the meat roll. Put in the butter and oil and turn on the heat to medium. When the butter foam subsides, put in the meat. Brown it well all over, using two spatulas to turn the roll to keep it from breaking up.

5. When you have browned the meat, add the wine, and let it bubble until it is reduced to half its original volume. In the process, turn the roll carefully once or twice.

6. Turn the heat down to medium low and add the chopped reconstituted *porcini* mushrooms. Add the tomatoes and their juice to the pot together with the filtered mushroom liquid. Cover tightly and adjust heat to cook at a gentle, but steady simmer, turning and basting the meat from time to time. After 30 minutes, set the cover slightly ajar, and cook for another 30 minutes, turning the meat once or twice.

7. Transfer the meat roll to a cutting board. Let it settle for a few minutes, then cut it into slices about ⅜ inch thick. If the juices left in the pot are a little too runny, boil them down over high heat, scraping the pot with a wooden spoon to loosen any cooking residues stuck to the bottom and sides. Coat the bottom of a serving platter with a spoonful or so of the cooking juices, place the meat slices over it, arranging them so they overlap slightly, pour the remaining juices in the pot over the meat, and serve at once.

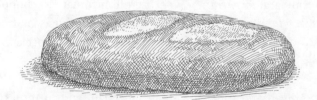

Bollito Misto—
Mixed Boiled Meat Platter

THE TIME MAY COME when *bollito misto* will become part of the heroic legends of our past and be a dish we only read about. And when we shall have to be satisfied with just reading, we won't do better than to look up Marcel Rouff's *The Passionate Epicure* and the episode of Dodin Bouffant's boiled beef dinner for the Prince of Eurasia.

In the meantime, if we travel to Northern Italy, we can still profit from a visit to those few restaurants where a steam trolley is rolled out to our table, and a waiter spears out of its vapors a moist round of beef, a whole buttery chicken, a breast of veal or even a satiny shin, a cut of tongue, or a *cotechino*—plump, rosy pork sausage soft as cream. Or we can gather a crowd of lusty eaters at home and produce a *bollito misto* of our own.

The recipe given below is for a complete *bollito* and will serve at least eighteen persons. You can reduce it by more than half simply by omitting the tongue and the *cotechino*. If any of the other meats are left over, they can be used in a salad. Leftover beef is, if anything, even more delicious than when it has just come out of the pot; see the recipe on page 568. And the greatest bonus of all may be the stupendous broth: You can freeze it as described on page 15 and use it for weeks to make some of the best *risotti* and soups you have ever had. *For 18 or more servings, if making the full recipe*

2 carrots, peeled
2 stalks celery
1 onion, peeled
½ red or yellow sweet bell
    pepper, its seeds and pulpy
    core removed
1 potato, peeled
1 beef tongue, about 3 to
    3½ pounds
2 to 3 pounds boneless beef
    brisket or chuck
¼ cup canned imported Italian
    plum tomatoes, drained

and cut up, OR 1 whole
    fresh, very ripe tomato
3 pounds veal breast with the
    short ribs in
A 3½-pound chicken
Salt
1 *cotechino* sausage, boiled
    separately as described on
    page 433, and kept warm in
    its own broth

1. Choose a stockpot that can contain all the above ingredients, except for the *cotechino*. The depth of flavor and aroma of a great *bollito misto*—and of

Mixed Boiled Meat Platter (continued)

its precious broth—comes from all the meats cooking together. If you don't have a single large pot to do it in, divide all the vegetables into two parts, cook the beef and tongue in one pot with half the vegetables, the other half with the veal and chicken in a second pot.

If using one pot, put in the vegetables, except for the tomatoes, with enough water to cover the meat later and bring it to a boil. If using two pots, start with the one in which you'll cook the beef and tongue.

2. When the water is boiling fast put in the tongue and beef and cover the pot. When the water resumes boiling, adjust heat so that it simmers gently, but steadily. Skim off the scum that surfaces during the first few minutes, then add the tomatoes. (Or half of them, if using two pots.)

3. After 1 hour of cooking at a slow simmer, take the tongue out to peel it. If you can handle the tongue while it is very hot, you'll find this easier to do. Slit the skin all around the tongue's edges and pull it off. The second skin beneath it will not come off, but can easily be cut away on one's plate after the tongue is fully cooked and sliced. Cut off and discard the gristle and fat at the base of the tongue, and return it to the pot.

4. If cooking in one pot, add the veal. If using 2 pots, bring water to a boil with the remainder of the vegetables, put in the veal, cover, and when the water returns to a full boil, adjust heat to cook at a steady, but slow simmer. Skim off any scum that may surface during the first minutes, then—if you are using a separate pot for the veal—add the remaining tomatoes.

5. Cook, always at a very gentle simmer, for another 1¾ hours, then put in the chicken. If using a separate pot, it goes with the veal. Add liberal pinches of salt to the single pot, or to both if using two. Cook until the chicken feels very tender when its thigh is prodded with a fork, about 1 hour.

If you are serving the *bollito* within 1 hour after turning the heat off, keep the pots covered, leave the meats in their broth, and they will still be warm enough to serve. If you are serving much later, keep the meats in their broth, and reheat at a very slow simmer for 10 to 15 minutes.

Serving notes ✿ Although a platter piled with steaming meat makes a hearty spectacle, the *bollito* will be much more succulent if kept submerged in its broth. Transfer to serving bowls or tureens, if you like, but pull out a piece of meat only to carve it and serve immediately. Keep the *cotechino* and its broth separate; the broth must not be mixed with that of the other meats and should be discarded when the sausage has been served.

Accompany *bollito misto* with an assortment of the following sauces:

❀Warm Red Sauce, page 43

❀Piquant Green Sauce, page 42, and variation, page 43

❀Horseradish Sauce, page 44

❀If your Italian specialties shop has it, or you are going to Italy, pick up a jar of *mostarda di Cremona,* sweet and spiced mustard fruits.

Ahead-of-time note ❀*Bollito misto* can be kept in its broth and refrigerated if you plan on serving it the following day. Please see remarks on page 15 on storing broth for longer than 3 days.

LAMB

Roast Easter Lamb with White Wine

In Italy, to eat lamb is to welcome the end of winter and hail the coming of spring, to celebrate renewal, to connect one's feelings with the Easter spirit of rebirth. For the Italian soul, as well as for the Italian palate, no other meat possesses the tenderness of roasted young lamb.

The recipe that follows is the simple and fragrant way that in Emilia-Romagna we do the first lamb of the season, at Easter. Every region follows a traditional approach of its own, another notable one being that of Rome, page 409.   *For 4 servings*

2 to 2½ pounds spring lamb
   (see note below), preferably
   the shoulder
2 tablespoons vegetable oil
1 tablespoon butter
3 whole garlic cloves, peeled
A sprig of fresh rosemary, cut
   into 2 or 3 pieces, OR

½ teaspoon dried rosemary
   leaves
Salt
Black pepper, ground fresh
   from the mill
⅔ cup dry white wine

Note ❀ The recipe given below works well with any lamb, but it is most successful with a very young, small one.

1. You'll be needing a heavy-bottomed or enameled cast-iron pot in which to roast the meat. If you don't have one that can accommodate the piece of meat whole, divide the lamb into 2 or 3 pieces. Wash it in cold running water and pat thoroughly dry with cloth or paper towels.

2. Put the oil and butter in the pot, turn the heat on to medium high, and when the butter foam begins to subside, put in the lamb, the garlic, and the rosemary. Brown the meat deeply all over, particularly the skin side. Check the garlic: If you find it is becoming very dark, remove it from the bottom of the pan and place it on top of the lamb.

3. Add salt, pepper, and the wine. Let the wine simmer briskly for about 15 or 20 seconds, turning the meat once or twice, then adjust heat to cook at a very gentle simmer and cover the pot, setting the lid on slightly ajar. Cook for about 1½ to 2 hours, until the lamb is cooked all the way through and begins to come off the bone. Turn the meat from time to time while it is cooking and, if the liquid in the pot has become insufficient, replenish it as often as needed with 2 or 3 tablespoons of water.

4. When done, transfer the lamb to a warm serving platter. Tip the pan to spoon off all but a small amount of fat. Add 2 tablespoons of water, raise the heat to high, and while the water boils away use a wooden spoon to scrape loose cooking residues from the bottom and sides. Pour the pot juices over the lamb and serve at once.

Abbacchio—Baby Lamb, Pan-Roasted Roman Style

THE DISH that Roman cooking is most famous for is month-old lamb, *abbacchio*. Rarely do butchers outside of Rome offer such young milk-fed lambs, but they can procure, usually on request, what is sometimes referred to in North America as hothouse lamb, a slightly older, but nonetheless very tender animal. You should try to obtain it for this dish, if you want to duplicate the special flavor of Roman *abbacchio*. If you must use older lamb, you can still count on excellent results from this recipe as long as you avoid anything more mature than young spring lamb.   *For 6 servings*

2 tablespoons cooking fat (see note below)

3 pounds shoulder, with some loin attached, of very young lamb, cut into 3-inch pieces, with the larger bones removed, if you like

Salt

Black pepper, ground fresh from the mill

½ teaspoon chopped garlic

6 to 8 fresh sage leaves OR ½ teaspoon dried leaves, chopped fine

A sprig of fresh rosemary OR 1 teaspoon chopped dried

1 tablespoon flour

½ cup wine vinegar

4 flat anchovy fillets (preferably the ones prepared at home as described on page 9), chopped to a pulp

Note ✹ In Rome, the fat traditionally used for roasting *abbacchio* is lard, and no other produces comparably fine flavor or the same light, crisp surface on

Baby Lamb, Pan-Roasted Roman Style (continued)

the meat. But if you prefer not to use lard, you can replace it with olive oil, or a combination of butter and vegetable oil, or all vegetable oil.

1. Choose a heavy-bottomed or enameled cast-iron pot that will comfortably contain all the meat. Put in the cooking fat and turn on the heat to medium high. It the fat is lard, put in the lamb pieces when it melts; if it is butter, when its foam subsides; or, if it is all oil, when hot enough that when you test it with a piece of meat, it sizzles. Brown the meat deeply on all sides, then add salt, pepper, the garlic, sage, and rosemary. Turn over all ingredients 2 or 3 times to coat them well.

2. After cooking for 1 minute, lightly dust the lamb with 1 tablespoon flour sifted through a sieve or fine wire strainer. Distribute the flour evenly over the meat. Cook long enough to turn each piece of meat once, then add the vinegar. When the vinegar has simmered briskly for 15 to 20 seconds, add ⅓ cup of water, and when the water begins to bubble, adjust heat to cook at a very gentle simmer, and cover the pot, setting the lid on slightly ajar.

3. Cook, turning the meat from time to time, until the lamb begins to come easily off any bone, and feels very tender when prodded with a fork. If very young, it may take 1 hour or less. If while it cooks, the liquid should become insufficient, replenish it with 2 to 3 tablespoons of water, as needed.

4. When the lamb is nearly done, put water in the bottom half of a small double boiler, and bring it to a boil. Place the upper half of the boiler over it, put into it a tablespoon or so of juice from the pot in which the lamb is cooking, add to it ½ tablespoon of water, and put in the chopped anchovies. Cook the anchovies, stirring constantly and mashing them with a wooden spoon against the sides of the pot until they dissolve into a paste. When the lamb is done, add the anchovies to it, turn the meat over for about 1 or 2 minutes, then transfer the entire contents of the pot to a warm platter and serve at once.

Ahead-of-time note ❀ The lamb tastes best when served the moment it is done, but it can be prepared several hours in advance, up to but not including the step with the anchovies. Reheat it gently, adding a little bit of water if its juices are skimpy. When it is warm all the way through, carry out the procedure with the anchovies as described above in Step 4.

Pan-Roasted Lamb
with Juniper Berries

THIS OLD LOMBARD recipe follows a procedure completely unlike that of most Italian roasts: The meat is not browned, no cooking fat is used because one relies on the juices supplied by the meat itself, and the vegetables do not undergo any preliminary sautéing, they cook from the start alongside the lamb.

Do not be discouraged by the gray appearance of the lamb during the early cooking phase. It is gray at first because it was not browned originally, but by the time it is done it will be as beautiful a glossy nut-brown as any roast. You will find that through this particular method of cooking even older lamb becomes tender, and its flavor rich and mellow. Allow about 3½ to 4 hours of cooking time.   *For 4 servings*

2½ pounds lamb shoulder, cut
  into 3- to 4-inch pieces,
  with the bone in
1 tablespoon chopped carrot
2 tablespoons chopped onion
1 tablespoon chopped celery
1 cup dry white wine
2 garlic cloves, mashed lightly
  with a knife handle, the
  skin removed

A sprig of fresh rosemary
  OR ½ teaspoon chopped
  dried
1½ teaspoons lightly crushed
  juniper berries
Salt
Black pepper, ground fresh
  from the mill

1. Choose a heavy-bottomed or enameled cast-iron pot that will contain all the ingredients. Put all the ingredients into it, cover the pot, and turn the heat on to medium low. Turn the lamb pieces over about twice an hour.

2. After 2 hours, the ingredients should have shed a considerable amount of juice. Set the pot's cover on slightly ajar, and continue cooking at slightly higher heat. Turn the meat from time to time. After an hour and a half more, the lamb should feel very tender when prodded with a fork. If there is still too much liquid in the pot, uncover, raise the heat, and reduce it to a less runny consistency. Taste the meat and correct for salt.

3. Tip the pot and spoon off as much of the liquefied lamb fat as you can. Transfer the entire contents of the pot to a warm platter and serve at once.

Ahead-of-time note ❀ If you are going to have it that same evening, the lamb can be prepared that morning. It could even be prepared a day in advance, but its flavor will acquire a sharp edge. When making it ahead of time, do not reduce the pot juices or spoon off the fat until after you have reheated it.

Thin Lamb Chops
Fried in Parmesan Batter

FRYING THEM in this batter is one of the most succulent ways to do lamb chops. The crust—crisp and delicious—seals in all the juiciness and sweetness of the lamb. The younger the lamb you use, the more delicate the flavor and texture of the dish will be, but you can successfully execute the recipe with standard lamb.

In order to fry them quickly, the chops should be no more than one rib thick. Have the butcher knock off the corner bone and remove the backbone, leaving just the rib. If he is cooperative, have him flatten the eye of each chop, otherwise flatten it yourself at home with a meat pounder, following the instructions for flattening *scaloppine* on page 38.   *For 6 servings*

12 single rib lamb chops, partly
   boned and flattened as
   described above
½ cup freshly grated
   parmigiano-reggiano cheese,
   spread on a plate
2 eggs, beaten lightly in a
   deep dish

1 cup fine, dry, unflavored
   bread crumbs, spread on
   a plate
Vegetable oil
Salt
Black pepper, ground fresh
   from the mill

1. Turn the chops on both sides in the grated Parmesan, pressing the chop firmly against the crumbs, using the palm of your hand to cause the cheese to adhere well to the meat. Tap the chops gently against the plate to shake off excess cheese. Dip them into the beaten egg, letting excess egg flow back into the dish. Then turn the chops in the bread crumbs, coating both sides, and tap them again to shake off excess.

Ahead-of-time note ❦ You can prepare the chops up to this point as much as 1 hour in advance or, if you refrigerate them, even 3 or 4 hours. If refrigerated, allow enough time for the meat to return to room temperature before cooking it.

2. Pour enough oil in a skillet to come ¼ inch up the sides, and turn on the heat to medium. When the oil is very hot, slip as many chops into the pan as will fit without crowding. As soon as one side forms a nice, golden crust, sprinkle it with salt and pepper, turn the chop, and sprinkle salt and pepper on the other side. As soon as the second side has formed a crust transfer to a warm platter, using a slotted spoon or spatula. Repeat the procedure, slipping more chops into the pan as soon as there is room for them. When all the chops are done serve promptly.

Note ✽ If the chops are as thin as directed, they will be cooked in the time it takes to form a crust on both sides. If they are much thicker, they need to be cooked a little longer.

Lamb Chops Pan-Roasted in White Wine, Finished Marches Style with Egg and Lemon

LIKE THE FRICASSEED chicken on page 335, this dish is finished with an uncooked mixture of beaten egg yolk and lemon juice that thickens on contact with the hot meat. It comes from the central Italian region known as The Marches. *For 4 to 6 servings*

1 cup onion sliced very thin
⅓ cup, about 1½ ounces, *pancetta,* cut into thin julienne strips
1 tablespoon lard OR vegetable oil
2½ pounds loin lamb chops
Whole nutmeg
Salt

Black pepper, ground fresh from the mill
1 cup dry white wine
1 egg yolk (see warning about salmonella poisoning, page 41)
2 tablespoons freshly squeezed lemon juice

1. Choose a sauté pan that can subsequently accommodate all the chops without overlapping, put in the onion, *pancetta,* and lard or vegetable oil, and turn on the heat to medium. Cook the onion, stirring, until it becomes colored a pale gold, put in the lamb chops, and turn up the heat to medium high. Brown the chops deeply on both sides, expecting in the process to see the onion becoming colored a dark nut brown.

Lamb Chops Pan-Roasted in White Wine (continued)

2. Add a tiny grating of nutmeg—about ⅛ teaspoon—salt, and liberal grindings of pepper. Add the white wine and while it simmers for about 10 or 15 seconds, quickly loosen the browning residues from the bottom of the pan, using a wooden spoon. Turn the heat down to cook at a slow simmer, and cover the pan, setting the lid on slightly ajar.

3. Cook for about 1 hour, until the lamb feels very soft when prodded with a fork. If during this period you should find that the liquid in the pan becomes insufficient, add 2 to 3 tablespoons of water as needed.

4. When the chops are done, remove from heat, tip the pan, and spoon off most, all but 1 or 2 tablespoons, of the fat they have shed. In a small bowl lightly beat the egg yolk with the lemon juice, then pour it over the chops. Turn the chops to coat both sides, then transfer to a warm platter with all the contents of the pan, and serve at once.

Lamb Stew
with Vinegar and Green Beans

For 6 servings

1 pound fresh green beans
¼ cup extra virgin olive oil
3 pounds lamb shoulder, cut
    into 2-inch cubes, with the
    bone in

½ cup chopped onion
Salt
Black pepper, ground fresh
    from the mill
½ cup good red wine vinegar

1. Snap the ends off the green beans, wash them in cold water, drain, and set aside.

2. Choose a heavy-bottomed or cast-iron enameled pot that can accommodate all the meat and green beans. Put in the olive oil, turn the heat on to medium high, and when the oil is hot, slip in as many pieces of lamb as will fit loosely, without crowding. Brown the meat deeply on all sides, then transfer it to a plate, using a slotted spoon or spatula, and put in more lamb pieces.

3. When you have browned all the meat and transferred it to a plate, put the onion in the pot. Cook the onion, stirring, until it becomes colored a pale gold, return the lamb to the pot, and then add salt, pepper, and the vinegar. Bring the vinegar to a brisk simmer for about 30 seconds, turning the meat and scraping loose browning residues from the bottom and sides of the pot with a wooden spoon. Turn the heat down to cook at a slow simmer, add the

green beans with a little more salt and pepper, and cover the pot, setting the lid on slightly ajar.

4. Cook for about 1½ hours, until the meat feels very tender when prodded with a fork. The juices in the pot ought to be sufficient, but if you find they are drying up, replenish when needed with 2 or 3 tablespoons water. At the end, the only liquid remaining in the pot should be the oil and the natural cooking juices. When the lamb is done, transfer it with all the contents of the pot to a warm platter and serve at once.

Ahead-of-time note ❀ The dish may be prepared entirely in advance and reheated gently just before serving. As with any dish with greens, it will taste best if consumed the day it is made without subjecting it to refrigeration.

Lamb Stew with Ham and Red Bell Pepper

UNLIKE MOST Italian stews in which the meat is put into hot fat, this one starts out *a crudo,* the meat and the oil heating up together, along with the garlic and herbs. There is also a difference to the ending: Strips of ham and raw sweet pepper are added when the lamb becomes tender, and the cooking continues just long enough to soften the pepper without dulling the freshness of its fragrance.   *For 6 servings*

¼ cup vegetable oil
3 pounds lamb shoulder, cut into 2-inch cubes, with the bone in
2 medium garlic cloves, peeled
A sprig of fresh rosemary OR ½ teaspoon dried rosemary leaves
4 or 5 fresh sage leaves OR 2 or 3 dried ones

½ cup dry white wine
Salt
Black pepper, ground fresh from the mill
1 red or yellow bell pepper
¼ pound boiled unsmoked ham, cut into thin strips

1. Put the oil, lamb, garlic, rosemary, and sage into a sauté pan and turn the heat on to medium high. Turn the meat several times for about 15 minutes, until it has become colored a deep brown on all sides. Add the wine, and let it simmer briskly for 15 to 20 seconds, while giving the lamb pieces a com-

Lamb Stew with Ham and Red Bell Pepper (continued)

plete turn. Add salt and pepper, adjust heat to cook at a slow simmer, and cover the pan, setting the lid slightly ajar.

2. Cook for about 1½ hours, until the meat feels very tender when prodded with a fork. If, in the interim, you find that the juices in the pan become insufficient, replenish them with 2 or 3 tablespoons water.

Ahead-of-time note ※ The stew can be prepared up to this point several hours or a day in advance. Reheat gently, but thoroughly before proceeding with the next step.

3. While the lamb is cooking, skin the raw bell pepper using a swiveling-blade peeler. Split the pepper into sections, remove and discard all the seeds and the pulpy core, and cut the sections into stubby strips about ½ inch wide and 1½ inches long.

4. When the lamb is cooked through and through and has become tender, add the strips of pepper and ham to the stew, and turn over all the contents of the pan. Cover and continue cooking over low heat for about 10 or 15 minutes, until the pepper is soft. If at this point, you find that the remaining juices in the pan are rather runny, uncover the pan, raise the heat, and boil them down briefly. Turn the contents of the pan out onto a warm platter and serve at once.

PORK

Pork Loin Braised in Milk, Bolognese Style

IF AMONG the tens of thousands of dishes that constitute the recorded repertory of Italian regional cooking, one were to choose just a handful that most clearly express the genius of the cuisine, this one would be among them. Aside from a minimal amount of fat required to brown the meat, it has only two components, a loin of pork and milk. As they slowly cook together, they are transformed: The pork acquires a delicacy of texture and flavor that lead some to mistake it for veal, and the milk disappears to be replaced by clusters of delicious, nut-brown sauce.   *For 6 servings*

1 tablespoon butter	Salt
2 tablespoons vegetable oil	Black pepper, ground fresh
2½ pounds pork rib roast (see	from the mill
note below)	2½ cups, or more, whole milk

Note ❧ The cut of meat specified above includes the rib bones to which the pork's loin is attached. Have the butcher detach the meat in one piece from the ribs and split the ribs into two or three parts. By having had the loin boned, you can brown it more thoroughly, and by cooking it along with the bones, the roast benefits from the substantial contribution of flavor the bones make.

Another cut of pork that is well suited to this dish is the boneless roll of muscle at the base of the neck, sometimes known as Boston butt. There is a layer of fat in the center of the butt that runs the length of the muscle. It makes this cut very juicy and tasty, but when you carve it later, the slices tend to break apart where the meat adjoins the fat. If you don't think this would be a problem, you ought to consider using the butt because of its excellent flavor and juiciness. Should you do so, substitute 2 pounds of it in one piece for the 2½-pound rib roast.

Pork Loin Braised in Milk (continued)

Do not have any fat trimmed away from either cut of meat. Most of it will melt in the cooking, basting the meat and keeping it from drying. When the roast is done, you will be able to draw it off from the pot, and discard it.

1. Choose a heavy-bottomed pot that can later snugly accommodate the pork, put in the butter and oil, and turn on the heat to medium high. When the butter foam subsides, put in the meat, the side with fat facing down at first. As it browns, turn it, continuing to turn the meat every few moments to brown it evenly all around. If you should find the butter becoming very dark, lower the heat.

2. Add salt, pepper, and 1 cup of milk. Add the milk slowly lest it boil over. Allow the milk to come to a simmer for 20 or 30 seconds, turn the heat down to minimum, and cover the pot with the lid on slightly ajar.

3. Cook at a very lazy simmer for approximately 1 hour, turning the meat from time to time, until the milk has thickened, through evaporation, into a nut-brown sauce. (The exact time it will take depends largely on the heat of your burner and the thickness of your pot.) When the milk reaches this stage, and not before, add 1 more cup of milk, let it simmer for about 10 minutes, then cover the pot, putting the lid on tightly. Check and turn the pork from time to time.

4. After 30 minutes, set the lid slightly ajar. Continue to cook at mini-mum heat, and when you see there is no more liquid milk in the pot, add the other ½ cup of milk. Continue cooking until the meat feels tender when prodded with a fork and all the milk has coagulated into small nut-brown clusters. Altogether it will take between 2½ and 3 hours. If, before the meat is fully cooked, you find that the liquid in the pot has evaporated, add another ½ cup of milk, repeating the step if it should become necessary.

5. When the pork has become tender and all the milk in the pot has thick-ened into dark clusters, transfer the meat to a cutting board. Let it settle for a few minutes, then cut it into slices about ⅜ inch thick or slightly less, and arrange them on a warm serving platter.

6. Tip the pot and spoon off most of the fat—there may be as much as a cup of it—being careful to leave behind all the coagulated milk clusters. Add 2 or 3 tablespoons of water, and boil away the water over high heat while using a wooden spoon to scrape loose cooking residues from the bottom and sides of the pot. Spoon all the pot juices over the pork and serve immediately.

Roast Pork with Vinegar
and Bay Leaves

For 6 servings

2 tablespoons butter	Salt
1 tablespoon vegetable oil	1 teaspoon whole black
2 pounds pork loin roast,	peppercorns
boneless, OR Boston butt,	3 bay leaves
in one piece	½ cup good red wine vinegar

1. Choose a heavy-bottomed or enameled cast-iron pot into which the pork can fit snugly. Put in the butter and oil, turn the heat on to medium high, and when the butter foam subsides, put in the meat, the side with the fat, if it has any, facing down. Brown the meat deeply all over, turning it when necessary. If you see the butter becoming colored a dark brown, turn the heat down a little.

2. Add salt, turning the meat to sprinkle all sides. Lightly crush the peppercorns with a mallet or meat pounder or even a hammer, then put them in the pot together with the bay leaves and vinegar. With a wooden spoon, quickly scrape loose browning residues from the bottom and sides of the pot, but do not let the vinegar simmer long enough for it to evaporate. Turn the heat down to low, cover the pot tightly, and cook, turning the pork occasionally, until the meat feels tender when prodded with a fork. If during this period the liquid in the pot becomes insufficient, replenish with 2 or 3 tablespoons water.

3. Transfer the pork to a cutting board. Let it settle for a few minutes, then cut it into slices about ⅜ inch thick or slightly less, and arrange them on a warm serving platter.

4. Tip the pot and spoon off most, but not all of the fat, and all the bay leaves. Add 2 tablespoons water, turn the heat on to high, and while the water boils away scrape loose with a wooden spoon any cooking residues from the bottom and sides. Pour the pot juices over the pork and serve at once.

Drunk Roast Pork

THIS TIPSY ROAST cooks at length in enough red wine to cover it, achieving extraordinary tenderness and acquiring a beautiful, lustrous, deep mahogany color. Without agonizing over the choice of wine, you should select one able to perform its crucial role in this preparation. A Barbera or Dolcetto from Piedmont would accomplish the job perfectly. So would one of the Tuscan wines made entirely from the *sangiovese* grape; or, from other countries, an Australian or South African Shiraz, or a well-made California Zinfandel, or a Côte du Rhône from France. Have an extra bottle or two on hand so you can serve it with the pork.   *For 6 to 8 servings*

3 medium carrots
3½ to 4 pounds pork center
    loin OR Boston butt,
    trussed up tightly with
    string
1 tablespoon vegetable oil
2 tablespoons butter
Flour, spread on a plate
2 tablespoons *grappa, marc,*
    calvados, or grape brandy
    (see note on page 365)

1½ cups or more dry red wine
    (see suggestions above in
    prefacing note)
Whole nutmeg
2 bay leaves
Salt
Black pepper, ground fresh
    from the mill

1. Peel and wash the carrots, then cut them lengthwise into sticks ⅜ inch thick or slightly less.

2. Take a long, pointed, fairly thick tool such as a meat probe, a knife-sharpening steel, a chopstick of the sturdy Chinese kind, or even an awl, and pierce the meat at both ends in as many places as you have carrot sticks, keeping the holes about 1½ inches apart. Stuff the carrot sticks into the holes.

3. Choose a heavy-bottomed or enameled cast-iron pot, preferably oval in shape, just large enough to contain the meat snugly later. Put in the oil and butter and turn on the heat to medium high. When the butter foam begins to subside, turn the meat in the flour, coating it all over, and put it in the pot. Brown it deeply all around, turning it to do so.

4. When you have browned the meat, add the *grappa* or other brandy. Allow it to simmer a few seconds, then pour in the wine until it is just shy of covering the meat. If the 1½ cups do not suffice—it will depend on the size pot you are using—add more.

5. Add a tiny grating of nutmeg—about ⅛ teaspoon—the bay leaves, several pinches of salt, and liberal grindings of pepper. Turn the pork once or twice. When the wine begins to simmer briskly, adjust heat to cook at a very gentle simmer, and cover the pot tightly. It's advisable to place a double sheet of heavy aluminum foil between the pot and its lid.

6. Cook at slow heat for 3 hours or more, occasionally turning the meat,

until it feels tender when prodded with a fork. After cooking for 2½ hours, check the pot to see how much liquid remains. If there is a substantial amount, remove the foil, set the lid ajar, and turn up the heat a little.

7. When done, the pork should be quite dark, and there should be a small amount of syrupy sauce in the pot. Transfer the meat to a cutting board, slice it thin, and arrange the slices on a warm serving platter. Spoon all the pot juices over it, together with any carrot sticks that may have slipped out, and serve at once.

Ahead-of-time note ✸ The roast can be finished several hours in advance, early in the day of the evening you plan to serve it. Reheat it gently in a covered pot, long enough for the meat to warm up all the way through, adding 2 or 3 tablespoons of water if it becomes necessary.

Braised Pork Chops with Tomatoes, Cream, and Porcini Mushrooms

For 4 to 6 servings

¼ cup vegetable oil
2 pounds pork chops, prefer-
    ably from the center loin,
    cut ¾ inch thick
½ cup dry white wine
½ cup canned imported Italian
    plum tomatoes, drained
    and cut up
½ cup heavy whipping cream
Salt
Black pepper, ground fresh
    from the mill

A small packet OR 1 ounce
    dried *porcini* mushrooms,
    reconstituted as described
    on page 27 and cut up
The filtered water from the
    mushroom soak, see page
    28 for instructions
½ pound fresh, white button
    mushrooms

1. Choose a sauté pan that can subsequently accommodate all the chops without overlapping. Put in 2 tablespoons of the vegetable oil, turn on the heat to medium high, and when the oil is hot, slip in the chops. Brown the meat deeply on one side, then do the other.

2. Add the white wine, letting it simmer briskly for 15 or 20 seconds, while using a wooden spoon to scrape loose any browning residues in the pan. Add the tomatoes, cream, salt, liberal grindings of pepper, and the cut-up

reconstituted *porcini* mushrooms. Turn the heat down to cook at a very gentle simmer, and cover the pan, setting the lid on slightly ajar.

3. Cook for 45 minutes or more, depending on the exact thickness and quality of the chops, until the meat feels tender when prodded with a fork. Turn the chops from time to time.

4. While the chops are cooking, put the filtered water from the *porcini* mushroom soak into a small saucepan, and boil it down to about ⅓ cup.

5. Wash the fresh white mushrooms rapidly under cold running water and wipe them thoroughly dry with a soft cloth towel. Cut them into very thin lengthwise slices without detaching the caps from the stems.

6. Choose a sauté pan that can contain the fresh mushrooms without crowding them. Put in the remaining 2 tablespoons of oil and turn on the heat to high. When the oil is hot, put in the mushrooms. Stir them frequently, adding salt and pepper. When the liquid they will shed has boiled away, add the reduced filtered water from the *porcini* soak, and continue to stir frequently until there is no more liquid in the pan. Take off heat.

7. When the pork chops are tender, add the cooked mushrooms to their pan. Turn the chops and mushrooms, cover the pan again, and continue cooking for 5 to 8 minutes always over moderate heat. Transfer the entire contents of the pan to a warm platter and serve at once.

Braised Pork Chops with Sage and Tomatoes, Modena Style

IN ITALY, one looks up to the cuisine of Emilia-Romagna for the most savory pork specialties in the country, and in Emilia-Romagna itself, one looks to Modena. The tasty way with fresh pork chops in the recipe that follows is an example of the Modenese touch.   *For 4 servings*

2 tablespoons butter	Black pepper, ground fresh
1 tablespoon vegetable oil	from the mill
4 pork loin chops, preferably	¾ cup canned imported Italian
bottom loin, ¾ inch thick	plum tomatoes, cut up,
Flour, spread on a plate	with their juice, OR fresh,
6 to 8 fresh sage leaves OR 3 to	ripe tomatoes, peeled and
4 dried ones	chopped
Salt	

1. Choose a sauté pan that can later contain all the chops without over-lapping. Put in the butter and oil, and turn on the heat to medium high. When the butter foam begins to subside, turn the chops on both sides in the flour, shake off excess flour, and slip them into the pan together with the sage leaves. Cook the chops to a rich brown on both sides, about 1½ to 2 minutes per side.

2. Add salt, several grindings of pepper, and the cut-up tomatoes with their juice. Adjust heat to cook at a slow simmer, and cover the pan, setting the lid on slightly ajar. Cook for about 1 hour, until the meat feels tender when prodded with a fork. Turn the chops from time to time while they are cooking.

3. By the time the pork is done, the sauce in the pan should have become rather dense. If it is too runny, transfer the chops to a warm serving platter, and reduce the pan juices over high heat for a few moments. Tip the pan and spoon off most of the fat. Pour the contents of the pan over the chops and serve at once.

Braised Pork Chops with Two Wines

THE TWO WINES required here are Marsala and a young red, a mixture that combines the aromatic intensity of the first with the vivacious sharpness of the latter. For the red wine, your preference should go to a Piedmontese Barbera or a Valpolicella or any young red from Central Italy, such as a non-*riserva* Chianti. It would be appropriate to serve the same wine with the chops.   *For 4 servings*

3 tablespoons extra virgin
    olive oil
4 pork loin chops, preferably
    bottom loin, ¾ inch thick
Flour, spread on a plate
1 teaspoon garlic chopped fine
1 tablespoon tomato paste,
    dissolved in a mixture of ½

cup dry Marsala and ½ cup
    dry young red wine (see
    remarks above)
Salt
Black pepper, ground fresh
    from the mill
¼ teaspoon fennel seeds
1 tablespoon chopped parsley

1. Choose a sauté pan that can later contain all the chops without over-lapping. Put in the oil, and turn on the heat to medium. When the oil becomes hot, turn the chops on both sides in the flour, shake off excess flour,

Braised Pork Chops with Two Wines (continued)

and slip them into the pan. Cook the chops to a rich brown on both sides, about 1½ to 2 minutes per side.

2. Add the chopped garlic, stirring it into the oil at the bottom of the pan. When the garlic becomes colored a pale gold, add the mixture of the two wines and tomato paste. Sprinkle generously with salt and pepper, and add the fennel seeds. When the wine has simmered briskly for about 20 seconds, turn the heat down to cook at a slow simmer, and cover the pan, setting the lid on slightly ajar.

3. Cook for about 1 hour, until the meat feels tender when prodded with a fork. Turn the chops from time to time while they are cooking. When they are done, add the parsley, turn the chops over 2 or 3 times, then transfer them to a warm serving platter, using a slotted spoon or spatula.

4. Tip the pan and spoon off all but a small amount of fat. Add ½ cup water, turn the heat up to high, and while the water boils away, scrape loose cooking residues from the bottom and sides of the pan, using a wooden spoon. When the pan juices become dense, pour them over the chops and serve at once.

Stewed Pork
with Porcini Mushrooms and Juniper

THE CHORUS of fragrances from the forest and the herb garden—*porcini* mushrooms, juniper berries, marjoram, bay—that accompany this stew echoes the flavors that one associates with furred game. And like game, the dish should go to the table in the company of steaming, soft Polenta (see page 274). The most suitable cut of pork for this recipe is the shoulder, sometimes known as Boston-style shoulder.   *For 4 servings*

20 juniper berries

1½ pounds boned pork
    shoulder, cut into pieces
    about 1 inch thick and
    2 inches wide

⅓ cup extra virgin olive oil

2 tablespoons chopped onion

½ cup dry white wine

2 tablespoons good red wine
    vinegar

A small packet OR 1 ounce
    dried *porcini* mushrooms,
    reconstituted as described
    on page 27 and cut up

The filtered water from the mushroom soak, see page 28 for instructions

3 flat anchovy fillets (preferably the ones prepared at home as described on page 90), chopped to a pulp

½ teaspoon fresh marjoram OR ¼ teaspoon dried

2 bay leaves, chopped if fresh, crumbled fine if dried

Salt

Black pepper, ground fresh from the mill

1. Wrap the juniper berries in a towel and crush them lightly using a mallet, a meat pounder, or even a hammer. Unwrap them and set aside.

2. Choose a sauté pan that can later contain the pork pieces stacked no deeper than two layers. Put in the oil and turn on the heat to medium high. When the oil is hot, put in as many pieces of meat as will fit without being crowded, and cook them, turning them, until they are deeply browned on all sides. Transfer them to a plate, using a slotted spoon or spatula, and repeat the procedure until you have browned all the pork.

3. Add the onion, and cook the onion, stirring, until it becomes colored a deep gold, then return the meat to the pan. Add the wine and vinegar and let them simmer briskly for about 30 seconds, then put in the cut-up mushrooms, their filtered liquid, the chopped anchovies, the marjoram, the bay leaves, and the crushed juniper berries. Turn the heat down to cook at a very slow simmer, and turn over all the ingredients in the pan. Add a few pinches of salt and several grindings of pepper, turn the ingredients over once again, and cover the pan tightly.

4. Cook for 1½ to 2 hours, until the meat feels tender when prodded with a fork. When it is done, transfer it with a slotted spoon to a warm serving platter. If the juices in the pan are thin and runny, raise the heat to high and reduce them. If the pork has shed a lot of fat in the pan, tip it and spoon most of it off, without discarding any of the good pan juices. Pour the remaining contents of the pan over the pork and serve at once.

Ahead-of-time note ✿ The dish can be completed 2 or 3 days in advance, but do not reduce the juices or discard any fat until after you have gently, but thoroughly reheated the stew.

Spareribs Pan-Roasted with Sage and White Wine, Treviso Style

IN WHAT WERE one time the poor regions of northern Italy, the eastern Veneto and Friuli, satisfaction and nourishment had to be found in the least expensive cuts of meat. No one in the Veneto goes hungry any longer, but the flavor of Treviso's ribs slowly pan-roasted with sage and white wine is as deeply gratifying now as it was then. Serve them with their pan juices, over Italian mashed potatoes, page 518, or hot, soft Polenta, page 274.

For 4 servings

A 3-pound rack of spareribs,
  divided into single ribs
¼ cup vegetable oil
3 garlic cloves, peeled and cut
  into very thin slices
2 tablespoons fresh sage leaves
  OR 2 teaspoons whole dried
  ones, chopped

1 cup dry white wine
Salt
Black pepper, ground fresh
  from the mill

1. Choose a sauté pan that can subsequently accommodate all the ribs without crowding them. Put in the oil and turn on the heat to medium high. When the oil is hot, put in the ribs, and turn them as they cook to brown them deeply all over.

2. Add the garlic and sage. Cook the garlic, stirring, until it becomes colored a very pale blond, then add the wine. After the wine has simmered briskly for 15 to 20 seconds, adjust heat to cook at a very slow simmer, add salt and pepper, and cover the pan, putting the lid on slightly ajar. Cook for about 40 minutes, turning the ribs occasionally, until their fleshiest part feels very tender when prodded with a fork and comes easily away from the bone. From time to time, as the liquid in the pan becomes insufficient, you will need to add 2 to 3 tablespoons of water to keep the ribs from drying.

3. Transfer the ribs to a warm serving platter, using a slotted spoon or spatula. Tip the pan and spoon off about one-third of the liquefied pork fat. Leave more fat than you usually would when degreasing a pan because you need it to season the recommended accompanying mashed potatoes or *polenta*. Add ½ cup water, turn up the heat to high, and while the water boils away, use a wooden spoon to scrape loose cooking residues from the bottom and sides of the pan. Pour the resulting dark, dense juices over the ribs and serve at once.

Spareribs with Tomatoes and Vegetables for Polenta

THESE SPARERIBS would certainly be most enjoyable even without *polenta*, with mashed potatoes say, but the juices they produce are exactly of the kind that yearn for a plump dollop of soft, hot *polenta* to sink into.

For 6 servings, if generously accompanied by polenta

3 tablespoons extra virgin
  olive oil
⅔ cup chopped onion
A 3-pound rack of spareribs,
  cut by the butcher into
  finger-size pieces
⅔ cup chopped carrot
⅔ cup chopped celery

1½ cups canned imported
  Italian plum tomatoes,
  chopped, with their juice,
  OR fresh, ripe tomatoes,
  peeled and cut up
Salt
Black pepper, ground fresh
  from the mill

1. Choose a sauté pan that can subsequently contain all the ribs no more than 2 layers deep. Put in the olive oil and the chopped onion, turn on the heat to medium, and cook the onion, stirring occasionally, until it becomes colored a pale gold. Put in the ribs, turning them several times to coat them well, and cook them long enough to brown them all over.

2. Add the carrot and celery, turning them 2 or 3 times, and cook until they are nearly tender.

3. Add the tomatoes, salt, and liberal grindings of pepper, put a lid on the pan setting it slightly askew, and cook at a slow, but steady simmer until the meat is very tender and comes easily off the bone, about 1 to 1½ hours. Check the pan from time to time. If the cooking liquid becomes insufficient and the ribs start to stick to the bottom, add ½ cup water as needed. On the other hand, if when the ribs are done the pan juices are too watery, uncover, turn up the heat, and boil them down until the fat floats free.

Ahead-of-time note 🐝 You can cook the ribs through to the end up to 1 day in advance. Reheat gently, but thoroughly before serving.

Note 🐝 If you like sausages, you can replace half the amount of ribs called for with 1 pound of sausages, and cook them together. It makes a very tasty dish. Cut the sausages in half before cooking, and use the plainest pork sausage you can buy, without fennel seeds, cumin, chili pepper, or other extraneous flavors.

Grilled Marinated Spareribs

The savory distinction of these grilled ribs is owed to the marinade of olive oil, garlic, and rosemary in which they must steep for at least 1 hour before cooking.   *For 4 servings*

¼ cup extra virgin olive oil	Salt
1 tablespoon garlic chopped very fine	Black pepper, ground fresh from the mill
1 tablespoon fresh rosemary leaves chopped very fine OR 2 teaspoons dried, chopped	A 3-pound rack of pork spareribs in one piece OPTIONAL: a charcoal grill

1. Put the olive oil, garlic, rosemary, liberal pinches of salt, and grindings of black pepper into a small bowl, and beat with a fork until the ingredients are evenly combined.

2. Place the rib rack on a platter, and pour the marinade from the bowl over it, rubbing it into the meat with your fingertips or brushing it on with a pastry brush. Allow to stand at room temperature for at least 1 hour, occasionally turning the rack, to allow the fragrance and flavor of the marinade to sink into the meat.

3. Preheat the broiler 15 minutes before you are ready to grill the ribs. If using charcoal, allow it time to form a full coating of white ash.

4. Place the broiler pan—or the grilling rack, if it is adjustable—about 8 inches away from the source of heat. Put the spareribs on the pan or grill, brushing them with what remains of the marinade in the platter. Cook for 25 minutes, turning the rack 3 or 4 times. The meat should be juicily tender, but well done, not pink. Serve at once when done.

Pork Sausages with Red Cabbage

CABBAGE DOES wonderful things for meat, especially sausages. Here the cabbage and the pork are cooked separately first; the cabbage in olive oil, the sausages in their own fat. They finish cooking together, engaging in a reciprocal and beneficial assimilation of flavors.   *For 4 servings*

1 tablespoon chopped garlic	1½ pounds red cabbage, cut into fine strips, about 8 cups
¼ cup extra virgin olive oil	

Salt

Black pepper, ground fresh
  from the mill

1 pound mild pork sausage,
  containing no herbs or
  strong spices

1. Put the garlic and olive oil into a large sauté pan, turn on the heat to medium, and cook the garlic, stirring, until it becomes colored a light gold, then add all the cabbage, turning it over several times to coat all of it well. Add salt and pepper and cook uncovered, turning the cabbage from time to time, while you proceed with the next step.

2. Put the sausages in a small skillet and pierce them in several places with a sharply pointed fork. The fat that will spill through as the sausages cook will be all the fat you require. Turn the heat on to medium, and cook the sausages, turning them, until you have browned them deeply all over. Transfer them to a plate, using a slotted spoon or spatula.

3. When the cabbage is nearly done—it should be reduced to half its bulk and limp, but not yet completely soft after about 45 minutes—sprinkle liberally with salt and pepper, and add the browned sausages. Continue cooking for 20 minutes or so, until the cabbage is very soft, turning the entire contents of the pan over from time to time. Transfer to a warm platter and serve at once.

Pork Sausages with Smothered Onions and Tomatoes

For 4 servings

3 tablespoons vegetable oil

2 cups onion sliced very,
  very fine

1 cup canned imported Italian
  plum tomatoes, chopped
  up, with just a little of their
  juice, OR fresh, ripe tomatoes, peeled and cut up

Salt

Black pepper, ground fresh
  from the mill

1 yellow or red sweet bell
  pepper

1 pound mild pork sausage,
  containing no herbs or
  strong spices

1. Put the oil and onion in a sauté pan, cover, and turn on the heat to medium. When the onion wilts and becomes much reduced in bulk, uncover the pan, turn up the heat to medium high, and cook the onion, turning it over from time to time, until it becomes colored a deep gold.

2. Add the tomatoes, salt, and pepper, stir to coat well, and turn the heat

Pork Sausages with Smothered Onions (continued)

down to cook, uncovered, at a steady, but gentle simmer for about 20 minutes, or until the oil floats free from the tomatoes.

3. Skin the pepper raw with a swiveling-blade peeler, split it, remove the seeds and pulpy core, and cut it into thin long strips.

4. Add the pepper to the tomato and onion. Put in the sausage, puncturing the skin in several places with a fork. Cover the pan and cook over medium heat for 20 minutes, turning the sausages and tomatoes over from time to time.

5. Tip the pan and spoon off most of the fat. Do not discard the fat; if sausages are left over, you will need it for other dishes, see note below. Transfer the contents of the pan to a warm platter and serve at once.

Leftover note ❀If sausage is left over, cut it into small pieces and combine it with the fat you had kept aside to form the flavor base of a *risotto*, see page 242 or crumble it, reheat it with a little of its reserved fat, and toss it with pasta; or drain it well of fat, combine it with grated Parmesan cheese, and add to a *frittata*, see page 278.

Ahead-of-time note ❀The sausages may be cooked all the way to the end several hours or a day or two in advance. Do not degrease until after they have been reheated.

Pork Sausages
with Black-Eyed Peas and Tomatoes

For 4 servings

2 tablespoons chopped onion
3 tablespoons extra virgin olive
    oil
¼ teaspoon chopped garlic
⅓ cup chopped carrot
⅓ cup chopped celery
1 cup canned imported Italian
    plum tomatoes, chopped
    coarse, with their juice, OR
    fresh, ripe tomatoes, peeled
    and cut up

1 pound mild pork sausage,
    containing no herbs or
    strong spices
1 cup dried black-eyed peas,
    soaked for at least 1 hour in
    lukewarm water
Salt
Black pepper, ground fresh
    from the mill

1. Choose a heavy-bottomed or enameled cast-iron saucepan, put in the onion and olive oil, and turn on the heat to medium. Cook and stir the onion until it becomes colored a light gold, then add the garlic, and when the garlic becomes colored a pale blond, add the carrot and celery, stir thoroughly to coat well, and cook for 5 minutes. Add the chopped tomatoes with their juice, stir to coat well, and adjust heat to cook at a gentle, but steady simmer for about 20 minutes, until the oil floats free of the tomatoes.

2. Add the sausages to the pot, puncturing them in several places with a fork. Cook at a steady simmer for about 15 minutes, turning the sausages from time to time.

3. Drain the peas and add them to the pot, together with enough fresh water to cover. Bring to a steady simmer and cover the pot tightly. Cook for about 1½ hours, until the peas are tender. Cooking times will vary because some peas cook faster than others. Check the level of cooking liquid in the pot; if it becomes insufficient, replenish with ⅓ cup of water as needed; if, on the other hand, when the beans are done, the juices in the pot are too watery, uncover, turn the heat up to high, and quickly boil away the liquid until it is reduced to a desirably dense consistency.

4. Tip the pot and spoon off as much fat as you can. Add salt and pepper to taste, stir thoroughly, then serve at once.

Oven note ❀ If you prefer to use the oven, after the peas have been added and the contents brought to a simmer as described in Step 3 you can transfer the pot to the middle level of a preheated 350° oven. Make sure the pot handles are ovenproof. If, when the peas are done, the juices need to be reduced, do so on top of the stove.

Ahead-of-time note ❀ The dish can be cooked entirely in advance several days ahead. If the cooking juices need to be reduced, do it only after thoroughly reheating the sausages and peas.

Pork Sausages with Red Wine and Porcini Mushrooms

For 4 to 6 servings

1 tablespoon extra virgin
  olive oil
1½ pounds mild pork sausage,
  containing no herbs or
  strong spices
½ cup dry red wine
A small packet OR 1 ounce
  dried *porcini* mushrooms,

reconstituted as described
  on page 27
The filtered water from the
  mushroom soak, see page
  28 for instructions

1. Choose a sauté pan that can subsequently accommodate all the sausages without overlapping. Put in the oil and sausages, puncture the sausages in several places with a fork, turn on the heat to medium, and cook, turning the sausages, until you have browned them deeply all over.

2. Add the red wine and adjust heat to cook at a gentle simmer. Turn the sausages from time to time while allowing the wine to evaporate completely. When the wine has completely evaporated, add the reconstituted mushrooms and the filtered liquid from their soak. Cook, always at a steady, but gentle simmer, turning the sausages occasionally and using a wooden spoon to scrape loose cooking residues from the bottom and sides of the pan until the mushroom liquid has evaporated.

3. Tip the pan and spoon off all the fat you can, unless mashed potatoes or *polenta* accompany the sausages, in which instance remove only part of the fat. Serve at once.

Cotechino—Boiled Large Sausage with Lentils

A SPECIALTY of Emilia-Romagna, and particularly of the town of Modena, *cotechino* is a fresh pork sausage about 3 inches in diameter and 8 to 9 inches long. The name comes from *cotica*, pork rind, a major component. The rind for *cotechino* is taken from the snout and jowl, to which one adds some meat from the shoulder and neck, together with salt, pepper, nutmeg, and cloves, the proportions and choice of seasonings varying according to the style of the maker. When the same mixture is stuffed into a casing made from the pig's trotter, it is called *zampone*. In the Veneto, a similar product is called *musetto*. It is made largely from the snout, or *muso*, and it is even softer than *cotechino*.

A properly cooked and skillfully made *cotechino* is exquisitely tender, with a succulent consistency that is almost creamy, and a sweeter taste than you might expect from any pork sausage. Butchers and delicatessens specializing in Italian food sell *cotechino*, but what sausage-makers outside Italy produce is leaner, drier, and saltier than the Modenese archetype, closer in style to a French *saucisson*. Nonetheless, when cooked and served as described below, it is a marvelously heartening dish. In Italy, it is believed that if *cotechino* with lentils is the first dish you eat on New Year's Day, it will bring luck for the whole year.   *For 6 servings*

1 *cotechino* sausage
1 tablespoon chopped onion
2 tablespoons vegetable oil
1 tablespoon chopped celery
1 cup lentils, washed in cold
    water and drained

Salt
Black pepper, ground fresh
    from the mill

1. *Cooking the cotechino:* Soak the sausage in abundant cold water a minimum of 4 hours, but better overnight.

2. When ready to cook, drain the *cotechino*, put it in a pot that can contain it roomily, add at least 3 quarts cold water or more if necessary to cover amply, and bring to a boil. Cook at a slow boil for 2½ hours. Do not prod with a fork, because the skin must not be punctured while it cooks. When done, turn off the heat and allow the *cotechino* to rest in its cooking liquid for a while, but not more than 15 minutes before serving. Do not remove it from the liquid until you are ready to slice it, but make sure it is still hot when you serve it.

3. *Cooking the lentils:* Wait until the sausage has boiled for 1½ hours, then in a saucepan bring 1 quart of water to a simmer.

4. Put the chopped onion and oil in a heavy-bottomed or enameled cast-iron pot, and turn the heat on to medium high. Cook and stir the onion until it becomes colored a pale gold, then add the chopped celery, stir to coat it well, and cook for 1 or 2 minutes.

5. Add the lentils to the onion and celery, and stir thoroughly to coat well. Add enough of the water simmering in the saucepan to cover the lentils, adjust heat to cook at the gentlest of simmers, cover the pot tightly, and cook until the lentils are tender, about 30 to 40 minutes. Add water from time to time as may be needed to keep the lentils fully covered. For more flavor, use some of the water in which the *cotechino* is cooking.

Boiled Large Sausage with Lentils (continued)

6. When the lentils begin to become tender, but are not yet done, stop adding liquid, because they must absorb all the liquid before you can serve them. If there is still liquid in the pot when they reach tenderness, uncover, turn the heat up to high, and boil it away, stirring the lentils as you do so. Do not worry if some of the lentils burst their skins and look mashed. Add salt and pepper to taste.

7. *Combining the cotechino and lentils:* Transfer the sausage to a cutting board and cut into slices ½ inch thick. Spoon the lentils onto a heated platter, spreading them out, arrange the sliced *cotechino* on top, and serve at once.

Pizza Rustica—Pork and Cheese Pie, Abruzzi Style

THERE ARE a great many dishes in Italy called *pizza* that do not coincide with any familiar image of pizza. This one is a meat and cheese pie from Abruzzi and is enclosed in *pasta frolla,* Italian sweet egg pastry. Combining sweet pastry with a salted filling is a practice that goes back centuries, and however startling it may sound, it is an appealing and lively coupling of flavors. I have adjusted the traditional pastry formula to one whose taste I am more comfortable with, using far less sugar. I have also eliminated the hard-boiled eggs that usually find their way into these fillings because I find the pork and cheese satiating enough, and, hallowed usage notwithstanding, there is no cinnamon, a spice I have an aversion to.   *For 6 servings*

FOR THE PASTA FROLLA, SWEET EGG PASTRY

2 cups all purpose flour	3 tablespoons ice water
2 egg yolks	2 tablespoons granulated sugar
Salt	
8 tablespoons (1 stick) butter, cut into small pieces	

Combine all the ingredients and knead them together, preferably on a cold surface such as marble. When they are amalgamated into a smooth, compact dough, wrap it in wax paper and put it in the refrigerator. Refrigerate for at least 1 hour, and up to 4 or 5, before proceeding with the rest of the recipe.

Food processor note: All the mixing and kneading can be done with the steel blade, spinning it on and off until balls of dough form on it. When taking the dough out of the processor bowl, shape it into a single compact ball before wrapping and refrigerating it.

MAKING THE FILLING AND COMPLETING THE PIE

2 egg yolks

¾ pound fresh *ricotta*

¼ pound prosciutto OR country ham OR boiled unsmoked ham, chopped rather coarse

¼ pound *mortadella,* chopped coarse

¼ pound mozzarella, preferably buffalo-milk mozzarella, cut up in small pieces

2 tablespoons freshly grated *parmigiano-reggiano* cheese

Salt

Black pepper, ground fresh from the mill

A 1-quart ceramic soufflé dish

Butter for smearing the dish

The cold sweet egg pastry made as directed above

1. Preheat oven to 375°.

2. Put the egg yolks in a bowl and beat them briefly with a whisk. Add the *ricotta* and beat until it becomes rather creamy. Add the chopped cold meats, the cut-up mozzarella, the grated Parmesan, salt, and pepper, and mix thoroughly until all ingredients are evenly combined.

3. Thickly smear the inside of the soufflé dish with butter.

4. Cut off ⅓ of the pastry dough, and over a sheet of wax paper or kitchen parchment, roll it into a circular sheet large enough to cover the bottom of the baking dish and come up its sides a little. Turn the sheet over into the dish, peeling the paper or parchment away. Fit the dough over the bottom of the dish, spreading it out evenly with your fingers.

5. Cut the remaining ball of dough in two, and, following the method described above, roll one half into rectangular strips about as wide as the soufflé mold is deep. Line the sides of the mold with the strips, overlapping where necessary, and filling in any gap with bits of dough, handling it like putty. Smooth with your fingers, evening off any unevenness. Where the sides meet the bottom, press the dough all around to seal the connection tightly.

6. Pour the mixture from the bowl into the mold and press it with the back of a spoon to force out any air bubbles trapped within it.

7. Roll out the rest of the pastry dough into a sheet large enough to cover the top of the pie amply. Place it over the filling and press it with your fingers where it meets the dough on the sides, making a tight seal. Trim the edge of the upper sheet of dough so that it does not extend more than ½ inch beyond the rim of the mold, and fold what remains over toward the center. Go over any rough connections with a moistened fingertip.

Pork and Cheese Pie (continued)

8. Place the dish on the upper rack of the preheated oven, and bake until the crust on top becomes colored a light golden brown, about 45 minutes. If at the end of 45 minutes the crust requires a little deeper browning, turn the oven up to 400° and bake for a few more minutes until the color looks right.

9. The pie can be served without unmolding, spooning it directly out of the baking dish. If you'd rather unmold it, when the dish has settled out of the oven for 10 minutes, run a knife all around the sides of the mold to loosen the pie. Put a dinner plate, bottom up, over the top of the mold. Grasp the plate and mold with a towel, holding them together tightly, and turn the mold upside down. Lift the mold away to leave the pie standing on the plate. Let cool at least another 5 to 10 minutes, or serve even a few hours later, at mild room temperature.

VARIETY MEATS

Sautéed Calf's Liver with Lemon, Piccata Style

Piccata is the term restaurants often use to describe sautéed veal *scaloppine* sauced with lemon juice. A similar procedure is here applied to calf's liver. If possible, it is an even more refined dish than the version with *scaloppine*. It is certainly one of the freshest and lightest things one can do with liver.

For 4 servings

1 pound choice, pale pink calf's liver, cut into slices no more than ¼ inch thick
1 tablespoon vegetable oil
3 tablespoons butter
Flour, spread on a plate

Salt
Black pepper, ground fresh from the mill
3 tablespoons freshly squeezed lemon juice
1 tablespoon chopped parsley

1. Remove any of the thin, stiff skin that may still be on the liver. It would shrink while cooking, and keep the liver from lying flat in the pan. If you find any large white gristly tubes, remove those also.

2. Put the oil and 2 tablespoons of butter in a large sauté pan and turn on the heat to medium high. When the butter foam subsides, rapidly turn the liver in the flour on both sides, and slip into the pan as many slices at one time as will fit loosely, without crowding or overlapping. Cook the liver about ½ minute on each side, then transfer to a warm plate, using a slotted spoon or spatula, and sprinkle with salt and pepper. Repeat the procedure until all the slices of liver are done and on the plate.

3. Add the lemon juice and the remaining 1 tablespoon butter to the pan over medium-high heat. Stir rapidly, 2 or 3 times, using a wooden spoon to scrape loose cooking residues from the bottom and sides of the pan. Return all the liver at one time to the pan, turn the slices over just long enough to coat them, then transfer the liver and the pan juices to a warm platter, sprinkle with parsley, and serve at once.

Sautéed Calf's Liver and Onions, Venetian Style

LIVER VENETIAN STYLE, *fegato alla veneziana,* is not just liver and onions. The onions are a necessary part of it, of course, but what really matters is that the liver be pale pink, creamy, and free of gristly, chewy tubes because it comes from a very young calf, that it be cut in even slices no thicker than ¼ inch, and that it be sautéed in a flash, at high heat. To cook the liver correctly, there should be no more than one layer of it at a time in the pan, because then it will stew, becoming stiff, bitter, and gray; it must be spread out in a broad pan, and cook so quickly at such fast heat that it has no time to lose any of its sweet juices.

There is one traditional feature of *fegato alla veneziana* it is possible to ignore without compromising the excellence of the dish. Venetian butchers cut the thin slices of liver into bite-size strips 1½ inches wide, and if you are having Venetians to dinner that is what you may want to do. I find it more practical to leave the slices whole; it makes them easier to turn when they are cooking, and it permits you to exercise more control to cook all the liver more uniformly.   *For 6 servings*

1½ pounds choice, pale pink calf's liver, cut into slices no more than ¼ inch thick	Salt
	Black pepper, ground fresh from the mill
3 tablespoons vegetable oil	
3 cups onion sliced very, very thin	

1. Remove any of the thin, stiff skin that may still be on the liver. It would shrink while cooking, and keep the liver from lying flat in the pan. If you find any large white gristly tubes, remove those also.

2. Choose your largest skillet or sauté pan, put in the oil, the onion, and salt, and turn on the heat to medium low. Cook the onion for 20 minutes or more until it is completely limp and has become colored a nut brown.

Ahead-of-time note ✿ You can complete the recipe up to this point several hours in advance.

3. Remove the onion from the skillet, using a slotted spoon or spatula, and set aside. Do not remove any oil. Turn the heat on to high, and when the oil is very hot, put in as many slices of liver as will fit loosely, without over-

lapping. They are not likely to fit in all at one time, so be prepared to do them in batches. The moment the liver loses its raw color, turn it, and cook for just a few seconds longer. Transfer the first batch when done to a warm plate, using a slotted spoon or spatula, and sprinkle with salt and pepper. Repeat the procedure until all the slices are done, then put the liver back into the pan.

4. Quickly put the onion back in the pan while the heat is still on, turn the onion and liver over once completely, then transfer the entire contents of the pan to a serving platter, and serve at once.

Breaded Calf's Liver

BREADING IS ONE of the most desirable things you can do with liver that is sliced thin in the Italian style. It protects the liver's precarious moisture, and the crisp coating contrasts very agreeably with the softness of young liver, when it is perfectly cooked. *For 6 servings*

2 tablespoons vegetable oil	toasted in the oven or in a
2 tablespoons butter	skillet
1½ pounds choice, pale pink	Salt
calf's liver, cut into slices no	Black pepper, ground fresh
more than ¼ inch thick	from the mill
¾ cup fine, dry, unflavored	Lemon wedges at table
bread crumbs, lightly	

1. Remove any of the thin, stiff skin that may still be on the liver. It would shrink while cooking, and keep the liver from lying flat in the pan. If you find any large white gristly tubes, remove those also.

2. Put the oil and butter in a large sauté pan and turn on the heat to medium high. Turn the liver slices in the bread crumbs on both sides, pressing the liver against the crumbs with the palm of your hands. Shake off excess crumbs and as soon as the butter foam begins to subside, slip the slices into the pan. Do not put in any more at one time than will fit loosely, without overlapping.

3. Cook the liver until it forms a crisp, brown crust on one side, then do the other side. Altogether, it should take about 1 minute. As you do one batch of slices, transfer them with a slotted spoon or spatula to a cooling rack to drain or to a platter lined with paper towels. Sprinkle with salt and pepper, and slip another batch into the pan, repeating the same procedure, until all the slices are done. Transfer to a warm platter and serve at once.

Grilled Calf's or Pork Liver
Wrapped in Caul

CAUL IS A SOFT, net-like membrane that envelops the pig's intestines. It dissolves slowly over a hot fire, eventually disappearing almost completely, thus acting as a natural basting agent for meats that need to be protected from drying. Liver grilled in a caul wrap is unequaled for its juiciness and sweetness.

Caul can be found at butchers that specialize in fresh pork, or it can be ordered from them. It is inexpensive and freezes perfectly, so that when you find it, it is worth buying a quantity of it. If when you freeze it, you divide it into several parts, it will be easier to use it on successive occasions.

For 6 servings

About 1 pound fresh or thawed caul, in one or several pieces

1½ pounds calf or pork liver, cut into pieces about 1 inch thick, 3 inches long and 2 inches wide

Salt

Black pepper, ground fresh from the mill

Whole bay leaves

Sturdy round toothpicks

Preferably a charcoal or gas-fired lava rock grill

1. If using an indoor broiler, preheat it 15 minutes before cooking. If using charcoal, light it in sufficient time for it to form a coating of white ash before cooking.

2. Soak the caul in lukewarm water for about 5 minutes until it becomes soft and loose. Rinse in several changes of water. Lay the membrane on a dry cloth and carefully spread it open. Cut the best parts into rectangles 5 by 7 inches. Do not waste time with small pieces that need patching.

3. Remove skin or tough, exposed tubes from the liver. Wash it in cold water and pat it thoroughly dry with cloth or paper towels. Sprinkle liberally with salt and pepper. Place a bay leaf on each piece, and wrap one of the caul rectangles around the liver, tucking under the ends. Fasten the wrapper to the liver with a toothpick.

4. Place the liver and caul bundles in the broiler or on the grill. Turn them after 2 to 3 minutes, and cook the other side another 2 minutes, depending on the intensity of heat. When done, the liver should still be pink and moist inside; if you are in doubt, cut into one piece to see. Serve piping hot, letting your guests remove the toothpicks themselves.

Sautéed Chicken Livers
with Sage and White Wine

For 6 servings

1½ pounds chicken livers
2 tablespoons butter
2 tablespoons onion chopped
   very fine
1 dozen fresh sage leaves

⅓ cup dry white wine
Salt
Black pepper, ground fresh
   from the mill

1. Examine the livers carefully for bile-green spots and cut them away. Remove any bits of fat, wash the livers in cold water, then pat thoroughly dry with cloth or paper towels.

2. Put the butter and onion in a skillet, and turn the heat on to medium. Cook and stir the onion until it becomes colored a pale gold. Then turn the heat up to high and add the sage leaves and chicken livers. Cook for 1 or 2 minutes, turning the livers over frequently, until they lose their raw, red color. Transfer them to a warm plate, using a slotted spoon or spatula.

3. Add the wine to the skillet, and let it simmer briskly for 20 or 30 seconds, while using a wooden spoon to scrape loose cooking residues from the bottom and sides of the pan. Add to the pan any liquid the livers may have shed on their plate, and boil it away.

4. Return the livers briefly to the pan, turning them over rapidly once or twice. Add salt and pepper, turn them once again, then transfer them with all the pan juices to a warm platter and serve at once.

Sautéed Sweetbreads
with Tomatoes and Peas

BREAD USED TO BE another way to say morsel, and sweet morsel is an accurate description of this most delectable portion of an animal's anatomy. Sometimes the coarser, stringier pancreas is passed off as sweetbread, but the real thing is the thymus, a gland in the throat and chest of young animals, which disappears as the animal matures. There are two parts to the gland, the "throat" and the "heart." The latter is the larger, more regularly formed, the less fatty of the two, and if there is a choice, it is the preferred one, but "throat" sweetbread is very nearly as good.

In the version given here, poached sweetbreads are sautéed in butter and oil, then cooked with tomatoes and peas. Many vegetables work well with this cream-like meat, but none more happily than peas, whose youth and sweetness are a natural match to the sweetbreads' own.   *For 4 to 6 servings*

1½ pounds calf's sweetbreads
A small carrot, peeled
1 celery stalk
1 tablespoon wine vinegar
Salt
3 tablespoons butter
1 tablespoon vegetable oil
2½ tablespoons chopped onion
⅔ cup canned imported Italian
    plum tomatoes, chopped
    coarse, with their juice

2 pounds unshelled fresh
    young peas OR 1 ten-ounce
    package frozen small, early
    peas, thawed
Black pepper, ground fresh
    from the mill

1. Working under cold running water, peel off as much of the membrane enveloping the sweetbreads as you can. It takes a little patience, but nearly all of it should come off. When done, rinse the peeled sweetbreads in cold water and drain.

2. Pour enough water into a saucepan to cover the sweetbreads amply later. Add the carrot, celery, vinegar, and salt, and bring to a boil. Add the sweetbreads and adjust the heat to cook at the gentlest of simmers. After 5 minutes, retrieve the sweetbreads and, while they are still as warm as you can handle, pull off any remaining bits of membrane. When cool and firmer, cut into small bite-size pieces, about 1 inch thick.

Ahead-of-time note ❀ You can complete the recipe up to this point even a day in advance, stopping short, however, of cutting the sweetbreads into pieces. Refrigerate tightly wrapped in plastic wrap or in an airtight plastic bag. Cut into pieces when cold out of the refrigerator, but let them come to room temperature before proceeding with the next step.

3. Put the butter, oil, and onion in a sauté pan, turn on the heat to medium, cook and stir the onion until it becomes colored a pale gold, then add the sweetbreads. Cook, turning them, until they become colored a light brown all over. Add salt and the chopped tomatoes with their juice, and adjust heat to cook at a very slow simmer.

4. If using fresh peas, shell them and add them to the pan after the tomatoes have simmered for 15 minutes. If using frozen peas, add the thawed peas

after the tomato has simmered for 30 minutes. Add pepper and turn over all ingredients thoroughly. Cover tightly and cook at a slow, but steady simmer, until the peas are tender if using fresh ones, or for 5 minutes, if using the frozen.

5. Transfer the entire contents of the pan to a warm platter and serve at once. If you find that the pan juices are too watery, transfer only the sweetbreads, using a slotted spoon or spatula, reduce the juices rapidly in the uncovered pan over high heat, then pour the contents of the pan over the sweetbreads.

Sautéed Lamb Kidneys with Onion, Treviso Style

THE METHOD that the cooks of Treviso use for this exceptionally simple and mild recipe for kidneys takes a step away from conventional procedure when it briefly heats up the kidneys in a pan all by themselves, before they are to be sautéed with onion. By this device they extract and discard some of the liquid responsible for the sharpness that is sometimes an objectionable component of kidney flavor.   *For 4 servings*

16 lamb kidneys	3 tablespoons parsley chopped
⅓ cup wine vinegar	very fine
1 tablespoon vegetable oil	Salt
3 tablespoons butter	Black pepper, ground fresh
½ cup onion chopped fine	from the mill

1. Split the kidneys in half and wash them in cold water. Put them in a bowl with the vinegar and enough cold water to cover amply. Soak them for at least 30 minutes, then drain.

2. Cut the kidneys into very thin slices that will resemble sliced mushroom caps. When you reach the whitish core, slice around it and discard the core.

3. Put the kidneys in a sauté pan and turn the heat on to medium. Cook them for about 2 minutes, stirring them almost constantly, until they lose their raw color and become grayish and they shed a dark red liquid. Remove the kidneys from the pan, discarding all the liquid. Put them in a wire strainer or colander and rinse them in fast-running cold water. Drain and pat thoroughly dry with paper towels.

Sautéed Lamb Kidneys, Treviso Style (continued)

4. Rinse the sauté pan and wipe it dry. Put in the oil, butter, and onion, and turn the heat on to medium. Cook, stirring the onion until it becomes colored a pale gold. Add the kidneys, stir 2 or 3 times to coat them well, then add the parsley. Cook for 1 or 2 minutes, stirring frequently. Add salt and pepper, stir again, turning over the kidneys completely, then transfer them to a warm platter with all the pan juices and serve at once.

Sautéed Lamb Kidneys with Onion, Garlic, and White Wine

For 6 servings

2 dozen lamb kidneys
⅓ cup wine vinegar
¼ cup extra virgin olive oil
3 tablespoons onion chopped
 very fine
½ teaspoon garlic chopped fine
3 tablespoons parsley chopped
 very fine

Salt
Black pepper, ground fresh
 from the mill
½ teaspoon cornstarch mixed
 into ¾ cup dry white wine

1. Split the kidneys in half and wash them in cold water. Put them in a bowl with the vinegar and enough cold water to cover amply. Soak them for at least 30 minutes, drain, and pat thoroughly dry with paper towels.

2. Cut the kidneys into very thin slices that will resemble sliced mushroom caps. When you reach the whitish core, slice around it and discard the core.

3. Put the oil and onion in a sauté pan, turn on the heat to medium high, and sauté the onion until it becomes colored a pale gold. Add the garlic. Stir rapidly 2 or 3 times, add the parsley, stir once, then add the kidneys. Stir thoroughly to coat the kidneys well, add salt and pepper, and stir again. The kidneys must be cooked swiftly at lively heat or they will become tough. As soon as they lose their raw, red color, transfer them to a warm plate, using a slotted spoon or spatula.

4. Add the wine and cornstarch to the pan and while the wine simmers briskly for 15 or 20 seconds, use a wooden spoon to scrape loose cooking residues from the bottom and sides of the pan. When the pan juices begin to thicken, return the kidneys to the pan, using a slotted spoon or spatula so as

to leave behind any liquid they may have shed. Turn the kidneys over once or twice to coat them well, then transfer them with all the pan juices to a warm platter and serve at once.

Fried Calf's Brains

THIS IS the most popular way of doing brains in Italy. The brains are first poached with vegetables, sliced when cool, and fried with an egg and bread crumb batter. Frying points up their exquisite texture: As one bites, the thin, golden crust gives way, yielding to the delectably tender core.   *For 4 servings*

1 calf's brains, about 1 pound	1 cup fine, dry, unflavored
1 medium carrot, peeled	bread crumbs, lightly
½ onion, peeled	toasted in a skillet or in the
½ stalk celery	oven, spread on a plate
1 tablespoon wine vinegar	Vegetable oil
Salt	Lemon wedges at table
1 egg	

1. Wash the brains thoroughly under cold running water, then let them soak in a bowl of cold water for 10 minutes. Drain, and patiently remove as much of the surrounding membrane as you can along with the external blood vessels.

2. Put the carrot, onion, celery, vinegar, and 1 teaspoon salt in a saucepan with 6 cups water, and bring to a boil. Put in the brains and as soon as the water returns to a boil, adjust heat to cook at a steady, but very gentle simmer, and cover the pan.

3. After 20 minutes, drain the brains, and allow them to cool completely. When cold, wrap them in plastic wrap and refrigerate for about 15 minutes, until they are very firm.

Ahead-of-time note ❀ You can prepare the brains up to this point several hours in advance on the same day you expect to fry them. Also see the alternative to frying in the variation below with poached brains.

4. Put the egg in a deep plate or small bowl, and with a fork or whisk beat it lightly together with 1 teaspoon salt.

5. When the brains are quite firm, cut them into pieces about ½ inch thick. Dip them into the beaten egg, letting the excess flow back into the plate or bowl, then turn them in the bread crumbs, coating them well all over.

Fried Calf's Brains (continued)

6. Put enough vegetable oil in a skillet to come ¼ inch up the sides, and turn on the heat to high. When the oil is very hot, slip the pieces of brains into the pan, putting in no more at one time than will fit loosely, without crowding. Cook until a fine, golden crust forms on one side, then turn and do the other side. Transfer to a cooling rack to drain or to a plate lined with paper towels. Repeat the procedure with the remaining pieces, until all are done. Serve immediately, with wedges of lemon on the side.

Poached Brains with Olive Oil and Lemon Juice Variation

The juices of those two quintessentially Mediterranean fruits, the olive and the lemon, have a beguilingly fragrant effect on poached brains. Poach the brains as described above, drain them, and let them cool partially. Do not refrigerate. When the brains are just slightly warmer than room temperature, cut into thin slices, and drizzle with extra virgin olive oil and freshly squeezed lemon juice. Sprinkle with salt and coarsely ground black pepper, and serve at once.

Oxtail, Vaccinara Style

Vaccinari is the old Roman word for butchers, and the dish they chose to make for themselves was oxtail, in a manner that came to be known as *alla vaccinara*, butcher's style. That they favored oxtail is not surprising, not merely because it was an inexpensive cut, but because it substantiated the adage that the meat with the most flavor is that near the bone.

Note ⊛ An ingredient of the traditional recipe is pork rind, which usually comes from the jowl. It makes an interesting contribution to the consistency as well as to the underlying flavor of the dish, but it is not an absolutely indispensable component, and if you cannot find it, it is preferable to omit it rather than forego making the oxtail. Also see, in this connection, the introductory remarks in the recipe for Beans and Sauerkraut Soup, page 106.

For 4 to 6 servings

OPTIONAL: ¼ pound fresh pork jowl OR pig's feet OR pork hock (see note above)

¼ cup extra virgin olive oil plus 1 tablespoon lard or ham fat OR 1 additional tablespoon olive oil

¼ cup chopped parsley

½ teaspoon chopped garlic

⅔ cup chopped onion

⅔ cup chopped carrot

2½ pounds oxtail (thawed, if frozen), severed at each joint

1½ cups dry white wine

½ cup canned imported Italian plum tomatoes, drained and chopped very coarse

Salt

Black pepper, ground fresh from the mill

1½ cups celery chopped very coarse

1. *If using fresh pork jowl or other fresh pork rind:* Put the pork rind in a soup pot with 1 quart of water and bring to a boil. Boil for 5 minutes, drain, discarding the cooking liquid, and cut the rind into ¾- to 1-inch-wide strips. Do not be alarmed if it is tough. It will soften to a creamy consistency in subsequent cooking.

If using fresh pig's feet or pork hock: Put the pork in a soup pot with enough water to cover by 2 inches, put a lid on the pot, and adjust heat so that the water bubbles at a slow, but steady boil for 1 hour.

Take the pork out of the pot, bone it, and cut it into ½-inch strips.

2. Choose a heavy-bottomed or enameled cast-iron pot that can later contain all the ingredients. Put in the olive oil, the lard or ham fat, if using it, the parsley, garlic, onion, and carrot, and turn on the heat to medium. Cook for 10 minutes, stirring frequently.

3. Turn the heat up to medium high, and add the oxtail and pork. Brown the oxtail, turning the pieces until you have browned them all around. Add the wine, let it simmer briskly for 20 to 30 seconds, then add the cut-up tomatoes, 1 cup water, salt, and pepper. Turn all the ingredients over to coat well. Bring to a steady simmer, cover the pot, putting the lid on slightly ajar, and cook for 1½ hours, turning the oxtail every 30 minutes.

Note ❀ If you prefer to use the oven, you can put the pot into a preheated 350° oven after adding the tomatoes and bringing them to a simmer.

Oxtail (continued)

4. When the meat has cooked for 1½ hours, add the chopped celery, stirring it thoroughly with the other ingredients. (If cooking in the oven, return the pot to the oven.) Cook for 45 minutes more, or until the meat feels very tender when prodded with a fork and comes easily off the bone. Turn the oxtail pieces from time to time while they are cooking.

5. Tip the pot and spoon off as much of the fat as possible, transfer the oxtail with the entire contents of the pot to a warm platter, and serve at once.

Ahead-of-time note ❀ You can complete the dish several hours or even 2 or 3 days in advance. Reheat it gently over the stove in a covered pot until the meat is very warm through and through; cold oxtail is not very appealing. If any meat is left over, it can be used with its juices to sauce pasta.

Honeycomb Tripe with Parmesan Cheese

AT ONE TIME tripe was so popular that restaurants used to specialize in it, preparing it in a score or more of different ways. One of the reasons it has become such a rare item may be that people no longer know how to prepare it. When you know how to go about it, tripe rewards you with tenderness so succulent, and a fragrance so appetizing, that more expensive cuts of meat cannot match.

Fortunately, we no longer need to go through all the preliminary soaking, scrubbing, and blanching that used to take up to twenty-four hours and made cooking tripe such a chore. It is now done by the packer, and the processed tripe you find in meat markets today, whether fresh or frozen, is all ready for the pot.

For 6 servings

2 pounds ready-to-cook honeycomb tripe, thawed if frozen
3 tablespoons butter
⅓ cup vegetable oil
½ cup onion chopped fine
½ cup celery chopped fine
½ cup carrot chopped fine
2 medium garlic cloves, mashed lightly with a knife handle and peeled

1 tablespoon chopped parsley
Chopped rosemary leaves, 1 teaspoon if fresh, ½ teaspoon if dried
1 cup dry white wine
1 cup canned imported Italian plum tomatoes, cut up, with their juice, OR, if very ripe and firm, fresh tomatoes, peeled and cut up

Chopped hot red chili pepper,
    to taste
Black pepper, ground fresh
    from the mill
Salt
1 cup Basic Homemade Meat
    Broth, prepared as directed

on page 15,
OR ½ cup canned beef
broth diluted with ½ cup
water
¾ cup freshly grated
    parmigiano-reggiano cheese

1. Rinse the tripe very thoroughly under cold running water, then drain and cut it into strips ½ inch wide and more or less 3 inches long.

2. Choose an enameled cast iron or other heavy-bottomed pot that can later contain all the ingredients. Put in 1 tablespoon of butter, all the oil, and the chopped onion, and turn on the heat to medium. Cook and stir the onion until it becomes colored a pale gold, then add the chopped celery and carrot, stir to coat them well, and cook for about 1 minute.

3. Add the garlic, parsley, and rosemary, cook for another minute, stirring once or twice, then add the cut-up tripe, turning it thoroughly to coat it well. Cook for about 5 minutes, stirring once or twice, then add the wine. Bring the wine to a brisk simmer for 20 to 30 seconds, then put in the tomatoes with their juice, the chili pepper, black pepper, salt, and broth, give all ingredients a thorough turning over, and bring the liquids in the pot to a slow boil.

4. Cover the pot and cook for about 2½ hours, until the tripe is tender enough to be cut easily with a fork and has an agreeably chewy consistency when tasted. Control heat to maintain a slow, but steady boil. While the tripe is cooking, check the liquid in the pot from time to time; if it should become insufficient, replenish with 2 or 3 tablespoons of water; on the other hand, if it is thin and watery, continue cooking with the lid slightly askew.

5. When the tripe has become very tender, transfer it to a warm bowl. If you should find the juices in the pot to be too watery, turn the heat up to high after removing the tripe, and boil them down to a satisfactory density. Pour the contents of the pot over the tripe, swirl in the remaining butter and all the grated Parmesan, and serve at once.

Ahead-of-time note ✹ It is fortunate, considering the long cooking time, that tripe tastes still better the day after it is cooked. It can even be prepared several days in advance and refrigerated in a tightly sealed container. Reheat over the stove, with the lid on slightly ajar, until the tripe is hot again. Replenish the cooking liquid if it becomes insufficient with 2 or 3 tablespoons of water. When preparing it ahead of time, swirl in the fresh butter and grated Parmesan only after reheating, just before serving.

Tripe with Beans Variation

For 6 servings

To the ingredients in the preceding recipe for tripe, add:

1½ pounds fresh cranberry beans, unshelled weight, OR ¾ cup dried cranberry or white *cannellini* beans, soaked and cooked as described on page 13, with their liquid, OR 2¼ cups drained canned cranberry or white *cannellini* beans

1. *If using fresh beans:* Shell them, wash them in cold water, and put them in a pot with enough water to cover by about 1½ inches. Do not add salt. Bring the beans to a very slow boil, then cover the pot. If the beans are very fresh, they will cook in about 45 minutes; if not, they may take up to 1½ hours. Taste to make sure. When completely tender, turn off the heat, letting them rest in the covered pot in their liquid. You can begin to cook the beans when you begin to cook the tripe.

If using cooked dried beans: Set them aside in their liquid and proceed to the next step.

If using drained canned beans: Proceed to the next step.

2. Follow the directions for making baked tripe as given in the preceding recipe, stopping short of swirling in the butter and grated cheese after the tripe is cooked.

3. When the tripe is fully cooked, but while it is still in the pot, put in the beans. If using cooked fresh or dried beans, add ½ cup of their cooking liquid; if using drained canned beans, add ¼ cup water. Keep the pot over the stove with the lid on slightly ajar, bring to a steady simmer, and cook for 10 minutes, turning all the ingredients over from time to time.

4. Swirl in the remaining 2 tablespoons of butter and the grated Parmesan as in the preceding recipe, transfer to a warm bowl, and serve at once.

Ahead-of-time note ❁ The comments appended to the tripe recipe, page 449, apply here. As in that recipe, swirl in the fresh butter and the grated cheese only after reheating, just before serving.

VEGETABLES

Braised Artichokes and Peas

For 4 to 6 servings

2 large globe artichokes
   OR 3 to 4 medium size
½ lemon
2 tablespoons chopped onion
3 tablespoons extra virgin
   olive oil
½ teaspoon garlic chopped
   very fine

2 pounds fresh unshelled peas
   OR 1 ten-ounce package
   frozen peas, thawed
1 tablespoon chopped parsley
Salt
Black pepper, ground fresh
   from the mill

1. Trim the artichokes of all their tough parts following the detailed instructions on pages 57–59. As you work, rub the cut artichoke with the lemon to keep it from turning black.

2. Cut each trimmed artichoke lengthwise into 4 equal sections. Remove the soft, curling leaves with prickly tips at the base, and cut away the fuzzy "choke" beneath them.

Detach the stems, but do not discard them, because they can be as good to eat as the heart if they are properly trimmed. Pare away their dark green rind to expose the pale and tender core, then split them in half lengthwise, or if very thick, into 4 parts.

Cut the artichoke sections lengthwise into wedges about 1 inch thick at their broadest point, and squeeze lemon juice over all the cut parts to protect them against discoloration.

3. Choose a heavy-bottomed or enameled cast-iron pot just large enough to accommodate all the ingredients, put in the chopped onion and olive oil, turn on the heat to medium high, cook and stir the onion until it becomes colored a very pale gold, then add the garlic. Cook the garlic until it becomes colored a light gold, then put in the artichoke wedges, ⅓ cup water, adjust heat to cook at a steady simmer, and cover the pot tightly.

Braised Artichokes and Peas (continued)

4. *If using fresh peas:* Shell them, and prepare some of the pods for cooking by stripping away their inner membrane as described on page 93. It's not necessary to use all or even most of the pods, but do as many as you have patience for. (The pods make a notable contribution to the sweetness of the peas and of the whole dish, but using them is an optional procedure that you can omit, if you prefer.)

5. When the artichokes have cooked for about 10 minutes, add the shelled peas and the optional pods, the chopped parsley, salt, pepper, and, if the liquid in the pot has become insufficient, ¼ cup water. Turn the peas over thoroughly to coat them well. Cover tightly again, and continue cooking until the artichokes feel very tender at their thickest point when prodded with a fork. Taste and correct for salt. Also taste the peas to make sure they are fully cooked. While the artichokes and peas are cooking, add 2 or 3 tablespoons of water if you find that there is not enough liquid.

If using frozen peas: Add the thawed peas as the last step, when the artichokes are already tender or nearly so, turning them thoroughly, and letting them cook with the artichokes for 5 minutes.

6. When both vegetables are fully cooked, should you find that the juices in the pot are watery, uncover, raise the heat to high, and quickly boil them away.

Ahead-of-time note ❀ The dish can be prepared any time in advance on the same day it will be served. Do not refrigerate or its flavor will be altered. Reheat gently in a covered pot, with 1 tablespoon water, if necessary.

Braised Artichokes and Leeks

For 6 servings

3 large globe artichokes
    OR 5 or 6 medium size
½ lemon
4 large leeks, about 1¾ inch
    thick, OR 6 smaller ones
	¼ cup extra virgin olive oil
	Salt
	Black pepper, ground fresh
	    from the mill

1. Cut the trimmed artichokes into 1-inch wedges and pare and split the stems as described on page 451. As you work, rub the cut artichokes with the lemon to keep them from turning black.

2. Trim away the roots of the leeks, any of their leaves that are blemished, and about 1 inch off their green tops. Slice the leeks in half lengthwise, then cut them into pieces about 2 or 3 inches long.

3. Choose a heavy-bottomed or enameled cast-iron pot just large enough to accommodate all the ingredients, put in the leeks, the olive oil, and sufficient water to come 1 inch up the sides of the pan. Turn on the heat to medium, cover tightly, and cook at a steady simmer until the leeks are tender.

4. Add the artichoke wedges, salt, pepper, and, if necessary, 2 or 3 tablespoons water. Cover again and cook until the artichokes feel very tender at their thickest point when prodded with a fork, about 30 minutes or more, very much depending on the artichokes. While the artichokes are cooking, add 2 or 3 tablespoons of water if you find that there is not enough liquid. When they are done, taste and correct for salt. If you should find, once the artichokes are cooked, that the juices in the pot are watery, uncover, raise the heat to high, and quickly boil them away.

Ahead-of-time note ❀ The note at the end of Braised Artichokes and Peas on page 452 is applicable here.

Braised Artichokes and Potatoes

For 4 to 6 servings

2 large globe artichokes	Salt
½ lemon	Black pepper, ground fresh
1 pound potatoes	from the mill
⅓ cup onion chopped coarse	1 tablespoon chopped parsley
¼ cup extra virgin olive oil	
¼ teaspoon garlic chopped	
very fine	

1. Cut the trimmed artichokes into 1-inch wedges, and trim and split the stems as described on page 451. As you work, rub the cut artichokes with the lemon to keep them from turning black.

2. Peel the potatoes, wash them in cold water, and cut them into small wedges about ¾ inch thick at their broadest point.

3. Choose a heavy-bottomed or enameled cast-iron pot just large enough to accommodate all the ingredients, put in the chopped onion and olive oil, and turn on the heat to medium high. Cook and stir the onion until it

Braised Artichokes and Potatoes (continued)

becomes translucent, but not colored, then add the garlic. Cook the garlic until it becomes colored a light gold, then put in the potatoes, the artichoke wedges and stems, salt, pepper, and parsley, and cook long enough to turn over all the ingredients 2 or 3 times.

4. Add ¼ cup water, adjust heat to cook at a steady, but gentle simmer, and cover tightly. Cook until both the potatoes and artichokes feel tender when prodded with a fork, approximately 40 minutes, depending mostly on the potatoes. While cooking, add 2 or 3 tablespoons of water if you find that there is not enough liquid in the pot. Taste and correct for salt before serving.

Ahead-of-time note ❧ The note at the end of Braised Artichokes and Peas on page 452 is applicable here.

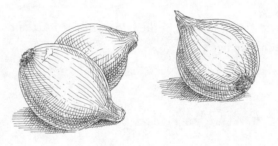

La Frittedda—Smothered Artichokes, Fava Beans, and Peas with Fennel, Palermo Style

FOR JUST SIX WEEKS in spring, between April and May, Sicilian cooks find vegetables young enough to make *frittedda*. Youth and freshness are the ideal components of this heavenly dish, the freshness of just-picked young artichokes, fava beans, and peas. I have seen *frittedda* made in Palermo when the vegetables were so tender they were cooked in hardly more time than it took to stir them in the pot.

If you grow your own, or if you have access to a good farmers' market, you can come very close to duplicating the gentle Sicilian flavor of this dish. But even if you must rely on produce from the average greengrocer, either limit yourself to the time of the year when the vegetables required here are at their youngest, or adopt the compromises suggested below, and enough of *frittedda*'s magic will come through to make it worth your while.

The aroma of fresh wild fennel is an important part of this preparation, as it is of many other Sicilian dishes. If the herb is not available to you, use fresh dill or ask your greengrocer to keep for you the leafy tops he usually cuts off the *finocchio*. *For 6 servings*

3 medium OR 5 small
  artichokes, very fresh, with
  no black spots or other
  discoloration
½ lemon
2 pounds fresh, small fava beans
  in their pods OR ⅔ of a
  15-ounce can "green *fave*,"
  drained
1 pound fresh small peas in
  their pods OR ½ of a

10-ounce package choice
  quality, frozen small peas,
  thawed
1 cup fresh wild fennel OR
  1½ cups leafy *finocchio* tops
  OR ⅔ cup fresh dill
1½ cups sweet raw onion sliced
  very thin (see note below)
⅓ cup extra virgin olive oil
Salt

Note ❀ Use the sweetest variety of onion available: Vidalia, Maui, or Bermuda. If you can obtain none of these, soak sliced yellow onion in several changes of cold water for 30 minutes, gently squeezing the onion in your hand each time you change the water; drain before using.

1. Cut the trimmed artichokes into ½-inch wedges, and trim, but do not split their stems, as described on page 451. As you work, rub the cut artichokes with the lemon to keep them from turning black.

2. If using fresh fava beans, shell them and discard the pods.

3. If using fresh peas, shell them, and prepare some of the pods for cooking by stripping away their inner membrane as described on page 93. It's not necessary to use all or even most of the pods, but the more you do, the sweeter the *frittedda* will taste.

4. Wash the wild fennel, *finocchio* tops, or dill in cold water, then chop into large pieces.

5. Choose a heavy-bottomed or enameled cast-iron pot just large enough to accommodate all the ingredients, put in the sliced onion and olive oil, turn on the heat to medium low, and cook until the onion becomes soft and translucent.

6. Put in the wild fennel, *finocchio* tops, or dill, the artichoke wedges and stems, stir thoroughly to coat well, and cover the pot tightly. After 5 minutes,

Artichokes, Fava Beans, and Peas with Fennel (continued)

check the artichokes. If they are at their prime, they should look moist and glossy, and the oil and the vapors from the onion and fennel should be sufficient to continue their cooking. But if they appear to be rather dry, add 3 tablespoons of water. If you are in doubt, add it anyway, it won't do too much damage. When not checking the pot, keep it covered tightly.

7. *If using fresh fava beans and peas:* Add them when the artichokes are about half done, approximately 15 minutes if very young and fresh. Add 2 or 3 tablespoons water if you doubt that there is sufficient moisture in the pot to cook them. Turn all ingredients over to coat them well.

If using fresh fava beans and frozen peas: Put the beans in first, cook for 10 minutes if very small, 15 to 20 if larger, then add the thawed peas and cook for 5 minutes longer, until both the artichokes and fava are tender.

If using fresh peas and canned fava beans: When the artichokes are half done, put in the peas and their trimmed pods. Cook until both peas and artichokes are tender, adding 2 or 3 tablespoons water when needed, then put in the drained canned "green *fave*" and cook 5 minutes longer.

If using frozen peas and canned fava beans: Put in both the thawed peas and the drained beans at the same time, when the artichokes have just begun to feel tender when prodded with a fork. Cook for 5 minutes longer.

8. Taste and correct for salt before serving. Let the *frittedda* settle for a few minutes, allowing its flavors to emerge from the heat, before bringing it to the table, but do not serve it cold. If possible, plan to serve it when done, without reheating.

Crisp-Fried Artichoke Wedges

HERE IS one instance where one needn't be too unbending about using frozen vegetables. Frozen artichoke hearts fry very well, and the contrast between their soft interior and the crisp egg and bread crumb crust is quite appealing. Not that one should pass up fresh artichokes, if they happen to be very young and tender.   *For 4 to 6 servings*

3 medium artichokes OR 1 ten-ounce package frozen artichoke hearts, thawed	1 egg
	1 cup fine, dry, unflavored bread crumbs, spread on a plate
If using fresh artichokes:	
½ lemon and 1 tablespoon freshly squeezed lemon juice	Vegetable oil
	Salt

1. *If using fresh artichokes:* Cut the trimmed artichokes into 1-inch wedges, and trim and split their stems as described on page 451. As you work, rub the cut artichokes with the lemon to keep them from turning black.

Bring 3 quarts of water to a boil. Put in 1 tablespoon of lemon juice together with the artichokes, and cook for 5 minutes or more after the water returns to a boil, until the artichokes are tender, but still firm enough to offer some resistance when prodded at their thickest point with a fork. Drain, let cool, and pat dry.

If using frozen artichokes: When thawed, if whole, cut in half, and pat thoroughly dry with paper towels.

2. Lightly beat the egg in a small bowl or deep saucer.

3. Dip the artichokes into the egg, letting the excess flow back into the bowl, then roll them in the bread crumbs to coat them all over.

Ahead-of-time note ✿ The recipe can be completed up to this point several hours in advance, but if refrigerating the crumbed vegetables, take them out in sufficient time to come fully to room temperature.

4. Put enough oil in a skillet to come ¾ inch up the sides, and turn the heat on to medium high. When the oil is hot enough to form a slight haze, slip the breaded artichokes into the skillet, cooking them long enough to form a crust on one side, then turning them and doing the other side. If they don't all fit at one time into the pan loosely, without crowding, fry them in two or more batches. As each batch is done, transfer it with a slotted spoon or spatula to a cooling rack to drain or to a plate lined with paper towels. When they are all done, sprinkle with salt and serve at once.

Gratin of Artichokes

For 4 servings

4 large OR 6 medium artichokes	Butter for smearing the dish
½ lemon	and dotting
1 tablespoon freshly squeezed	Salt
lemon juice	½ cup freshly grated
An oven-to-table baking dish	*parmigiano-reggiano* cheese

1. Cut the trimmed artichokes into 1-inch wedges, and trim and split their stems as described on page 451. As you work, rub the cut artichokes with the lemon to keep them from turning black.

2. Preheat oven to 375°.

3. Bring 3 quarts of water to a boil. Put in 1 tablespoon of lemon juice

Gratin of Artichokes (continued)

together with the artichokes, and cook for 5 minutes or more after the water returns to a boil, until the artichokes are tender, but still firm enough to offer some resistance when prodded at their thickest point with a fork. Drain and let cool.

4. Cut the artichoke wedges into very thin lengthwise slices.

5. Smear the bottom of the baking dish with butter, and cover it with a layer of artichoke slices and stems. Sprinkle with salt and grated Parmesan, and dot with butter. Repeat the procedure, building up layers of artichokes until all are used. Sprinkle the top layer generously with grated cheese and dot with butter.

6. Bake in the upper third of the preheated oven for 15 or 20 minutes, until a light crust forms on top. Allow to settle for a few minutes before serving.

Gratin of Artichokes, Potatoes, and Onions

IN THIS GRATIN, the artichokes are fully cooked before going into the oven with raw sliced potatoes and sautéed onions. While the potatoes cook, the thin artichoke slices become very soft, surrendering some of their texture in order to spread their flavor more liberally.   *For 6 servings*

2 large globe artichokes
   OR 4 medium size
	3 medium potatoes, peeled and
	   sliced potato-chip thin

1 lemon, cut in half	An oven-to-table baking dish

2 tablespoons butter plus more
   for dotting the baking dish
	Black pepper, ground fresh
	   from the mill

1 cup onion sliced thin	½ cup freshly grated
Salt	*parmigiano-reggiano* cheese

1. Cut the trimmed artichokes into 1-inch wedges, and trim and split their stems as described on page 451. Use half the lemon to moisten the cut parts with juice as you work. Put the artichoke wedges and stems into a bowl with enough cold water to cover and squeeze the juice of the other lemon half into the bowl. Stir and let stand until needed later.

2. Choose a sauté pan large enough to accommodate all the ingredients, put in the 2 tablespoons of butter and the onion, and turn on the heat to medium. Cook the onion at a slow pace, stirring occasionally, until it is very soft and becomes colored a deep gold. Take off heat.

3. Drain the artichoke wedges and stems, and rinse them in cold water to

wash away traces of their acidulated soak. Cut the wedges into the thinnest possible slices. Put the slices and the stems into the pan with the onion, sprinkle with salt, add ½ cup water, turn on the heat to medium, and cover the pot with the lid on slightly ajar. Cook at a slow, intermittent simmer, turning the artichokes from time to time, until they feel tender when prodded with a fork, about 15 minutes or more, depending on their youth and freshness.

4. While the artichokes are cooking, preheat oven to 400°.

5. When the artichokes are done, put the sliced potatoes in the pan, turn them over 2 or 3 times to coat them well, then remove from heat.

6. Pour the contents of the pan into a baking dish, preferably choosing one in which the ingredients, when they are all in, will not come more than 1½ inches up the sides. Add several grindings of pepper and a little more salt, and use the back of a spoon or a spatula to spread the artichoke and potato mixture evenly. Dot the top with butter, and place the dish in the upper rack of the preheated oven.

7. After 15 minutes, take the dish out of the oven, turn its contents 2 or 3 times, spread them out evenly again, and return to the oven. When the potatoes become tender, in another 15 minutes or so, take the pan out, sprinkle the top with grated Parmesan, and keep it in the oven until the cheese melts and forms a light crust. Allow the heat to subside for a few minutes before serving.

Artichoke Torta in a Flaky Crust

THE PASTRY SHELL for this vegetable pie is unusual because instead of the eggs that customarily go into making Italian flaky pastry it uses *ricotta*. It is very light, and the word that best describes its texture is, indeed, flaky.

The flavorful filling consists mainly of artichokes, which are sliced very thin and braised on a bed of carrot and onion. It is rounded out with eggs, *ricotta,* and Parmesan. *For 6 servings*

FOR THE FILLING

4 medium artichokes	Salt
1 lemon, cut in half	Black pepper, ground fresh
3 tablespoons extra virgin	from the mill
olive oil	¾ cup fresh *ricotta*
2 tablespoons chopped onion	½ cup freshly grated
3 tablespoons chopped carrot	*parmigiano-reggiano* cheese
1 tablespoon chopped parsley	2 eggs

Artichoke Torta (continued)

1. Trim the artichokes of all their tough parts, following the detailed instructions on pages 57–59. As you work, rub the cut artichoke with a lemon half, squeezing drops of juice over it to keep it from turning black. Cut the trimmed artichokes in half to expose and discard the choke and prickly inner leaves, then cut them lengthwise into the thinnest possible slices. Put in a bowl with enough water to cover and the juice of the other lemon half.

2. Pare the artichoke stems of their hard outer skin as described on page 451, and cut them lengthwise into very thin slices. Add them to the bowl with the sliced artichokes.

3. Put the oil, onion, and carrot in a sauté pan, and turn the heat on to medium. Cook and stir the onion until it becomes colored a pale gold. Then add the parsley, stirring it rapidly 2 or 3 times.

4. Drain the artichokes, rinse them well under cold water to wash away the lemon, pat them dry in a towel, then add them to the pan. Turn them over 2 or 3 times to coat them well, add salt and pepper, turn them over again another 2 or 3 times, then add ½ cup water, and put a lid on the pan. Cook until tender, from 5 to 15 minutes, depending on the youth and freshness of the artichokes. If in the meantime the liquid in the pan becomes insufficient, add 2 or 3 tablespoons water as needed. When the artichokes are done, however, there should be no water in the pan. If there is, remove the lid, raise the heat to high, and quickly boil it away. Pour the entire contents of the pan into a bowl and allow to cool completely.

5. When cool, mix in the *ricotta* and grated Parmesan.

6. Beat the eggs lightly in a deep dish, then swirl them into the bowl. Taste and correct the filling for salt and pepper.

MAKING THE PASTRY CRUST AND COMPLETING THE TORTA

1½ cups flour	½ teaspoon salt
8 tablespoons (1 stick) butter, softened to room temperature	Wax paper OR kitchen parchment
¾ cup fresh *ricotta*	An 8-inch springform pan
	Butter and flour for the pan

1. Preheat oven to 375°.

2. Mix the flour, butter, *ricotta,* and salt in a bowl, using your fingers or a fork.

3. Turn the mixture out onto a work surface and knead for 5 to 6 minutes until the dough is smooth. Divide the dough into 2 unequal parts, one twice as large as the other.

4. Roll out the larger piece of dough into a circular sheet no thicker

than ⅓ inch. To simplify transferring this to the pan, roll out the dough on lightly floured wax paper or kitchen parchment.

5. Smear the inside of the springform pan with butter, then dust it with flour and turn it over giving it a sharp rap against the counter to shake off loose flour.

6. Pick up the wax paper or kitchen parchment with the sheet of dough on it, and turn it over onto the pan, covering the bottom and letting it come up the sides. Peel away the wax paper or parchment, and smooth the dough, flattening and evening off any particularly bulky creases with your fingers.

7. Pour the artichoke filling into the pan and level it off with a spatula.

8. Roll out the remaining piece of dough, employing the same method you used earlier. Lay it over the filling, covering it completely. Press the edge of the top sheet of pastry dough against the edge of that lining the pan. Make a tight seal all around, folding any excess dough toward the center.

9. Place on the uppermost rack of the preheated oven and bake until the top is lightly browned, about 45 minutes. When you take it out of the oven, unlatch the pan's spring, and remove the hoop. Allow the *torta* to settle a few minutes before loosening it from the bottom and transferring to a serving platter. Serve either lukewarm or at room temperature.

JERUSALEM ARTICHOKES OR SUNCHOKES

Obscurity is often the fate of products that start out in life under a confusing name. This fine, but unjustly neglected, vegetable is not from Jerusalem, it is a native of North America; it is not an artichoke, it is the edible root of a variety of sunflower. Sunflower, in Italian, is *girasole,* which to non-Italian ears evidently sounded like Jerusalem. Even more strangely, its Italian name is not remotely related to *girasole* or sunflower. It is *topinambur,* the name of a Brazilian troupe that toured the country at apparently the same time the root was introduced. It may finally become better known to English speakers as "sunchoke," the name its producers have decided to coin for it, and which will be the one used henceforth here.

How to use ❀ When sliced very thin, raw sunchokes are crisp and juicy at the same time, with a nutty flavor that is most welcome in a salad. When sautéed or gratinéed, their texture is a blend of cream and silk, and their taste vaguely recalls that of artichoke hearts, but is sweeter, with none of the artichoke's underlying bitterness. The thin skin can be left on when they are to be eaten raw, but must be removed for cooking because it hardens.

How to buy ❦ Sunchokes are in season from fall through early spring. They are at their best when very firm; as they lose freshness, they become spongy.

Sautéed Sunchokes

For 6 servings

1½ pounds sunchokes	Black pepper, ground fresh
Salt	from the mill
¼ cup extra virgin olive oil	1 tablespoon parsley chopped
1 teaspoon garlic chopped	very fine
very fine	

1. Skin the sunchokes, using a small paring knife or a swiveling-blade peeler. Bring 3 quarts of water to a boil, add salt, then drop in the peeled sunchokes, the larger pieces first, holding back the smaller ones a few moments. When the water returns to a boil, take the sunchokes out. As soon as they are cool enough to handle, cut them into slices ¼ inch thick or less. They should still be quite firm.

2. Put the olive oil and garlic in a skillet, and turn on the heat to medium. Cook, stirring the garlic, until it becomes colored a very pale gold, then add the sliced sunchokes, turning them thoroughly to coat them well. Add salt, pepper, and chopped parsley, and turn them over completely once again. Cook until the sunchokes feel very tender when prodded with a fork, turning them from time to time while they are cooking. Taste and correct for salt and serve at once.

Sunchoke Gratin

For 4 servings

1 pound sunchokes	Black pepper, ground fresh
Salt	from the mill
An oven-to-table baking dish	¼ cup freshly grated
Butter for smearing and dotting	*parmigiano-reggiano* cheese
the baking dish	

1. Preheat oven to 400°.

2. Peel the sunchokes and drop them in salted, boiling water as described on page 462. Cook them until they feel tender, but not mushy when prodded with a fork. Ten minutes after the water returns to a boil, check them frequently because they tend to go from very firm to very soft in a brief span of time. Drain when done, and as soon as they are cool enough to handle, cut them into ½-inch thick slices.

3. Smear the bottom of a baking dish with butter, then place the sunchoke slices in it, arranging them so they overlap slightly, roof tile fashion. Sprinkle with salt, pepper, and the grated Parmesan, dot with butter, and place the dish on the uppermost rack of the preheated oven. Bake until a light golden crust begins to form on top. Allow to settle for a few minutes out of the oven before serving.

Smothered Sunchokes with Tomato and Onion

For 6 servings

1½ pounds sunchokes
¼ cup extra virgin olive oil
1 cup onion sliced very fine
½ teaspoon chopped garlic
2 tablespoons chopped parsley
⅔ cup canned imported Italian
    plum tomatoes, chopped,
    with their juice

Salt
Black pepper, ground fresh
    from the mill

1. Skin the sunchokes with a paring knife or a swiveling-blade peeler, wash them in cold water, and cut them into pieces about 1 inch thick.

2. Put the oil and onion in a sauté pan, and turn on the heat to medium high. Cook and stir the onion until it becomes colored a deep gold, then put

in the garlic. Stir rapidly, add the parsley, stir quickly 2 or 3 times, then put in the tomatoes with their juice. Stir to coat well, and adjust heat to cook at a steady simmer.

3. When the tomatoes have simmered for 5 minutes, add the cut-up sunchokes, salt, and pepper, turn the sunchokes over completely once or twice to coat them well, and adjust heat to cook at a very slow, intermittent simmer. Cook for about 30 to 45 minutes, stirring occasionally, until the sunchokes feel very tender when prodded with a fork.

Ahead-of-time note ❦ The dish may be cooked through to the end several hours or even a day in advance. Do not reheat more than once.

Braised Sunchokes and Scallions

For 6 servings

1 pound sunchokes	Salt
8 bunches scallions	Black pepper, ground fresh
3 tablespoons butter	from the mill

1. Skin the sunchokes with a paring knife or a swiveling-blade peeler, wash them in cold water, and pat thoroughly dry with paper towels. Cut them into very thin slices, preferably no more than ¼ inch thick.

2. Trim away the scallions' roots and any blemished leaves, but do not remove the green tops. Wash in cold water, pat dry, and make 2 short pieces out of each scallion, cutting it across in half. If some have thick bulbs, split them lengthwise in half.

3. Put the butter in a sauté pan and turn on the heat to medium high. When the butter has melted and is foaming, put in the scallions, turn them to coat them well, lower the heat to medium, and add ½ cup water. Cook until all the water evaporates, turning the scallions from time to time.

4. Add the sunchoke slices, salt, and pepper, and turn them over thoroughly to coat them well. Add another ½ cup water, and cook at a steady, but gentle simmer until the water evaporates completely, turning the scallions and sunchokes from time to time. Check the sunchokes with a fork while they cook. If very fresh, they may become tender before all the water evaporates. Should this happen, turn the heat up to high and boil away the liquid quickly. If, on the other hand, the water has evaporated and they are not yet fully tender, add 2 or 3 tablespoons of water and continue cooking. In most

cases, the sunchokes will be done within 20 or 25 minutes. Taste and correct for salt and serve at once.

Fried Sunchoke Chips

For 4 servings

1 pound sunchokes   Salt
Vegetable oil

1. Skin the sunchokes with a paring knife or a swiveling-blade peeler, and cut them into the thinnest possible slices. Wash them in several changes of cold water to rinse away traces of soil and some of the starch. Pat thoroughly dry with paper towels.

2. Pour enough oil in a skillet to come a little more than ¼ inch up the sides, and turn the heat on to high. When the oil is hot, slip in as many of the sunchoke slices as will fit loosely, without crowding the pan. When they become colored a nice russet brown on one side, turn them and do the other side. Transfer them with a slotted spoon or spatula to a wire cooling rack to drain or to a platter lined with paper towels. Put in the next batch and repeat the procedure until all the sunchokes are done. Sprinkle with salt and serve at once.

ASPARAGUS

How to buy ❀ The first thing to look at is the tip of the spear or the bud. It should be tightly closed and erect, not open and droopy. The hue of green asparagus should be fresh, bright, and with no hint of yellow. White asparagus should be a clear, even, creamy color. The stalk should feel firm and the overall look should be dewy. Although asparagus, like nearly everything else, is now marketed through most of the year, it is freshest in the spring, from April to early June. A thick spear of asparagus is not necessarily better than a

skinny one, but it is usually more expensive. If you will be cutting up asparagus for a pasta sauce, or a *risotto,* or a *frittata,* you certainly don't need to
pay a premium for size. If you are serving the asparagus whole, however, a
meatier stalk may sometimes be more satisfying.

How to keep ❀ Ideally, asparagus should go from the market into the pot,
but hours or even a day may elapse during which you'll want to keep it as fresh
as possible. Bunch the asparagus if loose, and stand it with its butts in a container with 1 or 2 inches of cold water. You can store it thus in a cool place,
unrefrigerated, for up to a day or a day and a half.

How to prepare for cooking ❀ All but a small woody portion at the bottom
of the stalk can be made edible, if the asparagus is properly prepared. Begin
by slicing off about 1 inch at the thick butt end. If you find that the end of
the stalk you exposed is parched and stringy, slice off a little more until you
reach a moister part. The younger the asparagus is, the less you will need to
trim from the bottom.

Even though the center of the stalk is juicy and tender, the darker green
fibers that surround it are not, and must be pared away. Hold the asparagus
with the tip pointing toward you, and using a small, sharp knife, strip away
the hard, thin, outer layer of the stalk, beginning at the base, at a depth of
about ¹⁄₁₆ th of an inch, and gradually tapering to nothing as you bring the
blade up toward the narrower section of the stalk at the base of the bud. Give
the stalk a slight turn and repeat the procedure until you have trimmed it all
around. Then remove any small leaves sprouting below the spear's tip.

Soak the spears for 10 minutes in a basin full of cold water, then wash in
2 or 3 changes of water.

How to cook ❀ Choose any pan that can later contain the trimmed spears
lying flat. Fill with water and bring it to a boil. Add 1 tablespoon salt for every
pound of asparagus, and as the water starts boiling rapidly again, put in the
asparagus. Cover the pan to hasten the water's return to a boil. When it does
so, you can uncover the pan. After 10 minutes, you can begin testing the asparagus by prodding the thickest part of the stalk with a fork. It is done when
easily pierced. (If very thin and exceptionally fresh, it may take a minute or
two less.) Drain immediately when cooked.

Gratinéed Asparagus with Parmesan

For 4 servings

2 pounds fresh asparagus
Salt
An oven-to-table baking dish
Butter for smearing and dotting
    the dish

⅔ cup freshly grated
    parmigiano-reggiano cheese

1. Preheat oven to 450°.
2. Trim and boil the asparagus as described on page 466.
3. Smear the bottom of a rectangular or oval baking dish with butter. Place the drained, boiled asparagus in the dish, laying them down side by side in partly overlapping rows, with all the buds pointing in the same direction. The tips of the spears in the top row should overlap the butt ends of the stalks in the row below. Sprinkle each row with salt and grated cheese, and dot with butter, before laying another row on top of it.
4. Bake in the uppermost rack of the preheated oven until a light, golden crust forms on top. Check after 15 minutes' baking. After taking it out of the oven, allow to settle for a few minutes before serving.

Variation with Fried Eggs

For 4 servings

To the ingredients in the preceding recipe, add:

2 tablespoons butter
4 eggs
Salt

Black pepper, ground fresh
    from the mill

1. Prepare Gratinéed Asparagus with Parmesan as directed in the recipe above.
2. Take the baking dish out of the oven, and divide the asparagus into 4 portions, putting each on a warm dinner plate.
3. Put the butter in a skillet, turn on the heat to medium high, and as the butter foam begins to subside, break the eggs into the pan and sprinkle with salt. Do not put any more eggs in at one time than will fit without overlapping. If the pan cannot accommodate all of them at once, fry them in two or more batches.
4. Slide a fried egg over each portion of asparagus, then spoon juices from the baking pan over each egg. Sprinkle with pepper and serve at once.

Asparagus and Prosciutto Bundles

For 6 servings

18 choice thick spears fresh
    asparagus
½ pound Italian *fontina* cheese,
    cut into thin slices (see note
    below)

6 large thin slices of prosciutto
2 tablespoons butter plus more
    for smearing and dotting a
    baking dish
An oven-to-table baking dish

Note ✹ If you cannot find true imported Italian *fontina,* rather than substituting bland imitation *fontina* from other sources, use *parmigiano-reggiano* cheese shaved into thin, long slivers. If you do so, substitute boiled unsmoked ham for the prosciutto because both Parmesan and prosciutto are salty and the two combined might make the asparagus bundles too salty.

1. Trim and boil the asparagus as described on page 466, cooking it more on the firm than on the soft side.

2. Preheat oven to 400°.

3. Set aside 12 slices of *fontina* (or 12 long slivers of Parmesan), and divide the rest of the cheese into 6 more or less equal mounds.

4. Spread open a slice of prosciutto (or boiled ham) and on it place 3 asparagus. In between the spears fit all the cheese from one of the 6 equal mounds. Add 1 teaspoon butter, then wrap the prosciutto tightly around the asparagus spears. Proceed thus until you have made 6 prosciutto- or ham-wrapped clusters of asparagus and cheese.

5. Choose a baking dish that will contain all the bundles without over-lapping. Lightly smear the bottom of the dish with butter and put in the asparagus bundles. Over each place 2 crisscrossed slices of *fontina* or slivers of Parmesan taken from the cheese you had earlier set aside. Dot every one of the sheaves lightly with butter and place the dish on the uppermost rack of the preheated oven. Bake for about 20 minutes, long enough for the cheese to melt and form a lightly mottled crust.

6. After taking it out of the oven, allow to settle for a few minutes before serving. When serving each bundle, baste it with some of the juices in the baking dish, and provide good, crusty bread for sopping them up.

FAVA BEANS

Until the discoverers of America came back home with beans, as well as with gold and silver, the only bean known to Europe up to then was the fava, or broad bean. Curiously, although it has been grown and consumed for close to 5,000 years, its popularity in Italy has never traveled above the south and center. Tuscans grow them by the acre and eat them by the bushel, even without cooking them, dipping them raw in coarse salt and chasing them down with *pecorino,* ewe's milk cheese. But in northern Italy, most people have never had them, and would have no idea what to do with them.

When and how to buy ❀ Their season lasts from April to June, but the best beans are the earliest and youngest. When shelled, they should be the size of lima beans or only slightly larger. Bigger fava are tougher, drier, and more starchy. Look for pods that do not bulge too thickly with overgrown beans.

How to cook ❀ When cooking fresh fava beans, the best advice is, do as the Romans do. The classic Roman preparation, which in the spring you can sample in every *trattoria* in the city, has few peers among great bean dishes. I have never gone through a single spring without cooking it at least half a dozen times, and no food I can put on the table is ever more warmly received. In Rome, the dish is known as *fave al guanciale,* because the beans are cooked with pork jowl, *guanciale.* In the version given here, *pancetta*—which is far easier to find—replaces pork jowl with total success.

Fava Beans, Roman Style

For 4 servings

Pancetta in a single slice ½ inch thick

3 pounds unshelled young fresh fava beans

2 tablespoons extra virgin olive oil

2 tablespoons onion chopped fine

Black pepper, ground fresh from the mill

Salt

1. Unroll the *pancetta* and cut it into strips ¼ inch wide.
2. Shell the beans, discarding the pods. Wash the fava in cold water.
3. Put the oil and onion in a sauté pan, and turn on the heat to medium. Cook and stir the onion until it becomes translucent, then add the *pancetta* strips. Cook for about 2 to 3 minutes, then add the beans and pepper, and stir to coat them well. Add ⅓ cup of water, adjust heat to cook at the slowest of simmers, and put a lid on the pan. If the beans are very young and fresh, they will cook in about 8 minutes, but if they are not in their prime, they may take 15 minutes or even longer. Test them with a fork from time to time. If the liquid becomes insufficient for cooking, replenish it with 3 or 4 tablespoons water. When tender, add salt, stir thoroughly, and cook another minute or two. If there should be any water left in the pan, uncover, raise the heat to high, and boil it away quickly. Serve at once, accompanied by thick slices of crusty bread.

GREEN BEANS

Spring and summer are generous with their gifts of vegetables, but none is more precious, or more characteristic of the Italian table, than young green beans at their freshest. When on a June day in Italy, you have let yourself fall in with the rhythm of an Italian meal and have had pasta, followed perhaps by *scaloppine* or chicken or fish, and then to the table comes a dish of still lukewarm boiled green beans, glistening with olive oil and lemon juice, you may well think, after a bite of those beans, that nothing could taste better.

There is no magic in making a dish of plain boiled beans look and taste wonderful. The quality of the olive oil is tremendously important, of course.

But it really starts with the beans, how they are chosen and how they are cooked.

How to buy ❀ Although they are now available throughout the year, the ones grown locally in spring and summer are still the best. Their color should be a uniform green, either light or dark, but even, without spots or yellowing patches. Their skin should be fresh looking, almost moist, not dull. And the beans should not be a mixed lot, but all of one size, preferably not too thick. If you can, take a bean from the basket and snap it: It should snap sharply and crisply.

How to cook ❀ Beans must be cooked long enough to develop a round, nutty, sweet flavor: They should not be overcooked, but not undercooked either. When undercooked, theirs is not the taste of beans, but the raw taste of grass. When boiling beans, you must add salt to the boiling water before dropping in the beans in order to keep their color a bright green. This principle applies to all green vegetables, particularly spinach and Swiss chard. The vegetable does not become salty because virtually all the salt remains dissolved in the water.

Boiling 1 pound of green beans

❀ Snap both ends off the beans, then soak the beans in a basin of cold water for 10 minutes.

❀ Bring 4 quarts water to a boil. Add 1 tablespoon salt, which will momentarily slow down the boil. As soon as the water is boiling rapidly again, drop in the drained green beans. When the water returns again to a boil, adjust heat so that it boils at a moderate pace. Cooking times will vary depending on the youth and freshness of the beans. If very young and fresh it may take 6 or 7 minutes; if not, it may take 10 or 12 minutes or even longer. Begin tasting the beans after they have been cooking 6 minutes. Drain when firm, but tender, when they have lost their raw, vegetal taste.

Sautéed Green Beans with Parmesan Cheese

For 6 servings

1 pound fresh, crisp green
   beans
3 tablespoons butter

¼ cup freshly grated
   parmigiano-reggiano cheese
Salt

1. Trim, soak, boil, and drain the green beans as described above.
2. Put the beans and the butter in a skillet and turn on the heat to medium. As the butter melts and begins to foam, turn the beans to coat them well. Add the grated cheese, turning over the beans thoroughly. Taste a bean and correct for salt. Turn them over once or twice again, transfer to a warm platter, and serve at once.

Smothered Green Beans with Carrot Sticks and Mortadella or Ham

For 6 servings

1 pound fresh, young
   green beans
3 or 4 medium carrots
Salt
¼ pound *mortadella* (see page
   18) OR boiled unsmoked

ham, diced into ¼-inch
   cubes
3 tablespoons butter

1. Trim, soak, boil, and drain the green beans as described on page 471. They will undergo more cooking later in the pan, so drain them when quite firm.
2. Peel the carrots, wash them in cold water, and cut them into sticks slightly thinner than the beans.
3. Choose a sauté pan that can accommodate all the ingredients without crowding them. Put in the beans, the carrots, salt, the diced *mortadella* or ham, and the butter. Turn on the heat to medium and cook, turning the beans and carrots over frequently to coat them well. When the butter begins to foam, cover the pan. Cook until the carrots are just tender, checking after 5 to 6 minutes, and turning them and the beans from time to time. Taste and correct for salt and serve promptly.

Green Beans and Potato Pie, Genoa Style

NOWHERE IN ITALY is the cooking of vegetables raised to greater heights than it is on the Genoese coast. The fragrance and the satisfying depth of flavor that characterize that cuisine is well represented by this savory pie that combines green beans with potatoes, marjoram, and Parmesan. It's a dish that will fit into any menu scheme, as an appetizer, a vegetable side dish, a light summer luncheon course, or as part of a buffet table.   *For 6 servings*

½ pound boiling potatoes
1 pound fresh green beans
2 eggs
1 cup freshly grated
   parmigiano-reggiano cheese
Salt
Black pepper, ground fresh
   from the mill

Chopped marjoram,
   2 teaspoons if fresh, 1
   teaspoon if dried
A 9-inch round cake pan
Extra virgin olive oil
Unflavored bread crumbs,
   lightly toasted

1. Wash the potatoes, put them with their peel on in a pot with enough cold water to cover amply, and bring to a boil.

2. Trim, soak, boil, and drain the green beans as described on page 471. They will undergo considerably more cooking in the oven later, so drain them when quite firm.

3. Chop the beans very fine, but not puréed, in a food processor, or pass them through the largest holes of a food mill, and put them into a bowl.

4. Preheat oven to 350°.

5. Drain the potatoes when tender, testing them with a fork, peel them, and pass them through a food mill or a potato ricer into the bowl containing the beans. Do not use a food processor because it makes potatoes gluey.

6. Break the eggs into the bowl, add the grated Parmesan, salt, a few grindings of pepper, and the marjoram. Mix thoroughly to blend all ingredients uniformly.

7. Lightly smear the baking pan with olive oil. Sprinkle bread crumbs over the entire inside surface of the pan, then turn the pan upside down and rap it on the counter to shake out excess crumbs.

8. Put the bean and potato mixture into the pan, distributing it evenly and leveling it with a spatula. Top with a sprinkling of bread crumbs and over them pour a thin and evenly spread stream of olive oil. Place in the upper third of the preheated oven, and bake for 1 hour. Allow to settle for a few

Green Beans and Potato Pie (continued)

minutes, then run a knife blade all around the pie to loosen it from the pan, invert it over a plate, then again over another plate. Serve warm or at room temperature.

Ahead-of-time note ❀ You can complete the recipe several hours in advance. Do not refrigerate. Finish and serve it the same day you start it.

Green Beans with Yellow Peppers, Tomatoes, and Chili Pepper

For 4 to 6 servings

1 pound fresh green beans
1 sweet yellow bell pepper
3 tablespoons extra virgin
   olive oil
1 medium onion sliced
   very thin
⅔ cup canned imported Italian
   plum tomatoes, chopped

coarse, with their juice,
  OR fresh, ripe tomatoes,
  peeled and cut up
Salt
Chopped hot red chili pepper,
  to taste

1. Snap both ends off the beans, soak them in a basin of cold water for 10 minutes, then drain and set aside.

2. Wash the pepper in cold water, split it lengthwise along its creases, remove the seeds and pulpy core, and skin it raw, using a swiveling-blade peeler. Cut it into long strips less than ½ inch wide.

3. Put the oil and onion in a sauté pan, turn the heat on to medium, and cook the onion, stirring, until it becomes translucent. Add the strips of pepper and the chopped tomatoes with their juice. Turn all ingredients over to coat them well, and adjust heat to cook at a steady, but gentle simmer for about 20 minutes, until the oil floats free of the tomatoes.

4. Add the raw green beans, turn them over 2 or 3 times to coat them well, add ⅓ cup water or less if you are using fresh tomatoes that turn out to be watery, salt, and chili pepper. Cover and cook at a steady simmer until tender, 20 to 30 minutes, depending on the youth and freshness of the beans. If the cooking liquid becomes insufficient, add 1 or 2 tablespoons water as needed. When the beans are done, if the pan juices are watery, uncover, turn the heat up to high, and rapidly boil them down. Taste and correct for salt and chili pepper, and serve promptly.

Ahead-of-time note ❀ The dish can be cooked through to the end several hours in advance and gently reheated before serving. Do not refrigerate.

Green Beans Pasticcio

A *pasticcio* can be one of two things in Italian. In everyday life it means a "mess," such as in "How did I ever get into this *pasticcio?*" When produced intentionally by a cook, however, it is a mix of cheese and vegetables, meat, or cooked pasta, bound by eggs or béchamel, or both. Sometimes it is baked in a pastry crust, sometimes not. The one given below could be made in a crust, but it is not and I think it is both lighter and better for it.

For 6 servings

1 pound fresh green beans
3 tablespoons butter
Salt
Béchamel Sauce, made as
    described on page 39,
    using 1¼ cups milk,
    2 tablespoons butter,
    2 tablespoons flour,
    and ⅛ teaspoon salt

3 eggs
3 tablespoons freshly grated
    parmigiano-reggiano cheese
Whole nutmeg
A 6- to 8-cup soufflé mold
½ cup unflavored bread
    crumbs, lightly toasted

1. Snap both ends off the beans, soak them in a basin of cold water for 10 minutes, drain, and cut into pieces about 1 inch long.

2. Choose a sauté pan that can contain all the beans snugly, but without overlapping. Put in 2 tablespoons butter, the green beans, 2 or 3 pinches of salt, just enough water to cover, and turn on the heat to medium high. Cook,

Green Beans Pasticcio (continued)

turning the beans from time to time, until all the water has simmered away. Continue to cook for a minute or two, turning the beans in the butter, then take off heat.

3. Preheat oven to 375°.

4. Make the béchamel sauce, cooking it to medium density.

5. Beat the eggs lightly in a mixing bowl, and swirl in the grated Parmesan and a tiny grating of nutmeg—about ⅛ teaspoon. Add the green beans and the béchamel, mixing thoroughly to obtain a uniform blend of all the ingredients.

6. Smear the inside of the soufflé mold with the remaining tablespoon of butter, and sprinkle with enough bread crumbs to coat the bottom and sides. Turn the mold upside down and give it a sharp rap against the counter to shake away loose crumbs. Pour the contents of the mixing bowl into the mold.

7. Place the mold on the uppermost rack of the preheated oven, and bake until a light crust forms on top, about 45 minutes.

8. To unmold, run a knife along the side of the *pasticcio* while it is hot, loosening it from the dish all the way around. Allow it to settle for a few minutes, then cover the mold with a dinner plate turned bottom up, grasp both the plate and the mold with a towel, holding them together tightly, and turn the mold upside down. The *pasticcio* should slip out onto the plate easily, with at most a little shake. Now you want to turn it right side up onto another plate. Sandwich the *pasticcio* between two plates and turn it over. Allow to settle for several minutes before serving.

BROCCOLI

We have come to expect broccoli to be in the market all year, but it does have a natural season, from late fall through winter, when it is at its best. When buying it, the florets or buds are the best guide to its freshness: They should be tightly closed, and their deep blue-green or purplish color must show no hint of yellow. The meatiest and tastiest part of the vegetable is its stem, which only needs be trimmed of its tough outer skin to become eminently edible. The leaves are also excellent, with a taste like that of kale, and in Italy, where broccoli comes to the market freshly picked and enveloped by its leaves, they are highly prized. Unfortunately, they are also highly perishable, and in North America the packer strips them away. If you grow your own, try the leaves in a vegetable or bean soup.

Sautéed Broccoli
with Olive Oil and Garlic

THE TECHNIQUE illustrated by this recipe—sautéing blanched green vegetables in olive oil and garlic—is analogous to that used for spinach and Swiss chard, and it is one of the tastiest ways to prepare broccoli.　　*For 6 servings*

1 bunch fresh broccoli (about 1
　　to 1½ pounds)
Salt
¼ cup extra virgin olive oil

2 teaspoons garlic chopped
　　very fine
2 tablespoons chopped parsley

1. Cut off about ½ to ¾ inch of the butt end of the stalk. Use a sharp paring knife to slice away the tough dark-green skin that surrounds the tender core of the main stalk and the branching-off stems. Dig deeper where the stalk is broadest because the skin is thicker there. Split the larger stalks in two or, if quite large, in four, without detaching the florets. Wash in 3 or 4 complete changes of cold water.

2. Bring 4 quarts water to a fast boil. Add 1 tablespoon salt and as the water returns to a boil, drop in the broccoli. Adjust heat to maintain a moderately paced boil, and cook until the broccoli stalk can be pierced by a fork, about 5 minutes, depending on the vegetable's youth and freshness. Drain at once when done.

Ahead-of-time note ✖ Prepare the broccoli up to this point several hours ahead of time on the same day you will be serving it, but do not refrigerate.

3. Choose a sauté pan or skillet that can accommodate all the broccoli without crowding it too tightly. Put in the olive oil and garlic, and turn on the heat to medium. Cook and stir the garlic until it becomes colored a pale gold, then add the broccoli, salt, and the chopped parsley. Turn the vegetable pieces over 2 or 3 times to coat them thoroughly. Cook for about 2 minutes, then transfer the contents of the pan to a warm platter and serve at once.

Variation with Butter and Parmesan Cheese

For 6 servings

1 bunch fresh broccoli,
　　trimmed, washed, cooked,
　　and drained as described
　　above

3 tablespoons butter
Salt
½ cup freshly grated
　　parmigiano-reggiano cheese

Sautéed Broccoli with Butter and Parmesan (continued)

Choose a skillet or sauté pan that will contain all the broccoli pieces without crowding them tightly, put in the butter, turn the heat on to medium, and when the butter foam begins to subside, add the cooked, drained broccoli and salt. Turn the broccoli over completely 2 or 3 times, and cook for about 2 minutes, then add the grated Parmesan. Turn the broccoli over again, then transfer the contents of the pan to a warm platter and serve at once.

Fried Broccoli Florets

ONLY THE FLORETS are used here because they lend themselves best to frying. The stalks are too good to throw away, however; after trimming them, use them in a cooked salad, or a vegetable soup, or sauté them with garlic and olive oil as described on page 477.   *For 6 servings*

1 medium bunch fresh broccoli (about 1 pound)	1 cup fine, dry, unflavored bread crumbs, spread on a
Salt	plate
2 eggs	Vegetable oil

Note ✸ The batter used here consists of eggs and bread crumbs. Another excellent batter for the florets is *pastella,* flour and water batter, used for fried zucchini on page 530.

1. Cut off the florets where their stems meet the stalk. Set the stalk aside, trimming it of its hard outer skin as described on page 477, and use it in another dish as suggested in the introductory remarks above.

2. Wash the florets in 2 or 3 changes of cold water. Bring 2 quarts water to a fast boil, add a large pinch of salt, and as the water resumes its boil, drop in the florets. From time to time, submerge any part of a floret that floats above the water line to keep it from turning yellow. When the water comes to a full boil again, retrieve the florets with a colander spoon and set aside to cool. When they are cold, cut the larger florets lengthwise into pieces about 1 inch thick. Try to have all the pieces more or less equal in size so that you can fry them evenly.

3. Break the eggs into a soup plate, and beat them lightly with a fork.

4. Dip the broccoli, one piece at a time, in the beaten egg, letting excess egg flow back into the plate, then dredge it in the bread crumbs, turning to coat it all over and patting it with your fingertips to cause the breading to

adhere securely. Put all the dipped and breaded pieces on a plate until you are ready to fry them.

5. Pour enough oil in a skillet or frying pan to come ½ inch up the sides, and turn on the heat to medium high. When the oil is very hot, slip in as many pieces of broccoli florets as will fit in at one time without crowding the pan. When they have formed a nice golden crust on one side, turn them and do the other side. Transfer them to a cooling rack to drain or to a platter lined with paper towels. Do another batch, and repeat the above procedure, until all the broccoli pieces are done. Sprinkle liberally with salt and serve at once.

Smothered Cabbage, Venetian Style

ANY VARIETY of cabbage—Savoy cabbage, red cabbage, or the common pale-green cabbage—works well in this recipe. It is shredded very fine and cooked very slowly in the vapors from its own escaping moisture combined with olive oil and a small amount of vinegar. The Venetian word for the method is *sofegao,* or smothered. *For 6 servings*

2 pounds green, red,
    or Savoy cabbage
½ cup chopped onion
½ cup extra virgin olive oil
1 tablespoon chopped garlic

Salt
Black pepper, ground fresh
    from the mill
1 tablespoon wine vinegar

Smothered Cabbage, Venetian Style (continued)

1. Detach and discard the first few outer leaves of the cabbage. The remaining head of leaves must be shredded very fine. If you are going to do it by hand, cut the leaves into fine shreds, slicing them off the whole head. Turn the head after you have sliced a section of it until gradually you expose the entire core, which must be discarded. If you want to use the food processor, cut the leaves off from the core in sections, discard the core, and process the leaves through a shredding attachment.

2. Put the onion and olive oil into a large sauté pan, and turn the heat on to medium. Cook and stir the onion until it becomes colored a deep gold, then add the garlic. When you have cooked the garlic until it becomes colored a very pale gold, add the shredded cabbage. Turn the cabbage over 2 or 3 times to coat it well, and cook it until it is wilted.

3. Add salt, pepper, and the vinegar. Turn the cabbage over once completely, lower the heat to minimum, and cover the pan tightly. Cook for at least 1½ hours, or until it is very tender, turning it from time to time. If while it is cooking, the liquid in the pan should become insufficient, add 2 tablespoons water as needed. When done, taste and correct for salt and pepper. Allow it to settle a few minutes off heat before serving.

Braised Carrots with Parmesan Cheese

I KNOW of no other preparation in the Italian repertory, or in other cuisines, for that matter, more successful than this one in freeing the rich flavor that is locked inside the carrot. It does it by cooking the carrots slowly in no more liquid than is necessary to keep the cooking going so that they are wholly reduced to their essential elements of flavor. When cooked, they are tossed briefly over heat with grated Parmesan.   *For 6 servings*

1½ pounds carrots
4 tablespoons butter (½ stick)
Salt

¼ teaspoon sugar
3 tablespoons freshly grated
    parmigiano-reggiano cheese

1. Peel the carrots, wash them in cold water, and slice them into ⅜ inch disks. The thin tapered ends can be cut thicker. Choose a sauté pan that can contain the carrot rounds spread in a single snug layer, without overlapping. Put in the carrots and butter, and enough water to come ¼ inch up the sides. If you do not have a single pan large enough, use two smaller ones, dividing

the carrots and butter equally between them. Turn on the heat to medium. Do not cover the pan.

2. Cook until the water has evaporated, then add salt and the ¼ teaspoon sugar. Continue cooking, adding from 2 to 3 tablespoons water as needed. Your objective is to end up with well-browned, wrinkled carrot disks, concentrated in flavor and texture. It will take between 1 and 1½ hours, during which time you must watch them, even while you do other things in the kitchen. Stop adding water when they begin to reach the wrinkled, browned stage, because there must be no liquid left at the end. In 30 minutes or a little more, the carrots will become so reduced in bulk that, if you have been using two pans, you will be able to combine them in a single pan.

3. When done—they should be very tender—add the grated Parmesan, turn the carrots over completely once or twice, transfer them to a warm platter, and serve at once.

Ahead-of-time note ❀ The carrots can be finished entirely in advance, except for the Parmesan, which you will add only when reheating, just before serving.

Braised Carrots with Capers

For 4 servings

1 pound choice young carrots
3 tablespoons extra virgin
    olive oil
1 teaspoon chopped garlic
2 tablespoons chopped parsley
Salt

Black pepper, ground fresh
    from the mill
2 tablespoons capers, soaked
    and rinsed as described on
    page 16 if packed in salt,
    drained if in vinegar

Braised Carrots with Capers (continued)

1. Peel the carrots and wash them in cold water. They ought to be no thicker than your little finger. If they are not that size to start with, cut them lengthwise in half, or in quarters if necessary.

2. Choose a sauté pan that can later accommodate all the carrots loosely. Put in the olive oil and garlic, and turn on the heat to medium high. Cook and stir the garlic until it becomes colored a pale gold, then add the carrots and parsley. Toss the carrots once or twice to coat them well, then add ¼ cup water. When the water has completely evaporated, add another ¼ cup. Continue adding water at this pace, whenever it has evaporated, until the carrots are done. They should feel tender, but firm, when prodded with a fork. Test them from time to time. Depending on the youth and freshness of the carrots, it should take about 20 to 30 minutes. When done, there should be no more water left in the pan. If there is still some, boil it away quickly, and let the carrots brown lightly.

3. Add pepper and the capers, and toss the carrots once or twice. Cook for another minute or two, then taste and correct for salt, stir once again, transfer to a warm platter, and serve at once.

CAULIFLOWER

How to buy ❀ A head of cauliflower must be very hard, with leaves that are fresh, crisp, and unblemished. The florets should be compact and as white as possible. If they are yellowish or speckled, it is preferable to look elsewhere or do without.

How to boil ❀

❀ Detach and discard most of the leaves, except for the small, tender inner ones, which are very nice to eat if you are serving the cauliflower as cooked salad. Cut a deep cross into the root end.

❀ Bring 4 to 5 quarts of water to a rapid boil. The more water you use the sweeter the cauliflower will taste and the faster it will cook. Put in the cauliflower and when the water returns to a boil, adjust heat to cook at a moderate boil.

❀ Cook, uncovered, until the cauliflower feels very tender when prodded with a fork, 20 minutes or more, depending on the freshness and size of the head. Drain immediately when done.

Ahead-of-time note ✼ If you are not serving boiled cauliflower lukewarm as salad, but are planning to use it in a gratin or for frying, you can cook it up to 1 day in advance.

Gratinéed Cauliflower with Butter and Parmesan Cheese

For 6 servings

1 medium head cauliflower,
    about 2 pounds
An oven-to-table baking dish
Butter for smearing and dotting
    the baking dish

Salt
⅔ cup freshly grated
    parmigiano-reggiano cheese

1. Preheat oven to 400°.

2. Boil and drain the cauliflower as described on page 482. When it has cooled enough to handle, divide the head into separate florets.

3. Choose a baking dish that can contain the florets snugly. Smear the bottom with butter and arrange the florets in it so that they overlap slightly, roof-tile fashion. Sprinkle with salt and grated Parmesan, and dot liberally with butter. Bake on the uppermost rack of the preheated oven until a light crust forms on top, about 15 to 20 minutes. After taking it out of the oven, let the cauliflower settle for a few minutes before serving.

Gratinéed Cauliflower with Béchamel Sauce

For 6 servings

1 medium head cauliflower,
    about 2 pounds
Salt
Béchamel Sauce, made as
    described on page 39,
    using 2 cups milk,
    4 tablespoons (½ stick)
    butter, 3 tablespoons flour,
    and ¼ teaspoon salt

¾ cup freshly grated
    parmigiano-reggiano cheese
Whole nutmeg
An oven-to-table baking dish
Butter for smearing and dotting
    the baking dish

Gratinéed Cauliflower with Béchamel Sauce (continued)

1. Boil and drain the cauliflower as described on page 482, but because baking it with the béchamel later will soften it up, cook only 10 minutes after the water returns to a boil. Separate the florets and cut them into bite-size slices about ½ inch thick. Put them in a bowl and toss them with a little salt.

2. Preheat oven to 400°.

3. Make the béchamel sauce as described on page 39. When it reaches a medium density, remove it from heat and mix in all but 3 tablespoons of the grated Parmesan and a tiny grating of nutmeg—about ⅛ teaspoon.

4. Add the béchamel to the bowl with the cauliflower and fold it in gently, coating the florets well.

5. Smear the bottom of a baking dish with butter. Put in the cauliflower and all the béchamel in the bowl. The dish should be able to contain the cauliflower pieces in a layer not more than 1½ inches deep. Sprinkle the top with the remaining 3 tablespoons of grated Parmesan and dot lightly with butter. Bake on the uppermost rack of the preheated oven until a light crust forms on top, about 15 to 20 minutes. After taking it out of the oven, let the cauliflower settle for a few minutes before serving.

Fried Cauliflower Wedges with Egg and Bread Crumb Batter

For 6 or more servings

1 medium head cauliflower,
   about 2 pounds
2 eggs
1 cup unflavored bread crumbs,
   lightly toasted, spread on a
   plate

Vegetable oil
Salt

1. Boil and drain the cauliflower as described on page 482. When it has cooled enough to handle, detach the florets from the head and cut them into wedges about 1 inch thick at their widest point.

2. Break the eggs into a small bowl and beat them lightly.

3. Dip the cauliflower wedges in the egg, letting excess egg flow back into the bowl, then turn them in the bread crumbs, coating them all over.

4. Pour enough oil in a frying pan to come ½ inch up the sides, turn the heat on to high, and when the oil is very hot, slip in as many cauliflower

pieces as will fit loosely, without crowding the pan. When a nice, golden crust has formed on one side, turn them and do the other side. Transfer with a slotted spoon or spatula to a cooling rack to drain or to a platter lined with paper towels. If there are more cauliflower pieces left to be fried, repeat the procedure. When they are all done, sprinkle with salt, and serve at once.

Fried Cauliflower
with Parmesan Cheese Batter

TRUE *parmigiano-reggiano* cheese makes marvelous frying batters because it is an ideal bonding agent, melting without becoming runny, stringy, or rubbery. And, of course, it also contributes its own unique flavor. The fluffy, tender crust this batter produces is ideal for such vegetable pieces as cauliflower. If you are pleased with it, try it with preboiled broccoli or *finocchio*.

For 6 or more servings

1 head young cauliflower, 2
    pounds or less
Salt
½ cup lukewarm water
⅓ cup flour

⅓ cup freshly grated
    parmigiano-reggiano cheese
1 egg
Vegetable oil

1. Boil and drain the cauliflower as described on page 482. When it has cooled enough to handle, detach the floret clusters from the head at the base of their stems, separate into individual florets, and cut each of them length-wise in two. Sprinkle lightly with salt.

2. Put the lukewarm water in a bowl, and add the flour to it gradually, shaking it through a strainer, not a sifter. Beat the mixture with a fork while you add the flour. Add the grated Parmesan and a pinch of salt and stir well.

3. Break the egg into a deep soup plate, beat it lightly with a fork, then mix it thoroughly into the flour and Parmesan mixture.

4. Pour enough vegetable oil in a skillet to come ¼ inch up its sides, and turn on the heat to high. When a speck of batter dropped into the pan stiffens and instantly floats to the surface, the oil is hot enough for frying.

5. Dip 2 or 3 florets in the batter, letting excess batter flow back into the bowl as you lift them out, and slip them into the pan. Add a few more batter-coated pieces to the pan, but do not put too many in at one time or the temperature of the oil will drop.

6. When the cauliflower forms a nice golden crust on one side, turn it and

Fried Cauliflower with Parmesan Cheese Batter (continued)

do the other side. Transfer with a slotted spoon or spatula to a cooling rack to drain or to a platter lined with paper towels. As room opens up in the pan, add more pieces of cauliflower. When they are all done, sprinkle with salt, and serve at once.

Braised and Gratinéed Celery Stalks with Parmesan Cheese

DESPITE THE SEQUENCE of cooking procedures—first the celery is blanched to fix its color; then it's sautéed with onion and *pancetta* to provide a flavor base; after that it is braised with broth to make it tender; and finally it is gratinéed with grated Parmesan to give it a savory finish—this is not a very complicated dish to prepare. You should find the means completely justified by the simply delicious end. *For 6 servings*

2 large bunches crisp, fresh celery

3 tablespoons onion chopped fine

2 tablespoons butter

¼ cup chopped *pancetta* OR prosciutto

Salt

Black pepper, ground fresh from the mill

2 cups Basic Homemade Meat Broth, prepared as directed on page 15, OR ½ cup canned beef broth diluted with 1½ cups water

An oven-to-table baking dish

1 cup freshly grated *parmigiano-reggiano* cheese

1. Cut off the celery's leafy tops, and detach all the stalks from their base. Save the hearts for a salad or for dipping in Pinzimonio, page 553. Use a swiveling-blade peeler to pare away most of the strings, and cut the stalks into pieces about 3 inches long.

2. Bring 2 or 3 quarts of water to a rapid boil, drop in the celery, and 1 minute after the water has returned to a boil, drain them and set them aside.

3. Preheat oven to 400°.

4. Put the onion and butter in a saucepan, and turn the heat on to medi-

um. Cook and stir the onion until it becomes translucent, then add the chopped *pancetta* or prosciutto. Stir to coat well, cook for 1 minute, then put in the celery, salt, and pepper, toss the celery to coat it well, and cook for about 5 minutes, stirring occasionally.

5. Add the broth, adjust heat to cook at a very gentle simmer, and cover the pan. Cook until the celery feels tender when prodded. Test the celery from time to time with a fork and when you find that it is nearly done— almost tender, but slightly firm—uncover the pan, raise the heat to high, and boil away all the liquid.

Ahead-of-time note ❀ The celery can be prepared up to this point several hours in advance on the same day that you will finish cooking it.

6. Remove only the celery to the baking dish and arrange it with the inner, concave side of the stalks facing up. Over the celery, spoon the onion and *pancetta* or prosciutto mixture still in the pan, then top with grated Parmesan. Place on the uppermost rack of the preheated oven for a few minutes until the cheese melts and forms a light crust. After taking the dish out of the oven, allow it to settle for several minutes before bringing it to the table.

Celery and Potatoes Braised in Olive Oil and Lemon Juice

For 4 to 6 servings

5 medium potatoes
1 large bunch celery
⅓ cup extra virgin olive oil

Salt
2 tablespoons freshly squeezed
lemon juice

1. Peel the potatoes, wash them in cold water, and cut them in half or, if large, in quarters.

2. Trim the celery stalks as described in Step 1 on page 486.

3. Choose a heavy-bottomed or enameled cast-iron pot that can subsequently contain all the ingredients, put in the celery, olive oil, salt, and enough water to cover, turn the heat on to medium, and put a lid on the pot.

4. Simmer the celery for 10 minutes, then add the potatoes, a pinch of salt, and the lemon juice, and cover the pot again. Cook until both the celery and potatoes are tender, testing them with a fork from time to time. It may take about 25 minutes. (Sometimes the celery lags behind while the potatoes

Celery and Potatoes Braised in Olive Oil (continued)

are already done. Should this happen, transfer the potatoes with a slotted spoon to a warm covered dish, and continue cooking the celery until it is tender.)

5. When the celery and potatoes are both cooked, the only liquid in the pot should be oil. If there is water, uncover the pot, raise the heat, and boil it away. (If the potatoes have been taken out of the pot earlier, put them back in after the water—if there was any—has been boiled away. Cover the pot again, turn the heat down to medium, and warm up the potatoes for about 2 minutes.) Taste and correct for salt, and serve promptly.

Braised Celery Stalks with Onion, Pancetta, and Tomatoes

For 4 to 6 servings

About 2 pounds celery
¼ cup extra virgin olive oil
1½ cups onion sliced very thin
⅔ cup *pancetta,* cut into
    thin strips
¾ cup canned imported Italian
    plum tomatoes, chopped
    coarse, with their juice

Salt
Black pepper, ground fresh
    from the mill

1. Trim the celery stalks as described in Step 1 on page 486.

2. Put the oil and onion in a sauté pan, and turn on the heat to medium. Cook and stir the onion until it wilts completely and becomes colored a light gold, then add the *pancetta* strips.

3. After a few minutes, when the *pancetta's* fat loses its flat, white uncooked color and becomes translucent, add the tomatoes with their juice, the celery, salt, and pepper, and toss thoroughly to coat well. Adjust heat to cook at a steady simmer, and put a cover on the pan. After 15 minutes check the celery, cooking it until it feels tender when prodded with a fork. If while the celery is cooking, the pan juices become insufficient, replenish with 2 to 3 tablespoons of water as needed. If on the contrary, when the celery is done, the pan juices are watery, uncover, raise the heat to high, and boil the juices away rapidly. Serve promptly when done.

SWISS CHARD

There is no green more useful than Swiss chard for Italian cooking. Its broad, dark green leaves, whose flavor is sweeter, less emphatic than spinach, can be used in pasta dough to dye it green, or together with cheese, for the filling in a variety of stuffed pastas. The leaves are good in soup, delicious boiled and served with olive oil and lemon juice, or sautéed with olive oil and garlic. The broad, sweet-tasting stalks of mature chard are magnificent in gratin dishes, or sautéed, or fried.

Swiss Chard Stalks
Gratinéed with Parmesan Cheese

For 4 servings

The broad, white stalks from 2 bunches mature Swiss chard	Salt
An oven-to-table baking dish	⅔ cup freshly grated *parmigiano-reggiano* cheese
Butter for smearing and dotting the baking dish	

Note ❀ This is an excellent recipe to keep in mind if you have used chard leaves in pasta, soup, or a cooked salad. You can keep the trimmed stalks in the refrigerator for 2 or 3 days. Or, if it is the leaves that are going to be left over after doing this dish, try to use them in one of the ways cited above within 24 hours.

1. Cut the chard stalks into pieces about 4 inches long, and wash them in cold water. Bring 3 quarts water to a boil, drop in the stalks, and cook at a moderate boil until they feel tender when prodded with a fork, approximately 30 minutes, depending on the stalks. Drain and set aside.

2. Preheat oven to 400°.

Swiss Chard Stalks Gratinéed with Parmesan Cheese (continued)

3. Smear the bottom and sides of a baking dish with butter, place a layer of chard stalks on the bottom, laying them end to end, and if necessary, trimming to fit. Sprinkle lightly with salt and with grated cheese, and dot sparingly with butter. Repeat the procedure, building up layers of stalks, until you have used them all. The top layer should be sprinkled generously with Parmesan and thickly dotted with butter.

4. Bake on the uppermost rack of the preheated oven until the cheese melts and forms a light, golden crust on top. You might begin to check after 10 or 15 minutes. After taking it out of the oven, let it settle for a few minutes before bringing it to the table.

Sautéed Swiss Chard Stalks with Olive Oil, Garlic, and Parsley

For 4 servings

2½ cups Swiss chard stalks, cut into pieces 1½ inches long

3 tablespoons extra virgin olive oil

1½ teaspoons chopped garlic

2 tablespoons chopped parsley

Salt

Black pepper, ground fresh from the mill

1. Wash the chard stalks in cold water. (See note on page 489 about using the chard leaves.) Bring 3 quarts water to a boil, drop in the stalks, and cook at a moderate boil until they feel tender when prodded with a fork, approximately 30 minutes, depending on the stalks. Drain and set aside.

2. Put the olive oil and garlic in a sauté pan, turn on the heat to medium. Cook and stir the garlic until it becomes very lightly colored, then add the boiled stalks, the parsley, salt, and pepper. Turn the heat up to medium high, tossing and turning the stalks to coat them well. Cook for about 5 minutes, then transfer the contents of the pan to a warm plate and serve at once.

Tegliata di Biete—Swiss Chard Torte with Raisins and Pine Nuts

THE TREASURES that Venice brought back from its trade and its wars with the empires of the East did not consist solely of silks and marbles, of gems and precious artifacts, but of ingredients and ways of cooking that were new to the West. Some examples, such as the fish *in saor* on page 63, are still part of the city's everyday fare. But in the seldom-explored recesses of Venetian cooking are others just as wonderful, like this tasty vegetable pie of young chard, onion, pine nuts, raisins, and Parmesan cheese.   *For 4 to 6 servings*

2½ pounds young Swiss chard with undeveloped stalks or 3¼ pounds mature chard

Salt

Extra virgin olive oil, ¼ cup for cooking the chard plus more for greasing and topping the pan

⅔ cup onion chopped fine

1 cup freshly grated *parmigiano-reggiano* cheese

2 eggs, lightly beaten

¼ cup *pignoli* (pine nuts)

⅓ cup seedless raisins, preferably of the muscat variety, soaking in enough water to cover

Black pepper, ground fresh from the mill

A 9½- or 10-inch springform baking pan

⅔ heaping cup unflavored bread crumbs, lightly toasted

1. If using mature chard, cut off the broad stalks and set aside to use in vegetable soup or bake as described on page 489. Cut the leaves and any very thin stalks into ¼-inch shreds. Soak the shredded chard in a basin with several changes of cold water, until the water runs completely clear of any soil.

2. Put about 1 quart water in a pot large enough to contain the chard later, and bring it to a boil. Add a liberal quantity of salt, wait for the water to resume a fast boil, then drop in the chard. Cook until tender, about 15 minutes depending on the youth and freshness of the chard, then drain and set aside to cool.

3. When cool enough to handle, take as much chard in your hand as you can hold and squeeze as much moisture out of it as you can. When you have done all the chard, chop it very fine—into pieces no bigger than ¼ inch—using a knife, not the food processor.

4. Preheat oven to 350°.

5. Choose a sauté pan that can subsequently contain all the chard, put in ¼ cup olive oil and the chopped onion, and turn on the heat to medium. Cook the onion, stirring frequently, until it becomes colored a light nut-brown.

6. Add the chopped chard, and turn up the heat to high. Cook, turning the chard over frequently, until it becomes difficult to keep it from sticking

Swiss Chard Torte (continued)

to the bottom of the pan, then transfer the entire contents of the pan to a bowl and set aside to cool.

7. When the chard has cooled down to room temperature, add the grated Parmesan, the beaten eggs, and the pine nuts. Drain the raisins, squeeze them dry in your hand, and add them to the bowl, together with a few grindings of pepper. Mix thoroughly until all ingredients are evenly combined, and taste and correct for salt and pepper.

8. Smear the bottom and sides of the springform pan with about 1 tablespoon olive oil. Put in a little more than half the bread crumbs, spreading them to cover the bottom and sides of the pan. Add the chard mixture, leveling it off, but not pressing it hard. Top with the remaining bread crumbs, and drizzle with about 1 tablespoon of olive oil poured in a thin stream. Put the pan in the preheated oven and bake for 40 minutes.

9. When you take the pan out, run a knife blade around the edge of the torte, loosening it from the sides of the pan, then unlatch the springform hoop and remove it. After 5 or 6 minutes, use a spatula to loosen the torte from the pan's bottom section and slide it, without turning it over, onto a serving platter. Serve at room temperature. Do not refrigerate.

EGGPLANT

When and what to buy ✺ Although you can walk into a market almost any time of the year and find eggplant, it never tastes quite so good the rest of the year as it does during its natural season, from mid- to late summer. It is at its best for a not too long period after it has been picked; beyond that, its underlying bitter flavor begins to be more prominent and most eggplant has to be purged of it by steeping in salt (see below). Do not buy eggplant that feels soft and spongy or whose skin is mottled, opaque, or wrinkled. It should feel firm in the hand, and the skin should be glossy, smooth, and intact.

The typical Italian eggplant is long, skinny, and dark purple, but Italians also use globe-like ones as well as the stout, pear-shaped variety prevalent in North America, and white eggplant is not uncommon. All of these can be found at one time or another in many markets, and for most recipes they are interchangeable. White eggplant seems to me to be the most dependable because of its usually mild flavor and firm flesh, and it is the kind I'd choose, if I had a choice. The pale purple Chinese eggplant found in Oriental markets is delicious, but its sweetness seems cloying when it is part of an Italian dish.

Purging eggplant ❀ As a preliminary to most recipes, you must purge eggplant of its harshness, which on occasion can be considerable. Proceed thus:

❀ Cut off its green, spiky top and peel the eggplant. You can omit peeling it if it is the young, skinny Italian variety sometimes known as "baby" eggplant.

❀ Cut lengthwise into slices about ⅜ inch thick.

❀ Stand one layer of slices upright against the inside of a pasta colander and sprinkle with salt. Stand another layer of slices against it, sprinkle it with salt, and repeat the procedure until you have salted all the eggplant you are working with.

❀ Place a deep dish under the colander to collect the drippings and let the eggplant steep under salt for 30 minutes or more.

❀ Before cooking, pat each slice thoroughly dry with paper towels.

Fried Eggplant

FRIED EGGPLANT slices are not only a delicious appetizer or vegetable dish on their own, but they are the indispensable component of Eggplant Parmesan, page 494, of pasta sauces with eggplant, pages 160 and 161, and of special combinations of vegetables and meat. To fry it so that the eggplant doesn't become sodden with oil, you must have a lot of very hot oil in the pan.

For 6 to 8 servings as a vegetable side dish or an appetizer

3 to 4½ pounds eggplant   Vegetable oil
Salt

1. Slice the eggplant and steep it in salt as described above.
2. Choose a large frying pan, pour enough oil into it to come 1½ inches up the sides, and turn the heat up to high. When you have dried the eggplant thoroughly with paper towels, test the oil by dipping into it the end of one of the slices. If it sizzles, the oil is ready for frying. Slip as many slices of eggplant into the pan as will fit loosely without overlapping. Cook to a golden brown color on one side, then turn them and do the other side. Do not turn them more than once. When both sides are done, use a slotted spoon or spatula to transfer them to a cooling rack to drain or to a platter lined with paper towels. Repeat the procedure until all the eggplant is done. If you find the oil

Fried Eggplant (continued)

becoming too hot, reduce the heat slightly, but do not add more oil to the pan.

If serving the eggplant on its own, you can choose to serve it immediately, when still hot, or allow it to cool to room temperature, when it may taste even better. Taste to see if it needs salt. The eggplant may already be salty enough from its preliminary steeping.

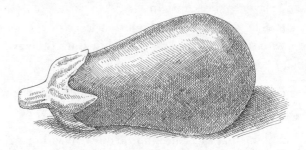

Eggplant Parmesan

NEXT TO SPAGHETTI with tomato sauce, this may well have been, for a certain generation or two, the most familiar of Italian dishes. Perhaps some cooks find it too commonplace to attract their serious attention, but at home I have never stopped making it, and I am pleased to see eggplant Parmesan continuing to appear in Italy, not just in pizza parlors, but even in rather fancy restaurants. No dish has ever been devised that tastes more satisfyingly of summer, and its popularity will no doubt endure long after many of the newer arrivals on the Italian food scene have had their day.   *For 6 servings*

3 pounds eggplant
Vegetable oil
Flour spread on a plate
2 cups canned imported Italian
   plum tomatoes, well
   drained and chopped coarse
1 tablespoon extra virgin olive
   oil
Salt
¾ pound mozzarella, preferably
   buffalo-milk mozzarella

8 to 10 fresh basil leaves
An oven-to-table baking dish,
   approximately 11 inches by
   7 inches or its equivalent
Butter for smearing and dotting
   the dish
½ cup freshly grated
   parmigiano-reggiano cheese

1. Slice the eggplant and steep it in salt as described on page 493.

2. Choose a large frying pan, pour enough oil into it to come 1½ inches up the sides, and turn the heat up to high. When you have dried the eggplant thoroughly with paper towels, dredge the slices in the flour, coating them on both sides. Do only a few slices at a time at the moment you are ready to fry them, otherwise the flour coating will become soggy. After coating with flour, fry the eggplant, following the method described in the basic recipe, page 493.

3. Put the tomatoes and olive oil in another skillet, turn the heat on to medium high, add salt, stir, and cook the tomato down until it is reduced by half.

4. Preheat oven to 400°.

5. Cut the mozzarella into the thinnest possible slices. Wash the basil, and tear each leaf into two or more pieces.

6. Smear the bottom and sides of the baking dish with butter. Put in enough fried eggplant slices to line the bottom of the dish in a single layer, spread some of the cooked tomato over them, cover with a layer of mozzarella, sprinkle liberally with grated Parmesan, distribute a few pieces of basil over it, and top with another layer of fried eggplant. Repeat the procedure, ending with a layer of eggplant on top. Sprinkle with grated Parmesan, and place the dish in the upper third of the preheated oven.

7. Occasionally eggplant Parmesan throws off more liquid as it bakes than you want in the pan. Check after it has been in the oven for 20 minutes by pressing down the layered eggplant with the back of a spoon, and draw off any excess liquid you may find. Cook for another 15 minutes, and after taking it out allow it to settle for several minutes before bringing it to the table.

Ahead-of-time note ✿ Eggplant Parmesan tastes best shortly after it has been made, but if you must, you can complete it from several hours to 2 or 3 days in advance. Refrigerate under plastic wrap when cool. Warm it up on the topmost rack of a preheated 400° oven.

Breaded Eggplant Cutlets

For 4 to 6 servings

A 1¼- to 1½-pound eggplant   Vegetable oil
Salt
1 egg
2 cups unflavored bread
     crumbs, lightly toasted,
     spread on a plate

1. Trim and peel the eggplant, cut it lengthwise into ⅛-inch-thick slices, and steep it in salt as described on page 493.

2. Lightly beat the egg in a deep plate or small bowl.

3. When the eggplant slices have finished steeping, pat them thoroughly dry with paper towels. Dip each slice in the beaten egg, letting excess egg flow back into the dish, then turn it in the bread crumbs, coating both sides. Press the bread crumbs onto each slice with the flat of your hand until your hand feels dry and the crumbs are sticking firmly to the surface of the eggplant.

4. Pour enough oil into a frying pan to come 1½ inches up the sides and turn the heat on to medium high. When you think the oil is quite hot, test it by dipping into it the end of one of the slices. If it sizzles, the oil is ready for frying. Slip as many slices of eggplant into the pan as will fit loosely without overlapping. Cook until the eggplant forms a crisp, golden brown crust on one side, then turn it and do the other side. When both sides are done, use a slotted spoon or spatula to transfer them to a cooling rack to drain or to a platter lined with paper towels. Repeat the procedure until all the eggplant is done. Sprinkle with salt and serve at once.

Eggplant Cubes, Al Funghetto

WHEN YOU SEE it listed on Italian menus as *al funghetto,* it means that the eggplant is cooked in olive oil with garlic and parsley, in an adaptation of the procedure traditionally associated with the cooking of mushrooms. At first, because eggplant has the structure of a sponge, you will see it soak up most of the oil. You mustn't be alarmed; as you continue cooking, the heat causes the spongy structure to cave in and release all the oil. Never add oil while cooking; simply make sure you have enough at the start.   *For 6 servings*

About 3 pounds eggplant
Salt
1 or 2 garlic cloves, lightly
    mashed with a knife handle
    and peeled

⅓ cup extra virgin olive oil
2 tablespoons parsley chopped
    very fine
Black pepper, ground fresh
    from the mill

1. Trim and peel the eggplant, and cut it into 1-inch cubes. Put the cubes in a pasta colander, sprinkle liberally with salt, toss to distribute the salt evenly, and set over a deep dish. Let steep for 1 hour, then take the eggplant pieces out of the colander and pat them thoroughly dry with paper towels.

2. Put the garlic and olive oil in a skillet or sauté pan, and turn on the heat to medium. Cook the garlic, stirring, until it becomes colored a pale gold. Remove it, add the eggplant, and turn the heat up to medium high. At first, when the eggplant soaks up all the oil, turn it frequently. When the heat causes it to discharge the oil, lower the flame to medium again. When the eggplant has cooked for about 15 minutes, add the parsley and pepper. Toss thoroughly and continue to cook another 20 minutes or so, until the eggplant feels very tender when prodded with a fork. Taste and correct for salt. Transfer to a serving platter, using a slotted spoon or spatula.

Sautéed Baby Eggplant Halves with Mozzarella

THE MOST SUITABLE eggplants for this recipe are the sweet, skinny ones not much larger than zucchini, but not miniature. They may be either the purple or white variety.   *For 8 servings*

8 thin, long "baby" eggplants
2 teaspoons garlic chopped
    very fine
2 tablespoons parsley chopped
    very fine
Salt
Black pepper, ground fresh
    from the mill

¼ cup unflavored bread
    crumbs, lightly toasted
⅓ cup extra virgin olive oil
½ pound mozzarella, preferably
    buffalo-milk mozzarella,
    sliced no thicker than
¼ inch

1. Trim the eggplants' green tops away, wash them in cold water, and split them lengthwise in two. Score the eggplant flesh in a cross-hatched pattern, cutting it deeply, while being careful not to pierce the skin.

Sautéed Baby Eggplant Halves (continued)

2. Choose a sauté pan large enough to accommodate all the eggplant halves without overlapping. If you need 2 pans, increase the olive oil to ½ cup. Place the eggplants in the pan, skin side down, cross-hatched side facing up.

3. Put the garlic, parsley, salt, pepper, bread crumbs, and 1 tablespoon of olive oil in a small bowl and mix well to combine the ingredients uniformly. Spoon the mixture over the eggplant halves, pressing it into and in between the cuts.

4. Pour the remaining olive oil in a thin stream, partly over the eggplants, partly directly into the pan. Cover, turn on the heat to medium low, and cook until the eggplant feels very tender when prodded with a fork, 20 or more minutes. Blanket each eggplant half with a layer of sliced mozzarella, turn up the heat to medium, cover the pan again, and cook until the mozzarella has melted.

Eggplant Patties with Parsley, Garlic, and Parmesan

THE TENDER FLESH of baked eggplant is chopped and mixed with bread crumbs, parsley, garlic, egg, and Parmesan to form patties. They are floured and browned in hot oil, and they taste very, very good.   *For 4 to 6 servings*

About 2 pounds eggplant
⅓ cup unflavored bread
    crumbs, lightly toasted
3 tablespoons parsley chopped
    very fine
2 garlic cloves, peeled and
    chopped very fine
1 egg

3 tablespoons freshly grated
    parmigiano-reggiano cheese
Salt
Black pepper, ground fresh
    from the mill
Vegetable oil
Flour, spread on a plate

1. Preheat oven to 400°.

2. When the oven is hot, wash the eggplants, keeping them whole and untrimmed. Place them on the uppermost rack of the preheated oven, with a baking pan on a lower rack to collect any drippings. Bake until tender, when a toothpick will penetrate them without resistance, about 40 minutes, depending on their size.

3. Take the eggplants out of the oven and as soon as they are cool enough to handle, peel them, and cut them into several large pieces. Put the pieces in a pasta colander set over a deep dish. The eggplant should shed most of its liquid, a process that should take about 15 minutes and one which you can encourage by gently squeezing the pieces.

4. Chop the eggplant flesh very fine and combine it in a bowl with the bread crumbs, parsley, garlic, egg, grated Parmesan, salt, and pepper. Mix thoroughly to obtain a uniform blend of ingredients. Taste and correct for salt and pepper. Shape the mixture with your hands into a number of patties about 2 inches in diameter and ½ inch thick, spreading them out on the counter or on a platter.

5. Pour enough vegetable oil into a frying pan to come ½ inch up the sides, and turn on the heat to high. When the oil is very hot, turn the patties on both sides in the flour, and slip them into the pan. Do not put in any more at one time than will fit loosely, without crowding the pan. When they have formed a nice dark crust on one side, turn them, do the other side, then use a slotted spoon or spatula to transfer them to a cooling rack to drain or to a platter lined with paper towels. Taste to correct for salt. Serve either hot or lukewarm.

Variation 1, with Onion and Tomatoes

The fried patties made using
    the basic recipe above
1½ cups onion sliced very fine
⅓ cup extra virgin olive oil
1½ cups canned imported
    Italian plum tomatoes,
    chopped, with their juice

Salt
Black pepper, ground fresh
    from the mill

1. Choose a sauté pan that can subsequently contain all the patties snugly, but without overlapping. Put in the onion and the olive oil, and turn on the heat to medium low. Cook the onion, stirring, until it becomes colored a deep gold, then add the chopped tomatoes. Continue to cook until the oil floats free from the tomatoes, about 20 minutes. Add salt and pepper, and stir thoroughly.

2. Add the fried eggplant patties to the pan. Turn them a few times in the onion and tomato sauce, and when they are completely reheated through and through, transfer the entire contents of the pan to a warm platter and serve at once.

Eggplant Patties (continued)

Variation 2, Baked with Mozzarella

The fried patties made using the basic recipe above

An oven-to-table baking dish

Butter for greasing the baking dish

Mozzarella, preferably buffalo-milk mozzarella, cut into as many ¼-inch slices as there are eggplant patties to cover

1. Preheat oven to 400°.

2. Choose a baking dish that can accommodate all the patties without overlapping, smear it with butter, and put in the fried eggplant patties. Cover each patty with a slice of mozzarella.

3. Place the dish on the uppermost rack of the preheated oven. When the mozzarella melts, take the dish out of the oven and bring to the table promptly.

Baked Escarole Torta

IN ITALIAN this might be called a pizza—*pizza di scarola*—but *torta,* "pie," is a more accurate name for it.

Escarole is related to chicory, with crisp, open, wavy leaves that form a pale green at their ruffled tips and fade to a creamy white at the base. While rather bland when raw, it acquires an appealingly tart, earthy taste cooked. (See the soup on page 90.) In the filling for this *torta,* escarole is sautéed with olive oil, garlic, olives, and capers, then anchovies and pine nuts are added. The shell is a simplified, savory bread dough that goes through one rising. The traditional shortening for the dough is lard, which produces the finest texture, but if the choice of lard causes concern, you can substitute olive oil. The 10-inch pan I like to use yields a *torta* about 2 inches deep.

For 8 servings

FOR THE DOUGH

2⅔ cups unbleached flour

1 teaspoon salt

Black pepper, ground fresh from the mill

⅓ package active dry yeast, dissolved in 1 cup luke-warm water

2 tablespoons lard, softened well at room temperature, OR 3 tablespoons extra virgin olive oil

FOR THE FILLING

3 pounds fresh escarole
Salt
⅓ cup extra virgin olive oil
2 teaspoons chopped garlic
3 tablespoons capers, soaked
    and rinsed as described on
    page 16 if packed in salt,
    drained if in vinegar
10 black, round Greek olives,
    pitted and each cut into 4
    pieces

7 flat anchovy fillets (prefer-
    ably the ones prepared
    at home as described on
    page 9), cut into
    ½-inch pieces
3 tablespoons *pignoli* (pine
    nuts)

TO BAKE THE TORTA

Wax paper OR kitchen parch-
    ment

A 10-inch springform pan
Butter for smearing the pan

1. To make the dough, pour the flour onto a work surface and shape it into a mound. Make a hollow in the center of the mound and put into it the salt, a few grindings of pepper, the dissolved yeast, and the softened lard or olive oil. Knead it for about 8 minutes. It is best if the dough is kept soft, but if you have difficulty handling it, either add another tablespoon or two of flour, or knead it in the food processor.

2. Shape the kneaded dough into a ball, and put it into a lightly floured bowl. Cover the bowl with a damp, doubled-up cloth towel, and put in a warm, protected corner of the kitchen until the dough has doubled in bulk, about 1 to 1½ hours.

3. Preheat oven to 375°.

4. While the dough is rising, prepare the filling. Trim the escarole of any bruised or discolored outer leaves, then cut it into 2-inch long pieces. Soak them in a basin filled with cold water, scooping them up, emptying the basin, refilling it with fresh water, and soaking them again, repeating the process 3 or 4 times.

5. Bring 3 to 4 quarts water to a boil, add salt, and drop in the escarole. Cook until tender, about 15 minutes, depending on its youth and freshness. Drain it and as soon as it is cool enough to handle, squeeze it gently to cause it to shed as much moisture as possible. Set it aside.

6. Put the olive oil and garlic in a large sauté pan, turn on the heat to medium, and cook the garlic, stirring, until it becomes colored a pale gold.

Baked Escarole Torta (continued)

Add the escarole, turning it over once or twice to coat it well. Reduce heat to medium low and cook for 10 minutes, turning the escarole from time to time. If the pan juices are watery, turn the heat up and reduce them quickly. Add the capers, turn them over with the escarole, then add the olives, turn over again, and remove from heat. Mix in the anchovies and pine nuts. Taste and correct for salt, then pour the entire contents of the pan into a bowl and set aside to cool.

7. When the dough has doubled in bulk, divide it into 2 unequal parts, one twice the size of the other. Roll out the larger piece of dough into a circular sheet large enough to line the bottom and sides of the springform pan. It should come out approximately ¼ inch thick. To simplify transferring this to the pan, roll out the dough on lightly floured wax paper or kitchen parchment.

8. Smear the inside of the springform pan with butter, pick up the wax paper or kitchen parchment with the sheet of dough on it, and turn it over onto the pan, covering the bottom and letting it come up the sides. Peel away the wax paper or parchment, and smooth the dough, flattening and evening off any particularly bulky creases with your fingers.

9. Pour all the escarole filling from the bowl into the pan, and level it off with a spatula.

10. Roll out the remaining piece of dough, employing the same method you used earlier. Lay it over the filling, covering it completely. Press the edge of the top sheet of bread dough against the edge of that lining the pan. Make a tight seal all around, folding any excess dough toward the center.

11. Place on the uppermost rack of the preheated oven and bake until the *torta* swells slightly, and the top becomes colored a pale gold, about 45 minutes. When you take it out of the oven, unlatch the pan's spring, and remove the hoop. Allow the *torta* to settle a few minutes before loosening it from the bottom and transferring it to a serving platter. Serve either lukewarm or at room temperature.

FINOCCHIO

Although there *is* an English equivalent for *finocchio*—Florence fennel—for many cooks it's the Italian word that has achieved everyday usage. Fennel is related to anise, but its cool, mild aroma has none of its kin's sharpness. People eat *finocchio* raw, in salads, but it is an exceptionally fine vegetable for braising, sautéing, gratinéing, and frying. The bulbous base is the part that is used, while the stems and leaves are usually discarded. When wild fennel is called for but not available, *finocchio*'s leafy tops are a tolerable substitute.

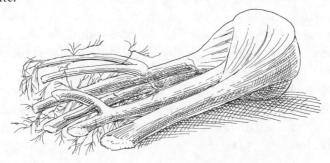

When and how to buy ❀ The best season for *finocchio,* when it is juiciest and its fragrance is sweetest and freshest, is from fall to spring, but it is also available in summer. Italians distinguish between male and female *finocchio,* the first with a stocky, round bulb, the latter flat and elongated. The "male" is crisper and less stringy, and it has a finer scent, qualities that are particularly desirable when it is to be eaten raw. For cooking, the flatter bulb is acceptable, but as long as it's equally fresh, the thicker, rounder one will always taste better.

Braised Finocchio with Olive Oil

For 4 servings

3 large *finocchi* OR 4 to 5 smaller ones

⅓ cup extra virgin olive oil
Salt

1. Cut the *finocchio* tops where they meet the bulb and discard them. Detach and discard any of the bulb's outer parts that may be bruised or discolored. Slice off about ⅛ inch from the butt end. Cut the bulb vertically into slices somewhat less than ½ inch thick. Wash the slices in several changes of cold water.

2. Put the *finocchio* and the olive oil in a large

saucepan, add just enough water to cover, and turn on the heat to medium. Do not put a lid on the pot. Cook, turning the slices over from time to time, until the *finocchio* becomes colored a glossy, pale gold and feels tender when prodded with a fork. Bear in mind that the butt end of the slice should be firm compared with the softer upper part of the slice. It should take between 25 and 40 minutes, depending on the freshness of the *finocchio*. If while cooking you find the liquid in the pan becoming insufficient, add up to ⅓ cup water. By the time the *finocchio* is done, all the water must be absorbed. Add salt, toss the slices once or twice, then transfer the contents of the pan to a warm platter and serve at once.

Variation with Butter and Parmesan

Omit the olive oil in the ingredients list of the preceding recipe, and add ¼ cup butter and 3 tablespoons freshly grated *parmigiano-reggiano* cheese. Follow the cooking procedure described in the recipe above, substituting butter for the olive oil. When the *finocchio* is done, sprinkle with salt, add the grated Parmesan, toss three or four times, then serve at once.

Breaded Fried Finocchio

For 4 to 6 servings

3 *finocchi*
2 eggs
1½ cups unflavored bread
    crumbs, lightly toasted,
    spread on a plate

Vegetable oil
Salt

1. Trim, slice, and wash the *finocchio* as described in Braised Finocchio with Olive Oil, page 503.

2. Bring 3 quarts of water to a boil, then drop in the sliced *finocchio*. Cook at a moderate boil until the butt end of the slice feels tender, but firm when prodded with a fork. Drain, and set aside to cool.

3. Beat the eggs with a fork in a deep dish or small bowl.

4. Dip the cooled, parboiled *finocchio* slices in the beaten egg, letting excess egg flow back into the dish, then turn it in the bread crumbs, coating both sides. Press the bread crumbs onto each slice with the palm of your hand until your hand feels dry and the crumbs are sticking firmly to the *finocchio*.

5. Pour enough oil into a frying pan to come ½ inch up the sides. When you think the oil is quite hot, test it by dipping into it the end of one of the slices. If it sizzles, the oil is ready for frying. Slip as many slices of *finocchio* into the pan as will fit loosely without overlapping. Cook until they form a crisp, golden brown crust on one side, then turn them and do the other side. When both sides are done, use a slotted spoon or spatula to transfer them to a cooling rack to drain or to a platter lined with paper towels. Repeat the procedure until all the *finocchio* is done. Sprinkle with salt and serve at once.

Sautéed Mixed Greens with Olive Oil and Garlic

THIS SOFT MIXTURE of greens is meant to be spread over wedges of *piadina,* the flat griddle bread on page 641, but it is so immensely satisfying that you should try it as a side dish on its own or with sausages or alongside any roast of pork.

A combination of both mild and slightly bitter greens is necessary to the successful balance of the mixture. Savoy cabbage and spinach are the mild components, *cime di rapa,* the bitter. For the spinach you can substitute Swiss chard. For *cime di rapa*—the long clusters of stalks with skinny leaves, topped with pale yellow buds, available from fall to spring—substitute Catalonia chicory or dandelion greens or other bitter field greens with which you may be acquainted.   *For 6 servings*

1 pound fresh spinach OR Swiss chard
½ pound *cime di rapa,* also called *rapini* or *broccoletti di rapa*
1-pound head Savoy cabbage

Salt
¼ cup extra virgin olive oil
1 tablespoon chopped garlic
Black pepper, ground fresh from the mill

1. Snap off the thicker, older stems from the spinach leaves, or detach the broadest, more mature stalks from the Swiss chard and soak either green in a

Sautéed Mixed Greens (continued)

basin filled with cold water. Scoop up the spinach or chard, empty out the water together with any soil, refill the basin with fresh cold water, and put the green back in to soak. Repeat the operation several times until you find no more soil settling to the bottom of the basin.

2. In a separate basin soak the *cime di rapa* in exactly the same manner.

3. Pull off and discard the darkest outer leaves of the Savoy cabbage. Cut off the butt end of the stem, and cut the head into 4 parts.

4. Bring 3 to 4 quarts water to a boil, add 1 tablespoon salt, and put in the *cime di rapa.* Put a lid on the pot, setting it ajar, and cook until tender, about 8 to 12 minutes, depending on the green's freshness and youth. Drain and set aside. Refill the pot with fresh water, and if using Swiss chard, cook it in the same manner. After draining the chard, refill the pot and cook the cabbage using the same procedure, *except* that you must omit the salt. Cook the cabbage until the thickest part of the head is easily pierced by a fork, about 15 to 20 minutes.

5. If using spinach, cook it in a covered pan with ½ tablespoon salt and just the moisture that clings to its leaves from the soak. Cook until tender, about 10 minutes or more, depending on the spinach. Drain and set aside.

6. Gently but firmly squeeze all the moisture you can out of all the greens. Chop them together to a rather coarse consistency.

Ahead-of-time note ✽ You can cook and prepare the greens up to this point several hours in advance of the time you are going to serve them. Do not keep overnight, and do not refrigerate.

7. Put the oil and garlic in a large sauté pan, and turn on the heat to medium. Cook and stir the garlic until it becomes colored a very pale gold, then put in all the chopped greens. Add salt and pepper and turn them over completely 3 or 4 times to coat them well. Cook for 10 to 15 minutes, turning the greens frequently. Taste and correct for salt. Serve promptly.

Braised Leeks with Parmesan Cheese

A FAVORITE with Italians from Roman times and earlier, the leek is often a part of soups, or of the vegetable background of some meat dishes. But this subtle relative of onion and garlic has merits enough to deserve a featured role, as in the preparation described below. As a tasty variant, you can follow exactly the same procedure using scallions in place of leeks. *For 4 servings*

4 large OR 6 medium leeks

3 tablespoons butter

Salt

3 tablespoons freshly grated
parmigiano-reggiano cheese

1. Pull off any yellow or withered leaves from the leeks. Trim away the roots from the bulbous end. Do not cut off the green tops. Cut each leek lengthwise in two. Wash the leeks very thoroughly under cold running water, spreading the tops with your hands to make sure any hidden bits of grit are washed away.

2. Put the leeks in a pan just broad or long enough so that they can lie flat and straight. Add the butter, salt, and enough water to cover, put a lid on the pan, and turn on the heat to medium low. Cook until the thickest part of the leeks feels tender when prodded with a fork, about 15 to 25 minutes, depending on the vegetable's youth and freshness. Turn them from time to time while they cook.

3. When done, uncover the pan, turn the heat up to high, and boil away all the watery juices in the pan. In the process the leeks should become lightly browned. Before removing from heat, add the grated Parmesan, turn the leeks over once or twice, then transfer to a warm platter and serve at once.

Smothered Boston Lettuce with Pancetta

For 4 servings

1½ pounds Boston lettuce

2 tablespoons vegetable oil

½ cup onion chopped fine

⅓ cup *pancetta* chopped fine

Salt

1. Detach all the leaves from the lettuce heads, saving the hearts to use raw in a salad. Soak the leaves in a basin filled with cold water. Scoop up the lettuce, empty out the water together with any soil, refill the basin with fresh cold water, and put the leaves back in to soak. Repeat the operation several times until you find no more soil settling to the bottom of the basin.

2. When you have drained the leaves for the last time, shake off all the water, either using a salad spinner or gathering them in a cloth towel and snapping it sharply 3 or 4 times.

3. Tear or cut each leaf into 2 or 3 pieces, depending on its size, and set them aside.

4. Put the oil, onion, and *pancetta* in a sauté pan, turn the heat on to

Smothered Boston Lettuce (continued)

medium, and cook the onion, stirring from time to time, until it becomes colored a deep gold.

5. Put in as many of the lettuce pieces as will not overfill the pan. If the lettuce doesn't all fit at first, you can add the rest when the first batch has cooked briefly and diminished in bulk. Add salt, cover the pan, and cook until the central rib of the leaves just reaches tenderness, about 30 to 40 minutes. Turn the lettuce over from time to time as it cooks. When it is done, if the juices in the pan are watery, remove the cover, raise the heat to high, and boil them away quickly. Serve promptly. Do not reheat or refrigerate.

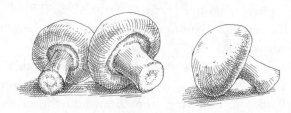

MUSHROOMS

Nearly all the fresh mushrooms available for cooking today are cultivated. The wild *boletus edulis*—Italy's highly prized *porcini*—has the richest flavor of any mushroom, but it is rarely found fresh in markets outside Italy and France. It is, however, widely distributed in dried form, and when properly reconstituted as described on page 27, its intense fragrance adds a powerful fillip to the flavor of sauces, of some soups and meats, and of dishes with fresh, cultivated mushrooms. Among the cultivated varieties available fresh, the following are the most useful in Italian cooking:

White mushrooms ❀ It is, by an overwhelming margin, the most common market mushroom. In Italy it goes either by the French name *champignon,* or its Italian equivalent, *prataiolo,* both words meaning "of the field." It is claimed that size does not affect taste, but I find the texture of the small, young mushroom called "button" to be distinctly superior to that of the more mature, larger examples.

Cremini ❀ This light- to dark-brown mushroom was the one cultivated variety available long before the white mushroom was developed. It has more depth of flavor than the white, but it is also more expensive. If cost is not a consideration, it can be used with success in any recipe that calls for white button mushrooms.

Shiitake ✿ The stems of this brown Japanese variety are too tough to use, but the caps give marvelous results when cooked by the method applied in Italy to fresh *porcini.*

How to buy and store ✿ Look for firmness as an indication of freshness, and avoid flabbiness, which is a signal of staleness. When buying white button or *cremini* mushrooms, choose those with smooth, closed caps, whereas the caps of *shiitake* are always open. Do not store mushrooms in plastic, which accelerates their absorption of moisture and deterioration, but in paper bags. If very fresh, they will stay in good condition in a refrigerator or a in a cold room in winter for 2 or 3 days.

Sautéed Mushrooms with Olive Oil, Garlic, and Parsley: Two Methods

THE CLASSIC flavor base for mushrooms in Italy is olive oil, garlic, and parsley. When mushrooms, or other vegetables, are sliced thin and cooked on such a base, they are known as *trifolati,* prepared in the manner of truffles.

The two methods that follow here both rest on the same traditional foundation of flavor, but differ in their objectives and results. The first has a more conservative approach, aiming at preserving firmness and texture. The second version is more radical, mixing white mushrooms with dried *porcini,* and cooking them slowly, as one would fresh wild *boletus,* bestowing on standard market mushrooms the musky aroma and the silky softness of *porcini.*

Method 1

For 6 servings

1½ pounds fresh, firm, white button OR *cremini* mushrooms

1½ teaspoons garlic chopped very fine

½ cup extra virgin olive oil

Salt

Black pepper, ground fresh from the mill

3 tablespoons parsley chopped very fine

1. Slice off and discard a thin disk from the butt end of the mushrooms' stem without detaching the stem from the cap. Wash the mushrooms rapidly in cold running water, taking care not to let them soak. Pat gently,

Sautéed Mushrooms, Method 1 (continued)

but thoroughly dry with a soft cloth towel. Cut them lengthwise into slices ¼ inch thick keeping stems and caps together.

2. Choose a sauté pan that can subsequently accommodate the mushrooms without crowding them, put in the garlic and olive oil, and turn on the heat to medium high. Cook and stir the garlic until it becomes colored a pale gold, then add all the mushrooms and turn up the heat to high.

3. When the mushrooms have soaked up all the oil, add salt and pepper, turn the heat down to low, and shake the pan to toss the mushrooms, or stir with a wooden spoon. As soon as the mushrooms shed their juices, which will happen very quickly, turn the heat up to high again and boil those juices away for 4 to 5 minutes, stirring frequently.

4. Taste and correct for salt. Add the chopped parsley, stir well once or twice, then transfer the contents of the pan to a warm platter, and serve at once.

Note ✸ If you allow the mushrooms to cool down to room temperature they will make an excellent *antipasto*. They can be served as part of a buffet or on their own, on thin slices of grilled or toasted bread.

Method 2

For 6 servings

To the ingredients in the preceding recipe add:

A small packet OR 1 ounce dried *porcini* mushrooms, reconstituted as described on page 27 and cut up

The filtered water from the mushroom soak, see page 28 for instructions

1. Trim, wash, towel-dry, and slice the white mushrooms as described in Step 1 of the preceding recipe.

2. Choose a sauté pan that can subsequently contain all the ingredients without crowding, put in the garlic and oil, and turn on the heat to medium. Cook and stir the garlic until it becomes colored a pale gold, then add the chopped parsley. Stir rapidly once or twice, add the chopped, reconstituted dried *porcini,* stir once or twice again to coat well, then add the filtered water from the *porcini* soak. Turn up the heat and cook at a lively pace until all the water has simmered away.

3. Add the sliced fresh mushrooms to the pan, together with salt and pepper, turn them over completely once or twice, turn the heat down to low,

and cover the pan. Cook, stirring occasionally, for 25 to 30 minutes, until the fresh mushrooms become very soft and dark. If, when they are done, the pan juices are still watery, uncover, raise the heat to high, and quickly boil them away. Transfer the contents of the pan to a warm platter, and serve at once.

Fresh Mushrooms with Porcini, Rosemary, and Tomatoes

For 4 to 6 servings

1 pound fresh, firm, white button OR *cremini* mush-rooms
⅓ cup extra virgin olive oil
1 teaspoon chopped garlic
Chopped rosemary leaves,
 1 teaspoon if fresh,
 ½ teaspoon if dried
A small packet OR 1 ounce dried *porcini* mushrooms, reconstituted as described on page 27 and cut up

The filtered water from the mushroom soak, see page 28 for instructions
Salt
Black pepper, ground fresh from the mill
½ cup canned imported Italian plum tomatoes, cut up, with their juice

1. Trim, wash, and towel-dry the fresh mushrooms as described in Step 1 of the recipe on page 509. Cut them lengthwise in half, or if large, in quarters, keeping the caps attached to the stems.
2. Choose a sauté pan that can subsequently contain all the ingredients loosely, put in the oil and garlic, and turn on the heat to medium high. Cook and stir the garlic until it becomes colored a pale gold, then add the rosemary and the chopped, reconstituted dried *porcini*. Stir once or twice again to coat well, then add the filtered water from the *porcini* soak. Turn the heat up and cook at a lively pace until all the water has simmered away.
3. Add the cut-up fresh mushrooms to the pan, together with salt and pepper, turn the heat up to high, and cook, stirring frequently, until the liquid shed by the fresh mushrooms has simmered away.
4. Add the tomatoes with their juice, toss thoroughly to coat well, cover the pan, and turn the heat down to low. Cook for about 10 minutes. If while cooking there should not be sufficient liquid in the pan to keep the mushrooms from sticking to the bottom, add 1 or 2 tablespoons of water, as

Fresh Mushrooms with Porcini, Rosemary and Tomatoes (continued)

needed. When done, transfer the contents of the pan to a warm platter and serve at once.

Fried Breaded Mushrooms, Tuscan Style

For 4 servings

¾ pound fresh, firm, white button OR *cremini* mushrooms
1 jumbo OR 2 smaller eggs
Black pepper, ground fresh from the mill

1½ cups unflavored bread crumbs, lightly toasted, spread on a plate
Vegetable oil
Salt

1. Trim, wash, and towel-dry the mushrooms as described in Step 1 of the recipe on page 509. Cut them into lengthwise sections about ¾ inch thick, or into halves if they are very small, keeping the caps attached to the stems.

2. Break the eggs into a deep dish or small bowl, add a few grindings of pepper, and beat lightly with a fork.

3. Dip the mushroom pieces in the beaten egg, letting excess egg flow back into the dish, then dredge them in the bread crumbs, coating both sides.

4. Pour enough oil into a frying pan to come ½ inch up the sides. When you think the oil is quite hot, test it by dipping into it one of the mushroom sections. If it sizzles, the oil is ready for frying. Slip as many pieces into the pan as will fit loosely without overlapping. Cook until they form a crisp, golden brown crust on one side, then turn them and do the other side. When both sides are done, use a slotted spoon or spatula to transfer them to a cooling rack to drain or to a platter lined with paper towels. Repeat the procedure until all the mushrooms are done. Sprinkle with salt and serve at once.

Sautéed Shiitake Mushroom Caps, Porcini Style

WHEN THEIR CAPS are sautéed slowly in olive oil and garlic as described below, *shiitake*—better than other market mushrooms—develop a flavor reminiscent of the forest scent of fresh *porcini*.

For 4 servings as a main course, 6 to 8 as a side dish

2 pounds fresh *shiitake* mushrooms with large caps	Black pepper, ground fresh from the mill
⅓ cup extra virgin olive oil	1 tablespoon chopped garlic
Salt	2 tablespoons chopped parsley

1. Detach the mushroom caps from the stems and discard the stems. Wash the caps quickly in running cold water without letting them soak. Pat dry gently, but thoroughly with a cloth towel.

2. Choose a skillet that can accommodate all the mushroom caps snugly, but without overlapping. (If necessary, use two pans, in which case increase the olive oil to ½ cup.) Coat the bottom of the pan with a few drops of olive oil, tilting the pan to spread it evenly. Put in the mushroom caps, top sides facing up, and turn on the heat to medium low.

3. After about 8 minutes, turn the caps over and sprinkle them with salt and pepper. When you find that the mushrooms have shed liquid, turn up the heat for as long as necessary to simmer the liquid away. When there are no more watery juices in the pan, turn the heat down again, sprinkle the caps with garlic and parsley, pour over them the remaining olive oil, and continue to cook for about 5 more minutes, until the mushrooms feel tender when prodded with a fork. Serve promptly with the oil, garlic, and parsley remaining in the pan.

Mushroom Timballo

A *timballo* is a traditional Italian mold, drum-like in shape. The name also applies to the dish cooked in that mold, and there are as many kinds of *timballi* as there are things that can be minced, sauced, and baked.

In this elegant and savory monument to the mushroom, the caps and stems are cooked separately. The caps are breaded and fried crisp, some are used to line the bottom of the mold, some to crown the *timballo,* and others in between. The stems, cooked with tomatoes and reconstituted dried *porcini,* are part of the filling, where they alternate with layers of fried caps and cheese. *For 6 to 8 servings*

Mushroom Timballo (continued)

A small packet OR 1 ounce
  dried *porcini* mushrooms,
  reconstituted as described
  on page 27
The filtered water from the
  mushroom soak, see page
  28 for instructions
2 pounds fresh, firm, white
  button OR *cremini* mushrooms with good-size,
  tightly closed caps
2 eggs
Unflavored bread crumbs,
  lightly toasted, spread on a
  plate
1¼ cups vegetable oil

⅓ cup extra virgin olive oil
½ teaspoon garlic chopped fine
2 tablespoons chopped parsley
Salt
Black pepper, ground fresh
  from the mill
½ cup canned imported Italian
  plum tomatoes, drained
  and chopped fine
A 1-quart ceramic soufflé mold
Butter for smearing the mold
½ pound imported *fontina* or
  Gruyère cheese, sliced thin
½ cup freshly grated
  parmigiano-reggiano cheese

1. Put the reconstituted mushrooms and their filtered water in a small saucepan, and turn on the heat to medium. When all the liquid has simmered away, take off heat and set aside for later.

2. Wash the fresh mushrooms quickly under cold running water, separate the caps from the stems, and pat both thoroughly dry with a soft cloth towel.

3. To even off and flatten the bottoms of the caps, cut off a thin slice straight across their base. These slices will look like rings. Cut them in two and set aside, leaving the caps whole. Cut the stems lengthwise into the thinnest possible slices, and set them aside, combining them with the slices cut from the bottom of the caps.

4. Break the eggs into a deep dish and beat them lightly with a fork. Dip the mushroom caps in the egg, letting the excess flow back into the dish as you pull them out. Turn them in the bread crumbs, coating them all over, and tapping the crumbs with your fingers against the mushrooms to make them stick firmly.

5. When all the caps have been breaded, put half the vegetable oil in a small frying pan, and turn on the heat to medium high. When the oil is hot, slip the caps into the pan, no more at one time than will fit very loosely. When they have formed a fine, golden crust on one side, turn them, do the other side, then transfer them to a cooling rack to drain or to a platter lined with paper towels. After you have done half the caps, the oil in the pan will prob-ably have turned black from the bread crumbs. Turn off the heat, carefully

pour out the hot oil into whatever container you keep waste oil in, and wipe the pan clean with paper towels. Put in the remaining vegetable oil, turn the heat on again to medium high, and finish frying the caps.

6. Preheat oven to 350°.

7. Put the olive oil and the garlic in a sauté pan, and turn on the heat to medium. Cook and stir the garlic until it becomes colored a pale gold, then put in the sliced mushroom stems and the chopped parsley. Turn the heat up to medium high, and cook for about 5 minutes, turning the mushrooms over frequently.

8. Add the cooked, reconstituted *porcini* mushrooms, a few pinches of salt, and several grindings of pepper. Stir once or twice, then put in the chopped tomatoes. Continue cooking, stirring from time to time, until the oil floats free of the tomatoes. Taste and correct for salt and pepper, and take off heat.

Ahead-of-time note ✸ You can prepare the *timballo* up to this point several hours in advance. Warm up the mushroom stems and tomatoes slightly before proceeding with the next step.

9. Smear the bottom of the soufflé dish with butter, and cover it with a layer of the fried mushroom caps, their bottoms (the underside) facing up. Sprinkle with salt, cover with a layer of sliced *fontina* or Gruyère, spread over it some of the mushroom stems and tomato mixture, then top with a sprinkling of grated Parmesan. Repeat the procedure in the same sequence, beginning with a layer of mushroom caps. Leave yourself enough mushroom caps to top the *timballo,* their bottoms always facing up. They will be facing right side up later, after you invert the *timballo.*

10. Place the dish in the upper third of the preheated oven and bake for 25 minutes.

11. Let the dish settle out of the oven for 10 minutes, then run a knife all around the sides of the mold to loosen the *timballo.* Put a dinner plate, bottom up, over the top of the mold. Grasp the plate and mold with a towel, holding them together tightly, and turn the mold upside down. Lift the mold away to leave the *timballo* standing on the plate. Let cool another 5 to 10 minutes before serving.

Sweet and Sour Onions

THE SECRET INGREDIENT in this delectable combination of tartness and sweetness is merely the patience it takes to nurse the onions through an hour or more of slow simmering. The actual preparation couldn't be simpler. If you can put it on while you are producing something else in the kitchen, you will find it well worth the time it demands, because there are few other vegetable dishes that please so many palates and that are a becoming adornment to so large a variety of meats and fowl.

For 6 servings

3 pounds small white boiling
    onions
4 tablespoons (½ stick) butter
2½ tablespoons good-quality
    wine vinegar

2 teaspoons sugar
Salt
Black pepper, ground fresh
    from the mill

1. Bring 3 quarts of water to a boil, drop in the onions, count to 15, then drain them. As soon as they are cool enough to handle, pull off the outside skin, detach any roots, and cut a cross into the butt end. Do not peel off any of the layers, do not trim the tops, handle the onions as little as possible so that they will remain compact and hold together during their long cooking.

2. Choose a sauté pan that can contain all the onions snugly, but without overlapping. Put in the onions, butter, enough water to come no more than 1 inch up the sides of the pan, and turn the heat on to medium. Turn the onions from time to time as they cook, adding 2 tablespoons of water whenever the liquid in the pan becomes insufficient.

3. In 20 minutes or so, when the onions begin to soften, add the vinegar, sugar, salt, and pepper, give the onions one or two complete turns, and turn the heat down to low. Continue to cook for 1 hour or more, adding a tablespoon or two of water whenever it becomes necessary. Turn the onions from time to time. They are done when they become colored a rich, dark, golden brown all over, and are easily pierced when prodded with a fork. Serve promptly with all the pan juices.

Ahead-of-time note ❧ Although the onions taste their best when cooked just before serving, they can be completely done several hours in advance. Reheat over slow heat adding 1 or 2 tablespoons of water if needed.

Sautéed Early Peas with Olive Oil and Prosciutto, Florentine Style

For 4 to 6 servings

2 pounds unshelled fresh, young peas OR 1 ten-ounce package frozen tiny peas, thawed

2 garlic cloves, peeled

2 tablespoons extra virgin olive oil

2 tablespoons prosciutto OR for a less salty taste, *pancetta,* diced into ¼-inch cubes

2 tablespoons parsley chopped very fine

Black pepper, ground fresh from the mill

Salt

1. *If using fresh peas:* Shell them, and prepare some of the pods for cooking by stripping away their inner membrane, as described on page 93. Try to do about 1 cup of pods.

If using frozen peas: Proceed to the next step.

2. Put the garlic and the olive oil in a sauté pan, and turn on the heat to medium high. Cook and stir the garlic until it has become colored a light nut-brown, then take it out, and add the diced prosciutto or *pancetta.* Stir quickly 5 or 6 times, then put in the fresh peas with their stripped-down pods or the thawed frozen peas, and turn them over completely once or twice to coat well. Add the parsley and a few grindings of pepper, and, if you are using fresh peas, ¼ cup water. Turn the heat down to medium and put a lid on the pan. If using frozen peas, cook for 5 minutes.

If using fresh peas, it may take from 15 to 30 minutes, depending entirely on their youth and freshness. If the liquid in the pan becomes insufficient, replenish with 1 or 2 tablespoons water as needed. When the peas are done, there should be no water left in the pan. Should the pan juices be watery when the peas are cooked, uncover, turn up the heat, and simmer them away.

Taste and correct for salt, stir well, then turn the entire contents of the pan onto a warm platter and serve at once.

Mashed Potatoes with Milk
and Parmesan Cheese, Bolognese Style

For 4 to 6 servings

1 pound round, waxy, old
   boiling potatoes
A double boiler
3 tablespoons butter,
   cut up small

½ cup milk or more if needed
⅓ cup freshly grated
   parmigiano-reggiano cheese
Salt
Whole nutmeg

1. Put the unpeeled potatoes in a large saucepan, add enough water to cover amply, put a lid on the pot, bring to a moderate boil, and cook until the potatoes feel tender when prodded with a fork. Refrain from puncturing them too often, or they will become waterlogged. Drain and peel while still hot.

2. Put water in the lower half of a double boiler and bring it to a simmer. Put the butter in the upper half of the pot. Mash the potatoes through a food mill or a potato ricer directly onto the butter.

3. Put the milk in a small saucepan and bring it almost to a boil—to the point when it begins to form tiny, pearly bubbles. Take it off heat before it breaks into a boil.

4. Begin beating the potatoes steadily with a whisk, or a fork, adding to them 2 or 3 tablespoons of hot milk at a time. When you have used half the milk, beat in all the grated Parmesan. When you have incorporated the cheese smoothly into the potatoes, resume adding milk. Do not cease to beat, unless you must rest your arm occasionally for a few seconds.

The potatoes must turn into a very soft, fluffy mass, a state that requires constant beating and as much milk as the potatoes will absorb before becoming thin and runny. Some potatoes absorb less milk than others: You must judge, by appearance and taste, when you have put in enough.

5. When there is no milk left, or you have determined that no more can be absorbed by the potatoes, add salt to taste and a tiny grating of nutmeg—about ⅛ teaspoon—swirling to distribute both evenly. Spoon the mashed potatoes onto a warm plate and serve at once.

Ahead-of-time note ❦ If you are really prevented from serving the mashed potatoes the moment they are done, when they are at their best, you can finish them up to 1 hour in advance. When ready to serve, reheat over simmering water in the double boiler, beating in 2 or 3 tablespoons of very hot milk.

If you are making one of the croquette recipes that follow, you can make them several hours or a full day in advance.

Potato Croquettes
with Crisp-Fried Noodles

WHEN TINY BALLS of mashed potatoes are fried with a coating of crumbled thin noodles, they look like some kind of thistle. The contrast between the crisp noodle surface and soft potato interior makes the croquettes as appealing in taste as in appearance. *For 6 servings*

1 cup very thin noodles, angel hair or thinner, hand-crushed into ⅛-inch fragments
⅓ cup flour
1 egg yolk

The mashed potatoes made from the recipe on page 518 (also see Ahead-of-time note on page 518)
Vegetable oil

1. Combine the crumbled noodles and flour in a dish.

2. Mix the egg yolk into the mashed potatoes. Shape them into 1-inch balls and roll them in the crumbled noodles and flour.

3. Put enough oil in a skillet to come ¼ inch up its sides, and turn on the heat to high. When the oil is quite hot—it should sizzle when you put in a croquette—slip in as many potato balls at one time as will fit loosely, but without crowding the pan. Cook, turning them, until a brown-gold crust forms all around. Transfer with a slotted spoon or spatula to a cooling rack to drain or to a platter lined with paper towels. Repeat the procedure until all the croquettes are done, and serve while still piping hot.

Potato and Ham Croquettes, Romagna Style

For 6 servings

The mashed potatoes made from the recipe on page 518 (also see Ahead-of-time note on page 518)
1 egg plus 1 yolk

6 ounces prosciutto, chopped very fine
Vegetable oil
Flour, spread on a plate

Potato and Ham Croquettes (continued)

1. Combine the mashed potatoes with the egg, the additional yolk, and the chopped prosciutto, working the ingredients into a uniform mixture.

2. Shape the mixture into small patties about 2 inches across and no more than ½ inch thick.

3. Pour enough oil into a skillet to come ¼ inch up its sides and turn the heat on to high.

4. Dredge the patties in the flour, one patty at a time on both sides, lightly pressing it into the flour with your palm and shaking off the excess. When the oil is quite hot—it should sizzle when you put in a croquette—slip in as many potato patties at one time as will fit loosely without crowding the pan. Cook, turning them, until a brown-gold crust forms all around. Transfer with a slotted spoon or spatula to a cooling rack to drain or to a platter lined with paper towels. Repeat the procedure until all the croquettes are done, and serve while still piping hot.

Pan-Roasted Diced Potatoes

THE IDEAL ROAST potato has a thin, crackly crust sheathing an interior of the most yielding tenderness. Dicing the potatoes smaller than bite-size, as in this recipe, speeds up the process and multiplies the benefits by producing from each potato many soft centers, each with its perfectly crisp crust.

For 4 to 6 servings

1½ pounds round, waxy,	Vegetable oil
boiling potatoes	Salt

1. Peel the potatoes, dice them into ½-inch cubes, wash them in two changes of cold water, and pat them dry with a cloth towel.

2. Choose a skillet that can accommodate all the potatoes fairly loosely, pour in enough oil to come ½ inch up its sides, and turn on the heat to medium high. As soon as the oil becomes hot enough to sizzle when you drop in a single potato dice, put in all the diced potatoes. Turn the heat down to medium and cook at a moderate pace until the potatoes feel tender when prodded with a fork, but are still pale, not having yet formed a crust. Take the pan off heat, remove the potatoes from the pan, using a slotted spoon or spatula, and allow them to cool completely. Do not empty out the oil from the pan.

Ahead-of-time note ✿ You can prepare the potatoes up to this point an hour or two in advance.

3. When you are nearly ready to serve, put the skillet with the oil over high heat, and when the oil is very hot, put the potatoes back in. Cook them until they form a light nut-brown crust on all sides, sprinkle with salt, transfer to a warm platter with a slotted spoon or spatula, and serve at once.

Baked Potatoes, Onion, and Tomatoes, Apulian Style

For 6 servings

2 pounds potatoes
2 cups onion sliced very thin
1 pound fresh, ripe, firm
    tomatoes, skinned raw with
    a peeler, all seeds removed,
    and cut into small dice
¾ cup freshly grated *romano*
    cheese (see page 32)
Oregano, 1½ teaspoons if fresh,
    ¾ teaspoon if dried

Salt
Black pepper, ground fresh
    from the mill
⅓ cup extra virgin olive oil
An oven-to-table baking dish,
    13 by 9 inches, or one of
    comparable size

1. Preheat oven to 400°.
2. Peel the potatoes, wash them in cold water, and cut them into slices no thicker than ¼ inch.
3. Put the potatoes in a bowl together with the onion, tomato, grated cheese, oregano, salt, pepper, and ½ cup water. Toss several times to mix the ingredients well.
4. Use about 1 tablespoon of olive oil to smear the baking dish. Turn out the entire contents of the bowl into the dish, and level off. Pour in the remaining olive oil.
5. Place the dish on the uppermost rack of the preheated oven and bake for about 1 hour, until the potatoes feel very tender when prodded with a fork. Turn the potatoes over every 20 minutes or so. After taking the dish out of the oven, let it settle for about 10 minutes before bringing to the table. The potatoes should be served warm, but not scalding hot.

Sliced Potatoes Baked with Porcini and Fresh Cultivated Mushrooms, Riviera Style

For 4 servings

A small packet OR 1 ounce dried *porcini* mushrooms, reconstituted as described on page 27

The filtered water from the mushroom soak, see page 28 for instructions

1 pound small, new, waxy, boiling potatoes

½ pound fresh, firm, white button OR *cremini* mushrooms

An oven-to-table baking dish, no larger than 11 inches by 7 inches or its equivalent

⅓ cup extra virgin olive oil

2 teaspoons garlic chopped very fine

2 tablespoons chopped parsley

Black pepper, ground fresh from the mill

Salt

1. Put the reconstituted mushrooms and their filtered water into a small saucepan, turn on the heat to medium high, and cook until all the liquid has boiled away. Set aside.

2. Preheat oven to 400°.

3. Peel the potatoes, or if very new rub their skins off, wash them in cold water, and cut them into ¼-inch slices.

4. Slice off and discard a thin disk from the butt end of the fresh mushrooms' stem without detaching the stem from the cap. Wash the mushrooms rapidly in cold running water, taking care not to let them soak. Pat gently, but thoroughly dry with a soft cloth towel. Cut them lengthwise into slices the same thickness as the potatoes, keeping stems and caps together.

5. Choose a baking dish in which all the ingredients will fit without being stacked any higher than 1½ inches. Put in the olive oil, garlic, potatoes, the *porcini* and the sliced, fresh mushrooms, the parsley, and several grindings of pepper. Toss several times to mix the ingredients evenly, and level them off with a spatula or the back of a spoon. Place the dish on the uppermost rack of the preheated oven. Bake for 15 minutes, then add salt, toss to distribute it well, return the dish to the oven and continue baking until the potatoes are tender, approximately another 15 minutes.

6. After taking the dish out of the oven, let it settle for a few minutes before bringing it to the table. If you find there is more oil in the dish than you'd like, spoon away the excess before serving.

Potatoes with Onions, Tomatoes, and Sweet Pepper

HERE IS A DISH that is as hearty and satisfying as a meat stew, without the meat. It begs for good, crusty bread to sop up the delicious juices.

For 6 servings

1 sweet yellow bell pepper
2 cups onion sliced very thin
⅓ cup extra virgin olive oil
1½ cups fresh, firm ripe toma-
    toes, peeled and chopped,
    OR canned, imported Italian
    plum tomatoes, cut up,
    with their juice

Black pepper, ground fresh
    from the mill
1½ pounds round, waxy,
    boiling potatoes
Salt

1. Split the pepper open, remove the seeds and pulpy core, and peel it, using a swiveling-blade peeler. Cut it lengthwise into ½-inch-wide strips.

2. Choose a sauté pan that can accommodate all the ingredients, put in the onions and the olive oil, and turn on the heat to medium. Cook, stirring, until the onions wilt and become colored a light gold, then put in the yellow pepper. Cook the pepper for 3 or 4 minutes, stirring occasionally, then add the cut-up tomatoes with their juice, adjusting the heat to cook at a slow, but steady simmer.

3. While the tomatoes are cooking, peel the potatoes, wash them in cold water, and cut them into 1-inch cubes.

4. When the oil floats free of the tomatoes, add the potatoes, turn the heat down to very low, and cover the pan. Cook until the potatoes feel tender when prodded with a fork, about 30 minutes, depending on the potatoes. While cooking, turn the contents of the pan over from time to time. Add several grindings of black pepper, taste and correct for seasoning, and serve at once.

Ahead-of-time note ❀ The dish can be prepared entirely a day in advance. Reheat gently and thoroughly in a covered pan.

Pan-Roasted Potatoes
with Anchovies, Genoa Style

For 6 servings

1½ pounds round, waxy,
    boiling potatoes
2 flat anchovy fillets (preferably
    the ones prepared at home
    as described on page 9)
3 tablespoons extra virgin
    olive oil

2 tablespoons butter
Black pepper, ground fresh
    from the mill
Salt
1 teaspoon chopped garlic
3 tablespoons chopped parsley

1. Peel the potatoes and cut them into ¼-inch-thick slices. Soak the slices in a bowl of cold water for 15 minutes, drain them, and pat thoroughly dry with a cloth towel.

2. Choose a sauté pan that can subsequently contain the potato slices stacked about 1½ inches high. Chop the anchovies to a pulp, put them in the pan together with the oil and butter, turn on the heat to very low, and cook the anchovies, using the back of a wooden spoon to mash them against the sides of the pan, until they begin to dissolve.

3. Add the sliced potatoes and a few grindings of pepper. Turn the potatoes over completely 2 or 3 times to coat them well. Turn the heat up to medium, cover the pan, and turn the potatoes occasionally while they cook. After about 8 minutes, uncover, and continue cooking, turning the potato slices from time to time, until they are tender and form a very light brown crust, another 15 minutes or so.

4. Taste and correct for salt, add the garlic and parsley, turn the potatoes over several times, then transfer the contents of the pan to a warm platter and serve at once.

Treviso Radicchio
with Bacon

OF THE SEVERAL varieties of red *radicchio* discussed in detail on pages 29–30, the sweetest, hence the most desirable for cooking, is the late-harvested one with spiky spear-like stalks that comes into season late in November. It is seldom seen outside Italy, where it is highly prized and rather expensive, so that one usually must turn to the elongated *variegato di Treviso*, whose shape resembles that of a small romaine lettuce. When even this kind is not available, one can use the far more common round Chioggia variety, preferably late in the year when it is less bitter.

Taste the *radicchio* raw: If you find it more bitter than you'd like, use ½ pound Belgian endive to 1 pound *radicchio,* a combination that will tip the balance toward milder flavor. *For 4 servings*

1½ pounds *radicchio*	Salt
1 tablespoon extra virgin olive oil	Black pepper, ground fresh from the mill
¼ pound bacon, cut into narrow strips	

1. If the *radicchio* root is very long, trim it down and pare the remaining stub all around to expose the tender core. Pull off and discard any blemished outer leaves. If using the elongated variety, or Belgian endive, cut it in half, lengthwise; if using round *radicchio,* cut it into 4 wedges. Make 3 or 4 parallel, lengthwise incisions in the root end. Wash in several changes of cold water, and spin or shake dry.

2. Choose a sauté pan or skillet that can subsequently accommodate all the *radicchio* and endive, if any, snugly, in a single layer. Put in the olive oil and bacon and turn on the heat to medium. Cook the bacon, turning it occasionally, until its fat dissolves, but without letting it become crisp.

3. Add the *radicchio* and optional endive, turn it over a few times to coat it well, turn the heat down to low, and cover the pan. Cook until the vegetable feels tender at the base when prodded with a fork, about 25 or 30 minutes, depending on its freshness. Turn it from time to time while it's cooking.

4. When done, add salt and pepper, turn it in the pan 2 or 3 times, then transfer the entire contents of the pan to a warm platter and serve at once.

Ahead-of-time note ❀ It's possible to cook the dish through to the end several hours in advance. Before serving, reheat gently, but thoroughly, in the pan or in the oven.

Baked Radicchio

The classic way of cooking *radicchio* is to grill it over charcoal or in a broiler, following the method used for grilling Belgian endive on pages 541–542. But grilling accentuates the bitterness of this vegetable, and one should restrict the procedure to the milder, elongated, late-harvested winter variety described on page 29. Baking in olive oil, on the other hand, is kinder to *radicchio,* and can be adopted even for the round, cabbage-like heads.

Baked Radicchio (continued)

If you wish, you can mitigate *radicchio*'s astringency by using it together with Belgian endive, 1 part of the latter to 2 parts of the former, as suggested in the immediately preceding recipe on page 525. Of course, you can replace *radicchio* altogether and use only Belgian endive, which you'll find to be quite delectable when cooked in this manner.   *For 6 servings*

About 2 pounds *radicchio,* preferably the long Treviso variety OR *radicchio* and endive, as suggested above	Salt Black pepper, ground fresh from the mill ⅓ cup extra virgin olive oil

1. Thirty minutes before you are ready to cook, preheat the oven to 400°.

2. Trim, split, score, wash, and shake dry the *radicchio,* or the Belgian endive, as described in the preceding recipe, page 525.

3. Choose a baking pan that can accommodate all the vegetable snugly in a single layer. Put it in with the cut side facing down, add salt and pepper, and all the oil, distributing it evenly.

4. Put the pan in the preheated oven. Turn the *radicchio* and optional endive over after 10 minutes, cook another 6 or 7 minutes, and turn it again. Cook it for about 10 minutes longer, until its base feels tender when prodded with a fork. Allow to settle a few minutes before serving. It is also good at room temperature.

Ahead-of-time note ❀ Baked *radicchio* can be made several hours in advance and reheated in the oven before serving.

Spinach Sautéed
with Olive Oil and Garlic

IF A SINGLE Italian vegetable dish deserves to be called classic, it is this version of spinach, which epitomizes the simplicity, directness, and heartiness that know no regional barrier and characterize good home cooking throughout the nation.

You should not easily settle for anything but fresh spinach, because that is what you really ought to have to achieve the flavor of which this dish is capable. On the other hand, if good, fresh spinach is not available, you can turn to frozen leaf spinach. However incomplete may be the satisfactions it brings, it is a tolerable alternative.   *For 6 servings*

2 pounds fresh, crisp spinach
   OR 2 ten-ounce packages
   frozen whole leaf spinach,
   thawed

Salt
2 large garlic cloves, peeled
¼ cup extra virgin olive oil

1. *If using fresh spinach:* If it is very young, snap off and discard just the hard end of the stems. If it is mature, or if you are in doubt, pull away and discard the entire stem. Soak and rinse the spinach leaves in several changes of cold water as described on page 89.

Cook the leaves in a covered pan with 1 tablespoon salt to keep their color bright and no more water than what clings to them from their soak. Cook until tender, about 10 minutes, depending on the spinach. Drain well, but do not squeeze it, and set aside.

If using thawed frozen spinach: Cook with a pinch of salt in a covered pan for 1 minute. Drain and set aside.

2. Put the garlic and olive oil in a skillet, and turn on the heat to medium high. Cook and stir the garlic until it becomes colored a nut brown, then take it out. Add the spinach, tasting and correcting it for salt. Cook for 2 minutes, turning it over completely several times to coat it well. Transfer the spinach with all its flavored oil to a warm platter, and serve at once.

Oven-Browned Tomatoes

IF YOU HAVE never seen how an Italian cook bakes tomatoes at home, you may be startled to find that these tomatoes cook down so long that they come out of the oven looking deflated and blackened around the edges. They are neither burnt nor dried out, however. They have shed the excess water that dilutes their flavor, and their juices are pure essence of tomato. They are delicious to eat on their own or together with other summer vegetables or with simple meat dishes. See serving suggestion on page 375.

For 4 to 6 servings

9 fresh, ripe, round tomatoes of
   medium size
3 tablespoons parsley chopped
   very fine
2 teaspoons garlic chopped very
   fine

Salt
Black pepper, ground fresh
   from the mill
3 tablespoons extra virgin olive
   oil

Oven-Browned Tomatoes (continued)

1. Preheat oven to 325°.

2. Wash the tomatoes and cut them in two at their widest point.

3. Choose a baking dish that can accommodate all the tomato halves snugly, but without overlapping. They can be squeezed in tightly because they will shrink considerably. Arrange them with their cut side facing up, and sprinkle them with the parsley, garlic, salt, and a few grindings of pepper. Pour the olive oil over them and place the dish on the uppermost rack of the preheated oven.

4. Cook for 1 hour or more, until the tomatoes have shrunk to little more than half their original size. The skins and sides of the pan should be partly blackened, but not burnt. Transfer to a serving platter, using a slotted spoon or spatula to leave the cooked oil behind. Serve hot, lukewarm, or at room temperature.

Fried Tomatoes

THERE IS no vegetable that does not take well to frying, and among them none that can surpass tomatoes. The combination of outer crispness and inner moistness that you can achieve only through this fastest of all cooking methods attains ideal proportions in a perfectly fried tomato.

For 4 servings

2 to 3 fresh, ripe, very firm, round tomatoes	Vegetable oil
	Salt
1 egg	
Flour, spread on a plate	
Unflavored bread crumbs, lightly toasted, spread on a plate	

1. Wash the tomatoes in cold water, and cut them horizontally into slices about ½ inch thick. Discard the tops. Gently pick out the seeds without squeezing the slices.

2. Beat the egg lightly in a deep dish or small bowl.

3. Turn the tomato slices over in flour, dip them in egg, letting the excess flow back into the dish, then dredge them in bread crumbs, coating both sides.

4. Pour enough oil in a skillet to come 1 inch up its sides, and turn on the heat to high. When the oil is very hot, slip in as many breaded slices of tomato as will fit loosely. When a dark, golden crust forms on one side, turn them and do the other side. Transfer them with a slotted spoon or spatula to a cooling rack to drain or to a platter lined with paper towels. Repeat the procedure until all the tomatoes are done. Sprinkle with salt and serve while piping hot.

ZUCCHINI

In appearance, zucchini is the most placid of vegetables. It has not the sensual furrows and crevices of the bell pepper, the bosomy exuberance of a ripe tomato, the playful ruffles of leafy greens. Yet it possesses more ways of beguiling the palate than can be counted. Riffle through Italian recipe books and everywhere you find zucchini, in appetizers, in pasta, in soup, in *risotto*, in *frittate*, in stews, and in vegetable dishes prepared by all the methods known to cooks. Zucchini can be boiled, baked, fried, sautéed, stewed, grilled; it can be cut into sticks, rounds, flat long slices, julienne strips, dice; it can be grated, mashed, or hollowed and stuffed. It is no exaggeration to say that when you explore all the ways of cooking zucchini, you reach for and bring within your grasp most of the processes that make up Italian cooking.

How to buy ✸ Good zucchini is available most of the year, but it has the most flavor during its natural season, late spring and early summer. Choose zucchini from a basket or vegetable bin whose contents seem to be all of a size, which indicates they come from a single lot rather than a mixed one of varying age and freshness. In Italy, zucchini is sometimes brought to market with the blossoms attached. The blossom wilts rapidly and drops off, so when it is still on and looks bright it is proof of the freshness of the zucchini.

The color of fresh zucchini may range from light to dark. What matters is for the skin to be glossy and free of blemishes. The vegetable should feel very firm in the hand. If it is flabby and bends with pressure, it isn't fresh.

Young, small zucchini are usually more desirable because of their compact flesh, small seeds, their tenderness and sweetness, but small does not mean the size of a finger. Young is one thing, undeveloped is another. Miniature zucchini, like other miniature vegetables, are undeveloped and taste of nothing.

How to clean ❀ The thin zucchini skin is easily penetrated by soil, which is hard to detect until you are eating. Although zucchini is occasionally fairly free of grit, the prudent course is to assume there is soil embedded in the skin and proceed to loosen it and remove it as described below.

❀ Soak in a large bowl or a basin filled with cold water for at least 20 minutes.

❀ Rinse the zucchini thoroughly under cold running water, rubbing briskly with your hands or a rough cloth to remove any grit still embedded in the skin.

❀ Trim away both ends and cut the zucchini as the recipe requires. When zucchini is to be boiled, omit this step, and leave the ends on.

Fried Zucchini
with Flour and Water Batter

ITALIANS CALL THIS frying batter made of flour and water *la pastella*. Those who like a crust on their fried vegetables that is thin and deliciously brittle, that does not soak up oil like a sponge, and that never falls off, need look no further than *pastella*. It is perfect for zucchini, but try it with such other vegetables as asparagus and broccoli, or with onion rings, following the procedure given below. *For 4 to 6 servings*

1 pound fresh zucchini   Vegetable oil
⅔ cup flour   Salt

1. Soak and clean the zucchini as directed above, trim away the ends, and cut it lengthwise into slices about ⅛ inch thick.
2. Put 1 cup water in a soup plate and gradually add the flour, shaking it through a strainer and, with a fork, constantly beating the mixture that forms. When all the flour has been mixed with water, the batter should have the consistency of sour cream. If it is thinner add a little more flour; if it is thicker, a little more water.
3. Pour enough oil into a skillet to come ¾ inch up its sides, and turn on

the heat to high. When the oil is quite hot, drop the zucchini slices, a few at a time, into the batter. Slip a fork under the zucchini, one slice at a time, lift it, and slide it into the pan. The oil should be hot enough to sizzle on contact with the zucchini. Do not put in any more of them at one time than will fit loosely.

4. Cook until a fine golden crust forms on one side, then turn the slices over and do the other side. Transfer them with a slotted spoon or spatula to a cooling rack to drain or to a platter lined with paper towels. Repeat the procedure until you have fried all the zucchini. Sprinkle with salt and serve while piping hot.

Fried Zucchini in Vinegar and Garlic

For 4 to 6 servings

1 pound fresh zucchini
Salt
2 garlic cloves
Vegetable oil
Flour

2 to 3 tablespoons good
   wine vinegar
Black pepper, ground fresh
   from the mill

1. Soak and clean the zucchini as directed on page 530, trimming away both ends, and cut it into sticks ¼ inch thick. Sprinkle these with salt, and stand them inside a pasta colander, letting them steep for 30 minutes or more. Place the colander over a plate to collect the drippings. When the zucchini sticks have shed a substantial amount of liquid, take them out of the colander and pat them thoroughly dry with cloth or paper towels.

2. Mash the garlic cloves lightly with a knife handle, just enough to split the skin, which you will pull off and discard. Set the garlic aside for later.

3. Pour enough oil into a skillet to come ¼ inch up its sides, and turn on the heat to high. When the oil is quite hot, put the zucchini sticks, a few at a time, into a strainer, pour some flour over them, shake off all excess flour, and slip them into the pan. The oil should be hot enough to sizzle on contact with the sticks. Do not put in any more of them at one time than will fit loosely.

4. Watch the zucchini sticks and turn them over when they become brown on one side. When they are brown all over, transfer them with a slotted spoon or spatula to a deep dish, and drizzle them with some of the vinegar. You will hear them crackle. Fry any remaining zucchini in the same manner and repeat the procedure with the vinegar.

5. When all the zucchini sticks are done, bury the garlic in their midst,

Fried Zucchini in Vinegar and Garlic (continued)

sprinkle with pepper, toss 2 or 3 times, and set aside to cool down to room temperature before serving.

Note ❧ Adjust the vinegar and garlic to suit your taste. The longer you leave the garlic in, the more pervasive will be its aroma. I prefer to take it out after it has steeped with the zucchini for no more than 10 minutes.

Sautéed Zucchini Rounds with Onions

For 6 servings

1½ pounds fresh zucchini
3 tablespoons butter

1 cup onion sliced very thin
Salt

1. Soak and clean the zucchini as directed on page 530, trimming away both ends, and slice into the thinnest possible rounds.
2. Put the butter and onion in a sauté pan, turn the heat on to medium, and without ever covering the pan, cook, stirring occasionally, until the onion becomes colored a rich golden brown.
3. Add the zucchini rounds, several pinches of salt, turn them over completely to coat well, and turn the heat up to high. Stir frequently. The zucchini will be cooked when the rounds become tender, and turn a light brown at the edges. The time will vary widely, from 5 minutes to 15 or more, depending on the youth and freshness of the vegetable. Taste and correct for salt. Transfer the contents of the pan to a warm platter and serve promptly.

Ahead-of-time note ❧ It is preferable to serve these zucchini the moment they are done, but if it is imperative that the dish be prepared earlier, you can cook it completely a few hours in advance and reheat it gently before serving it that same day. Do not refrigerate.

Sautéed Zucchini Rounds with Oregano

For 6 servings

1½ pounds fresh zucchini
¼ cup extra virgin olive oil
1 tablespoon garlic chopped
    rather coarse
Salt

Black pepper, ground fresh
    from the mill
Oregano, ½ teaspoon if fresh,
    ¼ teaspoon if dried

1. Soak and clean the zucchini as directed on page 530, trimming away both ends, and slice into the thinnest possible rounds.

2. Choose a sauté pan that can subsequently accommodate all the zucchini without stacking them much more than 1 inch high. Put in the oil and garlic, and turn on the heat to medium. Cook and stir the garlic until it becomes colored a pale gold, then put in the zucchini, together with salt, pepper, and the oregano. Toss thoroughly to coat well, turn the heat up to medium high, and cook until the zucchini rounds are tender, but slightly firm to the bite. Turn them from time to time as they cook. When done, spoon off some, but not all the oil, then transfer the entire contents of the pan to a warm platter and serve at once.

Ahead-of-time note ❀ The note at the foot of the preceding recipe applies here as well.

Zucchini Gratin
with Tomato and Marjoram

For 6 servings

1½ pounds fresh zucchini	1 tablespoon chopped parsley
¼ cup extra virgin olive oil	Salt
½ teaspoon chopped garlic	Black pepper, ground fresh
½ cup chopped onion	from the mill
1 cup canned imported Italian	An oven-to-table baking dish
plum tomatoes, cut up,	3 tablespoons freshly grated
with their juice	*parmigiano-reggiano* cheese
Marjoram, ½ teaspoon if fresh,	
⅛ teaspoon if dried	

1. Soak and clean the zucchini as directed on page 530, trimming away both ends, and slice them into very thin disks.

2. Preheat oven to 400°.

3. Put half the oil and all the garlic in a sauté pan, turn the heat on to medium high, and cook the garlic, stirring, until it begins to be barely colored. Put in the zucchini rounds. Turn them over completely once or twice to coat well, and cook until they are limp, stirring occasionally. Take off heat.

4. Put the onion and remaining oil in a small saucepan, and turn on the heat to medium. Cook and stir the onion until it becomes translucent, then put in the tomatoes with their juice and the marjoram. Turn the tomatoes over completely once or twice to coat well, and cook at a steady, but gentle

Zucchini Gratin (continued)

simmer until the oil floats free of the tomatoes, about 20 minutes. Take off heat, and swirl in the parsley, salt, and several grindings of pepper.

5. Smear the bottom of the baking dish with a little of the oil in the saucepan. Spread half the zucchini in a level layer on the bottom of the dish, cover with half the tomato sauce from the saucepan, and sprinkle over it 1 tablespoon grated Parmesan. Make another layer with the remaining zucchini, topping it with the rest of the sauce and the last 2 tablespoons of Parmesan.

6. Place the dish on the uppermost rack of the preheated oven, and bake for 15 minutes or more, until the cheese melts, and the top becomes colored rather brown. After taking the dish out of the oven, allow it to settle for about 10 minutes before bringing it to the table.

Ahead-of-time note ❀ You can finish baking the zucchini several hours in advance the same day you are going to serve it. Do not refrigerate. Reheat the dish in the oven.

Zucchini with Tomato and Basil

For 6 servings

1½ pounds fresh zucchini	Salt
½ cup onion sliced thin	Black pepper, ground fresh
¼ cup extra virgin olive oil	from the mill
1½ teaspoons garlic	6 or more fresh basil leaves
chopped coarse	
2 tablespoons chopped parsley	
⅔ cup canned imported Italian	
plum tomatoes, chopped	
coarse, with their juice	

1. Soak and clean the zucchini as directed on page 530, trimming away both ends, and cut them into disks a little less than ½ inch thick.

2. Preheat oven to 350°.

3. Choose a flameproof oven-to-table pan, preferably enameled cast-iron ware, put in the onion and oil, and turn on the heat to medium. Cook and stir the onion until it becomes colored a light gold, then add the garlic. When the garlic becomes colored a very pale gold, add the parsley, stirring it quickly once or twice, then put in the tomatoes with their juice. Cook at a

steady, gentle simmer until the oil floats free of the tomatoes, about 20 minutes.

4. Add the sliced zucchini, salt, and pepper, and turn the zucchini over once or twice to coat well. Cook for 5 minutes on top of the stove, then transfer the pan to the uppermost rack of the preheated oven. Cook until the liquid shed by the zucchini dries out, and the zucchini rounds are tender.

Ahead-of-time note ❀ The dish may be completed up to this point several hours in advance on the day you are going to serve it. Do not refrigerate. Reheat in a hot oven before proceeding with the next step.

5. Take the pan out of the oven. Wash the basil in cold water, tear the leaves into one or two pieces by hand, distribute them over the zucchini, and bring to the table.

Baked Zucchini
Stuffed with Ham and Cheese

For 6 servings or more if served as an appetizer

8 to 10 fresh zucchini
1 tablespoon butter
1 tablespoon vegetable oil
1 tablespoon onion
    chopped fine
¼ pound boiled unsmoked
    ham, chopped fine
Salt
Black pepper, ground fresh
    from the mill
Béchamel Sauce, prepared as
    directed on page 39, using
    1 cup milk, 2 tablespoons

butter, 1½ tablespoons
    flour, and ⅛ teaspoon salt
¼ cup freshly grated
    parmigiano-reggiano cheese
Whole nutmeg
1 egg
An oven-to-table baking dish
Butter for smearing and dotting
    the baking dish
Unflavored bread crumbs,
    lightly toasted

1. Soak and clean the zucchini as directed on page 530, but do not cut off the ends.

2. Bring 3 to 4 quarts of water to a boil, put in the zucchini, and cook until partly tender, still somewhat resistant when prodded with a fork. Drain, and as soon as they are cool enough for you to handle, cut off both ends, cut each zucchini into 2 shorter pieces, then cut each piece *lengthwise* in half. Using a teaspoon, gently scoop out the zucchini flesh, taking care not to break

Baked Zucchini Stuffed with Ham and Cheese (continued)

the skin. Discard half the scooped out flesh, and coarsely chop the other half. Set both the chopped flesh and the hollowed zucchini aside.

3. Preheat oven to 400°.

4. Put the butter, oil, and onion in a skillet, turn on the heat to medium, and sauté the onion just until it becomes translucent. Add the chopped ham, and cook it for about 1 minute, stirring once or twice. Add the chopped zucchini flesh, turning it to coat it well, and turn the heat up to high. Cook, stirring from time to time, until the zucchini becomes colored a rich gold and acquires a creamy consistency. Add salt and pepper, stir quickly once or twice, then transfer the contents of the skillet to a small bowl, using a slotted spoon or spatula.

5. Prepare the béchamel, cooking it long enough to make it rather thick. Pour the béchamel into the bowl with the sautéed zucchini flesh, mix, then add the grated Parmesan, a tiny grating of nutmeg—about ⅛ teaspoon— and the egg, and mix quickly until you obtain a uniform blend of all the ingredients.

6. Smear the bottom of the baking dish with butter. Place the hollowed-out zucchini in the dish, skin side facing down. Fill each one with the béchamel and zucchini flesh mixture, sprinkle with bread crumbs, and dot with butter.

Ahead-of-time note ❀ You may complete the dish up to this point several hours in advance on the same day you are going to serve it. Do not refrigerate.

7. Place the dish on the uppermost rack of the preheated oven, and bake for 15 to 20 minutes, until a light golden crust forms on top. After taking the dish out of the oven, allow it to settle for 5 to 10 minutes before bringing it to the table.

Hollowed Zucchini Stuffed with Beef, Ham, and Parmesan Cheese

For 6 servings

10 fresh zucchini, about 1¼ to
   1½ inches in diameter
3 cups onion sliced thin
3 tablespoons vegetable oil
2 tablespoons chopped parsley
2 tablespoons tomato paste,
   diluted with 1 cup lukewarm water
3 tablespoons milk or more
⅔ slice good, firm white bread,
   crust trimmed away

½ pound ground beef,
   preferably chuck
1 egg
3 tablespoons freshly grated
   parmigiano-reggiano cheese
1 tablespoon chopped pro-
   sciutto OR boiled unsmoked
   ham
Salt
Black pepper, ground fresh
   from the mill

1. Soak and clean the zucchini as directed on page 530, slice off both ends, and cut each zucchini into 2 shorter pieces. Using a vegetable corer, or the blade of a peeler, or any narrow enough sharp tool, hollow out the zucchini pieces, taking care not to pierce the sides. Keep the thinned-out wall of the zucchini at least ¼ inch thick. The scooped out flesh is not needed in this recipe, but you can use it in a *risotto* or a *frittata*.

2. Choose a sauté pan that can subsequently accommodate all the zucchini pieces snugly, but without overlapping. Put in the onion and the oil, turn on the heat to medium low, and cook, stirring, until the onion wilts and becomes tender. Add the parsley, stir 2 or 3 times, then add the diluted tomato paste, turning it thoroughly with the onions, and continue cooking for 15 more minutes.

3. At the same time, put the milk in a small saucepan, warm it without bringing it to a boil, mash the bread into it, and set aside to cool.

4. Put the ground beef, the egg, the grated Parmesan, the chopped prosciutto or ham, the bread and milk mush, salt, and pepper into a bowl, and knead with your hands until you obtain an evenly blended mixture.

5. Stuff the mixture into the hollowed-out zucchini, packing it tightly, but being careful not to split the vegetable's fragile walls. Put the stuffed zucchini into the pan with the onion and tomato, cover, and cook at medium low heat until the zucchini are tender, about 40 minutes, depending on their youth and freshness. Turn them over from time to time while cooking.

6. When done, if the juices in the pan are watery, uncover, raise the heat

Zucchini Stuffed with Beef, Ham, and Parmesan Cheese (continued)

to high, and boil them down. Taste and correct for salt. Turn the zucchini once or twice, transfer the contents of the pan to a serving platter, and allow to settle for a few minutes before bringing to the table.

Ahead-of-time note ✹ Here is one of those dishes that has nothing to gain from being served the moment it's done. Its flavor improves when it is served several hours or even a day later. Reheat it gently in a covered pan, and serve warm, but not steaming hot.

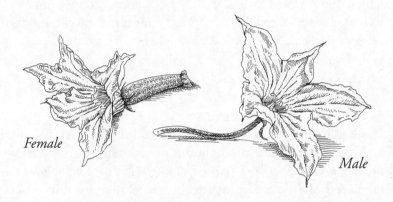

Female

Male

Crisp-Fried Zucchini Blossoms

THE LUSCIOUS orange-yellow blossoms of zucchini are very perishable, so you are likely to find them only in those markets that handle local, seasonal produce. There are both male and female blossoms, and only the male, those on a stem, are good to eat. The female blossoms, attached to the zucchini, are mushy and don't taste good.   *For 4 to 6 servings*

1 dozen male zucchini blossoms   Salt
Vegetable oil
The flour and water batter,
    pastella, on page 530

1. Wash the blossoms rapidly under cold running water without letting them soak. Pat them gently but thoroughly dry with soft cloth or paper towels. If the stems are very long, cut them down to 1 inch. Make a cut on one side of each blossom's base to open the flower flat, butterfly fashion.

2. Pour enough oil in a frying pan to come ¾ inch up its sides, and turn

on the heat to high. When the oil is very hot, use the blossoms' stems to dip them quickly in and out of the batter, and slip them into the skillet. Put in only as many as will fit very loosely. When they have formed a golden brown crust on one side, turn them and do the other side. Transfer to a cooling rack to drain or to a platter lined with paper towels, using a slotted spoon or spatula. If any blossoms remain to be done, repeat the procedure. When they are all done, sprinkle with salt, and serve immediately.

Mixed Baked Vegetable Platter

For 6 servings

4 medium round, waxy, boiling potatoes	4 medium yellow onions
3 sweet bell peppers, preferably yellow	A shallow baking dish
	¼ cup extra virgin olive oil
	Salt
3 fresh, firm, ripe, round OR 6 plum tomatoes	Black pepper, ground fresh from the mill

1. Preheat oven to 400°.

2. Peel the potatoes, cut them into 1-inch wedges, wash them in cold water, and pat dry with cloth towels.

3. Cut the peppers along their folds into lengthwise sections. Scrape away and discard the pulpy core with all the seeds. Skin the peppers, using a peeler with a swiveling blade.

4. If using round tomatoes, cut them into 6 to 8 wedge-shaped sections; if using plum tomatoes, cut them lengthwise in two.

5. Peel the onions and cut each one into 4 wedge-shaped sections.

6. Wash all the vegetables, except for the onions and the already washed potatoes, in cold water, and drain well.

7. Put the potatoes and all the vegetables into the baking dish. They should not be too snugly packed or they will steep in their own vapors and become soggy. Add the oil, salt, and several grindings of pepper, and toss once or twice. Place the dish in the upper third of the preheated oven. Turn the vegetables over every 10 minutes or so. The dish is done when the potatoes become tender, in about 25 to 30 minutes. If after 20 minutes you find that the tomatoes have shed a lot of liquid, turn up the oven to 450° or higher for the remaining cooking time. Do not be concerned if some of the vegetables become slightly charred at the edges. It is quite all right and even desirable.

8. When done, transfer the vegetables to a warm platter, using a slotted

Mixed Baked Vegetable Platter (continued)

spoon or spatula to drain them of oil. Scrape loose any bits stuck to the sides or bottom of the baking dish and add them to the platter, for they are choice morsels. Serve at once.

Charcoal-Grilled Vegetables

PLEASE READ this recipe through before you begin to cook. You will find that at any one time you may be handling several vegetables at different stages of their cooking. It is not at all a daunting procedure, it can be, in fact, rather a lot of fun to do, but it will all go much more smoothly if you first get a sense of its rhythm.   *For 4 to 6 servings*

2 fresh, glossy, medium
    zucchini
1 large flat Spanish onion
Salt
2 sweet yellow or red bell
    peppers
2 fresh, ripe, firm, large round
    tomatoes
1 medium eggplant
2 heads Belgian endive

Extra virgin olive oil
Crushed black peppercorns
1 teaspoon chopped parsley
⅛ teaspoon chopped garlic
½ teaspoon unflavored bread
    crumbs, lightly toasted
A charcoal-fired grill or gas-
    fired lava rocks
A pair of tongs

1. Soak the zucchini in cold water for 20 minutes, then wash them in several changes of water, rubbing their skins clean. Slice off both ends and cut the zucchini lengthwise into slices less than ½ inch thick.

2. Cut the onion in half at its middle, and score the cut sides in a crosshatch pattern, stopping well short of the skin. Do not remove the flaky outer skin or cut off the onion's point or root. Sprinkle the cut sides with salt.

3. Wash the peppers in cold water, keeping them whole.

4. Wash the tomatoes in cold water and divide them in two at their middle.

5. Wash the eggplant in cold water. Trim away its green top. Cut the eggplant lengthwise in two, and make shallow cross-hatched cuts on both cut sides, staying well short of the skin. Rub salt liberally into the cuts.

6. Split the endive heads lengthwise in two. Make 2 or 3 deep cuts at their base.

7. Light the charcoal or turn the gas-fired grill on to very hot.

8. When the coals have begun to form white ash, or the lava rocks are very hot, put the onion, cut side down, on the grill. Place the peppers alongside. Check the peppers after a few minutes; when the skin facing the fire is charred and the peppers begin to shrink, turn them with the tongs, bringing them closer together to make room for other vegetables as described below. Continue turning the peppers each time the skin facing the fire becomes charred, eventually standing them on end. When they are charred all over, put them into a plastic bag, twisting it tightly closed.

9. While cooking the peppers, check the onion. When the side facing the fire becomes charred, turn it over with a spatula, being careful not to separate any of the rings. Coat the charred side with olive oil, working it in between the cuts, and sprinkle with salt. Let the onion cook another 15 or 20 minutes, when it should feel tender, but firm when prodded with a fork. Remove its charred, outer skin, put the onion on the serving platter that will hold all the vegetables, cut each half into 4 parts, drizzle with olive oil, and sprinkle with cracked black pepper.

10. When you first turn the peppers and draw them closer together, use the space you made available on the grill for the tomatoes, placing them cut side facing down. Check them after a few minutes, and if they are already slightly charred, turn them over. Season each half with olive oil, salt, and some of the parsley, garlic, and bread crumbs. You needn't do anything else about the tomatoes until they have shrunk to nearly half their original size. Then transfer them to the serving platter.

11. When you put on the tomatoes also put the eggplant on the grill, its scored side facing the fire. Let that side become colored a light brown, then turn it over. Brush generously with olive oil, working the oil in between the cuts. You should soon see the oil begin to simmer. From time to time, drizzle a few drops of oil into the cuts. When the eggplant flesh feels creamy at the point of a fork, it is done. Transfer it to the serving platter.

12. At the same time that you put the eggplant on the grill, put on the endive, cut side facing down. If there is no room, put it on as soon as some

Charcoal-Grilled Vegetables (continued)

opens up. When the cut side of the endive becomes lightly charred, but not deeply blackened, turn it over. Sprinkle with salt, and brush it generously with olive oil, working it in between the leaves. You need do nothing else with the endive except test it from time to time with a fork. When it feels very, very tender, transfer it to the platter.

13. When you see that the eggplant is nearly done, and you have room on the grill, put on the sliced zucchini. These easily become burned, so you have to watch them. The moment the side facing the fire becomes mottled with brown spots, turn it over, and when the other side becomes similarly pockmarked, transfer it to the platter. Season immediately with salt, cracked black pepper, and olive oil.

14. By now, the peppers you've put in the plastic bag should be ready to be peeled. Take them out of the bag and have plenty of paper towels available for your hands, because the peppers will be very moist. Pull off all the charred skin, split the peppers open, remove the pulpy core with all its seeds, and add the peppers to the platter. Season with salt and a little olive oil.

Ahead-of-time note ❀ All the grilled vegetables are good at room temperature or the temperature of a warm day outdoors. They can be cooked, therefore, before whatever meat or fish you are planning to do on the grill.

SALADS

The salad course ✺ The literal meaning of the Italian for a salad—*un'insalata*—is "that to which salt has been added," but the word also enjoys popular metaphorical usage, applied disparagingly when describing, for example, an interior decor or a set of thoughts that appears to be rather mixed up. Then there is *L'insalata,* which specifically refers to the salad course, a course with a clearly defined role in an Italian meal's classic sequence. *L'insalata* is served invariably after the second course to signal the approaching end of the meal. It releases the palate from the grip of the cook's fabrications, leading it to cool, fresh sensations, to a rediscovery of food in its least labored state.

The principal, and usually only components of the salad course, are vegetables and greens, either raw or boiled, on their own or combined. The choice changes as the season does: raw *finocchio* or shredded Savoy cabbage or boiled broccoli in fall and winter; in the spring, boiled asparagus and green beans, followed by zucchini or new potatoes; in the fullness of summer, raw ingredients prevail, with tomatoes, peppers, cucumbers, lettuces, and an assortment of small greens. The broadened availability of many vegetables through much of the year has, of course, blurred some of the seasonal distinctions, but we still want the salad course to speak to us of the season that produced its components.

There are certainly a great many other kinds of salads, such as rice and chicken salads, rice and shellfish, tuna and beans, or any number of dishes that contain cold meats, fish, or chicken mixed with legumes or with raw or cooked vegetables. Such salads may be served as an appetizer, as a first course instead of pasta or *risotto,* as the principal course of a light meal, or as part of a buffet table. In fact, they may be served as anything except as *L'insalata,* the salad course.

Dressing the salad course ✺ Italian dressing is extra virgin olive oil, salt, and wine vinegar.

Many variations on the same proverb give us the formula for a perfectly seasoned salad. One version says, for a good salad you need four persons: A judicious one for the salt, a prodigal one for the olive oil, a stingy one for the vinegar, and a patient one to toss it. Olive oil is the dominant ingredient, and a properly made salad ought not to taste shy of it. Italians will never say, when savoring a well-tossed salad, "What a wonderful dressing!" They do say, "What marvelous oil!"

When washed raw greens go into a salad, they must first be shaken thoroughly dry because the water that clings to them dilutes the dressing. Salad spinners do the job, or you can wrap the greens in a large towel, gather all four corners of the towel in one hand, and give the towel several abrupt shakes over a sink.

The salad course is dressed at the table when ready to serve; it is never done ahead of time. The salad for the whole table should be in a single large bowl, with ample room in it for all the vegetables to move completely around when tossed. The components of the dressing are never mixed in advance, they are poured separately onto the salad.

First put in the salt and bear in mind that judiciousness does not mean very little salt, it means neither too much *nor* too little. Give the salad one quick toss to distribute the salt and begin to dissolve it, then pour in the oil liberally. From observation, I have found people outside Italy never use sufficient oil. There should be enough of it to produce a gloss on the surface of the vegetables. Add the vinegar last, just the few drops necessary to impart aroma, and never more than one skimpy part vinegar to three heaping parts oil. A little vinegar is sufficient to be noticed, a little too much monopolizes all your attention to the disadvantage of every other ingredient. Also bear in mind that the acid of vinegar, like that of lemon, "cooks" a salad, which explains why the oil is poured first, to protect the greens. As soon as you put in the vinegar, begin to toss. The more thoroughly a salad is tossed, and the more uniformly the salt, oil, and vinegar are distributed over every leaf and every vegetable, the better it will taste. Toss gently, turning the greens over delicately, to avoid bruising and blackening them.

Other seasonings ✱ Freshly squeezed lemon juice is an occasional, agreeable substitute for vinegar. It is excellent on cooked salads, such as boiled Swiss chard, which are then described as *all'agro,* in the tart style. Lemon is also welcome on carrots shredded very fine, or in summer on tomatoes and cucumbers.

Garlic can be exciting when you turn to it sporadically, on impulse, but on a regular basis, it is tiresome. Its presence should be an offstage one, as in the Shredded Savoy Cabbage Salad, page 550, or in the tomatoes on page 548.

Pepper is not common. It was probably too expensive a spice originally to become part of a humble, everyday dish like salad. But if you like it, there is certainly a place for it in Italian salads, as long as it is black pepper, because it has a more complete aroma than the white.

Balsamic vinegar, however unfamiliar it may have been until recently to other Italians, has been used in Modena for centuries to lift the flavor of the basic salad dressing. But the Modenese have never used it every day, and neither would I. Its sweetness and its dense fragrance are qualities that can be called upon, from time to time, to amaze the tastebuds, but call on them too often and they become cloying. When dressing a salad, balsamic vinegar is used to enrich regular wine vinegar, not to replace it.

Either basil or parsley will do most salads some good. The uses of mint, like those of marjoram and oregano, are more limited, as the recipes in this chapter will illustrate.

Sliced onion quickens the flavor of most raw salads, particularly those with tomatoes. To blunt its sharp bite, the onion must be subjected to the following procedure, beginning 30 minutes or more before preparing the other ingredients of the salad:

❀ Peel the onion, slice it into very thin rings, put it in a bowl, and cover amply with cold water.

❀ Squeeze the rings in your hand for 2 or 3 seconds, closing your hand tightly and letting go for seven or eight times. The acid you squeeze out of the onion will make the water slightly milky.

❀ Retrieve the onion rings with a colander scoop or strainer, pour the water out of the bowl, put fresh water in. Put the onion back into the bowl and repeat the above procedure 2 or 3 more times.

❀ After squeezing the onion for the last time, change the water again and put the onion in to soak. Drain and replace with a fresh change of water every 10 minutes, until you are ready to make the salad.

❀ Before putting the onion into the salad bowl, gather it tightly in a towel and squeeze out all the moisture you can.

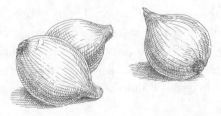

La Grande Insalata Mista—
Great Mixed Raw Salad

For 8 servings

½ medium onion, preferably of a sweet variety, such as Bermuda red, Vidalia, or Maui, sliced and soaked as described on page 545, OR 3 or 4 scallions

2 small carrots

1 squat, round *finocchio,* see page 502

½ yellow or red sweet bell pepper

1 celery heart

½ head curly chicory, Boston lettuce, or escarole, OR 1 whole head Bibb lettuce

½ small bunch *mâche* or field lettuce

½ small bunch *arugula*

1 medium artichoke

½ lemon

2 fresh, ripe, firm, medium round tomatoes

Salt

Extra virgin olive oil

Choice quality red wine vinegar

Note ❀ A mixed salad in the Italian style should reach for as great a variety of textures and flavors as the market can provide, and the ingredients suggested above take advantage of the year-round availability of many vegetables. The selection should be taken as a thoughtfully considered recommendation, but it is not ironclad and you can work within its guidelines to make substitutions that suit your taste and are adapted to the possibilities offered by your market and the season.

In a mixed salad such as this one you can also use Savoy, red cabbage, or green cabbage, shredded very fine; *radicchio;* romaine or any other variety of lettuce, save iceberg, which does not taste very Italian; small red or white radishes, sliced into thin disks; cucumber instead of carrot, but not the two together; very young zucchini, soaked, cleaned, and trimmed as described on page 530, cut into fine matchsticks and put into the salad raw.

1. Prepare the onion as suggested or, if you are using scallion, take a thin slice off the base, trimming it of its roots, and another slice off the tops, pull off and discard any blemished or discolored leaves, then cut the whole scallion into thin rounds and rings. Soak it in cold water a few minutes, then drain and shake dry in a towel. Put the onion when ready, or the scallion, in a large serving bowl.

2. Wash the carrots, take a thin slice off the tops and bottoms, peel them, then shred them on the largest holes of a grater, or in the food processor, or cut them into the thinnest possible rounds. Add them to the bowl.

3. Cut the *finocchio* tops where they meet the bulb and discard them. Detach and discard any of the bulb's outer parts that may be bruised or discolored. Slice off about ⅛ inch from the butt end. Cut the bulb horizontally, across its width, into very thin rings. Soak the rings in 2 or 3 changes of cold water, then shake dry in a towel or salad spinner. Add the *finocchio* to the bowl.

4. Scrape away and discard the inner pulp and all the seeds of the pepper. Skin it raw, using a swiveling-blade peeler, then cut it lengthwise into very thin strips, and add them to the bowl.

5. Cut away any leafy tops from the celery heart, take a thin slice off its base, slice the heart crosswise into narrow rings about ¼ inch wide, and drop them into the bowl.

6. If you are using curly chicory, Boston lettuce, or escarole, discard all the outer, dark green leaves. Detach the remaining leaves from the head and tear them by hand into small, bite-size pieces. Soak them in one or two changes of cold water for 15 to 20 minutes, until no trace of soil shows in the water. Drain and either spin-dry, or shake dry in a towel. If you are using Bibb lettuce, prepare it as described above but use special care in handling it because it bruises easily and discolors. Add to the bowl.

7. Pull off the stems of the *mâche* or field lettuce and the *arugula,* tear the larger leaves in two or more pieces, and soak, drain, and dry them as you did with the lettuce. Put them into the bowl.

8. Detach and discard the artichoke stem, and trim away all the hard portions as described on pages 57–59, taking a little more off the top of the leaves than you might if you were cooking it. Split the artichoke in half to expose the choke and spiky inner leaves, which you will scrape off and discard. Cut the artichoke lengthwise into the thinnest slices you can. Squeeze a few drops of juice from the lemon half over all cut parts to keep them from discoloring, and add them to the other ingredients in the bowl.

9. Skin the raw tomatoes, using a swiveling-blade peeler, cut them into wedges, remove some of the seeds, and put the tomatoes in the salad bowl.

10. Sprinkle liberally, if judiciously, with salt, toss once, pour in enough olive oil to coat all the vegetables, add a dash of vinegar, and toss repeatedly and thoroughly, but not roughly. Serve at once.

Garlic-Scented Tomato Salad

WHEN I GAVE a series of classes in Bridgehampton, Long Island, one summer, I had devised a curriculum of pasta sauces, *risotto,* and fish dishes that I hoped my students would find interesting and fitting vehicles for the extraordinary products of Long Island's farms and waters. As an afterthought one day, I included in the menu this tomato salad, done the way my father used to prepare it when I was a young girl. The response to the pastas and the fish was as enthusiastic as I could have wished, but it was the salad that stole the show. When all the tomato salad was gone, students fought for possession of the serving platter, to sop up the juices with bread. It seems difficult ever to make enough of this tomato salad, so you too may find it expedient, when you serve it, to send it to the table copiously accompanied by slices of good, crusty bread. *For 4 to 6 servings*

4 to 5 garlic cloves
Salt
Choice quality red wine vinegar
2 pounds fresh, ripe, firm,
    round or plum tomatoes

1 dozen fresh basil leaves
Extra virgin olive oil

1. Peel the garlic cloves and mash them rather hard with a knife handle. Put them in a small bowl or saucer together with 1 to 2 teaspoons salt and 2 tablespoons vinegar. Stir and let steep at least 20 minutes.

2. Skin the tomatoes raw, using a swiveling-blade peeler, cut them into thin slices, and spread the slices out in a deep serving platter.

3. When ready to serve the salad, wash the basil leaves in cold water, shake off their moisture, tear them by hand into 2 or 3 pieces each, and sprinkle them over the tomatoes.

4. Pour the garlic-steeped vinegar through a wire strainer, distributing it over the tomatoes. Add enough olive oil to coat the tomatoes well, toss, taste and correct, if necessary, for salt and vinegar, and serve at once.

Shredded Carrot Salad

SHREDDED CARROTS with lemon juice is one of the most refreshing of salads, and may well be the simplest to prepare.   *For 4 servings*

5 to 6 medium carrots, washed,
    trimmed, peeled, and
    shredded as described in the
    recipe for Great Mixed Raw
    Salad on page 546

Salt
Extra virgin olive oil
1 tablespoon freshly squeezed
    lemon juice

Combine all ingredients, using enough olive oil to coat the carrots well. Toss thoroughly, taste and correct for salt and lemon juice, and serve at once.

Variation with Arugula

To the ingredients in the preceding recipe, add ½ pound fresh *arugula,* and replace the lemon juice with red wine vinegar. Trim, soak, drain, and dry the *arugula* as described in the recipe for Great Mixed Raw Salad on page 546 Combine all ingredients in the manner described above.

Finocchio Salad

For 4 servings, if the finocchio *is a large one*

1 squat, round *finocchio,* see
    page 502
Salt

Extra virgin olive oil
Black pepper, ground fresh
    from the mill

Note ✽ No vinegar or lemon juice is used on raw *finocchio* when it is served alone.

1. Trim the *finocchio,* cut it into very thin slices, soak it, and dry it as described in the recipe for Great Mixed Raw Salad on page 546.

2. Toss in a serving bowl with salt, enough olive oil to coat it well, and liberal grindings of black pepper.

Sunchoke and Spinach Salad

For 4 servings

½ pound sunchokes
½ pound fresh, very young,
    crisp spinach
Salt

Black pepper, ground fresh
    from the mill
Extra virgin olive oil
Choice quality red wine vinegar

1. Soak the sunchokes for 15 minutes in cold water, then scrub them thoroughly under running water with a rough cloth or a brush. Cut them into paper-thin slices and put them in a serving bowl.

2. The spinach will be much more pleasant to eat if you free the tenderest part of each leaf from the stem and its chewy rib-like extention. With one hand fold the leaf lengthwise, folding it inward toward its top side, and with the other hand pull off the stem together with the thin rib protruding from the underside of the leaf. Soak the trimmed spinach in a basin with enough cold water to cover it amply. Drain and refill with fresh water as often as necessary until you find no more trace of soil. Spin-dry, or shake the leaves dry to drive away all the moisture possible, tear them into two or three smaller pieces, and add them to the bowl.

3. Toss thoroughly with salt, pepper, enough oil to coat well, and just a dash of vinegar. Serve immediately.

Shredded Savoy Cabbage Salad

YOU WILL FIND here another example of the way only the scent of garlic is used in Italian salads. Also see the tomato salad on page 548.

For 6 or more servings

1 Savoy cabbage,
    about 2 pounds

A slice of crusty bread
2 garlic cloves

Salt

Black pepper, ground fresh
from the mill

Extra virgin olive oil

Choice quality red wine vinegar

1. Pull off the green outer leaves from the cabbage and either discard or save for a vegetable soup. Shred all the white leaves very fine, and put them into a serving bowl.

2. Trim away the soft crumb from the bread, and from the crust cut two pieces about 1 inch long.

3. Lightly mash the garlic cloves with a knife handle, splitting the skin and removing it. Rub the garlic vigorously over both pieces of bread crust, put the crusts in the bowl and discard the garlic. Toss thoroughly and let stand for 45 minutes to 1 hour.

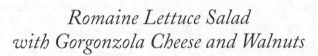

4. When ready to serve, put salt, pepper, enough olive oil to coat well, and a dash of vinegar into the bowl. Toss the cabbage repeatedly until it is uniformly coated with dressing. Take out and discard the bread crusts. Taste and correct for seasoning and serve at once.

Romaine Lettuce Salad
with Gorgonzola Cheese and Walnuts

For 6 to 8 servings

1 head romaine lettuce

5 tablespoons extra virgin
olive oil

1 tablespoon choice red wine
vinegar

Salt

Black pepper, ground fresh
from the mill

¼ pound imported *gorgonzola*
cheese, brought to room
temperature 3 to 4 hours
before using

½ cup shelled walnuts chopped
very coarse

Romaine Lettuce Salad (continued)

1. Pull off and discard any of the romaine's blemished outer leaves. Detach the rest from the core and tear them by hand into bite-size pieces. Soak in several changes of cold water, then spin-dry or shake dry in a towel.

2. Put the olive oil, vinegar, a pinch of salt, and several grindings of pepper into a serving bowl. Beat them with a fork until the seasonings are evenly blended.

3. Add half the *gorgonzola* and mash it thoroughly with a fork. Add half the chopped walnuts, all the lettuce, and toss thoroughly to distribute the dressing uniformly. Taste and correct for seasoning.

4. Top with the remaining *gorgonzola,* breaking it up over the salad, and with the remaining chopped walnuts. Serve at once.

Orange and Cucumber Salad

For 6 servings

1 cucumber	Salt
3 oranges	Extra virgin olive oil
6 small red radishes	The freshly squeezed juice of
Fresh mint leaves	½ lemon

1. If the cucumber is waxed or has a thick skin, peel it. If not, scrub it under cold running water. Slice the cucumber into very thin disks and put these on a serving platter.

2. Peel the oranges, removing all the white pith beneath the skin as well. Cut the oranges into thin rounds, pick out any seeds, and add the slices to the platter.

3. Cut off and discard the leafy tops from the radishes, wash the radishes in cold water, without peeling them, cut them into thin disks, and add them to the platter.

4. Wash half a dozen small mint leaves, tear them into 2 or 3 pieces each, and sprinkle them over the orange, radish, and cucumber slices.

5. Add salt, olive oil, and lemon juice, toss thoroughly to coat well, and serve at once.

Pinzimonio—Olive Oil, Salt, and Black Pepper Dip for Raw Vegetables

THE WORD *pinzimonio* is a contraction, facetious in origin but long since firmly established in respectable usage, of *pinzare,* to pinch, and *matrimonio,* matrimony. It describes the custom of holding a raw vegetable between thumb and forefinger—"pinching" it—and "marrying" it with a dip of olive oil, salt, and pepper.

In restaurants *pinzimonio* is sometimes brought to the table when one sits down, even before one looks at the menu, but its most appropriate and refreshing use is after the meat or fish course of a substantial and palate-taxing meal.

The usual assortment of raw vegetables for *pinzimonio* includes all or most of the following: carrots, sweet peppers, *finocchio,* artichokes, celery, cucumbers, radishes, and scallions. Here is how to prepare them:

1. Wash and peel the carrots. If they are small and they have fresh, leafy tops, leave the tops on to hold them by. If you have larger carrots, take a slice off the top, and split the carrot in two lengthwise.

2. Split the peppers in two to expose and remove the pulpy core with all the seeds. Cut the peppers lengthwise into strips about 1½ inches wide.

3. Trim away the leafy tops of the *finocchio,* take a thin slice off the butt end, discard any blemished outer leaves, cut the *finocchio* lengthwise into 4 wedges, and wash them in several changes of cold water.

4. Detach and discard the stems of the artichokes. Trim away all the tough parts as described on pages 57–59. Cut the artichoke lengthwise into 4 wedges, remove the choke and spiky, curly inner leaves, and squeeze a few drops of lemon juice over all cut parts to keep them from discoloring.

5. Separate the celery into stalks, keeping the heart whole but dividing it lengthwise in two. Pare away a thin slice all around the heart's butt end. Leave the leafy tops on the heart, but discard all the others. Wash in several changes of cold water.

6. Wash the cucumbers and split them lengthwise in two, or into 4 sections if very thick.

7. Wash the radishes and do nothing else to them, leaving their leafy tops on both for looks and to hold them by.

8. Choose scallions with thick, round bulbs, pull off and discard the outer leaves, and cut off the roots and about ½ inch off the tops. Wash in cold water.

9. Put all the vegetables in a bowl or jug where they will fit snugly.

Olive Oil, Salt, and Black Pepper Dip (continued)

There should be a saucer prepared for every guest with olive oil, salt, and a liberal quantity of cracked black pepper. Guests help themselves to the vegetable of their choice from the bowl, and dip it into the saucer, thus having a *pinzimonio*.

Panzanella—Bread Salad

Throughout Central Italy, from Florence down to Rome, the most satisfying of salads is based on that old standby of the ingenious poor, bread and water. Stale bread is moistened, but not drenched, with cold water, the other ingredients of the salad you'll find below are added, and everything is tossed with olive oil and vinegar. The bread, saturated with the salad's condiments and juices, dissolves to a grainy consistency like loose, coarse *polenta*. Given the right bread—not supermarket white, but gutsy, country bread such as that of Tuscany or Abruzzi—there is no change one can bring to the traditional version that will improve it. If you have a source for such bread, or if you have made the Olive Oil Bread on page 635 and have leftovers, make the salad with it in the manner I have just described. If you must rely on standard, commercial bread, the alternative solution suggested in the recipe that follows will yield very pleasant results. *For 4 to 6 servings*

½ garlic clove, peeled

2 or 3 flat anchovy fillets (preferably the ones prepared at home as described on page 9), chopped fine

1 tablespoon capers, soaked and rinsed as described on page 16 if packed in salt, drained if in vinegar

¼ yellow sweet bell pepper

Salt

¼ cup extra virgin olive oil

1 tablespoon choice quality red wine vinegar

2 cups firm, good bread, trimmed of its crust, toasted under the broiler, and cut into ½-inch squares (keep the crumbs)

3 fresh, ripe, firm, round tomatoes

1 cup cucumber, peeled and diced into ¼-inch cubes

½ medium onion, preferably of a sweet variety, such as Bermuda red, Vidalia, or Maui, sliced and soaked as described on page 545

Black pepper, ground fresh from the mill

1. Mash the garlic, anchovies, and capers to a pulp, using the back of a spoon against the side of a bowl, or a mortar and pestle, or the food processor.

2. Scrape away any part of the pulpy core of the sweet pepper together with the seeds, and dice the pepper into ¼-inch pieces. Put the pepper and the garlic and anchovy mixture in a serving bowl, add salt, olive oil, and vinegar, and toss thoroughly.

3. Put the bread squares together with any crumbs from the trimming in a small bowl. Purée 1 of the tomatoes through a food mill over the bread. Toss and let it steep, together with a little salt, for 15 minutes or more.

4. Skin the other 2 tomatoes, using a swiveling-blade peeler, and cut them into ½-inch pieces, picking out some of the seeds if there are too many of them. Add the soaked bread squares and the cut-up tomato to the serving bowl, together with the diced cucumber, the soaked and drained onion slices, and several grindings of black pepper. Toss thoroughly, taste and correct for seasoning, and serve.

Cannellini Bean Salad

ALL THE INGREDIENTS of this salad, except for the beans, are to be chopped so fine that they become creamy, blending with each other and clinging to the beans with the consistency of a sauce. It can be done by hand, but if a food processor is available it should be the instrument of choice.

The components of the salad develop better flavor if it is tossed while the beans are still quite warm. If you can arrange it, try to time the cooking of the beans so that they will become ready when you are about to make the salad.

For 6 servings

2 tablespoons chopped onion
3 fresh sage leaves
2 to 3 flat anchovy fillets
 (preferably the ones
 prepared at home as
 described on page 9)
⅓ cup extra virgin olive oil
1 tablespoon red wine vinegar
The yolks of 2 hard-boiled eggs

1 tablespoon chopped parsley
Salt
1 cup dried *cannellini* white
 beans, soaked and cooked
 as directed on page 13,
 and drained (see note)
Black pepper, ground fresh
 from the mill

Note ❦ If cooking the beans long in advance, keep them in their liquid and warm them up gently before using them.

Cannellini Bean Salad (continued)

1. Put all the ingredients, except for the beans and the black pepper, in a food processor and chop to a creamy consistency.

2. Toss the drained beans, preferably when they are still warm, with the processed ingredients. Add black pepper, toss again, and taste and correct for salt and other seasoning. Allow to steep at room temperature for 1 hour, then toss again just before serving. Do not refrigerate.

Radicchio and Warm Bean Salad

THE IDEAL COMPONENTS of this salad are long Treviso *radicchio* (see Radicchio on page 29), and fresh cranberry beans (described on page 102), but there are satisfactory substitutes for either or both. Instead of Treviso *radicchio* you can use the more common round one, or even Belgian endive, which is part of the same family. Instead of fresh beans you can use the dried, and if you can't find either fresh or dried cranberry beans, you can turn to dried *cannellini* beans.   *For 4 to 6 servings*

Cranberry beans, 2 pounds
  fresh, OR 1 cup dried,
  soaked and cooked as
  described on
  page 13
1 pound *radicchio,* either the
  long-leaf Treviso variety or

the round head OR Belgian
  endive
Salt
Extra virgin olive oil
Choice quality red wine vinegar
Black pepper, ground fresh
  from the mill

1. *If using fresh beans:* Shell them, put them in a pot with enough cold, unsalted water to cover by about 2 inches, bring the water to a gentle simmer, cover the pot, and cook at a slow, steady pace until tender, about 45 minutes to 1 hour. Time their preparation so they will still be warm when assembling the salad.

If using dried beans: Time their cooking, following the directions on page 13, so that they are still warm when you put together the salad.

2. *If using radicchio:* Detach the leaves from the head, discarding any blemished ones, shred them into narrow strips about ¼ inch wide, soak in cold water for a few minutes, drain, and either spin-dry or shake dry in a towel.

If using endive: Discard any blemished leaves, take a thin slice off the root end, then cut it across into strips ¼ inch wide, washing it and drying it as described above.

3. Drain the beans and put them, while they are still warm, into a serving bowl with the *radicchio* or endive. Add salt, toss once, pour in enough oil to coat well, add a dash of vinegar, liberal grindings of black pepper, toss thoroughly, and serve at once.

Asparagus Salad

WHEN ASPARAGUS is at its seasonal peak, the most popular way of serving it in Italy is boiled, as the salad course. It is served while it is still lukewarm or no cooler than room temperature. A little more vinegar than usual goes into the dressing. To keep the asparagus fresh, see suggestion on page 466.

For 4 to 6 servings

2 pounds fresh asparagus, peeled and cooked as described on page 466	Black pepper, ground fresh from the mill
Salt	Extra virgin olive oil
	Choice quality red wine vinegar

1. Cook the asparagus until tender, but still firm, drain, and lay it on a long platter, leaving one end of the platter free. Prop up the opposite end, to allow the liquid shed by the asparagus to run down toward the free end of the platter. After 15 to 20 minutes, pour out the liquid that has collected, and rearrange the asparagus, spreading it out evenly.

2. Add salt and pepper, coat generously with oil, and drizzle liberally with vinegar. Tip the platter in several directions to distribute the seasonings uniformly, and serve at once.

Green Bean Salad

For 4 servings

1 pound green beans, boiled as described on page 471	Choice quality red wine vinegar OR freshly squeezed lemon juice
Salt	
Extra virgin olive oil	

Green Bean Salad (continued)

Drain the beans when they are slightly firm, but tender, not crunchy. Put them in a serving bowl, add salt, and toss once. Pour enough oil over them to give them a glossy coat. Add a dash of vinegar or lemon juice, as you prefer. Toss thoroughly, taste and correct for seasoning, and serve while still lukewarm.

Baked Red Beets

THE VERY BEST WAY to cook beets is to bake them. It concentrates their flavor to an intense, mouth-filling sweetness that is to swoon over if you have never had them before. No other method compares favorably with baking in the oven—not boiling, not microwaving, certainly not buying them in cans. It takes time, but it doesn't take watching and it leaves you free to do whatever else you like. Sliced baked beets seasoned with olive oil, salt, and vinegar is one of the most delicious salads you can make.

One of the bonuses of buying raw beets is getting the tops. Both the stems

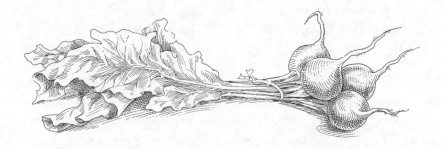

and leaves are excellent when boiled and served as salad. Look for the tops that have the smallest leaves, an indication of youth and tenderness. The spindly red stems strewn among the lush green leaves are delightful to look at, and delicious is the contrast between the crunchiness of the former and the tenderness of the latter. *For 4 servings*

1 bunch raw red beets with their tops, about 4 to 6 beets, depending on size	Salt Extra virgin olive oil Choice quality red wine vinegar

1. Preheat oven to 400°.
2. Cut off the tops of the beets at the base of the stems and save to cook as described in the recipe that follows. Trim the root ends of the beet bulbs.

3. Wash the beets in cold water, then wrap them all together in parchment paper or aluminum foil, crimping the edge of the paper or foil to seal tightly. Put them in the upper part of the oven. They are done when they feel tender but firm when prodded with a fork, about 1½ to 2 hours, depending on their size.

4. While they are still warm, but cool enough to handle, pull off their blackish skin. Cut them into thin slices.

5. When ready to serve, toss with salt, liberal quantities of olive oil, and a dash of vinegar.

Ahead-of-time note ❀ Baked beets taste best the day they are done, served still faintly warm from the oven. But they are very nice even if they must be kept a day or two. Refrigerate them whole, with the skin on, in a tightly sealed plastic bag. Take out of the refrigerator in sufficient time for them to come to room temperature before serving.

Beet Tops Salad

THE FRESHNESS of the stems and leaves is very short lived, and they should be cooked and eaten the day you buy them, if possible. You could make a nice mixed salad, combining the boiled tops with the sliced, baked beets. Or, you could put away the less perishable raw beet bulbs for two or three days and have just the tops in a salad while these are still fresh.   *For 4 servings*

The stems and leaves from 3 or   Extra virgin olive oil
  more bunches raw beets   Freshly squeezed lemon juice
Salt

Note ❀ If you are serving the tops and the sliced beets together, substitute vinegar for lemon juice.

1. Pull the leaves from the stems. Snap the stems into 2 or 3 pieces, pulling away any strings as you do so. Wash both the stems and the leaves in cold water.

2. Bring 3 to 4 quarts water to a boil, add salt, and as soon as it boils again put in just the stems. After 8 minutes or so—a little longer if the stems are rather thick—put in the leaves. They are done when tender to the bite, about 5 minutes or less. Drain well, shaking off all moisture.

3. When they have cooled down, but are still slightly warm, toss with salt, olive oil, and a dash of lemon juice. Serve at once.

Warm Cauliflower Salad

For 6 or more servings

1 head cauliflower, about 2 pounds, cooked as described on page 482	Salt Extra virgin olive oil Choice quality red wine vinegar

Note ❀ If you cannot use the entire head as salad, season only as much as you need to, and save the rest. It can be refrigerated and used a day or two later to make Gratinéed Cauliflower with Butter and Parmesan Cheese, Gratinéed Cauliflower with Béchamel Sauce, Fried Cauliflower Wedges with Egg and Bread Crumb Batter, or Fried Cauliflower with Parmesan Cheese Batter.

1. Drain the cauliflower when tender, but still slightly firm, and before it cools, detach the florets from the head, dividing all but the smallest into two or three pieces.

2. Put the florets in a serving bowl, and season liberally with salt, olive oil, and vinegar. Cauliflower needs ample quantities of all three. Toss gently so as not to mash the florets, taste and correct for seasoning, and serve at once.

Italian Potato Salad

IN TAKING the measure of a good home cook, many Italians might agree that among the criteria there would have to be the quality of the potato salad. Not that there is any mystery about what goes into it: It's just potatoes, salt, olive oil, and vinegar. No onions, eggs, mayonnaise, herbs, or other curiosities. But the choice of potatoes has to be right. Their flesh must be waxy smooth and compact, not crumbly; their color when cooked, warm and golden, like that of maize or country butter; their flavor fresh, sweet, and nutty, with no hint of mustiness. They should be boiled until fully tender, but without the least trace of sogginess. The slices must come off the potatoes whole, without breaking apart. They must be splashed with good wine vinegar when they are still hot so that they can soak up the aroma while their heat softens the vinegar's acetic edge.

For 4 to 6 servings

1½ pounds waxy, boiling potatoes, either new or mature, and all of a size	Choice quality red wine vinegar Salt Extra virgin olive oil

1. Wash the potatoes in cold water. Put them in a pot with their skins on and enough water to cover by at least 2 inches. Bring to a slow boil, and cook until tender, but not too soft. It should take about 35 minutes, less if you are using small, new potatoes. Refrain from prodding them too frequently with the fork, or they will become soggy, or break apart later when slicing them.

2. When done, pour out the water from the pot, but leave the potatoes in. Shake the pot over medium heat for just a few moments, moving the potatoes around, causing their excess of moisture to evaporate.

3. Pull off the potato skins while they are still hot.

4. Using a sharp knife and very little pressure, cut the potatoes into slices about ¼ inch thick, and spread them out on a warm serving platter. Sprinkle immediately with about 3 tablespoons of vinegar. Turn the potatoes gently.

5. When ready to serve, add salt and a liberal quantity of very good olive oil. Taste and correct for seasoning, adding more vinegar if required. Serve while still lukewarm or no colder than room temperature. Do not keep overnight, and do not refrigerate.

Boiled Swiss Chard Salad

Young Swiss chard has thin stems that must be discarded, but mature chard has broad, meaty stalks that are very good to eat. In the salad described here, both the leaves and the stalks are used. If, however, you prefer to utilize the stalks separately, such as in the gratinéed dish that you'll find on page 489, set them aside and make the salad solely from the leaves. *For 4 to 6 servings*

2 bunches Swiss chard	Extra virgin olive oil
Salt	Freshly squeezed lemon juice

1. If the chard is young, with skinny stems, detach and discard the stems. If it is mature chard with broad stalks, pull the leaves from the stalks, discarding any blemished leaves. Cut the stalks lengthwise into narrow strips a little less than ½ inch wide, and then trim these into shorter pieces about 4 inches long. Soak all the chard in a basin with several changes of cold water until there is no trace of soil in the water.

2. *If using just the chard leaves:* Put the leaves in a pan with only the moisture clinging to them, add 2 teaspoons salt, turn the heat on to medium, cover, and cook until fully tender, about 15 to 18 minutes from the time the liquid in the pan starts to bubble.

If using both stalks and leaves: Put the trimmed stalks in a pan with 2 to

Boiled Swiss Chard Salad (continued)

3 inches water, turn the heat on to medium, cover, and cook for 2 to 3 minutes after the water comes to a boil. Then add the leaves and 2 teaspoons salt and cook until tender.

3. Drain the chard in a colander, and gently press as much moisture out of it as possible, using the back of a fork. Transfer to a serving platter. When lukewarm or no cooler than room temperature, toss with salt, olive oil, and 1 or more tablespoons of lemon juice. Serve at once.

Boiled Zucchini Salad

For 6 servings

6 young, firm, glossy zucchini	2 tablespoons chopped parsley
3 large garlic cloves	Black pepper, ground fresh
Extra virgin olive oil	from the mill
Choice quality red wine vinegar	Salt

1. Soak and clean the zucchini as directed on page 530, but do not cut off the ends yet.

2. Bring 3 to 4 quarts of water to a boil, put in the zucchini, and cook until tender, but slightly resistant when prodded with a fork, about 15 minutes or more, depending on the vegetable's youth and freshness. Drain, and as soon as you can handle them, cut off both ends and slice each zucchini lengthwise in two.

3. While the zucchini is cooking, mash the garlic cloves with a knife handle, splitting the skin and removing it. As soon as you have cut the cooked, drained zucchini in half, rub each cut side while it is still hot with the crushed garlic.

4. Lay the zucchini on a long platter without spreading them out, but collecting them toward one end. Prop up that end, to allow the liquid shed by the zucchini to run down. After 15 to 20 minutes, pour off the liquid that has collected, and rearrange the zucchini, spreading it out evenly.

5. Season the zucchini with a liberal quantity of olive oil, a dash of vinegar, the parsley, and several grindings of pepper. Add salt only just as you are about to serve, otherwise the zucchini will begin to shed liquid again.

Variation all'Agro, with Lemon Juice

When served *all'agro,* zucchini is cooked exactly as described in the preceding recipe, but instead of slicing it in two long halves, it is cut into thin rounds.

The garlic is omitted, and lemon juice, to taste, replaces the vinegar. The zucchini rounds are tossed with all the condiments, including salt, only when ready to serve and preferably while still lukewarm. A popular late spring and summer salad in Italy combines the zucchini rounds with boiled green beans, page 471, and boiled sliced new potatoes, page 560. It is served *all'agro,* with lemon juice.

Insalatone—Mixed Cooked Vegetable Salad

IT TAKES a considerable amount of time to assemble all the components of this magnificent cooked salad, but the time it needs is mainly for cooking, not for watching, so you might plan on doing it when you have something else on the fire that requires lengthy cooking, such as a pot roast. Serve this salad the same day you make it, without refrigerating it, and with some of the ingredients still lukewarm, if that is possible.

The preparation of the ingredients is necessarily listed as a sequence, but in fact, except for the beets, which can be done a day or two earlier, they can all be done at the same time and taken in any order. *For 6 servings*

3 medium round, waxy, boiling
   potatoes
5 medium onions
2 yellow or red sweet bell
   peppers
½ pound green beans
3 medium or 2 large beets,
   baked as described on
   page 558

Salt
Extra virgin olive oil
Choice quality red wine vinegar
Black pepper, ground fresh
   from the mill

1. Preheat oven to 400°.
2. Boil the potatoes with their skins on as described on page 560. Drain when tender, peel while hot, and cut into ¼-inch slices. Put on a serving platter.
3. Meanwhile, bake the onions with their skins on on a baking sheet placed on the upper rack of the preheated oven. Cook until tender all the way through to the center when prodded with a fork. Pull off their skins, cut the onions into halves, and add them to the platter.
4. Char and peel the peppers as described on page 54, split them to

remove the pulpy core with all the seeds, and cut them lengthwise into 1-inch-wide strips. Add them to the salad platter.

5. Boil the beans as described on page 471, drain and put them on the platter.

6. Squeeze off the dark skin of the baked beets, cut them into thin slices, and add these to the salad.

7. Toss the salad with salt, enough olive oil to coat all ingredients, a dash of vinegar, and liberal grindings of pepper. Taste and correct for seasoning, and serve at once.

Beans and Tuna Salad

THE SALAD given here is basically a bean salad, enriched by tuna and flavored by onion. The proportions of the ingredients, however, can be adjusted to suit individual tastes. The balance can be tipped in favor of tuna, if that is what you prefer, particularly if you have access to very good tuna in olive oil sold in bulk. Nor would it do much damage to use a whole onion instead of a half; remember to slice it very thin, as described in the basic method for preparing onion for salads.   *For 4 servings*

1 cup dried *cannellini* white beans, soaked and cooked as directed on page 13, and drained, OR
3 cups canned *cannellini* beans, drained
½ medium onion, preferably of a sweet variety, such as Bermuda red, Vidalia, or Maui, sliced and soaked as described on page 545
Salt
1 seven-ounce can imported tuna packed in olive oil
Extra virgin olive oil
Choice quality red wine vinegar
Black pepper, cracked fairly coarse

Put the beans and onion into a serving bowl, sprinkle liberally with salt, and toss. Drain the tuna and add it to the bowl, breaking it into large flakes with a fork. Pour on enough oil to coat well, add a dash of vinegar and a generous quantity of cracked pepper, toss thoroughly, turning over the ingredients several times, taste and correct for seasoning, and serve at once.

Seafood Salad

IN SUMMER, in Italy, seafood salads are everywhere, on every buffet table, on every fish restaurant's list. They are hard to pass up because when they are good, they are very, very good. Unfortunately, they are sometimes trotted in and out of refrigerators more often than one would rather know, and are totally lacking in that vibrant, fresh taste that is their whole reason for being. The only road a seafood salad should travel is directly from the kitchen to the table with no overnight stops or detours through the icebox. The best reason for making it yourself at home may just be to be able to control that.

For 6 to 8 servings

½ pound whole squid
1 pound octopus tentacles (see
    note below)
2 medium carrots
2 medium onions
2 stalks celery
¾ pound unshelled small to
    medium shrimp
Wine vinegar
Salt
¼ pound sea scallops
1 dozen littleneck clams
1 dozen mussels

1 sweet red bell pepper
1 large garlic clove
6 black, round Greek olives and
    6 green olives in brine,
    pitted and quartered
¼ cup freshly squeezed lemon
    juice
Extra virgin olive oil
Black pepper, ground fresh
    from the mill
Marjoram, ½ teaspoon if fresh,
    ¼ teaspoon if dried

Note ⊛ Of the ingredients listed, octopus tentacles is the only one not regularly available at most fish markets. Fishmongers in Italian neighborhoods have it, and so do those who supply Oriental cooks. If possible, try to include it in your salad because its fine, firm consistency adds considerably to the variety of the dish. It is not indispensable, however, and if unavailable, proceed without it.

Seafood Salad (continued)

1. Clean the squid as described on pages 317–319, then cut the sacs into rings ½ inch wide or slightly less, and separate the tentacles into two clusters.

2. Separate the octopus tentacles into single strands, soak them in cold water, and peel off as much of their skin as will come off. Cut them into disks a little narrower than ½ inch.

3. Peel and wash the carrots, peel the onions, wash the celery.

4. Wash the shrimp in cold water, but do not shell it.

5. Using two separate pots, put 1 quart water, 2 tablespoons vinegar, 1 teaspoon salt, 1 carrot, 1 onion, 1 celery stalk into each pot, cover, and bring the water to a boil. When the water is boiling rapidly, drop the squid rings and tentacles in one pot, the octopus in the other. Drain the squid when its color changes from shiny and translucent to a flat white, which will take just a few minutes. The octopus will take a little longer. Drain it when it too is flat white in color, but first cut into one of the thicker pieces to make sure it is that flat color throughout.

6. Put 2 quarts water in a saucepan together with 2 tablespoons vinegar and 1 teaspoon salt, cover, and bring to a boil. Drop in the shrimp, and when the water resumes boiling, cook for 1 minute, or a few seconds less if they are very small. Drain, and as soon as they are cool enough to handle, shell and devein them. If they are very small, leave them whole; otherwise cut them into rounds about ½ inch thick.

7. Wash the scallops in cold water. Into a small saucepan put 2 cups water with 1 tablespoon vinegar and ½ teaspoon salt, cover, bring to a boil, and drop in the scallops. After the water resumes boiling, cook for 1½ to 2 minutes, depending on their size. Drain and cut into ½-inch cubes.

8. Wash and scrub the clams and mussels as described on page 81. Discard those that stay open when handled. Put them in a pan broad enough so that they don't need to be piled up more than 3 deep, cover the pan, and turn on the heat to high. Check the mussels and clams frequently, turning them over, and promptly remove them from the pan as they open their shells.

9. When all the clams and mussels have opened up, detach their meat from the shell. Use a slotted spoon to transfer the shellfish meat to a bowl. Tip the pan, gently spoon off the liquid from the top without stirring that on the bottom, and pour it over the clam and mussel meat. Add enough to cover.

10. Allow the clams and mussels to rest for 20 or 30 minutes, so that they may shed any sand still clinging to them, letting it settle to the bottom of the bowl. In the meantime, prepare the sweet pepper and the garlic. Split the pepper open to expose and remove the pulpy core with all the seeds. Skin the pepper raw with a swiveling-blade peeler, and cut it into strips about ½

inch wide and 1 inch long. Mash the garlic with a knife handle, splitting and removing the skin.

11. Retrieve the clam and mussel meat with a slotted spoon, and put it in a serving bowl together with the shrimp, squid, octopus, and scallops. Add the bell pepper, the quartered olives, the lemon juice, and enough oil to coat well, and toss thoroughly. Taste and correct for salt and lemon juice, add several grindings of pepper, the mashed garlic clove, and the marjoram. Toss again very thoroughly. Allow to steep at room temperature for at least 30 minutes. Before serving, take out the garlic, and toss the salad once or twice, turning over all the ingredients.

Rice and Chicken Salad

For 4 to 6 servings

Salt

1 cup long-grain rice

1 teaspoon mustard, Dijon or English style

2 teaspoons choice quality red wine vinegar

⅓ cup extra virgin olive oil

½ cup imported *fontina* cheese OR Swiss cheese diced very fine

½ cup round, black Greek olives, pitted and cut into fine dice

2 tablespoons green olives in brine, pitted and cut into fine dice

1 red or yellow sweet bell pepper, core and seeds removed, and cut into fine dice

3 tablespoons sour cucumber pickles, preferably *cornichons,* cut into fine dice

1 whole boiled breast of chicken, skinned and diced into ½-inch cubes

1. Bring 2 quarts water to a boil, add 1 tablespoon salt, then drop in the rice. When the water resumes boiling, cover, and adjust heat to cook at a gentle, but steady simmer. Stir the rice occasionally and cook until it is tender, but firm to the bite, about 10 to 12 minutes. Drain the rice, rinse in cold water, and drain well once more.

2. Put the mustard, salt, and vinegar into a serving bowl. Blend them well with a fork, then add the oil, beating with the fork to incorporate it into the mixture.

3. Add the drained rice and toss it with the seasonings. Add all the other ingredients, toss thoroughly, turning over the salad components 4 or 5 times, and taste and correct for seasoning. Serve at cool room temperature, but not out of the refrigerator.

Leftover Boiled Beef Salad

As FAR AS I am concerned, no beef dish is tastier than cold, leftover boiled beef. It may not satisfy quite the same wants as does a rib roast, a T-bone steak, or even the same cut when it was steaming in its broth, but it is light and fresh, and its flavor is wonderful.   *For 4 servings*

1 pound leftover boiled beef   Black pepper, ground fresh
Salt   from the mill
3 tablespoons extra virgin olive
   oil
1 tablespoon wine vinegar
   OR freshly squeezed lemon
   juice

1. Trim the meat of all loose bits of fat and skin. Put it in an airtight container just large enough to hold it, and refrigerate it. If the meat has already been sliced, fit one slice neatly above the other before putting it away, to leave as little surface exposed to the drying effects of air as possible. You can store it for as long as 3 days.

2. Take the beef out of the refrigerator at least 2 hours before you are going to use it. If the meat is still in one piece, slice it the very thinnest you can. Spread the slices on a serving platter, and season with salt, olive oil, turning the slices to coat them well, vinegar or lemon juice as you prefer, and several grindings of black pepper. Turn the slices over again, and serve when the beef has fully returned to room temperature.

Other Ways of Serving
Sliced Leftover Boiled Beef

❧ Over a bed of raw *finocchio* or celery sliced very, very thin. Season as described above.

❧ Over a bed of *arugula* and peeled orange or grapefruit sections. Season as described above, using lemon juice.

❧ With lukewarm *cannellini* beans. Season as described above, omitting the vinegar and lemon.

❧ With ¼ cup tuna and capers mayonnaise in the style of Vitello Tonnato, see page 382.

❀ With one of the green sauces, pages 42 and 43, or Horseradish Sauce, page 44. Let the meat steep in the sauce for 2 to 3 hours before serving.

❀ With mayonnaise and mustard.

DESSERTS

Croccante—Italian Praline

Croccante is the darkest, crunchiest, and least sweet of pralines, an irresistible candy that outshines most desserts and is astonishingly easy to make at home. Serve it alongside the after-dinner coffee, or to visitors at any time they may drop in, stash some in a bag when you are going on a trip, or crush it and grind it and use it as topping for ice cream or to mix with the frosting of other desserts. You can store it for weeks in a tightly closed jar or wrapped in aluminum foil, but once you start nibbling it doesn't last very long.

4 to 6 servings as candy, about 2½ cups if crushed

6 ounces, about 1½ cups, shelled almonds with their skins on
1 heaping cup granulated sugar
A large sheet of heavy-duty aluminum foil, spread flat on a counter and smeared with 1 teaspoon vegetable oil
A peeled potato

1. Drop the almonds into a pot of boiling water. Drain after 2 minutes, enclose them in a rough cloth dampened with cold water, and rub briskly for a minute or two. Open up the cloth, remove those almonds that have been skinned along with all the loose peels, and if there are still some nuts with their skins on, repeat the operation until they have all been peeled clean. Discard all the peels and chop the almonds very fine, using a knife, not the food processor, into pieces about half the size of a grain of rice.

2. Put the sugar and ¼ cup water into a small, preferably light-weight, saucepan. Melt the sugar over medium-high heat without stirring it, but tilting the pan occasionally. When the melted sugar becomes colored a rich tawny gold, add the chopped almonds and stir constantly until the almond and caramelized sugar mixture becomes a golden brown. Pour it *immediately* over the oiled aluminum foil. Cut the potato in two and use the flat side to spread the hot praline out very thin, to a thickness of about ⅛ inch.

3. *If you want to use it as candy:* Cut it into 2-inch diamond shapes before it cools. When completely cold, lift the pieces off the foil and put them in a screw-top jar, or into packets of foil, wrapped tightly, and store in a dry, cool cupboard.

If you want to use it for toppings: When it is completely cold, break it up into pieces, and grind them fine in the food processor. Store in an airtight jar, but do not refrigerate.

Bolognese Rice Cake

In Bologna, rice cake used to be made only at Easter, an occasion for lively rivalry among those families that claimed to have the most delicious and authentic recipe. The one given here came to me from those well-known Bolognese bakers, the Simili sisters, who unhesitatingly assured me theirs was the most delicious and authentic version. I leave the question of authenticity to those more willing than I to discuss it, but it is a fact that I have never had a better-tasting example of rice cake.   *For 6 to 8 servings*

1 quart milk
¼ teaspoon salt
2 or 3 strips lemon peel, the skin only, with none of the white pith beneath it
1¼ cups granulated sugar
⅓ cup rice, preferably imported Italian Arborio rice
4 eggs plus 1 yolk
½ cup almonds, blanched, skinned, and chopped, as described on page 570

⅓ cup chopped candied citron
A 6-cup square or rectangular cake pan
Butter for smearing the pan
Fine, dry, unflavored bread crumbs
2 tablespoons rum

1. Put the milk, salt, lemon peel, and sugar in a saucepan and bring to a moderate boil.

2. As soon as the milk begins to boil, add the rice, stirring it quickly with a wooden spoon. Adjust heat to cook at the slowest of simmers, and cook for 2½ hours, stirring from time to time. When done, the mixture will have become a dense, pale-brown mush. Most of the fine lemon peel should have dissolved, but if you find any pieces of it, take them out. Set the rice mush aside to cool.

3. Preheat oven to 350°.

Bolognese Rice Cake (continued)

4. Beat the 4 eggs and the yolk in a large bowl until all the yolks and whites are evenly blended. Add the rice mush, beating it into the eggs a spoonful at a time. Add the chopped almonds and the candied citron, mixing them in uniformly.

5. Generously smear the bottom and sides of the cake pan with butter. Sprinkle the pan with bread crumbs, then turn the pan over and give a sharp rap against the counter to shake off loose crumbs. Pour the mixture from the bowl into the pan, leveling it off. Place the pan on the middle rack of the preheated oven, and bake for 1 hour.

6. As soon as you take the pan out of the oven, while the cake is still hot, pierce it in several places with a fork, and pour the rum over it. When the cake is lukewarm, turn the pan over onto a serving platter and shake or tap it against the counter to work the cake loose. Serve rice cake no sooner than 24 hours after making it; if you let it mature for 2 to 3 days longer, its flavor will become even deeper and richer. To serve it in the traditional Bolognese fashion, cut the cake, before bringing it to the table, in a diagonally cross-hatched pattern that will produce diamond-shaped pieces about 2½ inches long.

Glazed Semolina Pudding

For 6 to 8 servings

Granulated sugar, ½ cup for the caramel plus ⅔ cup for the pudding

A 6-cup round, flameproof metal baking mold

2 cups milk

¼ teaspoon salt

⅓ cup *semolina*

1 tablespoon butter

1 tablespoon rum

¼ cup assorted candied fruit, chopped into ¼-inch pieces

The grated peel of 1 orange

Heaping ⅓ cup seedless raisins, preferably of the muscat variety, soaking in enough water to cover

All-purpose flour

2 eggs

1. Put ½ cup sugar and 2 tablespoons water in the mold, and bring to a boil on the stove over medium heat. Do not stir, but tilt the mold forward and backward to move the melted sugar until it becomes colored a light nut-brown. Take off heat immediately and quickly tip the mold in all directions, while the caramelized sugar is still liquid, to coat the mold evenly. Keep turning the mold until the caramel congeals, then set aside.

2. Preheat oven to 350°.

3. Put the milk and salt in a saucepan and turn on the heat to low. When the milk comes just to the edge of a boil, add the *semolina,* pouring it in a thin stream, and stirring rapidly with a whisk. Continue cooking, stirring constantly, until the *semolina* and milk mixture comes easily away from the sides of the pan. Take off heat, but continue to stir for another half minute or so until you are sure that the *semolina* mixture is not sticking to the pan.

4. Add the ⅔ cup sugar, stir, then add the butter and rum and stir thoroughly. Add the candied fruit and grated orange peel, stirring to distribute them evenly.

5. Drain the raisins and pat them dry in a cloth towel. Put them in a strainer and sprinkle them with flour while shaking the strainer. When the raisins have been evenly and lightly coated with flour, add them to the mixture in the pan.

6. Break the eggs into the *semolina* mixture, beating them in rapidly with a whisk. Pour the mixture into the caramelized mold and place it on the middle rack of the preheated oven. Bake for 40 minutes.

7. Take the pan out of the oven and allow the pudding to cool down. Then refrigerate it overnight. The following day, place the mold briefly on the stove over low heat, just long enough to soften the caramel. Take off heat, place a dish over the top of the mold, grasp the two tightly together with a dish towel, turn them over, and give the pan a few abrupt jerks against the dish until you feel the pudding loosen. Pull the pan away, unmolding the pudding onto the dish.

Glazed Bread Pudding

For 6 to 8 servings

Granulated sugar, 1 cup for the caramel plus ⅓ cup for the pudding

An 8-cup rectangular flameproof, metal cake pan or loaf pan

2½ cups good-quality stale white bread, trimmed of its crust, lightly toasted, and cut up

4 tablespoons (½ stick) butter

2 cups milk

½ cup seedless raisins, preferably of the muscat variety, soaking in enough water to cover

All-purpose flour

¼ cup *pignoli* (pine nuts)

3 egg yolks

2 egg whites

¼ cup rum

Glazed Bread Pudding (continued)

1. Put 1 cup sugar and 3 tablespoons water in the pan, and caramelize it, following the directions in Step 1 of the preceding recipe for Semolina Pudding.

2. Preheat oven to 375°.

3. Put the cut-up bread and the butter in a mixing bowl.

4. Put the milk in a small saucepan, turn the heat on to medium, and as soon as the milk forms a ring of tiny bubbles, pour it over the bread and butter. Do not stir, let the bread steep in the milk, and allow it to cool. When cool, beat it with a whisk or a fork until it becomes a soft, uniform mass.

5. Drain the raisins and pat them dry in a cloth towel. Put them in a strainer and sprinkle them with flour while shaking the strainer. When the raisins have been evenly and lightly coated with flour, mix them with the beaten bread mass.

6. Add ⅓ cup sugar, the pine nuts, and the egg yolks to the bowl, and mix thoroughly with the other ingredients.

7. In a separate bowl beat the egg whites until they form stiff peaks, then fold them gently into the bread mixture.

8. Transfer the bread mixture to the caramelized pan, level it off, and place the pan on the middle rack of the preheated oven. After 1 hour, turn the thermostat down to 300° and bake for 15 more minutes.

9. As soon as you take the pan out of the oven, while the pudding is still hot, pierce it in several places with a fork, and pour 2 tablespoons of rum over it. When the rum has been absorbed, turn the pan over onto a serving platter and shake or tap it against the counter to work the pudding loose. Lift the pan, unmolding the pudding onto the platter, pierce the pudding in several places, and pour the remaining 2 tablespoons of rum over it. Allow the pudding to mature for at least a day before serving it. You can refrigerate it for several days, but allow it to come to room temperature before bringing to the table.

Sbricciolona—Ferrara's Crumbly Cake

Sbricciolona—literal meaning of which is "she that crumbles"—is a dry, biscuity cake that is delicious after dinner with a glass of *vin santo* or Port, and it is equally welcome between meals, as a mid-morning nibble for example, or with an afternoon cup of tea or coffee.

It really does crumble and part of its charm is the irregularity of the pieces it breaks into. If you prefer to serve it in neat wedge-shaped sections, however, cut it while it is warm, before it hardens. *Sbricciolona* keeps beautifully for days and days, wrapped in foil or kept in a tin biscuit box.

My first acquaintance with *sbricciolona* took place in Ferrara, whose university I was attending. But when you travel in northern Italy you will find *sbricciolona* elsewhere, particularly in Mantua, and also in Piedmont's Langhe wine country, where they make it with hazelnuts instead of almonds.

For 6 servings

¼ pound almonds, blanched and skinned as described on page 570
1½ cups all-purpose flour
⅔ cup cornmeal
⅝ cup granulated sugar
The peel of 1 lemon grated without digging into the white pith beneath

2 egg yolks
8 tablespoons (1 stick) butter, softened to room temperature, plus more for smearing the cake pan
A 12-inch round cake pan

1. Preheat oven to 375°.

2. Grind the skinned almonds to powder in the food processor, turning the motor on and off.

3. Put the flour, cornmeal, granulated sugar, grated lemon peel, and powdered almonds in a bowl, and mix well. Add the 2 egg yolks, and work the mixture with your hands until it breaks up into little pellets. Add the softened butter, kneading it in with your fingers until it is completely incorporated into the mixture. (At first it may seem improbable that all the ingredients can ever be combined, but after working them for a few minutes, you will find they do hang together, forming a dry, crumbly dough.)

4. Smear the bottom of the cake pan with butter. Crumble the dough through your fingers into the pan until it is all uniformly distributed. Place the pan in the upper third of the preheated oven, and bake for 40 minutes. Serve when completely cold and hard (see prefatory note above).

Sweet Pastry Fritters

KNOWN BY a variety of names—*chiacchiere della nonna,* "grandmother's small talk," and *frappe* are the most common—these fritters are ribbons of dough twisted into bows and fried. The flavor and the fine, crisp texture of traditional versions depend on the use of lard, both in the dough and for frying.

If you have insurmountable objections to lard, butter and vegetable oil can be substituted, as indicated below. *For 4 to 6 servings*

1⅔ cups all-purpose flour
¼ cup lard OR butter
1 tablespoon granulated sugar
1 egg

2 tablespoons dry white wine
¼ teaspoon salt
Lard or vegetable oil for frying
Confectioners' sugar

1. Combine the flour with ¼ cup of either lard or butter and the granulated sugar, egg, white wine, and salt, kneading them into a smooth, soft dough. Put the dough in a bowl, cover with plastic wrap, and let it rest for at least 15 minutes.

2. On a lightly floured surface, roll out the dough to a thickness of ⅛ inch, then cut it into ribbons about 5 inches long and ½ inch wide. Twist and loop the ribbons into simple bows.

3. Melt enough lard in a skillet—or pour in enough vegetable oil—to come 1 inch up the sides of the pan. Have the heat turned to high. When the fat is very hot, put in as many pastry bows as will fit loosely in the pan. Fry them to a deep gold color on one side, then turn them and do the other side. Transfer them to a cooling rack to drain. (If you are using lard, make sure it does not overheat. If you detect the beginning of a burning smell, turn the heat down.) Repeat the procedure until all the remaining bows are done. Sprinkle with confectioners' sugar, and serve either piping hot or at room temperature. The fritters usually disappear so quickly that how best to keep them may remain purely theoretical, but in case some are left over, stack them on a plate and store them in a cupboard. They keep very well for several days.

Apple Fritters

For 4 to 6 servings

3 apples of any firm, but not
    sour, cooking variety
¼ cup granulated sugar
2 tablespoons rum
The peel of 1 lemon grated
    without digging into the
    white pith beneath

⅔ cup all-purpose flour
Vegetable oil
Confectioners' sugar

1. Peel and core the apples, and cut them into slices about ⅜ inch thick.
2. Put the granulated sugar, rum, and grated lemon peel into a bowl to-

gether with the apple slices. Turn the slices once or twice and let steep for at
least 1 hour.

3. Use the flour and about 1 cup water to make a *pastella* batter as
described on page 530.

4. Pour enough oil into a skillet to come ½ inch up the sides, and turn on
the heat to high.

5. Take the apple slices out of the bowl and pat them dry with paper
towels. When the oil is very hot, dip them in the batter and slip as many of
them into the skillet as will fit loosely. Fry them to a golden brown on one
side, then turn them and do the other side. Transfer them to a cooling rack
to drain. Repeat the procedure until all the remaining slices are done. Sprinkle with confectioners' sugar and serve while hot.

Diplomatico—A Chocolate Dessert with Rum and Coffee

Is THERE any other dessert like *diplomatico,* I wonder, that rewards such little
effort with such gratifying results? You never even have to turn on the oven
because you utilize ready-made pound cake. Slices of rum- and coffee-soaked
cake are alternated with a simple mousse-like mixture of melted chocolate
and eggs, and basically that is all there is to it. You can't go wrong: Put in a
little less rum, add a little more chocolate, add or subtract an egg, and it will
still be a great success. *For 6 to 8 servings*

FOR THE RUM AND COFFEE SOAK

5 tablespoons rum
1¼ cups strong espresso coffee

5 teaspoons granulated sugar
5 tablespoons water

Note ❀ Some pound cakes absorb more than others, and the rum and coffee
mixture may not suffice for soaking all the slices; have additional coffee and
rum available and prepare more, if you need to, guided by the proportions
given above.

A 16-ounce pound cake
Cheesecloth
A 9-inch rectangular cake pan
  (if you like your dessert to

be tall rather than broad,
use a narrow loaf pan)

Diplomatico (continued)

FOR THE CHOCOLATE FILLING

4 eggs
1 teaspoon granulated sugar
A double boiler

6 ounces semisweet chocolate in
  drops or chopped up or
  grated squares

THE FROSTING

(If you prefer chocolate)
4 ounces semisweet chocolate in
  drops or chopped up or
  grated squares

1 teaspoon butter
1 tablespoon heavy whipping
  cream

(If you prefer whipped cream)
1 cup very cold heavy whipping
  cream
1 teaspoon granulated sugar

A copper or other mixing bowl
  kept in the freezer

THE GARNISH

Fresh berries OR walnuts and
  candied fruit for either the

chocolate or whipped cream
  frosting

1. *For the rum and coffee soak:* In a small bowl combine the rum, espresso, sugar, and water. Cut the pound cake into slices ¼ inch thick. Moisten cheesecloth with water and use it to line the inside of the cake pan with enough left over to extend beyond the pan and cover the cake later. Soak the pound cake, slice by slice in the rum and coffee mixture, then use the slices to line the bottom and sides of the pan. Leave no gaps, patching where necessary with pieces of soaked pound cake. Dip the cake slices in and out of the mixture rather quickly, otherwise they become too soggy to handle. If you run out of rum and coffee, mix some more.

2. *For the chocolate filling:* Separate the eggs, and beat the yolks with 1 teaspoon sugar until they turn pale yellow.

3. Put water in the bottom of a double boiler, bring it to a gentle, but steady simmer, then put the chocolate drops or chopped or grated semisweet chocolate into the top of the double boiler. When the chocolate has melted, pour it, a little at a time, over the egg yolks, mixing rapidly, until all the chocolate has been thoroughly amalgamated into the egg yolks.

4. Beat the egg whites in a bowl until they form stiff peaks. Mix 1 table-

spoon of egg white into the chocolate and egg yolk mixture, then add the remainder, folding them in gently so as not to collapse them.

5. Spoon the chocolate filling into the pan, over the rum- and coffee-soaked cake slices. Top and cover with more slices of cake soaked in rum and coffee, and over them fold the moistened cheesecloth extending over the rim of the pan. Refrigerate until the following day at least.

Ahead-of-time note ✿ You can leave the *diplomatico* in the refrigerator for up to a week before proceeding with the next step.

6. When you take the cake out of the refrigerator, unfold the cheesecloth, pulling it away from the top. Turn the pan over on a platter, and shake it abruptly to loosen the cake, letting it drop onto the platter. Pull off the cheesecloth covering it.

7. *If frosting with chocolate:* Bring water to a simmer in the bottom of a double boiler. In the top put the 4 ounces of chocolate drops or chopped or grated semisweet chocolate together with 1 teaspoon butter. When the chocolate has melted, stir in the 1 tablespoon of heavy cream. Spread the frosting evenly over the top and sides of the *diplomatico*. Refrigerate for an hour or so until the chocolate hardens.

If frosting with whipped cream: Put 1 cup very cold heavy cream and 1 teaspoon sugar into the bowl you had been keeping in the freezer. Whip it with a whisk until it is stiff. Use it to cover the top and sides of the cake.

Garnish the cake with a simple arrangement of either walnuts and candied fruit or fresh raspberries and blueberries or other berries.

Zuccotto

THAT THIS dome-shaped dessert is a Florentine specialty appears certain; what there is no general agreement upon is whether the name is an affectionate reference to the cupola that dominates Florence's skyline, or a less than reverent allusion to the clergy, inasmuch as in the Tuscan dialect, a cardinal's skullcap is also called a *zuccotto*. However it may have come by its name, *zuccotto* is another of those delightful confections that is so easy to take, and happily, just as easy to make. It may look like a pastry chef's triumph, but the greatest demand its preparation makes on you is that of assembling a far from daunting list of mostly ready-made components.   *For 6 servings*

2 ounces shelled almonds, blanched and skinned as described on page 570
2 ounces shelled whole hazelnuts
A 1½-quart bowl, its bottom as perfectly round as possible
Cheesecloth
A 10- to 12-ounce pound cake
3 tablespoons Cognac
2 tablespoons Maraschino liqueur (see note below)

2 tablespoons Cointreau or white Curaçao liqueur
5 ounces semisweet chocolate in drops or squares
A mixing bowl kept in the freezer
2 cups very cold heavy whipping cream
¾ cup confectioners' sugar
A double boiler

Note ☞ Maraschino is a fine Italian liqueur made from the pulp and crushed pits of the Dalmatian *marasca* cherry, with a distinctive flavor that no other fruit cordial duplicates. One of its most appealing uses is with marinated fresh fruit. Do not confuse the liqueur with the cherries that go by the same name; the latter are quite ordinary preserved and artificially colored cherries. There's no perfect substitute for Maraschino, but if you must use something else, look for a not too sweet cherry liqueur.

1. Preheat oven to 375°.

2. When the oven reaches the preset temperature, put the peeled almonds on a baking sheet, and place it on the uppermost rack of the preheated oven for 5 minutes. Watch the nuts to make sure they don't burn. (Do not turn the oven off when you take the almonds out.) Chop the almonds rather coarse by hand, or in the food processor, turning the blade on and off.

3. Put the shelled hazelnuts on the baking sheet, and roast them in the hot oven for 5 minutes. Take them out and use a dry, rough towel to rub off as much of their skin as comes easily away. Chop rather coarse, as you did the almonds.

4. Line the inside of the round bowl with a layer of moistened cheese-cloth.

5. Cut most of the pound cake into slices ⅜ inch thick. Divide each slice diagonally in half, making two triangular pieces, each with crust on two sides.

6. Combine the Cognac, Maraschino, and Cointreau in a small bowl or deep saucer. Use a spoon to sprinkle some of the liqueur mixture over each piece of cake, reserving some of the mixture for later. Line the inside of the bowl with moistened pound cake, the narrow end of each piece facing the bottom of the bowl. As you lay the pound cake triangles side by side, have a side with crust next to one without. When you unmold the *zuccotto,* the thin crust lines will form a sunburst pattern. Make sure the entire inner surface of the bowl is lined with cake. If you need to slice more of the cake, do so. If there are gaps, fill them with small pieces of moistened cake without worrying about the pattern they form. A certain measure of irregularity has its appeal as indication of the handmade character of the dessert.

7. If using chocolate drops split them, if using squares, chop them rather coarse.

8. Take the mixing bowl out of the freezer, put in the heavy cream and the confectioners' sugar, and whip with a whisk until the cream is stiff. Add to it 3 ounces of the chocolate, and all the chopped almonds and hazelnuts, distributing them evenly. Spoon one-half of the whipped cream mixture into the cake-lined bowl, spreading it uniformly with the back of the spoon or with a spatula over all the cake lining. You should be left with a hollow in the center.

9. Melt the remaining 2 ounces of chocolate in the top of a double boiler as described on page 578. Fold the melted chocolate into the remaining half of the whipped cream mixture, and spoon it over the cake, filling the hollow. Trim away any pieces of cake that protrude past the top edge of the bowl. Work out how many more slices of cake you will need to cover the top of the bowl, moisten them with the remaining liqueurs, and place them over the cream. Their outside edge must meet the top edge of the cake lining the sides of the bowl, thus sealing the *zuccotto.* Cover with plastic wrap and refrigerate overnight or up to 2 days.

10. Upon taking the bowl out of the refrigerator, remove the plastic wrap and turn the bowl upside down onto a platter. Lift the bowl away, leaving the *zuccotto* on the platter, and carefully pull off the cheesecloth. Serve while still cold.

Variation: Zuccotto with Ice Cream

From the ingredients and materials in the basic recipe above, omit the double boiler, the whipping cream, the confectioners' sugar, and the bowl in the

Zuccotto with Ice Cream (continued)

freezer. Have on hand 1 cup premium-quality dark chocolate ice cream (see *Marcella's Italian Kitchen,* page 320), and 1 cup homemade egg custard ice cream (page 612) or premium-quality vanilla ice cream.

❈ Follow the directions in the basic recipe through Step 7, until you have split the chocolate drops or chopped the squares. Mix the chocolate drops or chopped squares together with the almonds and hazelnuts. Divide the mixture into 2 equal parts.

❈ Put the chocolate and the vanilla ice creams in separate small bowls or saucers, and soften them to spreading consistency with a fork, but do not allow them to melt.

❈ Add the chocolate ice cream to one half of the chopped nut mixture, and the vanilla or egg custard ice cream to the other half.

❈ Spread the vanilla or egg custard ice cream mixture over the cake lining the bowl, leaving a hollow in the center. Fill the hollow with the chocolate ice cream.

❈ Seal the *zuccotto* with cake slices as described in the basic recipe, cover with freezer paper, and place in the freezer for at least 3 hours. Transfer to the refrigerator for 30 minutes before serving. Unmold as described in the basic recipe, and serve at once.

CHESTNUTS

Fresh chestnuts become available at the beginning of fall and continue to come to the market through the winter. Preserved chestnut meat is sold throughout the year in cans and jars, but it is no substitute for good quality fresh nuts.

How to choose ❈ In Italy one distinguishes between two types of edible chestnuts; one is small and flat, each prickly bur that contains them bears two, and it is known as *castagna comune,* or common chestnut; the other is  larger and much plumper, each bur contains just one, and it is known as *marrone.* The latter is the kind to look for, because its flesh is much juicier and sweeter. When truly fresh, chestnut skins should be glossy, unwrinkled, and the nut should feel heavy in the hand.

How to prepare ❀ The whole secret of cooking fresh chestnuts successfully rests in learning how to cut their shell, so that when they are cooked both the shell and the tough thin skin beneath will easily come away.

❀ After washing the nuts in cold water, soak them in lukewarm water for about 20 minutes; this step softens their shell and makes it easier to slash.

❀ When the nuts have finished soaking, make a horizontal cut that partly rings the middle of each one, starting at one edge of the flat side, circling the bulging belly side of the chestnut, and stopping just past the other edge of the flat side. Do not cut into the flat side itself, and keep the slash shallow so that you do not dig into the chestnut meat.

Monte Bianco—Puréed Chestnut and Chocolate Mound

ON THOSE DAYS when Milan's veil of gray air miraculously dissolves, and through gaps in the city skyline one can see the mountains lined up on the horizon, the eye is irresistibly drawn up to the perpetually white summit of Mont Blanc, gleaming like a frosty mirage in the northern sky. *Monte Bianco,* to call the mount by its Italian name, has a namesake that, in the fall, makes its appearance on demand on Milanese tables: It is a pyramid of dark chocolate and puréed fresh chestnuts, topped by a snowy peak of whipped cream. We can be deeply—even if only momentarily—consoled for the end of summer and the approach of winter by the heartwarming aroma and flavor of fresh chestnuts, and in *monte bianco* they find their most succulent employment.

For 6 servings

1 pound fresh chestnuts, soaked and gashed as described on page 583	A double boiler ¼ cup rum A mixing bowl kept in the freezer
Milk	
Salt	2 cups very cold heavy whipping cream
6 ounces semisweet chocolate in drops or chopped squares	2 teaspoons granulated sugar

1. Put the gashed chestnuts in a pot, cover amply with water, put a lid on the pot, bring the water to a boil, and cook for 25 minutes after the boil begins. Scoop the chestnuts out of the water a few at a time, peeling them while still very warm. Make sure you remove not only the outer shell, but also the wrinkled inner skin, but do not worry about keeping the chestnuts whole because you'll be puréeing them later.

2. Put the peeled nuts in a saucepan with just enough milk to cover and a pinch of salt. Cook at a steady simmer without covering the pan until all the milk has been absorbed, about 15 minutes.

3. Melt the chocolate in a double boiler as described on page 578.

4. Purée the chestnuts into a bowl, passing them through a food mill fitted with the disk with large holes. Add the melted chocolate and rum, mixing the ingredients well. Cover the bowl tightly with plastic wrap and refrigerate for at least 1 hour.

Ahead-of-time note ☙ The chestnut and chocolate mixture can be prepared up to this point a day in advance and refrigerated until you are ready to proceed.

5. Pass the chestnut purée and chocolate mixture through the food mill, fitted with the same disk, letting it drop onto a round serving platter. At first hold the food mill close to the edge of the dish; as you pass the mixture through it and as it piles up, bring the food mill gradually toward the center of the dish in an upward spiral direction. What you want to do is distribute the chestnut and chocolate on the platter so that it forms a cone-shaped mound. Do not pat it, or shape it in any way, but leave it looking exactly the way it did when it dropped from the mill.

6. Put the cream and sugar in the bowl you had been keeping in the freezer and whip it with a whisk until it stiffens. Use half the whipped cream to

cover the top of the chestnut mound, coming about two-thirds of the way down. It should have a natural, "snowed-on" look, so let the cream come down the mound at random in peaks and hollows.

Ahead-of-time note ❀ The *monte bianco* can be completed as described above, and served up to 4 to 6 hours later. Refrigerate it, but do not cover it. Also refrigerate the remaining half of the whipped cream.

7. Serve the dessert with the remaining whipped cream on the side for those who would like their *monte bianco* with a little more "snow."

Chestnuts Boiled in Red Wine, Romagna Style

How PROVIDENTIAL of chestnuts to be on hand when days are short, and evenings long and cold. As a university student living in an unheated room, I remember almost looking forward to winter, to those days that would end sitting by a fireplace with friends, a pot of boiled chestnuts, and a flask of rough, young wine. My father would say that chestnuts and wine make one tipsy. It hasn't been demonstrated that the nuts make wine more inebriating, but it is true that a taste of one leads irresistibly to a sip of the other, and vice versa, and it may take a long time to decide, while you continue to try both, whether you want to bring the evening to a close with a bite of chestnut or a swallow of wine.

For 4 servings

1 pound fresh chestnuts, soaked and gashed as described on page 583
1 cup dry red wine, preferably Chianti

Salt
2 whole bay leaves

1. Put the gashed chestnuts in a pot with the wine, a tiny pinch of salt, the bay leaves, and just enough water to cover. Put a lid on the pot, and turn on the heat to medium.

2. When the chestnuts are tender—it depends greatly on the freshness of the nuts, it may take 30 minutes or 1 hour—uncover the pot, and allow all but 1 or 2 tablespoons of wine to simmer away. Bring the chestnuts to the table at once, preferably in the pot, or in a warm bowl. Everyone will peel his or her own, which is part of the fun.

Roasted Chestnuts

THERE MAY BE no food scent more enticing than that of chestnuts roasting over hot coals. Unfortunately, the roasted chestnuts most of us are acquainted with are of the street corner variety, hard, dry, half-cooked, and often as not, cold. Yet it is easy to roast chestnuts at home in the oven that will taste just as good as they smell.   *For 4 servings*

1 pound fresh chestnuts, soaked
    and gashed as described on
    page 583

1. Preheat oven to 475°.
2. Spread the gashed chestnuts on a baking sheet, and when the oven reaches the preset temperature, put it in on the middle rack. Turn the nuts over from time to time, but not so often to lose heat in the oven.
3. When the chestnuts are tender—it will take between 30 and 45 minutes, depending on their freshness—take them off the baking sheet and wrap them tightly in a cloth towel. They will steam a bit inside the towel, causing the skins to come loose much more easily. After 10 minutes, unwrap and serve.

Roasting Chestnuts over a Fire

IF YOU HAVE the perforated skillet made for the purpose, or a similar pan, you can roast chestnuts over a gas flame or a charcoal fire. Don't put in any more at one time than will fit without stacking. If you are doing it over the stove, use medium heat; if it is over charcoal, there should be enough very hot, but not flaming, coals to provide constant heat for about 40 minutes. If the heat is too hot, the nuts will be charred on the outside, and undercooked on the inside. If there is not enough heat, they won't be cooked at all. Move the chestnuts around frequently to prevent their being burned on one side.

They are done when tender all the way through, when their centers are no longer floury and dry. It will take from 30 minutes to 45 minutes, depending on the freshness and size of the nuts. When done, wrap them in a cloth towel for 10 minutes to help the skins come away easily.

Almond Cake

THE ALMOND is by a wide margin the most favored nut in Italian cakes, particularly in the Veneto, and a comprehensive anthology of Italy's almond desserts would require a substantial volume. There are no egg yolks and there is no butter in this recipe, which uses only the whites instead of whole eggs, and produces a firm, but fairly light cake.   *For 6 to 8 servings*

10 ounces shelled, but unpeeled
   almonds, about 2 cups
1⅓ cups granulated sugar
8 egg whites
Salt
The peel of 1 lemon grated
   without digging into the
   white pith beneath

6 tablespoons flour
An 8- or 9-inch springform pan
Butter for greasing the pan

1. Preheat oven to 350°.

2. Put the almonds and sugar in a blender or food processor and grind to a fine consistency, turning the motor on and off.

3. Beat the egg whites together with ½ teaspoon salt until they form stiff peaks.

4. Add the ground almonds and the grated lemon peel to the egg whites, a little bit at a time, folding them in gently, but thoroughly. The whites may deflate a bit, but if you mix carefully there should be no significant loss of volume.

5. Add the flour, shaking a little of it at a time through a strainer, and again, mixing gently.

6. Thickly smear the pan with butter. Put the cake batter into the pan, shaking the pan to level it off. Place the pan in the middle level of the preheated oven and bake for 1 hour. Before taking it out of the oven, test the center of the cake by piercing it with a toothpick. If it comes out dry, the cake is done. If it does not, cook a little longer.

7. When done, unlock the pan and remove the hoop. When the cake has cooled somewhat, and it is just lukewarm, loosen it from the bottom of the pan. Serve when it is completely cold. It will keep quite a while if stored in a tin biscuit box.

Walnut Cake

For 8 servings

½ pound shelled walnuts
⅔ cup granulated sugar
8 tablespoons (1 stick) butter,
    softened at room tempera-
    ture
1 egg
2 tablespoons rum

The peel of 1 lemon grated
    without digging into the
    white pith beneath
1½ teaspoons baking powder
1 cup flour
An 8- or 9-inch springform pan

1. Preheat oven to 325°. When it has reached the preset temperature, spread the walnuts on a baking sheet and place in the middle of the oven. After 5 minutes, take the walnuts out of the oven and turn the thermostat up to 350°.

2. When the walnuts are cold, put them in a food processor together with 1 tablespoon of sugar, and grind fine, but not to a powder, turning the motor on and off. Take them out of the processor bowl and set aside.

3. Set aside 1 tablespoon butter for smearing the pan later. Put the remaining 7 tablespoons into the processor together with the rest of the sugar and process to a creamy consistency. Add the egg, rum, lemon peel, and baking powder, and process briefly until all ingredients are uniformly combined. Transfer the contents of the food processor to a mixing bowl.

4. Add the ground walnuts to the bowl, working them uniformly into the mixture with a spoon or spatula. Add the flour, shaking it through a strainer and combining it with the other ingredients to form a fairly compact and evenly blended cake batter.

5. Smear the cake pan with the 1 tablespoon butter, sprinkle lightly with flour, then turn the pan over, tapping it against the counter to shake off excess flour. Put in the batter, leveling it off with a spatula. Place the pan in the upper level of the oven. After 45 minutes, before taking it out of the oven, test the center of the cake by piercing it with a toothpick. If it comes out dry, the cake is done. If it does not, cook 10 minutes or so longer.

6. When done, unlock the pan and remove the hoop. When the cake has cooled somewhat, and it is just lukewarm, loosen it from the bottom of the pan. Serve after 24 hours, when its flavor has fully developed. It will keep quite a while if stored in a tin biscuit box.

Note ❀ The concentrated flavor of this walnut cake makes a modest slice amply satisfying. It goes perfectly with tea or coffee in the morning or afternoon. If served after dinner, it should be topped with freshly whipped cream.

A Farm Wife's Fresh Pear Tart

THIS TENDER, FRUITY CAKE has been described as being so simple that only an active campaign of sabotage could ruin it. It is indeed simple, but the choice of pears will considerably affect its flavor. It is not half so appealing when made with Bartlett pears as it is when made with a winter variety such as the Bosc or the Anjou. In Italy one would choose a long, slim brownish yellow pear known as Conferenza. *For 6 servings*

2 eggs
¼ cup milk
1 cup granulated sugar
Salt
1½ cups all-purpose flour
2 pounds fresh pears

A 9-inch round cake pan
Butter for greasing the pan and
    dotting the cake
½ cup dry, unflavored bread
    crumbs
OPTIONAL: 1 dozen cloves

1. Preheat oven to 375°.
2. Beat the eggs and milk together in a bowl. Add the sugar and a tiny pinch salt, and continue to beat. Add the flour, mixing it in thoroughly to produce a compact cake batter.
3. Peel the pears, cut them lengthwise in two, scoop out the seeds and core, then cut them into thin slices about 1 inch wide. Add them to the batter in the bowl, distributing them evenly.
4. Smear the pan generously with butter, sprinkle lightly with bread crumbs, then turn the pan over and give it a sharp rap against the counter to shake loose excess crumbs.
5. Put the batter into the pan, leveling it off with the back of a spoon or a spatula. Make numerous small hollows on top with a fingertip and fill them with little bits of butter. Stud with the optional cloves, distributing them at random, but apart. Place the pan in the upper third of the preheated oven and bake for 50 minutes, or until the top has become lightly colored.
6. While it is still lukewarm, carefully loosen the tart from the bottom of the pan, lift it with spatulas, and transfer to a platter. It is very nice served while still a little warm, or at room temperature.

Polenta Shortcake with Raisins, Dried Figs, and Pine Nuts

WHEN JAMES BEARD sojourned in Venice many years ago, he was fascinated by this local specialty, whose nuts and dried fruits are redolent of imperial Venice's trading days with the Near East, and he asked me to provide the recipe.

Jim was surprised to find it contained only one egg, but it does rise to about 2 inches, which is not inconsiderable for this rich and dense dessert. It can be quite good served with a dollop or two of fresh whipped cream, but, then, what isn't?   *For 6 to 8 servings*

1 cup coarse cornmeal
Salt
1½ tablespoons extra virgin
   olive oil
Heaping ½ cup granulated
   sugar
⅓ cup *pignoli* (pine nuts)
⅓ cup seedless raisins, preferably of the muscat variety
1 cup dried figs, cut into ¼-
   inch pieces

2 tablespoons butter plus more
   for smearing the pan
1 egg
2 tablespoons fennel seeds
1 cup all-purpose flour
A 9-inch round cake pan
Fine, dry, unflavored bread
   crumbs

1. Preheat oven to 400°.

2. Bring 2 cups water to a boil in a medium-size saucepan, then adjust heat to medium and add the cornmeal, pouring it in a thin stream. Let it run through the fingers of your partly clenched fist. With your other hand, stir constantly with a wooden spoon. When all the cornmeal is in, add the salt and the olive oil. Continue to stir for about 15 seconds until the mush thickens and pulls away from the sides of the pan when you stir it. Take off heat.

3. To the cornmeal mush add the sugar, pine nuts, raisins, figs, butter, egg, and fennel seeds, and mix thoroughly to combine all ingredients uniformly. Add the flour, and mix well to form a smoothly amalgamated cake batter.

4. Smear the cake pan with butter, sprinkle lightly with bread crumbs, then turn the pan over tapping it against the counter to shake off excess bread crumbs. Put in the batter, leveling it off with a spatula. Place the pan in the upper level of the oven and bake for 45 to 50 minutes.

5. While the cake is still warm, loosen its sides from the pan with a knife, and invert the pan over a plate, shaking it a little to cause the cake to drop onto the plate. Then turn the cake over again onto a serving platter. Serve when it has become completely cold.

Pisciotta—Olive Oil Cake

IN THE COUNTRY north of Verona, the grape and olive growers share the hills with the stone cutters, the latter taking the elevations too high for the vines and olive trees to thrive. Many of the farmers and stonemasons also share a table at the Trattoria Dalla Rosa, in the ancient town of San Giorgio, perched under the brow of one of the tallest hills. Alda Dalla Rosa, the matriarch, is in command of the kitchen, but her daughter Nori is the baker. This surprising and savory cake that uses only the local olive oil—possibly Italy's finest—for shortening comes from an undatable recipe Nori salvaged from the family's few preserved written records.   *For 6 servings*

2 eggs

½ cup plus 2 tablespoons granulated sugar

The peel of 1 lemon grated without digging into the white pith beneath

Salt

⅓ cup dry Marsala wine

⅓ cup milk

¾ cup extra virgin olive oil for the batter plus more for the pan

1 tablespoon baking powder

1½ cups all-purpose flour

A 2¼-quart tube pan

1. Preheat oven to 400°.
2. Break the eggs into a bowl and beat them with all the sugar until they become pale and foamy.
3. Add the grated lemon peel, salt, Marsala, milk, and the ¾ cup olive oil.
4. Mix the baking powder with the flour, add to the other ingredients, and mix thoroughly.
5. Smear the inside of the pan with a thin coating of olive oil, pour the batter into the pan, and bake in the upper third of the preheated oven for 50 minutes.
6. Let the cake cool for about 10 minutes, loosen it from the tube and sides of the pan with a knife blade, turn it over, unmolding it, and place it on a cooling rack until it comes to room temperature.

Ciambella—Grandmother's Pastry Ring

MOST ITALIAN DESSERTS are purchased from the local pastry shop, but some are habitually baked at home, and each region has one or two that are its specialty. *Ciambella* is my native Romagna's traditional home-baked cake, and as with other home-nurtured traditions, every household has its own version. Some use anise along with, or in place of, the lemon peel; others add white wine to the batter. Each is as "authentic" as the next. The one below is the recipe my grandmother used and like all tastes one grows up with, it is the one I like best.

At home, there seems to be no time of the day that is not appropriate for having a slice of *ciambella*. My mother, at ninety-seven, still has it every morning with her *caffelatte*, a big cup of weak espresso diluted with hot milk. The old farmers' way is to dunk the cake at the end of the meal into a glass of sweet wine. In this, as in many other instances where Italian food and drink is concerned, the farmers' way amply rewards emulation.   *For 8 to 10 servings*

8 tablespoons (1 stick) butter
4 cups unbleached flour
¾ cup granulated sugar
2½ teaspoons cream of tartar, available in pharmacies as potassium bitartrate, and 1 teaspoon bicarbonate of soda OR 3½ teaspoons baking powder
Salt

The peel of 1 lemon grated without digging into the white pith beneath
¼ cup lukewarm milk
2 eggs
A heavy baking sheet
Butter and flour for smearing and dusting the baking sheet

1. Preheat oven to 375°.

2. Put the butter in a saucepan and melt it without getting it too hot.

3. Put the flour in a large mixing bowl. Add the sugar, melted butter, cream of tartar, bicarbonate, a tiny pinch of salt, grated lemon peel, and the lukewarm milk. Add 1 whole egg and the white of the second egg. Add the yolk of the second egg less 1 teaspoonful of it, which you will set aside for "painting" the ring later. Thoroughly mix all the ingredients, then turn them out onto a work surface and knead the mixture for a few minutes.

4. Shape the dough into a large sausage roll about 2 inches thick, and make it into a ring. Pinch the ends together to close the ring. Brush the surface with the teaspoonful of yolk you have set aside and 1 teaspoon water, and score with a few shallow diagonal cuts.

5. Smear the baking sheet with butter, sprinkle it with flour, then turn it over and give it a rap on the counter to shake off excess flour. Put the ring in its center and place the sheet in the upper level of the preheated oven. Bake for 35 minutes. It should rise to nearly double its original size. Transfer to a cooling rack. When cold, wrap in foil or store in a tin biscuit box, but do not refrigerate. It tastes best served the following day.

Brutti Ma Buoni—Piedmontese Almond Cookies

55 to 60 cookies

11 ounces almonds, blanched and skinned, as described on page 570	4 egg whites
	Salt
	½ teaspoon pure vanilla extract
1 cup plus 3 tablespoons granulated sugar	Butter for smearing the cookie sheet

1. At least 30 minutes before you are ready to bake, preheat oven to 300°.

2. If using a food processor, pulverize the peeled almonds together with the sugar, turning the processor on and off.

If using a knife, chop the almonds very fine by themselves, preferably while they are still warm, then combine them with the sugar.

3. Whip the egg whites in a bowl together with a pinch of salt until they form stiff peaks.

4. Fold the egg whites into the almond and sugar mixture together with the vanilla extract.

5. Smear a baking sheet or shallow pan with butter. Scoop up some of the

cookie batter with a tablespoon, and use another spoon to push it off onto the baking sheet or pan. Keep the mounds of batter about 1½ inches apart. Don't worry if they seem shapeless: Their Italian name means ugly, but good; they are expected to be very irregular.

6. Bake on the middle rack of the preheated oven for 30 minutes. Spread them out on a cooling rack. These cookies keep for a very long time if stored in a tin biscuit box.

Calabresi—Almond and Lemon Cookies

About 4 dozen cookies

4 ounces almonds, blanched
    and skinned, as described
    on page 570
½ cup granulated sugar
2 egg yolks
2 heaping cups unbleached
    flour
Salt
The peel of 1 lemon grated
    without digging into the
    white pith beneath

¼ cup freshly squeezed lemon
    juice
Butter for smearing the cookie
    sheet or pan
1 egg, lightly beaten with 1
    tablespoon water
A pastry brush

1. At least 30 minutes before you are ready to bake, preheat oven to 400°.

2. If using a food processor, pulverize the peeled almonds together with the sugar, turning the processor on and off.

If using a knife, chop the almonds very fine by themselves, preferably while they are still warm, then combine with the sugar.

3. If using the food processor, add the 2 egg yolks, the flour, a pinch of salt, the grated lemon peel, and the lemon juice. Run the steel blade until the batter forms a smooth lump.

If doing it by hand, put the almond and sugar mixture into a bowl, and add the ingredients as above. Work the batter with your hands for 8 to 10 minutes, until the ingredients are smoothly amalgamated.

4. Smear a cookie sheet or shallow pan with butter.

5. Lightly flour a work surface, a rolling pin, and your hands. Pull a piece the size of an apple from the batter, and roll it out to a thickness of ¼ inch. Use a 2-inch cookie cutter, or a glass of similar diameter, to cut the dough into disks, and place the disks not quite edge to edge on the

baking sheet or pan. Knead dough scraps together, roll out, and cut into more disks.

6. When you have rolled out and cut all the dough, brush all the disks on top with beaten egg. Bake for 10 minutes on the middle rack of the pre-heated oven.

7. When done, transfer to a cooling rack. Once cold, store in a biscuit box or cookie jar, where they will keep well for weeks.

Gallette—Salt and Pepper Biscuits

THESE are excellent apéritif cookies. *3½ dozen biscuits*

2 extra-large eggs
¼ cup extra virgin olive oil
1½ cups unbleached flour
1½ teaspoons salt
½ teaspoon black pepper
    ground coarse

2½ teaspoons baking powder
Butter for greasing the pan
A pastry brush

1. Preheat oven to 375°.

2. Beat the eggs lightly and pour all but ½ tablespoon—which you will set aside for brushing the biscuits later—into a bowl. Add all the remaining ingredients and mix thoroughly with a wooden spoon. Turn the batter out onto a lightly floured work surface, dust your hands with flour, and work it for a few minutes into a smooth, compact mass. If you prefer, you can execute the entire step with the food processor. Wrap the dough tightly in plastic wrap or aluminum foil, and set it aside to rest at room temperature for at least 30 minutes.

3. Divide the dough in two. Dust a work surface and a rolling pin with flour, and flatten the dough, one piece at a time, to a thickness of no more than ¼ inch. Use a 2-inch cookie cutter, or a glass of comparable diameter, to cut the dough into disks. Keep the trimmings.

4. Smear a baking sheet or pan with butter, and place the rounds of dough on it, keeping them about 1½ inches apart.

5. Briefly knead the trimmings into a ball, roll it out, and cut it into disks to be added to the others.

6. Brush the top of all the disks with egg, then put the sheet or pan on the middle rack of the preheated oven. Bake for 12 minutes.

7. Remove the biscuits from the pan, and let them cool completely on a rack. They will be even tastier a day later.

Crema—Italian Custard Cream

Crema, or *crema pasticcera* to use its full name, is the basic custard used as a filling in many Italian desserts, most famously, perhaps, in *zuppa inglese.* It is not difficult to do, if you are a patient cook. It must not boil, yet the flour must be given sufficient heat and time to dissolve without leaving any trace of graininess. When the custard is lumpy or has a doughy flavor, it means the flour has either been cooked too hurriedly or not thoroughly enough or a combination of both causes.

You can make *crema* directly over the flame in a heavy-bottomed saucepan, but if you are concerned about how to keep the heat under control, use a double boiler, making sure that the water in the lower half stays at a brisk boil.

About 2½ cups

4 egg yolks	The peel of ½ lemon grated
¾ cup confectioners' sugar	without digging into the
¼ cup flour	white pith beneath
2 cups milk	

1. Put the egg yolks and sugar into a heavy-bottomed saucepan or in the top of a double boiler. Off heat, beat the yolks until they become pale yellow and creamy. Add the flour gradually, beating it in 1 tablespoon at a time.

2. In another saucepan bring all the milk just to the brink of a boil, when the edge begins to be ringed with little bubbles.

3. Always off heat, add the hot milk very slowly to the beaten egg yolks, stirring the entire time to avoid the formation of lumps.

4. Put the saucepan over low heat, or over the bottom part of the double boiler in which the water has been brought to a boil, and cook for about 5 minutes, stirring steadfastly with a wooden spoon. Do not let the cream come to a boil, but it's all right for an occasional bubble to break the surface. The custard cream is done when it clings to the spoon, coating it with medium density.

5. Remove from heat, place the pan with the cream into a bowl with ice water, and stir for a few minutes. Mix in the grated lemon peel, and stir a while longer until the cream cools off.

Ahead-of-time note ✪ You can make the cream a day or two in advance, if necessary. Transfer to a steel or ceramic container, press plastic wrap against the surface of the cream, and refrigerate.

Zuppa Inglese

If there is a wholly convincing explanation of why the dessert is described as *inglese,* English, I have never come across it, but there is no doubt why it is called a soup: It is so steeped in custard that it resembles the bread soaking in peasant soups. And like soup, it should be eaten with a spoon.

The version given here is based on the dense *zuppa inglese* we make in Emilia-Romagna. There the cordial used to dampen the sponge cake is *alchermes* mixed with rum. *Alchermes,* a vaguely spicy liqueur with a flowery scent, derived its red color from the bodies of dried cochineal bugs in which it was steeped. I am told it's no longer made that way, but it is, in any event, unavailable outside Italy, so we all must look for substitutes that please us. My combination of cordials is given below, but as long as you don't omit the rum, which is essential to the character of the dessert, you can devise your own formula.

Do, however, have the spirits mixture ready and the pound cake cut before you make the custard cream so you can use the latter the moment it's done. *For 6 servings*

The custard cream made with the recipe on page 596

A 10-ounce pound cake, sliced ¼ inch thick

A pastry brush

1 tablespoon rum mixed with 2 tablespoons Cognac, 2 tablespoons Drambuie, and

4 tablespoons Cherry Heering

2 ounces semisweet chocolate squares, chopped up

A double boiler

OPTIONAL TOPPING: 1 ounce chopped toasted almonds

1. Choose a deep dish or a bowl from which you will be serving the *zuppa.* Smear the bottom of the dish with 4 to 5 tablespoons of hot custard cream.

2. Line the bottom of the dish with a layer of pound cake slices set edge to edge. Dip a pastry brush into the liqueur mixture and saturate the cake with it. Top with one-third the remaining custard cream. Cover with another layer of sliced cake, and brush it with half the remaining liqueur mixture.

3. Bring water to a simmer in the lower part of a double boiler. In the top of the double boiler put the 2 ounces of chopped chocolate. When the chocolate has melted, divide the remaining custard cream into two parts, mix the melted chocolate with one part, and spread it over the layer of pound cake in the dish.

Zuppa Inglese (continued)

4. Add another layer of cake slices to the *zuppa,* soak it with the remaining liqueurs, and cover with the last of the custard cream. Top with the optional toasted almonds.

5. Cover with plastic wrap, and refrigerate for a minimum of 2 to 3 hours, and up to a day in advance. Serve chilled.

Sandro Fioriti's Variation

Sandro's in New York is where I go when, after I've been on the road a while, I am overcome by desire for the unaffected flavors of an Italian home kitchen. Before covering the *zuppa* with the last of the custard cream, spread 3 tablespoons of sour cherry preserves—imported Italian *amarene* preserve, if you can find it, or English *morello,* or other sour cherry—over the uppermost layer of pound cake, then cover with the custard cream. Omit the chopped almonds.

Zabaglione

THE WARM, wine-scented froth we call *zabaglione* may be the only dish made of whipped egg yolks. I don't know of another. Because egg yolks harden quickly over strong heat, it is easier to make *zabaglione* off direct heat in a double boiler, as in the instructions that follow. If, however, you know how to control this kind of cooking, you can do it directly over the flame, possibly using the traditional, round-bottomed, unlined copper *zabaglione* pot.

For 6 servings

4 egg yolks	A double boiler
¼ cup granulated sugar	½ cup dry Marsala wine

Note ❀ The egg yolk mixture increases considerably in volume as you beat it and cook it. If your double boiler is not a large one, you'd be better off improvising one by putting one good-size pot into a larger one that contains simmering water. There are trivets made especially to support the inner pot (a useful gadget to own), but you can use any small metal trivet for the purpose.

1. Put the egg yolks and sugar in the top of the double boiler, or in the inner pot as described above, and whip the yolks with a whisk, or electric mixer, until they are pale yellow and creamy.

2. In the bottom of the double boiler, or in the larger pot, bring water to the brink of a simmer.

3. Fit the two double-boiler pans together, or place the smaller pot with the yolks inside the one with the water. Add the Marsala, beating constantly. The mixture will begin to foam, then swell into a soft, frothy mass. The *zabaglione* is ready in 15 minutes or less, when it has formed soft mounds.

Zabaglione is usually served warm, either spooned into glass cups on its own, or over sliced ripe fruit, such as peaches or mango, or with plain cakes. It is delicious with the Ciambella on page 592. A cold version of *zabaglione* made with red wine follows.

Cold Zabaglione with Red Wine

Use the ingredients of the basic recipe above, substituting 1 cup dry red wine for the ½ cup Marsala. Ideally, the red wine should be Barolo; it would be almost as ideal if it were Barbaresco, but you could substitute other reds with full flavor, such as a Tuscan all-Sangiovese, a good Valpolicella, or even a California Zinfandel, or a Côte du Rhône.

Make the *zabaglione* following the instructions in the preceding recipe. Spoon it into individual serving cups and refrigerate for 4 to 6 hours before serving.

Italian Chocolate Mousse

For 6 servings

A double boiler

6 ounces semisweet chocolate, chopped fine

4 eggs (see warning about salmonella on page 41)

2 teaspoons granulated sugar

¼ cup strong espresso coffee

2 tablespoons dark rum

A mixing bowl kept in the freezer

⅔ cup very cold heavy whipping cream

1. Put water in the bottom of the double boiler, bring it to a gentle, but steady simmer, set the top of the double boiler over it, and put the chopped chocolate in to melt.

2. Separate the eggs, put the yolks in a bowl together with the sugar, and beat them until they become pale yellow and creamy. Add the melted chocolate, coffee, and rum, and mix them in with a spatula until the ingredients are uniformly combined.

Italian Chocolate Mousse (continued)

3. Take the bowl out of the freezer, put in the cream, beat it with a whisk until it stiffens, then fold it into the chocolate and egg yolk mixture.

4. Put the egg whites into a bowl, whip them until they form stiff peaks, then fold them gently, but thoroughly into the chocolate mixture.

5. Spoon the mousse into 6 individual serving cups or goblets, cover with plastic wrap, and refrigerate overnight. It can be kept even 3 or 4 days, but after the first 24 hours it may wrinkle and lose some of its creamy consistency.

Ricotta and Coffee Cream

THIS INTRIGUINGLY good combination of *ricotta*, rum, and coffee may be the easiest dessert I have ever learned to make. It can all be done in less than 3 seconds in the food processor or, for a firmer consistency, by beating the mixture with 2 forks held in one hand. Please note that the cream needs to set in the refrigerator overnight before serving.   *For 6 servings*

1½ pounds fresh *ricotta*
⅔ cup granulated sugar
5 tablespoons dark rum
½ cup plus 2 tablespoons very
    strong espresso coffee

Garnish: 36 espresso coffee
    beans

1. Put the *ricotta*, sugar, rum, and coffee into the food processor and process to a creamy consistency.

2. Pour the mixture into 6 individual glass dessert coupes, and store in the refrigerator overnight.

3. Just before serving, arrange 6 fresh, crisp coffee beans in a circular or other pleasing pattern over the cream. Serve cold.

Note ✿ Do not refrigerate with the beans or they will become soggy.

Crema Fritta—Fried Custard Cream

ALTHOUGH *crema fritta* makes a fine sweet morsel with which to end a meal, it is also served in Italy alongside breaded meats, such as veal cutlets, liver, or lamb chops. It is a classic component of a large *fritto misto,* the Bolognese mixed fry in which you would find not only several breaded fried meats, but vegetables, cheese, and fruit.

The custard for *crema fritta* must be made with more flour than the one on page 596 that goes with *zuppa inglese,* otherwise it would be too soft for frying. To blend in the flour evenly and smoothly, you must cook it over very slow heat and stir virtually without interruption the entire time. But it can be conveniently prepared earlier in the day for that evening, or even a day in advance.   *For 6 servings*

2 eggs plus 1 egg for breading the cream	2 small strips lemon peel with none of the white pith beneath
A double boiler	
½ cup granulated sugar	Fine, dry, unflavored bread
½ cup flour	crumbs, spread on a plate
2 cups milk	Vegetable oil

1. Off heat, break 2 eggs into the top of the double boiler, add the sugar, and beat the eggs until they are evenly blended and the sugar has dissolved almost completely. Mix in the flour, 1 tablespoon at a time, until all of it has been incorporated into the eggs.

2. Bring the milk to a boil in a small saucepan, and when it just begins to form a ring of tiny bubbles, add it to the eggs, beating it in ¼ cup at a time. When you have added all the milk, put in the lemon peel.

3. In the bottom of the double boiler bring water to the gentlest of simmers, then set the upper part over it. Begin to stir slowly, but steadily. After 15 minutes, you may raise the heat slightly. Continue to cook and stir until the cream is thick and smooth and does not taste of flour, about 20 minutes more. When done, pour the cream out onto a moistened platter, spreading it to a thickness of about 1 inch. Allow it to become cold before proceeding.

Ahead-of-time note ❀ You can store the cream at this point for several hours or until the following day. Refrigerate it under plastic wrap.

4. Cut the cold cream into diamond-shaped pieces 2 inches long. Beat the remaining egg in a soup dish or small bowl. Dredge the pieces of cream in bread crumbs, dip them in the beaten egg, then dredge them in bread crumbs again.

5. Pour enough vegetable oil in a frying pan to come 1 inch up its sides, and turn the heat on to medium high. When the oil is very hot, slip in as many pieces of the breaded cream as will fit loosely. When they have formed a nice golden crust on one side, turn them and do the other

Fried Custard Cream (continued)

side. Transfer to a cooling rack to drain. Repeat the procedure if there are more pieces left over to fry. Serve piping hot or no cooler than lukewarm. If serving as dessert, you may want to sprinkle the cream with a little confectioners' sugar.

Ricotta Fritters

THIS IS ONE of the desserts I have nearly always included in my courses. My students love to eat them, but they are also delighted to find that they can make the batter hours ahead of time, and to see how easy and quick the fritters are to make, even when doubling or tripling the recipe for a crowd.

For 4 servings

½ pound fresh *ricotta*
2 eggs
⅓ cup flour
1½ tablespoons butter, softened
    to room temperature
The peel of 1 lemon grated
    without digging into the
    white pith beneath

Salt
Vegetable oil
Honey of runny consistency

1. Put the *ricotta* in a bowl and crumble it, using two forks held in one hand.

2. Break the eggs into the bowl, and mix them with the *ricotta.*

3. Add the flour a little at a time, working it into the ricotta and egg mixture with the two forks held in one hand or with a spatula. Add the butter, lemon peel, and a tiny pinch of salt, swirling them into the mixture and beating until all ingredients of the fritter batter are evenly combined.

4. Set the batter aside and allow it to rest for at least 2 hours, but no more than 3½ hours.

5. Pour enough oil into a frying pan to come ½ inch up its sides, and turn on the heat to medium high. When the oil is quite hot—if a driblet of batter dropped in floats instantly to the surface, it is ready—put in the batter, a tablespoonful at a time. Push the batter off the spoon using the rounded corner of a spatula. Do not put in any more at one time than will fit loosely, without crowding the pan.

6. When the fritters have become colored a golden brown on one side,

turn them. If they are not puffing slightly into little balls, the heat is too high. Turn it down a little. When the fritters are brown on both sides, transfer them with a slotted spoon or spatula to a cooling rack to drain. If there is batter left over, repeat the procedure until it is all used.

7. Place the fritters on a serving platter, dribble honey liberally over all of them, and bring to the table. They are best perhaps while still hot, but they are very good even when lukewarm or at room temperature.

Baked Apples with Amaretti Cookies

Amaretti, the Italian macaroons with the bitter-almond, fruit-pit flavor, are a classic accompaniment with Italian baked apples. They come wrapped in pairs, and in two sizes, standard and miniature. The recipe below is based on the standard size.   *For 4 servings*

4 crisp, tart-sweet apples
9 pairs imported Italian
    amaretti cookies
4 tablespoons (½ stick) butter,
    completely softened at
    room temperature

¼ cup granulated sugar
½ cup water mixed with ½ cup
    dry white wine

1. Preheat oven to 400°.

2. Wash the apples in cold water. Use any suitable tool, from an apple corer to a pointed vegetable peeler, to core them from the top, stopping short of the bottom. Create a hole in the center that is ½ inch broad. Prick the apples' skin in many places, every inch or so, using a pointed knife blade.

3. Double a sheet of wax paper around 7 pairs of the *amaretti,* and pound them with a heavy object, such as a mallet or meat pounder, until they are crushed to a coarse consistency, but not pulverized. Mix them thoroughly with the very soft butter. Divide the mixture into 4 parts, and pack one part tightly into each apple cavity.

4. Put the apples in a baking pan, right side up. Sprinkle a tablespoon of sugar over each, and pour over them the water and white wine. Place the pan on the uppermost rack of the preheated oven and bake for 45 minutes.

5. Transfer the apples to a serving platter or individual dishes, using a large metal spatula.

6. There will be some liquid left in the baking pan. Separate the remain-

Baked Apples with Amaretti Cookies (continued)

ing 2 pairs of *amaretti,* and dip each cookie in the pan, but do not let it become too soggy or it will crumble. Put one of the cookies over the opening of each apple.

7. If the baking pan cannot go over direct heat, pour its contents into a saucepan, and turn the heat on to high. When the liquid has cooked down to a syrupy consistency, pour it over the apples. Serve at room temperature.

Ahead-of-time note ✸ The apples can be completed 2 or 3 days in advance and refrigerated, but return them to room temperature before serving.

Chilled Black Grape Pudding

For 4 servings

1 pound fresh black grapes
2 tablespoons flour
2 tablespoons granulated sugar
A mixing bowl kept in the
    freezer

½ cup very cold heavy
    whipping cream

1. Pull off all the grape berries from their stems and wash in cold water. Insert the disk with the smallest holes in your food mill, and purée all the grapes through the mill into a bowl. If you prefer to use a blender or food processor, first cut the berries open and remove their seeds.

2. Put 1 cup of the puréed grapes into a small saucepan. Add the flour, shaking it through a strainer. Mix thoroughly until the flour is smoothly combined with the grape purée.

3. Add the sugar to the puréed grapes remaining in the bowl, stirring it until it dissolves completely. Slowly pour the contents of the bowl into the saucepan, stirring constantly all the while.

4. Turn the heat under the saucepan on to low. Stir constantly, cooking until the grape mixture has simmered gently for about 5 minutes and has become rather dense. Adjust heat if necessary to keep the simmer from turning into a boil.

5. Empty the pudding from the pan into a bowl, letting it cool completely at room temperature. Spoon the pudding into 4 individual glass bowls, cover with plastic wrap, and refrigerate for at least 4 hours, but not overnight, before serving.

6. Just before serving, take the bowl out of the freezer, put in the cream, beat it with a whisk until it is stiff, and distribute it among the 4 bowls.

Macerated Orange Slices

AMONG ALL THE WAYS in which a meal can be brought to a fragrant close, none surpasses in refreshment these sliced oranges macerated in lemon peel, sugar, and lemon juice.   *For 4 servings*

6 sweet juicy oranges	5 tablespoons granulated sugar
The peel of 1 lemon grated without digging into the white pith beneath	The freshly squeezed juice of ½ lemon

1. Using a sharp paring knife, peel 4 of the 6 oranges, stripping away all the white spongy pith and as much as possible of the thin skin beneath it.

2. Cut the peeled oranges into slices less than ½ inch thick. Pick out all seeds. Put the slices into a deep platter or a shallow serving bowl, and sprinkle with the grated lemon peel. Add the sugar. Squeeze the remaining 2 oranges and add their juice to the platter or bowl. Add the lemon juice, then toss rather gently several times, being careful not to break up the orange slices as you turn them over.

3. Cover with plastic wrap, and refrigerate for at least 4 hours, or even overnight. Serve chilled, turning the orange slices over two or three times after taking them out of the refrigerator.

Note ✽ I find the oranges quite perfect as they are, but if you want to vary them or give them a more celebratory and emphatic accent, you could toss them, shortly before serving, with 2 tablespoons of one of the following liqueurs: Cointreau, white Curaçao, or best of all, Maraschino (see note on page 580).

Macedonia—Macerated Mixed Fresh Fruit

GEOGRAPHICALLY SPEAKING, Macedonia is a region in southeastern Europe divided among what used to be Yugoslavia, Greece, and Bulgaria. The mixture of peoples that inhabit it must have suggested the name that has become

Macerated Mixed Fresh Fruit (continued)

attached to this famous fruit dish, whose success in fact depends on the greatest possible variety of ingredients.

Indispensable to fruit *macedonia* are apples, pears, bananas, and the juice of oranges and lemons. To these you should add as full a sampling of seasonal fruits as you can assemble, choosing them for diversity of textures, balancing succulence with firmness, giving ripeness the preference, but avoiding mushiness.   *For 8 or more servings*

1½ cups freshly squeezed orange juice

The peel of 1 lemon grated without digging into the white pith beneath

2 or 3 tablespoons freshly squeezed lemon juice (only 1 tablespoon if using the optional liqueur)

2 apples

2 pears

2 bananas

1½ pounds other fruit, such as cherries, grapes, apricots,

plums, peaches, berries, mango, melon, and tangerine sections in as varied an assortment as possible

⅓ cup to ½ cup granulated sugar, to taste

OPTIONAL: ½ cup Maraschino liqueur (see note page 580)

OPTIONAL: 3 tablespoons walnuts or peeled almonds, toasted in the oven and chopped coarse

1. In a tureen or punch bowl or other large serving bowl put the orange juice, grated lemon peel, and the lemon juice.

2. All the fruit, save for cherries, tangerine sections, grapes, and berries, must be washed, peeled, cored when applicable, and diced into ½-inch cubes. Add each fruit to the bowl as you prepare it, so that the citrus juices will keep it from discoloring.

3. Wash the cherries, grapes, and berries. Divide the cherries and grape berries in half, pitting the cherries and picking out the grape seeds, if any. Leave the other berries whole, if they are blueberries, raspberries, or currants. Put any blueberries or currants in the bowl. If you are using raspberries or strawberries, which become mushy when they steep in a marinade, add them 30 minutes before serving. Stem the strawberries, and cut the berries in half before adding them to the *macedonia*.

4. Put in the sugar and the optional liqueur and nuts, and toss thoroughly, but gently, taking care not to mash the more delicate fruits. Cover with plastic wrap and refrigerate for at least 4 hours, but not overnight. Serve chilled, tossing all the fruit gently 2 or 3 times before serving.

Mangoes and Strawberries
in Sweet White Wine

MANGOES ARE NOT native to Italy, and absolute fidelity to indigenous ingredients would suggest you do this dish with peaches. If you can buy peaches
that were picked ripe and are succulently sweet, forget the mangoes. I never
see such peaches, except for a week or two in August, so for the rest of the year
mangoes, their exotic flavor and texture notwithstanding, are a more desirable
choice. They are usually least expensive when already ripe and ready to use. If
they are still firm, let them ripen for 2 to 4 days at home at room temperature, until they begin to give under light pressure from your thumb.

For 6 servings

2 small, ripe mangoes OR
   1 large one OR peaches
1½ cups fresh strawberries
2 tablespoons granulated sugar
The peel of 1 lemon grated
   without digging into the
   white pith beneath

1 cup good sweet white wine
   (see note below)

Note ❦ The ideal wine for macerating fruit is one made from *moscato,* the
most aromatic of all grapes. Throughout the Italian peninsula, and beyond it
to the Sicilian islands, ravishing sweet muscat wines are made, and if you
chance upon one of these, do not pass it by. If you are obliged to choose a substitute, any fine, natural, late-harvest sweet white wine from Germany, South
Africa, or California will do.

1. Peel the mangoes (or peaches), and slice the flesh off the pits. If using
peaches, split them in half and remove the pit. Cut the fruit into bite-size
pieces of about 1 inch, and put them in a serving bowl.

2. Wash the strawberries in cold water, remove stems and leaves, and slice
them lengthwise in half, unless they happen to very small. Add them to the
bowl.

3. Add the sugar, lemon peel, and wine to the bowl, and toss the fruit
thoroughly, but gently to avoid bruising it. Refrigerate and let steep for 1 to
2 hours. Serve chilled, tossing the fruit once or twice before bringing it to
the table.

Black and White Macerated Grapes

THIS IS A BEAUTIFUL bowl of fruit. The purple spheres of the black grapes are divided in half and seeded, and the seedless elongated ovals of the white grapes are left whole. Macerated with orange juice and lemon peel, their fragrance and freshness are irresistible.   *For 6 to 8 servings*

1 pound seedless white grapes
1 pound large black grapes, not
    the pale purple seedless
    ones
The peel of 1 lemon grated
    without digging into the
    white pith beneath

3 tablespoons granulated sugar
The freshly squeezed juice
    of 3 oranges

1. Detach all the grape berries from their stems and wash them in cold water. Put only the white ones into a serving bowl.

2. You must halve the black grapes to extract their seeds. (Seedless red grapes are very bland and are not recommended for this dish.) Hold each berry with the stem end facing up. Use a sharp paring knife, or preferably a small vegetable knife with a serrated blade, to cut the berry horizontally around its middle, cutting it all around, but not all the way through. With your fingertips, hold the upper half of the grape, and with your other hand twist off the bottom half. From the exposed center of one of the halves seeds will protrude; pick them out, and add both halves of the seeded berry to the bowl. Repeat the procedure until all the black grapes are done.

3. Add the lemon peel, sugar, and orange juice to the bowl. If the juice is insufficient to cover the grapes, squeeze some more. Toss thoroughly, cover with plastic wrap, and refrigerate for 2 to 3 hours before serving. Do not keep overnight because the grapes may begin to ferment.

Frullati—Fresh Fruit Whips

A *frullato* could be described as an adult milk shake, laced with just enough liqueur to make it not merely refreshing, but interesting as well. In summer in Italy, it is something that one orders at an espresso bar, but there is no reason one shouldn't have it at home, and enjoy it at any time of day. You can make *frullati* in a food processor, but if you have a blender, it will do a better job.   *For 2 servings*

1 banana OR an equivalent
    amount of fresh peaches OR
    strawberries OR raspberries
⅔ cup milk
1½ teaspoons sugar

3 tablespoons crushed ice
2 tablespoons Maraschino
    liqueur (see note on
    page 580)

All fruit must be washed in cold water, except for the banana. Bananas or peaches must be peeled, the latter pitted, and cut into pieces. Put the fruit and the other ingredients into the bowl of the blender or processor, and whip— at high speed if using the blender—until the ice has completely dissolved, and the fruit has been liquefied. Serve immediately.

GELATO

The most widely accepted explanation for the difference between ice cream and *gelato* is that there is less air in *gelato;* hence it is denser. Whether there is less air or not I don't really know, but it seems beside the point. I started consuming *gelato* the moment I learned to walk and hold a cone at the same time, and to me it is hardly density that characterizes it, but lightness and freshness of flavor. There is far less fat, less cream, fewer eggs, and no butter in *gelato*. It is never oversweet or overrich. Mrs. Marshall in a nineteenth-century gem of a book, *Ices Plain and Fancy,* may not have been thinking of *gelato,* but she nonetheless perfectly summed up its aim: ". . . [to] convey to the palate the greatest possible amount of pleasure and taste, whilst . . . in no way [be] suggestive of nourishment and solidity."

Freezing the gelato mixture 🟎 Pour the mixture, making sure it is already cold, into the container of your ice-cream maker, and freeze it following the manufacturer's instructions. When done, the *gelato* is ready to eat, but if you want to serve it later, or prefer it when it's more compact, transfer it to a container that closes tightly and place it in the freezer. If you are going to leave it in the freezer overnight or longer, let the *gelato* soften a little before serving by putting it in the refrigerator for 30 minutes.

Strawberry Gelato

For 4 servings

½ pound fresh strawberries   An ice-cream maker
¾ cup granulated sugar
¼ cup cold heavy whipping
    cream

1. Pull off the leaves and stems from the strawberries, and cut the berries in half, unless they are exceptionally small. Wash the berries in cold water.

2. Put the strawberries with all the sugar in the bowl of a food processor, process for a few moments, then add ¾ cup water and continue to process until liquefied.

3. Whip the cream until it thickens slightly, to the consistency of buttermilk. Put the cream and the puréed strawberries in a bowl, and mix thoroughly.

4. Freeze as described above.

Prune Gelato

For 4 servings

14 large OR 18 smaller dried   ½ cup cold heavy whipping
    prunes   cream
2 tablespoons granulated sugar   An ice-cream maker

1. Put the prunes, sugar, and 1½ cups water in a saucepan, and bring the water to a simmer over medium heat. Cover and cook until the prunes are very soft, 10 to 15 minutes, depending on their size.

2. Let the prunes cool off in the liquid in the saucepan, then retrieve them without emptying out the pan, and pit them. Put the pitted prunes into the bowl of a food processor, run the steel blade for a moment or two, then add the liquid from the pan and continue processing until the prunes are completely puréed.

3. Whip the cream until it thickens slightly, to the consistency of buttermilk. Put the cream and the puréed prunes in a bowl, and mix thoroughly.

4. Freeze as described on page 610.

Black Grape Gelato

For 4 servings

⅔ cup granulated sugar
1 pound large black grapes, not
    the pale purple seedless
    ones

¼ cup cold heavy whipping
    cream
An ice-cream maker

1. Put the sugar and ½ cup water into a small saucepan, turn on the heat to medium, and stir from time to time, until the sugar has melted completely. Pour the sugar syrup into a bowl.

2. Detach the grape berries from their stems and wash them in cold water. Fit the disk with the smallest holes into your food mill, and purée the grapes through the mill into the bowl with the sugar syrup. If a few shreds of grape skin go through the mill it is not a problem, but make sure none of the seeds get into the bowl. Do not use a food processor, because it will chop up the seeds, releasing their astringent oil. Mix the puréed grapes with the sugar syrup, and allow to cool completely.

3. Whip the cream until it thickens slightly, to the consistency of buttermilk. Add the cream to the grape and sugar syrup and mix thoroughly.

4. Freeze as described on page 610.

Banana and Rum Gelato

RUM GIVES THIS *gelato* a consistency somewhat between dense slush and soft ice cream, a quality that seems quite appropriately matched to the rich, intense banana flavor.

For 6 servings

¾ to 1 pound ripe bananas
⅔ cup granulated sugar
⅔ cup milk

2 tablespoons dark rum
An ice-cream maker

Banana and Rum Gelato (continued)

1. Peel the bananas, cut them up, put them in a food processor, and purée them.

2. Add the sugar, milk, and rum to the processor bowl and run the steel blade for another minute.

3. Freeze as described on page 610. It does not need any tempering when you take it out of the freezer because this is a particularly soft *gelato*.

Egg Custard Gelato

I HAVE BORROWED this recipe from *Marcella's Italian Kitchen* because no view of the Italian ice-cream maker's art, however cursory, can fail to include Italy's favorite flavor, *gelato di crema*—egg custard ice cream. And I know no finer version than this one which comes from Bologna's great classic restaurant, Diana.

For 6 to 8 servings

6 egg yolks
¾ cup granulated sugar
2 cups milk
The peel of ½ orange, with
    none of the white pith
    beneath

1 tablespoon Grand Marnier
    liqueur
An ice-cream maker

1. Put the egg yolks and sugar into a bowl and beat the yolks until they become pale yellow and form soft ribbons.

2. Put the milk and orange peel in a saucepan, turn the heat on to medium, and bring the milk to a slow simmer, being careful not to let it break into a boil.

3. Add the hot milk to the beaten yolks, pouring it in a thin stream through a fine strainer. Add a little at a time, stopping each time to beat it into the yolks.

4. Add the Grand Marnier, stirring well.

5. Transfer the mixture to a saucepan, turn on the heat to medium, and beat constantly for about 2 minutes without letting it boil, then take off heat and allow it to become completely cold.

6. Freeze as described on page 610.

The Chimney Sweep's Gelato

WHEN CUSTARD *gelato* is dusted with powdered espresso and bathed with whisky, it is not just another clever way of dressing up ice cream: It is a combination of unexpected textures and aromas that quicken each other and thrill the palate.

The deep, doubly roasted taste of espresso coffee is essential. You can use it straight out of the can, but it is finer when ground to a powder in a high-speed blender.

If you are rushed and have no time to make the *gelato,* you can substitute very good quality vanilla ice cream. *For 8 servings*

The egg custard *gelato,* made with the recipe on page 612 OR enough premium-quality vanilla ice cream for 8 portions

½ cup ground espresso coffee
Scotch OR Bourbon, about 1 tablespoon per person

Scoop the *gelato* or vanilla ice cream into 8 individual bowls, sprinkle 1 teaspoon ground espresso coffee over each portion, and pour into each bowl enough whisky to pool at the bottom, about 1 tablespoon. Serve at once.

Sgroppino—Venetian Lemon and Strawberry "Slush" with Sparkling Wine

IF YOU RATE highly with a Venetian restaurant, at the end of the meal the waiter may ask if you'd care for a *sgroppino.* Should you say yes, he will set up on the serving trolley by your table two bowls, one with lemon ice cream and one with cold puréed strawberries, a whisk, and a bottle of sparkling wine. He'll beat the ice cream, strawberries, and wine into a mixture as refreshing as whipped snow, but infinitely tastier. *Sgroppino* is poured into wide-mouthed goblets and served in place of, or in addition to, dessert. *For 8 servings*

Venetian Lemon and Strawberry "Slush" (continued)

FOR THE LEMON ICE CREAM
(To be prepared and frozen at least 2 hours in advance.)

The peel of 4 lemons with none
of the white pith beneath,
about ½ tightly packed cup
1 cup plus 2 tablespoons
granulated sugar

⅔ cup freshly squeezed lemon
juice
⅔ cup heavy whipping cream

1. Put 1½ cups water, the lemon peel, sugar, and lemon juice in a small saucepan, and bring to a boil. After 2 minutes, take off heat, remove the lemon peel, and pour the syrup into a bowl. Let it become completely cold.

2. Add the heavy cream, stirring to incorporate it evenly into the lemon syrup, then pour the mixture into your ice-cream maker and freeze it following the manufacturer's instructions. Store in the freezer in a tightly sealed container until you are ready to use it.

FOR THE STRAWBERRY PURÉE
(To be prepared and refrigerated at least 2 hours in advance.)

⅔ pound fresh, very ripe strawberries

Pull off the stems and leaves of the strawberries, wash them in cold water, put them in the food processor, and purée them. You should have about 2 cups strawberry purée. Transfer it to a bowl and refrigerate for at least 2 hours before using.

TO MAKE THE SGROPPINO

The lemon ice cream and cold
strawberry purée from
above

1¼ cups sparkling wine (see
note below)

Note 🌼 The ideal wine to use for *sgroppino* is Venice's fresh and fruity native sparkler, Prosecco, which is available abroad in many shops that sell Italian wine. If you cannot obtain it in America, look for a substitute among non-Champagne-method wines, such as some of California's or Germany's bulk-produced sparkling wines, or a Crémant from France. A true Champagne-method sparkler has a yeastier, more complex flavor than is desirable for this preparation.

1. Put the lemon ice cream in a bowl, and break it up with a spoon. Add half the strawberry purée, beating it into the ice cream with a whisk.

2. Add half the sparkling wine, briefly whipping it in with the whisk.

3. Add the remaining purée and wine, beating them in to form a soft, foamy mixture. Do not work it too long or it will become too liquid.

4. Pour the *sgroppino* into glass coupes, individual dessert bowls, or wide-mouthed stemmed glasses, and serve at once.

Frozen Tangerine Shells Filled with Tangerine Sorbet

For 6 to 8 servings

FOR THE TANGERINE SHELLS

6 large or 8 small tangerines with unblemished, intact skins

1. Wash the tangerines in cold water. Neatly slice off their tops in one piece, leaving enough of an opening for you to extract the fruit, and later to stuff the shell. Set the tops aside. With your fingers, pull out all the fruit sections, working carefully in order not to tear the fragile tangerine rind. Part of the fruit may be pressed to provide the juice needed for the ice, or you can add it to a *macedonia*, page 605, or simply eat it as is.

2. Put the hollowed-out shells and their tops in the freezer. Freeze for at least 2 hours or for as long as you need to until you are ready to use them.

Frozen Tangerine Shells (continued)

FOR THE TANGERINE SORBET

1 cup granulated sugar

The peels of ½ orange and ½ lemon grated without digging into the white pith beneath

The freshly squeezed juice of 2 large or 4 small tangerines,

1 large or 2 small oranges, and 1 lemon

1 egg white

An ice-cream maker

3 tablespoons rum

1. Put the sugar and 1 cup water into a small saucepan, turn on the heat to medium, and stir from time to time until the sugar has melted. Pour the syrup into a bowl.

2. Add the grated orange and lemon peels, and the tangerine, orange, and lemon juices to the bowl, and mix well with the syrup. Allow the mixture to become completely cold.

3. Lightly beat the egg white until it begins to foam, then stir it into the mixture in the bowl.

4. Pour the mixture into the container of your ice-cream maker, and freeze it following the manufacturer's instructions. When done, transfer it to a tight-sealing container, stir in the rum, distributing it thoroughly, close the container, and place it in the freezer for 1 hour or even much longer, until you are ready to fill the tangerine shells and serve them.

FILLING THE TANGERINE SHELLS

2 bright, unblemished fresh mint leaves for every tangerine

1. Take out the frozen tangerine shells and their tops.

2. Take the tangerine sorbet out of the freezer and stir to redistribute some of the rum that may have separated from it. Spoon the sorbet into the hollowed-out shells. There should be enough sorbet in each shell to come up slightly above the rim.

3. Place 2 mint leaves on each sorbet, with their tips draped over the edge of the frozen shell. Put the tops over the shells, setting them slightly askew, to show both the mint and some of the sorbet.

4. Return the filled shells to the freezer, and serve after 45 minutes.

Granita—Coffee Ice with Whipped Cream

Granita di caffè con panna was the most welcome sign that Italian cafés used to put out in summer. On an afternoon slowed down by the southern sun, it was one of the best ways to while away the time, watching life dawdle by as you let the *granita*'s crystals melt on the tongue, spoonful by spoonful, until the roof of your mouth felt like an ice cavern pervaded by the aroma of strong coffee. Unfortunately and inexplicably, *granita* has largely disappeared. You can easily make it at home, however, and with the food processor it is even easier to do than it used to be.   *For 6 to 8 servings*

1½ cups very strong espresso coffee, more concentrated than you would usually make it

1 tablespoon sugar or more, to taste, plus 2 teaspoons sugar

A bowl kept in the freezer

1 cup very cold heavy whipping cream

1. Make the coffee and while it is still hot, dissolve the tablespoon or more of sugar in it. When the coffee is cold, pour it into ice-cube trays, filling them to a depth no more than ½ inch.

2. When the coffee has frozen into cubes, and you are ready to serve, take the bowl out of the freezer, put in the cream and the 2 teaspoons sugar, and whip it with a whisk until it becomes stiff.

3. Unmold the coffee cubes and put them in the food processor bowl. Run the metal blade, turning it on and off 4 or 5 times, until the frozen cubes have been ground to fine crystals, *granita*. Put the *granita* into individual glass bowls or stemware, top with the whipped cream, and serve at once.

FOCACCIA, PIZZA, BREAD, AND OTHER SPECIAL DOUGHS

Focaccia

BEFORE THERE WAS an oven, there was bread. It was baked in the hearth, where the dough was flattened over a stone slab and covered with hot ashes. From this hearth bread—*panis focacius* (*focus* is Latin for hearth)—comes today's soft, leavened *focaccia*.

Focaccia always starts out with an olive-oil enriched, salted dough, which may either be baked plain, or topped with onion, rosemary, sage, olives, bacon, and other flavorings. *Focaccia* is most closely associated with Liguria, the Italian Riviera, and with its principal city, Genoa. In many cities of the north, in fact, it is not called *focaccia* at all, but *pizza genovese,* Genoese-style pizza. In Bologna, however, if you are looking for *focaccia,* the appropriate word to use is *crescentina;* in Florence, Rome, and a few other parts of central Italy, it is *schiacciata.* If you ask for *focaccia* in Bologna or Venice, you will be given a very sweet *panettone*-like cake, studded with candied fruit and raisins.

Focaccia with Onions, Genoese Style

THE DOUGH in the recipe given here produces a thick, tender *focaccia* with a crisp surface, which you can top with sautéed onion in the Genoese style, as described below, or vary in one of the alternative ways indicated, or devise a suitable variation of your own.

For 6 servings

FOR THE DOUGH

1 package active dry yeast
2 cups lukewarm water
6½ cups unbleached flour

2 tablespoons extra virgin
   olive oil
1 tablespoon salt

FOR BAKING THE FOCACCIA

A heavy-duty rectangular metal
baking pan, preferably
black, about 18 by 14
inches or its equivalent
Extra virgin olive oil for
smearing the pan

A baking stone
A mixture of ¼ cup extra virgin
olive oil, 2 tablespoons
water, and 1 teaspoon salt
A pastry brush

FOR THE ONION TOPPING

2 tablespoons extra virgin
olive oil

4 cups onion sliced very,
very thin

1. Dissolve the yeast by stirring it into ½ cup lukewarm water, and let it stand about 10 minutes or slightly less.

2. Combine the yeast and 1 cup of flour in a bowl, mixing them thoroughly. Then add the 2 tablespoons olive oil, 1 tablespoon salt, ¾ cup water, and half the remaining flour. Mix thoroughly until the dough feels soft, but compact, and no longer sticks to the hands. Put in the remaining flour and ¾ cup water, and mix thoroughly once again. When putting in flour and water for the last time, hold back some of both and add only as much of either as you need to make the dough manageable, soft, but not too sticky. On a very damp, rainy day, for example, you may need less water and more of the flour.

3. Take the dough out of the bowl, and slap it down very hard several times, until it is stretched out lengthwise. Reach for the far end of the dough, fold it a short distance toward you, push it away with the heel of your palm, flexing your wrist, fold it, and push it away again, gradually rolling it up and bringing it close to you. It will have a tapered, roll-like shape. Pick up the dough, holding it by one of the tapered ends, lift it high above the counter, and slap it down hard again several times, stretching it out in a lengthwise direction. Reach for the far end, and repeat the kneading motion with the heel of your palm and your wrist, bringing it close to you once more. Work the dough in this manner for 10 minutes. At the end, pat it into a round shape.

Food processor note ❀ The preceding 2 steps may be carried out in the food processor, but the hand method, aside from the physical satisfactions it provides, produces a *focaccia* with better texture.

4. Smear the middle of the baking sheet with about 2 tablespoons olive oil, put the kneaded, rounded dough on it, cover it with a damp cloth, and leave it to rise for about 1½ hours.

Focaccia with Onions (continued)

5. *For the topping:* Put the 2 tablespoons of olive oil and all the sliced onion in a sauté pan, turn the heat on to medium high, and cook the onion, stirring it frequently, until it is tender, but not too soft. It should still be slightly crunchy.

6. When the indicated rising time has elapsed, stretch out the dough in the baking pan, spreading it toward the edges so that it covers the entire pan to a depth of about ¼ inch. Cover with a damp towel and let the dough rise for 45 minutes.

7. At least 30 minutes before you are ready to bake, put the baking stone in the oven and preheat oven to 450°.

8. When the second rising time for the dough has elapsed, keeping the fingers of your hand stiff, poke the dough all over, making many little hollows with your fingertips. Beat the mixture of oil, water, and salt with a small whisk or a fork for a few minutes until you have obtained a fairly homogeneous emulsion, then pour it slowly over the dough, using a brush to spread it all the way out to the edges of the pan. You will find that the liquid will pool in the hollows made by your fingertips. Spread the cooked onion over the dough, and place the pan on the middle rack of the preheated oven. Check the *focaccia* after 15 minutes. If you find it is cooking faster on one side than another, turn the pan accordingly. Bake for another 7 to 8 minutes. Lift the *focaccia* out of the pan with spatulas, and transfer it to a cooling rack.

Serve *focaccia* warm or at room temperature that same day. It is preferable not to keep it longer, but if you must, it is better to freeze than to refrigerate. Reheat in a very hot oven for 10 to 12 minutes.

Variation, Focaccia with Salt

From the ingredients for the preceding recipe for Focaccia with Onions, omit the onions and their cooking oil, and omit the salt in the mixture of oil and water. Follow all the other steps of the recipe. After brushing the dough with oil and water, sprinkle over it 1½ teaspoons coarse sea salt. Bake as directed in the basic recipe.

Variation, Focaccia with Fresh Rosemary

From the ingredients for the recipe for Focaccia with Onions on page 618, omit the onions and their cooking oil, and add several short sprigs of rosemary. Make the *focaccia* as directed in the basic recipe. When you check its progress in the oven after 15 minutes, spread over it the small sprigs of rosemary, and finish baking.

Variation, Focaccia with Fresh Sage

From the ingredients for the recipe for Focaccia with Onions on page 618, omit the onions and their cooking oil, and add 20 fresh sage leaves, chopped rather fine, and several whole leaves. When stretching out the dough in the pan prior to its second rising, as directed in the basic recipe, work the chopped sage into the dough, distributing it as uniformly as possible. Bake the *focaccia* as directed in the basic recipe. When you check its progress after 15 minutes, spread over it a thin scattering of fresh whole sage leaves, and finish the baking.

Variation, Focaccia with Black Greek Olives

From the ingredients for the recipe for Focaccia with Onions on page 618, omit the onions and their cooking oil, reduce the salt in the oil and water mixture to ½ teaspoon, and add 6 ounces black Greek olives. They should be the thin-skinned round ones that vary in color from dark brown to black. Do not use the purple, tapered Kalamata variety. Cut the olives all the way around their middle and loosen them from the pit, producing 2 detached halves from each olive. After you have poked hollows into the dough in the pan, as directed in the basic recipe, push the olives, cut side facing down, into the hollows, embedding them deeply into the dough, then brush the dough with the oil, water, and salt mixture. Bake the *focaccia* as directed in the basic recipe.

Crescentina—Bolognese Focaccia with Bacon

THERE IS a restaurant in Bologna whose tables, for nearly a century, have always been full. Their secret is solidly traditional cooking that satisfies that most solidly traditional of palates, the Bolognese. The restaurant is Diana, and the women in the kitchen there still roll out pasta by hand with the long Bolognese rolling pin, making incomparable *tortellini, tagliatelle,* and *lasagne.* While you wait for the *tortellini,* a waiter will put on your table a plate of thick *mortadella* cubes and sliced Parma ham, and squares of what is probably the most subtly savory of all *focaccia,* Bologna's *crescentina* with bacon. The following recipe is adapted from Diana's version. Here is an instance in which I prefer to use the food processor, because it does the best possible job of chopping the bacon and distributing it uniformly in the dough.

For 6 to 8 servings

Crescentina (continued)

¼ pound bacon, preferably
    choice quality slab bacon
1¼ teaspoons active dry yeast
1¼ cups lukewarm water
3¼ cups unbleached flour
1¼ teaspoons salt
A tiny pinch sugar
Extra virgin olive oil for oiling a
    bowl and pan

A baking stone
A 9- by 13-inch rectangular
    baking pan, preferably
    black
A pastry brush
1 egg, lightly beaten

1. Cut the bacon into pieces without stripping away any of the fat, put it into the food processor, and chop very fine. Do not take it out of the processor bowl.

2. Dissolve the yeast, stirring it into ¼ cup lukewarm water. When completely dissolved, in 10 minutes or less, put it into the processor bowl together with 1 cup of the flour, ½ cup lukewarm water, the salt, and the sugar. Turn on processor. While the blade is running, gradually add the rest of the flour and the remaining ½ cup water. Stop the processor when the dough masses together into a lump.

3. Use about 1 tablespoon olive oil to film the inside of a large bowl. Put the dough into the bowl, cover with plastic wrap, and place in a warm, protected corner to rise until it doubles in bulk, about 3 hours or slightly more.

4. When the dough has doubled in bulk, put the baking stone in the oven and preheat oven to 400°.

5. Thinly oil the bottom of the baking pan. Put the risen dough in the center, and gently spread it out with your fingers toward the sides until it completely covers the pan. Be careful not to make any thin spots, or they will burn through when baked. Cover the pan with plastic wrap, and put in a warm, protected corner for 30 to 40 minutes, until the dough rises some more.

6. Use a razor blade to cut a broad diamond-shaped, cross-hatched pattern into the top of the dough, then brush it with beaten egg. Don't attempt to use all the egg. Place the pan on the preheated baking stone, and bake for 30 minutes, until the dough becomes colored a deep gold on top. Take out the pan and turn off the oven, but leave its door closed. Loosen the *focaccia* from the bottom of the pan with a long metal spatula, lift it out of the pan, and slide it onto the baking stone in the oven. Take the *focaccia* out after 5 minutes, and place on a cooling rack. Serve warm or at room temperature.

Pizza

THE RECIPES for pizza dough are beyond numbering. Although some formulas are certainly better than others, none may credibly claim to be the ultimate one. What matters is knowing what you are looking for. I like pizza that is neither too brittle and thin nor too thick and spongy, a firm, chewy pizza with crunch to its crust. The dough that has satisfied my expectations most consistently is the single-rising one given below. I have never succeeded in getting the texture I like from pizza baked in pans, so I prefer to do mine directly on a baking stone.

Basic Pizza Dough

For 2 round pizzas, about 12 inches wide,
depending upon how thin you make them

1½ teaspoons active dry yeast
1 cup lukewarm water
3¼ cups unbleached flour
Extra virgin olive oil,
   1 tablespoon for the dough,
   1 teaspoon for the bowl,

and some for the finished
   pizza
½ tablespoon salt
A baking stone
A baker's peel (paddle)
Cornmeal

1. Dissolve the yeast completely in a large bowl by stirring it into ¼ cup lukewarm water. When dissolved, in 10 minutes or less, add 1 cup flour and mix thoroughly with a wooden spoon. Then, as you continue to stir, gradually add 1 tablespoon olive oil, ½ tablespoon salt, ¼ cup lukewarm water, and 1 cup more flour. When putting in flour and water for the last time, hold back some of both and add only as much of either as you need to make the dough manageable, soft, but not too sticky.

2. Take the dough out of the bowl, and slap it down very hard against the work counter several times, until it is stretched out to a length of about 10 inches. Reach for the far end of the dough, fold it a short distance toward you, push it away with the heel of your palm, flexing your wrist, fold it, and push it away again, gradually rolling it up and bringing it close to you. Rotate the dough a one-quarter turn, pick it up and slap it down hard, repeating the entire previous operation. Give it another one-quarter turn in the same direction and repeat the procedure for about 10 minutes. Pat the kneaded dough into a round shape.

Basic Pizza Dough (continued)

Food processor note 🏵 The previous two steps may be carried out in the food processor. Bear in mind that the hand method produces better dough, that it doesn't take appreciably longer than does using and cleaning the processor, and it can be more enjoyable.

3. Film the inside of a clean bowl with 1 teaspoon olive oil, put in the dough, cover with plastic wrap, and put the bowl in a protected, warm corner. Let the dough rise until it has doubled in volume, about 3 hours. It can also sit a while longer.

4. At least 30 minutes before you are ready to bake, put the baking stone in the oven and preheat oven to 450°.

5. Sprinkle the baker's peel generously with cornmeal. Take the risen dough out of the bowl and divide it in half. Unless *both* your peel and your baking stone can accommodate two pizzas at once, put one of the two halves back into the bowl and cover it while you roll out the other half. Put that half on the peel and flatten it as thin as you can, opening it out into a circular shape, using a rolling pin, but finishing the job with your fingers. Leave the rim somewhat higher than the rest. An alternate method—and the best way to thin the dough, if you can emulate it, is the pizza maker's technique. First roll out the dough into a thick disk. Then stretch the dough by twirling it on both your upraised fists, bouncing it from time to time into the air to turn it. When it is the desired shape, put the circle of dough on the cornmeal-covered peel.

6. Put the topping of your choice on the dough, and slide it, jerking the peel sharply away, onto the preheated baking stone. Bake for 20 minutes or slightly more, until the dough becomes colored a light golden brown. As soon as it is done, drizzle lightly with olive oil. (While the first pizza is baking, follow the same procedure for thinning the remaining dough and topping it, slipping it into the oven when the first pizza is done.)

Classic Pizza Toppings

PIZZA IS MADE for improvisation and brooks no dogmas about its toppings. Throughout Italy and the world, armies of *pizzaioli*—pizza bakers—each day are forming new combinations, conscripting mushrooms, onions, chili pepper, exotic vegetables and fruits, ham, sausages, cheeses, seafood, whatever seems to stray within their reach. Some ingredients are less congenial than others, however, and some, such as goat cheese, for example, produce flavor that is wholly incongruous when judged by Italian anticipations of taste. Without smothering spontaneity, it may be helpful, when one wants to make pizza in an idiomatic Italian style, to refer from time to time to those few blends of ingredients that represent, in the place where the dish was created, the broadest and longest-established consensus on what tastes best on pizza.

Margherita Topping: Tomatoes, Mozzarella, Basil, and Parmesan Cheese

Although some food historians, as historians are wont to do, dispute it, this most popular of all toppings is believed to have been created to please Italy's Queen Margherita when she visited Naples, late in the nineteenth century. The colors, tomato red, mozzarella white, and basil green, are evidently the patriotic ones of the then still-new Italian flag. Incidentally, Margherita's consort, Umberto I, seems to have been the only ruler among hundreds in the peninsula's nearly three-thousand-year recorded history to have had his name graced by the suffix The Good. Without any reservations, one can attach it to the topping that bears the name of his queen.

Topping for 2 twelve-inch pizzas made with the dough on page 623

THE TOMATOES

1½ pounds fresh, ripe, firm plum tomatoes (see note below) OR 1½ cups canned imported Italian plum tomatoes, drained and cut up
2 tablespoons extra virgin olive oil

Note ❧ The authentic flavor of Naples's pizza owes much to the very ripe, firm, fresh San Marzano plum tomatoes that go raw into the topping. In the brief season when local tomatoes of exceptional ripeness and firmness are available, omit the preliminary cooking procedure described in steps 1 and 2 below and use them as follows:

Margherita Topping (continued)

Skin the tomatoes raw with a swiveling-blade peeler, cut them into ½-inch-wide strips, discarding all seeds and any runny matter, and distribute them as they are over the pizza dough when you are ready to top it and bake it.

When working with tomatoes that do not quite meet that description, cook them down briefly, following the instructions that follow.

1. If using fresh tomatoes, wash them in cold water, skin them raw with a peeler, cut them into 4 pieces each, and discard all seeds and any runny matter. If using cut-up canned tomatoes, begin with the next step.

2. Put the tomatoes in a medium sauté pan together with the olive oil, put a lid on the pan, and turn on the heat to medium. After 2 to 3 minutes, uncover the pan and cook for another 6 to 7 minutes, stirring frequently, until the tomatoes have lost all their watery liquid.

THE MOZZARELLA

½ pound mozzarella, preferably imported buffalo-milk mozzarella

OPTIONAL: depending on the mozzarella, 1 tablespoon extra virgin olive oil

If you are using buffalo-milk mozzarella, which is very high in cream content, or a high-quality, moist, locally made fresh mozzarella, omit the olive oil, and slice the cheese as thin as you can.

If you are using commercial quality, supermarket mozzarella, grate it on the large holes of a grater, or with the shredding disk of the food processor. Put it into a bowl with the olive oil, mix thoroughly, and let steep for 1 hour before using it in the topping.

THE OTHER INGREDIENTS

Salt

3 tablespoons extra virgin olive oil

2 tablespoons freshly grated *parmigiano-reggiano* cheese

14 fresh basil leaves

1. *Applying the topping:* If using this topping for 2 pizzas, divide all ingredients in two equal parts, and use one part, following the instructions below, to top the dough that is about to go into the oven.

2. Spread the tomatoes evenly over the top, sprinkle with a little salt, and drizzle with olive oil. Slide the dough in the oven and bake for 15 minutes.

3. Use 2 metal spatulas, one in each hand, to take the dough out of the oven, quickly top the tomato with mozzarella and grated Parmesan, in that order, then return to the oven.

4. In about 5 minutes, when the cheese has melted, take out the pizza,

drizzle with a little olive oil, as described in Step 6 of the basic pizza recipe on page 624, and spread the basil leaves over it. Serve at once.

Variation with Oregano

Oregano so frequently takes the place of basil in a Margherita topping that its pungent and stirring fragrance has become identified with pizza itself. Use fresh oregano if possible, 1 teaspoon of it, or ½ teaspoon if dried. Sprinkle it on the partly baked pizza at the same time you add the mozzarella and grated Parmesan. Omit the basil.

Marinara Topping: Garlic, Tomatoes, and Olive Oil

Marinara means sailor style. It signifies cooked in the manner used aboard ship, therefore, "yes" to olive oil and garlic, but "no" to cheese, which would be incompatible with the fresh food most available at sea, fish. Marinara is the most traditional of all pizza toppings, and when the tomatoes are ripe and meaty, the garlic fresh and sweet, and the olive oil dense and fruity, it probably can't be surpassed.

Topping for 2 twelve-inch pizzas made with the dough on page 623

2 pounds fresh, ripe, firm plum tomatoes (see note on page 625) OR 3 cups canned imported Italian plum tomatoes, drained and cut up	Salt
	6 garlic cloves, peeled and sliced very thin
Extra virgin olive oil, 3 tablespoons for the tomatoes plus more for the pizza	Oregano, 1 teaspoon if fresh, ½ teaspoon if dried

1. Prepare the tomatoes, following the instructions in the Margherita topping recipe on page 625.

2. If using this topping for 2 pizzas, divide all ingredients in two equal parts, and use one part, following the instructions below, to top the dough that is about to go into the oven.

3. Spread the tomatoes evenly over the top, sprinkle with a little salt, add the sliced garlic, and drizzle generously with olive oil. Slide the dough into the oven and bake until done, as described on page 624. When you take out the pizza, drizzle with a little olive oil, and sprinkle the oregano over it. Serve at once.

Alla Romana Topping: Mozzarella, Anchovies, and Basil

Pizza topped in this manner, without tomatoes, is called *pizza bianca,* white pizza. In Naples it is further qualified as *alla romana,* Roman style, because of the anchovies, whereas, in the paradoxical Italian manner, in Rome and everywhere else in the country, it is called *alla napoletana,* Neapolitan style.

Topping for 2 twelve-inch pizzas made with the dough on page 623

1 pound mozzarella, preferably imported buffalo-milk mozzarella
Extra virgin olive oil, 2 table-spoons optional, depending on the mozzarella, plus 2 tablespoons for the pizza
4 flat anchovy fillets (preferably the ones prepared at home as described on page 9), cut up not too fine
½ cup fresh basil leaves, torn into 2 or 3 pieces
2 tablespoons freshly grated *parmigiano-reggiano* cheese
Salt

1. See the comments on mozzarella in the Margherita topping recipe on page 626 and follow the instructions there for its preparation, using the optional olive oil, if appropriate.

2. If you have grated the mozzarella, mix the cut-up anchovies with it; if you have sliced it, keep the anchovies separate. If using this topping for 2 pizzas, divide all ingredients in two equal parts, and use one part, following the instructions below, to top the dough that is about to go into the oven.

3. Top the dough with half of the mozzarella and anchovies that you have set aside for one pizza. Slide the dough in the oven and bake for 15 minutes.

4. Take the dough out of the oven, quickly top with the remainder of the mozzarella and anchovies reserved for that pizza, add the basil, the grated Parmesan, 1 tablespoon of olive oil, a pinch or two of salt, and return to the oven.

5. In about 5 minutes, when the cheese has melted, take out the pizza, drizzle with a little olive oil as described in Step 6 of the basic pizza recipe on page 624, and serve at once.

Sfinciuni—Palermo's Stuffed Pizza

Sfinciuni is to Palermo what pizza is to Naples and to the rest of the world. A coarse version of *sfinciuni* is indistinguishable from pizza in appearance, a layer of baked dough supporting a topping. A finer and more fascinating rendition is known as *sfinciuni di San Vito,* after the nuns of that order who are credited with creating it. It has two thin, round layers of firm dough that enclose a stuffing—called the *conza*—which are sealed all around. The San Vito *conza* has meat and cheese, but one can also make other excellent stuffings with vegetables instead of meat.

Dough for a thin 10- to 12-inch double-faced sfinciuni

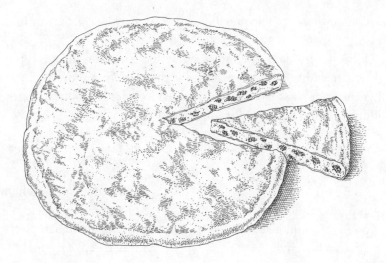

SFINCIUNI DOUGH

1 teaspoon active dry yeast
¾ cup lukewarm water
2 cups unbleached flour
A tiny pinch sugar
1 teaspoon salt

Extra virgin olive oil, 1 tablespoon for the dough plus some for the bowl
2 tablespoons whole milk

1. Dissolve the yeast completely in a large bowl by stirring it into ¼ cup lukewarm water. When dissolved, in 10 minutes or less, add 1 cup flour and mix thoroughly with a wooden spoon. Then, as you continue to stir, add ¼ cup lukewarm water, a small pinch of sugar, 1 teaspoon salt, 1 tablespoon olive oil, and 2 tablespoons milk. When all the ingredients have been smoothly amalgamated, add ¼ cup lukewarm water and the remaining 1 cup flour,

Sfinciuni (continued)

and mix thoroughly once again, until the dough feels soft, but compact, and no longer sticks to the hands.

2. Take the dough out of the bowl, and slap it down very hard against the work counter several times, until it is stretched out into a long and narrow shape. Reach for the far end of the dough, fold it a short distance toward you, push it away with the heel of your palm, flexing your wrist, fold it, and push it away again, gradually rolling it up and bringing it close to you. Rotate the dough a one-quarter turn, pick it up, and slap it down hard, repeating the entire previous operation. Give it another one-quarter turn in the same direction and repeat the procedure for about 10 minutes. Pat the kneaded dough into a round shape.

Food processor note ❀ The previous two steps may be carried out in the food processor.

3. Film the inside of a clean bowl with 1 teaspoon olive oil, put in the dough, cover with plastic wrap, and put the bowl in a protected, warm corner. Let the dough rise until it has doubled in volume, about 3 hours. While the dough is rising you can prepare the *conza*.

CONZA DI SAN VITO—MEAT AND CHEESE FILLING

3 tablespoons extra virgin
    olive oil
½ cup onion sliced very thin
½ pound ground beef,
    preferably chuck
Salt
Black pepper, ground fresh
    from the mill

½ cup dry white wine
⅓ cup cooked unsmoked ham
    chopped rather coarse
½ cup imported Italian *fontina*
    cheese diced very fine
¼ cup fresh *ricotta*

Note ❀ Palermo's *primo sale* and fresh *caciocavallo* cheeses that are both part of this stuffing are not yet, as I write, available outside Sicily. I have replaced them with a combination of *fontina* and *ricotta* to achieve mild flavor with a tart accent. I think it works, but if you have other ideas, try them out.

1. Put the olive oil and onion in a sauté pan and turn on the heat to medium high. Stir occasionally, and cook until the onion becomes colored a deep, dark gold. Add the ground beef, salt, and a few grindings of pepper. Crumble the meat with a fork and cook it, stirring frequently, until it loses its raw, red color.

2. Add the wine, turn the heat down a little, and continue cooking until

all liquid has simmered away. Transfer the contents of the pan to a bowl, and set aside to cool.

3. When cool, add the ham, *fontina,* and *ricotta* to the bowl and toss thoroughly until all ingredients have been evenly combined.

ASSEMBLING AND BAKING THE SFINCIUNI

A baking stone
Cornmeal
A baker's peel (paddle)
2 tablespoons plain, unflavored
    bread crumbs, lightly
    toasted

1 tablespoon extra virgin
    olive oil
A pastry brush

1. At least 30 minutes before you are ready to bake—the dough will have been rising for about 2½ hours—put the baking stone in the oven, and preheat oven to 400°.

2. Sprinkle cornmeal on the baker's peel.

3. When the dough has doubled in volume, divide it in half. Wrap one half in plastic wrap, and put the other half on the peel. Use a rolling pin to flatten it out into a circle at least 10 inches in diameter. The rim should be no thicker than the rest of the disk.

4. Distribute 1 tablespoon of bread crumbs over the dough and 1 teaspoon olive oil, stopping about ½ inch short of the edge. Spread the meat and cheese *conza* over it, again stopping short of the edge, and top the filling with 1 tablespoon bread crumbs and 2 teaspoons olive oil.

5. Unwrap the remaining dough, put it on a lightly floured work surface, and roll it out into a disk large enough to cover the first. Place it over the stuffing and crimp the edges of the two circles of dough securely together, bringing the edge of the lower one up over that of the top one.

6. Brush the top of the dough with water, then slide the *sfinciuni* off the peel and onto the preheated baking stone. Bake for 25 minutes. After removing it from the oven, let it settle for 30 minutes to allow the flavors of the stuffing sufficient time to come together and develop. Cut into pie-shaped wedges and serve.

OTHER FILLINGS FOR SFINCIUNI

Sfinciuni are exceptionally good with vegetables in the *conza*, or filling. A few particularly apt combinations are described below. They all must be cooked in advance, which you should plan on doing sometime during the 3 hours the dough needs to rise.

Tomato and Anchovy Conza

Filling for 1 ten- to twelve-inch sfinciuni

1 pound fresh, ripe, firm plum
  tomatoes OR 1½ cups
  canned imported Italian
  plum tomatoes, drained of
  juice and chopped
2 cups onion sliced very thin
3 tablespoons extra virgin
  olive oil
Salt

Black pepper, ground fresh
  from the mill
6 flat anchovy fillets (preferably
  the ones prepared at home
  as described on page 9),
  chopped to a pulp
Oregano, 1 teaspoon if fresh,
  ½ teaspoon if dried

LATER, ON THE SFINCIUNI

1 tablespoon extra virgin
  olive oil

¼ cup plain, unflavored bread
  crumbs, lightly toasted

AND

The dough made using the recipe on page 629

PLUS

A baking stone
Cornmeal

A baker's peel (paddle)
A pastry brush

1. Use fresh tomatoes only when they are truly ripe, sweet, and meaty. If they answer that description, wash them in cold water, skin them raw with a swiveling-blade peeler, discard the seeds and all watery pulp, cut them into strips ½ inch wide, and set them aside. If using canned tomatoes, proceed to the next step.

2. Put the onion and 3 tablespoons olive oil in a medium sauté pan, turn on the heat to medium, and cook the onion, stirring occasionally, until it becomes colored a light gold. Add either the strips of fresh tomatoes or the

drained, chopped canned tomatoes, salt, 2 or 3 grindings of pepper, turn over the ingredients 2 or 3 times, and turn the heat up to medium high. Cook, stirring from time to time, until the oil floats free of the tomatoes, about 15 minutes.

3. Turn the heat down to the minimum, add the chopped anchovy pulp, stir for a minute or a little less, then turn off the heat completely. Add the oregano, stir, and set aside to cool.

4. At least 30 minutes before you are ready to bake—the dough will have been rising for about 2½ hours—put the baking stone in the oven, and pre-heat oven to 400°.

5. Sprinkle cornmeal on the baker's peel, then proceed to roll out the dough and assemble the *sfinciuni* as described on page 631, with the following adjustments for this particular stuffing:

❋ Sprinkle 2 tablespoons of bread crumbs over the bottom round of dough.

❋ Use a slotted spoon or spatula to lift the tomato and anchovy mixture out of the pan so that as much cooked oil as possible is left behind.

❋ When you have spread the tomato and anchovy over the dough, top it with 2 tablespoons of bread crumbs and drizzle over it 1 table-spoon of fresh olive oil.

Cover the filling with the remaining dough, seal the *sfinciuni,* brush the top layer of dough with water, bake it, and serve it as described in the basic recipe on page 629.

Broccoli and Ricotta Conza

Filling for 1 ten- to twelve-inch sfinciuni

1 medium bunch fresh broccoli, about 1 pound
Salt

2 teaspoons chopped garlic
¼ cup extra virgin olive oil

LATER, ON THE SFINCIUNI

2 tablespoons plain, unflavored bread crumbs, lightly toasted
¾ cup fresh *ricotta*

¼ cup freshly grated *parmigiano-reggiano* cheese
1 tablespoon extra virgin olive oil

Broccoli and Ricotta Conza (continued)

AND

The dough made using the recipe on page 629

PLUS

A baking stone   A baker's peel (paddle)
Cornmeal   A pastry brush

1. Cut off ½ inch of the tough butt end of the broccoli stalks. Pare away the dark green skin from the stalks and the thicker stems.

2. Bring 3 quarts of water to a boil, add salt, and put in the broccoli. Cook for 5 to 7 minutes after the water returns to a boil, depending on the size and freshness of the broccoli. It will undergo additional cooking later, so it should be quite firm at this stage.

3. Drain and chop the broccoli stems and florets into pieces no larger than 1 inch.

4. Put the garlic and ¼ cup olive oil in a medium sauté pan, turn on the heat to medium, and cook the garlic, stirring once or twice, until it becomes colored a light gold. Add the chopped broccoli, sprinkle with salt, and cook for 5 minutes, turning the vegetable over frequently to coat it well. Take off heat and set aside to cool completely.

5. At least 30 minutes before you are ready to bake—the dough will have been rising for about 2½ hours—put the baking stone in the oven, and preheat oven to 400°.

6. Sprinkle cornmeal on the baker's peel, then proceed to roll out the dough and assemble the *sfinciuni* as described on page 631, with the following adjustments for this particular stuffing:

❀ Sprinkle 1 tablespoon of bread crumbs over the bottom round of dough.

❀ Spread the *ricotta* over the bread crumbs.

❀ Use a slotted spoon or spatula to lift the broccoli out of the pan so that as much of the cooking oil as possible is left behind. Spread the broccoli out over the *ricotta,* then sprinkle the grated Parmesan over it. Follow it with 1 tablespoon of bread crumbs, and top by drizzling 1 tablespoon of olive oil over the crumbs.

Cover the filling with the remaining dough, seal the *sfinciuni,* brush the top layer of dough with water, bake it, and serve it as described in the basic recipe on page 629.

Variation: Broccoli Conza Without Ricotta

For a more explicit broccoli flavor than the filling in the preceding recipe, omit the *ricotta* entirely and increase the grated Parmesan to ½ cup. Sprinkle the Parmesan over the broccoli after spreading the vegetable over the dough.

Mantovana—Olive Oil Bread

IF YOU FOLLOW the eastern-bound course of the Po river, Italy's largest, as it slices much of northern Italy in two, with parts of Lombardy and the Veneto on its left bank, and Emilia-Romagna on its right, you will be traveling across some of the country's best bread territory, once studded with flour mills powered by the river's currents.

These handsome loaves, notable for their fine, crisp, tasty crust, and soft crumb are popular on both the Emilia and the Lombardy side, but take their name from the ancient ducal town of Mantua, in Lombardy.

2 mantovane loaves

2 teaspoons active dry yeast
2 cups lukewarm water
¼ teaspoon sugar
About 5 cups unbleached flour
2 teaspoons salt
1 tablespoon extra virgin
   olive oil

A baking stone
A baker's peel (paddle), 16 by
   14 inches, OR a cookie sheet
   OR large piece of stiff
   cardboard
Cornmeal
A pastry brush

1. Dissolve the yeast completely in a large bowl by stirring it into ¼ cup lukewarm water with the ¼ teaspoon sugar added. When dissolved, in 10 minutes or less, add 2 cups flour and ¾ cup water, and mix thoroughly with a wooden spoon.

2. *If kneading by hand:* Pour the contents of the bowl onto a lightly

Olive Oil Bread (continued)

floured work surface, and knead steadily for about 10 minutes. Push forward against the dough, using the heel of your palm and keeping your fingers bent. Fold the mass in half, give it a quarter turn, press hard against it with the heel of your palm again, and repeat the operation. Make sure that you keep turning the ball of dough always in the same direction, either clockwise or counterclockwise as you prefer. Add a little more flour, if you find it necessary to make the dough workable, and dust your hands with flour if they stick to the dough. Knead until the dough is no longer sticky, but smooth and elastic. It should spring back when poked with a finger. Shape it into a ball.

If using the food processor: Pour 2 cups flour into the processor bowl, with the steel blade running add the dissolved yeast gradually, together with ¾ cup water. When the dough comes together forming a lump on the blades, take it out and finish kneading it by hand for 1 or 2 minutes.

3. Choose an ample bowl, dust the inside lightly with flour, and put in the dough. Wring out a wet cloth towel, fold it in two, and cover the bowl with it. Place the bowl in a warm, draft-free place, and let it rest for about 3 hours, until it has doubled in bulk.

4. *If kneading by hand:* Pour the remaining 3 cups flour onto the work surface. Place the risen ball of dough over the flour, punching it down and opening it with your hands. Pour the remaining 1 cup lukewarm water over it, and add the salt and the olive oil. Knead steadily as described above.

If using the food processor: Pour the remaining flour into the processor's bowl. Put in the risen dough, and the salt, and gradually add first the 1 cup lukewarm water, then the salt and the olive oil, while running the steel blades. Take out the dough when it forms a lump on the blades, and finish kneading it by hand for 1 or 2 minutes.

5. Return the kneaded dough to the floured bowl, cover it with a damp towel, and let it rest until it has doubled in bulk again, about 3 more hours.

6. Thirty or more minutes before you are ready to bake, put the baking stone in the oven and preheat oven to 450°.

7. When the dough has again risen to double its bulk, take the dough out of the bowl, and slap it down very hard several times, until it is stretched out lengthwise. Reach for the far end of the dough, fold it a short distance toward you, push it away with the heel of your palm, flexing your wrist, fold it, and push it away again, gradually rolling it up and bringing it close to you. It will have a tapered, roll-like shape. Pick up the dough, holding it by one of the tapered ends, lift it high above the counter, and slap it down hard again several times, stretching it out in a lengthwise direction. Reach for the far end, and repeat the kneading motion with the heel of your palm and your wrist, bringing it close to you once more. Work the dough in this manner for 8 minutes.

8. Divide the dough in half, shaping each half into a thick, cigar-shaped roll, quite plump at the middle and tapered at the ends. Sprinkle the peel (or the suggested alternatives) thinly with cornmeal, making sure the meal is well distributed over the surface. Place both shaped loaves on the peel, cover with a damp towel, and let them rest 30 to 40 minutes.

9. With a sharp knife or a razor blade, make a single lengthwise slash 1 inch deep along the top of each loaf. Brush the upper surface of the dough with a pastry brush dipped in water. Slide the loaves from the peel onto the preheated baking stone. Bake for 12 minutes, then turn the oven down to 375° and bake for 45 minutes more. When done, transfer the loaves to a cooling rack, and let the bread cool completely before cutting and serving it.

Pane Integrale—Whole-Wheat Bread

THE ITALIAN adjective *integrale* shares the same root as "integrity" in English, and it is customarily applied to whatever can be described as whole and unmixed. When applied to bread it means whole-wheat bread, which is, however, as you will find here, not unmixed at all, but made only partly from whole wheat.

Use all the ingredients from the recipe for Olive Oil Bread on page 635, except for the following proportions of flour:

1 round loaf Italian whole-wheat bread

1¾ cups stone-ground fine whole-wheat flour, free of any coarse bits of bran or kernel

About 3¼ cups unbleached flour

Whole-Wheat Bread (continued)

Follow the exact procedure given in the recipe for Olive Oil Bread on page 635, using whole-wheat and white flour in the proportions given here. Instead of shaping the dough into 2 tapered loaves, form it into a slightly domed round loaf. When it has rested, cut a shallow cross on top. Brush with water and bake as directed in the basic recipe.

Pane di Grano Duro— Hard-Wheat Bread

THE GOLDEN FLOUR of hard or *durum* wheat is in the opinion of many, among them the late James Beard, the choicest of bread flours because of its high proportion of gluten. It makes a very fine-textured and fragrant bread, with a biscuity quality, that tastes even better when reheated and used a day after it is made.

Use all the ingredients from the recipe for Olive Oil Bread on page 635, substituting 5 cups fine hard-wheat flour for the unbleached white flour.

1 ring-shaped loaf hard-wheat bread

Follow the exact procedure given in the recipe for Olive Oil Bread on page 635. Instead of shaping the dough into 2 tapered loaves, form it into a doughnut-like large ring with a hole the center about 3½ inches in diameter. When it has rested, put in a row of small diagonal cuts all around the top of the ring. Brush with water and bake as directed in the basic recipe.

Apulia's Olive Bread

AMONG THE SAVORY riches of regional Italian cooking, nothing can excite our wonder more than the toothsome diversity of its country breads. In this field, which few have yet broadly explored, one of the most talented researchers is Margherita "Mita" Simili, who is famous in Bologna, along with her sister Valeria, for the bakery they both used to run and for the baking classes they now teach. We have made pizza, *focaccia,* and bread together, developing doughs that are in this chapter.

Some of the best bread flour in the world is produced in Apulia, the spur and heel of the boot-shaped Italian peninsula. It was on a visit there that Mita acquired the recipe for Apulian olive bread, a product of the baker's craft that proves irresistible from the first bite. The method makes use of a starter dough known as *biga*. *Biga,* made from a small quantity of yeast and flour that is given an overnight rising, is the foundation on which Italian country bakers often build their breads. It acts upon the dough to which it is added in a manner similar to that of natural, ambient yeast, bestowing on the finished loaf exceptional flavor, fragrance, and airiness.

Food processor note: ❀ In this recipe, the dough is worked entirely by hand. It is not at all a lengthy process, just rather sticky because of the consistency of the dough, but it produces bread with better texture than the food processor does. If you must, you can use the processor for all the kneading steps, after you have made the starter.   *1 round loaf Apulian olive bread*

FOR THE STARTER (BIGA)

½ teaspoon active dry yeast   1¼ cups unbleached flour
½ cup lukewarm water   Extra virgin olive oil

FOR THE DOUGH

5 ounces black, round Greek   1½ teaspoons active dry yeast
   olives, see description in   3¾ cups unbleached flour
   Focaccia with Black Greek   2 teaspoons salt
   Olives, page 621   1 tablespoon extra virgin
1½ cups lukewarm water   olive oil

PLUS

A baking stone   Cornmeal
A baker's peel (paddle)

1. *For the starter:* In a bowl dissolve the ½ teaspoon yeast by stirring it into ½ cup lukewarm water. When it has dissolved completely, about 10 minutes or less, add the 1¼ cups flour and stir thoroughly with a wooden spoon to distribute the yeast uniformly in the flour.

2. Transfer the dough to a bowl lightly filmed with olive oil, cover tightly with plastic wrap, and place the bowl in a place protected equally from cold draughts and heat. Let it rise overnight for 14 to 18 hours, until it has more than doubled in volume.

3. When ready to proceed, start to prepare the dough by cutting the olives all the way around their middles and loosening them from the pits. Pull the olives apart any way they come.

Apulia's Olive Bread (continued)

4. Put ½ cup of the lukewarm water in a large bowl and stir into it the 1½ teaspoons dry yeast. When it has completely dissolved, add to the bowl half the *biga* (starter), 1¼ cups of the flour, and the 2 teaspoons salt, and mix with a spatula until all ingredients are well integrated. Then add the remaining 2½ cups flour and the remaining 1 cup lukewarm water, pouring it in gradually, while mixing steadily with the spatula. Add the pitted olives and continue to mix the dough, occasionally lifting it out of the bowl with the spatula, then slapping it back in. Mix the dough in this manner until it comes easily loose from the bowl, about 8 minutes or so.

5. Dust a work counter lightly with flour, and turn out the dough from the bowl onto the counter. Work the dough for a few minutes with the spatula, slipping the spatula under the edges and folding them over toward the center. Move the spatula over each time until you have circled the whole mass of dough and folded the edges over at least once. Dust the work surface with flour occasionally if necessary to keep the dough from sticking.

6. Put 1 tablespoon olive oil in a clean bowl, put the dough into the bowl, and turn it in all directions until it is evenly coated with oil. Dampen a towel, wring out excess moisture, and cover the bowl with it. Put the bowl in a warm, protected corner for about 3 hours, until it has approximately doubled in volume.

7. Dust the work counter with flour, and turn the dough in the bowl out on it. Dust your hands with flour and use the palms to flatten the dough to a thickness of about 1½ inches. With both hands, lift the edge of the dough furthest from you and fold it toward you, stopping about one-third of the way from meeting the edge close to you. Stick your thumbs out straight and horizontally, parallel to your body, bringing their tips together, and use them to push out the folded-over dough toward its original position. Perform this operation 3 times, then rotate the dough a one-quarter turn, and repeat the step 3 more times. Periodically you will need to dust the counter and your hands with flour.

8. Rotate and pat the dough to form a more or less round shape. Turn a bowl upside down over it, covering it entirely, and let it rise for 1 full hour. At least 30 minutes before you will be ready to bake, put the baking stone in the oven and preheat oven to 425°.

9. When the final rising time is over, spread cornmeal thinly over the baker's peel, put the ball of dough on the peel, and slide it into the oven onto the preheated stone. After 3 minutes, turn the oven down to 400°. In 20 minutes, turn the oven down again, to 375°. Bake for another 40 minutes. Let the bread cool down completely on a rack before using. When it has cooled off,

you can freeze it, if you like. This bread seems to mature in the freezer and once it is reheated in a very hot oven, it tastes even better, if possible, than when it was just baked.

Piadina—Flat Griddle Bread

Piadina is a thin flat bread, chewy, but tender and not brittle. Until quite recently, it was the everyday bread for Romagna's farmers, whose women baked it in the hearth on a terra-cotta slab over hot coals. It goes well with prosciutto or country ham, with salami, with pan-fried sausages, but it is at its surpassing best with the garlicky, sautéed greens on page 505.

Farm women in Romagna—the narrow, fertile plain between the hills and the sea on the northern Adriatic—still make *piadina.* Sometimes, on a Sunday, they make it for themselves, but more frequently they cook it on street corners for the summer people who crowd the seaside towns of Rimini, Riccione, and Cesenatico. It has now become the smart thing for Italian families in Romagna to dine in nostalgically rustic style at some converted farmhouse, where the standard menu of homemade pasta and roast chicken or rabbit is invariably preceded by platters piled high with wedges of *piadina,* accompanied by thick, hand-cut slices of salami or *coppa.* It is the kind of meal I put together for my own family from time to time, and for those friends on whose appreciation of casual, earthy food I can count.

What to cook piadina *on* ❀ Even in Romagna, the original, but fragile terra-cotta slab called *testo* on which the thin disk of dough was grilled, is being replaced with heavy, flat steel griddles. At home, one can use a heavy, black, cast-iron skillet. Heat it up gradually until it becomes very hot, but not fiery. It must be hot enough to cook *piadina* quickly, but not so hot that it merely scorches it.

For this purpose, however, metal can't quite match earth or stone. If you travel to Italy, traditional housewares shops in the towns of Romagna, and in Emilian cities such as Bologna, still carry the terra-cotta *testo.* Since it is fragile, but cheap, it is a good idea to buy at least two. In North America, Vermont soapstone griddles do the job every bit as well as terra-cotta, and are much sturdier. One mail-order source that Julia Child originally put me on to is the Vermont Country Store, Weston, Vermont 05161.

For 6 servings

Flat Griddle Bread (continued)

⅓ cup shortening, preferably
    lard, but extra virgin
    olive oil is an acceptable
    substitute
4 cups unbleached flour
⅓ cup milk

2 teaspoons salt
½ teaspoon bicarbonate of soda
½ cup lukewarm water
A 10-inch cast-iron skillet or a
    soapstone griddle (see
    introductory remarks)

1. If using lard, heat it gently in a small saucepan until it has melted completely, but do not let it simmer. If using olive oil, proceed to the next step.

2. Pour the flour onto a work surface, shape it into a mound, make a hollow in its center, and pour into it the melted lard or the olive oil together with all the other ingredients. Draw the sides of the mound together, mixing thoroughly with your hands, and knead for 10 minutes as described in the recipe for Olive Oil Bread on page 635.

3. When the dough is no longer sticky and has become smooth and elastic, you can either wrap it tightly in plastic wrap and return to it 1 or 2 hours later, or else proceed at once, as follows: Cut it into pieces each about the size of an extra-large egg, about 6 to 7 pieces for the quantity of dough produced with this recipe. Roll out each piece of dough into a very thin disk about ¹⁄₁₆ inch thick.

4. Over medium heat, heat up the cast-iron skillet or the soapstone griddle until it is hot enough to make a drop of water skip. If you are using a skillet, you will need to adjust the heat periodically because iron does not retain heat as steadily and evenly as stone. Place one of the disks of dough on it, cook without moving it for 10 seconds, then turn it over with a spatula and cook the other side, without moving it, another 10 seconds. (The side that was next to the grilling surface should be speckled with a scattering of black spots; if it is blackened over a large area, turn the heat down a little.) When the *piadina* has cooked for 10 seconds on each side, prick it here and there with a fork, and continue cooking for 3 or 4 minutes, rotating it frequently to keep it from being scorched and flipping it over from time to time to cook it evenly on both sides. When done it should have a dull, parched, white surface mottled by random burn marks.

5. Take the *piadina* off the fire, cut it into 4 pie-like wedges, and prop them up anywhere where they can stand on their curved edge, letting air circulate around the wedges while you cook another *piadina*. Repeat the procedure until all the disks of dough are done. Serve as promptly as possible, preferably while still warm. If necessary, *piadina* wedges can be reheated in a very hot oven.

Consum—Griddle Dumplings

Consum, both the word and the dumpling it designates, are not to be found outside of Romagna. The dough closely resembles that of another native Romagna product, *piadina,* on page 641, and the cooking method is identical, over the same sort of flat griddle. The robustly savory stuffing is a mixture of greens sautéed in garlic and olive oil.   *For 6 servings, 6 or 7 dumplings*

FOR THE STUFFING

Make the Sautéed Mixed Greens with Olive Oil and Garlic from the recipe on page 505, using 3 pounds of greens divided as follows:

2 pounds "sweet" greens, such as Swiss chard, spinach, or Savoy cabbage
1 pound "bitter" greens, preferably *cime di rapa,* also known as *broccoletti di rapa* or *rapini,* OR Catalonia chicory OR dandelion

FOR THE DOUGH

All the ingredients required for making Piadina, page 641

FOR COOKING

A cast-iron skillet or a soapstone griddle (see note on page 641)

1. Follow the directions in the *piadina* recipe on page 642 to prepare the dough and roll it into thin disks about 6 to 7 inches in diameter.

Griddle Dumplings (continued)

2. Over one-half of each disk spread a ½-inch thick layer of sautéed greens, drained of their cooking oil. Fold the other half of the disk over the greens, to meet the edge of the lower half, thus making a large half-moon–shaped dumpling. Seal the edges tightly together, pressing them down with your thumb or using a pastry crimper.

Note ❀ The dough for *consum* can be thinned out through the rollers of a pasta machine set to obtain a thickness no greater than ⅛ inch. If it is easier for you, you can cut the dough into squares and make the dumplings triangular in shape, or even rectangular. As long as the dough is all the same thickness, and the dumplings are more or less the same size, the shape is not important.

3. Heat up the skillet or griddle as described in Step 4 of the *piadina* recipe on page 642. When hot, put on it 2 dumplings, or 3 if they fit. Cook them 4 to 5 minutes altogether, turning them frequently, and using a pair of tongs to stand them on edge briefly. They are done when the dough is a dull, parched, white mottled by random burn marks. Serve promptly.

Variation: Cassoni

When *consum* are fried they become *cassoni,* and they are very, very good. Prepare them exactly as described above, but if you are using melted lard in the dough, reduce it to 1½ tablespoons. Fry the dumplings in vegetable oil, if you prefer, but they are most delicious and crisp when fried in hot lard.

Focaccette—Cheese-Filled Pasta Fritters

THERE IS no exact equivalent abroad for the fresh, tart, savory cheese one would use in Italy as the filling of these *focaccette.* I have tried to come close by combining *fontina,* for its silkiness and delicacy, Parmesan, for flavor and fullness, and *ricotta,* for its tart accent. If you have access to other cheeses that you think would produce a similar or possibly even more appealing mixture of soft, rich flavor and piquant freshness, try them.   *For 4 to 5 servings*

FOR THE DOUGH

1 cup flour	½ teaspoon salt
1 tablespoon extra virgin olive oil	5 tablespoons warm water

FOR THE FILLING

3 tablespoons imported Italian
    fontina cheese, chopped
    fine
7 tablespoons fresh *ricotta*
2 tablespoons freshly grated
    parmigiano-reggiano cheese

Salt
Black pepper, ground fresh
    from the mill

PLUS

1 egg white

Vegetable oil

1. *For the dough:* Pour the flour onto a work surface, shape it into a mound, and push down its center to form a hollow. Into the hollow put the olive oil, salt, and lukewarm water, and draw the sides of the mound together, mixing all ingredients well with your hands. Knead for 8 minutes. Shape the dough into a ball, and put it in a bowl. Cover the bowl with a plate or a cloth towel, and let the dough rest for about 2 hours.

2. *For the filling:* Combine the three cheeses in a bowl, adding to them a pinch of salt and a few grindings of pepper.

3. When the dough has rested the 2 hours, flatten it into a not too thin sheet with a rolling pin. At first it may fight you, but it should soon relax and open out easily. If you prefer, you can thin it through the rollers of a pasta machine, stopping at the setting that produces dough 1/16 inch thick.

4. Cut the sheet of dough into rectangles about 3¼ to 4 inches wide and 6 to 7 inches long. Over half of each rectangle, spread a thin layer of the cheese mixture, about 2 teaspoonfuls. Fold the other half of the rectangle over the cheese, joining it edge to edge with the lower half. Pinch the edges together, then dip a fingertip into the egg white and brush it over the edges to ensure a tight seal.

5. As you finish filling and sealing each fritter, lay it on a clean, dry cloth towel spread out on the counter. If you are not ready to fry them immediately, turn them from time to time to keep them from sticking to the towel. Do not overlap them or stack them.

6. Pour enough oil into the frying pan to come ½ inch up its sides, and turn on the heat to high. When the oil is very hot, slip in as many *focaccette* at one time as will fit loosely without crowding the pan. Fry them to a golden color on one side, then turn them and do the other side. Often the fritters will puff up and parts of them may jut above the oil level. Use a long-handled wooden spoon to tip them over and dunk them under the hot oil so that they fry as evenly as possible all over.

Cheese-Filled Pasta Fritters (continued)

7. With a slotted spoon or spatula, transfer them to a cooling rack to drain or to a platter lined with paper towels. If there are more *focaccette* left to fry, repeat the procedure until they are all done. Serve promptly.

Note ✸ Use caution when you take your first bite: The cheese oozes out quickly and it may be scalding.

I Ripieni Fritti—
Fried Stuffed Dumplings

A GREAT VARIETY of savory fillings can be put into these dumplings that look like large triangular *ravioli*. One of the tastiest combinations is strips of raw tomatoes with anchovies and capers. Another is cheese and chopped parsley. Once you have tried the basic versions and seen how they work, you can devise your own fillings. You might try putting in thin strips of fried eggplant and roasted peppers. Or mushrooms sautéed in garlic and olive oil. With taste and imagination, you can easily dream up many more.

TOMATO FILLING FOR 20 DUMPLINGS

⅓ cup fresh, ripe, firm tomatoes, skinned raw, seeded, and cut into strips about ½ inch wide and 1½ inches long

2 tablespoons capers, rinsed if packed in salt, drained if in vinegar, chopped unless very small

10 flat anchovy fillets (preferably the ones prepared at home as described on page 9), cut in two

CHEESE FILLING FOR 20 DUMPLINGS

2 tablespoons chopped parsley

3 ounces mild cheese and 2 ounces savory cheese, cut into very thin strips, or

slivers, or grated, or crumbled, depending on the cheese

Suggested Cheese Combinations

❀ Mozzarella and Parmesan

❀ *Ricotta* and *Gorgonzola*

❀ Smoked Mozzarella and *Fontina*

❀ Gruyère and *Taleggio*

Note ❀ When using either the tomato or the cheese filling, keep all the ingredients separate in individual small bowls or saucers.

THE DOUGH FOR ABOUT 20 DUMPLINGS

1½ cups unbleached flour
½ teaspoon salt
½ teaspoon baking powder

1 tablespoon extra virgin olive
oil
⅓ cup lukewarm water

PLUS

Vegetable oil for frying

1. *For the dough:* Pour the flour onto a work surface, shape it into a mound, and push down its center to form a hollow. Into the hollow put the salt, baking powder, olive oil, and lukewarm water. Draw the sides of the mound together, mixing all ingredients well with your hands. Knead for 10 minutes, until the dough loses its stickiness and is smooth and elastic.

2. Flatten the dough into a not too thin sheet with a rolling pin or, if you prefer, you can thin it through the rollers of a pasta machine, stopping at the setting that produces dough ¹⁄₁₆ inch thick. Trim the sheet of dough along the edges to give it a regular, rectangular shape. Briefly knead the trimmings into a small ball, and roll it out or thin it in the pasta machine. Trim it to give it the same rectangular shape as the rest of the dough.

3. Cut the dough into 3-inch squares, or as close to it as you can. Take a little bit of each of the components of the filling you are using from the individual bowls or plates and place it in the center of each square. Try to judge how much you are going to have to put into each square to make the filling come out evenly distributed. Fold the squares over on the diagonal, forming triangles. Seal the edges securely tight, pressing them with your fingers or with a pastry crimper. It is essential to stuff and seal the dumplings as soon as the dough has been rolled out, otherwise it will dry out. If it has begun to do so and you are having difficulty sealing the edges, moisten them very lightly with water.

Fried Stuffed Dumplings (continued)

4. As you finish filling and sealing each dumpling, lay it on a clean, dry cloth towel spread out on the counter. If you are not ready to fry them, turn them from time to time to keep them from sticking to the towel. Do not overlap them or stack them.

5. Pour enough oil into the frying pan to come ½ inch up its sides, and turn on the heat to high. When the oil is very hot, slip in as many dumplings at one time as will fit loosely without crowding the pan. Fry them to a golden color on one side, then turn them and do the other side. Often the dumplings will puff up and parts of them may jut above the oil level. Use a long-handled wooden spoon to tip them over and dunk them under the hot oil so that they fry as evenly as possible all over.

6. With a slotted spoon or spatula, transfer them to a cooling rack to drain or to a platter lined with paper towels. If there are more left to fry, repeat the procedure until all the dumplings are done. Serve while hot, but not scalding.

AT TABLE

The Italian Art of Eating

A PERFECT DISH of pasta or an impeccable *risotto* or a succulent chicken can, by itself, be so powerfully satisfying that we may reasonably ask, what else does one need? Just add a salad on the side, a slice of good bread, finish with a ripe fruit to sweeten one's mouth, and we have a complete Italian meal. Or do we?

Having Italian food may often amount to no more than that, or to a pizza, or a platter of cold cuts, or a rice and chicken salad. There are times we simply do not want more. Yet, food has many ways of nourishing us, and there is more to a well-planned Italian meal than a single satiating dish.

In an Italian meal, there is no main course. With some rare exceptions—such as *ossobuco e risotto,* which is served as one dish, in the Milanese style—a single dominant course goes against eating in the Italian way, which consists of working one's way through an interesting and balanced succession of small courses. Of these, two are principal courses that are never served side by side.

The first course may be pasta served either sauced or in broth, or it can be a *risotto,* or a soup. The Italian word for soup, *minestra,* is also the word often used in naming the first course, because even if it is a sauced pasta or *risotto,* it is served in a soup dish and, like any soup, always precedes and never accompanies the meat, fowl, or fish course.

When there has been time to relish and consume the first course, to salute its passing with some wine and to regroup the taste buds, the second course comes to the table. If one is ordering in a restaurant, a restaurant that caters to Italians, not to tourists, the choice of a second course is made after one has had the first course. This doesn't mean that one has made no plans, but that one waits to confirm them to make sure that one's original intentions and present inclinations coincide.

At home, of course, the entire meal will have been planned in advance by whoever makes such decisions. Here, the second course is usually a development of the theme established by the first. The reverse may also be true, when the first course is chosen in relation to the second. If the second course is going to be beef braised in wine, you will not preface it with *spaghetti* in clam sauce or with a dish of *lasagne* thickly laced with meat. You might prefer a *risotto* with asparagus, with zucchini, or plain, with Parmesan cheese. Or a dish of green *gnocchi*. Or a light potato soup.

If you are going to start with *tagliatelle alla bolognese,* homemade noodles with meat sauce, you might want to give your palate some relief by following it with a simple roast of veal or chicken. On the other hand, you would not choose a second course so bland, such as poached fish, that it could not sustain the impact of the first.

An Italian meal is a lively sequence of sensations, alternating the crisp with the soft and yielding, the pungent with the bland, the variable with the staple, the elaborate with the simple. It may take for its theme "fish," and announce it very gently with a simple *antipasto* of tiny, boiled shrimp, delicately seasoned with olive oil, parsley, and lemon juice, and served still warm. Subsequently, a squid and clam *risotto* can make peppery comments on the theme, which might then be resoundingly proclaimed by a magnificent turbot baked with potatoes and garlic. All will subside in a brisk, slightly bitter salad of *radicchio* and field greens, to close on the sweet, liquid note of fresh sliced fruit in wine.

The second course is often accompanied by one or two vegetable side dishes, which sometimes develop into an independent course of their own. The pleasures of the Italian table are never keener than when the vegetables come on the scene. The word for a vegetable dish is *contorno,* whose literal translation is "contour." It's a good description of the role vegetables play because it is the choice of vegetables that defines an Italian meal, that gives it shape, that circles it with the flavors, texture, and colors of the season.

In planning an Italian menu, choosing the vegetables is often the most critical decision you will have to make. It will probably determine what kind of a pasta sauce or *risotto* you are going to make, which in turn affects plans for the second course, the vegetable *contorno,* and the all-important salad. It's not a choice you should make abstractly, if you can help it. The most successful Italian menu plan is one that takes shape in the market, when you come face to face with your materials.

Salad is always served after the second course and its *contorno* are cleared away. It is the meal's next to last act, gently letting the palate recoup its freshness, allowing it to deal with dessert and come away from the table without fatigue.

A baked dessert is rarely served at home after a meal of two or more courses. The traditional and sensible preference is for a bowl of fruit, sometimes substituted by marinated fruit slices.

It is not expected that every Italian meal one takes or makes will be full scale. Nor should we feel guilty when all we have the time or capacity to handle is pasta, or even just a seafood salad. But we ought not to be quite ready yet to dismiss the established practices of Italians at table.

In the relationships of its parts, the pattern of a complete Italian meal is very like that of a civilized life. No dish overwhelms another, either in quantity or in flavor, each leaves room for new appeals to the eye and palate, each fresh sensation of taste, color, and texture interlaces a lingering recollection of the last. To make time to eat as Italians still do is to share in their inexhaustible gift of making art out of life.

Composing an Italian Menu: Principles and Examples

WHEN DEVISING A MENU, we can chart the basic guidelines we need to follow by drawing on plain good sense. Courses served side by side ought not to have sauces whose flavors and consistencies are repetitive or at odds with each other: If the second course is a fricassee or a stew with a tomato base, obviously tomato should not be a large presence in the accompanying vegetable course, or vice versa; if one is boldly flavored with garlic and olive oil, we'll think twice before matching it with a subtle dish whose base might be cream or butter. Nor are we likely to enjoy a sequence of courses that are equally runny, or dense, or starchy, or spicy, or that are strongly accented with the same herb, unless we are deliberately restating and developing a theme.

If the flavors and aromas of one course are exuberant, we shan't want to follow it with one whose gentle, soft-spoken approach would, by comparison, become imperceptible. Whenever two or more courses precede the salad or dessert, their progress must move upward, climbing toward more prominent sensations of weight, of richness, of pungency if any, of palate-gripping flavor. It is the same principle people follow when serving more than one wine.

From the practical point of view of organizing time, space, and equipment to pull together the components of a meal, clearly we must avoid an assemblage of dishes whose preparation can become mutually obstructive, nor can we fail to take into account the last-minute attention each may require to reach the table at its peak of flavor.

Once the general and commonsensical principles of menu planning become apparent, the choices remaining before us provide an infinite number of agreeable and workable combinations. A representative selection that encompasses different occasions for an Italian meal is illustrated by the specimen menus that follow, of which all but a few are based on the classic Italian sequence of courses. I am aware that, judged by contemporary usage, some of them will appear to be rather densely packed. Actually, if you keep the portions small, you might find that a full-scale Italian meal is a less stultifying, more interesting event at table than one based on a sufficiently filling single course. If you feel you absolutely must simplify, you can always drop either the first or the second course. Moreover, even when you cannot reproduce the menus in full, you should find their examples a helpful guide to choosing dishes that go well together.

The role of bread ❦ One of the Italian words for a meal is *companatico*—that which you eat with bread. At an Italian table, food and bread are inseparable. In Italy, you will notice people begin to nibble on bread the moment they sit down to eat, just bread alone, without butter. No bread is eaten with pasta, but it will be used to wipe the dish clean of any sauce that might be left over. Morsels of bread punctuate the consumption of the second course, sop up the juices of a stew, or of a vegetable gratin. The bread is removed from the table only after you have finished the salad, whose most delectable part many claim are the tiny puddles of lightly salted and vinegary olive oil that, at the end, you soak up with bread.

AN ELEGANT MENU WITH HOMEMADE PASTA

The thread connecting the first three courses of this menu is the richness of the cooking based on butter and originating in Italy's great northern plain.

Baked Zucchini Stuffed with Ham and Cheese, page 535

❧

Fettuccine, page 134, with Cream and Butter Sauce, page 193,
blanketed if possible with shaved white truffles, see page 193

❧

Sautéed Veal Chops with Sage and White Wine, page 375

or

Sautéed Sweetbreads with Tomatoes and Peas, page 441

or

Asparagus and Prosciutto Bundles, page 468

(You can omit vegetable, because it is present elsewhere in the meal, and follow one of the above second courses with a simple, refreshing salad of field greens such as *mâche* and *arugula* dressed with olive oil and vinegar as described on page 543.)

Macedonia—Macerated Mixed Fresh Fruit, page 605

A CLASSIC MENU IN THE BOLOGNESE STYLE

Mushroom, Parmesan Cheese, and White Truffle Salad, page 60

or

Prosciutto slices over very ripe melon or figs

Tagliatelle, page 136, with Bolognese Meat Sauce, page 203

or

Any of the *lasagne* dishes, pages 214–220, except the one with *pesto*

Pork Loin Braised in Milk, Bolognese Style, page 417

or

Drunk Roast Pork, page 419

or

Pan-Roasted Breast of Veal, page 354

ACCOMPANIED BY

Spinach Sautéed with Olive Oil and Garlic, page 526

or

Swiss Chard Stalks Gratinéed with Parmesan Cheese, page 489

or

Breaded Fried Finocchio, page 504

AND

Pan-Roasted Diced Potatoes, page 520

❧

Bolognese Rice Cake, page 571

or

Egg Custard Gelato, page 612

A HOLIDAY MENU WITH ROAST BIRDS

Carciofi alla Romana—Artichokes, Roman Style, page 56

❧

Risotto with Porcini Mushrooms, page 247

or

Green Tortellini with Meat and Ricotta Stuffing, page 208

or

Spaghettini with Black Truffle Sauce, page 178

❧

Pan-Roasted Squab Pigeons, page 346

or

Roast Duck, page 347

ACCOMPANIED BY

Sautéed Shiitake Mushroom Caps, Porcini Style, page 512

or

Sweet and Sour Onions, page 516

and/or

Sunchoke Gratin, page 462

PLUS

Boiled Zucchini Salad all'Agro, with Lemon Juice, page 562

✧

Monte Bianco: Puréed Chestnut and Chocolate Mound, page 583

A FISH FEAST

Probably no cuisine surpasses the Italian, if indeed any equals it, in the vivacity and ease with which it handles seafood. The following menu draws on just some of the riches to be found in doing fish *all'italiana*.

Cold Trout in Orange Marinade, page 64

or

Gamberetti all'Olio e Limone—Poached Shrimp with Olive Oil
and Lemon Juice, page 65

✧

Fettuccine, page 134, and Pink Shrimp Sauce with Cream, page 191

or

Fettuccine, page 134, with Pesto, page 176

or

Tortellini with Fish Stuffing, page 209

✧

Halibut Sauced with White Wine and Anchovies, page 300

or

Baked Sea Bass or Other Whole Fish Stuffed with Shellfish, page 304

or

Bass or Other Whole Fish Baked with Artichokes, page 308

FOLLOWED BY

Orange and Cucumber Salad, page 552

✧

Zuppa Inglese, page 597

or

Sgroppino, page 613

A WINTER MENU

Acquacotta—Tuscan Peasant Soup with Cabbage and Beans, page 104

or

Barley Soup in the Style of Trent, page 114

or

Minestrone alla Romagnolla—Vegetable Soup, Romagna Style, page 84

or

Spinach or Escarole Soup with Rice, page 90

❧

Beef Stew with Red Wine and Vegetables, page 398

or

Veal Stew with Sage, White Wine, and Cream, page 377,
or Mushrooms, page 379

or

Cotechino, page 432, served with Mashed Potatoes with Milk
and Parmesan Cheese, Bolognese Style, page 518

FOLLOWED BY

Shredded Savoy Cabbage Salad, page 550

or

Romaine Lettuce Salad with Gorgonzola Cheese and Walnuts, page 551

or

Warm Cauliflower Salad, page 560

❧

Glazed Bread Pudding, page 573

or

A Farm Wife's Fresh Pear Tart, page 589

or

Pisciotta—Olive Oil Cake, page 591

A RUSTIC MENU, I

Bagna Caôda, page 77

Chicken Fricassee with Red Cabbage, page 333

or

Polenta, page 274

with

Spareribs with Tomatoes and Vegetables, page 427

or with

Sautéed Calf's Liver and Onions, Venetian Style, page 438

Chestnuts Boiled in Red Wine, Romagna Style, page 585

A RUSTIC MENU, II

Piadina—Flat Griddle Bread, page 641, with Sautéed Mixed Greens with
Olive Oil and Garlic, page 505

Pork Sausages with Smothered Onions and Tomatoes, page 429

FOLLOWED BY

Shredded Carrot Salad, page 549

or

Baked Red Beets, page 558

Ciambella—Grandmother's Pastry Ring (served with *vin santo*
or other sweet wine), page 592

or

Polenta Shortcake with Raisins, Dried Figs, and Pine Nuts, page 590

A LUNCH MENU FOR SUMMER

Even in summer, lunch in the Italian style can be a complete and leisurely meal, but it needn't be weighty, as the fresh and sprightly flavors of the dishes in this menu demonstrate.

Panzanella—Bread Salad, page 554

Spaghettini with Eggplant Sauce with Tomato
and Red Chili Pepper, page 160
or with
Sardinian Bottarga Sauce, page 183

Vitello Tonnato—Cold Sliced Veal with Tuna Sauce, page 382

FOLLOWED BY

Italian Potato Salad, page 560 (made with new potatoes)

Lemon Ice Cream from the recipe for Sgroppino, page 614

A SUMPTUOUS SUMMER DINNER

An appetite-arousing active summer day spent on the tennis courts or by the ocean could scarcely come to a more satisfying close than this.

Crostini Bianchi—Ricotta and Anchovy Canapés, page 52
or
Poached Tuna and Spinach Roll, page 71

Pappardelle broad noodles, page 135, with Red and Yellow Bell Pepper
Sauce with Sausages, page 197

or

Penne with Roasted Red and Yellow Pepper Sauce with Garlic
and Basil, page 165

❈

Roast Chicken with Lemons, page 327

or

Pan-Roasted Veal with Garlic, Rosemary, and White Wine, page 351

or

Sautéed Veal Chops with Garlic, Anchovies, and Parsley, page 376

FOLLOWED BY

Green Bean Salad, page 557

or

Boiled Zucchini Salad, page 562

❈

Black and White Macerated Grapes, page 608

or

Mangoes and Strawberries in Sweet White Wine, page 607

A MENU FOR THE CHARCOAL GRILL

Bruschetta, page 73

❈

Grilled Fish, Romagna Style, page 288

or

Grilled Chicken alla Diavola, Roman Style, page 336

or

La Fiorentina—Grilled T-Bone Steak, Florentine Style, page 385

❈

Charcoal-Grilled Vegetables, page 540

❈

A basket of fresh seasonal fruit

or

Mixed berries marinated with fresh mint and sugar
and tossed with lemon juice before serving

FAMILY-STYLE PASTA AND CHICKEN

Spaghetti and Tomato Sauce with Onion and Butter, page 152

❦

Pan-Roasted Chicken with Rosemary, Garlic,
and White Wine, page 329

ACCOMPANIED BY

Braised Artichokes and Potatoes, page 453

or

Crisp-Fried Artichoke Wedges, page 456

or

Braised Carrots with Parmesan Cheese, page 480

FOLLOWED BY

La Grande Insalata Mista—
Great Mixed Raw Salad, page 546

❦

Diplomatico—A Chocolate Dessert with Rum and Coffee, page 577

or

Any of the fresh fruit or *gelati* in this book

A 45-MINUTE MENU WITH BEEF

Butter and Rosemary Sauce, page 169, with Spaghetti,
or with Tonnarelli, page 134, made and dried on a previous occasion

or

Boiled Rice with Parmesan, Mozzarella, and Basil, page 258

❧

Pan-Broiled Thin Beef Steaks with Tomatoes and Olives, page 387

or

Beef Tenderloin with Red Wine, page 397

FOLLOWED BY

Finocchio Salad, page 549

❧

A bowl of fresh fruit

A 45-MINUTE SEAFOOD MENU

Spaghettini with Scallop Sauce with Olive Oil, Garlic,
and Hot Pepper, page 185

❧

Grilled Swordfish Steaks, Sicilian Salmoriglio Style, page 289

FOLLOWED BY

Garlic-Scented Tomato Salad, page 548

❧

The Chimney Sweep's Gelato, page 613

A SIMPLE FISH MENU

Spaghettini with Clam Sauce, either Red, page 180,
or White, page 182

or

Risotto with Clams, page 253

FOLLOWED BY

Pinzimonio, page 553

❊

Macerated Orange Slices, page 605

AN EASY AND HEARTY
LAMB-STEW DINNER

On those occasions that call for just a single satisfying meat course, this menu
can offer a lot of comfort.

Lamb Stew with Vinegar and Green Beans, page 414

FOLLOWED BY

Radicchio and Warm Bean Salad, page 556

or

Baked Radicchio, page 525

❊

Glazed Semolina Pudding, page 572

A VEGETARIAN MENU I

Roasted Eggplant with Peppers and Cucumber, page 55

❊

Risotto with Zucchini, page 250, or with Asparagus, page 248
(in cooking, substitute water for broth, if desired)

or

Fusilli with Eggplant and Ricotta Sauce, Sicilian Style, page 161

❧

Swiss Chard Torte with Raisins and Pine Nuts, page 490

❧

Ricotta Fritters, page 602

A VEGETARIAN MENU II

Peppers roasted as described on page 54 (omit the anchovies)

❧

Spaghetti "Aio e Oio", page 170

or

Potato Gnocchi, page 260, with Pesto, page 176

❧

Mushroom Timballo, page 513

or

Eggplant Patties with Parsley, Garlic, and Parmesan, page 498

or

Eggplant Parmesan, page 494

❧

Sunchoke and Spinach Salad, page 550

❧

Strawberry Gelato, page 610

COLD BUFFET PARTY MENU

A seafood theme runs through this buffet, pausing only to make room for a cool and welcome rice and chicken salad. Except for dessert, all the dishes can be put on the table at the same time.

Tomatoes Stuffed with Shrimp, page 61

In Carpione—Fried Marinated Fresh Sardines
(or other fish), page 63

Poached Tuna and Potato Roll, page 70

Seafood Salad, page 565

Rice and Chicken Salad, page 567

Insalatone—Mixed Cooked Vegetable Salad, page 563

Zuccotto, page 579

Cold Zabaglione with Red Wine, page 599

HOT BUFFET PARTY MENU

I see no reason why the dishes of an Italian hot buffet cannot be put on the table in the same sequence that one would follow in a sit-down meal, first course first and second courses second. They will taste fresher and better, and they will be spared the ignominy of being piled all on the same plate. When serving a hot buffet in this manner, I write out a list of the dishes and put it in a picture frame on the table. It informs the guests of what is coming, so they can pace themselves.

FIRST COURSES

Cannelloni with Meat Stuffing, page 222

Sliced Pasta Roll with Spinach and Ham Filling, page 224

or

Layered Crespelle with Tomato, Prosciutto, and Cheese, page 270

SECOND COURSES AND VEGETABLES

Pan-Roasted Lamb with Juniper Berries, page 411

Stinco—Braised Whole Veal Shank, Trieste Style, page 359

Chicken Cacciatora, New Version, page 331

Gratinéed Asparagus with Parmesan, page 467

Green Beans and Potato Pie, Genoa Style, page 473

or

Sliced Potatoes Baked with Porcini and Fresh Cultivated Mushrooms,
Riviera Style, page 522

DESSERTS

Ricotta and Coffee Cream, page 600

Walnut Cake, page 588, and a bowl of whipped cream on the side

✿ *Index* ✿